ANSWER BOOK

10,001 FAST FACTS ABOUT OUR WORLD

ANSWER BOOK

10,001 FAST FACTS ABOUT OUR WORLD

FOREWORD BY KATHRYN THORNTON

NATIONAL GEOGRAPHIC

WASHINGTON, D.C.

CONTENTS

How many answers?

THAT'S 1,482—AND THAT IS JUST THE BEGINNING . . .

ANSWER BOOK | CONTENTS

ANSWER BOOK | CONTENTS

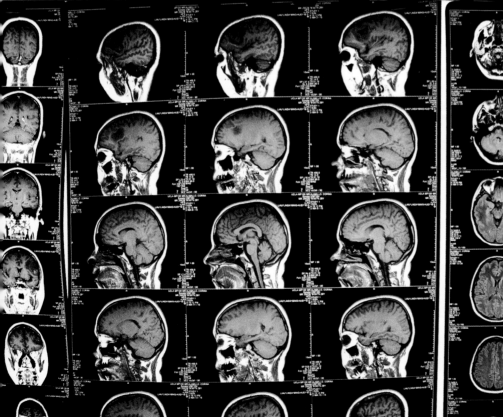
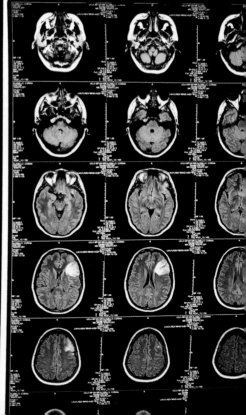

A VIEW of the WORLD

FOREWORD BY KATHRYN THORNTON

When I launched into space for the first time, I expected to see a beautiful and fragile blue gem on the black velvet background of space. That image of Earth—the extraordinarily powerful image of a little blue marble wrapped in white swirls of cloud cover, the image that became the icon of the environmental movement in the 1970s—that was my mental picture of our planet, a passive host for living things that needed protection from human-induced damage and degradation. And yet that was not at all what I saw. In fact, I was completely unprepared for my first glimpse of the beautiful and dynamic planet that we call our home.

Almost painfully bright, the Earth I saw showed little evidence of human activity when compared with abundant evidence of its own natural processes. During the shuttle's daylight passes over the oceans, we could see the churning motion of the oceans, visible in the sun's reflection on the water, evidence of the immense energy in the turbulent water that covers 70 percent of the Earth's surface. We could clearly distinguish the Himalaya, the highest mountain range on Earth, proof of an ongoing collision between the Indian subcontinent and

the Asian continent. From orbit, its peaks and ridges resemble crinkled wrapping paper. Volcanoes appear as the tiniest pimples on the face of the Earth.

Imagine how much energy is involved in all that wrinkling, folding, lifting, and melting—in the continuous creation of Earth's new crust! I did not see a fragile planet, but rather a living, breathing, powerful Earth.

The night side of Earth gave me a different perspective, though. On night passes in orbit, evidence of human activity is abundantly clear. Densely populated landmasses are lit up brilliantly, whereas sparsely inhabited deserts are almost completely dark. Lights outline continents, particularly in the Northern Hemisphere, where people live along the coastlines. Strings of lights illuminate rivers and, in some places, even highways, where densely populated towns and cities have grown up along these transportation arteries.

All this made it abundantly clear how much geography and climate influence where people have chosen to live. And it strikes me that this remarkably comprehensive book contains within it these same two divergent views of the planet: the powerful Earth, largely unaffected by its human inhabitants, and the fascinating world, glowing with human activity. I imagine looking through a zoom lens, starting with a wide field of view of Earth and the universe and then zooming in to a microscopic view of Earth's inhabitants and how they have modified their surroundings to suit their needs.

This book begins with the broadest possible view of the Earth as just one planet in the universe, reinforcing the apparent insignificance of our species. Spread by spread, detail by detail, it progresses from that view through chapters on the forces and variety of nature on Earth, and then to chapters on the remarkable story of our human family, cultures, and history.

Painting such a comprehensive picture, this *National Geographic Answer Book* reminds us of our insatiable thirst for knowledge—that uniquely human quest that has brought us through thousands of years to the amazing moment in time and technology when we can fly out of the atmosphere, view Earth from above, and marvel at this beautiful planet.

KATHRYN THORNTON was a NASA astronaut from 1985 to 1996 and is now a professor of engineering at the University of Virginia.

Below, left: Italian beach scene; below, right: Traffic in Ahmedabad, India. Preceding pages: 1, Chicago at night; 2, Parade in Delhi, India; 3, Frost on window; 4-5, Harvesting tea in Japan; 6, Grevys zebras; 7, Rice plantation in Costa Rica; 8, Marching band; 9, Brain x-rays.

ABOUT this BOOK

National Geographic Answer Book divides the world of nature and the universe of humankind up into more than 200 vivid spreads, each one containing a different combination of illustrations, text, and interactive details. Every page in this book is an eye-opener, with bits of information and nuggets of knowledge at every turn.

STRIKING CHAPTER OPENERS

Chapter topics divide the world and all that is in it into realms of knowledge, from the physical to the cultural world, from natural history to human history.

Tabs offer easy reference tools within the book.

Every chapter opener introduces you to the topics to come with a list of its contents.

NEW IDEAS ON EVERY SPREAD

Spreads begin with an illustrated introduction that orients you to the subject and introduces the major ideas.

Yellow bars highlight interesting dates, statistics, superlatives, categories, or other items related to the subject of the spread.

SCIENCE & TECHNOLOGY

LIFE-FORMS

WHAT DID DARWIN LEARN IN THE GALÁPAGOS?

Captions running along the side identify the primary illustration.

Glossary items define key words used in the spread or introduce new ideas closely related to those discussed in the spread.

Click It boxes recommend websites for you to visit to learn more about the subject of that spread.

Etymologies are offered in yellow type if they contribute to a sense of the word's use and meaning.

Biographies provide brief portraits of important people from history and the present day, always with portraits and sometimes with memorable quotations.

Fast Fact boxes highlight interesting pieces of information related to the subject.

Handy cross-references guide you to other sections of the book where related information can be found.

COUNTRIES of the WORLD

CHAPTER 9:
AN ALMANAC OF COUNTRIES OF THE WORLD

Chapter 9 provides comprehensive information about every country of today's world, organized in a way to pack lots of knowledge into a small space.

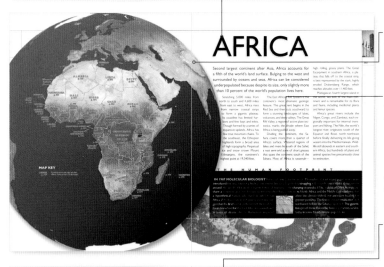

AFRICA

Sections within the chapter are organized by continent. Every continent is featured on its own spread, with information about its geography.

Each section opens with a labeled map of that continent. For further information on a country of interest, look up its name and page number on the continent map.

For each continent, you will also find a special feature, "The Human Footprint," that traces the migration of the human species through that region over time.

Within a section, countries are organized by region. Those near one another geographically are near one another in the pages of this book.

Country listings begin with the national flag, the commonly used name for that country, and the official name for that country.

Each country is represented with a set of demographics and trade statistics. This opening text box includes the following: the country's area in square miles; an up-to-date count of the country's population; the country's capital city and its population; the country's most recently reported literacy rate and life expectancy; the national currency; the country's per capita gross domestic product; and the primary products of that country, designated Industrial (IND), Agricultural (AGR), and Export (EXP).

Each country is represented by a brief overview of its geography, history, and government.

Locator maps at the bottom of each page help you find a country of interest on the continent map. Each country featured on the page is outlined in red on a detail map of the continent. Compare the detail map with the continent map on the opener to get the bigger geographical picture.

MAPS

& GLOBES

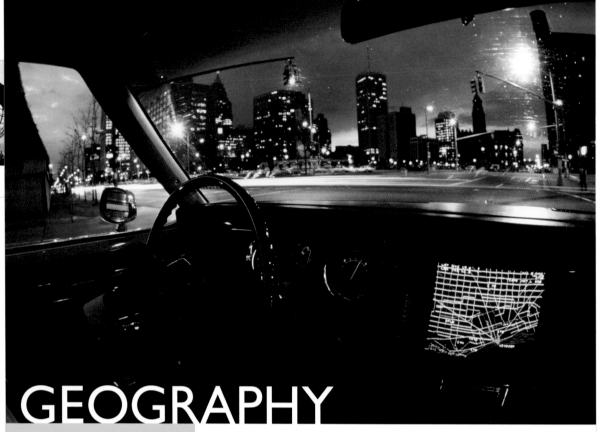

Electronic dashboard navigation, Detroit, Michigan

GEOGRAPHY

ince their earliest presence on Earth, humans have sought to make sense of their surroundings. Survival depended on understanding the behavior of a volcano, the flood cycles of a river, or the optimum time to cross a mountain pass—and humans developed ways to record and pass on such information. As they ventured from their places of origin, by land and by sea, people acquired a broader perspective of Earth's processes and of the patterns and impact of human settlement throughout the world.

Ancient cultures such as the Egyptian, Phoenician, and Chinese amassed geographical understanding, but few of those records survive, and so the Greeks have become today's main source of early knowledge. Homer's epics, *The Iliad* and *The Odyssey*, written in the ninth century B.C., reveal the Greeks as intrepid travelers and keen observers of distant lands. They also excelled in scientific inquiry. Aristotle, for example, sought to determine the size and nature of Earth in the fourth century B.C.

Geographic knowledge advanced exponentially during the heyday of

FOR MORE FACTS ON...

ANCIENT GREEK CIVILIZATION, HISTORY & CULTURE see *Greece & Persia*, CHAPTER 7, PAGES 274-5

THE RISE OF EARLY EUROPEAN EXPLORERS & THEIR EXPEDITIONS see *World Navigation*, CHAPTER 7, PAGES 292-3

exploration by both European and Asian explorers in the 15th, 16th, and 17th centuries. Mapping, surveying, and specimen collecting became stock activities on every voyage.

In the 21st century, a few computer clicks can bring up photo images or map information for much of Earth's surface. We take for granted the ability to get directions to almost anywhere we need to go, without our needing to plot the course on a map.

Modern science and information gathering have given geographers more insight than ever before, and modern technology allows it to be shared worldwide, but for many people the facts and terms lack a context. An understanding of geography, both physical and cultural, provides that context—ever more necessary and important, as global interactions and shared responsibility for Earth's future connect us all.

GLOSSARY

Geography: From the Greek *geo*, Earth, + *graphia*, write about or describe. The systematic study of the physical Earth and its human population—where things are and how they got there. The field is divided into two major areas: physical geography and human geography.

PTOLEMY / ANCIENT GEOGRAPHER

Born in Egypt of Greek ancestry, Claudius Ptolemy (ca A.D. 90–168) created a body of work synthesizing the Greco-Roman world's knowledge of cartography, mathematics, and astronomy. His eight-volume *Geography* offered instructions and information for preparing a world atlas, including a world map and 26 regional maps. He also refined a number of map projections and provided a list of some 8,000 place-names and their coordinates. *Almagest*, his 13-volume treatise on astronomy, posited a geocentric model of the solar system, and his four-book *Tetrabiblos* tried to reconcile astrology with more scientific matters. Ptolemy's influence on geography and cartography spread through Arabic translations made by Islamic scholars and influenced Near Eastern and Western geographic and cartographic thought for centuries.

THE SCOPE OF GEOGRAPHY

Today geography is rooted in location, but it involves more than the position of place-names on a map. It integrates methods and knowledge from many different disciplines and encompasses both the physical and the social sciences. It links all these disciplines to determine why things happen in a particular location or according to particular spatial patterns.

Physical geography incorporates geology, climatology, biology, ecology, hydrology, and other natural sciences. Human geography includes cultural anthropology, economics, political science, history, demography, and other social sciences. Cartography, which is the art and science of mapmaking, provides graphic representations of geographic settings.

Geographers also use other tools in their data gathering, analysis, and representation—tools including statistics, photographs, remotely captured images (such as satellite photos), and computer-generated graphics.

CLICK IT: National Geographic www.nationalgeographic.com

FAST FACT Trusting Ptolemy's concept of Earth's circumference, Columbus did not venture beyond the Caribbean.

FOR MORE FACTS ON...

THE DEVELOPMENT OF MODERN MAPPING METHODS *see Advances in Mapping*, CHAPTER 1, PAGES 28-9

HOW CONCEPTS OF THE WORLD HAVE EVOLVED THROUGH HISTORY *see Scientific Worldviews*, CHAPTER 8, PAGES 326-7

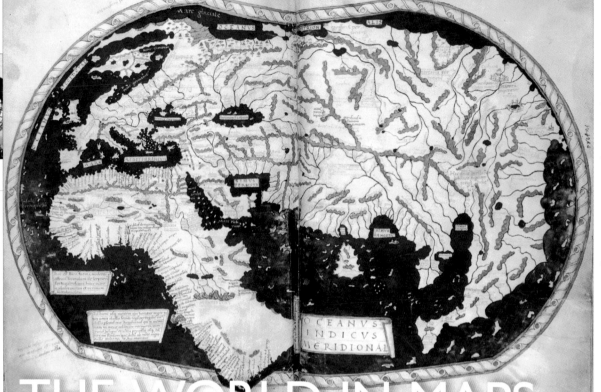

15th-century Venetian map of the known world: Europe, Africa, and Asia

THE WORLD IN MAPS

Think of how hard it is to peel an orange and press the resulting pieces of peel down flat on a table. That analogy represents the challenge faced by the mapmaker, who attempts to turn the spherical planet Earth into a flat visual representation. To tackle the challenge—getting the surface of a sphere to lie flat—cartographers use shapes that lend themselves to flattening, such as planes, cones, and cylinders, known as developable surfaces.

By applying mathematical calculations to the developable surfaces, they can transform Earth's features into flat forms. Those forms are called projections, and they represent the challenge of mapmaking through the centuries.

Projections inevitably result in distortions. Those distortions can be controlled to some degree by the choice of map shape, which depends on which part of the planet is of most interest to the cartographer.

Only where the surface directly touches the globe will the map be completely accurate. Away from these points of contact, Earth's features become stretched or squeezed in order to become flat.

FOR MORE FACTS ON...

ENVIRONMENTAL MAPPING, FROM BIOMES TO ECOREGIONS *see Biomes,* **CHAPTER 5, PAGES 194-5**

HOW MEASUREMENT DEVELOPED THROUGH HISTORY *see Counting & Measurement,* **CHAPTER 8, PAGES 322-3**

CHANGING FASHIONS IN WORLD MAPS

No one world map projection can do it all—accurate distance, direction shape, and area. Over the years, different projections have come to the forefront.

The Winkel Tripel projection, adopted in 1998 by the National Geographic Society, is most often chosen today for general reference.

The Robinson projection was favored for classrooms and textbooks from 1988 to 1998.

The Van der Grinten projection was used by the National Geographic Society for most of its political maps from 1922 into the 1980s.

The Mercator projection, centuries old and yet still broadly used, also distorts the relative sizes of landmasses in high latitudes.

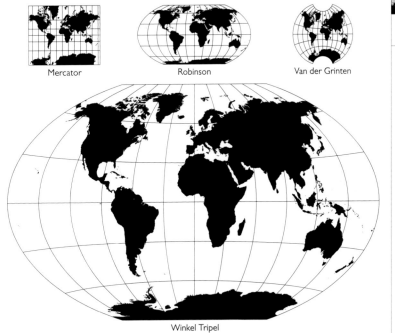

Mercator · Robinson · Van der Grinten

Winkel Tripel

G L O S S A R Y

Azimuth: In astronomy, gunnery, navigation, and other fields, two coordinates describing the position of an object above the Earth.

STANDARD MAP PROJECTIONS

CONICAL PROJECTIONS are made as if a large paper cone rested on the top of the globe, with its point above the North Pole and its bottom edge touching the globe somewhere north of the Equator. When the cone is cut, a flat map unfolds, shaped like a fan. Conical projections are best for showing areas in the middle latitudes.

CYLINDRICAL PROJECTIONS show the globe as if it were projected onto a large sheet of paper surrounding it. Those points around the center, near the Equator, appear accurately, but areas near the Poles are stretched, causing landmarks far to the north and south to look much larger than they really are.

AZIMUTHAL PROJECTIONS are also called plane or zenithal projections. To create these, the mapmaker designates one point of the globe as the center of the map—the point can be anywhere—and projects an image as if a flat piece of stiff paper were resting there.

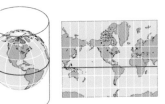

FOR MORE FACTS ON...

MAPPING THE IMPACT OF HUMANS ON THE ENVIRONMENT see *Human Impact*, **CHAPTER 6, PAGES 214-5**

SHIFTING BOUNDARIES AMONG THE WORLD'S COUNTRIES see *Nations & Alliances*, **CHAPTER 9, PAGES 358-9**

Gerardus Mercator, ca 1590

EARLY MAPPING

CIRCA 6000 B.C.
Earliest known map created in Iraq

1500 B.C.–A.D. 1000
Polynesians navigate Pacific Ocean

A.D. 1136
Map of China with grid system engraved on stone

1420–1460
Prince Henry the Navigator of Portugal advances navigation science

1540–1552
Münster maps continents

1569
Mercator introduces world projection

1570
Ortelius makes portable atlas

THE HISTORY OF MAPPING

Some form of mapmaking—whether scribbles in sand, measurements on chiseled stone, or sacred geography in songs and art—is common to all cultures. The earliest surviving maps and charts come from ancient Babylonia and Egypt. By the third millennium B.C., both possessed the necessary mathematical and drafting skills and the bureaucracy for surveying and mapping. Babylonian cartography was mostly practical, whereas Egyptian maps rendered mythical lands and routes to the afterlife.

The Greeks laid the scientific foundation of Western cartography while investigating the nature of the Earth and the universe. The Romans mostly mapped properties, town plans, and roads. At the same time, the Chinese incorporated art and verbal narrative into their maps, yet they also were concerned with military planning and state security. Japan and Korea tended to rely on China for their world maps, adding themselves to the fringes.

Religious cartography held sway in the Middle Ages, although the Arabs maintained classical intellectual traditions and developed their own Islamic mapmaking traditions as well.

The invention of the printing press and the rediscovery of Ptolemy's *Guide to Geography* sparked a revival in scientific cartography in western Europe, accelerated by voyages by the Spanish and Portuguese to Africa, the Americas, and the Spice Islands. The French became the first to conduct an official national land survey, producing 182 map sheets by 1787. The British adapted French techniques to produce the Great Trigonometrical Survey of India in the late 19th century.

FAST FACT America was first named on Waldseemüller's 1507 world map.

FOR MORE FACTS ON...

ANCIENT CHINESE DYNASTIES see China 2200 B.C.-A.D. 500, **CHAPTER 7, PAGES 272-3**

DEVELOPMENTS DURING THE MIDDLE AGES see Middle Ages 500-1000 & Middle Ages 1000-1500, **CHAPTER 7, PAGES 278-81**

ORTELIUS & MERCATOR, PIONEERING MAPMAKERS

As a young man, Flemish scholar and geographer Abraham Ortelius (1527–1598) was known for skillfully illuminating manuscripts and for his collection of books and coins. Once established as a cartographer, he revolutionized the Renaissance world with the publication in 1570 of *Theatrum Orbis Terrarum,* or *Theater of the World.* It is known as the first modern atlas.

The *Theatrum* proved a huge success and helped transfer the center of the European map trade from Rome and Venice to Antwerp, his home. Some 7,300 copies were printed in 31 editions and seven languages and sold at a cost equivalent to about $1,630 today, making Ortelius very wealthy.

The *Theatrum* included a one-page reduction of the world projection drawn by Ortelius's friend and fellow Flemish cartographer Gerardus Mercator (1512–1594). First published in 1569, Mercator's projection was designed to aid navigation. With all lines of latitude and longitude depicted as straight lines, mariners could more easily plot a course over a long distance.

Despite its original nautical purpose, the Mercator projection, with modifications, became a standard two-dimensional representation of the world until well into the 20th century. Generations of schoolchildren have studied Mercator's projection, which led them to believe that Greenland and Africa were roughly the same size—although Africa is in fact some 14 times larger.

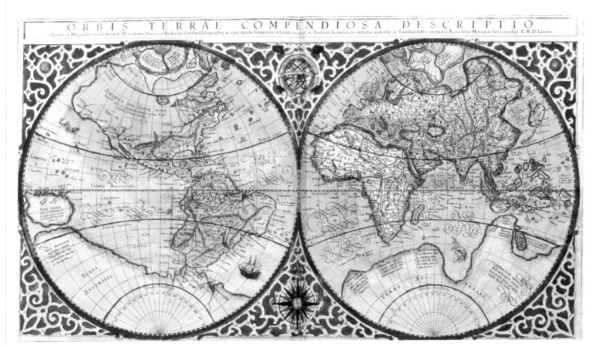

MERCATOR'S GROUNDBREAKING MAP OF 1585 used techniques that distorted the size and shape of landmasses but created a set of lines and angles that allowed sailing ships to navigate the world's oceans. His maps and globes were works of art as well, with elegant calligraphy and ornaments.

G L O S S A R Y

Atlas: Named after Atlas, figure in ancient Greek mythology, believed to hold Earth on his shoulders. A collection of maps or charts, usually bound together, and often containing pictures, tabular data, facts about areas, and indexes of place-names keyed to coordinates of latitude and longitude or to a locational grid with numbers and letters along the sides of maps.

FOR MORE FACTS ON...

MAPPING TECHNIQUES INCLUDING THE MERCATOR PROJECTION see *The World in Maps* **CHAPTER 1, PAGES 18-19**

EARLY EXPLORATIONS OF EARTH'S OCEANS see *World Navigation 1492-1522,* **CHAPTER 7, PAGES 292-3**

The Unisphere, built for the 1964 World's Fair in New York: world's biggest globe

GLOBES

GREAT GLOBES

FIRST
Made by Crates of Mallus, ancient Greek philosopher, in 150 B.C.

OLDEST SURVIVING
Marble celestial globe on the Roman sculpture "Farnese Atlas," circa A.D. 150

OLDEST SURVIVING TERRESTRIAL
Behaim's Erdapfel, Nürnberg, 1492

POPULAR PAIR
Mercator's matching terrestrial and celestial globes, sold throughout Europe, 1541–1551

GLOBES FOR A KING
Two, each 13 feet tall, made for Louis XIV by Coronelli, 1680

A globe can be terrestrial—a spherical representation of the Earth—or celestial—a spherical representation of the heavens. Both types were constructed in ancient Greece and China. The earliest globes were small and made of marble, metal, or wood, with etched or painted surfaces. The earliest known celestial globe forms part of the "Farnese Atlas," a Roman copy of a Greek statue. Atlas holds a sphere some 25 inches across showing the constellations.

In 1492 the Nürnberg mapmaker Martin Behaim made a globe from a mold using wood strips, plaster, and fiber. Soon other mapmakers were covering balls with map segments called globe gores, printed map segments with tapered points. Dutch artist Albrecht Dürer published rules for preparing globe gores in 1525. A more formal illustrated guide appeared in 1527, published in Basel by Henricus Glareanus. He proposed using 12 globe segments, each representing 30 degrees of longitude and extending from Pole to Pole.

Antonio Florian's 1555 world map portrays the Northern and Southern

FOR MORE FACTS ON...

EARLY METHODS OF CARTOGRAPHY see How Could the Ancients Measure the Earth?, **CHAPTER 1, PAGE 31**

THE HISTORY, EMPERORS & WORLD OF ANCIENT ROME see Rome 500 B.C.-A.D. 500, **CHAPTER 7, PAGES 276-7**

Hemispheres, both subdivided into 36 gores of ten degrees. It may have been intended as a flat map or as the surface cover for a globe, each segment to be cut, moistened, stretched, and pasted over a ten-inch sphere. Today terrestrial globes depict Earth's physical features and may include features on the ocean floor as well. Most globes commonly show political features such as countries and cities. Globes typically are mounted with the axis tilted at 23½°, to simulate Earth's inclination as it orbits the sun. Globes also depict other spheres, such as the moon.

G L O S S A R Y

Geocentric: From Greek *ge*, earth + *kentron*, center. Any theory of the structure of the solar system or the universe in which Earth is assumed to be at the center of all. **/ Heliocentric:** From Greek *helios*, sun + *kentron*, center. A cosmological model in which the sun is assumed to lie at or near a central point while Earth and other bodies rotate around it.

WHAT IS AN ARMILLARY SPHERE?

An armillary sphere is a globe made of movable, concentric rings that depict such things as horizon, meridian, Equator, tropics, and polar circles. The earliest known complete armillary is attributed to the Greeks in the early second century A.D. Ptolemy created one to promote his geocentric vision of the cosmos. In 1543, German mathematician Caspar Vogel constructed an armillary sphere that supported Ptolemy's theory. In the same year, Copernicus published his revolutionary treatise placing the sun at the center of the solar system.

Afterward, Ptolemaic and Copernican spheres were exhibited together to display the differences between the two versions of the cosmos.

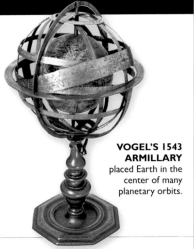

VOGEL'S 1543 ARMILLARY
placed Earth in the center of many planetary orbits.

 The Egyptian Nile surpasses all rivers of the earth in sweetness of taste, length of course, and utility. **— IBN BATTUTA, 1325**

IBN BATTUTA / CHRONICLER OF TRAVELS

Among the wide-ranging Arab historian-geographers of the Middle Ages, Ibn Battuta (1304–1369) covered more distance than anyone. For all his journeys he earned the epithet Traveler of Islam. His 29 years of travels began in 1325, when at the age of 21 he undertook the pilgrimage to Mecca on the Arabian peninsula—some 3,000 miles from his birthplace in Morocco, in western Africa. For most of the rest of his life, his wanderlust kept him on the move through the continents of Asia, Africa, and Europe. In all, he traveled 75,000 miles, three times the distance covered by Marco Polo. The narrative of his journeys, titled *Rihlah*, or *Travels*, remains one of the premier sources of early cultural geography.

CLICK IT: Yale University Library Map Collection www.library.yale.edu/mapcoll

FOR MORE FACTS ON...

THE ANCIENT CULTURES OF AFRICA see *Africa 500-1500*, **CHAPTER 7, PAGES 282-3**

THE PTOLEMAIC AND COPERNICAN VISIONS OF THE COSMOS see *Scientific Worldviews*, **CHAPTER 8, PAGES 326-7**

MAPMAKING

MODERN MAPS

1768-1779
Capt. Cook maps Pacific lands

1801-1803
England's Flinders charts Australian coastline

1803-1806
Lewis and Clark receive cartography help from Shoshone chief Cameahwait

1838-1843
Frémont maps U.S. west of Mississippi

1940s & 1950s
Pruitt encourages remote sensing and use of satellites in mapmaking

1950s & 1960s
Tharp creates seafloor maps that become basis for plate tectonics theory

apmaking involves accurate measurement. Today almost every inch of Earth's land area has been mapped—some areas in greater detail than others. Oceans and seafloors have been extensively charted, too, though generally in less detail than the land. Maps must also be continuously revised to reflect changes in boundaries, place-names, human structures, and natural phenomena.

Surveying in the broad sense is the science of determining the exact size, shape, and location of a given land or undersea area. Some surveying still is done on the ground using mathematical methods such as triangulation and traditional instruments such as theodolites and tellurometers—or their electronic equivalents.

Mapping coasts and charting the open seas involves another set of measuring techniques that use some of the same mathematical methods as land-based surveying. Data gathering also relies on instruments that have enabled navigators and cartographers to take readings of celestial bodies to determine location and distance.

FOR MORE FACTS ON...

THE HISTORY OF CELESTIAL BODY OBSERVATION *see Observation,* **CHAPTER 2, PAGES 68-9**

THE EXPANSION OF URBAN POPULATIONS & CITY PLANNING *see Cities,* **CHAPTER 6, PAGES 260-1**

MAPS TELL STORIES

Maps reveal a lot about their makers. Cartographers may often favor their own countries or regions in map portrayals. On his 1402 world map, Chinese cartographer Kwon Kun noted that "the world is very wide," extending "from China in the center to the four seas at the outer limits." This could be seen as a form of persuasive cartography—using maps to create an impression, prove a point, or promote propaganda. Propaganda maps proliferated during World Wars I and II and in the intervening years, as well as during the Cold War. Such maps still are being created, but broader access to worldwide information makes it more difficult to sustain such false impressions.

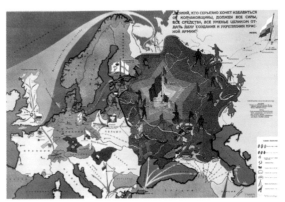

WITH AREAS OF BOLSHEVIK CONTROL blazing red and stalwart soldiers patrolling the territory, this state-printed 1928 map tells Russia's version of the Civil War of 1919–1921.

G L O S S A R Y

Meridian: An imaginary north-south line that connects Earth's Poles; it is used to indicate longitude. **/ Theodolite:** Basic surveying instrument used to measure horizontal and vertical angles, consisting of a mounted, swiveling telescope with a level; a transit is a theodolite mounted so that it can be reversed. **/ Tellurometer:** A device that measures the round-trip travel of reflected microwaves to calculate distance.

TIME-TESTED MAPMAKING INSTRUMENTS

Although GPS and electronic equipment have supplanted traditional surveying and navigational equipment, masses of fundamental knowledge were collected through the use of these tools through many centuries.

THE MAGNETIC COMPASS was perfected at the end of the 13th century and, paired with a card bearing cardinal directions, allowed for the development of nautical sailing charts and, in later years, terrestrial maps.

TELESCOPES were not invented by Galileo, but he was likely the first to use one for astronomical observations. Newton's telescope used mirrors and reflected light. Now astronomers view a screen or photograph.

THE ASTROLABE originated in the sixth century as a tool to tell time and observe the heavens. Medieval astrolabes helped calculate the position of the sun and stars with respect to the horizon and the meridian.

A SEXTANT measures the angle between the horizon and a celestial body in order to determine latitude and longitude. Angle readings, paired with the exact time of day, are correlated with data in published tables.

CLICK IT: National Geodetic Survey www.ngs.noaa.gov

FAST FACT The world's first astrolabes were used by Muslims to determine prayer times and the direction of Mecca.

FOR MORE FACTS ON...

TRAVEL & MOVEMENT AROUND THE WORLD AS PART OF HUMAN CULTURE see Transportation, **CHAPTER 6, PAGES 252-3**

EXPLORATION IN HUMAN HISTORY see World Navigation 1492-1522, **CHAPTER 7, PAGES 292-3**

MAPMAKING
MODERN MAPS

Scientific methods of surveying and mapping expanded greatly in the 17th, 18th, and 19th centuries, in part due to more sophisticated mathematical applications as well as rigorous, comprehensive surveys of large areas.

Surveying today often employs elements of remote sensing—obtaining information about an object or an area from a distance. Looking down on a city from the top of a tall building or on a village from the top of a tall mountain is a form of remote sensing. Mapmakers use more sophisticated methods to get similar results.

Aerial photography, used to some extent during World War I, became widespread during World War II as a remote-sensing tool in mapmaking. It eliminated much of the legwork for surveyors and allowed precise surveying of some otherwise inaccessible places.

Remote sensing by radar, or radio waves, and sonar, or sound waves, provides another way to record surface features of the land or the ocean floor. In both methods, distance is calculated from the time it takes the waves to travel to and from the target area.

Remotely sensed images vary by the kind of resolution they portray.

Spatial resolution refers to how sharp an image is. Greater distance usually equates with fuzzier images.

Spectral resolution refers to which part of the light spectrum is being captured and can include such wavelengths as visible light or infrared light.

Temporal resolution refers to the time frame represented. This technique uses sequential images of an area to show changes over a period of time.

Fires
Fishing fleets
Human settlement lights
Natural gas flares

LIGHTS OF THE WORLD, detected by satellite and imaged on a world map, show the concentrated use of electricity but not necessarily the concentration of human habitation. Many people—in China and Africa, for example—live in close quarters but do not have electric lighting.

FOR MORE FACTS ON...

THE VISIBLE SPECTRUM & THE PHENOMENON OF LIGHT ON EARTH see *Light*, **CHAPTER 3, PAGES 108-9**

THE CHANGING DEMOGRAPHICS OF HUMANS ON EARTH see *World Population*, **CHAPTER 6, PAGES 250-1**

AERIAL MAPPING

Wilbur Wright took the first aerial photographs from an airplane during a flight over Italy in 1909. By 1918, during World War I, French aerial units were taking 10,000 aerial photos daily, mostly for interpretation. The British Expeditionary Force in Egypt experimented with using aerial photographs to prepare maps. By mid-century, aerial photographers and cartographers were preparing basic topographic map coverage for much of the world.

Measurements were taken directly from photographs, which became substitutes for costly and time-consuming ground surveys. Later, with the introduction of sensing devices beyond the normal visual range of film, many new kinds of maps were produced.

WINGED COMBAT during World War I pushed the development of photography forward and inspired imaging techniques that advanced mapmaking tremendously for decades after.

CLICK IT: MapMachine maps.nationalgeographic.com/map-machine

G L O S S A R Y

Photogrammetry: Technique that uses terrestrial and aerial photographs for mapmaking and surveying. **/ Trimetrogon Method:** System of aerial photography using three wide-angle cameras to photograph territory from horizon to horizon across line of flight from 20,000 feet.

MAPPING THE OCEANS

Sonar plays the major role in surveying the ocean floor—taking measurements on the depth and form of features on the seabed. Sonar is based on the principle of the echo: Sound waves are bounced to the ocean bottom and back, with distance determined by the time this process takes.

In multibeam sonar, the sound source and receiver are built into the hull of the ship, and the sonar system scans a wide area as the ship moves along. In sidescan sonar, the sound originates in a towed source.

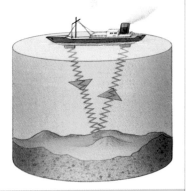

SONAR in its simplest form: Sound waves emanate from a ship, bounce off the ocean floor, and are picked up on their return by a receiver on the ship.

CLICK IT: National Atlas nationalatlas.gov

FAST FACT From the deepest ocean bottoms, sound waves take fewer than 15 seconds to return to the surface.

FOR MORE FACTS ON...

THE DEVELOPMENT OF AERIAL PHOTOGRAPHY IN WORLD WAR I see World Wars: Depression 1929-39, **CHAPTER 7, PAGE 313**

WHAT WE KNOW ABOUT EARTH'S OCEANS see Oceans, **CHAPTER 3, PAGES 112-5**

ADVANCES IN MAPPING

Recent developments in mapping have redefined cartography. Personal computers and GPS equipment, remote-sensing satellites, and the Internet have changed the ways map data are collected, manipulated, shared, and used.

The cartographic applications of remote sensing are nearly limitless, what with mapping and charting from space using satellites, space telescopes, and spacecraft in combination with many-layered software such as geographic information systems (GIS) and numerous databases. The surface of Earth is now pictured daily by numerous remote-sensing satellites, producing vast archives of mappable data that are received, analyzed, and maintained by cartographers, scientists, and technicians around the world.

Today most natural processes and the effects of many human activities can be rendered into map form as well, revealing Earth's secrets and giving a good picture of where the planet has been and where it is headed.

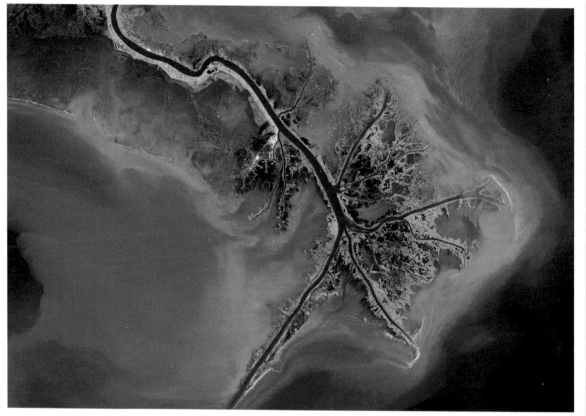

THE MISSISSIPPI RIVER DELTA, as imaged by the Landsat 7, spreads out in a filigree of blue and green. First launched by NASA and the U.S. Geological Survey in 1972, Landsat represents the world's longest continuously acquired collection of space-based remote-sensing landform data.

FOR MORE FACTS ON...

THE GEOGRAPHY OF RIVERS ON PLANET EARTH see Rivers, **CHAPTER 3, PAGES 116-7**
+
HOW THE INTERNET WORKS AROUND THE WORLD see The Internet, **CHAPTER 8, PAGES 348-9**

WHAT IS LANDSAT?

Landsat is a series of unmanned scientific satellites equipped with cameras, launched by the United States beginning in 1972. With a primary mission of collecting information about Earth's natural resources and monitoring atmospheric and oceanic conditions, Landsat collects surface images in bands of 115 miles square and has the capability to rephotograph each area every 18 days. Overall, the Landsat system provides low- and medium-resolution mapping.

Newer Landsat satellites have more data-gathering equipment, including a thematic mapper with resolution in seven spectral bands, or wavelengths of light.

In 1985 Landsat became private but was transferred back to government control in 1992. New satellites are planned, including in 2012 Landsat Data Continuity Mission (Landsat 8).

CLICK IT: NASA Landsat Program landsat.gsfc.nasa.gov

HOW DOES GPS WORK?

GPS—global positioning system—is a space-age version of triangulation. Originally developed for military use, GPS has three components: satellites orbiting Earth, master control stations around the world, and receivers installed in locations ranging from naval destroyers to private golf carts.

In the U.S. GPS system, two dozen Navstar satellites orbit the planet every 12 hours, following six different orbits. Three additional satellites orbit as backup. The satellites contain atomic clocks that send precise times with each signal. The control stations monitor the satellites, using remote-controlled on-board thrusters to manage their positions.

When a GPS user on land or sea calls for location information, signals pass from orbiting satellites to that user's receiver. The length of time taken by the transmissions—usually a fraction of a second—helps determine distance to a point on an imaginary sphere, and the user's latitude and longitude can be calculated by using the mathematics of triangulation. Three satellites would suffice, but more provide redundancy and compensate for inaccuracies.

GPS signals are broadcast on two different frequencies, one for military use and one for civilian use. Civilian augmentation can provide precise location to within 0.4 of an inch.

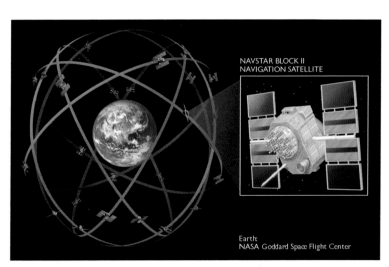

NAVSTAR BLOCK II
NAVIGATION SATELLITE

Earth:
NASA Goddard Space Flight Center

THE NAVSTAR SATELLITE SYSTEM contains 24 orbiting satellites, similar to Block II (above, right). Signals from Earth-based GPS equipment send and receive information from these satellites, thus ascertaining latitude and longitude position.

CLICK IT: Real-Time Satellite Tracking science.nasa.gov/realtime

FAST FACT At any time or place on Earth, a Navstar GPS receiver gets signals from 6 of the system's 24 satellites.

FOR MORE FACTS ON...

SPACE TELESCOPES TODAY see *Observation: Modern Methods,* **CHAPTER 2, PAGES 70-1**

METHODS FOR GATHERING INFORMATION ABOUT THE WEATHER see *Weather: Predictions,* **CHAPTER 5, PAGES 184-5**

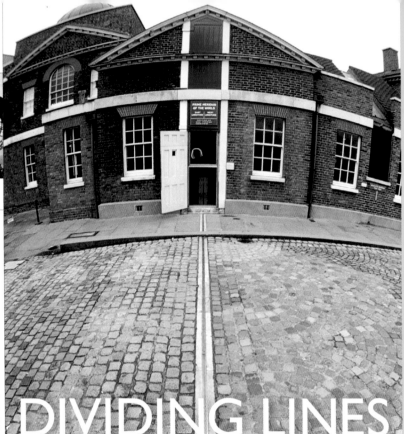

LONGITUDE

1514
Werner proposes lunar distance method

1530
Frisius suggests importance of clock

1598
Philip III of Spain offers prize

1616
Galileo calculates by Jupiter's moons

1634
Morin plans moon observatory

1657
Huygens invents pendulum clock

1714
English Parliament offers prize

1727-1761
Harrison perfects clock for use at sea

DIVIDING LINES

Cartographers need lines of reference to locate places on maps. Their reference system, which originated with the ancient Greeks, uses a grid of lines known as latitude (parallels) and longitude (meridians), with distances between them measured in degrees of a circle. Latitude measures angular distance north and south of the Equator, which is assigned 0° latitude.

All lines of latitude are parallel to the Equator. Latitude divides Earth into the Northern and Southern Hemispheres. Longitude measures angular distance east and west of the prime meridian, which is assigned 0° longitude. An 1884 international agreement set the prime meridian in Greenwich, England. All lines of longitude converge at the North and South Poles.

The measure of a degree of latitude or longitude varies according to distance from the Equator. Longitude varies more than latitude. At the Equator, a degree of latitude is equal to 68.708 miles and a degree of longitude equals 69.171 miles.

There are other sorts of dividing lines in maps and globes of the world. The world is divided politically into independent countries, delineated by boundary lines. International boundaries only occasionally mark true geographical or cultural boundaries; they are a complex artifact of territorial rights, colonialism, conquest, religious conversions, conflicts, and alliances.

The lines on maps and globes can describe many other features: transportation routes such as roads, railroad tracks, and ferry lines; water features such as rivers and wetlands; and other physical features including cliffs, hills, mountains, and valleys that represent changes in elevation.

FAST FACT A map needs only four colors to ensure that regions with common borders do not have the same color.

FOR MORE FACTS ON...

EARTH'S DEFINING FEATURES & THE FORCES THAT INFLUENCE THEIR SHAPE see *Landforms*, CHAPTER 3, PAGES 98-101

THE ROLE OF GEOGRAPHY IN THE MEASUREMENT OF TIME see *Telling Time*, CHAPTER 8, PAGES 324-5

WHY ARE THERE 360 DEGREES IN A CIRCLE?

A degree is a fraction of a circle, and there are 360 degrees in each of the imaginary circles that describe the surface of the Earth. The number 360 in this context usually is attributed to the Babylonians, who devised a base-60 number system. (Our modern system is base 10.) They probably were the first to divide a circle into 360 degrees (6 x 60). Some historians think that the base-60 system derives from the approximate length in days of a calendar year, but others claim that the Babylonians probably chose 60 because it is divisible by so many other numbers. Hipparchus, who invented the formal system of latitude and longitude, divided each Earth circle into 360 degrees, each degree having 60 minutes and each minute having 60 seconds.

G L O S S A R Y

Great circle: The shortest course between two points on the surface of a sphere. It lies in a plane that intersects the sphere's center.

HOW COULD THE ANCIENTS MEASURE THE EARTH?

The early geographer Eratosthenes (ca 276-194 B.C.), head of the great library at Alexandria in Egypt, created maps of the known world, from the British Isles to Sri Lanka and from the Caspian Sea to Ethiopia. He devised a mapping system using meridians and parallels and thus presaged latitude and longitude, which was conceived a century later.

Eratosthenes also accurately estimated the circumference of the Earth: His calculation was fewer than 4,000 miles off from the actual measurement of 24,840 miles. He noted the position of the sun at the summer solstice at two different locations, and, assuming that the Earth was a sphere, multiplied the distance between the two by the portion of a circle represented by that distance. Minor errors, compounded, contributed to his overestimation.

Few geographers accepted his calculation, preferring a smaller number generated by another geographer. To Eratosthenes, however, a larger Earth circumference suggested that all the known seas must be connected into one large ocean.

Greek astronomer Hipparchus (ca 190-126 B.C.) contributed significantly to the science of mapmaking as well. After plotting the position of bright stars using latitude and longitude, Hipparchus developed a measurement system using 360° as a baseline from which to plot positions on the Earth's surface.

1544 WORLD MAP, painted on vellum with ink and watercolor by Battista Agnese in Genoa, Italy, displays the route taken by Ferdinand Magellan's expedition around the world, 1519-1521.

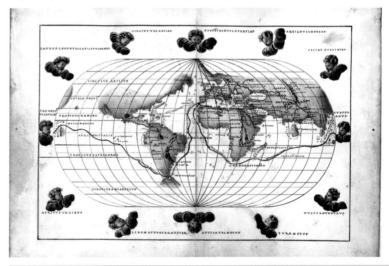

CLICK IT: Perry-Castañeda Map Collection www.lib.utexas.edu/maps

FOR MORE FACTS ON...

THE HISTORY & CULTURE OF ANCIENT GREECE see *Greece & Persia 1600 B.C.-A.D.500,* **CHAPTER 7, PAGES 274-5**

EARLY METHODS OF CALCULATION see *Counting & Measurement,* **CHAPTER 8, PAGES 322-3**

TIME ZONES

The concept of time is built into the biological rhythm of living things. In this scheme, time and sunlight are inextricably linked: Morning glories open and roosters crow at dawn, night-blooming jasmine unfurls and fireflies begin their amatory signaling at dusk. Time operates on a larger, seasonal scale as well. Geese and other birds migrate at the same time each year; bears hibernate at the onset of winter.

Early humans responded to the same kinds of biological rhythms, but over time they developed ways to standardize measures of time in order to predict and gain control over events. The positions of the sun and the other stars in the sky during Earth's rotation provide the fundamental unit: the day. The Earth does not rotate at a uniform speed, so the length of all solar days in a year have been averaged, giving us a 24-hour day.

Back when there was little communication among different areas, each town set its clocks by observing the sun's position. When it was noon in Washington, D.C., it was 12:12 p.m. in New York City. As transportation systems advanced, especially the railroads, the need for a standardized time system increased. In the United States, this happened in 1883, when the country's 60° of longitude was divided into four time zones. All the localities in a zone would observe the time at the center of the zone. These four zones still broadly define today's eastern, central, mountain, and Pacific time zones.

Soon a system of global time zones was created, using the longitudinal line that runs through Greenwich, England, as the prime meridian. Since then, continuing small adjustments have been made to national and international time-zone systems.

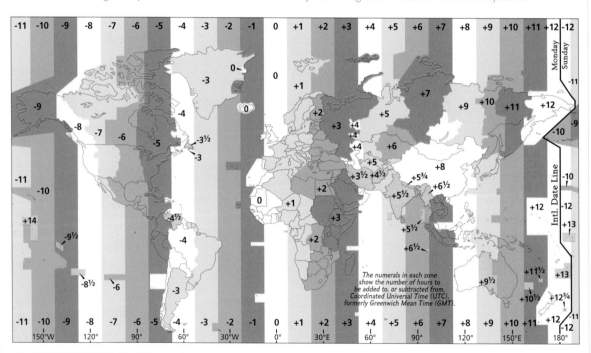

AN INTERNATIONAL TIME-ZONE SYSTEM, established in 1884, divided the globe into 24 zones with meridians at 15° intervals. The prime meridian, 0° longitude, was set at Greenwich, England, with an international date line at 180°, halfway around the world from Greenwich.

FOR MORE FACTS ON...

THE PRIME MERIDIAN & LONGITUDE & LATITUDE see *Dividing Lines,* **CHAPTER 1, PAGES 30-1**

GLOBALIZATION AS A DEVELOPMENT IN WORLD HISTORY see *Globalization 1991-Present,* **CHAPTER 7, PAGES 318-9**

WHERE DOES ONE DAY END AND THE NEXT BEGIN?

In theory, the international date line represents the 180° meridian of longitude. When this meridian is crossed from west to east, the date advances by one day. In crossing the line in the opposite direction, from east to west, the date reverts by one day. In reality, however, a number of situations cause adjustments to the international date line. Political frontiers, such as Russia's Kamchatka Peninsula, push out the line to keep a nation's territory intact, datewise. Similarly, the line takes detours to keep together all islands in some Pacific Ocean groups. These local modifications move the international date line off the 180° meridian for much of its length.

CAN CLOCKS SAVE DAYLIGHT?

During World War I, a number of countries pushed their clocks forward an hour to extend daylight as an energy-saving measure. This concept was expanded during World War II, with many countries observing a one-hour advancement year-round.

In the United States, the adjustment of daylight hours lasted continuously, from February 9, 1942, to September 30, 1945. To gain an even greater benefit during the war, Britain instituted a two-hour extension known as "double summer time" in the summer that reverted to a single-hour extension in the winter.

Many countries retained a partial-year daylight adjustment after the war, and others adopted it. Congressional measures in the United States, beginning in 1966 and continuing to 2005, have instituted the plan nationally. Currently daylight saving time in the U.S. starts the second Sunday in March and ends the first Sunday in November.

Today, some 70 countries worldwide observe summer daylight saving time. Some have adopted and then rejected the plan, including Japan and China. Numerous social, economic, and political influences affect the decision to keep, extend, or discontinue daylight saving time.

GLOSSARY

Greenwich Mean Time: Former name for mean solar time at the longitude 0°, or Greenwich meridian. Now officially called Universal time, although GMT is still used widely, especially in English-speaking countries.

WHY DO WE NEED LEAP YEARS?

Since it takes Earth approximately 365¼ days to orbit the sun, an extra day's worth of time accumulates every four years. In a leap year, February receives an extra day to compensate for the difference between the astronomical year and the calendar year.

If no adjustment were made, the calendar and the seasons would drift apart by 24 days every 100 years. The plan of adding a day every four years was devised by the Egyptians. The Romans created a standard leap day, February 29, in 46 B.C.

Adding one day per four years didn't perfectly correct the problem, however, because Earth orbits in 11 minutes and 14 seconds less than 365¼ days. A correction, established in 1582, adds a leap day only to century years divisible by 400. Thus 2000 was a leap year, but 2100, 2200, and 2300 will not be.

CLICK IT: World Clock www.timeanddate.com/worldclock

FAST FACT Legend has it that Benjamin Franklin invented daylight saving time in order to extend his evening chess games. He advocated that adjusting the clocks seasonally would help economize on candles.

FOR MORE FACTS ON...

DEVELOPMENTS IN THE MEASUREMENT OF TIME & THE MODERN CALENDAR see *Telling Time*, **CHAPTER 8, PAGES 324-5**

COOPERATION AMONG THE WORLD'S COUNTRIES see *Nations & Alliances*, **CHAPTER 9, PAGES 358-9**

DIVIDING LINES

THE POLES

The Earth rotates around an axis, an invisible line passing from one end of the sphere, symmetrically through its center, and out the other end of the sphere. The ends are known as the North and South Poles. The Poles exist in three forms—geographic, magnetic, and geomagnetic—each slightly different in location.

Geographic poles are fixed by the axis of Earth's rotation and indicated on globes and maps at the congruence of lines of latitude and longitude. Magnetic poles are indicated by compass needles that line up with Earth's magnetic field. Geomagnetic poles are points where the axis of the magnetic field intersects with Earth's surface.

The location of the Poles also changes because of the nature of planet Earth. Earth's spin on its axis is not stable: The planet experiences wobbling, a side-to-side motion. Some wobbling, attributable to the flattening of the planet as it rotates, occurs over a 14-month period and is likely reinforced in its momentum by atmospheric and oceanic events. Because of this wobble, the geographic location of the Poles moves by some 9 to 18 feet. Another wobble is probably caused by a yearly high-pressure weather system that settles over Siberia and unbalances the Earth, creating a wobble of about 9 feet.

Yet another kind of wobble probably emanates from gravity pulling on the Earth's inner core. Earth's wobble, the changes in geomagnetic fields, and the rotation of the inner core all seem to be tied together in ways that are not fully understood. Nevertheless, they make the Poles hard to pinpoint.

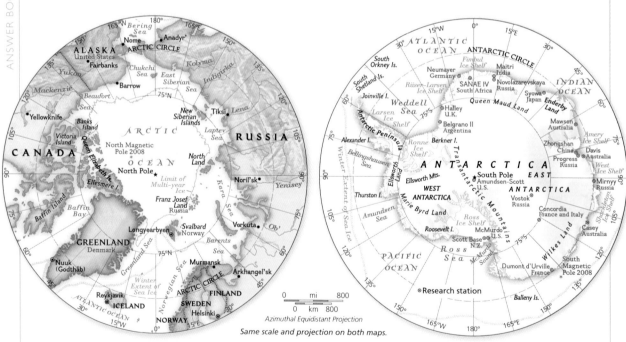

Azimuthal Equidistant Projection
Same scale and projection on both maps.

NOT UNTIL THE EARLY 20TH CENTURY did explorers reach the North and South Poles and gather information needed to map them.

FOR MORE FACTS ON...

THE BIOME FOUND AT EARTH'S POLAR EXTREMES see *Tundra & Ice Cap*, **CHAPTER 5, PAGES 210-1**

ANTARCTICA & ITS POLITICAL STATUS IN THE WORLD TODAY see *Nations & Alliances*, **CHAPTER 9, PAGE 359**

WHAT IS GEOMAGNETISM?

Scientists believe that Earth's magnetism arises from electric currents generated by the movement of hot liquid iron in its core. The currents create a magnetic field with invisible lines of force flowing between Earth's geomagnetic poles. These are not the same as the North and South Poles and, more significant, they are not stationary. The geomagnetic poles mark the ends of the axis of Earth's magnetic field.

In 1971 a group of scientists investigating a 30,000-year-old aboriginal campsite in Australia discovered that the fire's heat had allowed iron particles in the stones to realign with Earth's magnetic field at the time. What's more, the iron particles pointed south, indicating that magnetic north at that time must have been somewhere in the Antarctic. The discovery confirmed other recent reversals of the Earth's magnetic field.

It is now understood that major reversals in Earth's magnetic field occur about every half million years. Shorter flips, lasting a few thousand to 200,000 years, occur at other times. These reversals are clearly recorded in the rocks created in the seafloor's Mid-Ocean Ridge, which are carried away from the ridge by shifting ocean-floor plates.

Earth's magnetic field dominates a region called the magnetosphere, which wraps around the planet and the atmosphere.

Solar wind—charged particles flowing from the sun—presses the magnetosphere against Earth on the side facing the sun and stretches it on the shadow side.

Nevertheless, some particles of solar wind do leak through and are trapped in the Van Allen belts. When they hit atoms of gas in the upper atmosphere near the geomagnetic poles, they produce the eerie light displays that are called auroras.

CLICK IT: Polar History www.south-pole.com

G L O S S A R Y

Van Allen belts: Named for American physicist James Van Allen. Two doughnut-shaped magnetic rings around Earth that contain charged particles trapped from the solar wind, discovered in 1958 by the Explorer I satellite.

 East, west, and north had disappeared for us. Only one direction remained, and that was south.
— **ROBERT E. PEARY, 1910**

ROBERT PEARY / ARCTIC EXPLORER

A career naval officer, Robert Edwin Peary (1856–1920) had a passion for Arctic exploration. In 1891 he accepted an American flag from the President of the fledgling National Geographic Society, who told him to "place it as far north on this planet as you possibly can!" Peary made five tries for the Pole. In 1909, with his African-American sledger Matthew Henson, four Eskimos, and 40 dogs, he left base camp on northern Ellesmere Island and reported reaching the Pole on April 6, where he spent 30 hours of study and photography. Peary was an instant hero, but his achievement evoked skepticism. Investigators ultimately concluded that Peary got within 60 miles of the North Pole.

FAST FACT The weight of the Antarctic ice cap deforms the shape of the Earth.

FOR MORE FACTS ON...

GEOGRAPHIC SOCIETIES AROUND THE WORLD see *The World in Maps*, **CHAPTER 1, PAGE 18**

THE CAUSE & EFFECTS ON EARTH OF SOLAR WIND see *The Sun: Solar Details*, **CHAPTER 2, PAGE 57**

EQUATOR & TROPICS

The Equator and the tropics are represented by imaginary lines that geographers over the centuries have assigned to positions on the Earth that correspond to certain mathematical, astronomical, and climatological phenomena.

The Equator is an imaginary line circling the Earth, halfway between and always equidistant from the North and South Poles. It is assigned the latitude of 0°, the only line of latitude, or parallel, that is a great circle. (All other great circles are lines of longitude, or meridians.)

Locations along the Equator receive the sun's rays most directly year-round and therefore are always warm, except in high mountains.

Any great circle around the Earth divides it into two equal halves called hemispheres. The Equator divides the Earth into the Northern and Southern Hemispheres. The Earth also can be divided into hemispheres along specific lines of longitude. For example, the 20° W meridian and the 160° E meridian divide the planet into the Eastern and Western Hemispheres. The Eastern Hemisphere is commonly defined as Europe, Africa, Asia, Australia, and New Zealand, and the Western Hemisphere as North and South America.

The tropics is the name given to the region that lies between the 23° 30' line of latitude north of the Equator and the line of latitude 23° 30' south of the Equator. These lines of latitude, or parallels, are known as the Tropic of Cancer and the Tropic of Capricorn, respectively.

The tropics encompass 36 percent of the Earth's land, including parts of North and South America, Africa, Asia, and Australia. The term subtropics refers to the zones between the Tropics of Cancer and Capricorn and 40° north and south of the Equator.

The tropics generally experience warm temperatures year-round, with monthly averages between 77° and 82°F. The warm temperatures primarily result from the fact that the tropics receive the sun's rays more directly than other places as the Earth orbits the sun.

The amount of precipitation in the tropics, however, varies greatly between one area and another. Wet climates and habitats that include rain forests, with their wide variety of plant and animal species, are common in the region. Yet some areas experience a tropical wet-and-dry climate with three main seasons: cool and dry, hot and dry, and hot and wet. Life in these zones depends on abundant rain in the wet seasons.

YEAR-ROUND WARMTH, thanks to Earth's orientation to the sun, makes the region between the tropic lines—such as Icacos Island, off Puerto Rico—the planet's playground.

FOR MORE FACTS ON...

TROPICAL REGIONS OF THE WORLD see Rain Forests, **CHAPTER 5, PAGES 198-9**

+

GEOGRAPHY & ECONOMICS OF COUNTRIES IN THE CARIBBEAN see North America, **CHAPTER 9, PAGES 418-23**

WHAT CAUSES THE SEASONS?

The changing seasons occur because the Earth, tilted on its axis, orbits the sun. Thus, the plane of the Equator is tilted with respect to the plane of the Earth's orbit. Since the Earth is always tilted in the same direction, the latitude at which the sun appears directly overhead at noon changes as the Earth orbits the sun.

The sun appears to follow a yearly pattern of northward and southward motion in the sky. If the equatorial plane and the orbital plane were the same, the sun would always be directly overhead at noon to an observer at the Equator, and there would be no change of seasons. However, since the planes are tilted about 23° 30' from each other, the latitude at which the sun appears directly overhead at noon varies throughout the year.

Following centuries of tradition, astronomers divide the year into seasons according to equinoxes and solstices. The equinoxes occur when the Earth reaches the points in the orbit where the equatorial and orbital planes intersect, causing the sun to appear directly overhead at noon at the Equator. During equinoxes, the periods of daylight and darkness are nearly equal all over the world. One equinox occurs about March 21. In the Northern Hemisphere, this is the vernal, or spring, equinox; in the Southern Hemisphere it is the autumnal. The other equinox, which occurs around September 23, is the autumnal equinox in the Northern Hemisphere and the vernal in the Southern.

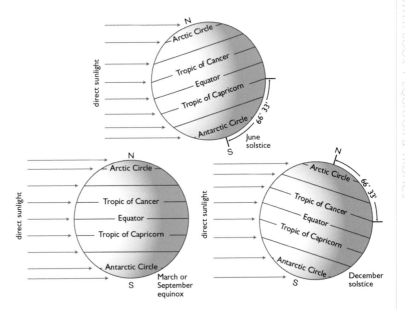

EARTH'S TILT as it orbits the sun means that direct light reaches different regions of the globe during the course of the year, causing seasons.

WHAT CITIES ARE ON THE TROPIC LINES?

THE TROPIC OF CANCER RUNS THROUGH	THE TROPIC OF CAPRICORN RUNS THROUGH
Guangzhou, China	Longreach, Australia
Bhopal, India	Toliara, Madagascar
Muscat, Oman	Rehoboth, Namibia
Little Exuma, Bahamas	São Paulo, Brazil
Mazatlán, Mexico	Tubuai, French Polynesia

FAST FACT About a third of the world's people live in latitudes between the Tropics of Cancer and Capricorn.

FOR MORE FACTS ON...

THE SUN & ITS RELATION TO PLANET EARTH see *The Sun*, CHAPTER 2, PAGES 54-7

WATCHING THE MOVEMENT OF CELESTIAL BODIES see *Observation*, CHAPTER 2, PAGES 68-71

NAVIGATION

Navigation is the process of directing the course of a craft such as a boat, ship, plane, or spacecraft to a destination. It requires, among other things, ongoing knowledge of the position, direction, and distance of the vessel and an understanding of astronomy, meteorology, mathematics, ocean currents, and features of coastlines and harbors. Early navigators relied on their direct experiences with all the physical phenomena involved and knowledge passed on by others.

Celestial navigation requires accurate calculations based on the position of the sun, moon, and stars. By the heyday of European voyages of exploration, instruments such as the compass, the sextant, and the chronometer aided mariners, as did an ever expanding collection of maps, charts, tables, and almanacs. Modern navigation, based on traditional principles, uses electronic instrumentation—such as radio, radar, and global positioning systems—to determine position and to set course.

Tens of centuries before Europeans explored and mapped the Pacific

FOR MORE FACTS ON...

THE RELATIVE POSITIONS OF SUN, MOON & STARS see *The Sun,* **CHAPTER 2, PAGES 54-7**

HOW DOES A GLOBAL POSITIONING SYSTEM (GPS) WORK? see *Advances in Mapping,* **CHAPTER 1, PAGE 29**

Ocean, islanders there sailed nearly 20 million square miles in double-hulled canoes by means of wayfinding, a system of observation that incorporated patterns in nature and allowed the sailors to find their way with great accuracy. The ancient Pacific navigators dedicated a lifetime to the mastery and application of such knowledge as the shape and sequence of waves, the rising and setting of stars, the color of sunrises and sunsets, island-influenced cloud cover, and even the flight patterns of birds.

Lacking charts and maps to carry as their guides, they repeated sailing chants that incorporated the names of stars, winds, rains, and key navigational reference points. Sky lore and tribal mythology also added to their practical knowledge. In recent decades these traditional navigational skills have been revived and tested in long-distance sea trials.

G L O S S A R Y

Dead reckoning: Determination without the aid of celestial navigation of the position of a ship or aircraft from the record of the courses sailed or flown, the distance made (estimated from velocity), the known starting point, and the known or estimated drift.

JAMES COOK / PACIFIC NAVIGATOR

Young James Cook (1728–1779) joined the Royal Navy in 1755 and rose quickly through the ranks at a time when the vast Pacific, covering more than one-third of Earth's surface, was the primary focus of European discovery and exploration. During three long expeditions, Cook discovered and charted more of the Pacific Basin than any other explorer. Between 1768 and 1779, he crossed the South Pacific three times, twice venturing into the Antarctic Circle. He also cruised the North Pacific, entering the Arctic Sea through the Bering Strait, and sailed to Hawaii, where he was slain with four of his men. Cook's expeditions produced the first accurate charts of the Pacific, based on thousands of astronomical sightings. He had perfected his skills by surveying the coasts of Newfoundland, skills that had to be adapted in the immense Pacific.

NAVIGATION BEFORE WRITING

The ancient Hawaiians highly revered those among them who could navigate the vast Pacific Ocean, so much so that they called them navigator-priests. These navigators combined observation, learning, and intuition.

Along coastlines, ancient Pacific navigators used the stick chart, a method of recording landmarks and coastline geography. Surviving examples of these charts are made of coconut palm or pandanus reeds and cowrie shells: The reeds represent ocean currents and sea swells; the shells are islands. Stick charts were used as teaching tools for navigation apprentices, as were more impromptu arrangements of fronds and shells fashioned during the course of lessons by instructors. Navigators consulted these devices before they set sail, and then left them behind for others.

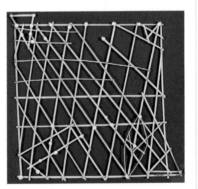

WITH PALM STICKS and cowrie shells, Marshall Islanders reconstructed this chart, conveying wisdom dating back to A.D. 300.

FAST FACT In 1769 Capt. James Cook asked a Tahitian sailor to navigate his ship, the *Endeavour,* in the South Pacific.

FOR MORE FACTS ON...

THE HUMAN URGE TO TRAVEL see *Transportation,* **CHAPTER 6, PAGES 252-3**
+
THE HISTORY OF EARLY PACIFIC CULTURES see *Oceania & North America Prehistory to 1500,* **CHAPTER 7, PAGES 286-7**

Cosmic Beginnings / Stars / C
Holes & Dark Matter / New
Terrestrial Planets / Outer Plan
& Meteors / Ancient Observa
Exploration / Space Collab

THE

nstellations / Galaxies / Black

olar System / Sun / Planets /

s / Moons / Asteroids, Comets

on / Modern Methods / Space

ation / Expanding Universe

UNIVERSE

42

Galaxies as seen by Hubble Space Telescope, 2003-2004

COSMIC BEGINNINGS

AFTER THE BIG BANG

10^{-35} SECONDS LATER
Big bang's energy turns into matter

10^{-5} SECONDS LATER
Universe's natural forces take shape

3 SECONDS LATER
Nuclei of simple elements formed

10,000 YEARS LATER
Universe's energy becomes radiation

300,000 YEARS LATER
Energy in form of matter equals energy
in form of radiation

300,000,000 YEARS LATER
Gas pocket density increases; stars form

e on Earth think of the universe as a vastness containing everything we know of—and much that we cannot even imagine. For millennia, humans have struggled to make sense of what they see all around them. They have observed, calculated, and conjectured, trying to articulate an explanation for a puzzle whose pieces are slowly being revealed with each scientific breakthrough.

The investigations of astronomy, astrophysics, and mathematics join the cosmological inquiries of seeking minds in all cultures and at all times—those of philosophers, scientists, religious scholars, and poets. Questions about the universe have always involved beginnings and endings. Now science is finding answers to questions long answered only by means of myth.

FAST FACT Astronomers can map the temperature of cosmic microwave background radiation as it was only 400,000 years after the big bang.

FOR MORE FACTS ON...

THEORIES ON EARTH'S BEGINNINGS see *Formation of the Earth*, **CHAPTER 3, PAGES 80-1**

HOW PICTURES OF THE COSMOS HAVE CHANGED THROUGH HISTORY see *Scientific Worldviews*, **CHAPTER 8, PAGES 326-7**

THE BIG BANG

Accepted astrophysical theories posit that at one point there was nothing: no stars, planets, or galaxies—not even space itself. The matter that makes up everything that now exists was concentrated in a single, extremely dense point known as a singularity.

The force of gravity in a singularity is so great that the fabric of space-time curves in on itself. In an instant known as the big bang, however, the contents of the primordial singularity escaped—and formed the universe.

The big bang is catchy shorthand for a complex astrophysical theory, backed up with sophisticated calculations. The term was coined in the 1950s by British astronomer Fred Hoyle, a proponent of a theory of the universe as a steady state. In fact, Hoyle used the term derisively. Though the name stuck, it gives a false impression, making it seem as though the event that unleashed all the energy of the universe almost 14 billion years ago was an explosion. Astro-

SCHEMATIC OF ALL TIME shows the big bang to the left and then a progression from particles to atoms, atoms to molecules, and molecules to life-forms.

physicists see the big bang more as an instantaneous expansion that within a few seconds created nuclear reactions and produced the protons, neutrons, and electrons that form the structure of matter today. Not long after, the nuclear reactions stopped. The universe was roughly one-quarter helium, three-quarters hydrogen—a ratio exhibited in the universe's oldest stars today. The formation of the universe played out over billions of years. Our own Earth, along with our solar system, is a product of a stellar explosion almost five billion years ago.

The story of the universe still is being written and refined. By all scientific accounts, it continues to expand, and the question of an eventual end looms large in current investigations.

The universe itself provides some concrete support for the big bang theory in the form of cosmic background radiation, the "afterglow" of the cosmic inflation. In 1965, engineers looking for the source of the static interfering with satellite communications found a consistent signal emanating from every point in the sky at the wavelength predicted for this radiation.

CLICK IT: NASA's Imagine the Universe imagine.gsfc.nasa.gov

G L O S S A R Y

Space-time: Single entity that relates space and time in a four-dimensional structure, postulated by Albert Einstein in his theories of relativity. /
Steady state theory: Concept of an expanding universe whose average density remains constant, in which matter is continuously created to form new stars and galaxies at the same rate that old ones recede from sight.

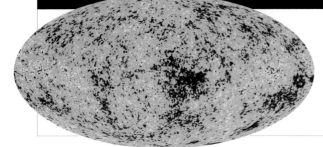

COSMIC MICROWAVE BACKGROUND RADIATION, as mapped by satellites, validates the big bang theory. Pictures taken by the Cosmic Background Explorer (COBE) showed hot spots that could be correlated to the gravitational field of the fledgling universe: the seeds of galaxy clusters hundreds of millions of light-years away. The 2001 Wilkinson Microwave Anisotropy Probe (WMAP) brought out even more details, as shown here. Telltale hot spots show as red flecks in the image.

FOR MORE FACTS ON...

THE LIFE & WORK OF EDWIN HUBBLE see *Observation: Modern Methods,* **CHAPTER 2, PAGE 71**

THE EVOLUTION OF PHYSICS & CONTEMPORARY KEY THEORIES see *Physics,* **CHAPTER 8, PAGES 330-1**

New star forming in Carina Nebula

BRIGHTEST

SIRIUS, THE DOG STAR
Blue-white dwarf
in constellation Canis Major

CANOPUS
Yellow-white supergiant
in constellation Carina

ARCTURUS
Orange-colored giant
in constellation Boötes

ALPHA CENTAURI
Triple star
in constellation Centauris

VEGA
Blue dwarf
in constellation Lyra

CAPELLA
Four-star cluster in
constellation Auriga

STARS

When we look at stars in the night sky, we are looking back in time. Many stars formed millions, if not billions, of years ago. Furthermore, the starlight that reaches our eyes left those faraway stars some time ago—ranging from a few minutes ago (the sun) to four years ago (Alpha Centauri, the sun's nearest star neighbor) to a much longer time ago (objects at the edges of our galaxy).

We measure these distances in light-years. One light-year is equivalent to approximately 6 trillion miles, or the distance light travels in one 365-day Earth year. Alpha Centauri, at 24 trillion miles from Earth, is 4 light-years away. The light we see today from the Andromeda Galaxy left it two million years ago: Andromeda is two million times 24 trillion miles away.

Stars, which are balls of gas (mostly the gases hydrogen and helium), emit radiation. They create energy by fusing hydrogen and turning it into helium in their cores. We see the resulting energy as starlight.

Astronomers classify stars based on their size, temperature, and color. Size in this case relates to mass rather than linear measurement, such as diameter. Stars start the same way, but their lives play out according to their size and mass. The mass of a star determines all of its other characteristics, including how hot it is, what color it is, and how long it will live. Massive stars are hot and blue, whereas small stars are cool and red.

FAST FACT A neutron star ten miles in diameter could have more mass than three stars comparable in size to our sun.

FOR MORE FACTS ON...

GALAXIES IN OUR SOLAR SYSTEM, INCLUDING THE MILKY WAY see *Galaxies*, CHAPTER 2, PAGES 48-9

THE STAR THAT IS CLOSEST TO PLANET EARTH see *The Sun*, CHAPTER 2, PAGES 54-7

IN STARS, SIZE MATTERS

Small stars continue to burn for hundreds of billions of years. The largest stars, about a hundred times the mass of the sun, live shorter lives, burning out after a few million years and dying with a bang. They become exploding supernovae that may leave behind a remnant of glowing gas. Shock waves from supernovae tend to compress interstellar gas, which may ignite and become a new star: stellar recycling.

G L O S S A R Y

Light-year: The distance traveled by light moving in a vacuum in the course of one year, at its accepted velocity of 186,282 miles per second; used as a unit to describe distances between objects in the universe. **/ Neutron star:** A body of densely packed neutrons, formed after the explosion of a supernova. **/ Supernova:** The violent, luminous explosion at the end of a massive star's life.

NEBULAE: BIRTHPLACE OF STARS

Stars are born in an enormous cloud of interstellar dust and hydrogen gas called a nebula. Nebulae represent the building blocks for stars, galaxies, and planets in the universe.

Emission nebulae are hot, discrete clouds of primarily ionized hydrogen that glow with their own light. Reflection nebulae emit a bluish glow by reflecting the scattered light of nearby stars. Absorption nebulae, or dark nebulae, comprise dense clouds of gas and dust. They appear as silhouettes against the light of brighter objects.

Nebulae form when stars die. When the end comes for our sun, for example, its outer layers will heat, swell, and eventually blow off. The hot, dead core will create a glowing nebula, which will in turn become a nursery for new stars.

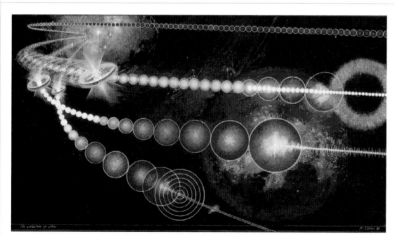

THE DEATH OF NEARBY STARS triggered the birth of our planet and other contents of our galaxy. The arms of a spiral galaxy such as ours are rich in stellar debris (upper left), cooled clouds of gas and dust out of which new generations of stars are born. Different physical phenomena result in (top to bottom) brown dwarfs, white dwarfs, neutron stars, and black holes.

Stars range in size from a white dwarf (bottom) to an O star (top)—both tiny compared with a red giant such as the one filling the lower right-hand corner. Our sun is a G star, fourth from the bottom.

CLICK IT: StarDate stardate.org

FOR MORE FACTS ON...

THE DEFINITION & DIFFERENT CLASSIFICATIONS OF BLACK HOLES see Black Holes & Dark Matter, **CHAPTER 2, PAGES 50-1**

+

THE BIRTH OF OUR PLANET see Formation of the Earth, **CHAPTER 3, PAGES 80-1**

The Pleiades star cluster

CONSTELLATIONS

CONSTELLATIONS OF THE ZODIAC

♈ ARIES

♉ TAURUS

♊ GEMINI

♋ CANCER

♌ LEO

♍ VIRGO

♎ LIBRA

♏ SCORPIO

♐ SAGITTARIUS

♑ CAPRICORN

♒ AQUARIUS

♓ PISCES

Stars seem to move across the sky through the night, but that movement is due to Earth's rotation. As Earth spins on its axis, objects appear to rise in the east and set in the west. In the Northern Hemisphere, some stars never appear to set. Called circumpolar stars, they circle at a point projected in the sky above the North Pole near Polaris, the Pole Star. A corresponding situation exists above the South Pole near the star Sigma Octantis.

In ancient cultures, sky-watching played an important role in navigation, agriculture, religion, and even entertainment. Those who observed the heavens connected stars to form patterns that related to the heroes, gods, and legends of their culture—what we refer to today as constellations. Most cultures named constellations and attached cultural meaning to their patterns. Native American sky lore, for instance, often used constellations to teach moral lessons.

Today, the Western world acknowledges the constellations that originated in Mesopotamia more than

FOR MORE FACTS ON...

THE NORTH & SOUTH POLES see *The Poles,* **CHAPTER I, PAGES 34-5**
+
THE CATEGORIES, ORIGIN & NATURE OF STARS IN THE SKIES see *Stars,* **CHAPTER 2, PAGES 44-5**

5,000 years ago. Babylonian, Egyptian, and Greek astronomers also made contributions during the classical ages of their cultures.

In 1928 the International Astronomical Union (IAU) determined which constellations would be officially recognized. Of the 88 constellations on the IAU list, 48 were identified in ancient times with just the naked eye. The remaining 40 were added in more recent centuries.

The IAU also defined each constellation's border so that the groupings represent not only star patterns but specific regions of the sky. These borders ensured that each star would be restricted to only one constellation.

Constellations change over time as the stars in them move through space. The dipper part of the Big Dipper in the constellation Ursa Major (Great Bear) appeared much more square in the past. Now the dipper's bowl is starting to elongate. About 100,000 years from now, it will look more like a soup bowl with a handle.

G L O S S A R Y

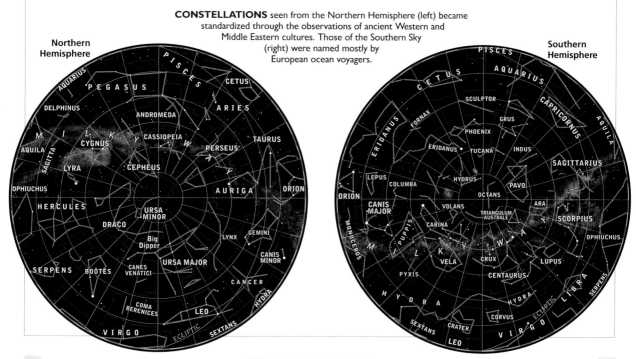

CLICK IT: Constellations www.iau.org/public_press/themes/constellations/

Asterism: Pattern of stars that is not a constellation but may contain stars from one or more constellations.

THE ZODIAC

The zodiac is a band of constellations that extends roughly nine degrees on each side of the ecliptic, the sun's apparent yearly path through our sky.

Ancient Greek astronomers divided the zodiac into 12 parts.

Over time, Earth's slight rotational wobble has shifted the ecliptic by more than 30 degrees against the backdrop of stars. The 18-degree-wide zodiac now also includes parts of Cetus (the Whale) and Orion (the Hunter).

CONSTELLATIONS seen from the Northern Hemisphere (left) became standardized through the observations of ancient Western and Middle Eastern cultures. Those of the Southern Sky (right) were named mostly by European ocean voyagers.

FOR MORE FACTS ON...

CURRENT DEFINITIONS OF PLANETS see *The New Solar System*, **CHAPTER 2, PAGES 52-3**
+
CHANGING METHODS OF ASTRONOMICAL OBSERVATION see *Observation*, **CHAPTER 2, PAGES 68-71**

MILKY WAY FACTS

TYPE OF GALAXY
Spiral

TOTAL MASS
400 billion solar masses
including dark matter
(1 solar mass = 1.99 x 10^{30} kg)

DISK DIAMETER
100,000 light-years

NUMBER OF STARS
100 billion

AGE OF OLDEST STAR CLUSTERS
14 billion years

DISTANCE OF NUCLEUS FROM SUN
26,000 light-years

GALAXIES

The universe contains more than 125 billion galaxies, immense aggregations of stars, gas, dust, and dark matter bound by their own gravity. Galaxies vary in size, luminosity, and mass. The largest are a million times brighter than the faintest. Galaxies take one of three primary shapes: elliptical, spiral, and irregular.

Galaxy names begin with the letter M followed by a number. This naming tradition began when French astronomer Charles Joseph Messier (1730-1817) cataloged stellar bodies and gave them numbers in sequence following an M for his name. Galaxies often have a common name as well.

M31 (above), for example, is also known as the Andromeda galaxy.

Our solar system resides in an arm of the Milky Way, a spiral galaxy some 100,000 light-years long from end to end. Our sun and planets revolve once around the center of the Milky Way every 250 million years.

Scientists studying galaxies have recently discovered that they are not randomly distributed but rather clump together in clusters, lined up at the same distance from one another, forming a kind of great wall. The Milky Way belongs to a cluster called the Local Group, which contains the Andromeda and M33 galaxies as well as about 30 dwarf galaxies. "Local" is a relative term here. The cluster's diameter is more than 10 million light-years, which means our neighbors in the Local Group are millions of light-years from the Milky Way. Gravity holds the galaxies together even as clusters, groups, and individual galaxies fly away from each other as the universe expands.

FAST FACT Light from the center of the Milky Way takes 25,000 years to reach us on Earth.

FOR MORE FACTS ON...

ENLIGHTENMENT THINKERS IN 18TH-CENTURY EUROPE *see Revolutions 1600-1800,* CHAPTER 7, PAGES 298-9

THE FORCE THAT HOLDS THINGS TOGETHER *see Physics,* CHAPTER 8, PAGES 330-1

THE MANY DIFFERENT SHAPES OF GALAXIES

Investigators have collected images of galaxies as far as 10 to 13 billion light-years away. Galaxies are classified according to the shape they present to telescopes on Earth or in space. A small galaxy can have a diameter of a few thousand light-years and contain a billion stars or fewer, while a large galaxy can have a diameter of half a million light-years and contain more than a trillion stars. Our galaxy, the Milky Way, is a medium-size galaxy: It is estimated to have a diameter of about 100,000 light-years and to contain about 100 billion stars.

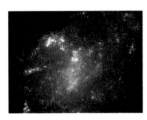

THIS SPIRAL GALAXY has older red stars in its center, younger blue ones in its arms.

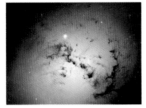

AN ELLIPTICAL GALAXY, this giant was formed when two gas-rich galaxies merged.

STARBURST GALAXY Messier 82 includes a blue disk and glowing red plumes of hydrogen.

A BARRED SPIRAL GALAXY near the Milky Way includes star-forming clouds and bands of dust.

G L O S S A R Y

Mass: The total quantity of material in an object, determining its gravity and resistance to movement.

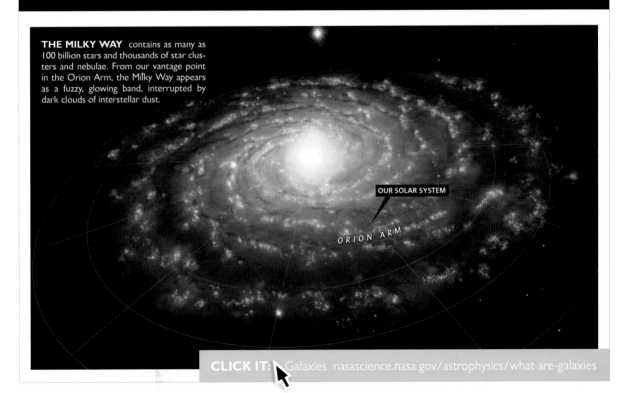

THE MILKY WAY contains as many as 100 billion stars and thousands of star clusters and nebulae. From our vantage point in the Orion Arm, the Milky Way appears as a fuzzy, glowing band, interrupted by dark clouds of interstellar dust.

OUR SOLAR SYSTEM

ORION ARM

CLICK IT: Galaxies nasascience.nasa.gov/astrophysics/what-are-galaxies

FOR MORE FACTS ON...

HOW GALAXIES CHANGE THROUGH TIME see *Expanding Universe,* **CHAPTER 2, PAGES 76-7**

THE ORIGIN & ESTABLISHMENT OF PLANET EARTH see *Formation of the Earth,* **CHAPTER 3, PAGES 80-1**

Black hole sucking in gas and dust, forming accretion disk

BLACK HOLES & DARK MATTER

THREE TYPES OF BLACK HOLE

STELLAR MASS
• Formed from collapsed cores of giant stars
• Mass a few times greater than that of Earth's sun
• Examples: A0620-00 and Cygnus X-1

INTERMEDIATE MASS
• Thousands of times bigger than Earth's sun
• Only a few identified and confirmed
• Examples: G1 and M74

SUPERMASSIVE
• Largest type
• Inhabits cores of galaxies
• From a few million to a few billion times larger than the sun
• Examples: Milky Way Sagittarius A and RX J1242-111

What we can observe in our sky—planets, stars, gas, dust, galaxies, nebulae, asteroids, meteors, and more—is a small fraction of what exists. Bright matter, the visible stuff of the universe, forms only about a sixth of its mass. What forms the rest, and how do we know it's there?

Scientists know there must be more out there than meets the eye because the unseen substance has gravity and appears to be holding together the parts of the universe that we can see, galaxies in particular. Because the unseen matter does not emit radiation, scientists call it dark matter.

Believed to constitute about 90 percent of the universe's total mass, dark matter may comprise unfathom-able numbers of tiny subatomic particles. Candidates for dark matter include cold dark matter (CDM), sluggish elementary particles; weakly interacting massive particles (WIMPS), heavy hypothetical particles that rarely interact with other matter; and massive compact halo objects (MACHOS), known objects such as planets, neutron stars, and white dwarfs that are presumed to be in the halos of galaxies.

FOR MORE FACTS ON...

A DEFINITION OF DARK ENERGY AS THE REVERSE OF GRAVITY see Expanding Universe, CHAPTER 2, PAGE 77

CURRENT IDEAS IN PHYSICS see Physical Science: Physics, CHAPTER 8, PAGES 330-1

WHAT IS A BLACK HOLE?

A black hole forms when a large, dying star collapses. The gravity created by this condensing matter completely overpowers any outward forces, including light. Although a black hole emits no light, its presence is detectable by radioastronomy equipment. Its extremely strong gravitational pull sucks gas and dust toward itself, forming a whirling accretion disk around the hole. The disk heats any matter that crosses it, emitting x-rays (opposite).

G L O S S A R Y

Black hole: Extremely dense object of such strong gravitational force that nothing passing within a certain distance can escape, not even light. /
Dark matter: Unknown substance detected only by the gravity it exerts; makes up five-sixths of the universe's total mass.

STEPHEN HAWKING / ASTROPHYSICS VISIONARY

Appropriately enough, British theoretical physicist Stephen W. Hawking (b. 1942) was born on the 300th anniversary of the death of Galileo. Since 1979 Hawking has held the chair in mathematics at Cambridge University once held by Isaac Newton. Hawking studies basic questions of the origins, nature, and future of the universe, and he seeks a unified theory able to reconcile Einstein's general theory of relativity and quantum theory. Early in his career, at age 21, Hawking was struck with amyotrophic lateral sclerosis (ALS)—a degenerative neuromuscular disorder commonly known as Lou Gehrig's disease. Despite his ALS, he remains vitally invested in his work, sharing ideas with scientists and the public through books, on the Internet, and on television.

WHAT IS A WORMHOLE?

A highly speculative idea of modern astrophysics, wormholes are theoretical possibilities allowed within the mathematical framework of Einstein's general theory of relativity. A wormhole is a short-lived portal, lasting only a brief moment, that joins two black holes in different locations.

Wormholes could connect two points in the present-day universe or, perhaps, in different times. In wormhole theory, matter falling into a black hole at one point should emerge through a proposed "white hole"—the reverse of a black hole—at the other end.

Neither wormholes nor any evidence of them has yet been observed. Scientists cannot determine how they would be created, although astrophysicists such as Hawking continue to work on this intriguing notion.

TRAVELERS COULD GO from point to point in time or space through wormholes, as imagined here in glowing purple.

CLICK IT: Black Hole Encyclopedia blackholes.stardate.org

FAST FACT The largest black hole on record weighs as much as 18 billion suns and is orbited by another, small black hole.

FOR MORE FACTS ON...

THEORIES OF THE EVOLUTION OF THE UNIVERSE see *Cosmic Beginnings*, **CHAPTER 2, PAGES 42-3**

THE INFLUENCE OF EINSTEIN'S IDEAS ON OUR WORLDVIEW see *Scientific Worldviews*, **CHAPTER 8, PAGES 326-7**

Saturn, as seen by the Cassini spacecraft, 2005

HOW MANY MOONS?

MERCURY: 0

VENUS: 0

MARS: 2
Phobos & Deimos

JUPITER: AT LEAST 63
*including Io, Europa,
Ganymede & Callisto*

SATURN: AT LEAST 60
*including Mimas, Enceladus,
Tethys & Dione*

URANUS: 27
*including Miranda, Ariel,
Umbriel & Titania*

NEPTUNE: 13
*including Naiad, Thalassa,
Despina & Galatea*

THE NEW SOLAR SYSTEM

ncient observers watched the celestial bodies move regularly against the starry sky. Those movements inspired the word "planet," from the Greek for wanderer. The ancients named and honored the sun, moon, and five planets that they believed revolved around Earth: Mercury, Venus, Mars, Jupiter, and Saturn.

In the 16th century, Nicolaus Copernicus disputed the notion that most heavenly bodies orbited Earth with his proposal of a heliocentric universe. Uranus was discovered—rather, it was identified as a planet and not a star—by British astronomer William Herschel in 1781. In 1846, German astronomer Johann Gottfried Galle identified Neptune. Tiny Pluto turned up on a photographic plate at Arizona's Lowell Observatory in 1930.

The list of our solar system's nine planets was challenged in 2005 when the discovery of a large body in the Kuiper belt reopened rigorous discussion among astronomers about planetary classification.

The International Astronomical Union (IAU) met in Prague in August 2006 and, though only a fraction of its members were present for the vote, arrived at a new definition of planet. The effect of this decision changed the lineup of our solar system, leaving the number of planets an "elite eight." The IAU classified Pluto with two other smallish bodies as dwarf planets. Ongoing discoveries no doubt will continue to change our view of the solar system.

FAST FACT Our address in the universe looks something like this: Earth, third planet from the sun, solar system, local interstellar cloud, local bubble, Orion arm, Milky Way, Local Group, Virgo supercluster, visible universe, universe.

FOR MORE FACTS ON...

ANCIENT & MODERN ASTRONOMICAL METHODS see *Observation*, **CHAPTER 2, PAGES 68-71**
+
HOW COPERNICUS'S IDEAS SHAPED OUR VIEW OF EARTH see *Globes*, **CHAPTER 1, PAGE 23**, & *Scientific Worldviews*, **CHAPTER 8, PAGES 326-7**

MORE NEW PLANETS?

The definition of a planet and the list of the planets in our solar system may keep changing. At one point during the great planetary shake-up of 2006, the IAU briefly proposed a definition that would have included more than a hundred objects belonging to the category of "planet."

Ceres, Pluto, and Eris are dwarf planets; the latter two and their moons are further designated as plutoids, dwarf planets found beyond Neptune in the Kuiper belt. Likely additions to the list of plutoids include the unusual body known as EL61. This egg-shaped object, also described as a squashed football, spins rapidly, completing one rotation every four hours.

CLICK IT: Science & Space nationalgeographic.com/science/space

FAST FACT In 2008 Maryn Smith, ten years old, from Great Falls, Montana, won the National Geographic Society's contest for a mnemonic for the 11 planets: **M**y **V**ery **E**xciting **M**agic **C**arpet **J**ust **S**ailed **U**nder **N**ine **P**alace **E**lephants.

A PLANET is a celestial body that (1) orbits a star; (2) has acquired a roughly round shape by its own gravity; and (3) contains enough mass that its gravitational field has cleared its orbit of debris. A dwarf planet meets only the first two of these requirements.

ELEVEN PLANETS, including dwarf planets, now constitute our solar system, seen below from left to right: Mercury, Venus, Earth, Mars, Ceres, Jupiter, Saturn, Uranus, Neptune, Pluto, and Eris. Ceres, Pluto, and Eris are dwarf planets.

CERES, the largest known asteroid in the asteroid belt, was discovered in 1801 by Italian astronomer Giuseppe Piazzi. Shaped like a flattened sphere and having a volume approximately 27 percent that of Earth's moon, Ceres contains a rocky core surrounded by a thick layer of ice.

ERIS, another of the three dwarf planets in Earth's solar system, circles the sun much farther out than even Neptune and Pluto. Discovered in 2005, Eris has a diameter larger than that of Pluto. It has its own moon, Dysnomia.

FOR MORE FACTS ON...

PLUTO'S DEMOTION TO DWARF PLANET see *The Planets,* **CHAPTER 2, PAGES 58-9**

+

THE PLANETS IN OUR SOLAR SYSTEM see *The Planets: Terrestrial & The Planets: Outer,* **CHAPTER 2, PAGES 60-3**

54

Sunrise, Magdalena Island, Baja California, Mexico

THE SUN

SUN FACTS

DIAMETER
879,000 miles

**AVERAGE DISTANCE
FROM EARTH**
93,000,000 miles

**AVERAGE SURFACE
TEMPERATURE**
9932°F

PERIOD OF ROTATION
(measured in Earth days)
25.4 days

SURFACE GRAVITY
28
(Earth's surface gravity = 1)

AGE
4.6 billion years

The sun, the star closest to Earth, anchors our solar system. It seems immense to us, but compared with other stars, it is only average in size. For example, Alpha Orionis in the constellation Orion, commonly known as Betelgeuse, is almost 400 times bigger than—and 10,000 times brighter than—the sun. Still, if the sun were hollow, a hundred Earths could fit inside.

Like all stars, the sun is a ball of hydrogen gas that radiates heat and light. It generates power by nuclear fusion: Atoms are rammed together, producing nuclear energy. Every second, the sun converts some four million tons of matter into energy.

Earth orbits the sun at a distance ideal for terrestrial life, provided that Earth's atmosphere protects us from the sun's heat and deadly radiation.

The sun is a third-generation star, composed of recycled elements from two previous stars. It is about 74 percent hydrogen and 25 percent helium, with traces of iron, carbon, calcium, and sodium. These same elements are found in planet Earth and our bodies.

FOR MORE FACTS ON...

THE MASS & CHARACTERISTICS OF STARS *see Stars,* **CHAPTER 2, PAGES 44-5**

HARNESSING SOLAR ENERGY FOR USE ON EARTH *see Alternative Technologies,* **CHAPTER 8, PAGES 354-5**

WHAT ARE SUNSPOTS?

Visible features on the sun's surface, sunspots are dark regions on the photosphere where a particularly strong portion of the sun's magnetic field has slowed the gas that is rising to the surface.

The center of a sunspot, depressed a little below the level of the surrounding gas, exhibits a lower temperature than the surrounding photosphere, creating a visible spot.

Sunspots measure up to several times Earth's diameter. Sunspot activity increases and decreases in an 11-year cycle. Early in each cycle, most sunspots appear near the sun's 30° N and 30° S latitudes. Later in the cycle, they occur closer to its equator. During the low point in the cycle, called the solar minimum, the sun goes for days or even weeks without flaring.

SUNSPOT 536, just left of center, can flare and affect Earth. The spot itself is six times wider than our planet.

G L O S S A R Y

Photosphere: Visible surface of the sun, from which is emitted most of the sun's light that reaches Earth directly. **/ Chromosphere:** Layer of the sun's atmosphere located above the photosphere and below the corona.

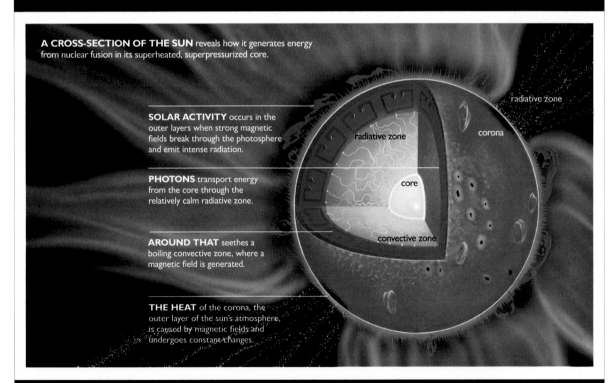

A CROSS-SECTION OF THE SUN reveals how it generates energy from nuclear fusion in its superheated, superpressurized core.

SOLAR ACTIVITY occurs in the outer layers when strong magnetic fields break through the photosphere and emit intense radiation.

PHOTONS transport energy from the core through the relatively calm radiative zone.

AROUND THAT seethes a boiling convective zone, where a magnetic field is generated.

THE HEAT of the corona, the outer layer of the sun's atmosphere, is caused by magnetic fields and undergoes constant changes.

radiative zone

corona

radiative zone

core

convective zone

FAST FACT The sun accounts for 99 percent of the total matter in our solar system.

FOR MORE FACTS ON...

THE SUN'S ROLE IN EARTH'S BEGINNINGS see Formation of the Earth, **CHAPTER 3, PAGES 80-1**
+
THE INFLUENCE & EFFECT OF SUNLIGHT ON EARTH see Earth's Atmosphere, **CHAPTER 3, PAGES 104-5**

THE SUN

SOLAR DETAILS

The sun's influence extends to the limits of the solar system. Its teardrop-shaped heliosphere, created by solar wind and filled with its magnetic field, stretches through the solar system, past Pluto.

Regions of this magnetic field rise through the photosphere—the part of the sun that is visible to the unaided human eye—into the transparent corona, forming tangled loops that constantly break and reconnect. This field is probably responsible for many of the sun's most dramatic features.

Dark regions known as sunspots and bright active areas appear where the field breaks through the photosphere. Enormous loops of gas called prominences and filaments, some of them many times larger than Earth, also shoot forth (as shown below). Huge explosions that are known as solar flares erupt.

The sun is now about halfway through its life. In another five billion years or so, it will run out of hydrogen to fuel its fusion. When that happens, the sun's core will collapse and its outer layers will cool and expand, turning it into a red giant star. Eventually, the outer layers will float away from the core, leaving behind a white dwarf star.

SOLAR FLARES rise up in loops as big as ten Earths. Such images come to us thanks to missions such as SOHO (Solar and Heliospheric Observatory), a joint venture of NASA and the European Space Agency.

FAST FACT Calendar of solar eclipses: E. Pacific and Asia, July 22, 2009; S. South America, July 11, 2010; N. Australia and S. Pacific, November 13, 2012; N. Atlantic, Faroe Islands, and Svalbard, March 20, 2015.

FOR MORE FACTS ON...

THE CHARACTERISTICS & INNER WORKINGS OF THE SUN see The Sun, **CHAPTER 2, PAGES 54-5**

THE SUN'S ROLE IN THE ORIGIN OF EARTH'S LIGHT see Light, **CHAPTER 3, PAGES 108-9**

WHAT ARE SOLAR FLARES?

Solar flares are sudden eruptions on the surface of the sun, such as those shown below and opposite. Typically occurring during the peak of the

DRAMATIC SOLAR FLARES spurt fiery gases beyond the sun's corona and into space.

sunspot cycle, these violent releases of energy eject billions of tons of charged particles at more than 600 miles per second into space, as well as spewing out radiation ranging from radio waves to x-rays.

A flare usually lasts only a few minutes. In that time, its temperature can reach several million kelvins. (For comparison, note that the highest recorded temperature on Earth, 136°F, is equal to only about 331°K.)

The charged particles of a solar flare sometimes extend to Earth's magnetic field, which can cause auroras and geomagnetic storms, disrupt

satellite communications, and endanger astronauts in space.

Unusually large solar flares can have broader consequences on Earth. For example, on October 28, 2003, a huge solar flare shot highly charged energetic particles right at our planet. Airplanes were diverted away from the Poles because passengers would have been exposed to increased radiation. A power blackout occurred in Sweden, and some satellites were damaged. Even the Hubble Space Telescope had to be placed in its "safe" mode to protect its delicate electronics.

G L O S S A R Y

Kelvin: Named for Scottish physicist William Thomson, Baron Kelvin of Largs. The unit of an absolute temperature scale with its zero point at absolute zero (-459.67°F). **/ Corona:** Outermost region of the sun's atmosphere, consisting of plasma (hot ionized gas).

WHAT IS SOLAR WIND?

Solar wind occurs when atomic particles stream out from the sun's corona. A gust can amount to one million tons of matter per second.

Solar wind consists mostly of protons and electrons, with tiny amounts of silicon, sulfur, calcium, chromium, nickel, neon, and argon ions. It travels up to 540 miles a second—fastest when escaping through coronal holes.

Where solar wind encounters planetary magnetic fields, it can cause auroras. It also makes the tails of comets point away from the sun.

PARTICLES ESCAPE the sun's corona, shown at left, and streak past Earth. Heavy solar winds can disrupt telecommunications on Earth. Solar winds increase when solar flares peak.

CLICK IT: Solar News solar-center.stanford.edu

FAST FACT It takes the sun up to 250 million years to complete one revolution around the Milky Way.

FOR MORE FACTS ON...

WHAT CAUSES SEASONAL CHANGES ON EARTH see *Equator & Tropics,* **CHAPTER I, PAGES 36-7**

SUNLIGHT & ITS INTERACTION WITH EARTH'S ATMOSPHERE see *Earth's Atmosphere,* **CHAPTER 3, PAGES 104-5**

Artist's rendition of outer space as seen from surface of Pluto

THE PLANETS

DISTANCE FROM SUN

MERCURY
35,983,606 miles

VENUS
67,232,363 miles

EARTH
92,957,130 miles

MARS
141,635,996 miles

JUPITER
483,426,788 miles

SATURN
886,696,691 miles

URANUS
1,783,950,479 miles

NEPTUNE
2,795,082,966 miles

What does it take for something to be considered a planet? According to the definition established by the International Astronomical Union, a planet is a spherical object larger than 600 miles in diameter that orbits a star and has a strong enough gravitational pull to clear the neighborhood around its orbit of debris. Critics of this definition point out that Earth, Mars, Jupiter, and Neptune all travel with an entourage of debris.

The eight classical planets fall into two different categories: terrestrial planets and gas giants. The terrestrial planets, which are the four innermost planets in our solar system—Mercury, Venus, Earth, and Mars—are primarily composed of silicate rocks.

Jupiter, Saturn, Uranus, and Neptune are the gas giants. These large planets are composed mostly of frozen hydrogen and helium. Unlike terrestrial planets, they have no solid surface. They also are called Jovian planets, referring to Jupiter.

FOR MORE FACTS ON...

REPRESENTATIONS OF THE PLANETS AS CELESTIAL GLOBES see *Globes*, **CHAPTER 1, PAGES 22-3**

HOW TO DETERMINE THE DEFINITION OF A PLANET see *The New Solar System*, **CHAPTER 2, PAGES 52-3**

WHAT ELSE IS OUT THERE?

Dwarf planets are smaller round objects that orbit the sun. Because their gravitational pull is weak, they have debris within their orbits. They are not, however, satellites of other planets. Pluto, Ceres (found in the asteroid belt), and Eris (located in the Kuiper belt) are dwarf planets. More will likely soon be identified.

Two other types of planets are known as super-Earths and hot Jupiters. These are called exoplanets (short for extrasolar planets) because they may exist outside our solar system. Super-Earths measure two to three times the size of Earth and are made of rock and ice. They orbit cooler red stars about half the size of our sun but do so at distances too close to allow life. A super-Earth that orbits its star at a safe distance might be able to support life. Hot Jupiters, which are larger than Jupiter, are made of gas and orbit extremely close to their stars. Because of their size, they are quite easy to detect.

CLICK IT: Catalog of Exoplanets exoplanets.org

WHAT ABOUT PLUTO?

Pluto's status as a full-fledged planet was revoked in 2006. Many people, scientists and laypersons alike, grieved Pluto's demotion. This tiny planet at the far reaches of our solar system has many admirers. Even a beloved Disney cartoon character had been named after it.

But as astronomers discovered other objects about the size of Pluto out in the Kuiper belt, beyond Neptune's orbit, they came to regard Pluto as one of a group of orbiting bodies and not as a solitary planet. The question of whether to classify such objects as planets or to reassign Pluto formed the basis of intense argument among members of the International Astronomical Union (IAU) in 2006. The vote at the IAU convention was not in Pluto's favor, so 76 years after this orbiting body was discovered and heralded as the ninth planet, it was downgraded to dwarf planet status.

G L O S S A R Y

Asteroid belt: A nearly flat ring orbiting the sun between the orbits of Mars and Jupiter composed of a host of rocky small bodies, each about 600 miles or less in diameter. **/ Kuiper belt:** Named for the Dutch-American astronomer Gerard P. Kuiper. A flat ring of icy small bodies that revolve around the sun beyond the orbit of the planet Neptune.

MICHAEL E. BROWN / ASTRONOMER

Since his childhood, Michael E. Brown (b. 1965) has kept his sights on the solar system's outer edges. In 2005 he and two colleagues discovered in the Kuiper belt an object officially classified as 2003 UB313, the largest discovered in 150 years. Brown nicknamed it Xena, for the pop culture superhero, although it was eventually renamed Eris.

His discovery was a catalyst for the great debate about the planets in our solar system. Accordingly, Eris's moon was named Dysnomia, after the goddess of lawlessness and the daughter of Eris in Greek mythology. Although Brown, a professor at the California Institute of Technology, has dozens more discoveries to his credit, he will go down in history as the man responsible for Pluto's demotion.

FOR MORE FACTS ON...

DEFINITIONS OF THE DIFFERENT TYPES OF PLANETS see The Planets: Terrestrial & The Planets: Outer, **CHAPTER 2, PAGES 60-3**

CHANGING METHODS OF ASTRONOMICAL OBSERVATION see Observation, **CHAPTER 2, PAGES 68-71**

TERRESTRIAL

The first five planets nearest the sun are known as the terrestrial planets because of their Earthlike characteristics, especially their rocky composition. But each of the four terrestrial planets—Mercury, Venus, Earth, and Mars—has distinctive features that set it apart from its neighbors in the solar system.

Mercury, closest planet to the sun, orbits the sun in only 88 Earth days, but it revolves on its axis so slowly that one Mercurian day lasts 59 Earth days. It has a large iron core, suggesting that it lost most of its surface in an ancient collision. Mercury appears to be shrinking still as its iron core grows cold.

Venus has the densest atmosphere of any planet in the solar system, composed largely of clouds of carbon dioxide some 40 miles thick. These clouds trap incoming sunlight, which heats the planet's surface to 864°F day and night. No trace of water has been found on Venus. It shines luminously, making it the third brightest object in our sky after the sun and the moon.

Earth has a unique blue-and-white appearance because more than 70 percent of its surface is covered with water and its atmosphere is filled with clouds rich in oxygen. Both its optimum distance from the sun and the presence of water in three states—liquid, solid, and vapor—make Earth conducive to life. Earth's terrain varies more than that of any other planet, and its life-forms thrive on land and in water.

Mars's iron-rich soil gives it a reddish glow. Half the size of Earth, Mars is known for the oversize features of its terrain. Its Valles Marineris canyon stretches some 2,500 miles, equivalent to the distance from Los Angeles to New York City. Its Olympus Mons volcano stands at least 15 miles high, more than twice the height of Mount Everest. Despite Mars's inhospitable atmosphere, the United States still hopes to send a manned spacecraft to this, Earth's closest neighbor.

Ceres, a dwarf planet, resides in the asteroid belt that orbits the sun between Mars and Jupiter. About one-fourth the size of Earth's moon, Ceres is the largest object in that belt of solar system leftovers.

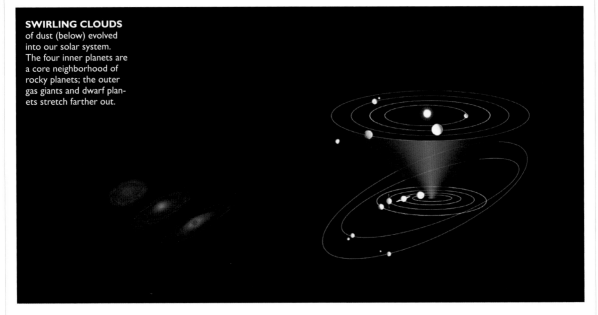

SWIRLING CLOUDS of dust (below) evolved into our solar system. The four inner planets are a core neighborhood of rocky planets; the outer gas giants and dwarf planets stretch farther out.

FOR MORE FACTS ON...

THE COMPOSITION & LAYERS OF EARTH'S ATMOSPHERE see Earth's Atmosphere, **CHAPTER 3, PAGES 104-5**
+
THE ELEMENTS THAT COMPOSE THE PLANET EARTH see Earth's Elements, **CHAPTER 3, PAGES 90-1**

BETWEEN MARS (reddish planet, center) and Jupiter (large planet, right), a wide belt of asteroids orbits our sun.

WHAT IS THE ASTEROID BELT?

The asteroid belt, located between the orbits of Mars and Jupiter, is a wide belt of material orbiting the sun that contains perhaps millions of asteroids. Ceres, an asteroid recently upgraded to a dwarf planet, is also found here. These asteroids are spread out over such a large swath of space that a spacecraft traveling through the belt would rarely encounter one. They tend to collect in orbiting groups separated from one another by significant gaps, called Kirkwood gaps, which are caused by the gravitational pull of Jupiter. Jupiter's gravity occasionally pulls an asteroid out of orbit and sends it hurtling to the sun. A rare asteroid veers out of the belt and rockets to Earth.

FAST FACT Like our moon, Mercury and Venus go through phase changes when viewed from Earth.

WHAT DOES AN ASTEROID LOOK LIKE?

The image to the right was created from a composite of four photographs of asteroid 433, also known as Eros, in our solar system's asteroid belt. The photographs were taken by the Near Earth Asteroid Rendezvous (NEAR) mission in February 2000.

The NEAR spacecraft entered Eros's orbit about 200 miles from the asteroid and about 160,000,000 miles from Earth. A year later, the NEAR spacecraft landed on Eros and confirmed that it is without atmosphere or water.

This asteroid is heavily cratered, suggesting that it is relatively old. The large crater visible here measures about four miles across. In its depression can be seen a boulder, equivalent in size to a single-family house.

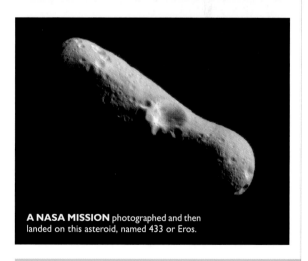

A NASA MISSION photographed and then landed on this asteroid, named 433 or Eros.

CLICK IT: Mars Exploration mars.jpl.nasa.gov

FOR MORE FACTS ON...

ASTEROIDS & RELATED HEAVENLY OBJECTS see Asteroids, Comets & Meteors, **CHAPTER 2, PAGES 66-7**
+
THE HISTORY OF THE HUMAN INVESTIGATION OF OUTER SPACE see Space Exploration, **CHAPTER 2, PAGES 72-5**

THE PLANETS

OUTER

The planets that orbit the sun on the other side of the asteroid belt are called the outer planets. Four of them—Jupiter, Saturn, Uranus, and Neptune—are also known as gas giants.

Jupiter, the innermost planet among the gas giants, is larger than all the other planets in our solar system combined—and then some. This giant planet was fittingly named for the premier Roman god. With at least 63 orbiting moons, Jupiter can almost be likened to a sun at the center of its own miniature solar system. Much about the planet remains a mystery, however, because even powerful space-based telescopes cannot see its surface, which is obscured by perpetual cloud cover with streaks caused by raging storms.

Saturn, the most distant planet visible to the naked eye, is noted for its brilliant rings—the remains of a torn-apart moon or asteroid—which shine more brightly than the planet itself. Composed mostly of hydrogen and helium gas, Saturn has such a low density that it would float like a cork if dropped into water.

Uranus gets its blue-green glow from methane gas in its atmosphere and is composed almost entirely of hydrogen and helium. Its axis is uniquely tilted at 98°, possibly the result of a collision with an immense object. Its rings tilt sideways as well.

Neptune, the smallest gas giant, has the most extreme weather of any planet in our solar system, with winds stronger than 1,200 miles an hour. The existence of Neptune was predicted mathematically before it was observed, since gravity from a large body seemed to be affecting the orbit of Uranus. Neptune takes 164.8 Earth years to orbit the sun.

Pluto was counted as the ninth planet from the sun for 76 years, but it now ranks as the tenth (albeit dwarf) planet. Its orbit is oval shaped, so sometimes it crosses inside the orbit of Neptune and temporarily becomes the ninth planet from the sun again. Some astronomers consider Pluto and Charon, its largest moon, a double-planet system.

Eris, a dwarf planet discovered in 2005, caused a scientific reconfiguration of the solar system. Cold, rocky, and extremely remote, Eris travels with its moon, Dysnomia, through the Kuiper belt.

VOYAGER 1, launched in 1977, transmitted data that was then compiled to create this colorful image of the surface of Jupiter.

FOR MORE FACTS ON...

VARIOUS SPACE TELESCOPES & THEIR CAPABILITIES see *Observation: Modern Methods,* **CHAPTER 2, PAGES 70-1**

THE DEFINITION OF A MOON see *Moons,* **CHAPTER 2, PAGES 64-5**

JUPITER'S FOUR MAIN MOONS

Of Jupiter's 63 moons, four can be viewed from Earth through binoculars. These moons were first discovered by Galileo Galilei, looking through a newly refined telescope around 1610, and they still are called the Galilean moons.

Galileo was astonished to find that these four moons—Ganymede, Io, Europa, and Callisto—form a perfect line with the planet. Each has its own distinctive features.

With more than 150 volcanoes, Io is the most geologically active moon in the solar system. Europa has an icy surface that may cover liquid water, offering the possibility that we may one day discover some kind of life-form there. Ganymede is the largest moon in the solar system, larger even than the Earth's moon. Callisto, heavily pockmarked, is the most cratered object in the solar system.

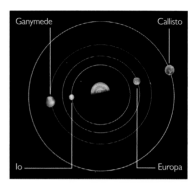

Ganymede   Callisto

Io   Europa

G L O S S A R Y

Dwarf planet: A spherical or nearly spherical rocky body that is in orbit around the sun, is not the satellite of another body, and is smaller than most of the other planets in our solar system.

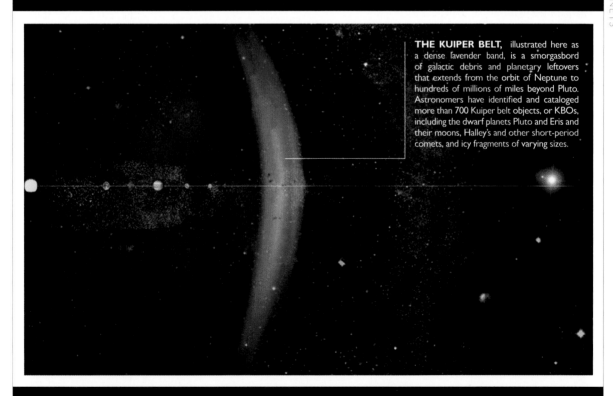

THE KUIPER BELT, illustrated here as a dense lavender band, is a smorgasbord of galactic debris and planetary leftovers that extends from the orbit of Neptune to hundreds of millions of miles beyond Pluto. Astronomers have identified and cataloged more than 700 Kuiper belt objects, or KBOs, including the dwarf planets Pluto and Eris and their moons, Halley's and other short-period comets, and icy fragments of varying sizes.

FAST FACT Voyager 2, traveling on average 42,000 miles an hour, reached Neptune in 12 years.

FOR MORE FACTS ON...

ANOTHER ASTEROID BELT see *The Planets: Terrestrial,* **CHAPTER 2, PAGE 61**

THE NATURE OF OBJECTS FOUND IN THE KUIPER BELT see *Asteroids, Comets & Meteors,* **CHAPTER 2, PAGES 66-7**

MOON FACTS

DIAMETER
2,160 miles

**AVERAGE DISTANCE
FROM EARTH**
240,000 miles

**AVERAGE SURFACE
TEMPERATURE**
-4°F

PERIOD OF ROTATION
(measured in Earth days)
27 days, 4 hours, 43 minutes

SURFACE GRAVITY
0.17
(Earth's surface gravity = 1)

ESTIMATED AGE
4.5 billion years

MOONS

Moons are natural satellites, celestial bodies that orbit other bodies such as planets or large asteroids that are large enough to have their own gravitational pull. Planets acquire moons in a number of ways. Satellites that orbit close by, near a planet's equatorial plane, and in the same direction—such as Jupiter's moons— were likely created at the same time as the planet.

Moons in retrograde to a planet appear to have formed separately and been captured by the planet's gravity. Neptune's Triton is one such moon. Moons can also come into being when large objects collide with planets, chipping off matter that becomes an orbiting body: Earth's moon, for example.

All the planets and dwarf planets except Venus, Mars, and Ceres have moons; some of them have more than one. Altogether, our solar system contains at least 137 moons. Until the invention of the telescope, only Earth's moon was visible.

Moons interest astronomers because they seem the most promising places to look for evidence of extraterrestrial life-forms. A few moons, such as Neptune's Triton and Jupiter's Io, have atmospheres as well as other notable features. Triton has polar ice caps and geysers; Io has huge volcanic eruptions. Jupiter's moon Europa may be the only body in the solar system apart from Earth to have liquid water.

FAST FACT Upcoming lunar eclipses: Americas, Europe, E. Asia, Australia, Pacific: December 21, 2010; South America, Europe, Africa, Asia, Australia: June 15, 2011; North America, Europe, E. Africa, Asia, Australia, Pacific: December 10, 2011; Americas, Australia, Pacific: April 15, 2014; Americas, Asia, Australia, Pacific: October 8, 2014, and April 4, 2015.

FOR MORE FACTS ON...

HEAVENLY BODIES OTHER THAN MOONS & PLANETS see Asteroids, Comets & Meteors, CHAPTER 2, PAGES 66-7
+
THE SEARCH FOR LIFE ELSEWHERE IN THE UNIVERSE see Expanding Universe, CHAPTER 2, PAGE 76

EARTH'S MOON

Earth's moon took form in a cosmic collision about 4.5 billion years ago, shortly after our planet formed. An object about the size of Mars struck Earth, blasting large fragments of the planet into orbit. This orbiting matter eventually coalesced into the moon, which has a composition very similar to that of Earth's crust.

The moon's original molten surface cooled over time and then was intensely bombarded by space debris, which created the many craters visible on its surface today. Next, molten rock welled up from the moon's interior and flooded the impact basins, creating the moon's seas, called maria. Eventually the tumult died down and the moon turned into the quiet, dusty, rocky world that greeted the Apollo astronauts in 1969, when Earth's moon became the first extraterrestrial body visited by humans.

Our planet's sole natural satellite, the moon is one-fourth the size of Earth and the fifth largest satellite in the solar system. Some astronomers have suggested that Earth and its moon are close enough in size that they should be considered a double-planet system.

The Lunar Reconnaissance Orbiter, dubbed "NASA's first step back to the moon," will add to our lunar knowledge.

THE MOON'S SPIN has been slowed by gravitational interactions with both the sun and Earth, so that its rotational speed equals that at which it revolves around Earth. Thus, the same side of the moon consistently faces Earth. Astronomers could only speculate about the landscape of the far side of the moon until the images brought back by the Soviet space probe Luna 3 in 1959.

WHO IS THE MAN IN THE MOON? Some cultures see a hare, whereas others see a frog, a moose, or a woman's silhouette. But many people see a man's face: eyes, nose, and mouth. The topography results from events some four billion years ago. Fierce bombardment by asteroids on the far side of the moon caused volcanic action on the near side. Magma flooded the surface and hardened into the features we see today.

WHY DO ECLIPSES HAPPEN?

A solar eclipse (shown at right, with the moon to the left of Earth) occurs when the moon passes directly between Earth and the sun, blocking the sun from view.

A lunar eclipse (shown at right, with the moon to the right of Earth) occurs when Earth passes directly between the sun and the moon. The moon passes into Earth's shadow, or umbra, and dims temporarily.

A total solar eclipse can last up to 7.5 minutes. A total lunar eclipse can last up to 100 minutes.

ECLIPSES occur when the alignment of the sun, the moon, and Earth results in shadows cast by one on another.

CLICK IT: Lunar & Planetary Science nssdc.gsfc.nasa.gov/planetary

G L O S S A R Y

Crater: A circular depression in the surface of a planet caused by a meteorite impact or by volcanic activity. **/ Retrograde motion:** The actual or apparent motion of a body in a direction opposite to that of the predominant motions of similar bodies.

FOR MORE FACTS ON...

THE ROLE PLAYED BY THE MOON IN CREATING TIDES see *Oceans,* **CHAPTER 3, PAGE 115**

+

THE DEVELOPMENT OF CALENDARS THROUGH HISTORY see *Telling Time,* **CHAPTER 8, PAGES 324-5**

Perseid meteor shower, Amman, Jordan, 2005

ASTEROIDS, COMETS & METEORS

VISIBLE METEOR SHOWERS

QUADRANTIDS
Peak January 3, in constellation Boötes

DELTA AQUARIDS
Peak July 29, in Aquarius

CAPRICORNIDS
Peak July 30, in Capricorn

PERSEIDS
Peak August 12, in Perseus

ORIONIDS
Peak October 21, in Orion

GEMINIDS
Peak December 4, in Gemini

Asteroids, comets, and meteors are forms of interplanetary debris—rocky and icy fragments left from the formation of the solar system. They usually travel at a great distance from Earth, but we see them, even with the naked eye, when they near our planet.

Millions of asteroids orbit the sun, usually in a belt between the orbits of Mars and Jupiter. A few brush past the planet Earth. Generally larger than comets and meteors, asteroids are chunks of rock and metal that can range from 100 yards to almost 600 miles in width.

Comets, sometimes likened to big, dirty snowballs, are made of rock, ice, dust, carbon dioxide, methane, and other gases. They originate in the Kuiper belt. As comets journey toward the sun, they begin to defrost. Solar heat vaporizes ice, which forms a halo of gas and dust, called a coma, around the comet's nucleus. Approaching Mars, comets may form tails, some hundreds of millions of miles long.

Meteors, more commonly seen from Earth than asteroids or comets, are known to most as shooting stars, but they are actually not stars at all.

FOR MORE FACTS ON...

THE FORMATION OF THE SOLAR SYSTEM see *Cosmic Beginnings*, **CHAPTER 2, PAGES 42-3**

THE KUIPER BELT & ITS POSITION IN OUR SOLAR SYSTEM see *The Planets: Outer*, **CHAPTER 2, PAGE 63**

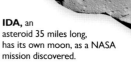

WILL AN ASTEROID HIT SOON?

If an asteroid hit Earth, its effect on our planet would depend upon its size. Earth's atmosphere protects the planet from asteroids less than 150 feet in diameter.

Objects up to 3,000 feet across create intense, localized damage. Such impacts occur every few centuries. Asteroids more than 5,000 feet across would kick up dust and cause an "impact winter." Such hits occur once or twice every million years. The Chicxulub crater in Mexico was probably the result of an asteroid impact 65 million years ago. The dust produced may have caused a climate change that led to the extinction of the dinosaurs.

IDA, an asteroid 35 miles long, has its own moon, as a NASA mission discovered.

To date, astronomers have cataloged some 960 potentially hazardous asteroids (PHAs), though none are believed to be on a collision course with Earth.

HALLEY'S COMET is the most famous and brightest comet reliably visible on Earth. Its reappearance in 1758 confirmed British astronomer Edmond Halley's 1750 prediction of a 75- or 76-year period. This color image is an enhancement of a 1910 black-and-white photograph.

VARIATIONS ON THE METEOR

Meteoroids, meteors, and meteorites all represent different stages of interplanetary debris. Meteoroids are small chunks of rock and metal—pieces of asteroids, bits of comets, and, rarely, pieces of the moon or Mars—that orbit the sun. Earth's gravity sweeps up millions of meteoroids. Most of them vaporize in our atmosphere, leaving a visible trail of glowing dust we call a meteor or shooting star.

Meteorites are meteors that make it through Earth's atmosphere and reach the ground.

Meteors appear on a regular basis in the night sky, but they also occur with great reliability in large numbers at certain times of the year. Known as meteor showers, they are often named for the background constellations against which they appear.

GLOSSARY

CLICK IT: Asteroids www.nasm.si.edu/etp/asteroids

Short-period comet: A comet that makes regular orbits around the sun every 200 years or less. Halley's comet, with its 75- or 76-year period, is a short-period comet. **/ Long-period comet:** A comet that makes regular orbits around the sun every 200 years or more.

FOR MORE FACTS ON...

THE APPEARANCE & LOCATION OF ASTEROIDS see *The Planets: Terrestrial,* **CHAPTER 2, PAGE 61**

THE CHICXULUB CRATER IN MEXICO see *Ages of the Earth,* **CHAPTER 3, PAGE 95**

Sunset at Stonehenge, Wiltshire, England

OBSERVATION

LANDMARKS IN ASTRONOMY

CIRCA 2250 B.C.
Sumerians record constellation names and positions

CIRCA 1300 B.C.
Egyptians track 43 constellations and 5 planets

250 B.C.
Greece's Eratosthenes measures Earth's circumference

A.D. 1054
Chinese note a supernova

1609
Galileo uses first telescope

1610
Kepler discovers the laws of planetary motion

n ancient times, everyone was a lay astronomer. Shepherds guarding their flocks, for instance, had unimpeded views of the night sky and spent long hours observing it. Everything in the sky, day or night, was of great interest. Time, impending weather, and signs of the passage of the seasons could be discerned from a close watch of the heavens.

Keen early astronomers noticed patterns in the movement of heavenly objects. The oldest known astronomical records were made some 5,000 years ago by the Sumerians, living in modern-day southern Iraq. They catalogued star patterns and named them according to their suggested shapes, including the bull, lion, and scorpion seen now in the zodiac.

Stargazing evolved into systematic observation, and ancient cultures began to chart the movements of the sun, moon, and planets more methodically. Much of this record-keeping tied into astrology and the belief that the movement and position of celestial bodies can predict or influence events. While now regarded as pseudoscientific, these observations and records helped build the foundation of astronomical knowledge.

FOR MORE FACTS ON...

THE ZODIAC & HOW ANCIENT CULTURES VIEWED STAR PATTERNS see *Constellations,* **CHAPTER 2, PAGES 46-7**

WHAT CAUSES THE SEASONS ON EARTH see *Equator & Tropics,* **CHAPTER 1, PAGE 37**

ROYAL OBSERVATORY OF THE 18TH CENTURY

Jantar Mantar in Jaipur, India, was built by Maharajah Jai Sawai Singh II between 1727 and 1734. The world's largest stone observatory, it houses 14 instruments used to predict astronomical events such as eclipses. In 1948 it was declared a national monument; in 2004 efforts began to recalibrate and restore the equipment.

EQUIPMENT at Jantar Mantar includes the world's largest sundial, 90 feet tall.

FAST FACT Early astronomers thought that stars were positioned between Earth and the moon.

TYCHO BRAHE / FOREFATHER OF ASTRONOMY

Tycho Brahe (1546–1601) was born into an aristocratic family in a part of Denmark that now belongs to Sweden. At 17 he observed the conjunction of Jupiter and Saturn, keeping meticulous records. He went on to describe and chart a brilliant supernova in the constellation Cassiopeia, now known as Tycho's star. His fame brought him to the attention of the Danish king, who helped him build two observatories and obtain superior instruments. Altogether Tycho measured the position of 777 stars without the aid of a telescope. He became imperial mathematician to the Holy Roman Emperor in Prague in 1599. There he hired a number of assistants, including Johannes Kepler, who furthered Tycho's observations of the skies.

ASTRONOMY CIRCA 500 B.C.

Astronomy among the ancient Babylonians involved observation, record-keeping, and links between heavenly objects and the mythic powers. The Babylonians identified constellations with mythological characters and natural objects, as well as establishing the 12-constellation zodiac.

These ancient astronomers took note of the first and last appearance of planets in the sky, caused by seasonal cycles. They kept such good records that by about 600 B.C. they were able to predict future first and last appearance dates.

BABYLONIAN TABLET, a slab of clay impressed with hash marks, represents astronomical observations circa 500 B.C.

FOR MORE FACTS ON...

THE HISTORY OF MESOPOTAMIA & THE BABYLONIANS see *Mesopotamia 3500 B.C.-500 B.C.,* **CHAPTER 7, PAGES 266-7**

THE GEOGRAPHY & ECONOMICS OF THE COUNTRY OF INDIA see *Asia,* **CHAPTER 9, PAGE 386**

MODERN METHODS

In the 1800s, scientists discovered the realm of light beyond what is visible. Electromagnetic radiation, often simply called radiation, extends on either end of the spectrum from visible light. Much of the story of the universe—past, present, and future— is written in these wavelengths of the electromagnetic spectrum, which are not visible on Earth's surface. Even as it lets in visible light, radio waves, and some infrared waves, Earth's atmosphere blocks many other waves.

The 20th century saw dramatic improvements in observation technologies. Today's scientists observe stars, galaxies, and other celestial objects in the full electromagnetic spectrum by sending up planes, balloons, rockets, spacecraft, and satellites carrying equipment that can capture the more elusive wavelengths such as gamma rays, x-rays, and ultraviolet rays.

Orbiting observatories have truly expanded our astronomical senses. Space-based observatories can see into radiation wavelengths that Earth-based instruments find difficult to image. These include far-infrared wavelengths, which reveal the secrets of relatively cool objects such as planets, comets, and infant stars. Space-based observatories also can examine high-energy processes in the nuclei of galaxies or near black holes.

GROUND-BASED OBSERVATORIES

Our atmosphere interferes with light coming from distant astronomical objects, so most observatories sit on carefully selected mountaintops. High altitude helps eliminate atmospheric distortions, the air here is thinner and more transparent, and these mountaintops experience smooth airflow, creating stable skies for steady viewing. Because of the exacting criteria and expense of establishing ground-based observatories, international astronomical communities cooperate in their administration. Hawaii's Mauna Kea Observatory, for example, contains more than a dozen telescopes operated by more than ten countries.

STARS PASS BY, time-lapsed, over one of the telescopes at Hawaii's Mauna Kea Observatory, the world's largest.

FOR MORE FACTS ON...

THE IMPORTANCE OF TELESCOPES IN CARTOGRAPHY see *Mapmaking,* **CHAPTER 1, PAGE 25**

THE HAWAIIAN ARCHIPELAGO & ITS GEOLOGIC FORMATION see *Islands,* **CHAPTER 3, PAGES 102-3**

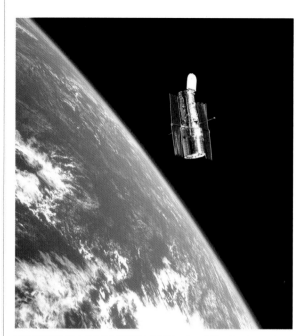

THE HUBBLE SPACE TELESCOPE orbits 375 miles above Earth. Its huge mirrors, cameras, and spectrographs seek—and sometimes find—distant glimmers from the big bang. Computer-controlled adaptive optics help prevent distortions. Spectrographs taken from the Hubble can also distinguish different gases by color.

THE JAMES WEBB SPACE TELESCOPE will replace the Hubble. A longer instrument (72 feet, while Hubble is 43), it will explore both the visible and infrared spectra of the universe from a vantage point a million miles from Earth. It is named for NASA's second administrator, a key leader of the space program in the 1960s.

CLICK IT: HubbleSite www.hubblesite.org

G L O S S A R Y

Infrared spectra: That portion of the electromagnetic spectrum that extends from the long wavelength, or red, end of the visible-light range to the microwave range. Invisible to the eye, it can be detected as a sensation of warmth on the skin. **/ Spectrograph:** Instrument that enables astronomers to analyze the chemical composition of planetary atmospheres, stars, nebulae, and other celestial objects.

EDWIN HUBBLE / OBSERVER OF GALAXIES

Born in Missouri, Edwin Powell Hubble (1889–1953) originally researched nebulae, little understood in his time. He announced in 1924 his surprising discovery that some objects thought to be nebulae were in fact other galaxies. In 1927, Hubble measured the spectra of 46 newly identified galaxies and found that their light had redshifted; that is, these spectra had shifted toward longer wavelengths at the red end of the spectrum. This shift indicated that the galaxies were receding—moving away from Earth. Hubble hypothesized that the universe was expanding at a rate that could be calculated based on a constant, now known as the Hubble constant. He also devised a classification system for galaxies based on their shape.

FOR MORE FACTS ON...

THE HISTORY OF ASTRONOMY & EARLY OBSERVATION METHODS see Observation, **CHAPTER 2, PAGES 68-9**

THEORIES OF HOW THE GALAXIES ARE RECEDING see Expanding Universe, **CHAPTER 2, PAGES 76-7**

72

Lunar Roving Vehicle on the moon during Apollo 15 mission

MILESTONES IN SPACE EXPLORATION

1957
First Soviet satellite, Sputnik I

1958
First U.S. satellite, Explorer I

1961
First men in space

1963
First woman in space

1969
First people on moon

1969
First Soyuz space station

1972
Apollo 17, last moon mission

SPACE EXPLORATION

enturies of scientific breakthroughs—from Chinese rockets to Newtonian physics—laid the groundwork for 20th-century spaceflight. Serious impetus took hold in mid-century and played out actively amid Cold War politics, as the Soviet Union and the United States staged a game of orbital one-upmanship, sending satellites and humans into space.

Since the end of the Cold War, international cooperation has largely replaced competition. It has become common for countries to pool resources and share technology.

Even the most advanced methods of spaceflight continue to conform to the basic principles that Newton laid out some 400 years ago, however.

Every voyage into space, whether manned or unmanned, obeys the law of gravity. Rocketry forms the backbone of space exploration, and Newton's third law of motion governs the principle behind the rocket: The action is the high-speed escape of gas through the rocket's nozzle, and the reaction is the forward movement of

the rocket. In 1957 a Soviet rocket launched the first artificial satellite, Sputnik I, into space. The United States responded with Explorer I the following year.

Once satellites were successful, it was only a short wait until the first manned flight into space took place. Various animals, from mice to dogs to a chimp, were enlisted for preliminary tests.

Cosmonaut Yuri Gagarin edged out American astronauts with his pathbreaking launch in 1961. Inaugurating the Apollo program in 1961, the United States took the lead in the moon race in 1969, landing Apollo 11 there on July 20. The U.S. remains the sole nation to have accomplished manned extraterrestrial landings.

FOR MORE FACTS ON...

RECENT INVESTIGATIONS & EXPLORATION ON THE PLANET MARS see *Space Exploration: Collaboration*, **CHAPTER 2, PAGES 74-5**

THE HISTORY OF THE COLD WAR see *Cold War 1945-1991*, **CHAPTER 7, PAGES 316-7**

WHAT DOES IT MEAN TO BE AN ASTRONAUT?

In 1959 seven handpicked pilots became the first U.S. astronauts, or "star sailors." Initially, all were to be qualified test pilots. Professional scientists were included in 1965, and more joined when NASA began the space shuttle program in 1978. Women and minorities were also added to the roster, eventually commanding shuttle flights. The U.S. space program now has more than a hundred active astronauts.

Astronauts' duties include walking in space, flying the shuttle, and constructing the International Space Station. They also conduct experiments, make observations, maintain and repair equipment, and contribute to the design and testing of new space vehicles.

In 2001 private citizen Dennis Tito paid a reported $20 million to board a Russian spacecraft for a "vacation" that included a stay aboard the International Space Station. The U.S. and Russian space agencies refer to space tourists as "spaceflight participants."

MOONWALKER Edwin E. "Buzz" Aldrin, Jr., makes history on July 20, 1969. He was photographed by Cmdr. Neil A. Armstrong from the lunar landing module, while fellow astronaut Michael Collins continued orbiting the moon in Apollo 11.

YURI GAGARIN / FIRST INTO SPACE

Yuri Gagarin (1934-1968) was the first human being to travel in space when he successfully completed a single orbit in a one-man space capsule, Vostok I. The son of a carpenter, Gagarin joined the Soviet Air Force in 1955. Two years later his country, the Union of Soviet Socialist Republics, launched Sputnik, the world's first communications satellite.

Gagarin's historic spaceflight took place on April 12, 1961. Launched from Kazakhstan, his craft reached a speed of 17,000 miles an hour and a distance of 187 miles above Earth. Vostok I orbited Earth once; the flight lasted 108 minutes. Although Gagarin was scheduled for further spaceflights, he died in a jet crash in 1968. His Russian birthplace now bears his name.

FAST FACT: At its peak, some 400,000 people worked on the Apollo project, at NASA headquarters and elsewhere.

FOR MORE FACTS ON...

THE BIOGRAPHY OF AN ASTRONAUT see *Space Exploration: Collaboration,* **CHAPTER 2, PAGE 75**

+

THE LAYERS OF GASES SURROUNDING EARTH see *Earth's Atmosphere,* **CHAPTER 3, PAGES 104-5**

SPACE EXPLORATION

COLLABORATION

The International Space Station (ISS) is a global collaboration in space engineering and technology and the largest scientific cooperative program in history. Canada, Japan, Russia, Brazil, the United States, and 11 European nations represent the core partnership at the heart of the operation. Involvement and interest comes from other countries of the world as well. ISS was first launched in 1998 and has been in operation ever since. It represents the first permanent human presence in space.

Powered by an array of solar photovoltaic cells spread like wings on a truss structure above the vessel, ISS is made up of a series of cylindrical cabins for work and habitation. Additional modules are launched and connected with each new mission.

Not only do the men and women living in the space station manage many different ongoing experiments, but they are themselves experimental subjects, as they learn how to conduct life and work in the weightless environment of an orbiting spacecraft.

THE INTERNATIONAL SPACE STATION uses Canadarm2 (in the foreground), a complex robotic arm, to manipulate large payloads and interact with the space shuttle.

SPACEFLIGHT TRAGEDIES

Considering all the potential dangers, manned spaceflight has been a remarkably safe undertaking. Those who have died on space missions (4.1 percent of American astronauts, 0.9 of Russian cosmonauts) have become heroes.

Although it occurred during a training procedure, the 1967 loss of the three-member Apollo 1 crew had a great impact in the United States.

No one who witnessed the launch of the space shuttle *Challenger* on January 28, 1986, will forget the horror of the explosion that occurred 73 seconds after liftoff, killing all seven crew members, including New Hampshire schoolteacher Christa McAuliffe. And on February 1, 2003, the entire crew of the space shuttle *Columbia* perished over the southwestern United States.

FOR MORE FACTS ON...

ALTERNATIVE ENERGY SOURCES INCLUDING SOLAR in *Power: Alternative Technologies*, **CHAPTER 8, PAGES 354-5**

INTERNATIONAL EFFORTS AT COLLABORATION IN OTHER REALMS see *Nations & Alliances*, **CHAPTER 9, PAGES 358-9**

PHOENIX LANDS ON MARS

"Phoenix is now on the surface of Mars, much to the joy of everyone here in Mission Control," wrote NASA blogger Brent Shockley on May 25, 2008. "As icing on the cake," he said, "we've landed nearly perfectly level."

After nearly ten months of travel, the exploratory spacecraft landed on the planet's north pole, a destination determined by NASA's overall strategy to "follow the water" on Mars. The mission will allow scientists to study materials dug from regions of high ice content on the planet's surface.

Two further objectives are to study the history of water in the Martian arctic plain and to search for evidence of a habitable zone. Phoenix will also aid in NASA's long-term goals: determining whether any form of life has arisen on Mars, characterizing Mars's climate and geology, and preparing for human exploration.

THE PHOENIX MARS LANDER, shown here in an artist's rendition, descended onto the surface of Mars in May 2008. Once landed, the spacecraft extended a mechanical arm connected to a rasp, which scrapes shavings from the hard-frozen surface of the red planet. By the end of June, the first samples of Martian soil had been analyzed. Results revealed similarities with the surface soils of the upper dry valleys in Antarctica, suggesting that the planet may once have contained water as we know it on Earth.

CLICK IT: Phoenix Mission phoenix.lpl.arizona.edu/index.php

G L O S S A R Y

Microgravity: A measure of the degree to which an object in space is subjected to acceleration, generally used to mean zero gravity and weightlessness experienced by humans in outer space.

JULIE PAYETTE / ASTRONAUT

Julie Payette (b. 1963) is a runner, a mother, a pianist and singer, a computer engineer, a deep-sea diver, a speaker of six languages, *and* a world-orbiting astronaut. Originally from Montreal, Quebec, she was one of four—from among 5,330 applicants— selected by the Canadian Space Agency (CSA) in 1992 to become an astronaut. She completed her training at NASA in 1998, specializing in robotics. Her first space mission took her on STS-96, a logistics and resupply mission, to the International Space Station in 1999. She has logged nearly 500 hours in space since then. One of the most remarkable moments, she recalls, was the first time she opened the hatch door to let crew members exit on an extravehicular assignment and she first smelled outer space.

FOR MORE FACTS ON...

THE SEARCH FOR LIFE ELSEWHERE IN THE UNIVERSE *see Expanding Universe,* **CHAPTER 2, PAGE 76**

THE FIELDS OF ENGINEERING & RECENT TECHNOLOGY *see Engineering,* **CHAPTER 8, PAGES 332-3**

76

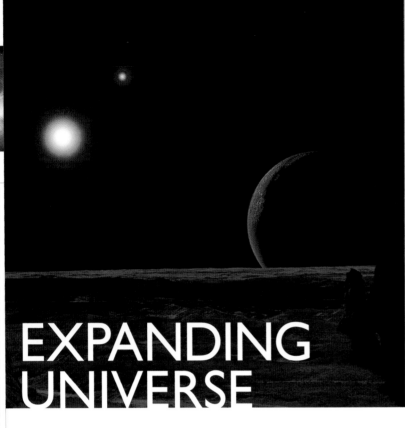

IS THERE LIFE ELSEWHERE?

1960
First SETI experiment examined two stars

1992
NASA begins High Resolution Microwave Survey, seeking short radio waves from stars like the sun

1993
Congress ends NASA's SETI funding

1998
Astronomers begin search for pulses of laser light

2006
Studies of Jupiter's moon Europa investigate possible biosphere beneath ice

2008
Phoenix mission finds ice on Mars, hence the possibility of water supporting life

EXPANDING UNIVERSE

A s galaxies race away from each other, they move not through but with space, for space itself is expanding. The image often used is a loaf of raisin bread. As the dough rises, the raisins (representing objects in space, such as galaxies) move away from each other—and so does the dough they rest in. Expansion is a property of the universe as a whole and not just of galaxies.

Edwin Hubble first discovered that the universe is expanding in 1927. In the decades since then, astronomers have turned their attention to the implications of this finding. It countered prevailing ideas about the future of the universe, presumed to be a slow-ing down due to the pull of gravity from all its matter, which would result finally in a collapse that some termed the "big crunch."

With Hubble's findings, astronomers had to grapple with the implications of a universe that is not only expanding but accelerating as it goes. Many astronomers believe the acceleration is tied to dark energy, a type of antigravity force radiating from deep space.

The nature of dark energy, about which we know very little, might determine the fate of the universe. If dark energy is stable, the universe might continue to expand and accelerate forever. If it is unstable, the universe could ultimately be pulled apart in a scenario dubbed the "big rip." If dark energy has the capacity to change, it could gradually decelerate and become an attractive force that contracts the universe in an implosion like a big crunch.

FAST FACT In a few billion years, the Milky Way and Andromeda galaxies will likely collide and form a combined galaxy.

FOR MORE FACTS ON...

EDWIN HUBBLE & HIS CONTRIBUTIONS TO SPACE EXPLORATION see *Observation: Moden Methods,* **CHAPTER 2, PAGES 70-1**
+
RECENT DEVELOPMENTS IN PHYSICS see *Physics,* **CHAPTER 8, PAGES 330-1**

WHAT'S DARK ENERGY?

Scientists have given the name dark energy to the expansion-generating force or substance of the universe.

Dark energy is the reverse of gravity: It pushes things away rather than pulling them together. It is unknown whether the laws of physics or the general theory of relativity can account for dark energy.

In 1998 astronomers studying supernovae found them dimmer than anticipated. This meant both they were farther away and the universe was expanding faster than expected.

The U.S. government's Joint Dark Energy Mission (JDEM) examines Type Ia supernovae, dying white dwarfs, because of their high and consistent luminosity. Three probes will investigate galaxies near and far, gathering data on the rate of expansion over time.

G L O S S A R Y

String theory: Any of a number of theories in particle physics that treat elementary particles as infinitesimal one-dimensional "stringlike" objects rather than dimensionless points in space-time. **/ White dwarf:** The small, dense core of a once larger star that has fused all the helium in its core.

WHAT'S A BRANE?

Mathematicians and astrophysicists considering the existence of other universes must entertain the possibility of more dimensions than the four we know as space-time: the three familiar dimensions plus the dimension of time, added by Einstein. In one version of string theory, physicists allow for eleven dimensions, including seven that remain imperceptibly "curled up."

The visible universe could be a four-dimensional membrane, or brane for short, moving through unseen dimensions. Other branes, or parallel universes, may also exist, floating through a fifth dimension that we cannot perceive.

Some scientists propose that our would-be universe existed as a brane into which another brane collided in a uniform fashion, generating the heat energy and expansion accounted for in the big bang.

But these theories now exist mainly as mathematical models that require much additional investigation.

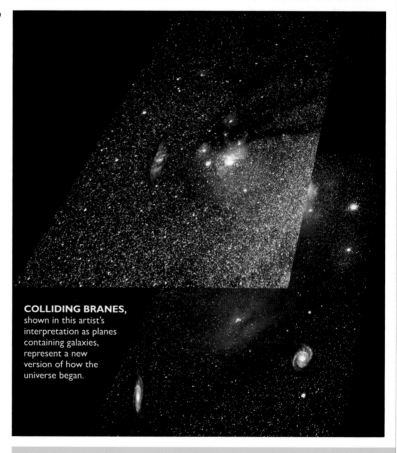

COLLIDING BRANES, shown in this artist's interpretation as planes containing galaxies, represent a new version of how the universe began.

CLICK IT: Sky Survey cas.sdss.org/dr6/en

FOR MORE FACTS ON...

THEORIES ON THE ORIGIN & TIME LINE OF OUR UNIVERSE see *Cosmic Beginnings*, **CHAPTER 2, PAGES 42-3**
+
KEY IDEAS IN ASTROPHYSICS see *Black Holes & Dark Matter*, **CHAPTER 2, PAGES 50-1**

PLANET

EARTH

Spiral galaxy, as seen by Hubble, about ten million light-years from Earth

FORMATION OF THE EARTH

EARTH FACTS

MASS
6.583 sextillion tons

DISTANCE AROUND EQUATOR
24,901 miles

AREA
196,938,000 square miles

LAND AREA
57,393,000 square miles

WATER AREA
139,545,000 square miles

For as long as human beings have observed and reflected on the natural world that they inhabit, they have told stories about the formation of Earth. Creation narratives occur in just about every system of belief. They may involve the actions of primeval deities, abstract powers, or—in our modern scientific worldview—physical objects and the forces that govern their interactions.

There is also a human urge to want to date the beginning of the world as we know it.

In the early 17th century, after carefully studying biblical chronologies that recounted the span of many kingships and long lists of family descendants, Anglican Archbishop James Ussher announced as a fact that the creation of the Earth had occurred at 9 a.m. on October 26 in the year 4004 B.C.

Ussher's calculations and their implications were widely accepted for more than a century, but then scientific study of rock formations and fossils suggested that Earth had existed longer than Ussher supposed.

We now know that Earth and the rest of our solar system formed

FOR MORE FACTS ON...

THE FORMATION AND EVOLUTION OF THE UNIVERSE see *Cosmic Beginnings*, **CHAPTER 2, PAGES 42-3**

HOW THEORIES OF THE COSMOS HAVE CHANGED THROUGH HISTORY see *Scientific Worldviews*, **CHAPTER 8, PAGES 326-7**

together about 4.6 billion years ago from a huge cloud of gas and dust following a gigantic star explosion within the universe. The sun formed at the center of some debris.

Chunks of matter coalesced into planets, including Earth. In a process known as accretion, Earth's gravity continued (and continues) to attract debris, which becomes incorporated into its surface. Over time the fledgling Earth took shape.

Repeated impacts, radiation from the sun, and internal processes caused our planet to settle into layers: an inner core, an outer core, a mantle, and a crust. A few fragments of the original crust remain.

Interior melting traveled to the surface, creating volcanic processes that spewed forth lava and gases. These gases, including water vapor, gave rise to Earth's primitive atmosphere. The resulting precipitation accumulated over time to form Earth's first oceans.

These materials and processes also set the stage for the appearance of life on planet Earth some 3.5 billion years ago.

G L O S S A R Y

Accretion: Growth or increase in size by incorporation of external materials; in astronomy or geology, the gradual building up of a body through inclusion of incoming matter. **/ Aggregation:** A mass composed of many distinct parts; in geology, growth or increase in size by combining many distinct pieces of material into one body through heat, pressure, or both.

EARTH'S FOUR LAYERS

Earth has four major layers. The crust floats on the mantle and is the thinnest and least dense of the four layers. The crust of the ocean floors ranges from 2 to 7 miles thick and is composed of igneous rock rich in iron and magnesium. Continental crust ranges from 6 to 45 miles thick—it is thickest under mountain ranges—and contains much feldspar and silica, making it less dense than oceanic crust. Over millions of years the crust has been shaped into a variety of landscapes, including both continental and oceanic mountain ranges and deep oceanic trenches.

Earth's mantle is denser rock that extends about 1,790 miles toward the core. The mantle incorporates both brittle and molten layers. Temperature and pressure increase with the depth of the mantle.

Earth's core lies beneath the mantle in two layers. The outer core, which is liquid, measures about 1,400 miles thick. The inner core, which is solid, lies at the center of the planet. It is spherical, with only a 750-mile radius. Iron is the most common element in the outer and inner cores. The core and mantle are nearly the same thickness, yet the mantle comprises 84 percent of Earth's volume and the core only 15 percent.

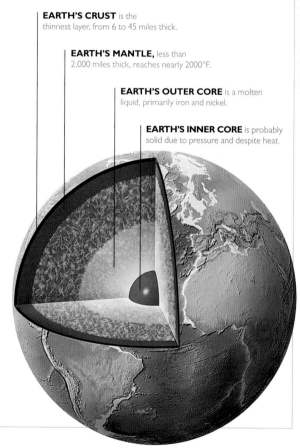

EARTH'S CRUST is the thinnest layer, from 6 to 45 miles thick.

EARTH'S MANTLE, less than 2,000 miles thick, reaches nearly 2000°F.

EARTH'S OUTER CORE is a molten liquid, primarily iron and nickel.

EARTH'S INNER CORE is probably solid due to pressure and despite heat.

FOR MORE FACTS ON...

THE INNER LAYER OF PLANET EARTH *see Earth's Interior,* **CHAPTER 3, PAGES 82-3**

THE CHARACTERISTICS AND DYNAMICS OF WATER ON PLANET EARTH *see Oceans,* **CHAPTER 3, PAGES 112-5**

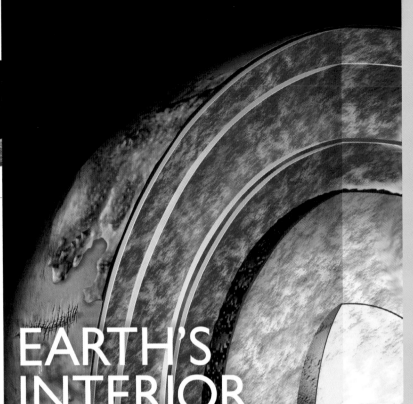

Illustration indicating the layers that make up the Earth's crust and core

LAYERS OF THE EARTH

CRUST
6-45 miles thick above sea level
2-7 miles thick on ocean floor
Thinnest and least dense layer
Composed of igneous rock

MANTLE
Approximately 1,790 miles thick
Includes both brittle and molten layers
Temperatures reach nearly 2000°F
Heat increases with depth

OUTER CORE
Approx. 1,400 miles thick
Composed of molten metal,
especially iron and nickel

INNER CORE
750-mile radius
Solid due to pressure
Composed primarily of iron

EARTH'S INTERIOR

Novelist Jules Verne imagined journeying to the center of the Earth in his 19th-century science fiction classic by that same name, but no human has really ventured deeper than Earth's crust—let alone all the way to the core at its center. Extremes of temperature and pressure make the almost 4,000-mile undertaking impossible. The deepest mine shaft extends no more than 2.5 miles beneath Earth's surface. Interior sample drilling has penetrated only 8 miles down.

Scientists gather information about Earth's interior by recording, imaging, and measuring vibrations, or seismic waves, caused by earthquakes or explosions. The movement and the speed of seismic waves as they travel through Earth provide data that inform us about the composition and structure of Earth's interior.

Earth may have started out as a cold planet and heated up, or it may have been a molten planet that eventually cooled on the outside. Scientists do not yet agree on those points. Either way, complex geologic events created the present structure of Earth's core.

The inner part of the core is made of superhot, iron-rich material. The temperature there may be as high as 10,000°F, as hot as scientists believe it gets on the surface of the sun. The pressure on the inner core is so intense that it remains solid and does not melt, despite such high temperatures.

The outer part of the core likely is molten iron and nickel.

The entire core is some 4,350 miles in diameter, more than half of Earth's diameter. Studies of Earth's interior suggest that the outer boundary of the core may be irregular, much like Earth's surface.

FAST FACT Earth's inner solid core spins at a different rate from Earth itself.

FOR MORE FACTS ON...

WHY AND HOW EARTHQUAKES OCCUR see *Earthquakes,* **CHAPTER 3, PAGES 88-9**

THE CHEMICAL COMPOSITION OF PLANET EARTH see *Earth's Elements,* **CHAPTER 3, PAGES 90-1**

THE MOHO AND GUTENBERG DISCONTINUITIES

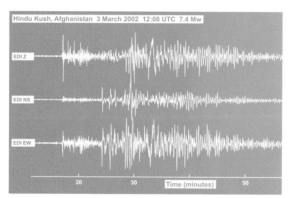

Hindu Kush, Afghanistan 3 March 2002 12:08 UTC 7.4 Mw

EDI Z

EDI NS

EDI EW

20   30   Time (minutes)   50

A SEISMOGRAM graphs Earth's motions through time, sensed by a seismograph, an instrument with electromagnetic sensors that detect movement in the Earth's surface. This seismogram shows a single earthquake tremor detected at three different locations.

Croatian physicist Andrija Mohorovičić (1857-1936), one of the first scientists to use seismographic equipment to study earthquakes, noticed that some seismic waves arrived at his observatory earlier than anticipated. From this, he calculated that Earth's crust and mantle had different densities. As seismic waves reach the denser mantle, they speed up. In his honor, the transition zone where this speedup occurs is named the Mohorovičić, or Moho, discontinuity.

Seismic waves also undergo changes in speed in the transition zone between Earth's mantle and the outer core. This zone is named the Gutenberg discontinuity, honoring American physicist Beno Gutenberg (1889–1960), who helped Charles Richter develop the Richter scale.

CLICK IT: Geology www.geology.com

GLOSSARY

Lithosphere: A rigid, rocky outer layer of Earth, consisting of the crust and the solid, outermost layer of the upper mantle; includes nearly all of the Moho discontinuity. **/ Asthenosphere:** A zone of Earth's mantle that lies beneath the lithosphere; it is believed to be much hotter and more fluid than the lithosphere. **/ Mesosphere:** A zone of the deep mantle that lies below the asthenosphere, where rocks are believed to be rigid again.

THE DEEPEST HOLE EVER DUG

On Russia's Kola Peninsula, near Norway, geologists have been drilling a well since 1970. Now at over 40,000 feet deep, it is the deepest hole in Earth. Next deepest is the Bertha Rogers well in Oklahoma, a gas well for which the drilling stopped at 32,000 feet, when molten sulfur was reached.

The Kola well is being dug to study Earth's crust. It now goes about halfway through the crust of the Baltic continental shield, penetrating to rocks 2.7 billion years old.

Scientists noted a change in seismic velocities at the bottom of a layer of metamorphic rock—formed by change in its composition, the effects of intense heat and pressure—that extends from about three to six miles

A SOVIET STAMP from 1987 celebrates the history and science of the world's deepest borehole.

down. It had been thoroughly fractured and was saturated with water. No one expected to find water at these depths.

The discovery could only mean that water that had originally been a part of the chemical composition of the minerals themselves—not groundwater—had been forced out of the crystals and prevented from rising by an overlying cap of impermeable rock. This phenomenon has never been observed anywhere else.

The Kola well discovery has a potential economic impact. No technology exists for mining these depths, but a drill bit could be turned by the mudflow itself, eliminating the need for the entire drill string above.

FOR MORE FACTS ON...

THE USE OF SONAR TECHNOLOGY TO PROBE OCEAN DEPTHS see Modern Maps, **CHAPTER 1, PAGE 27**

THE GEOGRAPHY OF THE COUNTRY OF RUSSIA TODAY see Europe, **CHAPTER 9, PAGE 407**

CONTINENTAL AREA

ASIA
17,208,000 square miles

AFRICA
11,608,000 square miles

NORTH AMERICA
9,449,000 square miles

SOUTH AMERICA
6,880,000 square miles

ANTARCTICA
5,100,000 square miles

EUROPE
3,841,000 square miles

AUSTRALIA
2,970,000 square miles

CONTINENTS

Earth's total landmass is exceeded by a factor of almost three to one by the surface of the oceans. Still, the major land divisions—the continents—are what give the shape and physical identity to the planet. The seven continents represent some 57 million square miles in area, portioned unequally among them. They range in size from Asia, the largest, to Australia, the smallest. Although Europe and Asia form one large landmass, they are usually regarded as two continents, due mainly to the cultural differences between their peoples.

The seven continents as they appear today represent just one episode in an ongoing scenario of wandering landmasses. It is a process whose history reaches back to the initial formation of continental material on Earth's crust almost four billion years ago—a process called plate tectonics.

The crust and the top portion of the mantle form a rigid shell around the planet that is broken up into 16 large sections known as plates. Heat generated inside Earth and distributed through convection currents causes the plates to move slowly. That same sort of movement has been going on for hundreds of millions of years.

Most geologists believe that the continents were created when vast plates of rock collided, forcing one to slide under another in a process called subduction. The crust then melted and formed magma, or molten rock. Erupting to the surface, the magma built volcanic islands that eventually fused with other islands on adjoining plates—becoming the first continental material.

FAST FACT Earth, not a sphere, bulges in the Southern Hemisphere.

FOR MORE FACTS ON...

THE CONTINENT OF ANTARCTICA see Nations & Alliances, **CHAPTER 9, PAGE 359**

THE CONTINENTS see Africa, Asia, Europe, Australia & Oceania, North America & South America, **CHAPTER 9, PAGES 360-1, 378-9, 394-5, 408-9, 414-5 & 424-5**

HOW DID THE CONTINENTS FORM?

As Earth's continental masses grew bigger, moving all the while, they shifted in relation to each other and coalesced into different arrangements over hundreds of millions of years. The current configuration of continents is just a temporary one in the eons-long process of plate tectonics.

Three times during the past billion years, drifting landmasses have merged to form supercontinents.

In between these stages of continental drift, they split into smaller landmasses before recombining again. Scientists predict that a new supercontinent, Pangaea Ultima, will eventually form, 250 million years from now.

500 MILLION YEARS ago, a chunk broke off a single continent. Shallow waters spawned the first multicellular creatures.

300 MILLION YEARS ago, some of today's mountains formed. A new ice age covered Earth's southern regions.

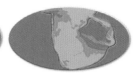

225 MILLION YEARS ago, the earliest dinosaurs roamed a single continent that stretched from Pole to Pole.

100 MILLION YEARS ago, cracks across the one continent, known as Pangaea, formed rifts that evolved into oceans.

50 MILLION YEARS ago, a climate-changing meteor crashed into Earth and the highest mountains began their uprise.

20,000 YEARS ago, ice sheets a mile deep gouged out the Great Lakes and then receded, raising sea levels.

GLOSSARY

Continent: From the Latin *continens*, "held together." One of Earth's seven large continuous masses of land. **/ Tectonics:** From the Greek *tekton*, "builder." Study of the changes in Earth's crust and the forces that produce such changes. **/ Subduction zone:** The oceanic trench area in which the seafloor underthrusts an adjacent plate, dragging accumulated sediments downward into Earth's upper mantle.

> " We have to be prepared always for the possibility that each new discovery, no matter what science furnishes it, may modify the conclusions we draw. "
> — **ALFRED WEGENER, 1929**

ALFRED WEGENER / EARTH SCIENTIST

German Alfred Wegener (1880–1930), among the first to use balloons to track air currents, participated in expeditions to Greenland to study polar air circulation but became better known for his theory of continental drift. People had already noticed that the coastlines of western Africa and eastern South America seemed to match, but Wegener found evidence that the continents had been joined: similar fossils from both sides of the Atlantic and tropical species in Arctic areas. He posited the existence of a supercontinent, Pangaea (All Lands), that eventually broke up, and he presented his ideas in *The Origins of Continents and Oceans*—but few believed him. In the 1950s and 1960s, studies of the ocean floor demonstrated a mechanism for crustal movement, and Wegener's theory of continental drift finally gained acceptance.

FOR MORE FACTS ON...

SHAPES & CONTOURS ON PLANET EARTH see *Landforms*, **CHAPTER 3, PAGES 98-101**
+
THE EVOLVING CONFIGURATION OF LAND ON PLANET EARTH see *Ages of the Earth*, **CHAPTER 3, PAGES 94-5**

Japan's Mount Fuji, a dormant volcano

VOLCANOES

DEADLIEST

TAMBORA
Indonesia / 1815 / 92,000 dead

KRAKATAU
Indonesia / 1883 / 36,417 dead

MONT PELEE
Martinique / 1902 / 29,025 dead

NEVADO DEL RIO
Colombia / 1985 / 25,000 dead

UNZEN
Japan / 1792 / 14,300 dead

LAKI
Iceland / 1783 / 9,350 dead

KELUT
Indonesia / 1919 / 5,110 dead

Volcanoes are produced when heat and pressure build up deep inside Earth. Material that makes up the mantle and the lower part of the crust reaches such high temperatures, the rock melts. This molten rock, called magma, collects in underground chambers where heat, pressure, and gases cause it to erupt to the surface.

Volcanoes most often appear at the edges of Earth's crustal plates, the 16 separate continental and oceanic segments that move in relation to each other. The action between the two plates determines the type of volcano.

Volcanoes also emerge in the middle of plates at hot spots, where the heat of interior molten rock burns through the crust. The Hawaiian Islands emerge from a hot spot that has moved over time with the Pacific plate.

Volcanoes spew not just lava but also poisonous gases, ash, cinders, and fragments of rock. This deadly combination of volcanic products, called pyroclastic flow, can produce more devastation than a lava flow.

FAST FACT Fewer than 8 percent of Earth's volcanoes are considered active.

FOR MORE FACTS ON...

THE LAYERS INSIDE PLANET EARTH see *Earth's Interior*, **CHAPTER 3, PAGES 82-3**

THE VOLCANIC FORMATION OF EARTH'S ISLANDS & ARCHIPELAGOS see *Islands*, **CHAPTER 3, PAGES 102-3**

Volcanoes take diverse shapes depending on the type of magma involved and the structure of the chamber and vents through which it erupts. Japan's Mount Fuji is a composite cone, built of alternating layers of lava and ash. Hawaii has shield volcanoes, formed from thin, runny lava that travels far before it hardens. A magma chamber in the northern Rockies, site of an ancient collapsed volcano, fuels Yellowstone's hot springs, vents, and geysers—the world's largest collection of these geothermal features.

About 1,900 active volcanoes can be found on Earth. Volcanoes that have not erupted in a long time are called dormant; volcanoes that once erupted but will never erupt again are called extinct.

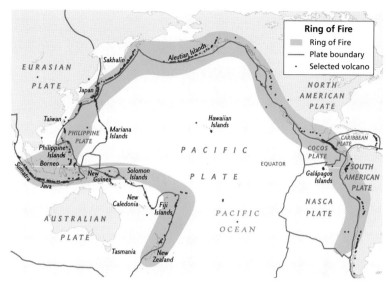

RING OF FIRE, EARTH'S VOLCANIC RIM, is home to more than half of the volcanoes on Earth. This configuration in the Pacific Ocean, an arc more than 24,000 miles long, follows the rim of the Pacific plate. In this zone of subduction, the Pacific plate dives under the edge of continental plates. As a result, rock melts and fuels volcanoes on the surface.

FAST FACT Dust after Tambora's eruption lowered temperatures worldwide: 1816 was a "year without summer."

TYPES OF VOLCANOES

Volcanoes vary in shape depending on the processes by which they were formed, the configurations of their eruptions, and the way they laid materials upon Earth's surface during their eruptions. Sometimes a volcano type can be identified from the ground or the air, but its underground form and composition is key to identification.

STRATOVOLCANOES are steep cones built of ash, rock, and lava spewed out during eruptions and deposited in layers.

SHIELD VOLCANOES are large dome-shaped mountains built of lava flows, usually composed of basalt.

CALDERAS are large bowl-shaped depressions with in-facing rims, often collapsed volcanic cones.

SOMMAVOLCANOES are calderas now partly filled with newly formed central cones.

COMPLEX VOLCANOES reveal volcanic structures formed of multiple craters and summits.

G L O S S A R Y

CLICK IT: Hawaii Volcano Observatory hvo.wr.usgs.gov

Magma: Melted rock; erupting to Earth's surface, it becomes lava. **/ Lahar:** Mudflow of volcanic material. **/ Pyroclastic flow:** In a volcanic eruption, fluidized mixture of hot rock fragments, gases, and entrapped air that moves at high speed in thick clouds that hug the ground.

FOR MORE FACTS ON...

VOLCANISM AS ONE OF THE FORCES THAT SHAPE THE SURFACE OF PLANET EARTH see *Landforms,* **CHAPTER 3, PAGE 99**

OCEANIA & THE ISLANDS OF THE PACIFIC see *Australia & Oceania,* **CHAPTER 9, PAGES 408-13**

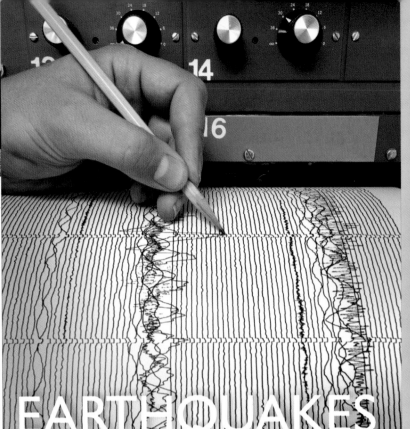

Taking notes on a seismograph

DEADLIEST SINCE 1900

CHINA / 1976 / 655,000 dead

SUMATRA / 2004 / 227,898 dead

HAITI / 2010 / 222,570 dead

CHINA / 1920 / 200,000 dead

JAPAN / 1923 / 142,800 dead

RUSSIA / 1948 / 110,000 dead

PAKISTAN / 2005 / 86,000 dead

ITALY / 1908 / 72,000 dead

PERU / 1970 / 70,000 dead

CHINA / 2008 / 69,000 dead

EARTHQUAKES

Earthquakes happen when vibrations are caused by the movement of rock along a fault, a fracture that exists in Earth's crust. As the tectonic plates push against, pull away from, grind past, or dive under one another, fault zones are created. Sometimes tension builds up along a fault, and further movement can cause the release of energy in the form of seismic waves, or vibrations in Earth's crust. Those vibrations ripple violently through the crust, causing an earthquake.

Faults in Earth's crust can take different forms, depending on the kind of tectonic stress involved, the strength of the rock, the presence of groundwater along the fault plane, and the area of contact between the plates. Movement along faults can be fast or slow. Abrupt movement causes earthquakes; movement so slow as to be imperceptible is called fault creep.

A severe earthquake can produce underground movements—forward and back, up and down, side to side—and wavelike ripples. Seismographs around the world sense at least a million earthquake movements a year. People barely perceive most of these.

Like volcanic eruptions, most earthquakes happen along the edges of tectonic plates. California's San Andreas Fault, for example, is a zone where the slow sideways movement of slabs has pushed rock formations some 350 miles from their sources.

Major earthquakes tend to produce dangerous side effects such as landslides and tsunamis, adding greatly to the destruction and casualties.

FAST FACT The average rate of motion across the San Andreas Fault is the same rate at which fingernails grow.

FOR MORE FACTS ON...

THE NATURE AND COMPOSITION OF EARTH'S CRUST see Earth's Interior, **CHAPTER 3, PAGES 82-3**

ALFRED WEGENER AND HIS THEORY OF CONTINENTAL DRIFT see Continents, **CHAPTER 3, PAGE 85**

WHAT IS A TSUNAMI?

A tsunami is a deadly series of seismic sea waves: ocean waves triggered primarily by the movement of the ocean floor during strong earthquakes. Volcanic eruptions in or near the ocean may also cause tsunamis. Tsunamis generally cause major damage to coastlines and can cause death.

The worst tsunami in history occurred after a 9.0 earthquake off the northwest coast of Sumatra, Indonesia, on December 26, 2004. The resulting oceanwide tsunami struck Thailand, Malaysia, Sri Lanka, India, the Maldives, and Africa. Nearly a quarter million people died as a result.

A tidal wave is an ocean wave of unusual strength caused by the same tidal forces that create the daily tidal ebb and flow. One such wave appears annually at China's Hangzhou Bay.

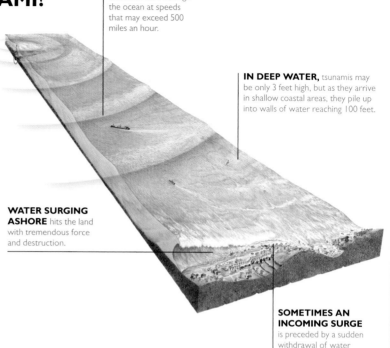

SEISMIC SEA WAVES race through the ocean at speeds that may exceed 500 miles an hour.

IN DEEP WATER, tsunamis may be only 3 feet high, but as they arrive in shallow coastal areas, they pile up into walls of water reaching 100 feet.

WATER SURGING ASHORE hits the land with tremendous force and destruction.

SOMETIMES AN INCOMING SURGE is preceded by a sudden withdrawal of water from the shore.

G L O S S A R Y

Seismic wave: Vibration generated by an earthquake, explosion, or similar phenomenon and propagated within the Earth or along its surface.

METHODS FOR MEASURING EARTHQUAKES

Until recently, scientists measuring earthquakes mostly used the Richter scale, developed by U.S. seismologists Charles F. Richter and Beno Gutenberg in the 1930s and 1940s.

In their logarithmic scale of earthquake magnitude, each number represents an intensity ten times greater than the previous one. No earthquake has exceeded a value of 9.5, which occurred in Chile on May 22, 1960.

The Richter scale measures only magnitude. Other scales categorize earthquakes by other criteria. The moment magnitude scale is based on the seismic moment: the area of rock displaced, the rigidity of that rock, and the average distance of displacement.

The Mercalli intensity scale (named for Giuseppe Mercalli, the Italian scientist who originated it) uses Roman numerals to rate an earthquake by its effects on the surroundings. During an earthquake rated I, people feel no Earth movement. During a V, almost everyone feels movement, trees might shake, and liquid might spill. During a X, most buildings and foundations are destroyed, dams break, and cracks in the ground show.

CLICK IT: Seismic Science at the Epicenter www.exploratorium.edu/faultline/index.html

FOR MORE FACTS ON...

WAVES IN EARTH'S OCEANS see *Oceans,* **CHAPTER 3, PAGE 114**
+
OTHER TYPES OF DISASTER INCLUDING TORNADOES & HURRICANES see *Storms,* **CHAPTER 5, PAGES 186-9**

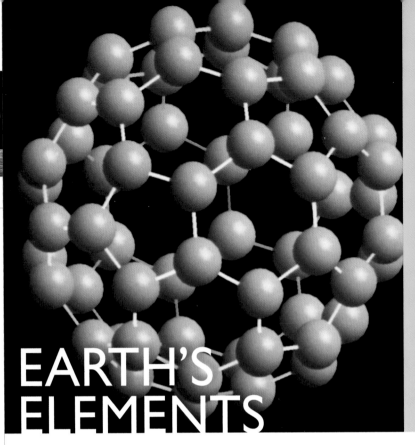

Molecule of 60 carbon atoms, commonly called fullerene or buckyball

MOST COMMON ELEMENTS
BY WEIGHT IN EARTH'S CRUST

OXYGEN
46.6%

SILICON
27.7%

ALUMINUM
8.1%

IRON
5.0%

CALCIUM
3.6%

SODIUM
2.8%

POTASSIUM
2.6%

EARTH'S ELEMENTS

Matter is composed of elements, substances that cannot be broken down chemically into simpler or more basic substances. To date, 117 elements have been discovered. Some of these, such as oxygen, silicon, aluminum, and iron, are abundant in Earth's makeup. Though it appears that Earth contains a limited number of naturally occurring elements, the number of compounds formed by the joining of one or more of these elements seems nearly limitless, especially when considering both natural and artificial compounds.

During the first billion years of the existence of Earth, heat from three sources—meteorite impacts, gravity's compression of magma and other material, and the radioactive decay of some elements—caused melting in the interior. Elements separated into layers based on their density. Heavy elements such as iron and nickel concentrated nearer Earth's center; lighter elements such as oxygen and silicon combined and formed surface rocks and minerals.

Earth's elements can be displayed in a chart called the periodic table. The periodic table arranges the elements into groups (vertically) of elements sharing common physical and chemical characteristics and into periods (horizontally) based on the atomic configuration of elements. Each element is given a number and a distinctive location on the chart. Elements 112–116 and 118 are reported to have been created experimentally but have not yet received permanent names.

FAST FACT The periodic table of elements contains placeholders for elements not yet discovered or created.

FOR MORE FACTS ON...

CURRENT ATOMIC THEORY & SUBATOMIC PARTICLES see *Physics*, **CHAPTER 8, PAGES 330-1**

RECENT DEVELOPMENTS & NEW IDEAS IN CHEMISTRY see *Chemistry*, **CHAPTER 8, PAGES 334-5**

ELEMENTS ESSENTIAL FOR LIFE ON EARTH

When scientists found evidence of simple living cells in rocks they have determined to be 3.5 billion years old, it gave them reason to wonder: How could life have begun on an irradiated, oxygen-starved Earth? In their laboratories, they duplicated Earth's primitive atmosphere. To simulate lightning and harsh sunlight, they seared gas mixtures with high-voltage sparks and ultraviolet light—forces that make and break chemical bonds. In the resulting brew they found amino acids, the building blocks of life. Now researchers believe that the same process occurred on Earth 3 to 4 billion years ago.

Another experiment showed that amino acids on a hot, dry surface—like that of a cooling rock—form cell-like spheres when splashed with water. If rain washed the spheres into a tidal pool, a place safe from ultraviolet radiation, more complex molecules could form. At last one appeared with the ability to reproduce itself: That molecule was similar to deoxyribonucleic acid, or DNA, the complex organic molecule that exists today in every living cell. And with the appearance of DNA, life on Earth began.

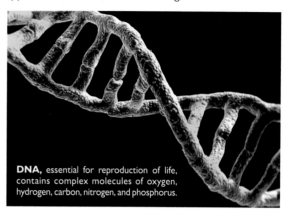

DNA, essential for reproduction of life, contains complex molecules of oxygen, hydrogen, carbon, nitrogen, and phosphorus.

CLICK IT: Interactive Periodic Table www.webelements.com

G L O S S A R Y

Atomic weight: Ratio of the average mass of a chemical element's atoms to some standard. Since 1961 the standard unit of atomic mass has been one-twelfth the mass of an atom of the isotope carbon-12. **/ Native element:** Any of 19 chemical elements that can occur as minerals and are found in nature uncombined with other elements; gold, for example, is a native element.

" The elements, if arranged according to their atomic weights, exhibit an apparent periodicity of properties. — **DMITRY MENDELEYEV, 1869** "

DMITRY MENDELEYEV / INVENTOR OF PERIODIC TABLE

Born in Siberia, the youngest of 14 children, Dmitry I. Mendeleyev (1834–1907) was working as a chemist in St. Petersburg in the early 1860s when he devised a visual scheme by which to organize Earth's elements. At the time, 63 elements were known, and Mendeleyev arranged them in a table by atomic weight, making groupings based on shared properties. He also used his principles to predict the existence of new elements. During his lifetime three new elements were recognized—gallium, scandium, and germanium. They fit his table according to plan. These discoveries went far to validate Mendeleyev's periodic table, which has become a fixture in the field of chemistry. Many other scientists have contributed to it since its invention, and it continues to help us understand how our planet and universe are put together.

FOR MORE FACTS ON...

THE PERIODIC TABLE OF ELEMENTS see Chemistry, **CHAPTER 8, PAGE 335**

THE DISCOVERY OF DNA & ITS ROLE IN RECENT GENETIC SCIENCE & ENGINEERING see Genetics, **CHAPTER 8, PAGES 344-5**

Sandstone, Colorado Plateau, Arizona

ROCKS & MINERALS

MINERAL HARDNESS
FROM SOFT TO HARD

1 / TALC

2 / GYPSUM

3 / CALCITE

4 / FLUORITE

5 / APATITE

6 / FELDSPAR

7 / QUARTZ

8 / TOPAZ

9 / CORUNDUM

10 / DIAMOND

arth's crust is composed of rock, a naturally occurring aggregate of one or more minerals. Minerals themselves consist of inorganic crystals, chemical building blocks arranged in patterns that form three-dimensional solids. Chemical composition and crystal structure determine the mineral's physical properties, such as its hardness, its resistance to weathering, and its uses.

The mineral quartz, for example, is formed from the elements silicon and oxygen. Quite hard and resistant to weathering, quartz is used as a source of silicon in computer chips.

More than 4,000 minerals have been identified, but few are common on Earth. Those—such as calcite, quartz, feldspar, and mica—tend to be combi-nations of the most common elements, such as silicon, oxygen, and iron.

Some kinds of rock are composed of a single kind of mineral. Pure marble, for example, is made only of calcite. Other rocks form from a combina-tion of minerals. Granite is a sedimen-tary rock that contains three common minerals: quartz, feldspar, and mica.

FOR MORE FACTS ON...

THE CHEMICAL COMPOSITION OF EARTH see Earth's Elements, **CHAPTER 3, PAGES 90-1**

HOW WEATHER HAS AN INFLUENCE ON EARTH'S TOPOGRAPHY see Weather, **CHAPTER 5, PAGE 182**

THREE TYPES OF ROCK

Rocks fall into three categories, based on their method of formation: igneous, sedimentary, and metamorphic.

Igneous rocks begin in Earth's core. Hotter and lighter than surrounding rock, magma moves up, cools, and crystallizes. Intrusive, or plutonic, igneous rocks usually reach the surface through tectonic processes, such as the formation of mountains. Extrusive igneous rocks, such as obsidian, have a crystal or glassy appearance and are usually found where volcanic activity has occurred.

Sedimentary rocks form when sediments settle in lakes, oceans, and locations such as sand dunes or glacial deposits. The sediments solidify in layers. Clastic rocks, such as sandstone, form from bits of other rocks. Chemical rocks, such as limestone, form when chemicals in solution evaporate. Organic rocks, such as chalk, form from dead plant and animal matter.

Metamorphic rocks take form when igneous, sedimentary, and even previously metamorphosed rocks are subjected to heat and pressure deep within the Earth. The metamorphosis, or change, of the state of the material may involve recrystallization of minerals or development of a new compound. Limestone metamorphoses into marble and granite into gneiss. Most of the oldest rocks on Earth are metamorphic.

PAHOEHOE LAVA from a Hawaiian volcano will harden into igneous rock.

SANDSTONE spires in Canyonlands National Park typify sedimentary rocks.

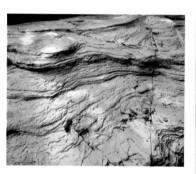

QUARTZITE, here found in North Carolina, is metamorphosed sandstone.

G L O S S A R Y

Crystal: Any solid material in which the component atoms are arranged in a definite pattern and whose surface regularity reflects its internal symmetry. **/ Fossil:** Remnant, impression, or trace of an animal or plant of a past geologic age that has been preserved in Earth's crust. **/ Lithification:** From Greek *lithos*, "rock." A complex process whereby freshly deposited loose grains of sediment are converted into rock.

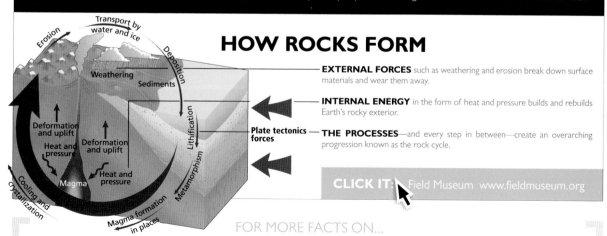

HOW ROCKS FORM

EXTERNAL FORCES such as weathering and erosion break down surface materials and wear them away.

INTERNAL ENERGY in the form of heat and pressure builds and rebuilds Earth's rocky exterior.

THE PROCESSES—and every step in between—create an overarching progression known as the rock cycle.

CLICK IT: Field Museum www.fieldmuseum.org

FOR MORE FACTS ON...

VOLCANOES see *Volcanoes,* **CHAPTER 3, PAGES 86-7**

THE CHANGING COMPOSITION OF EARTH THROUGH TIME see *Ages of the Earth,* **CHAPTER 3, PAGES 94-5**

Fish fossils found at Sihetun, Liaoning Province, China

GEOLOGIC AGES

PHANEROZOIC EON
542 million years ago to today

CENOZOIC ERA
65.5 million years ago to today

MESOZOIC ERA
251 to 65.5 million years ago

PALEOZOIC ERA
542 to 251 million years ago

PROTEROZOIC EON
2,500 to 542 million years ago

ARCHAEAN EON
3,800 to 2,500 million years ago

HADEAN EON
4,500 to 3,800 million years ago

AGES OF THE EARTH

Earth was formed some 4.6 billion years ago. The time that has elapsed since then seems unfathomable to us. We consider ancient the happenings in early civilizations, but they are only a few thousand years old. Our planet's geologic time recedes to the dawn of time, far outstretching any timeframe representing human habitation on Earth.

Geologists separate Earth's history into major units of time called eons. Generally, four are recognized: the Hadean, Archaean, the Proterozoic, and the Phanerozoic eons.

The earliest two, often called Precambrian time, cover the history of the Earth before the first complex life-forms appeared, from 4.6 billion to about 542 million years ago.

Sometimes the Hadean period is incorporated at the beginning of the Precambrian; it spans the early formation of the Earth and predates most of the geological record.

The Precambrian represents four-fifths of Earth's history. Little is known of it compared with the most recent eon, the Phanerozoic, which is known by its abundant fossil record.

Scientists separate the Phanerozoic eon into three subdivisions, or eras: the Paleozoic ("old life"), the Mesozoic ("middle life"), and the Cenozoic ("recent life").

The eras are separated according to the kinds of life-forms that existed at that stage. Animal life sprang into its diverse forms during the Paleozoic. Dinosaurs ruled during the Mesozoic, when flowering plants also evolved.

Humans appeared in the late Cenozoic, an era also known as the age of mammals.

FAST FACT Modern humans have lived on Earth for just over one-thousandth of a percent of the planet's existence.

FOR MORE FACTS ON...

BIODIVERSITY AMONG THE PLANT & ANIMAL SPECIES ALIVE ON EARTH see *Biodiversity*, **CHAPTER 4, PAGES 174-5**

EXTINCTION OF PLANT & ANIMAL SPECIES ON EARTH see *Extinction*, **CHAPTER 4, PAGES 176-7**

WHY DID THE DINOSAURS DISAPPEAR?

Something drastic happened on Earth about 65 million years ago. According to one theory, an asteroid more than 6 miles across struck just off the coast of Mexico's Yucatán Peninsula. The impact created the Chicxulub crater, more than 110 miles wide, and caused a gigantic dust cloud. The dust settled, forming the layer of iridium-rich clay now found in sedimentary rock under the Atlantic and Pacific Oceans and in most northern landmasses.

The cloud likely caused world temperatures to drop. Scientists link this global cooling to the extinction of dinosaurs and numerous other plant and animal species. The fossil record shows this disappearance in the significant differences between the remains from the Cretaceous (K) period of the Mesozoic era and those from the Tertiary (T) period of the Cenozoic era—a transition point called the K-T boundary.

Other geologic events caused atmospheric changes that may also have contributed to the mass extinctions.

CLICK IT: Palaeos: The Trace of Life on Earth www.palaeos.com

EARTH'S LIFE SPAN, pictured as spiraling back through time, shows the human world as just a sliver. The K-T boundary, middle right, is indicated by the words "65 million years ago."

FOR MORE FACTS ON...

DINOSAURS & THEIR RELATIONSHIP TO SPECIES TODAY see Birds, **CHAPTER 4, PAGE 164**

THE BRIEF PERIOD OF HUMAN HISTORY & ITS EFFECT ON EARTH see Human Impact, **CHAPTER 5, PAGES 214-5**

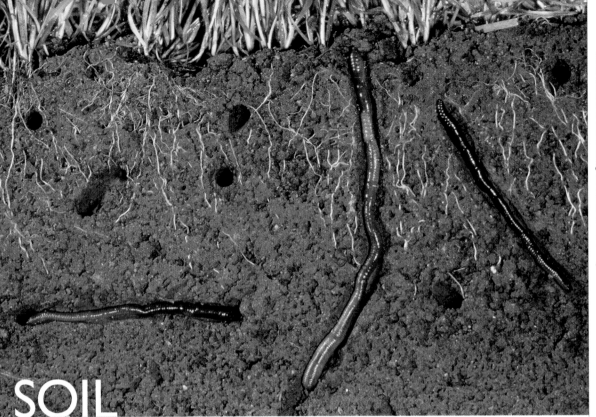

Cross-section of soil showing earthworms burrowing

SOIL

SOIL ORDERS

ALFISOLS in mild climates

ANDISOLS in volcanic sites

ARIDISOLS in deserts, arid lands

ENTISOLS in newly exposed spots

GELISOLS amid permafrost

HISTOSOLS (peats) in wetlands

INCEPTISOLS in former floodplains

MOLLISOLS in grasslands

OXISOLS in weathered tropical surfaces

SPODOSOLS are acidic, infertile

ULTISOLS in warmer climates

VERTISOLS in changeable climate zones

Soil is composed of layers of rock material, minerals, and organic matter—a combination capable of supporting the growth of rooted plants. Soil scientists classify soils into 12 different orders, distinguished by physical, chemical, and biological characteristics. Within each order, there are many soil types. In the United States alone, there are more than 20,000 different types.

The slow, continuous physical and chemical breakdown of rocks and minerals begins the process of making soil, along with the decomposition of organic matter and the incorporation of water and air.

The type of parent rock affects the overall chemical composition and texture of soil. For example, limestone creates soil rich in calcium, while shale develops a smooth, clayey soil that resists penetration by water and air.

The rate at which soil is formed depends on the environment. Less than an inch of soil may form during a century in a desert, whereas almost half an inch can form annually in the humid tropics.

FOR MORE FACTS ON...

THE LAYERS OF MATERIAL BENEATH EARTH'S CRUST see Earth's Interior, **CHAPTER 3, PAGES 82-3**

THE FORMATION AND CHARACTERISTICS OF ROCKS & MINERALS see Rocks & Minerals, **CHAPTER 3, PAGES 92-3**

HOW DO EARTHWORMS HELP THE SOIL?

Some 7,000 earthworm species live at all soil depths in most temperate and many tropical environments. They dominate the soil's invertebrate realm. They burrow through soil, aerate it, increase its porosity, and make channels for plant roots. They help turn rock to soil. Their biggest contribution, however, is their waste, called castings. Worm castings form a major organic component of soil and increase its fertility abundantly.

G L O S S A R Y

Humus: Nonliving, finely divided organic matter in soil, derived from microbial decomposition of plant and animal substances.

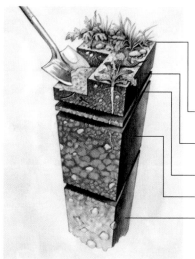

LAYERS OF SOIL

Soil layers, also called horizons, differ in composition and depth and are defined according to location. The soil profile shown here represents a clayey soil common in parts of the southeastern United States.

HORIZON O Up to 1 inch thick. Decomposing material such as leaf litter and humus, on its way to becoming topsoil.

HORIZON A 6–8 inches thick. The dark topsoil contains organic material and animals ranging from microscopic bacteria to worms and burrowing shrews.

HORIZON E A few inches thick. Lighter in color than Horizon A as a result of minerals leaching downward.

HORIZON B 1.5–2 feet thick. High iron content turns this layer red. Also called subsoil.

HORIZON C Soil is born here, where water and temperature join to break bedrock, volcanic ash, or sediment down into smaller particles. Little organic material is found here.

HORIZON R (not seen in illustration) Solid bedrock, unweathered, beneath the other layers.

WHY ORGANIC?

Adding biological materials—such as manure, compost, grass, straw, and crop residues—to agricultural land improves soil structure and nourishes soil life, which in turn nourishes plants. Chemical fertilizers, by contrast, feed plants directly and do not benefit the soil over time.

ORGANIC GARDENING is an age-old practice followed by farmers around the world, such as these in China's Sichuan Province.

CLICK IT: Orders of Soil soils.usda.gov/technical/soil_orders

FOR MORE FACTS ON...

THE MANY NATURAL HABITATS OF PLANTS & ANIMALS ON EARTH see Biomes, **CHAPTER 5, PAGES 194-5**

THE HUMAN ENTERPRISE OF GROWING & HARVESTING FOOD see Agriculture, **CHAPTER 6, PAGES 246-9**

Landslide near San Ricardo, Philippines, 2003

LANDFORMS

HIGHEST POINTS

ASIA / MOUNT EVEREST
29,035 feet above sea level

S. AMERICA / CERRO ACONCAGUA
22,834 feet above sea level

**N. AMERICA / MOUNT MCKINLEY
(DENALI)**
20,320 feet above sea level

AFRICA / KILIMANJARO
19,340 feet above sea level

EUROPE / EL'BRUS
18,510 feet above sea level

ANTARCTICA / VINSON MASSIF
16,067 feet above sea level

AUSTRALIA / MOUNT KOSCIUSZKO
7,310 feet above sea level

Two geologic forces are responsible for shaping most of Earth's major land formations: first, the movement of tectonic plates; and second, the processes of weathering and erosion, which occur over very long periods of time. Ice caps are an exception to these rules: They form when large amounts of water freeze and remain frozen for a long time.

Mountains often arise at the edges of tectonic plates; the most spectacular tend to occur where continental plates converge. The Himalaya thrust up, for instance, when the Indian subcontinent collided with Eurasia, a dynamic process that continues to this day.

Mountains also form in places where oceanic plates dive beneath continental ones, creating volcanic activity. This occurs, for instance, in the Pacific Ocean's Ring of Fire.

In the center of tectonic plates, areas of intense heat inside Earth known as hot spots burn through the crust and form volcanoes. The Hawaiian archipelago is an example of islands forming through this process.

FAST FACT Mountains beneath Antarctica's ice sheets rise 16,000 feet.

FOR MORE FACTS ON...

THE PACIFIC OCEAN'S VOLCANIC RING OF FIRE see Volcanoes, **CHAPTER 3, PAGE 87**
+
THE EARTH'S TOPOGRAPHY & ITS EFFECTS ON WEATHER see Weather, **CHAPTER 5, PAGES 182-3**

WHAT FORCES SHAPE LANDFORMS?

Weathering and erosion shape the Earth by removing surface features.

Widely spaced mountains result from the erosion of heavily faulted mountains—as seen in the Basin and Range region of the western United States. High plateaus, such as that found in Tibet, come about from the force of uplift, which shoves relatively flat land up and places it high above the surrounding area. Hills and low plateaus are lower, weathered elevations; North America's Ozark Mountains include examples of these features.

Depressions, like the Congo Basin in Africa, occur where basins are bounded by higher lands. Plains are level or rolling treeless expanses, such as the Indo-Gangetic Plain in India.

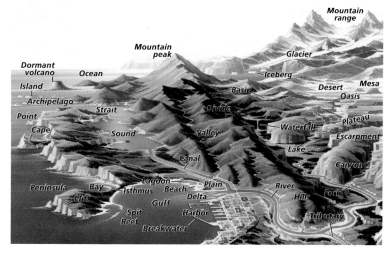

EARTH'S MANY LANDFORMS are the result of forces at work above and below the planet's surface. From the water's edge to the tallest peaks, physical forces work through time to shape the landforms of the planet. Wind, water, pollution, and gravity, together with the massive forces of change coming from underground, sculpt Earth's surface. The process continues every day, unseen aside from the occasional cataclysmic event such as a volcanic eruption or a landslide.

CLICK IT: Volcano World volcano.oregonstate.edu

G L O S S A R Y

Erosion: Removal of surface material from Earth's crust by natural agencies and transportation of the eroded materials from the point of removal.

SHAPING LANDFORMS FROM WITHIN

Forces such as the movement of tectonic plates, earthquakes, and volcanoes make lasting changes in the shape and composition of Earth's landforms.

IN VOLCANISM, magma rises to the surface where one tectonic plate pushes under another or a plate passes over a hot spot.

SUBDUCTION occurs when an oceanic plate dives under a continental plate. Mountains, volcanoes, and earthquakes can result from this geologic process.

FAULTS are cracks that form when two plates grind past each other. Movement along fault lines can be the cause of earthquakes.

SPREADING occurs as ocean plates move apart. The ocean floor cracks, allowing magma to rise. New crust forms this way.

COLLISIONS between two plates can cause their edges to break and fold. This geologic process can create mountains.

FOR MORE FACTS ON...

HOW LANDFORMS ON THE SURFACE OF EARTH GET THEIR SHAPES see Landforms: Taking Shape, **CHAPTER 3, PAGES 100-1**

VIOLENT WEATHER & ITS EFFECT ON LANDFORMS see Weather & Storms, **CHAPTER 5, PAGES 182-3 & 186-91**

TAKING SHAPE

Forces emanating from inside Earth create many of the planet's major landforms. Processes on Earth's surface or originating in the atmosphere account for others. Some of Earth's most exquisite natural forms result from the work of weathering agents, which can include a variety of mechanical or chemical means.

Wind, rain, snow, ice, and groundwater are strong mechanical influences that can shape Earth's surface.

Dissolved chemicals in water, rock minerals, atmospheric carbon dioxide, and decaying organic matter can change the mineral components of rocks and even wash them away.

Physical and chemical forms of weathering interact, and each increases the impact of the other. The rate of weathering will vary according to climate—especially in relation to levels of temperature and moisture. Limestone weathers rapidly in moist

climates and slowly in dry ones, for example. Vegetation also affects the weathering process: Root growth can physically break rock apart, and humic acids, which are a product of decomposition, act chemically on rock.

Wind-generated landforms are called eolian after Aeolus, the Greek god of the winds. The effects of wind erosion are seen in many parts of the world, particularly where there are large deposits of sand or loess. Sand dunes represent an eolian landform.

Erosion is the movement of weathered material from one place to another. Water, ice, wind, and gravity contribute greatly to erosion.

Water, ice, and wind can move rock fragments and particles of soil and deposit them in new locations. The deposited sediments may range in size from boulders to fine grains of sand, silt, and clay. Eventually they build up, form new features, and change the landscape.

Weathering and erosion also affect the human-made landscape. Buildings, bridges, monuments, and other structures all are affected by weathering. Consider, for instance, the softened edges of the Pyramids at Giza, in Egypt.

Some human activities also hasten weathering and erosion. Corrosive chemical emissions from energy use, clearing fields for farming, preparing sites for excavation and construction, deforestation, and mining are just a few examples. When compounded on a global scale, these activities cause immeasurable damage.

SPIRES OF ROCK called hoodoos, formed by uneven erosion in hard and soft rock, stand as tall as ten-story buildings in Utah's Bryce Canyon.

FAST FACT From base to rim, the Grand Canyon spans 1.7 billion years of geologic processes.

FOR MORE FACTS ON...

WIND & ITS INFLUENCE ON EARTH see Wind, **CHAPTER 3, PAGES 106-7**

THE INFLUENCE OF HUMANS ON EARTH'S ENVIRONMENT see Threatened Planet, **CHAPTER 3, PAGES 122-7**, & Human Impact, **CHAPTER 5, PAGES 214-5**

HOW DOES WIND SHAPE THE LAND?

Sand dunes are caused by wind working through three main actions: deflation, or the removal of dust and sand from dry soil; sandblasting, the erosion of rock by wind-borne sand; and deposition, the laying down of sediments.

Wind can move sediments uphill and down. Among desert landforms created by wind, sand dunes may be the most spectacular, their form depending on wind direction, the amount of sand available, and the presence of vegetation.

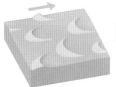 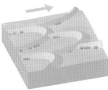 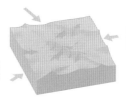 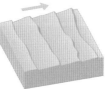 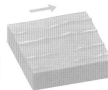

BARCHAN DUNES are crescents with arms pointing downwind.

PARABOLIC DUNES are crescents with arms that point upwind.

STAR DUNES have curving ridges that radiate from their centers.

TRANSVERSE DUNES are "waves" with crescents perpendicular to the wind.

LONGITUDINAL DUNES lie parallel to the wind.

FAST FACT Some migrating sand dunes can move in location more than 200 feet per year.

HOW DOES ICE SHAPE THE LAND?

Glaciers are landforms created by ice, legacies of Earth's most recent ice age. Glaciers are powerful forces and can topple or crush anything in their paths. There are two kinds of glaciers: valley or alpine glaciers, which occur in mountainous terrain and are constrained within valleys, and continental ice sheets, which extend across landmasses, unconstrained by topography.

ALPINE GLACIERS move downhill from a bowl-shaped depression called a cirque. Ice sculpts a horn and an arête from the mountain. Tributary glaciers flow from an adjoining valley. A ridge of loose rock (medial moraine) snakes through, with crevasses cracking the surface.

An active glacier (left) moves slowly through the landscape. Centuries later, the shapes it carved out of the land remain (right).

G L O S S A R Y

Loess: Recent unstratified deposit of silty or loamy material, usually buff or yellow-brown, deposited chiefly by the wind.

CLICK IT: Dynamic Earth science.nationalgeographic.com/science/earth/the-dynamic-earth

FOR MORE FACTS ON...

THE PLANTS & ANIMALS THAT INHABIT DESERT ENVIRONMENTS see Desert & Dry Shrubland, **CHAPTER 5, PAGES 208-9**
+
THE PLANTS & ANIMALS THAT INHABIT GLACIAL ENVIRONMENTS see Tundra & Ice Cap, **CHAPTER 5, PAGES 210-1**

ISLANDS

Quite simply, islands are bodies of land that are surrounded by water. The water can be a lake, a river, a sea, or an ocean. An island can be any size, from a tiny dot in the tropics to the two largest on the planet—Australia and Antarctica, more often considered continents.

Australia, the smallest continent, is more than three times the size of Greenland, the next largest island.

Islands measuring less than an acre are often referred to as islets.

Many islands sit in splendid isolation, thousands of miles from the nearest mainland. Others, such as the Aleutians of Alaska and the Cyclades of Greece, cluster together in closely spaced groups called archipelagoes.

Island coverings range from barren rock to permanent ice to lush, tropical vegetation. Island fauna can vary from microscopic—such as those that predominate in Antarctica—to the insect, bird, reptile, amphibian, and mammal-rich habitats of Indonesia. Islands differ in terms of human populations as well, from the uninhabited to the densely populated metropolitan areas of Tokyo and New York City on the islands of Honshu and Manhattan, respectively.

Islands can be classified into three major groups: continental, oceanic, and barrier. A fourth group, coral, forms as part of an atoll (see opposite).

Continental islands were once connected to a continent. They can form in one of several ways. Some, notably Greenland and Madagascar, broke off from their continental base as a result of continental drift over millions of years. Others came into being as low-lying areas flooded when sea levels rose at the end of ice ages: The British Isles, for example, were isolated from mainland Europe. Weathering and erosion over time can also separate a piece of land from a continental mainland. The flow of the Orinoco River severed the island of Trinidad from the rest of South America, for instance.

Oceanic islands form when undersea volcanoes erupt. Spewed lava builds up over time, increasing in height, until the layers break the ocean's surface. The Hawaiian Islands grew this way.

A LIMESTONE ISLAND, topped with misty rain forest growth, emanates from Phang Nga Bay on Thailand's southwestern coast.

FOR MORE FACTS ON...

THE TROPICAL RAIN FOREST BIOME AROUND THE WORLD see *Rain Forests,* **CHAPTER 5, PAGES 198-9**

THE GEOGRAPHY OF THE COUNTRY OF AUSTRALIA see *Australia & Oceania,* **CHAPTER 9, PAGES 408-10**

Barrier islands are long, narrow strips of land that lie parallel to coastlines. They are made up of sediment—sand, silt, or gravel—and are separated from the shore by a channel or sound. They usually contain sand dunes, barriers that protect the coast from the buffeting of storm waves and winds. Barrier islands can form from the accumulation of sand on sandbars, from the isolation of oceanfront dunes by rising sea levels, or from deposits of rock, soil, and gravel left as moraines by melting glaciers—as Long Island, off the coast of New York, did.

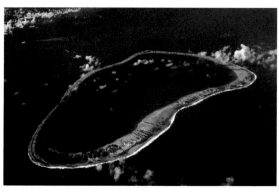

A CLEARLY VISIBLE ATOLL rises up from the South Pacific, part of the Tuamoto Archipelago in French Polynesia.

WHAT IS AN ATOLL?

An atoll starts with an undersea volcanic eruption in the warm tropics, which builds a mid-ocean island. Coral then begins to build an encircling reef around the island, just below the water's surface.

Over millions of years the volcano erodes and sinks, while the encircling coral reef continues to rise ever higher. The constant buffeting of the waves eventually breaks the reef, making channels that link the central water, called a lagoon, with the ocean.

As the reef itself crumbles, sand and other material piles on top, forming an island or islets.

FAST FACT The Midway Islands, which also rose out of the Hawaiian Ridge, are estimated to be 20 million years old.

HOW DID HAWAII FORM?

The Hawaiian archipelago stretches above the Hawaiian Ridge, a line of volcanoes running 1,865 miles along the floor of the Pacific Ocean. Islands form over a hot spot beneath the tectonic plate. Volcanoes build underwater peaks that eventually reach above sea level.

As the Pacific plate continues moving northwest, the islands age. At the same time, new islands are always forming. At the current southeast end of the chain, Loihi, now a seamount, will one day become the newest Hawaiian island.

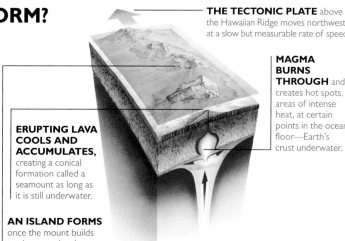

THE TECTONIC PLATE above the Hawaiian Ridge moves northwest at a slow but measurable rate of speed.

MAGMA BURNS THROUGH and creates hot spots, areas of intense heat, at certain points in the ocean floor—Earth's crust underwater.

ERUPTING LAVA COOLS AND ACCUMULATES, creating a conical formation called a seamount as long as it is still underwater.

AN ISLAND FORMS once the mount builds to above sea level.

CLICK IT: Encyclopedia of Earth www.eoearth.org

FOR MORE FACTS ON...

EARTH'S OCEANS see Oceans, **CHAPTER 3, PAGES 112-5**
+
THE QUESTION OF WHO OWNS THE CONTINENT OF ANTARCTICA see Nations & Alliances, **CHAPTER 9, PAGE 359**

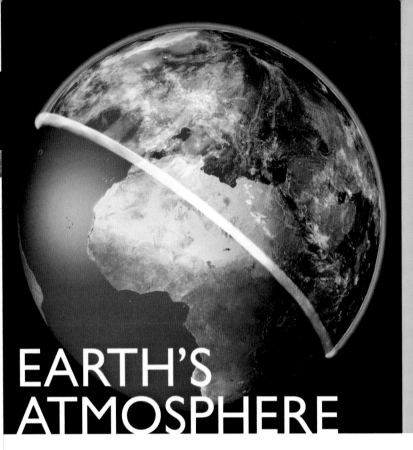

ATMOSPHERIC GASES

NITROGEN
78.1 percent

OXYGEN
20.9 percent

ARGON
0.9 percent

NEON
0.002 percent

HELIUM
0.0005 percent

KRYPTON
0.0001 percent

HYDROGEN
0.00005 percent

EARTH'S ATMOSPHERE

Earth's atmosphere is an invisible layer of gases, plus water vapor and dust—all held close to the planet by the force of gravity. The atmosphere acts as a filter. It keeps out much of the sun's harmful ultraviolet radiation while still letting in solar heat, which warms the Earth and lower atmosphere. It also recycles Earth's precious supply of water.

The atmosphere extends from Earth's surface upward for almost 400 miles, where its outer reaches gradually merge into space.

The atmosphere has a five-layered structure (see opposite): The troposphere, stratosphere, mesosphere, thermosphere, and exosphere differ according to characteristics such as density, composition, and temperature. There are no definite boundaries between the layers of the atmosphere. In fact, these boundaries vary with latitude and season.

The troposphere accounts for almost all of the atmosphere's mass— some 98 percent—and forces within it account for most of its weather.

At sea level, air pressure measures 1,000 millibars. Air pressure decreases by approximately half with every four miles of altitude. Yet the atmosphere is so dispersed that its weight is barely perceptible, even though the weight of Earth's atmosphere equals that of a layer of water some 34 feet deep.

Our atmosphere likely evolved from gases spewed out from early volcanoes at the time of the formation of Earth's surface. Added to these gases was oxygen, most likely a by-product of photosynthesis and in very short supply. In fact, photosynthesis over millions of years may account for most of today's oxygen.

FAST FACT Gravity holds the 5,000-trillion-ton atmosphere in place.

FOR MORE FACTS ON...

CHARACTERISTICS OF THE SUN see The Sun, **CHAPTER 2, PAGES 54-7**

THE PROCESS & BENEFITS OF PHOTOSYNTHESIS see Life Begins, **CHAPTER 4, PAGE 131**

JOSEPH PRIESTLEY / DISCOVERER OF OXYGEN

Educated to be a minister, Englishman Joseph Priestley (1733-1804) joined other natural philosophers, as they called themselves, in shaping a new view of the physical world. A 1766 encounter with Benjamin Franklin awakened his interest in electricity. Living next door to a brewery, Priestley became interested in gases. By 1772 he had identified carbon dioxide and nitrous oxide; two years later he revolutionized the field of chemistry by isolating oxygen and seven other individual gases, proving that air—for centuries considered a fundamental element of nature—was not a singular substance but a combination of gases, each with its own distinctive characteristics. Due to his radical politics, Priestley's home was mobbed and destroyed. He spent his last days in the United States.

 In the course of my inquiries, I was ... soon satisfied that atmospherical air is not an unalterable thing. —— **JOSEPH PRIESTLEY, 1775**

LAYERS OF THE ATMOSPHERE

Temperature, gaseous composition, and pressure change through the many layers of Earth's atmosphere. Beyond the thermosphere lies the exosphere, or outer boundary (not shown here), which extends into space and contains only wisps of hydrogen and helium.

THE THERMOSPHERE begins 50 miles up and extends 350 miles. X-rays and other short-wave radiation from the sun cause temperatures there to rise to more than 3100°F, but molecules are widely dispersed, so this layer would seem cold to humans.

THE MESOSPHERE extends from 30 to 50 miles above Earth's surface. Temperatures here drop sharply, down to almost -200°F.

THE STRATOSPHERE extends from about 6 to 30 miles. Strong, steady winds occur here, and this is the layer where most jets travel. The ozone layer in this level absorbs much of sun's ultraviolet radiation.

THE TROPOSPHERE starts at ground level and extends about 6 miles up. It is the densest layer, and except for thermosphere, it is also the warmest—with average surface temperature of 59°F. It is the source of most water vapor and the location of cloud formation and weather origination.

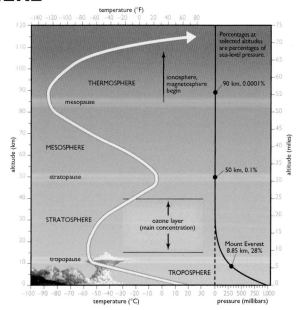

G L O S S A R Y

Ozone: From the Greek *ozon,* "to smell." Pale blue gas that is irritating, explosive, and toxic. **/ Ozone layer:** Region in the stratosphere with significant concentrations of ozone formed by the effect of solar radiation on oxygen.

CLICK IT: Explaining Ozone Layer Depletion www.epa.gov/ozone/science/process.html

FOR MORE FACTS ON...

THREATS TO THE QUALITY OF AIR ON EARTH see *Threatened: Air,* **CHAPTER 3, PAGES 124-5**

CLIMATE CHANGE & ITS IMPACT ON EARTH'S ATMOSPHERE see *Climate,* **CHAPTER 5, PAGES 192-3**

Hundred-mile-an-hour winds during Hurricane Allen, 1980

WIND

BEAUFORT SCALE

1 / Calm, winds 0 mph

2 / Light air, winds 1-3 mph

3 / Light breeze, winds 4-7 mph

4 / Moderate breeze, winds 8-12 mph

5 / Fresh breeze, winds 13-18 mph

6 / Strong breeze, winds 19-24 mph

7 / Near gale, winds 25-31 mph

8 / Gale, winds 32-46 mph

9 / Strong gale, winds 47-54 mph

10 / Storm, winds 55-63 mph

11 / Violent storm, winds 64-72 mph

12 / Hurricane, winds 73+ mph

Wind is the movement of air caused by the uneven heating of Earth by the sun. When atmospheric pressure is higher at one place than at surrounding locations at the same altitude, air flows equalize the imbalance and create wind. The great equalizer of the atmosphere, wind transports heat, moisture, pollutants, and dust around the globe.

There are three large-scale wind patterns that occur in each hemisphere (see map opposite).

The Equator receives more of the sun's warmth than the rest of the globe. The warm equatorial air rises higher into the atmosphere and migrates toward the Poles. At the same time, cooler, denser air moves toward the Equator to replace the heated air. The process of warm and cool air trading places is the main driving force for wind.

At about the 30° latitude line, most equatorial air cools and sinks. Some moves toward the Equator and some toward the Poles. At about 60° latitude, polar air heading toward the

FOR MORE FACTS ON...

THE POLES & THE EQUATOR see *The Poles,* **CHAPTER 2, PAGES 34-5,** & *Equator & Tropics,* **CHAPTER 2, PAGES 36-7**

THE USE OF WIND TO GENERATE POWER see *Power: Alternative Technologies,* **CHAPTER 8, PAGES 354-5**

Equator collides with the mid-latitude air, forcing that air to rise.

Generally, winds blow east and west rather than north and south, because Earth's rotation causes a pattern of deflections that is commonly known as the Coriolis effect. The Coriolis effect makes winds veer to the right in the Northern Hemisphere and makes winds veer to the left in the Southern Hemisphere.

Other forces, such as land and ocean topography and tempera-tures, can influence the winds as well. Winds are often described by their speed and the direction from which they blow. A southerly breeze, in other words, comes from the south.

To allow for easier comparisons between wind speeds, the Beaufort scale (opposite) was created in 1805 by Sir Francis Beaufort of the British Royal Navy. Also a member of the Royal Geographic Society, he commissioned Darwin's voyage on the *Beagle*.

Beaufort wanted a system for describing wind force that linked up with procedures for setting sails. The resulting scale indicates wind force by a series of numbers, from 0 to 12. The numbers correlate to wind speeds, to the appropriate sails to be used in given conditions, and also to the winds' visible effects on the ocean surface.

In 1955 the U.S. Weather Service increased the Beaufort scale to include numbers 13 through 17, to account for the highest of winds experienced during hurricanes.

CLICK IT: Beaufort Scale www.stormfax.com/beaufort.htm

G L O S S A R Y

Atmospheric pressure: Per force unit area exerted by air above the surface of the Earth. Standard sea-level pressure, by definition, equals one atmosphere, or 29.92 inches of mercury. **/ Coriolis effect:** Named for French mathematician Gustave-Gaspard Coriolis (1792-1843). Apparent deflection of the path of an object that moves within a rotating coordinate system.

WORLD-FAMOUS WINDS

Some predictable wind patterns bear local names.

THE BURAN is a strong northeasterly wind in Siberia and Central Asia that creates winter blizzards.

THE BRICKFIELDER is a hot, dusty wind blowing south from central Australia, named for brickfield dust near Sydney.

THE CHINOOK is a warm, dry wind that blows down the eastern slopes of North America's Rocky Mountains.

THE DOLDRUMS are a band of nearly still air along the Equator, where northerly and southerly trade winds meet.

LE MISTRAL is a violent southerly wind that lasts three months, winter into spring, in the French Mediterranean.

EL NORTE (THE NORTHER) is a cold, strong wind bringing a rapid temperature drop across Texas and the Gulf of Mexico and south through Central America.

EL PAMPERO is a dry, bitterly cold wind that blows across the pampas of Uruguay and Argentina.

SIROCCO WINDS are hot spring winds that blow from Africa's Sahara to the southern European coastline.

THE WILLIWAW is a brisk wind blowing down off mountains in coastal and central Alaska.

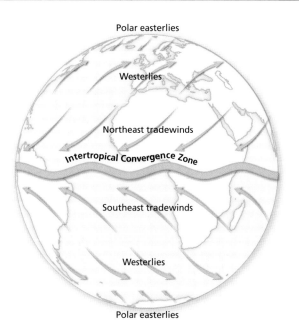

Polar easterlies
Westerlies
Northeast tradewinds
Intertropical Convergence Zone
Southeast tradewinds
Westerlies
Polar easterlies

GLOBAL WINDS move energy, moisture, and weather patterns around the world. Heat and moisture are also distributed by ocean currents, which interact with global winds.

FOR MORE FACTS ON...

NAVIGATION METHODS, BOTH ANCIENT & MODERN see *Navigation*, **CHAPTER 1, PAGES 38-9**
+
THE CAUSES & EFFECTS OF STORMS, TORNADOES & HURRICANES see *Storms*, **CHAPTER 5, PAGES 186-91**

COLORS OF A RAINBOW
BY WAVELENGTH

RED
650 nanometers

ORANGE
600 nanometers

YELLOW
580 nanometers

GREEN
550 nanometers

CYAN
500 nanometers

BLUE
450 nanometers

VIOLET
400 nanometers

LIGHT

olar energy results from nuclear fusion in the sun's core, which creates an enormous, continuous flow of radiant energy that travels throughout the solar system. The energy that reaches us from all the stars twinkling in our galaxy cannot compare with what we receive from the sun, the only significant source of energy for Earth's atmosphere.

This radiant energy is released in the form of electromagnetic waves, which travel unimpeded from the sun in straight lines at the speed of light—186,000 miles a second.

Although the intensity of the energy diminishes as it travels the 93 million miles from the sun to Earth's outer atmosphere, the amount of energy received by Earth from the sun in one second still is equivalent to all the electricity generated on the planet in one week.

Electromagnetic waves vary in length, which is measured as the distance between the crests of waves.

All the types of these waves together constitute the electromagnetic spectrum, which ranges from extremely short ultraviolet waves to very long radio waves. Visible light, which occupies a narrow band of that spectrum, comprises colors that vary in wavelength from short to long.

Shorter wavelengths scatter more effectively in the atmosphere, which is why the sky is blue—a color with a relatively short wavelength—on a sunny day.

At dawn and dusk, light must pass through more atmosphere, allowing the longer orange and red light waves to predominate over the widely scattered blue waves.

FAST FACT Only about 50 percent of the sun's energy arrives at the Earth's surface.

FOR MORE FACTS ON...

HOW SOLAR WINDS FORM ON THE SUN see *The Sun*, **CHAPTER 2, PAGES 54-7**

APPLICATIONS OF THE SCIENCE OF LIGHT IN OUR EVERYDAY WORLD see *Optics*, **CHAPTER 8, PAGES 336-7**

WHAT MAKES A RAINBOW?

The multicolored arc of a rainbow is produced by sunlight striking raindrops beneath a rain cloud.

Light refracts—bends—when it passes through drops of water. Each color of light refracts at a different angle: Violet bends more than blue, which bends more than green, and so on, with red refracting the least. If sunlight enters a raindrop at just the proper angle, it refracts, and its many colors spread into a visible array.

Sunlight refracted through millions of raindrops forms a rainbow.

On a primary rainbow, red is the outside color and violet the inside color. Occasionally a secondary rainbow appears slightly higher in the sky, and in it the colors of the rainbow are reversed (opposite).

A rainbow's position in the sky depends on the sun's altitude above the horizon—the lower the sun, the higher the rainbow appears.

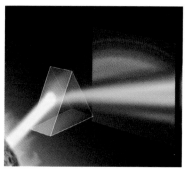

A PRISM reveals colors by refracting the constituents of white light at different angles.

G L O S S A R Y

Refraction: The change in direction of a wave passing from one medium to another caused by its change in speed. A ray of sunlight is composed of many wavelengths that in combination appear to be colorless; upon entering a glass prism or a raindrop, the different refractions (or changes in direction of light waves, of the various wavelengths, or colors) spread them apart, making all visible, as in a rainbow.

WHAT MAKES THE NORTHERN LIGHTS?

Named for the Roman goddess of dawn, an aurora is a colorful nightly light display in or near the Arctic and Antarctic Circles. In the north the display is called aurora borealis—northern lights. In the south, it is aurora australis—southern lights.

Gaseous elements in the sun split into electrically charged particles. The sun's surface continuously sheds these particles, some of which flow toward Earth as solar wind. Those particles that penetrate the Earth's magnetic field enter the upper atmosphere and bombard its gases. The resulting collisions produce energy visible as arcs, streaks, or curtains of colored light. With particularly intense solar wind, activity increases and the lights are seen from far away.

NORTHERN LIGHTS paint the sky in eerie shades of yellow, red, and green, upstaging the city lights of Whitehorse, capital of the Yukon territory of Canada. An active night display on Earth is a sign of intense solar wind activity on the sun.

FOR MORE FACTS ON...

SUNLIGHT AS A SOURCE OF ELECTRICITY & HEAT see *Power: Alternative Technologies,* **CHAPTER 8, PAGES 354-5**
+
THE GEOGRAPHY OF THE COUNTRY OF CANADA see *North America,* **CHAPTER 9, PAGE 416**

Hindu pilgrims in Narmada River waterfall, Kadil Dhara, India

WATER

CHINA
1931 / 3,700,000 dead

CHINA
1959 / 2,000,000 dead

CHINA
1939 / 500,000 dead

CHINA
1935 / 142,000 dead

CHINA
1911 / 100,000 dead

CHINA
1949 / 57,000 dead

GUATEMALA
1949 / 40,000 dead

Water, vital to all life, is Earth's most abundant substance. The oceans contain 97 percent of the planet's water. Of the other 3 percent, two-thirds is found as ice, in the form of glaciers, ice sheets, and ice caps. Most of the remaining one percent is found underground. A tiny fraction of Earth's water exists in streams, rivers, and lakes.

Water forms from atoms of hydrogen and oxygen at the ratio of two to one, thus the chemical symbol H_2O. It occurs naturally in three states, as a liquid, solid (ice), and gas (water vapor or steam).

Water is the only substance found in three forms within the average range of the Earth's temperatures. In fact, rain, snow or hail, and water vapor all can appear in the same area at the same time during a severe storm.

Water freezes at 32°F. When it freezes, it does not contract, as most substances do: It expands and forms ice. Ice, therefore, is lighter than liquid water, which is why ice cubes float in a glass of water.

FOR MORE FACTS ON...

CHARACTERISTICS OF EARTH'S OCEANS *see Oceans,* **CHAPTER 3, PAGES 112-5**

THE HABITATS OF PLANTS & ANIMALS THAT LIVE IN OR NEAR THE WATER *see Aquatic Biomes,* **CHAPTER 5, PAGES 212-3**

WATER: THE UNIVERSAL SOLVENT

Water can dissolve many substances, including most of the hardest rock. It has been a primary force in the shaping of Earth's surface since the first oceans formed billions of years ago.

Water is a solvent, which means it combines with other ingredients to form a solution, a new chemical substance whose composition is the same at every point in the mixture.

Water has also been an essential and defining element in the support of life. When astronomers seek planets capable of sustaining life, they first look for signs of water.

FAST FACT The total volume of water on Earth equals some 336 million cubic miles.

THE WATER CYCLE

The water cycle—which is also known as the hydrologic cycle, from the Greek for "knowledge about water"—represents the endless movement of water in all its forms, solid, liquid, and gas, around the planet, circulating through the atmosphere, the land and inland bodies of water, the groundwater, and the ocean.

The atmosphere contains only 0.001 percent of the Earth's water at any given time, yet it serves as the chief agent in the water cycle.

Water enters the atmosphere through evaporation, creating water vapor, or water in its gaseous form. Water vapor holds latent energy, released when the gas reverts to a liquid or solid during the processes called condensation or precipitation.

Since oceans contain most of the water in the planet, they make the largest contribution of water for evaporation into the atmosphere—some 85 percent. The rest comes mostly from the surface water evaporation and transpiration from plants.

As the sun warms the surface of the Earth, water rises: It turns to a gas, or evaporates. Water vapor forms clouds. Eventually the water returns to a liquid state and falls to Earth in the form of precipitation.

It takes about ten days for water to circulate through the entire cycle.

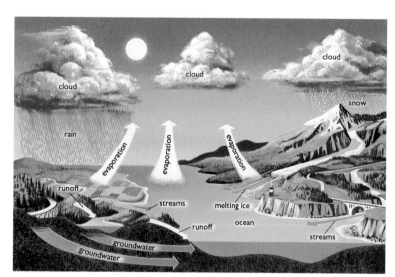

WATER CYCLES through all three phases—solid, liquid, and vapor—and through many locations—underground, in bodies of water, in soil, and in the atmosphere—all the time. The total volume of water on Earth has likely remained constant since the planet's formation.

G L O S S A R Y

Aquifer: A rock layer that contains water and releases it in appreciable amounts. **/ Transpiration:** From the Latin *trans-*, "through," + *spiritus*, "breath." In botany, a plant's loss of water, mainly through the stomates of leaves.

FOR MORE FACTS ON...

THE CHEMICAL COMPOSITION OF PLANET EARTH see *Earth's Elements*, **CHAPTER 3, PAGES 90-1**

+

THE POLLUTION OF BODIES OF WATER ON EARTH see *Threatened Planet: Water*, **CHAPTER 3, PAGES 126-7**

OCEANS

Oceans cover nearly three-fourths of Earth's surface. They surround all the continents and give Earth its blue appearance when viewed from space. Although the oceans are composed of a contiguous body of water measuring some 139 million square miles, geographers divide it into four entities: largest to smallest, Pacific, Atlantic, Indian, and Arctic.

About 3.5 percent salt, ocean water also contains traces of all the chemical elements found on Earth. It enables life on the planet as part of the water cycle. The oceans also regulate global temperatures by absorbing heat in the summer and releasing it in winter.

Currents, wind, density gradients, and Earth's rotation keep the ocean in motion. As Earth spins, wind and surface currents are deflected to the right in the Northern Hemisphere and to the left in the South Hemisphere. As a result, enormous gyres transport warm water from equatorial regions into the much colder polar regions.

The ocean floor contains myriad physical features, starting with the continental shelf, the submerged extension of the continents. The shelf descends gradually before dropping off sharply in the continental slope and then softening again in the continental rise. The deep-ocean floor, or abyssal plain, features hills and underwater volcanoes as well as the Mid-Ocean Ridge, a mountain chain more than 40,000 miles long. In the rift molten rock rises from Earth's interior, forming new seafloor.

Some areas of the ocean floor also have deep, narrow depressions called trenches. The deepest of all is the Challenger Deep in the Mariana Trench in the Pacific Ocean near Guam, more than 35,000 feet below the surface.

THIS HISTORIC 1977 MAP, sponsored by the U.S. Office of Naval Research, reveals the incredible topography of world's ocean floors including trenches, rifts, and seamounts. Some peaks underwater equal Mount Everest in height.

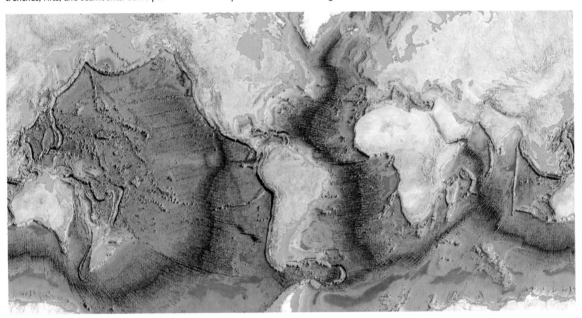

FAST FACT The Mid-Ocean Ridge on the Atlantic floor is Earth's largest geologic feature.

FOR MORE FACTS ON...

THE USE OF SONAR TO MAP THE OCEAN FLOOR see *Modern Maps,* **CHAPTER 1, PAGE 27**

EARTH'S CONTINENTS see *Africa, Asia, Europe, Australia & Oceania, North America & South America,* **CHAPTER 9, PAGES 360-1, 378-9, 394-5, 408-9, 414-5 & 424-5**

WHAT ARE EL NIÑO AND LA NIÑA?

Periodic shifts in wind speed and direction in the tropical eastern Pacific can affect sea-surface temperatures. In El Niño events, prevailing easterly winds weaken or give way to westerly winds. Surface temperatures rise and the upwelling of cool, nutrient-rich waters from deeper in the ocean stops. This creates an unfavorable habitat for many fish and often leads to increased rainfall along the west coast of the Americas and drought in Australia and Africa.

The opposite set of conditions is called La Niña. A stronger easterly wind flow increases upwelling and reduces the surface temperatures.

Both events affect weather: Strong El Niño events often result in a weak Atlantic hurricane season. La Niña events favor more Atlantic hurricanes. La Niña sometimes alternates with El Niño and causes opposite changes in weather around the world. In India, for example, monsoon rains decrease during an El Niño but increase during La Niña.

Most events start in December or January—hence the name, El Niño, the little boy, which refers to the Christ child. La Niña, the little girl, was chosen recently to match the other nickname.

 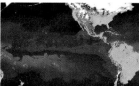  

TRADE WINDS usually blow Pacific warmth west, and nutrient-rich cold water wells up along South America.

DURING EL NIÑO, the trade winds relax and warm waters (shown as red) build off the American coastlines.

HOTTER SEA SURFACE temperatures mean less food for fish and more rain in South America.

A CONTINENT AWAY, hotter sea surface temperatures tend to cause drought in Australia and Africa.

G L O S S A R Y

Density gradient: Variations in temperature, sediment concentration, or the concentration of dissolved substances in bodies of water that produce layers of differing densities and can cause water movement. **/ Gyre:** A semiclosed ocean current system exhibiting spiral motion.

WILLIAM BEEBE / UNDERSEA EXPLORER

Naturalist William Beebe (1877–1962) began deep-sea diving when technology had not developed much beyond copper helmets and rubber hoses. To reach greater depths, he invented a diving sphere suspended by a cable. Otis Barton, an engineer and adventurer, helped see the project to completion. In June 1930, Beebe and Barton took their two-ton bathysphere ("deep ball") to Bermuda. On the deck of the mother ship, they squeezed themselves into the sea-blue ball, 4 feet 9 inches in diameter, along with oxygen tanks and chemicals for absorbing carbon dioxide and excess moisture. On their second try, they made it to a record-breaking 1,426 feet. The pair made a total of four dives in the bathysphere, the last two sponsored by the National Geographic Society. In August 1934 they reached 3,028 feet, a record they held for the next 15 years.

 As I peered down I realized I was looking toward a world of life almost as unknown as that of Mars or Venus. —— WILLIAM BEEBE, 1931

FOR MORE FACTS ON...

WINDS AROUND THE WORLD see Wind, **CHAPTER 3, PAGES** 106-7

WATER-DWELLERS see Mollusks, Fish, Reptiles, Amphibians & Sea Mammals, **CHAPTER 4, PAGES** 156-63, 168-9, & Aquatic Biomes, **CHAPTER 5, PAGES** 212-3

WATER
OCEANS

The surface of the ocean keeps in constant motion through the up-and-down motions of waves. Most waves originate from the action of the wind, although some are generated by earthquakes or volcanic eruptions. These megawaves, known as tsunamis, can cause a great deal of destruction on land.

Ocean waters also move as a result of currents—riverlike streams of water. Currents help distribute waters of different temperatures throughout the ocean. They also transport oxygen to living beings and distribute the nutrients that nourish ocean life.

Not all ocean currents are created equally. Some are much larger and stronger than others. One of the most powerful currents is the Gulf Stream, a warm surface current that originates in the tropical Caribbean Sea and flows northeast along the eastern coast of the United States. The Gulf Stream measures more than 50 miles across and is more than a half mile deep.

Like other ocean currents, the Gulf Stream plays a major role in climate. As the stream travels north, it transfers heat and moisture from its warm tropical waters to the air above. Westerly winds then carry the warm, moist air across the Atlantic to the British Isles and to Scandinavia, causing them to have milder winters than they otherwise would experience at their northern latitudes.

HOW DOES A WAVE FORM?

A wave begins as the wind ruffles the surface of the ocean. When the ocean is calm and glasslike, even the mildest breeze forms ripples, the smallest type of wave. Ripples provide surfaces for the wind to act on, which produces larger waves.

Stronger winds push the nascent waves into steeper and higher hills of water. The size a wave reaches depends on the speed and strength of the wind, the length of time it takes for the wave to form, and the distance over which it blows in the open ocean—known as the fetch. A long fetch accompanied by strong and steady winds can produce enormous waves.

The highest point of a wave is called the crest and the lowest point the trough. The distance from one crest to another is known as the wavelength.

Although water appears to move forward with the waves, for the most part water particles travel in circles within the waves. The visible movement is the wave's form and energy moving through the water, courtesy of energy provided by the wind. Wave speed also varies; on average waves travel about 20 to 50 mph.

As a wave enters shallow water and nears the shore, its up-and-down movement is disrupted and it slows down. The crest grows higher and begins to surge ahead of the rest of the wave, eventually toppling over and breaking apart. The energy released by a breaking wave can be explosive. Breakers can wear down rocky coast and also build up sandy beaches.

OCEAN WAVES VARY greatly in height from crest to trough, averaging 5 to 10 feet. Storm waves may tower 50 to 70 feet or more.

FOR MORE FACTS ON...

BASIC MECHANICAL PRINCIPLES INCLUDING FORCE & MOTION see *Physical Science*, **CHAPTER 8, PAGES 328-9**

THE DEFINITION OF A TSUNAMI see *Earthquakes*, **CHAPTER 3, PAGE 89**

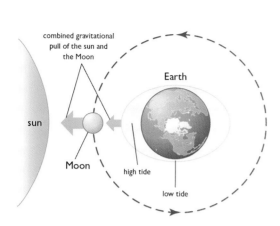

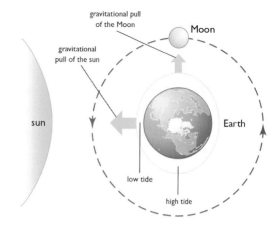

GRAVITY from the sun and moon influences tides. When both are in alignment, tides are extremely high or low—commonly called spring tides.

A WEEK LATER, when the sun and moon are at right angles to each other in relation to Earth, tides are moderate—called neap tides.

FAST FACT In Nova Scotia, waters at high tide can rise more than 50 feet higher than the low-tide level.

HOW DO TIDES FORM?

Tides are the regular daily rise and fall of ocean waters. Twice each day in most locations, water rises up over the shore until it reaches its highest level, or high tide. In between, the water recedes from the shore until it reaches it lowest level, or low tide.

Tides respond to the gravitational pull of the moon and sun. Gravitational pull has little effect on the solid and inflexible land, but the fluid oceans react strongly. Because the moon is closer, its pull is greater, making it the dominant force in tide formation.

Gravitational pull is greatest on the side of Earth facing the moon and weakest on the side opposite. Nonetheless, the difference in these forces, in combination with Earth's rotation and other factors, allows the oceans to bulge outward on each side, creat-

ing high tides. The sides of Earth that are not in alignment with the moon experience low tides at this time.

Tides follow different patterns, depending on the shape of the sea-coast and the ocean floor. They tend to roll in gently on wide, open beaches. In confined spaces, such as a narrow inlet or bay, the water may rise to very high levels at high tide.

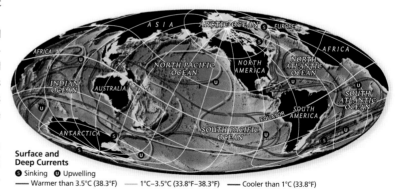

Surface and Deep Currents
S Sinking **U** Upwelling
—— Warmer than 3.5°C (38.3°F) —— 1°C–3.5°C (33.8°F–38.3°F) —— Cooler than 1°C (33.8°F)

WATER MOVES constantly through the oceans as if on a conveyor belt. Red arrows indicate the flow of warm waters, turquoise the flow of moderate waters, dark blue the flow of cool water.

CLICK IT: National Data Buoy Center www.ndbc.noaa.gov/

FOR MORE FACTS ON...

CHANGING TECHNIQUES IN MAPPING THE WORLD see The World in Maps, **CHAPTER 1, PAGE 19**

CLOCKING THE RHYTHMS OF NATURE see Time Zones, **CHAPTER 1, PAGES 32-3**; Telling Time, **CHAPTER 8, PAGES 324-5**

RIVERS

Rivers—large natural streams of flowing water—run through every continent. Wide rivers even flow beneath Antarctica's massive ice sheet.

Rivers are found in every kind of terrain. Some flow continuously with great force, some experience seasonal surges, and some dry up intermittently. South America's Amazon River carries more water than any other river on Earth.

Rivers vary widely in length. A river may have a fairly short course, or it can span much of a continent. The Mississippi River bisects most of the United States, from its source in Minnesota to its delta in Louisiana.

Rivers play a major role in the water cycle, discharging large amounts of fresh water into the oceans, where evaporation occurs. Clouds form from the resulting water vapor and travel inland, creating precipitation and a supply of fresh water to rivers and streams.

Since the beginning of human settlement, river valleys have been favored locations. They provide a reliable water supply for settlers and their crops and provide a means for moving people and goods. As industries developed, river waters were harnessed to power machinery. In flood, however, out-of-control rivers threaten lives and property.

THE ITAQUAI RIVER, a tributary of the Amazon, makes a meandering loop through remote rain forests in western Brazil.

FOR MORE FACTS ON...

THE EARLY SETTLEMENT STAGES OF HUMANKIND see *Human Migration,* **CHAPTER 6, PAGES 220-1**

WANDERLUST AND THE HUMAN TENDENCY TO TRAVEL see *Transportation,* **CHAPTER 6, PAGES 252-3**

JOHN WESLEY POWELL / EXPLORER OF THE WEST

A Civil War veteran who lost his right arm at the Battle of Shiloh, John Wesley Powell (1834–1902) taught geology at Illinois Wesleyan University and was curator of its museum. Before the war, he had explored the Mississippi, Ohio, and Illinois Rivers, collecting shells and minerals. After the war, he explored the Grand Canyon of the Colorado River. He set out on May 24, 1869, with nine other men and provisions for ten months. They rode the river's rapids, portaging where they could. By the end, half the crew had deserted. Powell's second expedition in 1871 produced a map and scientific articles about the Grand Canyon. In 1881 Powell became director of the U.S. Geological Survey. Later he devoted himself mostly to studying Indian languages and ethnography.

> " The wonders of the Grand Canyon cannot be adequately represented in symbols of speech, nor by speech itself. —— JOHN WESLEY POWELL, 1895 "

HOW DO RIVERS FORM THEIR SHAPES?

From its source in a melting mountain glacier, a river flows swiftly downhill, cutting a narrow valley. Smaller streams, called tributaries, flow in from springs and lakes. Where the river tumbles over rocks and down steep bluffs, rapids and waterfalls occur. Farther downstream the terrain flattens out and the river flows more slowly, winding from side to side.

A mature river meanders, creating large, lazy loops that sometimes curve so much, only a narrow neck of land separates either side of the loop. The river gradually widens and forms a floodplain, and as it nears the ocean it may form a marsh.

Shedding the heavy load of sand, silt, and clay it has been moving along, the river creates an expanse of flat, fertile land called a delta.

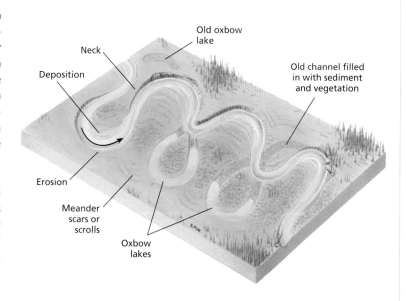

A MEANDERING RIVER may overflow and cut through a neck of land, opening up a new channel and forming a crescent-shaped body of water known as an oxbow lake. Typically shallow, oxbow lakes often fill with sediment and then dry up.

FAST FACT Each year the Amazon sends 20 percent of the Earth's available fresh water into the Atlantic.

FOR MORE FACTS ON...

THE POLLUTION OF VARIOUS BODIES OF WATER ON EARTH see *Threatened Planet: Water,* **CHAPTER 3, PAGES 126-7**

PLANTS & ANIMALS THAT LIVE IN OR NEAR THE WATER see *Aquatic Biomes,* **CHAPTER 5, PAGES 212-3**

LAKES

Bodies of water surrounded by land, lakes are found on every continent and in every kind of environment, totaling in the millions throughout the world. Lakes vary in size, from small ones typically called ponds to bodies of water so large they are known as seas.

Lakes form in basins, depressions in the Earth's surface, which are created in a number of ways. Many lakes, especially those found in the Northern Hemisphere, trace their origins to the work of glaciers at the height of the last ice age. The glaciers ground out pits and hollows in the land they traveled over. When the ice retreated, the depressions filled with water. Glaciers also carved valleys and then dammed them with the deposits they left behind, forming lakes.

Shifts in Earth's crust create depressions that may fill with water from rainfall or streams. When crustal movement occurs near the ocean, a part of that ocean may be cut off by an uplifted block of land. Volcanoes also participate in the formation of lakes. The crater of an inactive volcano may fill with water, as will a caldera, the depression formed when a volcano blows its top and collapses. Meandering rivers, landslides, and the dam-building work of beavers also create lakes. Artificial lakes are created as water-supply reservoirs or for recreational purposes.

Lakes receive their water from rain, ice- and snowmelt, streams, and groundwater. Lakes can be open or closed. An open lake discharges water by an outlet such as a stream or by seepage. A closed lake has no such outlet but loses water from evaporation. In some lakes evaporation greatly concentrates mineral content, creating salty bodies such as the Great Salt Lake in Utah, with waters saltier than the ocean.

The largest lake in the world is the Caspian Sea. Its salinity varies from one region to another. It was formed when tectonic movements created barricades that cut off and enclosed a portion of the ocean. No water flows out of the Caspian Sea into any ocean. Located at the nexus between Asia and the Middle East, it covers about 170,000 square miles.

Of the world's next largest lakes, three belong to the Great Lakes system of North America—Lake Superior, Lake Huron, and Lake Michigan—and two are found in Africa—Lake Victoria and Lake Tanganyika.

THIS CRATER LAKE is found amid volcanoes in Kamchatka, a peninsula in northeastern Russia full of extreme landscapes due to a long history of volcanic activity. Like other crater lakes, this one formed when precipitation accumulated in the depression of a caldera, or sunken volcanic cone.

CLICK IT Lakes & Reservoirs ga.water.usgs.gov/edu/earthlakes.html

FAST FACT Panch Pokhri—found at 17,758 feet on Mount Everest—is the highest named lake in the world.

FOR MORE FACTS ON...

FORCES THAT SHAPE THE SURFACE OF THE EARTH see *Landforms,* **CHAPTER 3, PAGES 98-101**
+
THE LOCATION AND CATEGORIES OF VOLCANOES AROUND THE WORLD see *Volcanoes,* **CHAPTER 3, PAGES 86-7**

HOW DO LOCKS WORK?

Locks on canals allow boats to travel inland waters by helping them adjust to differences in elevation from one body of water to another.

The Erie Canal, a 363-mile-long wonder, was completed by human-

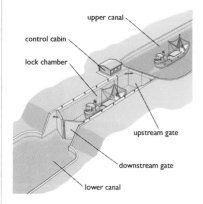

upper canal

control cabin

lock chamber

upstream gate

downstream gate

lower canal

and horsepower in 1825. It linked the Hudson River at Albany with Lake Erie at Buffalo—a rise of 568 feet—improving commerce and facilitating westward settlement in the growing United States.

On the Erie Canal, a boat approaching a lock was pulled in by a mule on the towpath and the downstream water gate was then closed. Sluices in the upstream gate allowed the lock's water level to rise.

When the water "topped out," the upstream gate was opened and the mule was allowed to pull the boat through. Today, boats "lock through"

A BOAT REMAINS in the lock chamber as the water level adjusts to the upper canal.

on their own power, but the principle is the same.

Locks operate around the world, from the canals of the Netherlands to the Panama Canal, from the Soo Locks at Sault Ste. Marie, Michigan, to the ship locks of China's Three Gorges Dam.

Most of the world's locks share three operating features: (1) a chamber in which boats sit as the water level changes; (2) gates at either end of the chamber; and (3) a valve, pump, or other water-moving device to change the level of water in the chamber.

A boat enters the chamber; the gates close; the water level is adjusted, and the boat exits, higher or lower than it was before.

HOW DO DAMS WORK?

A dam is a structure built across a river to control its flow. Sometimes a reservoir or lake is created behind the dam and can be used for recreation. Water flow controlled by a dam may be used to supply water to nearby communities, to power a hydroelectric plant, or to irrigate crops.

Dams can be built in different designs and of different materials such as earth, rock, or concrete. Most large dams are made of concrete. They are often designed to arch toward the incoming flow of water, a design that provides additional strength and distributes the weight of the water to the ends of the dam.

Dams typically have a valve built in to allow operators to release excess water from the upstream side. They also have spillways to release larger amounts of water in order to prevent unwanted flooding.

Dam building—as in the case of the construction of the Nile's Aswan Dam in the late 19th century or of China's Three Gorges Dam in the 20th century—sometimes floods land that has importance economically, culturally, or as wildlife habitat. Dams must be designed to withstand the challenge of floods or earthquakes. Enormous damage can occur when a major dam breaks, often including loss of life.

HOOVER DAM withstands pressures up to 45,000 pounds per square foot and generates over four billion kilowatt-hours of power a year.

FOR MORE FACTS ON...

THE HIGHEST POINTS ON EACH CONTINENT see *Landforms*, **CHAPTER 3, PAGE 98**
+
ENGINEERING EFFORTS PAST, PRESENT & FUTURE see *Engineering*, **CHAPTER 8, PAGES 332-3**

ICE

Ice, which is water in its frozen, solid state, will form when the water temperature reaches 32°F. In cold weather, ice appears on rivers, lakes, and the ocean. In areas where it is perpetually cold, ice becomes part of the landscape as features such as glaciers, ice caps, and ice sheets.

Glaciers form in locations where snow accumulates faster than it can melt, usually in mountainous areas. Over time the snow becomes compressed and recrystallizes into ice. When the ice reaches a solid mass of a certain thickness it can begin to move, or flow, under its own weight. Most glaciers move very slowly, perhaps only a few inches a year, but under some circumstances they can advance quickly.

An ice cap is a thick layer of ice and snow that has formed a permanent crust over areas of land. Such formations are found primarily in polar regions. Sometimes the term ice cap is used interchangeably with ice sheet, although an ice sheet usually is larger. Ice sheets that cover continents are known as continental glaciers.

The Antarctic ice sheet, for example, is a continental glacier. It covers almost 90 percent of the continent of Antarctica and contains about 85 percent of the world's ice and about two-thirds of the world's fresh water.

The area of the Antarctic ice sheet is shrinking at what many scientists consider an alarming rate for the future of the planet—as is also the case with the Greenland ice sheet.

MELTWATER on the Greenland ice sheet is a telltale sign of global warming.

EARTH'S ICE SHEETS

The Greenland ice sheet, which covers about 80 percent of the island of Greenland, is a remnant of one of the immense ice sheets that once blanketed much of the Northern Hemisphere at the height of the last ice age 18,000 years ago. Several decades ago it covered some 670,000 square miles. In the face of the world's changing climate, the melting rate of the Greenland sheet has increased, alarming scientists.

The Antarctic ice sheet serves as a global laboratory, yielding information about the Earth's geological and climatological history. Core samples of the ice provide a look at the layers that have built up over millions of years. Bubbles in the core samples contain clues about atmospheric conditions, including ash fallout from ancient volcanoes.

THE GREENLAND ICE SHEET offers 300-foot rappelling opportunities for climbers.

FOR MORE FACTS ON...

THE FORMATION AND CHARACTERISTICS OF SNOW & ICE see *Storms: Snow & Ice,* **CHAPTER 5, PAGES 190-1**

PLANTS & ANIMALS LIVING IN FROZEN TERRAINS see *Tundra & Ice Cap,* **CHAPTER 5, PAGES 210-1**

HOW DO GLACIERS SHAPE THE LAND?

Among the legacies of Earth's most recent ice age are landforms shaped by glaciers. Glaciers are powerful forces and can topple or crush anything in their paths. While they seem to be frozen still and solid, they are actually moving, carving and churning the land beneath and around them.

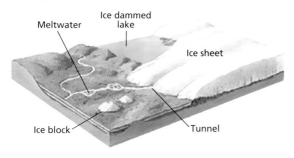

Meltwater — Ice dammed lake — Ice sheet — Ice block — Tunnel

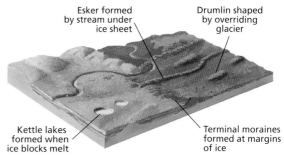

Esker formed by stream under ice sheet — Drumlin shaped by overriding glacier — Kettle lakes formed when ice blocks melt — Terminal moraines formed at margins of ice

DURING GLACIATION, an ice sheet prevents water flow except for trickles of meltwater through glacial tunnels.

AFTER GLACIATION, the landforms reflect an icy past, not only in structure but also in the composition of the soil.

WHAT IS AN ICEBERG?

An iceberg forms when a large chunk of ice calves, or breaks off, from a glacier and falls into the sea. The word comes from the Dutch *ijsberg,* ice hill.

Icebergs are formed of fresh water, not salt water. The water in icebergs is so pure that in some places chunks of iceberg are removed and melted, and the resulting water is used in cooking and brewing.

In the Northern Hemisphere, most icebergs originate from glaciers on Greenland, and they often drift southward into the North Atlantic Ocean. In the Southern Hemisphere, glaciers frequently calve from glaciers in Antarctica.

As little as one-tenth of a glacier is visible above the water—a phenomenon that inspired the familiar phrase "That's just the tip of the iceberg." Sharp ice on the hidden parts of an iceberg poses a threat to ships such as the historic cruise liner *Titanic,* whose hull was pierced by underwater ice in 1912, resulting in the swift sinking of the ship and the tragic death of more than 1,500 people.

AN ICEBERG TOWERS over *National Geographic Endeavour,* an expedition ship, in Antarctica.

CLICK IT: National Snow & Ice Data Center nsidc.org/glaciers

FOR MORE FACTS ON...

HOW GLACIERS PLAY A PART IN EARTH'S WATER CYCLE see *Water: Ice,* **CHAPTER 3, PAGES 120-1**

WHO OWNS THE CONTINENT OF ANTARCTICA see *Nations & Alliances,* **CHAPTER 9, PAGES 358-9**

Waste treatment water entering Volga River, Yaroslavl, Russia

THREATENED PLANET

CO$_2$ EMISSIONS
FROM FOSSIL FUELS

CHINA
7,706.826 million metric tons

UNITED STATES
5,424.530 million metric tons

INDIA
1,591.126 million metric tons

RUSSIA
1,556.661 million metric tons

JAPAN
1,097.965 million metric tons

GERMANY
765.562 million metric tons

CANADA
540.967 million metric tons

On every front—land, air, and water—human activities have consequences, many of them negative. Earth faces environmental stresses, some urgent and all needing attention. No part of the world remains untouched, no natural system untainted. Our forests regulate water flow, retain carbon, distribute nutrients, and produce soil—yet they are disappearing.

Cutting, burning, and leveling operations reduce forests, mostly tropical, by an area equal to Florida each year. Habitat loss threatens species. Coastal areas experience degradation. By 2060, erosion may claim a quarter of all homes in the U.S. within 500 feet of the shoreline. Our oceans are polluted and overexploited. More than 70 percent of marine fisheries are depleted. More than half of all coral reefs are threatened. The atmosphere itself has come under assault. Global warming is predicted to cause the loss of half the boreal forests, millions more malaria cases, and the displacement of millions of people by rising sea levels.

FOR MORE FACTS ON...

THE IMPACT OF HUMAN BEINGS & HUMAN SOCIETY ON THE PLANET see *Human Impact,* **CHAPTER 5, PAGES 214-5**

BIRTHRATES AROUND THE WORLD, PAST & PRESENT see *World Population,* **CHAPTER 6, PAGES 250-1**

PAPER OR PLASTIC?

Paper or plastic? If you're caught up in the paper versus plastic debate at the grocery store, don't assume that your choice of paper is the more environmentally sound decision.

Paper bags use more resources in their production, although they have a greater chance of being recycled and of breaking down when they do make it to the landfill.

Plastic bags, which are cheaper to manufacture, create less trash by weight but do not break down. Burning them to create electricity puts heavy metals into the air and toxic ash into solid waste. Today, some stores offer only paper, preferring recyclables.

GROCERY STORE CHOICES symbolize consumer quandaries. As to the choice between paper and plastic, the best is a reusable bag.

FAST FACT An area of tropical forest as large as 50 football fields is destroyed every minute.

WHAT IS THE FUTURE OF TRASH?

Humans today create a lot of garbage. In times past, there was less. People owned fewer things, used things longer, and much of their waste decomposed. Today, trash has staying power, made from materials that will still be intact when we no longer are.

In the United States, trash sometimes goes to a landfill, where it is dumped in a lined pit, compacted, and covered with soil in a sequence of layers. Other garbage is incinerated. More localities are requiring residents to separate recyclable materials. These are reprocessed or, sometimes, incinerated to produce energy.

Some areas of the planet face extreme waste disposal situations: Antarctica, for example, surprisingly. Decades of exploration there have produced 70 waste sites that contain solid waste of all kinds as well as chemicals and heavy metals that must be contained. Cycles of freezing and

thawing, paired with the logistics and expense of transporting waste or neutralizing contaminated land, pose formidable challenges. Charged chemical compounds that trap pollutants have shown some success and may have applications in similar habitats, such as northern Russia and Alaska.

LANDFILLS receive about 55 percent of all garbage in the United States. Researchers are investigating ways to turn trash to fuel, such as extracting cellulosic ethanol from paper refuse.

CLICK IT: Earth Day Network www.earthday.net

FOR MORE FACTS ON...

THE THREATS OF POLLUTION see *Threatened Planet: Air & Threatened Planet: Water,* **CHAPTER 3, PAGES 124-7**

THE FUTURE OF ANIMAL & PLANT SPECIES see *Biodiversity: Threatened Species,* **CHAPTER 4, PAGES 178-9**

AIR

As residents of Earth, most of us are more immediately aware of the state of our air than of our land or water. We live in the lower atmosphere and interact with the air for our daily survival. On a hot, hazy day in summer, pollution may hang low over our cities: We can feel it, breathe it in, and depending where one lives, perhaps actually smell it.

In recent decades our awareness of the toxins and particulates that have entered the atmosphere has grown. We also sense that the air from day to day is warmer, and we have learned that the 1990s were possibly the warmest decade of the last millennium.

The greenhouse gases in Earth's atmosphere are actually good for the planet. They have been there since the atmosphere first formed, and they keep our planet from becoming an icy mass. Without the natural greenhouse effect, the Earth would be more than 50°F colder than it is today, with an average global temperature of only 5°F—much less hospitable to life.

But in the case of greenhouse gases, too much of a good thing is not good. The planet has been experiencing an increase in carbon dioxide in the atmosphere, generated in large part from fossil fuel emissions and the proliferation of other greenhouse gases such as nitrous oxide and methane. What has caused this increase? By and large, human activities are to blame. At one level, greenhouse gases protect us, but when they reach a higher level, they become a threat to comfort, safety, and even life.

Global temperatures are predicted to increase by 2.5 percent to 10.4 percent on average through the end of the 21st century. Scientists who study the air and the atmosphere are not all in agreement about either the causes or the ramifications of the current trend toward global warming. Most do agree, however, that the trend began as far back as 1750, the beginning of the industrial revolution.

In the absence of definitive knowledge of the future, say many, we must plan for a worst-case scenario. The efforts begin by understanding the current science behind the changes in Earth's ozone layer and the resulting greenhouse effect.

LOS ANGELES, CALIFORNIA, notorious for its smog, experiences the confluence of physical geography and human behavior: The region's bowl-shaped topography traps intense auto exhaust.

CLICK IT: Worldwide Ozone Hole www.epa.gov/ozone/strathome.html/

FAST FACT The hole in Earth's protective ozone layer above Antarctica is now about the size of North America.

FOR MORE FACTS ON...

INDICATORS OF GLOBAL WARMING & IMPENDING CLIMATE CHANGE see *Climate,* **CHAPTER 5, PAGES 192-3**

THE TREND TOWARD URBANIZATION AND CITY GROWTH see *Cities,* **CHAPTER 6, PAGES 260-1**

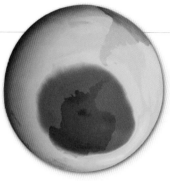

THE OZONE LAYER

The ozone layer is a region in Earth's stratosphere that contains high concentrations of a bluish gas called ozone. Although ozone constitutes only about one-millionth of the atmosphere's gases, it absorbs most of the sun's ultraviolet radiation. Without the ozone layer, this radiation would destroy all life on the surface of the planet.

Ultraviolet radiation creates and perpetuates ozone. When an ozone molecule is struck by an ultraviolet ray, it falls apart, yielding free oxygen and an oxygen atom that combines with another free oxygen to form more ozone. This cycle absorbs most UV radiation.

THE ANTARCTIC OZONE HOLE develops every winter. In 1979, its size did not overshadow the continent itself.

TWENTY YEARS LATER, spectrometer analysis by satellite showed the hole had grown to 10.5 million square miles.

Some manufactured chemicals interfere with this cycle, thus reducing the amount of ozone in the stratosphere. Among the worst offenders are chlorofluorocarbons (CFCs), usually found in refrigerants and aerosol sprays and now generally banned.

Falling ozone levels have caused a thinning of the ozone layer above Antarctica, known as the ozone hole. The Antarctic ozone hole has increased dramatically in size over the past two decades. A smaller hole over the Arctic is now developing.

WHAT IS THE GREENHOUSE EFFECT?

The greenhouse effect allows the short-wave radiation of sunlight to pass through the atmosphere to Earth's surface but makes it difficult for heat in the form of long-wave radiation to escape. This effect blankets the Earth and keeps our planet at a reasonable temperature to support life.

Earth radiates energy, of which about 90 percent is absorbed by atmospheric gases: water vapor, carbon dioxide, ozone, methane, nitrous oxide, and others. Absorbed energy is radiated back to the surface and warms Earth's lower atmosphere. The gases have come to be called greenhouse gases because they hold in light and heat, just as a greenhouse does for the sake of the plants inside.

Greenhouse gases are essential to life, but only at an appropriate balance point. These gases increased during the 20th century due to industrial activity and fossil fuel emissions. For example, the concentration of carbon dioxide in the atmosphere has recently been growing by about 1.4 percent annually.

This increase in greenhouse gases is one of the contributors to the observed patterns of global warming.

LIKE A GREENHOUSE, the atmosphere holds in radiation—light and warmth. Without this greenhouse effect, Earth could not sustain life. So-called greenhouse gases intensify the effect, though, changing the chemistry of atmospheric layers and holding in more heat.

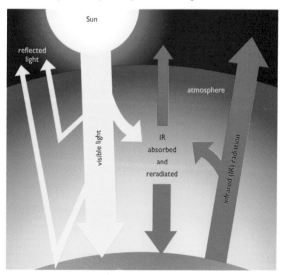

FOR MORE FACTS ON...

THE PHYSICAL CHARACTERISTICS OF EARTH'S ATMOSPHERE see *Earth's Atmosphere,* **CHAPTER 3, PAGES 104-5**
+
ENERGY SOURCES OTHER THAN FOSSIL FUELS see *Power: Alternative Technologies,* **CHAPTER 8, PAGES 354-5**

WATER

Earth's waters are threatened in contradictory ways: While the supply of fresh water for drinking for human use cannot keep up with demand, the level of water in the oceans continues to rise as a result of global warming. Shrinking polar region ice fuels this ocean surge. A predicted 23-foot surge in sea level in the coming centuries would wipe out New York City and South Florida and force millions of people from low-lying regions of Asia.

Less than one percent of Earth's fresh water is available for human use. Since 1970, the global water supply has declined by 33 percent. In the next 50 to 100 years, when the population is expected to reach 11 billion, the strain will be even greater.

At present, the freshwater crisis is mostly one of distribution. One-third of the world's people lack sufficient water for their use. Even though the United States is considered a water rich country—with 4 percent of the world's population and 8 percent of its fresh water—distribution is uneven. The southwestern states struggle to meet their growing needs, while northeastern states have more abundant resources. This situation has plagued the nation since the West was first settled and disputes arose over ownership and access to water. Rivers run dry due to diversion, and aquifers are being drained beyond their capacity to replenish.

In the developing world especially, water equity is even more skewed. The United Nations anticipates that by 2025 more than half the world's population will lack water for their basic needs.

When water nominally is available, nevertheless, it often is unfit for human consumption due to various types of pollution, both chemical and microbial. Throughout the world, up to 20,000 children die each day from diseases related to an unclean water supply.

Some hope is found in basic, low-tech means that can be carried out by individuals. Catching rainfall and road and roof runoff could improve agricultural production in sub-Saharan Africa and Southeast Asia. Desalinizing drinking water, normally an expensive, energy-intensive process, is improving with the use of nanotechnologies and models that mimic organic cell osmosis.

HUMAN LITTER mingles with natural flotsam on Natadola Beach in Fiji.

FAST FACT As many as four items of debris per square meter now float in the waters of Indonesia.

FOR MORE FACTS ON...

THE PROCESSES OF EARTH'S OCEANS see Water: Oceans, **CHAPTER 3, PAGES 112-5**

THE WORLDWIDE PROBLEM OF TRASH ACCUMULATION see Threatened Planet, **CHAPTER 3, PAGES 122-3**

HOW DO WE CLEAN OIL SPILLS?

Of the various kinds of pollution that affect the ocean, spills from oil tankers rank as one of the most challenging to clean up. There is no one method for handling all situations, but there are general techniques that apply to many kinds of spills.

Aerial reconnaissance often is necessary to determine the extent of an oil spill, whether it occurs in the open ocean or near the coast. The aerial survey provides information about the nature of the spill and sites along the coast in immediate danger.

To directly deal with the spill, floating barriers called booms are placed around the spill to contain it. These allow skimmers, which can be boats, vacuum machines, or oil-absorbent ropes, to collect the oil into containers. Chemical dispersants also may be applied to break down the oil and render it less harmful. In some situations, it may be best for the fresh spill to be ignited, although burning poses its own hazards and creates pollution.

If the oil reaches the shore, other cleaning methods are deployed. These

A KOREAN OIL SPILL in 2007 brought out volunteers and environmental specialists to join soldiers in cleaning the coastline near Taean, southwest of Seoul.

include pressurized water hoses and vacuum trucks, as well as the dispersal of absorbent materials. At times the sand is removed to another site, cleaned, and returned to the beach.

Rescue efforts on behalf of oil-coated sea and shore birds and mammals requires carefully washing them with a mild detergent, such as a dishwashing liquid. This painstaking job involves much human effort, often by dedicated volunteers, and offers no guarantee for the survival of the affected animals.

CLICK IT: Water Resources water.usgs.gov

FAST FACT The oil released during the 2010 Deepwater Horizon spill equals one-quarter of one day's U.S. use.

THE TRASH FLOATING IN OUR OCEANS

The Pacific Ocean contains a plastic soup of waste that covers an area twice the size of the continental United States. Plastic trash from land, ships, and oil platforms travels in a vortex just below the surface of the

ocean and often deposits itself on beautiful Hawaiian beaches.

Fanning out from either side of Hawaii are the Western and Eastern Pacific Garbage Patches. Waste in them ranges from tiny plastic pellets

to footballs and kayaks. Such ocean trash is not limited to the Pacific, though. The United Nations estimates that every square mile of the ocean contains an average of 46,000 pieces of floating plastic.

FOR MORE FACTS ON...

PLANTS & ANIMALS THAT LIVE IN OR NEAR WATER see *Aquatic Biomes,* **CHAPTER 5, PAGES 212-3**

THE GROWING WORLD POPULATION & ITS INFLUENCE ON PLANT EARTH see *World Population,* **CHAPTER 6, PAGES 250-1**

Life Begins / Life-Forms / Fungi &
Shrubs / Trees / Medicinal Plants /
Archaea / Insects / Butterflies & M
Fish / Reptiles / Amphibians / Bird
Curiosities / Migration / Biodivers

LIFE ON

ichens / Plants / Flowering Plants
ant Curiosities / Bacteria, Protists &
hs / Spiders & Their Kin / Mollusks
Mammals / Sea Mammals / Animal
/ Extinction / Threatened Species

EARTH

Splendid leaf frog, Costa Rica

LIFE BEGINS

EARLIEST FORMS

PROKARYOTES
Single-celled bacteria
Archaean eon / 3.9-3.5 billion years ago

BLUE-GREEN ALGAE
First plants; photosynthesis
Archaean eon / 3.5-2.5 billion years ago

EUKARYOTES
Multicellular organisms; cells have nucleus
with chromosomes
Proterozoic eon / 2.5-1 billion years ago

METAZOANS
Soft, multicellular marine organisms
Proterozoic eon / 2 billion-540 million
years ago

TRILOBITES
Segmented marine arthropods
Cambrian period / 540 million years ago

n three and a half billion years, life on Earth has transformed from single cells to complex multicellular organisms. Life permeates all environments on Earth and is a defining characteristic of our planet. It occurs in the biosphere, a thin layer between the upper part of Earth's troposphere and the topmost layers of porous rocks and sediments. The size and nature of the biosphere has grown and changed over time, as has the relationship between organic and inorganic elements in the biosphere.

In the beginning, the conditions on Earth were limiting, and the first cells formed from molecular building blocks reflected this. Early organisms were single-celled prokaryotes, such as bacteria, that lacked a defined nucleus. A billion and a half years later, eukaryotes, such as amoebas, appeared: single-celled organisms that possess a bounded nucleus and rely on oxygen to function. These two categories of cells have persisted through time in an unbroken sequence, while also evolving into the myriad and astonishingly diversified life-forms found on the planet today.

FOR MORE FACTS ON...

EARLY AGES OF THE PLANET EARTH see Formation of the Earth, **CHAPTER 3, PAGES 80-1**
+
THE AMAZING DIVERSITY OF LIFE-FORMS ON EARTH see Biodiversity, **CHAPTER 4, PAGES 174-9**

Humans should not be viewed as the culmination of life on Earth. Like all situations involving natural selection, the pathway that led to *Homo sapiens* was not predetermined, but variable. A sequence of many favorable circumstances was necessary for the human species to evolve. Had not a cataclysmic event occurred some 65 million years ago, dinosaurs still might be the dominant vertebrates on the planet, as they had been for the 100 million years during which they coexisted with early mammals. If one group of organisms is to be singled out for its longevity and adaptability, it is bacteria. Bacteria have been here since the beginning and in all likelihood will be here at the end.

GLOSSARY

Eukaryote: From Greek *eu-*, good, + *karyon*, nut or kernel. Any organism composed of one or more cells, each of which contains a clearly defined nucleus enclosed by a membrane, along with organelles—small, self-contained, cellular parts that perform specific functions. **/ Prokaryote:** From Greek *pro-*, before, + *karyon*, nut or kernel. Any cellular organism that lacks a distinct nucleus.

WHAT IS PHOTOSYNTHESIS?

Photosynthesis is a life process powered by the sun. Directly or indirectly through the food chain, it fuels most life on Earth. Photosynthesis is carried out by green plants and some types of algae as well as by cyanobacteria (formerly known as blue-green algae) and related organisms, which are responsible for most of the photosynthesis in oceans.

In the process of photosynthesis, plants capture sunlight and absorb carbon dioxide from the atmosphere. The light and CO_2 combine with water, brought in by plant roots. The end product is sugars, food for the plant; a waste product is oxygen, respired out through the plant leaves.

Thus plants use the carbon dioxide that animals breathe out and provide the oxygen that animals breathe in.

Photosynthesis provides all the food we eat—plants and animals that eat plants—and the oxygen we breathe. If photosynthesis were to cease, the atmosphere's oxygen would likely be depleted within several thousand years.

Photosynthesis also created the raw materials for the fossil fuels we so depend on. Green plants formed the bulk of the organic deposits that through geological processes were transformed into coal, oil, and natural gas.

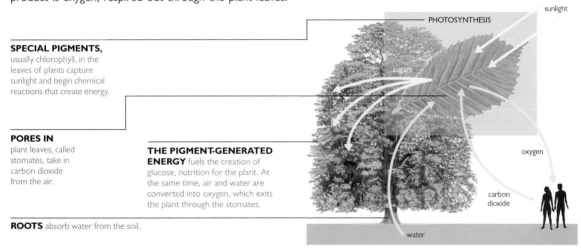

PHOTOSYNTHESIS

sunlight

sugars

oxygen

carbon dioxide

water

SPECIAL PIGMENTS, usually chlorophyll, in the leaves of plants capture sunlight and begin chemical reactions that create energy.

PORES IN plant leaves, called stomates, take in carbon dioxide from the air.

THE PIGMENT-GENERATED ENERGY fuels the creation of glucose, nutrition for the plant. At the same time, air and water are converted into oxygen, which exits the plant through the stomates.

ROOTS absorb water from the soil.

FAST FACT Half of all oxygen comes from photosynthesizing phytoplankton, one-celled plants on the ocean surface.

FOR MORE FACTS ON...

ANCIENT LIFE-FORMS INCLUDING BACTERIA see *Bacteria, Protists & Archaea,* **CHAPTER 4, PAGES 148-9**

THE EARLIEST ERAS OF THE HUMAN SPECIES see *Human Origins,* **CHAPTER 6, PAGES 218-9**

LINNAEAN TAXONOMIC CATEGORIES

KINGDOM

PHYLUM

CLASS

ORDER

FAMILY

GENUS

SPECIES

LIFE-FORMS

any systems of classification and description have been invented to help catalog and discuss the vast number of life-forms on Earth. In the fourth century B.C., Aristotle suggested grouping organisms by nature rather than by superficialities in form. He separated vertebrates and invertebrates and—in a step advanced for the time—recognized that whales and other marine animals were mammals and not fish.

The Aristotelean system of classification of animals remained paramount until the 18th century, when Swedish botanist Carolus Linnaeus devised a taxonomic system for flora and fauna, assigning to each type of plant or animal a two-part name that distinguished it from all others by species. The Linnaean system of taxonomy has since been expanded and refined. We still use the two-part name for genus and species.

Traditional taxonomy provides a useful tool for organizing Earth's nearly two million known and named organisms. Recently, scientists have begun looking to evolutionary relationships between species as a new way of classifying and organizing life-forms. A focus on evolutionary ancestry has generated a field of taxonomy known as cladistics.

A German entomologist, Willi Hennig (1913-1976), originated the methods of cladistics, which relies heavily on data derived from DNA and RNA sequencing and produces computer-generated genetic evolutionary trees known as cladograms. As more data become available and are evaluated, evolutionary pathways are refined.

FAST FACT The approximately 1.75 million identified plants and animals represent only a fraction of all species.

FOR MORE FACTS ON...

STAGES IN GEOLOGIC TIME see Ages of the Earth, **CHAPTER 3, PAGES 94-5**
+
DNA & GENETIC SCIENCE see Earth's Elements, **CHAPTER 3, PAGES 90-1, &** Genetics, **CHAPTER 8, PAGES 344-5**

WHAT DID DARWIN LEARN IN THE GALÁPAGOS?

Charles Darwin's first understanding of evolution blossomed in 1835 on the Galápagos Islands, a thousand miles off the coast of Ecuador. This remote 19-island archipelago is located at the confluence of three ocean currents, giving it a unique climatic situation in which species such as the penguin and the flamingo can coexist. Fully one-third of Galápagos vascular land plants are endemic, as are most of the reptiles, half of the breeding land birds, and almost a third of the marine species.

The highly challenging conditions of the Galápagos, with its arid climate, poor soil, and rugged terrain, afforded Darwin a chance to witness how species—such as the giant tortoise and the Galápagos finches—adapt in an

A GIANT GALÁPAGOS TORTOISE lives to 100 years old on its Pacific island. These reptiles have differentiated into 14 or more different subspecies—a fascinating study in evolution.

almost laboratory-type setting. Such far-reaching observations and connections underpinned his theory of evolution.

Today, the archipelago is under threat from various stresses, despite its U.N. designation as a World Heritage site.

CLICK IT: Taxonomic Information www.itis.gov

G L O S S A R Y

Endemic: Limited in distribution to a particular area; a specific organism, for example. **Species:** Related organisms that share common characteristics and are capable of interbreeding. **/ Cladistics:** From Greek *klados,* "branch." Taxonomy, or science of organizing and categorizing living things, based on genetic and evolutionary information.

CAROLUS LINNAEUS / FATHER OF CLASSIFICATION

Carolus Linnaeus (1707–1778) studied botany and medicine in his native Sweden and then moved to the Netherlands in 1735, where he swiftly passed his medical exams. He soon published a book, *Systema Naturae (The System of Nature),* in which he presented his scheme of a hierarchical classification for the three kingdoms of nature: plants, animals, and stones. Linnaeus's taxonomy replaced others based on dichotomy, and he built its foundation from the individual species on up, through genera, classes, and kingdoms. Additional ranks were added later by other scientists. His binomial nomenclature (genus, species) was considered a real breakthrough, as it provided a recognizable shorthand, especially in publications. His writings greatly influenced both Charles Darwin and Gregor Mendel, the father of modern genetics.

FAST FACT Linnaeus was the first to use the scientific name *Homo sapiens* for human beings.

FOR MORE FACTS ON...

THE GEOLOGY OF ISLANDS see *Landforms: Islands,* **CHAPTER 3, PAGES** 102-3

EVOLUTION & VARIETY AMONG ANIMAL SPECIES see *Animal Curiosities & Biodiversity,* **CHAPTER 4, PAGES** 170-1, 174-9

Fungi growing on tree stump, Gifford Pinchot National Forest, Washington State

FUNGI & LICHENS

USEFUL FUNGI

ASPERGILLUS NIGER
Used to produce citric acid for flavoring
sweets and beverages

ASPERGILLUS ORYZAE
Used in making sake

CEPHALOSPORIUM ACREMONIUM
Source for cephalosporin antibiotic

PENICILLIUM CHRYSOGENUM
Used to manufacture penicillin antibiotic

PENICILLIUM ROQUEFORTI
Used to ripen blue cheeses

SACCHAROMYCES CEREVISIAE
Used in baking and making beer and wine

TOLYPLOCLADIUM INFLATUM
Source for cyclosporine, drug used in
organ transplants

fungus is a member of the kingdom Fungi—a grouping of some 80,000 organisms that range from single-celled yeasts to mushrooms and molds to large slabs of bracket fungus growing up the sides of trees. Many fungi live freely in soil or water and many more engage in parasitic or symbiotic relationships with plants and animals. Most species are composed of strands of cells called hyphae that combine to form a fungal body or mass known as a mycelium.

Fungi, like algae, once were taxonomically grouped with plants. In most classification systems today, fungi appear as a separate kingdom, and what sometimes are called the lower fungi, such as slime molds, are grouped with the protists. Algae fall in with the protists as well. Some kinds of fungi have entered into a symbiotic partnership with some colonies of algae to create organisms known as lichen.

Most fungi are saprophytes; in other words, they feed on dead or decaying plant matter. Fungi digest their food externally by sending out their hyphae—single-celled

FOR MORE FACTS ON...

THE CLASSIFICATION OF LIVING THINGS see Life-forms, **CHAPTER 4, PAGES 132-3**

CHARACTERISTICS & GROWING HABITS OF TREES see Plants: Trees, **CHAPTER 4, PAGES 142-3**

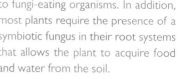

filaments—through the substances they devour. The hyphae then dispense enzymes that break down the food, allowing the nutrients to be absorbed by the fungus. Unlike green plants, fungi lack chlorophyll and therefore do not photosynthesize.

In a forest, fungi serve as important and efficient recyclers of plant debris, making these nutrients available to fungi-eating organisms. In addition, most plants require the presence of a symbiotic fungus in their root systems that allows the plant to acquire food and water from the soil.

G L O S S A R Y

Saprophyte: From Greek *sapro-*, "dead," + *phyton*, "plant." An organism that lives on dead or decaying organic matter.

ALEXANDER FLEMING / DISCOVERER OF PENICILLIN

Scottish bacteriologist Alexander Fleming (1881–1955) studied substances that could ward off bacterial infections. His efforts redoubled after World War I, when bacterial infection in the form of trench fever and other afflictions took more lives than combat. In 1928, while investigating the *Staphylococcus* bacterium, he discovered a bacteria-free zone in a culture where a patch of the mold *Penicillium notatum* had formed. Fleming was able to obtain enough of the mold, which had the property of inhibiting bacterial growth, for topical treatment of skin and eye infections in humans. He shared the Nobel Prize for physiology or medicine in 1945 with Ernst Chain and Howard Florey, who completed the work leading to the mass production of penicillin.

FAST FACT Most dandruff seems to be caused by a fungus, *Malassezia furfur*.

THE LICHEN PARTNERSHIP

A lichen may resemble a single plant-like organism, but it is really a colony of algae embedded in a matrix formed by the filaments of a fungus—a good example of symbiosis.

This partnership between algae and fungi benefits from the combination of two different methods of getting food for energy. The algae in lichens make food through photosynthesis, while the fungi absorb food and water from their environs.

With both methods available to it, a lichen can survive in challenging habitats such as rocks or snow.

There are at least 15,000 varieties of lichens. They provide a major food source for reindeer and caribou and are used commercially as foods and dietary supplements and in dyes.

LICHENS called British soldiers (center) and pixie cups (bottom center) survive in bleak settings because of a botanical partnership between algae and fungi.

CLICK IT: Fungi & Mycology www.doctorfungus.org

FOR MORE FACTS ON...

ADVANCES IN MEDICINE & PHARMACEUTICALS see *Medical Science,* **CHAPTER 8, PAGES 338-45**

THE DIVERSITY OF EARTH'S SPECIES see *Biodiversity,* **CHAPTER 4, PAGES 174-5**

PLANT EVOLUTION

SEEDLESS VASCULAR PLANTS
Ferns, horsetails
410 million years ago

EARLY SEED-BEARING PLANTS
Precursors to conifers
360 million years ago

BRYOPHYTES
Mosses
320 million years ago

GINGKOS
286 million years ago

CYCADS
275 million years ago

ANGIOSPERMS
Flowering plants
130 million years ago

PLANTS

ost paleobotanists believe that land plants evolved about 430 million years ago from predominantly freshwater green algae. Living members of these groups seem more evolved today, so it is assumed that some of their traits were developed after they transitioned to land. Primitive plants were simple structures that did not look like modern plants.

The earliest plants had upright stems but no roots and leaves, to say nothing of flowers, a development that would come much later.

Nonflowering plants fall into two groups: bryophytes and vascular plants. Bryophytes lack a system for the transport of water and food. They tend to be small and lack true roots. They photosynthesize and mostly reproduce by means of alternating nonsexual and sexual generations, in a fashion similar to the ferns.

Early nonflowering vascular plants include the ferns and horsetails. These plants reproduce by means of spores and alternating generations. Also included in this group are the gymnosperms ("naked seeds"), plants whose seeds are not enclosed, as in flowering plants, but sit on the scales of cones.

Conifers, including pines, firs, and spruces, create both male and female cones. The male cone makes fine pollen that is blown onto a female cone and unites with an egg inside, producing a seed. When the seeds ripen, the scales loosen and spread out, allowing the seeds to disperse.

Some 200 million years ago, gigantic gymnosperms formed the dominant plant life on Earth. As such they also satisfied the appetites of the Jurassic herbivores.

FAST FACT Giant horsetail plants formed a large part of the plant life that turned into coal deposits millions of years ago.

FOR MORE FACTS ON...

THE LIFE SPAN OF PLANET EARTH see Ages of the Earth, **CHAPTER 3, PAGES 94-5**

EXTREMES AMONG THE PLANT SPECIES ON PLANET EARTH see Plant Curiosities, **CHAPTER 4, PAGES 146-7**

PLANTS WITH A PAST

A number of plants today appear little changed from their prehistoric predecessors: mosses, horsetails, and ferns, found especially in moist environments, for example. Others are found among the cycads, a group that goes back 245 million years.

Cycads have a columnar trunk and a crown of leaves, much like a palm tree, and are either male or female. They are found in the tropics and subtropics of both the Eastern and Western Hemispheres. Both sexes of cycads in most species bear outsize cones. Today's gingko, a lone survivor of a once large group, no longer appears in the wild. It formerly was limited to southeastern China, although as a cultivated plant it is known worldwide. Gingkos are recognized by their clusters of fan-shaped leaves.

By about 380 million years ago, plants were diversifying into the forms we know today. As specialized tissues to transport water and nourishment and provide strength in the stems developed, tree-size and treelike species were able to thrive. Seedlike structures soon appeared, leading to the development of flowering plants.

CYCAD TREES of Western Australia are probably little different from those that sprouted during the age of the dinosaurs.

HOW DO FERNS REPRODUCE?

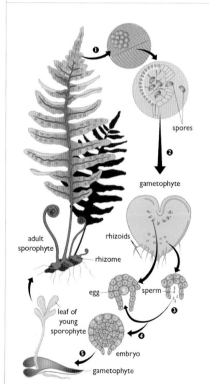

- ❶
- spores
- ❷
- gametophyte
- adult sporophyte
- rhizoids
- rhizome
- egg
- sperm
- ❸
- leaf of young sporophyte
- ❹
- ❺
- embryo
- gametophyte

Ferns reproduce differently from the flowering plants that bear seed. Under a fern frond, or leaf, are often found rows of small brown dots called sporangia. Inside these sporangia, spores develop and release into the air when they are ripe.

Fallen spores sprout into tiny, often heart-shaped plants that anchor themselves in the ground with root-like rhizoids. Under their leaves are separate structures where eggs and sperm develop and mature.

Rain swells the sperm structures and they burst, releasing flagellated sperm that travel to the egg in water droplets. Fertilization of an egg by sperm results in a new fern plant with a core of fronds that usually start out tightly coiled and eventually unfurl.

Fern species have existed on Earth for some 300 million years. They thrived on Earth from 359 to 299 million years ago during the Carboniferous period, which is sometimes called the age of ferns, since they were then the dominant vegetation.

The ferns that grew during the Carboniferous period are now extinct, but some of them likely evolved into the ferns we know today. As many as 12,000 species of ferns have been identified worldwide.

FERNS REPRODUCE not by seed but by spore, a more primitive method than found in flowering plants.

CLICK IT: American Fern Society www.amerfernsoc.org

FOR MORE FACTS ON...

REPRODUCTION AMONG FLOWERING PLANTS see Plants: Flowering, **CHAPTER 4, PAGE 139**

THE CONTINENT OF AUSTRALIA & ITS GEOGRAPHY see Australia & Oceania, **CHAPTER 9, PAGES 408-10**

FLOWERING

Any vascular plant in which flower parts mature after fertilization into seed-bearing fruit is considered an angiosperm, or flowering plant. Flowering plants first appeared about 145 million years ago and today represent more than 80 percent of all green plants. Directly or indirectly, they represent the major source of food for all the animal species on Earth, from insects to humans.

Flowering plants also supply the raw materials for clothing such as cotton and linen, a large number of drugs and remedies, and important building materials. The flowering plants in our gardens and homes also add priceless aesthetic pleasure to our lives.

Angiosperms come in two basic forms: woody and herbaceous. Trees and shrubs represent the woody forms; herbaceous plants, which include many more species than we normally think of as herbs, are categorized as annuals, biennials, and perennials. Annuals complete their whole growth cycle in one year. Biennials use the first year to grow from seed and the second to develop flowers and fruit for the next generation. Perennials grow for many years and often produce flowers every year. While they may die back in winter, perennials produce new shoots each growing season from underground structures such as bulbs, rhizomes, corms, and tubers.

Pollination—the transfer of male reproductive cells to the female reproductive parts of a plant of the same species—occurs by a number of methods, some random and some more orchestrated. Some flowers require pollinators—mostly insects, but also birds, reptiles, and mammals—that transport the pollen to other plants of the same species. These flowers often entice with strong scent and even landing guides on their petals. The pollinator's reward is the nutritious pollen itself or nectar, a sweet liquid produced in the flowers.

FOR THE PLANT, flowers serve reproductive purposes. For humans, they bring beauty and joy. Here a field worker harvests sunny calendula flowers in Arizona.

FAST FACT Wind can carry pollen grains as far as 3,000 miles from a parent plant.

FOR MORE FACTS ON...

THE IMPORTANCE OF POLLINATION IN PLANT REPRODUCTION see *Plants: Shrubs,* **CHAPTER 4, PAGE 141**

CLOTHING & SOURCES FOR FIBER see *Clothing,* **CHAPTER 6, PAGES 242-3**

WHAT IS PHOTOTROPISM?

Many plants, and some other organisms such as fungi, exhibit a tendency to grow toward a light source. Known as phototropism, this movement is very pronounced in some species. Plants' responses also vary according to the wavelength of the light to which they are exposed, with red light often evoking the strongest response.

Plant hormones called auxins trigger cellular changes and swelling inside the plant, causing it to move toward the light.

The shoots of some vines may purposefully grow away from the light. They seek instead dark solid objects to climb; this process is called negative phototropism, or skototropism—growing toward darkness. Plant roots also exhibit this negative motion, but they also respond strongly to gravity.

Some plants move in response to the daily motion of the sun. This action, called heliotropism, does not involve plant growth and is therefore not considered a form of phototropism.

FLOWERS PREPARE FOR FRUIT. After pollination and fertilization, a flower's petals fall off, and the structure remaining develops into fruit, in which the plant's seeds mature.

CLICK IT: Plants in Motion plantsinmotion.bio.indiana.edu

G L O S S A R Y

Vascular plant: Any plant that has a specialized conducting system consisting mostly of phloem (food-conducting tissue) and xylem (water-conducting tissue), collectively called vascular tissue. **/ Auxin:** Any of a group of hormones that regulate plant growth, particularly by stimulating cell elongation in stems and inhibiting it in roots.

HOW DOES A FLOWER WORK?

In many species of flowering plants, each flower produced contains both male and female parts; in others, male and female flowers grow separately, sometimes even on separate plants.

The male flower part is known as the stamen. The female flower part is known as the pistil. The anther, part of the stamen, produces pollen, the male reproductive cells. The stigma, part of the pistil, receives the pollen.

The pollen migrates inside the flower to the ovary, where it fertilizes the ovules, or egg cells, inside. The fertilization process initiates the production of seeds by the flower.

PARTS OF A FLOWER

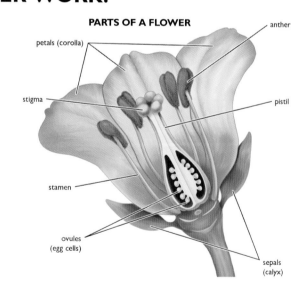

petals (corolla)
stigma
stamen
ovules (egg cells)
anther
pistil
sepals (calyx)

FAST FACT Southeast Asia's rafflesia has blossoms as big as Hula-Hoops that can weigh 15 pounds.

FOR MORE FACTS ON...

THE CHARACTERISTICS & CLASSIFICATIONS OF INSECTS see *Insects*, **CHAPTER 4, PAGES 150-3**
+
THE NATURE & VARIETY OF BIOMES WORLDWIDE see *Biomes*, **CHAPTER 5, PAGES 194-5**

SHRUBS

Shrubs are perennial woody plants that grow several or many stems, usually fairly low to the ground, and can reach up to about 20 feet tall. In some woody plant species, the outcome can be either a shrub or a tree, depending on the environment. A dominant stem or trunk may form in place of multiple stems, and the speci-

men will usually grow taller than the average shrub. Both deciduous and evergreen shrubs are common.

Ornamental shrubs include lilacs and hydrangea. Coffee and tea are economically important shrubs. Hedges, used for centuries as green borders around yards and fields, are shrubs too.

Woody vascular plants, shrubs de-

velop a system of secondary vascular tissue in addition to that found in herbaceous vascular plants. This secondary tissue includes extra xylem, the tissue that transports water and minerals absorbed by the roots, as well as extra phloem, tissue that transports the food made by photosynthesis.

Bushes and shrubs are not the same, according to horticulturists. A bush is usually a low, dense, and extremely multibranched woody plant. Woody plants that are more treelike in structure and taller than the average shrub are called arborescences.

COFFEE, SIPPED AROUND THE WORLD, begins on shrubs or small trees that grow in tropical and subtropical regions. Here a woman stretches to harvest the beans from an Indonesian coffee tree. Naturally shade loving, coffee bushes are sometimes forced into sunny plantations for increased yield.

FOR MORE FACTS ON...

FOODS THAT FEED THE WORLD see Food, **CHAPTER 6, PAGES 244-5**

AGRICULTURAL METHODS, PAST & PRESENT see Agriculture, **CHAPTER 6, PAGES 246-9**

WHAT IS POLLINATION?

The essential reproductive act in the plant world is pollination: the distribution of male reproductive cells in the form of pollen to join with female reproductive cells in the ovary, deep within a plant's flower.

Pollination often involves a partnership between a flowering plant and an animal that carries the pollen on its body. Insects are the most frequent pollinators, but birds, butterflies, reptiles, and even mammals such as bats participate.

PURPLE-THROATED MOUNTAIN-GEM —a hummingbird seen in Costa Rica's Monteverde Cloud Forest Reserve—sips nectar from orchids. At the same time, it distributes pollen.

CLICK IT: Making Your Backyard into a Wildlife Habitat www.nwf.org/backyard

DECIDUOUS OR EVERGREEN?

Deciduous shrubs and trees lose their leaves for part of the year, usually in the fall, followed by a dormant period in which biological processes rest except for limited root growth. Prior to leaf drop, many species of trees and shrubs exhibit brilliant fall color. Some examples of deciduous shrubs include viburnum, hydrangea, and forsythia.

Evergreen shrubs and trees hold their leaves or needles through the year. They do lose leaves more or less continuously, although not noticeably. In temperate climates, evergreens grow at a slower rate and photosynthesize at a slower pace during winter than summer.

Most of the conifers—pines, spruce, hemlock, and fir—are evergreen, although two conifer species—larch and bald cypress—are deciduous.

HOLLY (ABOVE) AND SMOKE BUSH are typical evergreen and deciduous shrubs: Both shed leaves, but hollies maintain full foliage all year long.

FAST FACT The coffee shrub commonly grows to a height of 30 feet.

FOR MORE FACTS ON...

WHY & HOW LEAVES CHANGE COLORS SEASONALLY see Trees, CHAPTER 4, PAGE 143
+
THE EVOLUTION OF BIRDS see Birds, CHAPTER 4, PAGES 164-5

TREES

WOODPECKER HOLES mottle the trunk of a York apple tree in Virginia.

Trees form by far the bulk of Earth's biomass. In life and in death trees contribute to the biosphere by making oxygen, moving water, storing carbon dioxide, enriching soil with dead and decaying parts, and recycling the nutrients that life on Earth depends on.

Trees are vascular plants that develop a single main woody stem known as a trunk. Generally, trees grow to 15 feet or taller. Trees differ from shrubs, which are shorter and usually have multiple stems. Trees span the three botanical groups that represent vascular plants—pteridophytes, gymnosperms, and angiosperms.

Gymnosperms and angiosperms propagate by seeds. In the former type seeds are exposed, or naked, on a structure such as a cone; on the latter, they are within the ovary of a flower. Pteridophytes, on the other hand, are seedless vascular plants such as the tree fern.

Not all parts of a tree are alive at one time, especially in mature trees. Keeping so much mass alive all the time would require more energy than a tree's system could handle. The inner core of the trunk, called the heartwood, is composed of out-of-commission xylem that no longer transports water throughout the tree. Similarly, the oldest layers of phloem, which transports the food manufactured through photosynthesis, form the outer, dead bark of the tree's surface.

In between the heartwood and bark lies the tree's sapwood, its living energy-storage tissue.

FAST FACT Over the course of its life, an average tree can absorb a ton of carbon dioxide.

FOR MORE FACTS ON...

HOW PHOTOSYNTHESIS WORKS & WHY IT'S NECESSARY *see Life Begins,* CHAPTER 4, PAGE 131

PLANTS & TREES WITH EXTRAORDINARY CHARACTERISTICS *see Plant Curiosities,* CHAPTER 4, PAGES 146-7

WHY DO LEAVES CHANGE COLOR?

As days grow shorter and temperatures cooler, deciduous trees prepare for winter dormancy. Lacking sufficient light and water, photosynthesis shuts down, and trees must live off food stored during the growing season.

In spring, leaves lay the groundwork for their demise. A special layer of cells forms at the base of each leaf, called the abscission or separation layer. Its work is to transport water to the leaf and take food, created by photosynthesis, back to the tree.

In autumn, the cells of this layer begin to swell and the bottom of this layer forms a corklike substance that eventually cuts off all transfer between leaf and tree. Meanwhile, the top of the layer begins to disintegrate, making it easy for the leaf to detach.

As photosynthesis ceases, the leaves lose their chlorophyll, which gives them their green color. With-

AUTUMNAL HUES reflect twofold in the waters of the Ellicott River in Alaska's Wrangell-St. Elias National Park. Tree leaves take on distinctive colors: yellow, orange, red, or brown.

out chlorophyll, other colors emerge. Yellow and orange, for example, are normally present in the leaves but are overshadowed by the chlorophyll. Maple-leaf red occurs because glucose remains when photosynthesis shuts down. Drab oak-leaf brown represents wastes left in the leaves.

GLOSSARY

Cambium: In plants, a layer of actively dividing cells between xylem (fluid-conducting) tissue and phloem (water-transporting) tissue.

A TREE FROM AGES PAST

The long-needled Wollemi pine is a survivor from the age of the dinosaurs. While fossil records made the 200-million-year-old species known to us, it was believed to be extinct. Then, in 1994, an Australian parks officer found a single tree in the Blue Mountains in Wollemi National Park. Subsequently, a hundred adult trees were counted there. Conservation efforts funded in part from the sale of saplings go to save and strengthen the species.

FOSSIL REPLICA of a Wollemi pine recalls the 200-million-year history of this Australian tree. About 100 survive in the wild—the world's oldest existing species of tree.

FAST FACT Only about one in a million acorns makes it all the way to becoming a mature oak tree.

FOR MORE FACTS ON...

EARTH IN PREHISTORIC TIMES see Ages of the Earth, **CHAPTER 3, PAGES 94-5, & Life Begins, CHAPTER 4, PAGES 130-1**

THE DIFFERENCE BETWEEN DECIDUOUS & EVERGREEN PLANTS see Plants: Shrubs, **CHAPTER 4, PAGE 141**

MEDICINAL

Nature provides a bountiful pharmacopoeia through its plant life. Plants were humankind's original medicines, and even with the birth of modern medicine, plants remain an important source of medicinal help.

In all traditional cultures, certain members accrue specialized knowledge of medicinal plants and their applications. These are the healers, midwives, shamans, and other individuals who dispense cures and remedies through their understanding of healing plants and their applications. Women in their roles as mothers and grandmothers also command this knowledge, sometimes in the form of "old wives'" remedies that, more often than not, have a firm basis in herbal medicine.

Today countless people still use medicinal plants, whether in traditional ways, in alternative and complementary medicine, or as building blocks for new research and innovative drugs. Pharmaceutical companies and government research programs routinely screen plants, focusing especially on species with potential anticancer and anti-HIV benefits. And today's burgeoning use of dietary supplements carries on a tradition that is millennia old.

As to the importance of medicinal plants, the statistics are telling. A full 50 percent of prescription drugs are based on molecules found naturally in plants. Some 25 percent of prescription drugs are derived directly from plants or modeled on plant molecules. These percentages have held steady for nearly 60 years, a testament to plants' enduring medicinal powers.

A NATIVE AMERICAN HERBALIST in Winslow, Arizona, gathers the wild plants from which he will derive teas, salves, and smudges to use as medicinal and spiritual treatments. Many herbal remedies harvested and prepared by indigenous peoples have inspired modern medicine.

FAST FACT The aroma of lavender has been shown to enhance sleep.

FOR MORE FACTS ON...

THE TRADITIONS OF KIN & FAMILY AROUND THE WORLD see The Human Family, CHAPTER 6, PAGES 222-3

EMERGING DEVELOPMENTS IN MODERN MEDICINE see Medical Science, CHAPTER 8, PAGES 338-45

THE VALUE OF CHOCOLATE

For the ancient cultures of the Americas, chocolate, or cacao, was a sacred plant. Its use began with the Olmecs around 1200 B.C. and continued with the Maya and Aztec. The Aztec restricted drinks made from cacao seed to ceremonial use and consumption by high-ranking adult males—priests, government officials, and warriors.

Mesoamericans recognized the general properties of cacao (later called cocoa) and used it to treat intestinal complaints, to calm the nerves, and as a stimulant. Mixed with maize and other herbs, cacao treated fever, shortness of breath, and heart palpitations. Cacao flowers were ingested to treat fatigue; cocoa butter, the creamy fat in the beans, soothed burns, irritated skin, and chapped lips. European explorers brought cocoa and chocolate to Western cultures, where it became very popular as a delicacy and as a medicinal plant. Its assigned scientific genus name, *Theobroma,* means "food of the gods."

Today studies show that cacao seeds contain more than 300 different chemical compounds. These include the stimulant caffeine as well as theobromine, an alkaloid that has a calming effect on the brain and an energizing effect on the nervous system. Cacao also contains compounds that tend to reduce depression and may induce a slight sense of euphoria, as well as powerful antioxidant compounds that may help protect against cancer and heart disease. Some medical professionals even recommend a daily "dose" of about an ounce and a half of dark chocolate for its cardiovascular benefits.

CACAO BEANS ripen inside pods dangling off abundant trees in the Ivory Coast, the world's largest producer of cocoa.

CLICK IT: Green Medicine nps.gov/plants/medicinal/plants.htm

G L O S S A R Y

Antioxidant: Chemical compound that protects cells against damage by molecules called oxygen-free radicals, major causes of disease and aging.

WHAT PLANTS TREAT MODERN AILMENTS?

THIS MEDICINE	FROM THIS PLANT	IS USED TO TREAT
Theophylline	Cacao	Asthma
Ephedrine	Ephedra	Respiratory congestion
Vinblastine, vincristine	Madagascar periwinkle	Tumors, leukemia
Taxol	Pacific yew	Tumors
Morphine, codeine	Poppy	Pain
Digoxin	Foxglove	Heart disease
Quinine	Quinine tree	Malaria
Thymol	Thyme	Skin fungus
L-dopa	Velvet bean	Parkinson's disease
Aspirin	White willow	Pain, other ailments

FOXGLOVE, OR DIGITALIS, which grows wild in North America and Europe, provides one of the many plant-derived compounds used in Western pharmacology.

Some 70 percent of plants found to have anticancer properties grow only in rain forests, yet fewer than 5 percent of tropical species have been screened for their medicinal properties.

FOR MORE FACTS ON...

FOOD PLANTS AROUND THE WORLD see *Food,* **CHAPTER 6, PAGES 244-5**

PLANTS & ANIMALS IN THE TROPICAL RAIN FOREST BIOME see *Rain Forests,* **CHAPTER 5, PAGES 198-9**

Baobab trees, Madagascar

PLANT CURIOSITIES

EXTREMES

LARGEST FLOWER
3 feet wide, weighing up to 24 pounds
Rafflesia arnoldii
Found in Sumatra & Borneo

SMALLEST FLOWER
0.04 to 0.1 inch across
Lemnaceae, Duckweeds
Floating aquatic plants, found worldwide

TALLEST TREE
378.1 feet tall
Sequoia sempervirens, California redwood
Found in Redwood National Park, 2006

OLDEST LIVING TREE
Root system 9,550 years old
Picea abes, Norway spruce
Found in Sweden, 2004

Some plant species have evolved unusual appearances or surprising methods of obtaining nutrients, achieving reproduction, or adapting to their environments. These plants have evolved in ways that make them stand out from their counterparts—making them curiosities in human eyes—and attest to the fine-tuned intricacy of adaptation for survival.

Plants may take on unexpected and very unplantlike shapes or coloration to blend in with their environments, often to avoid consumption by animals. Where nutrition is not easily available, some plants act as parasites, freeloading off other plants, or tap unusual sources of nutrients, such as insects.

Certain flowering plants have developed extreme propagation techniques. Flowers may waft out scents of rotting flesh, as the arum does, attracting flies that will accomplish its pollination. Thermogenic plants, a curious type of plant found mainly in the tropics, create a heated interior environment that disseminates scent to attract pollinating insects such as beetles.

FAST FACT The baobab tree of Africa can store 25,000 gallons of water in its trunk and lower branches.

FOR MORE FACTS ON...

THE ROLE OF FLOWERS IN PLANT REPRODUCTION see *Plants: Flowering,* **CHAPTER 4, PAGE 139**

ANIMALS WITH UNUSUAL & EXTREME CHARACTERISTICS see *Animal Curiosities,* **CHAPTER 4, PAGES 170-1**

PLANTS THAT PREY ON ANIMALS

Some plants that live in areas poor in nutrients or sunshine get energy in other ways. Carnivorous plants live, at least part of the time, off the nutrition they ingest from the insects they lure and devour. These carnivores are more specifically insectivores, and they often live in bogs and swamps.

One of more than 400 known insectivorous plants, the Venus flytrap is common to swamps in North and South Carolina. The plant's hinged leaves form traps that snap shut on insects alighting there. Trigger hairs on the inside of the leaves sense the presence of the insect. The insect must touch the hairs more than once for the trap to close—that way, the plant doesn't react to a single touch,

which might be from an inanimate object such as a windblown leaf. Once the flytrap has captured the prey, fluids inside the leaf dissolve the insect into a nourishing liquid that the plant absorbs. It takes about ten days for the flytrap to reopen after a meal.

Other insectivores include pitcher plants and sundews. The pitcher plant traps and drowns insects in a cuplike cavity of liquid and then dissolves them. The stalks of sundews are covered with supersticky, glistening drops of liquid that attract insects. The sticky surface traps the insect, and then the plant's leaves bend around it to start the digestion process.

A FLY TRAPPED inside sticky leaves will supplement the nutrients that this carnivorous Venus flytrap generates by photosynthesis.

CLICK IT: Carnivorous Plant Society www.carnivorousplants.org

FAST FACT One ragweed plant can produce one billion pollen grains; a grain can travel one hundred miles by wind.

PLANTS THAT PREY ON PLANTS

THE AUSTRALIAN CHRISTMAS TREE, a mistletoe, grows haustoria—or root parts—that draw nutrients from host plants. Like other parasitic plants, it does not photosynthesize.

Parasitic plants commandeer the resources of other plants. Some tap into the root systems of other plants; some attach directly into trunks or branches. Many do not even photosynthesize, relying on the host plant for all their nutrition. Dodder, an aggressive parasitic vine, has no leaves or chlorophyll.

Other plants, known as hemiparasites, do photosynthesize but still take nutrients from host plants. Members of the mistletoe family belong to this category. Mistletoe's sticky seeds attach to a tree or other host plant and

send out a root, which taps into the tree's sap for nutrients.

Some parasitic plants don't distinguish, at least initially, between potential plant and non-animate hosts. The Western Australian Christmas tree, a type of freestanding mistletoe, has become the bane of cable installers. Its roots can reach a hundred yards out, tapping into surrounding tree roots for moisture. Along the way, they tap into communication cables, causing frequent, costly disruptions. Only extremely thick—and expensive—cables seem to thwart the plant.

FOR MORE FACTS ON...

THE VARIETY OF EARTH'S INSECTS see Insects, **CHAPTER 4, PAGES 150-2**

DIVERSITY AMONG EARTH'S LIVING CREATURES see Biodiversity, **CHAPTER 4, PAGES 174-7**

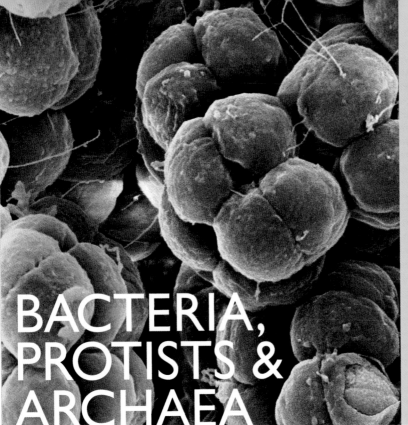

Halobacteriales, a type of salt-loving bacteria

TYPES OF BACTERIA

SPHERICAL / COCCUS
Examples:
Streptococcus (includes species that cause scarlet and rheumatic fever)
Staphylococcus (includes species that cause food poisoning)

ROD-SHAPED / BACILLUS
Examples:
Bacillus subtilis (used to make bacitracin, an antibiotic)
Bacillus anthracis (causes anthrax)

CURVED / VIBRIO, SPIRILLUM, SPIROCHETE
Examples:
Vibrio cholerae (causes cholera)
Borrelia burgdorferi (causes Lyme disease)

BACTERIA, PROTISTS & ARCHAEA

acteria, protists, and archaea belong to the world of microbes—mostly unicellular organisms. Bacteria are prokaryotes, organisms with DNA that is not enclosed within a nucleus, whereas protists are eukaryotes, organisms with a bounded nucleus. Archaea, an ancient life-form recognized only in the late 1970s, are prokaryotes but are different from bacteria. They are the extremists in the bunch, able to survive in the most challenging environmental conditions.

Despite their small size and single-cell structure, bacteria exhibit an amazing range and complexity of characteristics and behaviors. Along with archaea, they were the earliest forms of life on the planet. Cyanobacteria, also known as blue-green algae,

date back some three billion years and contributed to the formation of Earth's atmosphere by developing photosynthesis.

Protists are a diverse group that includes protozoans, algae, and lower fungi. They share characteristics with

both animals and plants. Protozoans are prevalent in soils and aquatic habitats worldwide, and most maintain symbiotic and even parasitic relationships with other organisms. Algae dominate many aquatic habitats and range dramatically in size—from organisms only millimeters long to strands of sea kelp up to 200 feet long.

Archaea resemble bacteria under a microscope but are biochemically and genetically different. These are the organisms that live in thermal vents in the deep ocean and even in petroleum deposits underground. But they also thrive in more normal conditions, including with the plankton of the open sea.

FAST FACT There are approximately ten times as many bacteria as human cells in the human body.

FOR MORE FACTS ON...

THE DISCOVERY OF PENICILLIN & ITS ROLE IN FIGHTING BACTERIAL INFECTION see *Fungi & Lichens,* **CHAPTER 4, PAGE 135**

EARTH'S OCEANS AS HABITATS see *Aquatic Biomes,* **CHAPTER 5, PAGES 212-3**

WHAT IS A VIRUS?

A virus is a microscopic infectious agent that enters animal, plant, or bacteria hosts. A single virus particle, called a viron, is little more than a bundle of genetic material—DNA or RNA—that does not take the form of a cell. Instead it is encased in a shell called a viral coat, or capsid, made of bits of protein. Some viruses have an additional enclosure around the capsid called an envelope.

Viruses cannot function without their hosts. They cannot synthesize proteins without essential ingredients from their host cells, and they can neither generate nor store energy on their own. In fact, viruses depend on host cells for all their metabolic functions.

Some scientists decline to count viruses among living organisms, since they cannot survive on their own and cannot reproduce outside of a host cell. Not usually counted among plants, animals, or prokaryotic bacteria, viruses are instead classified in a group of their own.

What viruses can do, however, is infect, or cause disease. Fortunately, the immune systems of most animal species can fend off infection from

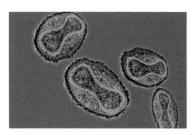

SMALLPOX IS CAUSED when variola virus particles (above) enter the cells of a host. Extinct since 1977, smallpox is maintained in cultures by the U.S. and Russia for research.

many kinds of viruses. Antibiotics cannot cure viral illnesses, but vaccines can prevent them, and many widespread life-threatening viral outbreaks, such as smallpox, have been controlled or eliminated with vaccines.

CLICK IT: Microbe World www.microbeworld.org

GLOSSARY

Microbe: Microorganism; one of a diverse group of minute, simple life-forms that include bacteria, archaea, algae, fungi, protozoans, and viruses. **/ Cytoplasm:** Portion of a eukaryotic cell outside the nucleus. **/ Fermentation:** Process that allows respiration to occur in the absence of oxygen. Biologically, it allows cells to obtain energy from molecules (e.g., glucose) anaerobically.

LOUIS PASTEUR / PIONEER MICROBIOLOGIST

Louis Pasteur (1822–1895) earned four university degrees by the time he was 25. As dean of a new science program at the University of Lille, France, he created evening classes for factory workers and included industrial applications of science. He also started his own experiments on fermentation in alcohol and milk. Moving in 1867 into a laboratory of physiological chemistry set up for him by Emperor Napoleon III, Pasteur began to tackle the question of spontaneous generation: Did organisms grow spontaneously from certain substances, such as maggots from dead flesh or weevils from wheat? Knowing fermentation was hastened by exposure to air, Pasteur proved that microbes in the air caused putrefaction. He invented the process named after him, pasteurization, which destroys harmful microbes so food can be stored.

66 I am persuaded that life, as it is known to us, is a direct result of the 99 asymmetry of the universe. — **LOUIS PASTEUR, 1874**

FAST FACT The amoeba moves by its pseudopod, or false foot, the most primitive form of animal locomotion.

FOR MORE FACTS ON...

CHALLENGE OF PROVIDING SAFE FOOD FOR WORLD see Food, **CHAPTER 6, PAGES 244-5,** & Agriculture: Modern, **CHAPTER 6, PAGES 248-9**

ATTENTION TO VIRUSES IN MEDICAL SCIENCE see Medical Science, **CHAPTER 8, PAGES 338-9**

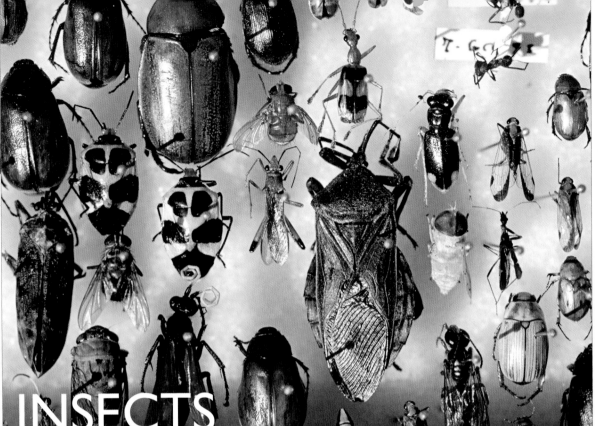

Insect collection, Hitoy-Cerere Biological Reserve, Costa Rica

INSECTS

INSECT ORDERS

ODONATA / Dragonflies

DICTYOPTERA / Cockroaches & mantids

ORTHOPTERA / Grasshoppers & crickets

ISOPTERA / Termites

HEMIPTERA / True bugs

COLEOPTERA / Beetles

SIPHONAPTERA / Fleas

DIPTERA / Flies

LEPIDOPTERA / Butterflies & moths

HYMENOPTERA / Ants, bees & wasps

rthropods, the phylum of animals that includes insects, spiders, and crustaceans, represent 84 percent of all animal life on the planet. More than one million species of creeping, crawling, and flying creatures are included in the order, and they inhabit every continent and biome throughout the world—in and on the ground, in the water, and in the sky. And scientists are identifying new species all the time.

All arthropods, including insects, are invertebrates—they have no backbones. Insects have exoskeletons (outside skeletons) made of chitin, a light, flexible material containing protein. An insect has a three-part body—head, thorax, and abdomen—and six legs. Many insects also have antennae and wings. Most insects hatch from eggs and undergo some form of metamorphosis, or life cycle transformation. Often metamorphosis involves molting, the shedding of a too-small exoskeleton as the insect grows.

FAST FACT A square mile of field may be home to almost six billion insects.

FOR MORE FACTS ON...

CLASSIFICATION OF LIVING THINGS see *Life-forms*, **CHAPTER 4, PAGES 132-3**

THE CHARACTERISTICS & LIFE CYCLES OF BUTTERFLIES & MOTHS see *Insects: Butterflies & Moths*, **CHAPTER 4, PAGES 152-3**

Beetles form the most numerous insect group, with about 350,000 known species. Hard-bodied with firm front wings that protect their bodies and rear wings, beetles typically morph from egg to larva to pupa before attaining the adult stage.

People often use the words "bug" and "insect" interchangeably, but in fact, bugs are a particular kind of insect and make up only about 10 percent of all insects. They usually have front wings that are thick and hard near the body, thin and clear at the tip. Their rear wings are thin and clear, and their wings fold over their backs in a characteristic X shape.

Spiders are not insects but arthropods, as are centipedes, millipedes, ticks, and mites. Worms form a different group altogether—the annelids.

G L O S S A R Y

Larva: From Latin *laurua,* "ghost" or "specter." Early active, feeding stage in the development of some animals, occurring after birth or hatching and before the adult form is reached. **/ Metamorphosis:** Change in structure by an animal that has more than one body form during its lifetime. **/ Pupa:** From Latin *pupa,* "girl," "doll," or "puppet." The resting stage of an insect as it transforms from larva to adult.

WHERE ARE ALL THE BEES?

In October 2006, U.S. beekeepers began noticing that they were losing some 30 to 90 percent of the populations of their hives. The phenomenon has become known as colony collapse disorder. An affected hive will still have a live queen and often some honey and some immature bees, but no adult worker bees are to be found, dead or alive.

Possible causes include pesticides, the appearance of a new parasite or pathogen, or a combination of stress factors: hive overcrowding or poor nutrition. Researchers have also found that pollution can reduce the range of a flower's scent by 75 percent—another possible factor in colony collapse.

The loss of honeybee hives could severely affect U.S. agriculture, especially the production of nuts and other orchard crops, where bees are used to promote pollination, which guarantees an abundant crop. In areas affected by colony collapse disorder,

HONEYBEES are social insects, living in colonies that number in the tens of thousands of individuals.

growers are trucking in hives of unaffected bees from long distances to accomplish pollination.

FAST FACT The trap-jaw ant snaps shut its mandibles 2,000 times faster than the blink of an eye.

HOW OLD ARE COCKROACHES?

Most insects descend from long, hardy lineages. One of the most durable is the cockroach, which has changed very little in more than 300 million years. Fossils from the Paleozoic era (left) include cockroaches virtually identical in shape and size to today's pests. One coal mine in eastern Ohio contained fossil specimens not only of cockroaches with three-inch wings but also of centipedes, millipedes, and spiders.

CLICK IT: Insect Appreciation www.insects.org

FOR MORE FACTS ON...

SPIDERS see *Spiders & Their Kin,* **CHAPTER 4, PAGES 154-5**

PREHISTORIC LIFE ON EARTH see *Ages of the Earth,* **CHAPTER 3, PAGES 94-5,** & *Life Begins,* **CHAPTER 4, PAGES 130-1**

BUTTERFLIES & MOTHS

Butterflies and moths belong to the order Lepidoptera, which means "scale wings." Butterflies and moths fly with two pairs of wings covered with tiny, overlapping, powdery scales that often rub off.

Almost all butterflies and moths have a long, tubular mouthpart called a proboscis, which they use to feed on plant nectar. They spend their larval stage as caterpillars, voraciously consuming plant matter, then undergo metamorphosis into the adult forms.

There are several ways to tell a butterfly from a moth. On the whole, butterflies are brightly colored whereas moths are more drab. Butterflies flutter about in the day, but moths tend to be nocturnal. Butterflies have knobs on the ends of their threadlike antennae; moth antennae are wider and often feathery. At rest, butterflies keep their wings closed, while moths usually hold theirs out flat. Also, moth bodies are usually plumper than those of the butterfly. In the pupal stage, a butterfly makes a smooth, shiny chrysalis, while a moth makes a woolly cocoon.

The feeding habits of moths can prove destructive to the natural and human-constructed world. The larvae of the European pine shoot moth have devastated large swaths of pine forests there by eating the tree's tender shoots. Carpet moth larvae munch on fabric made from plants and animals, such as cotton and wool, making holes in clothing and carpets.

Studies of moth mating behavior have shown the role of pheromones, chemical attractants involved in enticing the opposite sex across a large number of animal species. Even the male silk moth, a domesticated species used in silk production that has only stumpy, flightless wings, demonstrates the allure of these potent chemicals.

In one famous experiment, a male is alerted of a female's presence by the airflow of an ordinary household fan. As soon as the scent reaches the male's antennae, he beats his stubby wings and runs—since flying is not an option—toward the female to mate with her. A pheromone-laced piece of paper can produce the same effect.

MONARCH BUTTERFLIES commune at a watering hole in central Mexico, preparing for their long annual migratory flight north.

FAST FACT The atlas moth, found in Asia's tropical regions, has a wingspan of 8 to 12 inches.

FOR MORE FACTS ON...

INTERESTING ANIMAL MATING BEHAVIOR see Animal Curiosities, **CHAPTER 4, PAGES 170-1**
+
THE VARIETY AND HISTORY OF TEXTILES IN HUMAN CULTURE see Clothing, **CHAPTER 6, PAGES 242-3**

THE YUCCA CONNECTION

Of the many plant-animal connections in the natural world, that of the yucca plant and the yucca moth is one of the most specialized. These species have evolved a relationship in which one depends on the other for survival: Only the yucca moth can pollinate the plant, whose seeds provide the moth's only food source.

In this symbiosis, the moth lays its eggs at the base of the yucca flowers. When the caterpillars hatch, they feed on some of the seeds. Those remaining seeds grow into the next generation of yucca plants. Meanwhile, the caterpillars drop off the plant and pupate in the cocoon stage in soil, transforming into the next generation of yucca moth. The moths that emerge begin the process all over again.

A FEMALE YUCCA MOTH seeks nectar on the tip of a stamen inside a fragrant yucca flower, one step in the complex symbiosis between plant and insect.

CLICK IT: Butterflies & Moths of North America www.butterfliesandmoths.org

FAST FACT Butterfly wings often exhibit eyespots—bold circles that may startle enemies.

FROM CATERPILLAR TO BUTTERFLY

Moths and butterflies undergo a maturational transformation so remarkable it has become the stuff of myth and poetry around the world.

A butterfly begins as an egg. Soon the larva—a caterpillar—bites through the egg and exits. It consumes its former shell and goes on to feed on leaves and shed its skin several times. Then it attaches itself to a twig or other object and enters the pupal stage when it forms a chrysalis. Inside, the caterpillar's body re-forms as a butterfly. When the transformation is complete, the adult butterfly crawls out of the chrysalis and flexes its wings to pump blood into them. With wings firm and dry, it flies away.

THE TIGER SWALLOWTAIL, like all moths and butterflies, assumes three forms after it hatches from an egg: larva (or caterpillar), chrysalis, and mature insect. The entire process takes about one month. Moths undergo a similar metamorphosis.

G L O S S A R Y

Chrysalis: From the Greek for "golden sheath." The pupal stage when a caterpillar is transforming into an adult butterfly. **/ Cocoon:** Protective covering made by a moth caterpillar from its own silk in which it rests and transforms into an adult moth.

FOR MORE FACTS ON...

THE DIVERSITY OF LIFE-FORMS ON EARTH see Biodiversity, **CHAPTER 4, PAGES 174-7**

+

THE HUMAN TRADITION OF TELLING MYTHS AND LEGENDS see Language, **CHAPTER 6, PAGES 228-9**

Black-and-yellow argiope spider with katydid trapped in its web

SPIDERS & THEIR KIN

ARACHNIDS

ACARI / Mites & ticks

AMBLYPYGI / Whipscorpions

ARANEAE / Spiders

OPILIONES / Daddy longlegs

PALPIGRADI / Micro-whipscorpions

PSEUDOSCORPIONES / False scorpions

SCORPIONES / Scorpions

SOLIFUGAE / Wind scorpions, camel spiders, sun spiders

UROPYGI / Whip-tailed scorpions, vinegaroons

Within the arthropods, spiders occupy a taxonomic class called the arachnids, a group comprising a diverse array of other creatures including mites, ticks, and scorpions. The horseshoe crab is closely related as well. Arachnids have a two-part body and eight legs. Spiders in particular have silk glands and use the contents to spin webs and to encase their eggs or prey.

Most spiders produce venom and inject it into their prey through one pair of mouthparts, the chelicerae, which act like fangs. The other pair of mouthparts, called pedipalps or pincers, are used to sense prey.

Tenacious predators, spiders and other arachnids are unable to ingest prey whole and must liquefy it by squirting it with digestive juices before sucking up the mushy contents.

The pedipalps in scorpions have developed into claws. Scorpions also have stingers at the end of their tails and use them to inject highly toxic venom into their prey. Scorpions occupy crevices and burrows during the day and come out at night to hunt.

FOR MORE FACTS ON...

THE DIVERSITY OF PLANT & ANIMAL SPECIES see Biodiversity, **CHAPTER 4, PAGES 174-7**

THE CONCEPT OF NATURAL HABITAT OR BIOME see Biomes, **CHAPTER 5, PAGES 194-5**

Mites and ticks occur in almost every habitat. Many of these abundant species are parasites, feeding on the fluids of other animals. Crustaceans belong to a subphylum of arthropods and represent some 39,000 species that display a wide variety of features. Lobsters, crabs, and shrimp are the most well known of the group.

Some crustaceans live on land, but most live in salt or fresh water. Their heads usually sport two pairs of antennae, stalked eyes, and three pairs of biting mouthparts.

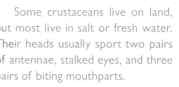

FAST FACT South America's tarantula, up to 12 inches across, eats insects, frogs, bats, rodents, and even baby birds.

VARIETIES OF SPIDERWEBS

Spiders create webs by extruding silk from glands. Some spiders have as many as seven specialized glands, each of which manufactures a different protein-rich silk strand specialized for a dragline, a web frame, an egg case, and other purposes. Spiders can be classified according to the type of web they weave.

ORB WEBS are circular in pattern.

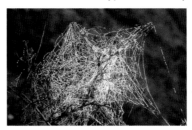

SHEET WEBS spread out in flat planes.

FUNNEL WEBS include a hole for hiding.

FAST FACT Of the world's some 40,000 spider species, only about 30 have venom that causes illness in humans.

HORSESHOE CRABS: LIVING FOSSILS

A close relative of the spider—and not a crab at all—the horseshoe crab bears a long lineage. Vestiges of similar animals date back 200 million years. Horseshoe crabs have hinged bodies, a horseshoe-shaped head, and a long tail-spine. They can grow up to two feet long. They live on the east coasts of Asia and North America.

Horseshoe crabs feed on true crabs, mollusks, worms, and other prey. They swim along the ocean floor and can also travel along the mud by pulling up their body and pushing with the spine and rear legs.

Spring tides bring horseshoe crabs onto the land by the thousands. Females scoop out depressions in the sand and fill them with hundreds of eggs. Males follow and cover the eggs with sperm. Within two weeks tiny hatchlings, about an eighth of an inch long, wash out to sea with the tide to complete their life cycle.

MALE HORSESHOE CRABS converge on a single female during early June, breeding season on the New Jersey shoreline.

FOR MORE FACTS ON...

EARTH'S OCEANS & THEIR TIDES see *Water: Oceans,* **CHAPTER 3, PAGES 114-5**

THE EVOLUTION OF PREHISTORIC LIFE-FORMS in *Life Begins,* **CHAPTER 4, PAGES 130-1**

Tawny fringed sea slug, Oregon

LONGEST

GIANT SQUID
Architeuthis species
660 inches (estimated)

GIANT CLAM
Tridacna gigas
51 inches

AUSTRALIAN TRUMPET SNAIL
Syrinx aruanus
30 inches

SEA SLUG
Hexabranchus sanguineus
20 inches

HETEROPOD
Carinaria cristata
19 inches

STELLER'S COAT OF MAIL SHELL
Cryptochiton stelleri
18 inches

MOLLUSKS

he beautiful seashells collected by people the world over are actually protective coverings for a vast array of invertebrates known as mollusks. A mollusk is an animal covered in a thin layer of tissue called a mantle, which produces a calcium carbonate shell. Mollusks occur in varied habitats, sea and land, from ocean bottom to mountaintop.

Typical shelled mollusks divide into four categories: bivalves, chitons, gastropods, and tusk shells.

Bivalves, such as oysters, clams, and mussels, have a two-part hinged shell. Most burrow into sediment and some attach to a firm surface.

Chitons are oval in shape and have an interlocking eight-part upper shell. Most of a chiton's body is a single, flat foot that it uses to pull itself along and to cling to surfaces.

Gastropods (which means "stomach feet"), the largest mollusk group, include snails, slugs, and limpets. Most have a spiral shell, but some, such as slugs, have no exterior shell.

Tusk shells have a long, tubelike shell that is open at both ends. The larger end contains the foot, head, and tentacles; the smaller end admits water to breathe and removes waste.

Octopuses, squid, cuttlefish, and nautiluses, also mollusks, are called cephalopods (literally, head feet). Their feet are located close to their heads in a modification of tentacles. Among these animals, only the nautilus has a full shell. The squid and cuttlefish have a shell remnant inside the body. The octopus has no shell at all.

Cephalopods are predators that also scavenge. They draw food into their mouths and crush it with their sharp, parrotlike beaks. Cephalopods travel by means of jet propulsion. They squirt water from their bodies to move forward and back. The octopus deftly manipulates its eight suctioned tentacles to travel.

FOR MORE FACTS ON...

THE OCEANS OF PLANET EARTH see *Oceans*, **CHAPTER 3, PAGES 112-5**

PLANTS & ANIMALS IN UNDERWATER LIVING ENVIRONMENTS see *Aquatic Biomes*, **CHAPTER 5, PAGES 212-3**

HOW SMART ARE CEPHALOPODS?

Three cephalopods—octopus, squid, and cuttlefish—have shown apparently deliberate, cunning, and even subversive behavior, causing even the most skeptical researchers to take notice. All three have demonstrated puzzle-solving abilities, a capacity for boredom that can be relieved by making up games, and the ability to deceive prey, fellow members of their species, and even their keepers in order to get what they want.

For instance, octopuses in aquariums have been known to dismantle the pumps in their tanks and to use amazing escape techniques to sneak out at night, visit other tanks and gorge on fish, and then be back in place by daybreak, having left behind a telltale watery smear on floor and walls.

SQUID LOCOMOTION occurs thanks to a mantle, a flap of tissue surrounding its head. In slow motion, the mantle helps the squid stabilize and turn. For quick moves, the squid effects a watery sort of jet propulsion, sucking in water, locking the mantle shut, and then spewing the water out in a focused stream. Squid can swim backward or forward.

CLICK IT: Mollusks www.ummz.umich.edu/mollusks

NAUTILUS: NATURE'S PERFECT GEOMETRY

Related to the squid, the octopus, and the cuttlefish, the nautilus is the only cephalopod with an exterior shell. The shell starts out with only a few chambers. The animal itself resides in the innermost chamber. As the animal grows, new chambers are added, always following the same proportion. The resulting spiral of the nautilus shell closely approximates the golden mean, a ratio of 1:1.618.

NAUTILUS POPULATIONS concentrate in the tropical West Pacific. They are now endangered, primarily because their shells are prized by collectors and curio purchasers.

FAST FACT Giant clams embed themselves in the seafloor and never move; they can weigh up to 700 pounds.

FOR MORE FACTS ON...

HUMAN METHODS OF LOCOMOTION see Transportation, **CHAPTER 6, PAGES 252-3**

THE IMPORTANCE OF PROPORTIONS IN MATHEMATICAL THINKING in Counting & Measurement, **CHAPTER 8, PAGES 322-3**

Fairy basslet, Papua New Guinea

FISH

ENDANGERED FOOD FISH

ATLANTIC BLUEFIN TUNA

CHILEAN SEA BASS

GROUPER

ORANGE ROUGHY

ATLANTIC COD

ATLANTIC HALIBUT

SNAPPER

SHARK

ish account for more than half of all the vertebrate species known in the world, with more than 24,000 species identified so far. They are found in almost every watery habitat—salt, fresh, or brackish— from large puddles to polar seas. They range in size from gobies, less than an inch long, to whale sharks, 59 feet long. Fish come in all colors and in thousands of patterns, but some are colored drably to blend in with their surroundings.

Fish fall into three main groups: jaw-less, cartilaginous, and bony. The category of jawless fish includes hag-fish and lampreys; the category of cartilaginous fish includes sharks and rays; and the category of bony fish, to which the largest number of fish belong, includes both the lobe-finned and the ray-finned fish species.

Most fish have scales that protect their bodies. Nearly all fish have fins, used for swimming. Flying fish can launch themselves into the air for brief periods, and some fish, such as walking catfish, use their fins to drag themselves along on land.

Most fish reproduce by means of eggs laid by the female and fertilized

FOR MORE FACTS ON...

WATER & OCEANS ON PLANET EARTH see Water, **CHAPTER 3, PAGES 110-9**

UNDERWATER LIVING ENVIRONMENTS see Aquatic Biomes, **CHAPTER 5, PAGES 212-3**

by the male, outside the female's body. Many sharks, however, reproduce by internal fertilization and live birth from the mother's body.

Many fish eat algae or insect larvae and other small animals, but some, such as sharks, are tireless predators that hunt even large sea mammals.

Fish frequently travel in large groups called schools or shoals. Using low-frequency sonar, researchers detected a shoal of some 20 million fish.

HOW DO FISH BREATHE?

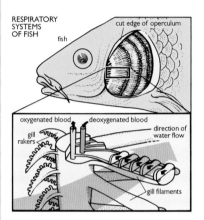

RESPIRATORY SYSTEMS OF FISH

fish
cut edge of operculum

oxygenated blood   deoxygenated blood
gill rakers
direction of water flow
gill filaments

Most fish breathe with gills, arched structures on either side of the body that contain features known as filaments and lamellae. Water, which contains oxygen, flows in through the fish's open mouth and then out across the gills. Rakers filter out particles as the water flows through.

Blood coursing through the filaments and lamellae delivers oxygen into the bloodstream. The filaments and lamellae also dump carbon dioxide from the body into the gills, and water carries it out of the body. Many species, including sharks and bony fish, have a pumping mechanism that aids respiration.

A fish out of water suffocates because its gill structures collapse and the oxygen exchange cannot continue.

CLICK IT: All About Fish nationalgeographic.com/animals/fish

THE LIFE STORY OF A SALMON

Every sockeye salmon undertakes a life journey with distinctive changes in form and location. One of the smaller species of Pacific salmon, the sockeye is also called the red or blueback salmon. "Sockeye" is an early mispronunciation of a Native American name.

The adult female lays her eggs in river gravel. When the eggs hatch, the nourishing yolk sac remains attached to the young fish. Within a few days, the fish consume the attached yolk sac and become free-swimming fry.

Juvenile sockeyes will stay in their natal habitat for up to three years,

more than any other salmon. Then, called smolt, they make a transition to salt water. They stay in the ocean for one to four years.

Finally they return upriver to breed. Seagoing sockeyes have silver flanks with black speckles and a bluish top, but as they return to their spawning grounds, their bodies turn bright red and their heads take on a greenish color. Breeding-age males have a distinctive look, developing a humped back and hooked jaws filled with tiny, easily visible teeth. Males and females both die a few weeks after spawning.

SOCKEYE SALMON, third most abundant of seven Pacific salmon species, may swim 600 miles upriver to reach their spawning grounds.

FAST FACT Some kinds of fish change sex multiple times to increase chances of reproductive success.

FOR MORE FACTS ON...

THREATS TO EARTH'S WATERY ENVIRONMENTS see *Threatened Planet: Water,* **CHAPTER 3, PAGES 126-7**

THE FUTURE OF FISH & FISH FARMING see *Agriculture: Modern,* **CHAPTER 6, PAGE 249**

Day-old Nile crocodile, Luango National Park, Gabon

MAJOR SNAKE FAMILIES

COLUBRIADAE

1,700 species / 1-10 feet long; many species lay eggs / Includes garter snakes, corn snakes, black snakes, rat snakes

BOIDAE

45 species / 3-25 feet long; bear living young / Includes pythons, boas, and anacondas

ELAPIDAE

315 species / 2-20 feet long; venom-conducting fang; may bear live young or lay eggs / Includes cobras, mambas, coral snakes, taipans

VIPERIDAE

260 species / 1-12 feet long; eye with vertical pupil; movable jaw bones; venom-injecting fang that folds against roof of mouth / Includes rattlesnakes, vipers, adders, copperheads, water moccasins

REPTILES

eptiles form an ancient line of vertebrates that have lived on Earth for more than 300 million years. They include four main groups: crocodilians, snakes, lizards, and turtles. Cold-blooded animals, reptiles most commonly inhabit the world's temperate and tropical regions, in salt and fresh water, on and under the ground, and in trees. A few species live in the Arctic and survive by sunning themselves for warmth. Reptiles in very hot climates often remain in the shade or underground during the day.

Like mammals and birds, reptiles engage in internal fertilization. In most species, the female lays eggs after fertilization, but some snakes give birth to live young. Although female crocodiles are caring mothers, few reptiles raise their young or even feed them; most are long gone by the time the eggs hatch.

Turtles are renowned for their longevity. The American box turtle is known to live up to 30 years, and some giant tortoises are reported to have lived for a century or more in captivity. Many sea turtles take between 20 and 40 years to reach sexual maturity.

Generally, reptiles do not need to eat as often as birds and mammals. They may go for days, even weeks, without food. Flexible jaws enable snakes to ingest prey that is much wider around than they are.

All snakes are carnivores, and some are aggressive predators with venomous bites. Venom potency varies. In some snake species the venom merely stuns prey; in others it kills quickly. A few lizard species, such as the Gila monster, also have a venomous bite.

A rare, fifth type of reptile, the tuatara, is the last of a large group of beak-headed reptiles that lived before the dinosaurs.

FOR MORE FACTS ON...

EQUATORIAL & TROPICAL REGIONS OF THE WORLD see Dividing Lines: Equator & Tropics, **CHAPTER 1, PAGES 36-7**

PLANTS & ANIMALS IN THE DESERT BIOMES see Desert & Dry Shrubland, **CHAPTER 5, PAGES 208-9**

HOW DO SNAKES MOVE?

Snakes may lack arms and legs, but their supple bodies squeeze through narrow openings and slither—a motion that depends on the combination of a flexible spinal column, strong muscles, and specialized scales on their undersides called scutes.

Adult humans have 26 vertebrae in their spines; a snake may have more than 400. Each pair of ribs is attached to a vertebra. Overlapping scutes on the snake's belly attach by muscles to the animal's ribs.

When the snake is moving, the back edges of the scutes catch and hold the ground as the muscles pull the snake forward. Snakes move according to the terrain they travel through. Sidewinding snakes in sandy habitats have ways to keep from slipping: The snake swings its head and upper body forward and sideways. Its lower body and tail follow, with the belly raised above the hot sand, leaving a J-shaped pattern in the sand.

Some snakes climb trees. To do that, a snake coils up like an accordion, anchors with its tail, then stretches its head forward, gathering momentum, so the rest of the body catches up.

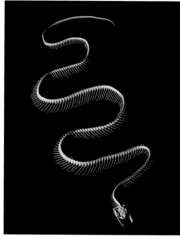

SNAKE SPINES are long and supple, thanks to the large number of vertebrae they contain, more than any other vertebrate.

G L O S S A R Y

CLICK IT: Reptiles nationalgeographic.com/animals/reptiles

Cold-blooded: Having a variable body temperature that is usually only slightly higher than the environmental temperature. / **Vertebrate:** From the Latin for "joint" or "articulation of the body"; perhaps from Latin *vertere,* "to turn." Any animal of the subphylum Vertebrata, having a backbone, a muscular system consisting primarily of bilaterally paired masses, and a central nervous system partly enclosed within the backbone.

CROCODILE OR ALLIGATOR?

Crocodilians can be distinguished by the shapes of their snouts and jaws. Crocodile teeth line the entire jawline and are visible even when their mouths are closed. They inhabit saltwater environments. Their color tends toward olive green. Alligator teeth cluster in the front of the jaw and disappear when the animals' mouths are shut. Freshwater creatures, inhabiting swamps and rivers, alligators are brownish gray.

Crocodillian species inhabit all the world's continents except Europe. They are carnivores, but their diets vary by species and surroundings. Crocodiles and alligators are known to eat insects, slugs, snails, and crustaceans frequently, but birds and small mammals also sometimes fall prey to them.

CROCODILES AND ALLIGATORS, both reptiles, can be distinguished through a few key observations, particularly the V-shaped snout of the crocodile (top) compared with the U-shaped snout of the alligator (bottom).

FAST FACT In 2006 a Komodo dragon in an English zoo laid a fertile egg without its being fertilized by a male.

FOR MORE FACTS ON...

DEFINITION & GEOGRAPHY OF RIVERS see Water: Rivers, **CHAPTER 3, PAGES 116-7**

CLASSIFICATION OF ANIMAL & PLANT SPECIES see Life-forms, **CHAPTER 4, PAGES 132-3**

Northwestern salamander embryos

AMPHIBIANS

ENDANGERED AMPHIBIANS

COLOMBIA / 209 species

MEXICO / 196 species

ECUADOR / 162 species

BRAZIL / 110 species

CHINA / 88 species

PERU / 81 species

GUATEMALA / 76 species

VENEZUELA / 69 species

INDIA / 66 species

COSTA RICA / 61 species

Descendants of fish, amphibians were the first vertebrates to leave the water and live on land. The name amphibian means "double life," and most amphibians live part of their lives in water and part on land. Amphibians reproduce from eggs, which are usually laid in water. They hatch in a larval stage and breathe through gills before transforming into air-breathing adults that live mostly on land.

Amphibians have scaleless skin kept moist by mucus glands. Many species breathe through the skin, even though they have lungs for breathing, too. The skin of some amphibians produces toxins that thwart predators or even kill them.

There are three main groups of amphibians: frogs and toads, newts and salamanders, and legless creatures called caecilians.

Frogs form the largest group of amphibians. They differ from toads by having longer and more slender bodies, being better jumpers, and having smoother, moister skin. Frogs were the first land animals with vocal cords, and their songs still punctuate many

FOR MORE FACTS ON...

HOW ANIMALS BREATHE THROUGH GILLS see Fish, CHAPTER 4, PAGE 159
+
PLANTS & ANIMALS IN THE RAIN FOREST BIOME see Forests: Rain Forests, CHAPTER 5, PAGES 198-9

an evening around the world. Strictly speaking, toads are frogs, but there is a family called true toads.

Salamanders and newts, the second largest group of amphibians, are quite secretive. Most species emerge from eggs laid underwater. They then transform to gilled larvae, spend a terrestrial phase as efts, and head back to the water as adults to breed.

Legless caecilians look like worms and are the only amphibians with scales, found underneath their skin. Most are blind and live underground, excavating with their hard heads.

CLICK IT: National Geographic Amphibians nationalgeographic.com/animals/amphibians.html

WHERE DO DART FROGS GET THEIR POISON?

Poison dart frogs inhabit the rain forests of Central and South America. Their brilliant colors make them look like children's playthings, but they represent some of the most naturally toxic animals on Earth. Humans have learned to make use of their poison.

The golden poison dart frog, for example, grows only two inches long but contains enough venom to kill ten human beings. The Emberá people of western Colombia use this frog's venom for hunting, spreading a tiny amount on a dart that they propel by blowgun into their prey.

Scientists suspect that poison dart frogs gain their toxicity from alkaloids in the food they eat, including ants and mites. Poison dart frogs raised in captivity and isolated from their native diet do not develop venom.

HARVESTING POISON for hunting, a Colombian native touches the tip of his arrow to the body of a colorful golden poison dart frog.

ENDANGERED AMPHIBIANS

Amphibians—frogs in particular—are considered a bellwether of environmental health. Recent reports from many locations tell of frogs with extra limbs, misplaced limbs, and other abnormalities occurring at a higher rate than expected. Many researchers lay blame on a parasite infection and pesticide runoff.

Frog tadpoles pick up parasites in ponds where infected snails live. The parasites form hard cysts in the tadpoles' bodies and interfere with limb development. Pesticide runoff increases the tadpoles' vulnerability.

More amphibian species have been disappearing since the 1970s, too. Kihansi spray toads, for example, inhabit only ten acres in Tanzania's Kihansi River gorge. When a new dam there diverted 90 percent of water flow in 2000, the toad population began to plummet. Today these toads—along with other endangered species—are being nurtured in captivity in zoos, with the idea that populations could eventually be reestablished in the wild.

THE GOLDEN TOAD, once native to Costa Rica but now extinct, may have succumbed to climate change as rain forest mist dwindled over the highland forests near Monteverde.

FAST FACT Dart frogs have only one predator: a snake, *Leimadophis epinephelus,* that is immune to their poison.

FOR MORE FACTS ON...

ENDANGERED ANIMAL SPECIES see *Biodiversity: Threatened Species,* **CHAPTER 4, PAGES 178-9**

THE GEOGRAPHY & ECONOMICS OF COLOMBIA see *South America,* **CHAPTER 9, PAGE 426**

Male peacock's feather display, Henry Doorly Zoo, Omaha, Nebraska

ENDANGERED AMERICAN BIRDS

CALIFORNIA CONDOR
Raised in captivity, reintroduced into wild, numbers slowly increasing

WHOOPING CRANE
Wild population slowly increasing

GUNNISON SAGE-GROUSE
Population estimated 2,000-6,000

KIRTLAND'S WARBLER
Cowbirds disturb nests; human controls improving situation

PIPING PLOVER
Human activities disturb beach nesting

FLORIDA SCRUB-JAY
Numbers declined precipitously in the 20th century

BIRDS

irds descended from dinosaurs more than 150 million years ago. Like their reptile ancestors, birds have scales on their legs and lay eggs. Unlike dinosaurs, birds are warm-blooded. The recent discovery of featherlike fibers preserved in amber for 100 million years raises the question of whether dinosaurs had feathers or whether these ancient feathers came from flightless birds.

There are about 10,000 bird species worldwide. Scientists continue to find previously undiscovered species even as other species face extinction.

Most birds are built aerodynamically, with bullet-shaped bodies, muscular wings, and lightweight bones. Some birds—such as the penguin, the kiwi, and the ostrich—have lost the ability to fly over the course of their evolution.

Birds range in size from the ostrich—nine feet tall and 300 pounds—to the bee hummingbird, which measures two inches and weighs a mere tenth of an ounce.

Many bird species migrate. Most move in and out of winter and summer ranges to take advantage of favorable weather and food supplies, but some take this to the extreme, traveling thousands of miles between destinations.

Birds originally were grouped by morphology: their outward form and features. Today, studies of bird DNA support much of this classification but give a truer picture of bird evolution and relationships.

Bird morphology, however, still remains the key to identification among the vast numbers of people worldwide who enjoy birdwatching as a pastime.

FAST FACT The alarm call of the Southern Screamer, related to ducks and geese, can be heard two miles away.

FOR MORE FACTS ON...

MIGRATORY HABITS AMONG ANIMALS see Migration, **CHAPTER 4, PAGES 172-3**
+
EXTINCT ANIMALS INCLUDING DINOSAURS see Biodiversity: Extinction, **CHAPTER 4, PAGES 176-7**

THE NATURAL HISTORY OF BIRDSONG

Birdsong is an exceedingly complex and sophisticated communication system. It is produced from the bird's syrinx, a sound box at the junction of the two bronchi, which lead to the lungs. Air from the lungs is passed over membranes in the syrinx, which then vibrate, producing sound waves. Because there are two bronchi with membranes, sound can emanate from each and combine higher in the vocal tract, producing a large variety of sounds.

Complexity in the vocal muscles also translates into more complex songs. Birds sing to defend territory and to attract mates. Some species even sing when pursued by predators to convey how robust they are. On the whole, males sing more than females. The male brown thrasher has command of some 2,000 different songs. Male and female birds sometimes sing duets, and groups of birds may sing together to defend a territory.

Some species are especially adept at mimicry. Some Scottish starlings reproduce the sounds of sheep; some English starlings even mimic city buses.

MIGRATORY SONGBIRDS of North America, including the Baltimore oriole (top), the rose-breasted grosbeak (lower left), and the whip-poorwill (lower right), are declining in number.

CLICK IT: Birds of the World www.birdlist.org

G L O S S A R Y

Warm-blooded: Distinguishing characteristic of animals able to maintain a relatively constant internal temperature (about 99°F for mammals, about 104°F for birds), regardless of the environmental temperature; this capability distinguishes these animals from cold-blooded animals, which usually have a body temperature close to that of their environment.

IDENTIFYING BIRDS

There are millions of bird-watchers in the world—people who look for, identify, and catalog bird species. Some participate in organized events, competing and mutually cataloging their observations. Many keep life lists, recording all the birds they have seen over the years. To confirm a bird's identity, bird-watchers note the distinctive appearance of certain body parts.

chin
throat
breast
side
belly
secondary wing feathers
tertial wing feathers

crown
nape
back
tail

primary wing feathers

CLICK IT: National Geographic Birds nationalgeographic.com/animals/birds

FAST FACT Some 150 million years ago *Archaeopteryx*, a bird ancestor, had four feathered limbs, teeth, and claws.

FOR MORE FACTS ON...

BIOLOGICAL CLASSIFICATION SYSTEMS see *Life-forms*, CHAPTER 4, PAGES 132-3

THE HUMAN IMPULSE TO SING & MAKE MUSIC see *Music*, CHAPTER 6, PAGES 240-1

Research boat alongside a blue whale, world's largest mammal

MAMMALS

LONGEST GESTATION

AFRICAN ELEPHANT / 660 days

ASIATIC ELEPHANT / 600 days

BAIRD'S BEAKED WHALE / 520 days

WHITE RHINOCEROS / 490 days

WALRUS / 480 days

GIRAFFE / 460 days

TAPIR / 400 days

DROMEDARY / 390 days

FIN WHALE / 370 days

LLAMA / 360 days

Mammals are vertebrates distinguished by their ability to produce milk to feed their young. They grow hair—sometimes a full-body covering of fur and sometimes just a few whiskers here and there. Mammals are typically considered warm-blooded, although the naked mole rat, an African species, may present an exception to this rule.

Mammals are divided into three large groups based on methods of reproduction: monotremes, marsupials, and placental mammals. Monotremes lay eggs, marsupials give birth to underdeveloped young that mature in a pouch of skin on the mother's abdomen, and placental mammals give birth to developed young that are nourished during gestation by a placenta.

There are about 5,000 species of mammals, which evolved from reptiles some 200 million years ago. Rodents represent almost half of these species.

Mammals live on the land and underground, in the air, and in both salt and fresh water. They inhabit all the continents except Antarctica, although even there, marine mammals live in surrounding waters.

FOR MORE FACTS ON...

WATER-DWELLING MAMMALS see *Sea Mammals*, **CHAPTER 4, PAGES 168-9**
+
A DEFINITION OF THE BIOME AS GEOGRAPHIC UNIT OF NATURE ON EARTH see *Biomes*, **CHAPTER 5, PAGES 194-5**

PRIMATE KIN

Primates as a group are intelligent, largely tree-dwelling mammals with forward-looking eyes that allow them to see in three dimensions. They possess opposable thumbs, enabling them to grasp objects well. Primates form two main groups: the lower primates, or prosimians, including lemurs, bush-babies, and tarsiers; and the higher primates, or monkeys and apes.

Humans are primates: Recent investigations suggest that only about one percent of the human genome differs from that of chimpanzees. Socially and physically, we seem to be most like the bonobo. Chimps, bonobos, and other primates—and a number of other mammal species including elephants and dolphins—exhibit

A BONOBO, also called a pygmy chimpanzee—the primate most closely resembling a human—mirrors his keeper at play in the ABC Sanctuary of the Democratic Republic of the Congo.

significant intelligence, but relative to body size, humans have the largest brain and the greatest surface area of the cerebral cortex, an anatomical difference that results in distinctive functions such as language.

Wild primates live in rain forests, mainly in the tropical and subtropical regions of Africa, Asia, and South America. Among the higher primates, monkeys are classified as Old and New World monkeys, based on range and physical characteristics. Apes' distinguishing features include upright posture, shorter spine, no tail—and profound differences in intelligence.

GLOSSARY

Placenta: Organ in most mammals that develops in the uterus along with a fetus to mediate metabolic exchange. **/ Genome:** All the genetic content contained within an organism, made up of molecules of deoxyribonucleic acid (DNA).

EGGS, POUCHES, WINGS: EXCEPTIONAL MAMMALS

Monotremes and marsupials present exceptions to certain mammalian rules. Like reptiles and birds, monotremes lay eggs; but like mammals, female monotremes nurse their young. Marsupials give birth to extremely immature young that complete their development in a pouch or fold of skin, complete with a milk source, on the mother's body.

Bats are the only mammals that truly fly. Flying squirrels simply glide.

THE PLATYPUS, a monotreme, has a genetic code as mixed up as its physical traits.

THE KANGAROO symbolizes Australia—the continent with the most marsupials.

THE FLYING FOX BAT of the Philippines can have a wingspan more than five feet wide.

FAST FACT In Mozambique, trained giant pouched rats detect explosives and land mines.

FOR MORE FACTS ON...

TROPICAL RAIN FORESTS see Forests: Rain Forests, **CHAPTER 5, PAGES 198-9**

UNUSUAL REPRODUCTIVE STRATEGIES AMONG ANIMALS see Spiders & Their Kin, **CHAPTER 4, PAGES 154-5,** & Animal Curiosities, **CHAPTER 4, PAGES 170-1**

SEA MAMMALS

Whales, dolphins, and porpoises are sea mammals known as cetaceans. Some scientists believe these animals descend from a land-dwelling ancestor that resembled a small semiaquatic deer. Over time, bodies became streamlined, rear legs were lost, front legs became flippers, and a powerful, fluked tail developed.

Cetaceans spend their entire lives in the water. They form two groups, based on how they feed: toothed whales and baleen whales. Among the toothed whales, orcas hunt in pods and consume fish as well as other marine mammals.

Baleen whales represent the sea's largest creatures, although they feed on tiny prey such as plankton. Bony, meshlike plates hang from their top jaws and filter the prey from ingested water. The blue whale can take in up to 8 tons of food each day.

When sailors of yore glimpsed the manatee in warm, murky tropical waters, their eyes sometimes tricked them into seeing a beautiful maiden with a long fishlike tail. Thus may have begun the legend of the mermaid, reflected in the class name for manatees and dugongs—Sirenians. These large, slow mammals with vestigial parts from their land-based ancestors graze sea grasses and other plants in tropical and subtropical waters.

Sea otters, relatives of the weasel, inhabit the Pacific coastal waters of North America and Asia. They lack the layer of blubber that other sea mammals have for warmth but compensate with the thickest fur of any mammal. Their numbers have declined drastically due to the fur trade.

Many species of sea mammals appear on the endangered species list. Sea otters carry protected status in the United States.

THE BOTTLENOSE DOLPHIN, its face appearing to wear a perpetual smile, can reach swimming speeds of up to 18 miles an hour.

FAST FACT The Weddell seal dives to 1,900 feet and can stay underwater for up to an hour.

FOR MORE FACTS ON...

OCEAN DYNAMICS see Water: Oceans, **CHAPTER 3, PAGES 112-5**

THE EARTH'S MANY UNDERWATER HABITATS see Aquatic Biomes, **CHAPTER 5, PAGES 212-3**

SEA OTTERS AND THEIR TOOLS

One of the smallest sea mammals, the sea otter has mastered the shallow coastal waters of the northern Pacific Ocean. It lives most of its life in the water, where it feeds on sea urchins, abalone, mussels, clams, crabs, snails, fish, octopus, and other sea creatures.

The sea otter belongs to an exclusive club of tool-users that includes only a small number of animal species such as primates, elephants, and some birds. Diving more than 300 feet to obtain food, the sea otter may bring a clam or other mollusk to the surface along with a rock. Floating on its back, it rests the rock on its chest and repeatedly bangs the clam against the rock until it opens. After the meal, the sea otter will roll over to wash bits of shell and food off its fur.

Mothers raise their young totally offshore. A mother's body serves as a bed, playpen, dining room, and diving platform for the young pup as it learns

CALIFORNIA'S SEA OTTERS feast on snails, urchins, and abalones, now hard to find.

the ways of the ocean. To keep her young from floating away, a mother will wrap kelp around herself and her pup.

CLICK IT: American Cetacean Society www.acsonline.org

FAST FACT Sea otters have up to a million hairs per square inch of skin.

WHAT HAPPENS WHEN A BLUE WHALE DIES?

The largest animal species, the blue whale can weigh 200 tons. When a blue whale dies, other animals may feast on its remains for more than a century.

When the carcass sinks to the ocean floor, it is first swarmed by mobile scavengers such as sleeper sharks, hagfish, and king crabs who nibble away at soft tissue—for up to a decade. When they finish, worms, snails, clams, and limpets settle in on the lipid-rich carcass for another ten years or so. Joining them are recently discovered gutless zombie worms that bore into the bones and mine the lipids, assisted by bacteria inside their bodies.

Then more clams, snails, crustaceans, and worms feed on sulfides released by bacteria that have invaded the bones of the carcass. This stage may last a hundred years. Even after all the nutrients are depleted, the blue whale's crumbled carcass provides a reeflike home for filter feeders.

BLUE WHALE REMAINS on King George Island, Antarctica, undergo a transformation different from those that sink to the ocean bottom.

G L O S S A R Y

Plankton: From Greek *planktos,* "wandering" or "drifting." Marine and freshwater organisms that exist in a drifting, floating state. **/ Vestigial:** From Latin *vestigium,* "footprint" or "trace." A small or partially developed body part that remains from a fully developed example in an earlier generation of a species or earlier stage of an individual organism.

FOR MORE FACTS ON...

THE NATURE OF BACTERIA & RELATED ORGANISMS see *Bacteria, Protists & Archaea,* **CHAPTER 4, PAGES** 148-9

WHALES & THEIR MIGRATION PATTERNS see *Migration,* **CHAPTER 4, PAGES** 172-3

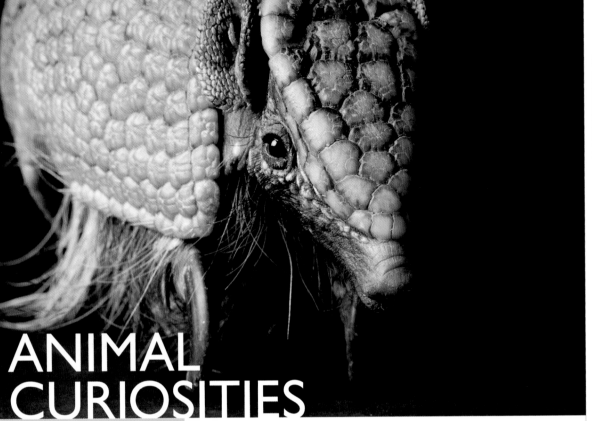

Three-banded armadillo, found in South America

ANIMAL CURIOSITIES

SUPERLATIVES

LAND ANIMAL WITH BIGGEST BRAIN
Elephant / 13 pounds 4 ounces

HEAVIEST BIRD
Male ostrich / 343 pounds

BIRD WITH LARGEST WINGSPAN
Great white pelican / 141 inches

LONGEST SNAKE
Royal python / 35 feet

HEAVIEST TERRESTRIAL ANIMAL
African elephant / 7,500 pounds

LARGEST MOTH OR BUTTERFLY
Atlas mother / 11.8-inch wingspan

MOST OFFSPRING
Prairie vole / 17 litters, 150 young a year

The animal kingdom is extraordinarily diverse. Many species display physical features or behaviors so unusual or specialized that they raise the question why. No matter how strange, comical, or exaggerated these animal features seem to us, they usually serve the species in some way relevant to day-to-day survival or the drive to reproduce.

Much colorful animal behavior occurs during mating. Many birds and fish take elaborate measures to appeal to the opposite sex: painstaking collection and construction projects combined with flamboyant bodily displays and dancelike movements. Usually the males mount the display and the females choose the most impressive. The reward? The winning male's genetic line survives and proliferates.

Throughout the world, there are extremophiles—animals that survive extreme conditions. Acidophiles prefer acidic environments; alkaliphiles prefer alkaline. Anaerobes grow without oxygen. Halophiles require high concentrations of salt. Hyperthermophiles thrive in temperatures of 176°F and above. Toxitolerants withstand toxic elements. Xerophiles grow in low moisture.

FOR MORE FACTS ON...

CHEMICAL CONSTITUENTS OF PLANET EARTH see *Earth's Elements*, **CHAPTER 3, PAGES 90-1**

THE DIVERSITY OF PLANT & ANIMAL SPECIES see *Biodiversity*, **CHAPTER 4, PAGES 174-5**

THE BOWERBIRD: CHECK OUT MY CRIB

In many bird species, the male sports brighter and more elaborate plumage than the female. The fancier feathers serve as a means of getting noticed and attracting females as mates. Male bowerbirds of Australia and New Guinea lack eye-catching plumage, but they increase their chances of success by constructing complex and often highly decorated bowers in which to woo the females. Interested visitors are treated to a full mating display that furthers the cause.

Male bowerbirds choose natural objects for decorating their bowers, such as silvery leaves, flowers, berries, and shells, but they will also seek out and add manufactured ones to their displays. Plastic bits, including bottle

A MALE BOWERBIRD (right) puts on a show for a female, tucked inside a grassy bower in the Australian bush. Once this male finishes, the female may visit another. Research suggests that mating decisions include assessment of the decorations collected by the male in his bower.

caps, straws, and lids, are prized. Blue seems to be a favored color. One bower cataloged by a researcher even included a prosthetic glass eye.

G L O S S A R Y

Phenols: From Greek *phainein*, "to shine," because they were first used in production of gases for illumination. A class of organic compounds with a hydroxyl group attached to a carbon atom in a ring of an aromatic compound; similar to alcohols, they are highly acidic.

THE BOMBARDIER BEETLE: DON'T COME CLOSE

Many animals have developed defensive features, but the bombardier beetle packs a wallop unlike any other.

Just half an inch in length, these insects live under rocks and logs and feed on the larvae of moths and other insects. When disturbed, they blast out irritating chemicals from their

flexible abdomens. They produce the irritant as needed, mixing hydrogen peroxide and phenols in an enzyme chamber, where oxidation produces heat and an explosive pop.

A BOMBARDIER BEETLE cannot easily take to flight when attacked, and so it protects itself against predators by spraying.

CLICK IT: Cave Extremophiles www.pbs.org/wgbh/nova/caves/extremophiles.html

FAST FACT Bee flight patterns, conveying directions to hive mates, are so complex and efficient that they have helped engineers improve algorithms for robotic assembly lines.

FOR MORE FACTS ON...

THE WIDE ARRAY OF INSECT SPECIES see *Insects*, CHAPTER 4, PAGES 150-1
+
VARIETIES OF BIRDS & FEATURES USED TO IDENTIFY THEM see *Birds*, CHAPTER 4, PAGES 164-5

Canada geese, Wisconsin

WHO MIGRATES?

ARCTIC TERN
Between northern Canada & Antarctica
Round-trip 22,000-30,000 miles
90 days each way

CARIBOU
"Porcupine herd": Between Yukon/Alaska
& the Arctic Circle
Round-trip about 800 miles
Total distance traveled can exceed 3,000
miles per year

GRAY WHALE
Between Baja Mexico & the Arctic Circle
Round-trip 10,000-14,000 miles
2-3 months each way

RUBY-THROATED HUMMINGBIRD
Between Mexico/Panama & northern
U.S./Canada
Round-trip about 5,000 miles
In 500-mile stretches, 18-22 hours each

MIGRATION

ome animal species make epic journeys over extraordinary distances as part of their annual routine. They migrate to escape very cold or very hot weather, to leave a dry place for a wetter one, to find more food, and to return to a favored place to reproduce and raise young. Migrating animals may change latitude, moving north to south, or altitude, moving up or down a mountain, for example, with the changing seasons. Sometimes migration is nomadic—simply a search for new food sources.

Birds, insects, fish, and mammals migrate. Even some crustaceans do: The spiny lobster migrates significant distances across the floor of the Caribbean Sea by forming a conga line of creatures attached loosely to each other by their front legs.

Migration is a dangerous undertaking. Birds on the wing have to battle the elements and avoid predators such as hawks while they keep their bodies aloft for days. Wildebeest making their annual migration in search of greener pastures must cross crocodile-infested waters where the predators lie in wait for one to stumble and be separated from the herd. As salmon return to their spawning grounds, they swim vulnerably near the paths of grizzlies, who only have to wade into rivers to grab them. Migration also depletes fat stores, as many species forgo eating while on the move.

In complete migration, all the members of a species relocate seasonally. In partial migration, many but not all members move. In irruptive migration, members of a species may move in some years and stay put in others, depending on such factors as food supply. The snowy owl, for example, may move south of its normal range when populations of lemmings, its food source, drop in Canada.

FOR MORE FACTS ON...

THE PHENOMENA THAT CAUSE SEASONS see Dividing Lines: Equator & Tropics, CHAPTER 3, PAGE 37

THE HISTORY OF HUMAN MIGRATION see Human Migration, CHAPTER 6, PAGES 220-1

HOW DO THEY KNOW WHEN AND WHERE TO GO?

Why does migration happen when it does, and how do the various species know the routes? Animals can easily sense the changing seasons. They note shorter daylength in fall at many latitudes, for example, and they become immediately aware when food supplies dwindle. Sometimes too many animals congregating in the same area triggers the need to move on.

But how do they know the route to follow? There are several possible answers. Many species inherit the knowledge of the routes from their parents genetically. Some bird species use the sun and the stars to orient themselves as they fly. And a wide range of species make use of the Earth's magnetic field for navigation.

Sea turtle hatchlings emerge on moonlit beaches, head for the sea, and join the regular migration route. They

WILDEBEEST OF THE SERENGETI migrate northwest from grass plains, crossing the Grumetic River and traveling into Kenya's Masai Mara, where they cross another crocodile-infested river to reach the Mara grasslands in late autumn. They return to breeding grounds in the spring, completing the circle that they travel.

appear to be using the geomagnetic field for orientation. A recently identified molecule in the brains of birds may be a chemical connection for detecting geomagnetic energy, and a patch of nerve cells in the brains of Zambian mole rats is thought to process magnetic information for navigation.

CLICK IT: Monarch Butterfly Conservation www.fs.fed.us/monarchbutterfly/conservation

MONARCH MIGRATION

Each fall millions of fragile monarch butterflies undertake an amazing journey. They travel from southern Canada and the northern United States to the mountains of Mexico and the coast of California, covering up to 180 miles a day. Some monarchs make a round-trip and travel 4,000

IN MEXICO, a 217-square-mile preserve now protects the southernmost habitat of migrating monarch butterflies.

miles in a year. They spend the winter resting and conserving fat stores in their southern locations.

When spring comes, monarchs head north, laying eggs along the way. The eggs hatch, turning into caterpillars and then butterflies that will join the migration, following a route they have never traveled before. Those that complete the round-trip migration expire after mating.

FAST FACT The sooty shearwater migrates 40,000 miles a year, between the Southern and Northern Hemispheres.

FOR MORE FACTS ON...

THE LIFE CYCLES OF BUTTERFLIES & MOTHS see *Insects: Butterflies & Moths,* **CHAPTER 4, PAGES** 152-3

EARTH'S GRASSLAND & SAVANNA BIOME see *Grassland & Savanna,* **CHAPTER 5, PAGES** 206-7

Zebra mussels, native to Black and Caspian Seas, brought to Europe and North America

BIODIVERSITY

NOW EXTINCT

GIANT MOA / Last seen in 1500

AUROCH / Last seen in 1527

CHINESE ELEPHANT / Last seen in 1530

DODO / Last seen in 1681

ATLANTIC GRAY WHALE / Last seen in 1750

STELLER'S SEA COW / Last seen in 1768

SPECTACLED CORMORANT / Last seen in 1832

QUAGGA / Last seen in 1883

PORTUGUESE IBEX / Last seen in 1892

RIGHT WHALE / Last seen in 1900

PASSENGER PIGEON / Last seen in 1914

n the natural scheme of things, the Earth harbors tens of millions of plant and animal species, although we have identified and given names to slightly less than two million of them. Biodiversity refers to the number and variety of species and natural communities in a geographic area, and it directly correlates with the ecological health of a region. No plant or animal species operates in a vacuum; each is part of an ecological system.

By nature, these systems are built on a resilient web of interacting organisms. When connections break down—when imbalances develop due to species endangerment or habitat destruction—the system becomes vulnerable to further weaknesses, making even naturally occurring disturbances hard for remaining species to tolerate.

Biodiversity knows no political boundaries, as nature does not recognize political distinctions. The rich biodiversity of our planet has long been under threat, and any successful solution will be an international one. The richness and livelihood of all our planet's biological species represent a heritage and responsibility of all Earth's citizens.

FOR MORE FACTS ON...

GEOLOGIC & BIOLOGICAL EVOLUTION see Ages of the Earth, **CHAPTER 3, PAGES 94-5**

THE EFFECT OF HUMAN CULTURE ON NATURE see Human Impact, **CHAPTER 5, PAGES 214-5**

NON-NATIVE SPECIES: EARTH'S INVASIVE ALIENS

The introduction of non-native species can threaten biodiversity, but it has gone on since human migration began. In North America, non-native plants and animals include starlings, dandelions, earthworms, and honeybees. Some species work out in the long run; introduced agricultural crops and animals provide important food sources. But other species overtake native species, having an irreversible effect on flora and fauna.

Not all invasive species are deliberately introduced: weed seeds may arrive among crop seeds, for example, or organisms may be discharged when ships empty tanks of ballast water.

English ivy was likely introduced to North America for sentimental reasons. It spreads aggressively, and its vines smother a host tree's limbs, prevent sunlight from reaching its leaves, and can add considerable weight to a host, making it more likely to blow over in a storm.

CRITICAL AND ENDANGERED AREAS of biodiversity appear in every continent. Leading causes of extinction are loss of habitat and the introduction of non-native plants and animals.

CLICK IT: Encyclopedia of Life www.eol.org

G L O S S A R Y

Pheromone: Any chemical compound secreted by an organism in minute amounts to elicit a particular reaction from other organisms of the same species. **/ Sociobiology:** Systematic study of the biological basis of social behavior.

E. O. WILSON / SOCIOBIOLOGIST

Edward Osborne Wilson (b. 1929) was from the start an avid entomologist. At 13, he came upon the first known colonies of fire ants in the United States, near the docks of Mobile, Alabama. Ants became his specialty in his studies and as a professor of biology at Harvard. He used his expertise of ant physiology and social behavior to develop pathbreaking theories, often collaborating with others. He is best known for a general theory he called sociobiology, which proposes that behavioral patterns over time can influence genetics. An ardent ecologist and conservationist, Wilson heads the Biodiversity Foundation, an organization he founded to safeguard the planet's astounding but ecologically fragile variety of life-forms and habitats.

FAST FACT The isolated island of Madagascar serves as a laboratory of evolution, with one of the greatest concentrations of unique plant and animal species on the planet.

FOR MORE FACTS ON...

VARIETY OF LIFE-FORMS ON EARTH see Life Begins, **CHAPTER 4, PAGES 130-1,** & Life-forms, **CHAPTER 4, PAGES 132-3**

INTERNATIONAL TRADE & COMMERCE see Commerce, **CHAPTER 6, PAGES 254-7**

EXTINCTION

Extinction, the permanent loss of a species of plant or animal, occurs when a species fails to reproduce at replacement levels and ultimately dies out. Extinction often comes with environmental change. Inability to adapt to changes, say, in climate or food supply can force a species either to die out or to evolve into a new species.

Extinction serves as a natural part of the evolutionary process and often ties in to major environmental impacts. Such a case likely occurred in the Cretaceous period 65 million years ago, when an asteroid impact caused catastrophic climate change, leading to the extinction of dinosaurs and many other land and sea species. Some scientists think these mass extinctions occur at 26-million-year intervals.

Human actions have sped up the process of extinction through habitat degradation, hunting, fishing, collecting, and other activities. This is not just a recent phenomenon. The disappearance of megafauna such as mammoths in the Americas coincided with the appearance of humans there.

Clearly, however, human actions have caused or hastened extinctions in recent centuries at a rate up to a thousand times higher than expected. The International Union for Conservation of Nature (IUCN) estimates that more than 15,000 species currently are threatened with extinction.

SOME SPECIES are known only from fossil remains, such as the mammoth (right), whose bones are displayed at Morrill Hall in Lincoln, Nebraska.

FAST FACT One in every four mammals faces a high risk of extinction in the near future.

FOR MORE FACTS ON...

THREATS TO PLANET EARTH see *Threatened Planet*, **CHAPTER 3, PAGES 122-7**
+
THE EFFECT OF HUMAN CULTURE ON PLANET EARTH see *Human Impact*, **CHAPTER 5, PAGES 214-5**

DINOSAURS: CELEBRITIES OF EXTINCTION

Dinosaurs dominated life on Earth for some 135 million years, from their beginnings in the Triassic period 200 million years ago until their abrupt exit during the Cretaceous period, more than 65 million years ago. They flourished during the Jurassic period, when there were only two basic continents, but by the beginning of the Cretaceous period, 145 million years ago, they inhabited a seven-continent planet—albeit a warmer and wetter one where many species, both plant and animal, were gigantic.

Based on the evidence studied by paleontologists, dinosaurs fell into two basic physiological categories: those with bird hips and those with lizard hips, determined by the angle at which the pelvis tilted. Most had long tails; most laid eggs. Dinosaurs could be either carnivorous or herbivorous. Little is known about their temperature-regulating mechanisms.

A catastrophic event occurred at the end of the Cretaceous period, believed to be a giant asteroid that hit the Yucatán Peninsula and formed the Chicxulub crater, still recognizable today. Such an event would have caused huge environmental changes leading to mass extinctions. Yet dinosaurs seem to have been on the decline for 20 million years before that. In any case, by the beginning of the Cenozoic era, about 65.5 million years ago, dinosaurs were history.

DINOSAUR SPECIES continue to emerge from the prehistoric past, as paleontologists unearth fossil evidence for ever new evolutionary variations. Styracosaurus, for example, the horned dinosaur at lower right in this fantasy assemblage, was a rhinoceros-size herbivore that may have blushed, its blood filling and reddening the fleshy frill above its forehead.

FAST FACT Passenger pigeons, now extinct, once migrated across the United States in flocks of up to two billion.

CAN SPECIES EVER COME BACK?

Occasionally a species considered extinct reappears. Recently a rare giant turtle believed to be extinct in the wild was found in northern Vietnam. The Swinhoe's soft-shelled turtle, which can weigh up to 300 pounds and live for more than 100 years, was discovered and photographed by zoologists. A second sighting in southern China has been confirmed, so the species likely has survived a brush with extinction.

Bird enthusiasts live in hope of the same outcome for the ivory-billed woodpecker, last photographed in northeastern Louisiana in 1938 and last reliably sighted in 1944.

It lived in the southeastern forests of the United States and the upland pine forests of Cuba. It is presumed extinct by many ornithologists, but sightings in 2004 and 2005 have given bird lovers cause for optimism.

THE IVORY-BILLED WOODPECKER was painted by John James Audubon in the early 19th century, but since then the bird has disappeared and possibly become extinct.

CLICK IT Endangered Species www.endangeredspeciesinternational.org

FOR MORE FACTS ON...

DINOSAURS & WHY THEY BECAME EXTINCT see Ages of the Earth, **CHAPTER 3, PAGE 95**

SPECIES FACING POSSIBLE EXTINCTION see Biodiversity: Threatened Species, **CHAPTER 4, PAGES 178-9**

THREATENED SPECIES

Some people see a trade-off between protecting nature and advancing economically; they often view these as mutually exclusive. Yet we all benefit from biodiversity. Environmental stewardship and the promotion of biodiversity is part of an overall global strategy to reverse many of the potentially disastrous trends facing us in the 21st century, including global warming.

Worldwide, many organizations contribute to awareness and action for the cause of threatened species. One of the large umbrella organizations is the International Union for Conservation of Nature (IUCN), headquartered in Gland, Switzerland. The IUCN serves as a global clearinghouse for information on all threatened animal and plant species. It evaluates and assesses the plight of thousands of species each year and publishes the Red List, which is the standard reference for conservation work.

One of the most threatened groups of species in the world is that nearest to our own: the great apes. Across all their habitats, populations of gorilla, chimpanzees, bonobos, and orangutans have declined dramatically in recent decades. The great apes are currently under siege from poachers, trophy hunters, and tribal peoples seeking bushmeat; from pathogens such as the Ebola virus; and from general habitat loss and degradation, caused by encroaching human development. As a result, many of our closest evolutionary kin may soon carry on their lines only in the confines of zoos and conservation research centers.

PROPAGATING ITS KIND, an adult bald eagle brings food to a chick, first of two to hatch in a nest of sticks and grasses built high in Newfoundland treetops.

THE BALD EAGLE: A SUCCESS STORY

Just a few decades ago, the United States stood in danger of losing its national bird. In 1963, only 417 breeding pairs of bald eagles were known to inhabit the lower 48 states. Hunting and the use of the pesticide DDT were both to blame. DDT exposure caused the eagles to lay eggs with shells so thin the unborn birds did not survive.

DDT was banned in 1972. The bald eagle was placed on the endangered species list in almost all states in 1978. Today, there are almost 10,000 nesting pairs in the lower 48 states. And in June 2007, the U.S. government removed the species from the threatened list.

FOR MORE FACTS ON...

THREATS TO PLANET EARTH see *Threatened Planet,* **CHAPTER 3, PAGES 122-7**

PRIMATE SPECIES & THEIR RELATIONSHIP TO HUMANS see *Mammals,* **CHAPTER 4, PAGE 167**

THE POLAR BEAR: VICTIM OF GLOBAL WARMING

In May 2008, the United States added the polar bear to the list of threatened species protected under the U.S. Endangered Species Act. Activists had supported the listing for a number of years, recognizing that the polar ice cap was melting at even a greater rate than predicted—with new estimates that it might melt completely by 2099.

Polar bears rely on the ice cap to stage their hunting of ringed seals and other prey, so the loss of the ice poses a distinct threat to their survival.

While a robust male polar bear can measure 11 feet tall and weigh up to 1,200 pounds, there is evidence that the species is losing its vigor and suffering a decline in size. There has also been a noticeable decline in the survival rate of cubs, which usually are born as twins in the winter.

A POLAR BEAR LEAPS across gaps in the pack ice in Norway's Northeast Svalbard Nature Preserve. As polar ice floes melt and shrink, polar bears are losing precious habitat. In 2008 the U.S. declared polar bears a threatened species, citing sea ice loss due to global warming as the cause.

CLICK IT: Red List of Threatened Species www.iucnredlist.org

THREATS TO SPECIES ON EVERY CONTINENT

Biodiversity is decreasing at a rapidly increasing rate. Some fear that as many as a quarter of the world's species could be lost in the next quarter century.

Continents around the world are experiencing extinction differently. Asia in particular stands to lose many species, particularly mammals, birds, reptiles, and fish. Species are experiencing extinction because of loss of habitat and introduction of non-native plants and animals. Both effects correlate with high human populations.

AS THE 21ST CENTURY BEGAN, every type of animal was facing the threat of extinction to one or more of its species.

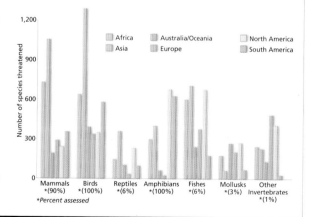

FAST FACT International fisheries discard some 30 million tons of accidentally caught animals each year.

FOR MORE FACTS ON...

PLANTS & ANIMALS THAT LIVE IN EARTH'S ICIEST BIOMES see *Tundra & Ice Cap,* **CHAPTER 5, PAGES 210-1**

THE WORLD'S CONTINENTS in *Africa, Asia, Europe, Australia & Oceania, North America & South America,* **CHAPTER 9, PAGES 360-1, 378-9, 394-5, 408-9, 414-5, 424-5**

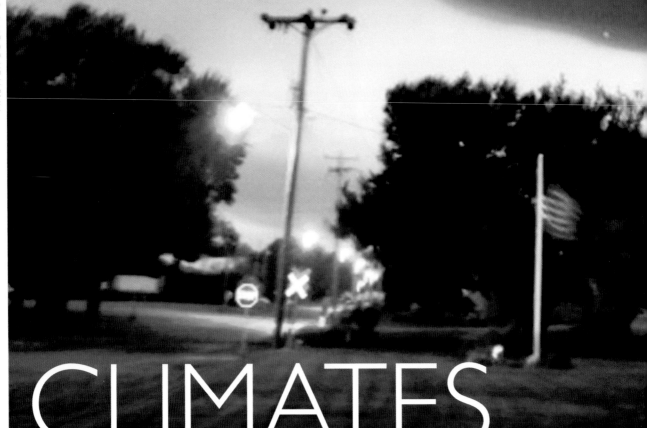

CLIMATES

Storms / Hurricanes / Snow &
/ Rain Forests / Boreal Forests
/ Grassland & Savanna / Desert &
Aquatic Biomes / Human Impact

& HABITATS

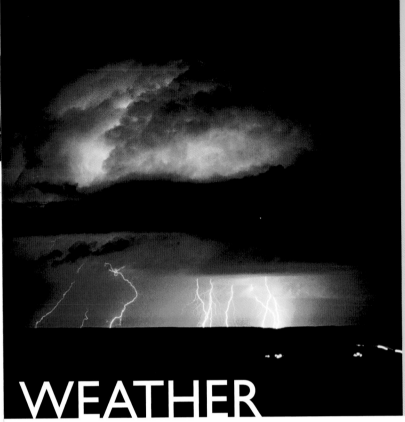

EXTREMES
AVERAGE TEMPERATURES CITED

HOTTEST INHABITED PLACES
Djibouti, 86.0°F
Timbuktu, Mali, 84.7°F
Tirunelevi, India, 84.7°F
Tuticorin, India, 84.7°F

COLDEST INHABITED PLACES
Norilsk, Russia, 12.4°F
Yakutsk, Russia, 13.8°F
Yellowknife, Canada, 22.3°F
Ulan-Bator, Mongolia, 23.9°F

WETTEST INHABITED PLACES
Buenaventura, Colombia, 265.47 in/yr
Monrovia, Liberia, 202.01 in/yr
Pago Pago, American Samoa,
196.46 in/yr

DRIEST INHABITED PLACES
Aswan, Egypt, 0.02 in/yr
Luxor, Egypt, 0.03 in/yr
Arica, Chile, 0.04 in/yr

WEATHER

Combine the heat of the sun with the rotation of a planet covered mostly in water, and the product is what we call weather: the day-to-day changes in the quality of the atmosphere near the surface of the Earth. Fundamentally, weather is caused by the sun, which heats the air at the planet's bulging equatorial regions more than at either Pole.

Because hotter air rises and cooler air falls, the difference in temperature across the planet causes masses of air to begin to move. We feel that moving air as wind. The movement of the air becomes even more dynamic because of Earth's rotation, while the steady evaporation of surface water leads to the formation of clouds, and eventually precipitation.

Weather is the result of a global system of moving air and moisture, but it can also be shaped by local features such as mountain ranges or nearby bodies of water. Weather occurs only in the lower atmosphere.

The differences in temperature and pressure that cause such profound day-to-day shifts at ground level smooth out higher in the atmosphere, where the air is cold and "thin," a term referring to lower oxygen levels. The highest winds that shape weather are the jet stream air currents, which roar around the globe five to nine miles above its surface at speeds of up to a hundred miles per hour.

The effects of humidity—another word for the saturation of air with evaporated water—can be felt at warmer temperatures. Cooler air has a lower saturation point than warmer air. As warm, water-soaked air molecules rise, they also cool. Their saturation point drops. Eventually the excess

FAST FACT Lightning can reach temperatures of around 54,000°F.

FOR MORE FACTS ON...

THE POLES, THE EQUATOR & THE TROPICS see *The Poles*, **CHAPTER 1, PAGES 34-5, &** *Equator & Tropics*, **CHAPTER 1, PAGES 36-7**

THE FORCES ON EARTH THAT CREATE WIND see *Wind*, **CHAPTER 3, PAGES 106-7**

water condenses into clouds and falls back to Earth.

Atmospheric pressure is another factor watched closely by scientists who monitor the weather. Changes in air pressure—which can be thought of as the weight of the air pressing down on the ground—often herald a change in the weather. High-pressure systems bring air toward the ground, prevent moisture from rising, and are usually associated with clear skies. In low-pressure systems, rising air draws moisture up with it, forming clouds as the air cools.

TYPES OF CLOUDS

Clouds, which are condensed water vapor, are one of the most visible marks of the weather. They form in distinctive patterns and often give a quick clue to what weather might happen in the near future.

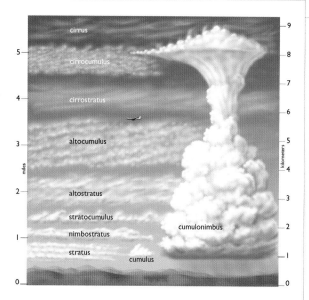

HIGH-FLYING CIRRUS CLOUDS form from ice crystals four miles above the planet's surface, and their sparse, wispy streaks are usually a sign of clear weather.

STRATUS CLOUDS are flat, broad, and close to the ground, and they usually prompt observers to grab a raincoat. The lowest stratus clouds touch the Earth in the form of fog.

NIMBOSTRATUS CLOUDS stretched out like a blanket usually fore-shadow extended precipitation.

CUMULUS CLOUDS can be playfully puffy components of a high-pressure system, but they can also build into towering cumulonimbus thunderheads, accompanying a squall or thunderstorm.

G L O S S A R Y

Front: The boundary between large air masses of differing temperature and moisture content. **/ Lightning:** The violent leveling of an electrical imbalance between the Earth and a storm cloud.

HOW DOES TOPOGRAPHY AFFECT WEATHER?

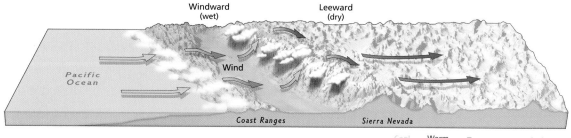

MOUNTAIN RANGES BLOCK AIR MOVEMENT, as on the California coastline (above), where precipitation collected from the ocean falls in the Sierra Nevada, leaving the leeward slopes dry.

FOR MORE FACTS ON...

THE CONTINENTS ON PLANET EARTH see Continents, **CHAPTER 3, PAGES 84-5**

+

HOW ELEMENTS AFFECT THE SHAPING OF EARTH'S LANDFORMS see Landforms: Taking Shape **CHAPTER 3, PAGES 100-1**

PREDICTIONS

K nowing the weather in advance is an obvious benefit—for farmers wondering about rainfall, sailors wondering about navigation, or, in modern times, pilots and passengers wondering whether inclement weather may affect air travel. With data gathered from networks of balloons, satellites, radar, and other equipment, meteorologists can create reasonable short-term predictions and can monitor local conditions closely enough to give advance notice of when tornadoes, hailstorms, or other dangerous events are likely to occur.

Though casual observation can provide an idea of where a weather system is heading, systematic analysis was not possible until the mid-19th century. Tools to measure basic variables like temperature and pressure were developed well before then, but the development of the telegraph provided a missing link in the 1800s— the ability to assemble data quickly from different geographic locations and compare it for patterns of change.

At Washington's Smithsonian Institution, Joseph Henry was preparing daily weather maps using telegraphed reports by 1849; early meteorologists at the Cincinnati Observatory began preparing forecasts in 1869. Two years later, the U.S. Army Signal Corps began operation of the first network of national weather stations.

By the 1930s radio had replaced the telegraph for communication, and observation balloons had replaced the naked eye for observation. A global network of radiosonde balloons—so named for the observation equipment attached to them—were launched from different spots around the globe each day, feeding back data about atmospheric conditions and allowing meteorologists to see what was happening at ever higher heights. That system is in place today, with balloons launched every 12 hours from some 700 locations around the world.

Coupled with data from about 25,000 ground stations, this information goes into supercomputers that, using complex models, forecast the weather for the coming days. Since 1960, the system has been augmented by satellites that give a view of cloud patterns and the movement of storms. Radar supplements the readings with more local data.

A WEATHER BALLOON drifts upward from an icebreaker in the Bellingshausen Sea, Antarctica, released on its mission to sense and deliver data on atmospheric pressure and temperature.

FAST FACT The first known photograph of a tornado was taken on August 28, 1884, near Howard, South Dakota.

FOR MORE FACTS ON...

WIND CHARACTERISTICS & DYNAMICS ON PLANET EARTH see Wind, **CHAPTER 3, PAGES 106-7**

WEATHER & CLOUD FORMATIONS see Weather, **CHAPTER 5, PAGES 182-3**

WHAT IS DOPPLER RADAR?

By tracking changes in the speed and direction of wind and precipitation, Doppler radar helps detect when dangerous rotational patterns are developing—precursors to things like tornadoes and hurricanes. The installation of short-range Doppler radar at airports has given air traffic controllers the ability to know when conditions are ripe for microbursts or wind shear, a phenomenon that has caused planes to crash at takeoff and landing.

Astronomers have applied the Doppler effect—the change in the wavelength of light emitted by a moving star—to show that galaxies are moving away from one another. Meteorologists use the phenomenon to improve their ability to warn of imminent weather.

A DOPPLER RADAR ANTENNA tracks storms in the Texas Panhandle. Weather radar tools sense precipitation's intensity and motion; the information is projected onto maps for the general public, using colors to distinguish different types of precipitation.

G L O S S A R Y

Cyclones: From the Greek *kykloun,* "whirl" or "move around in a circle." Swirling air masses that converge around low-pressure areas, often associated with storms. **/ Anticyclones:** Swirling air masses that converge around high-pressure areas, often associated with clear weather. **/ Synoptic forecasting:** General overview of changes in temperature and pressure drawn from data across a wide area.

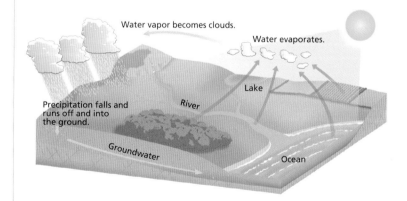

Water vapor becomes clouds.

Water evaporates.

Lake

Precipitation falls and runs off and into the ground.

River

Groundwater

Ocean

WHAT IS RAIN?

Rain is one of the stages in the planet's hydrologic cycle (also called the water cycle), the constant circulation of moisture through levels in Earth and its atmosphere. Evaporation transports water vapor from land and ocean to the atmosphere. Water returns to Earth in the form of precipitation. On land, water constantly seeks lower ground and ultimately flows into the ocean.

CLICK IT: National Oceanic & Atmospheric Administration www.noaa.gov

FOR MORE FACTS ON...

ASTRONOMICAL OBSERVATION METHODS TODAY see *Observation: Modern Methods,* **CHAPTER 2, PAGES 70-1**

WATER & THE WATER CYCLE ON EARTH see *Water,* **CHAPTER 3, PAGES 110-1**

Thunderstorm, Ardmore, Oklahoma

STORMS

DEADLIEST U.S. TORNADOES

MARCH 18, 1925 / MS, IL, IN
695 dead

MAY 6, 1840 / NATCHEZ, MS
317 dead

MAY 27, 1896 / ST. LOUIS, MO
255 dead

APRIL 5, 1936 / TUPELO, MS
216 dead

APRIL 6, 1936 / GAINESVILLE, GA
203 dead

APRIL 9, 1947 / WOODWARD, OK
181 dead

MAY 22, 2011 / JOPLIN, MO
est. 151 dead

Storms result from imbalances—such as warm air colliding with cold air, low-pressure areas feeding so much moisture into the atmosphere that it pours back as rain, or the friction of rising air creating a static charge that gets released as lightning—and can be among nature's most violent and catastrophic events. Thunderstorms develop when the usual pattern of rising warm air becomes intensified and concentrated in a shaft.

As the moisture in the cell of rising air condenses, it releases heat that pushes the air higher still. From a puffy cumulus cloud, a towering cumulonimbus thunderhead can build, accumulating moisture and electric charge until the imbalance becomes too much to sustain. Rain may fall in torrents, and fall-

ing cold air can translate into vicious winds. As electricity is discharged in the form of lightning, the shock wave of thunder can be heard miles away.

Thunderstorms can also spawn tornadoes, which form when large air masses with sharply different temperatures, wind directions, and wind

FAST FACT Between 700 and 1,000 tornadoes occur annually in the U.S.

FOR MORE FACTS ON...

THE ATMOSPHERE & ITS COMPONENTS see *Earth's Atmosphere*, **CHAPTER 3, PAGES 104-5**
+
FAMOUS WIND PATTERNS FROM AROUND THE WORLD see *Wind*, **CHAPTER 3, PAGES 106-7**

speeds collide. The rising warm air may begin to spin, a process accelerated when higher, cooler air rushes downward. In its early stages, this spinning mass of air is called a mesocyclone. Under conditions, which storm researchers cannot yet fully explain, the spin can form into the well-known funnel shape.

Tornado intensity is measured by the six-degree enhanced Fujita scale, based on the damage caused. The majority rank low on the scale: They grow to perhaps 600 feet wide, traveling at about 30 miles an hour, and typically move no more than 6 miles before they dissipate.

The largest tornadoes may span more than a mile, travel at speeds of up to 70 miles an hour, and travel as far as 300 miles. Their winds may reach 300 miles an hour.

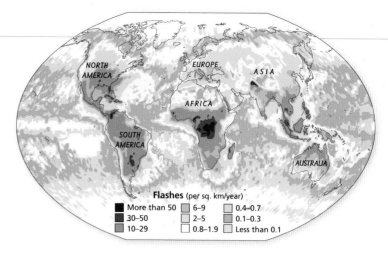

Flashes (per sq. km/year)

■ More than 50	■ 6–9	■ 0.4–0.7
■ 30–50	■ 2–5	■ 0.1–0.3
■ 10–29	□ 0.8–1.9	□ Less than 0.1

LIGHTNING FLASHES AROUND THE WORLD, but some regions see more than others, as shown in this world map generated by NASA scientists using five years of data—a total of more than 1.2 billion intracloud and cloud-to-ground flashes—and calculating mean annual distribution.

Both thunderstorms and tornadoes have the effect of quickly correcting differences in pressure and temperature between air masses. Those imbalances can also give rise to lingering storm systems, such as the "nor'easters" that howl along the Atlantic coast of the United States in winter. When warm low-pressure systems, fed by the waters off the coast of Florida, collide with cold high-pressure systems fed by Arctic air, the result can be feet of snow or long spells of cold, rainy weather.

FAST FACT About 16 million thunderstorms and 1.2 billion lightning strikes occur annually across the planet.

WHAT TO DO IN A TORNADO

Tornadoes kill roughly 100 people each year in the United States. Most die after being struck by flying or falling debris. If a storm is approaching, therefore, it's best to move to a confined space where the chances of being struck are minimized. That means moving to the basement and sheltering beneath a table or workbench. If there is no basement, move to a closet or bathroom and use a mattress or blankets for extra protection. Stay away from windows, since glass may fly. Anyone caught outside should lie low in a ditch or culvert, if possible, or near a tree or pole that can be grabbed. Don't stay in a car—it may be swept away by the storm. People in mobile homes should relocate to more secure structures.

A FAMILY LIES LOW, as recommended, in a highway underpass as a tornado rips through the Newcastle, Oklahoma, area.

CLICK IT: Tornadoes www.nssl.noaa.gov/edu/safety/tornadoguide.html

FAST FACT Relative to geographic size, Great Britain's average of 33 tornadoes annually ranks as the world's highest.

FOR MORE FACTS ON...

HURRICANES & TYPHOONS see Storms: Hurricanes, **CHAPTER 5, PAGES 188-9**

ENGINEERING MATERIALS DESIGNED TO WITHSTAND STORMS see Physical Science: Engineering, **CHAPTER 8, PAGES 332-3**

HURRICANES

The collision of warm and cold air often results in large rotating weather systems known as cyclones, low-pressure zones that can lead to days of cloudy weather and precipitation. When such systems develop over warm ocean water, typically between 5° and 25° above the Equator, they can produce the massive storms known as hurricanes, tropical cyclones, and typhoons. These three types of storm are the same—defined by a wind speed in excess of 74 miles per hour. But they occur in different parts of the world: The storm is called a hurricane if it develops over the Atlantic or eastern Pacific Ocean, a cyclone if it develops over the Bay of Bengal or the Indian Ocean, and a typhoon if it develops over the western Pacific.

Strong and deadly, these storms are dangerous not just for their winds, which can rage in excess of 150 miles per hour, but also for the massive amounts of water they dump from the sky and push inland through a storm surge—a wall of ocean water. On September 8, 1900, between 6,000 and 8,000 people drowned in Galveston, Texas, for example, when a 20-foot storm surge flooded the town in the deadliest natural disaster in U.S. history. In Asia, individual typhoons have claimed hundreds of thousands of lives—including a storm in 1970 in Bangladesh that killed 300,000 with an estimated 30-foot surge of water.

Hurricanes, cyclones, and typhoons form as winds from different directions meet over the ocean. Warmed by the ocean, moisture-laden, low-pressure air begins to rise. As cooler air rushes in, it is also warmed and hydrated, and it begins moving upward. Typically, this air movement leads to little more than thunderstorms, but sometimes the system will organize itself and begin to spin, gathering force as it moves across warm water. Now the system is classified as a tropical depression, because of its extreme low pressure. When its winds reach 39 miles per hour, it becomes classified as a tropical storm. At 74 miles per hour, it is reclassified as a hurricane or other serious storm. While these tropical storm systems may wander harmlessly at sea, they often do not fully dissipate until they reach land. The collision with land robs them of the warm ocean water that fuels them.

A MASSIVE STORM SURGE—a wall of water pushed on land by strong winds—accompanied Hurricane Katrina in August 2005. Reaching 20 feet above sea level, it pummeled the Louisiana and Mississippi coastlines and left many houses standing in water. The world's worst storm surge occurred in Bathurst Bay, Australia, in 1899, when a hurricane produced a 42-foot surge.

FOR MORE FACTS ON...

WATER IN ALL ITS FORMS ON PLANET EARTH see Water, **CHAPTER 3, PAGES 110-1**

THE INTERACTION OF OCEANS & ATMOSPHERE IN CAUSING WEATHER see Water: Oceans, **CHAPTER 3, PAGE 113**

KATRINA'S LEGACY

Hurricane Katrina raked the U.S. Gulf coastline in August 2005. It left about 75 percent of New Orleans underwater when levees built to protect the city from Lake Pontchartrain and Lake Borgne failed. A study soon after found at least three different types of levee breaches, some of which might have been prevented with minor design adaptations.

In several spots, the storm surge from the hurricane built up above the levee's concrete wall, spilling over the top, eroding the supporting earthen embankment on the other side, and eventually collapsing the wall itself. Elsewhere pressure from the storm surge pushed through the underlying soil and eroded the levee from beneath. Where levees of different design met, weak spots in one led to larger breaches overall.

SATELLITE IMAGERY OF KATRINA at 8:15 p.m. Sunday, August 28, 2005, reveals the intensity of the storm near peak strength.

CYCLONES: WHERE & WHEN?

Hurricanes, cyclones, and typhoons develop over tropical waters in summer and autumn, when ocean temperatures are warmest. The movement of these storms is governed by global and upper atmosphere winds and by the Coriolis effect, deflections created by Earth's rotation.

About a hundred storms form near the west coast of Africa every year. Of those, only 10 percent actually maintain their shape, travel across the Atlantic, and reach the coasts of the Caribbean and North America as hurricanes.

PREDICTABLE PATTERNS of season and location do not reduce the terror and devastation that tropical cyclonic storms can cause.

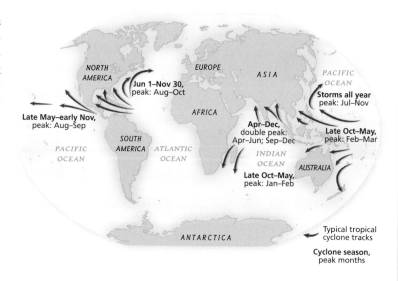

CLICK IT: National Hurricane Center www.nhc.noaa.gov

FAST FACT Eight of the world's ten worst tropical cyclones occurred in the Bay of Bengal.

FOR MORE FACTS ON...

THE DEFINITION OF TROPICAL REGIONS see *Dividing Lines: Equator & Tropics*, **CHAPTER 1, PAGES 36-7**

LAYERS OF THE ATMOSPHERE see *Earth's Atmosphere*, **CHAPTER 3, PAGES 104-5**

SNOW & ICE

Most precipitation begins as ice crystals in the cold upper reaches of cloud formations. As warm air rises, it begins to cool. Since colder air can hold less water, it eventually reaches a saturation point. Water vapor then begins to condense around microscopic "condensation nuclei," forming supercooled crystals around bits of salt, sand, dust, pollutants, and other material scattered through the upper atmosphere. Clouds form, and the particles of ice continue to grow until they become so heavy that they fall to the Earth.

What happens on the way down determines whether the precipitation reaches the ground in the form of snow, ice, sleet, or hail—all forms of frozen precipitation that can cause tremendous damage, even (in the case of snow) while offering recreational opportunities for winter sports enthusiasts.

If temperatures are above freezing near the ground, the ice crystals melt and turn into rain. But if ground level temperatures are below freezing, the crystals remain intact as they accumulate more water vapor or merge together to form snowflakes. Sometimes, the falling ice crystals pass through a band of warm air and melt, only to freeze again if lower level temperatures are cooler. Sleet is rain that has fully refrozen before it hits the ground. Rain that freezes as it comes in contact with the cooler surface of the Earth is called "freezing rain"—a particularly hazardous form of precipitation that can make driving treacherous and topple trees and power lines under the weight of the ice.

Water that freezes in the upper reaches of a thunderstorm can accumulate into large pellets of ice—hailstones—that can reach as much as four inches in diameter. In addition to being dangerous, hailstorms can cause damage to crops, automobiles, and other property.

WINTRY WEATHER meant snowy roads, requiring careful driving and daytime headlights, in southern Germany in January 2007.

FOR MORE FACTS ON...

ICE AS ONE FORM OF WATER ON PLANET EARTH see *Water: Ice,* **CHAPTER 3, PAGES 120-1**

PLANTS & ANIMALS THAT LIVE IN SNOW-FILLED & ICY BIOMES see *Tundra & Ice Cap,* **CHAPTER 4, PAGES 210-1**

HOW DO SNOWFLAKES FORM?

Snowflakes start as ice crystals that form high in the atmosphere, when water vapor either condenses around a solid nucleus or, under even colder conditions, freezes directly in a process called sublimation. The flakes, typically hexagonal, are infinite in design. Their individuality depends on the temperature and pressure at which freezing occurs. There are seven basic snow-flake shapes: plates, stellars, columns, needles, spatial dendrites, capped columns, and irregular crystals, each associated with temperatures ranging from freezing to -50°F.

NEEDLES, including these crossed needles, form at about -23°F.

STELLAR DENDRITES is one of the shapes visible with the naked eye.

CAPPED COLUMNS have crystals perpendicular to a central column.

CLICK IT: National Snow and Ice Data Center www.nsidc.org

FAST FACT Four inches of snow falling on a given area contain the same water as 0.4 inch of rain falling there.

WILSON A. BENTLEY / STUDENT OF SNOWFLAKES

Wilson A. "Snowflake" Bentley (1865-1931) was a farmer by trade, but from the snowy landscape of Vermont he drew inspiration for another calling: documenting the intricate and apparently nonrepetitive designs of snowflakes. Connecting a rudimentary bellows camera to a microscope, Bentley took the first photographs of snowflakes in 1885—showing them to be far more than simply frozen drops of water. Instead, he found them to be "miracles of beauty. . . . Every crystal was a masterpiece of design and no design was ever repeated." Over the years, Bentley produced some 5,000 photographs of snowflakes. Along with revealing their structure, his work pioneered the field of photomicrography—using photography to reveal what was invisible to the naked eye.

 The mysteries of the upper air are about to reveal themselves, if our hands are deft and our eyes quick enough. **— WILSON A. BENTLEY, 1902**

FOR MORE FACTS ON...

THE VARIETIES & CAUSES OF WEATHER PATTERNS ON EARTH see *Weather,* **CHAPTER 5, PAGES 182-3**

ADVANCES IN ELECTRON MICROSCOPY see *Optics,* **CHAPTER 8, PAGES 336-7**

Meltwater near Ilulissat, Greenland

CLIMATE

EARTH'S EXTREMES

HOTTEST PLACE
Dalol, Denakil Depression
Ethiopia
Annual average temperature:
93.2°F

COLDEST PLACE
Plateau Station
Antarctica
Annual average temperature:
-70°F

WETTEST PLACE
Mawsynram, Assam
India
Annual average rainfall:
467 in/yr

DRIEST PLACE
Atacama Desert
Chile
Rainfall barely measurable

Weather happens from day to day, whereas climate refers to average conditions over time. Climatologists look at trends over decades and centuries, including average precipitation, average temperature, prevailing winds, and the average amount of sunlight received. Climate shapes the surrounding environment and influences both the biology and the culture of a region.

Climate is determined by large-scale patterns and forces, beginning with the position of the Earth 93 million miles from the sun, close enough to receive a life-sustaining amount of solar radiation.

Since Earth tilts on its axis, much of the sun's heat falls on the tropical areas around the Equator. The resulting uneven distribution of sunlight—and of temperature in the atmosphere and throughout the world's oceans—establishes underlying sea current and wind patterns that, in turn, influence climate.

Latitudinal banding, from the Equator outward to the Poles, plays a central role in determining conditions in a given area. The steady flow of heat and sunlight to Earth's equatorial areas, for example, yields the hot, wet conditions associated with rain forests and other tropical regions. Toward the Poles, climate tends to get progressively drier and colder.

These general climate rules are affected greatly by the presence of mountains or nearby bodies of water. Immediately to the north of Africa's tropical zone, for example, precipitation practically disappears across the arid expanse of the Sahara. The Rocky Mountains in the U.S. and Canada bottle up moist air pushed inland from the Pacific on westerly breezes, increasing precipitation on the windward side of the mountains and creating drier conditions to the lee.

FOR MORE FACTS ON...

THE DETERMINATION OF EARTH'S LATITUDES *see Dividing Lines,* **CHAPTER 1, PAGES 30-7**

THE IMPORTANCE OF DIVERSITY AMONG LIFE-FORMS ON PLANET EARTH *see Biodiversity,* **CHAPTER 4, PAGES 174-5**

WHAT ARE INDICATORS OF GLOBAL WARMING?

Climatic conditions remain relatively constant when seen from the human perspective, but they have changed many times over the life of the planet. A warming trend in the last century raises the urgent question of whether human activity is now changing the climate. The United Nations' Intergovernmental Panel on Climate Change shared the 2007 Nobel Peace Prize for its work on climate change.

The panel studied the net change in heat entering or leaving the climate system and concluded that due to increased greenhouse gases like carbon dioxide—up from 280 parts per million in pre-industrial society to 379 parts per million in 2005—heat exchange had increased about 2.3 watts per square meter since 1750. That increase—unprecedented over the last

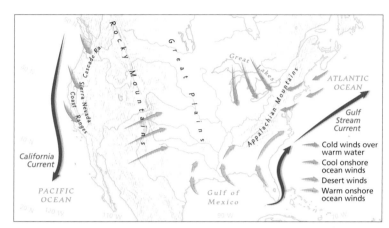

GEOGRAPHY INFLUENCES CLIMATE, as this map illustrates. Coastal areas are refreshed when cooler air moves ashore. South and east of the Great Lakes, "lake effect" snow falls when cold air sweeps over warmer waters. Spring and summer thunderstorms build where three types of air mass converge: cold and dry from the north, warm and dry from the southwest, and warm and moist from the Gulf of Mexico.

10,000 years—is leading to warmer ocean temperatures, higher sea levels, increased humidity, and shrinking snow pack and ice at the Poles. These climate changes could influence the weather worldwide.

GLOSSARY

Milankovitch theory: Named for Milutin Milankovitch, Serbian geophysicist. Theory relating historic global cooling patterns to cyclical changes in the Earth's tilt and orbit around the sun. **/ Microclimate:** Weather patterns affected by local features such as lakes or mountains.

WLADIMIR KÖPPEN / CLIMATE SCIENTIST

Born to a distinguished academic family in imperial Russia, Wladimir Köppen (1846-1940) noticed during trips to his family's coastal estate on the Black Sea how the plant life changed as he traversed plains, mountains, and the seaside landscape. His study of how flora was related to climate led him in 1884 to produce a map of global temperature bands ranging from the Poles to the Equator. Sixteen years later he refined that map into a mathematical formula, which defined five major climate types based on temperature and rainfall—ranging from the intense humidity of the tropics to the cold, dry polar caps. The system, still in use today, corresponds roughly to the classification system of biomes that describes the world's regions based on plant and animal life.

FAST FACT The temperature in the Arctic permafrost zone has risen by about 5.5°F since 1980.

FOR MORE FACTS ON...

THE DEFINITION OF GREENHOUSE GASES see *Threatened Planet: Air,* **CHAPTER 3, PAGE 125**
+
THE IMPACT OF HUMAN SOCIETY ON EARTH see *Human Impact,* **CHAPTER 5, PAGES 214-5**

Costa Rican rain forest

BIOMES

MAJOR BIOMES

TEMPERATE FOREST

RAIN FOREST

BOREAL FOREST

MEDITERRANEAN FOREST

MANGROVE

GRASSLAND & SAVANNA

DESERT & DRY SHRUBLAND

TUNDRA & ICE CAP

MARINE

FRESHWATER

L ife on Earth exists within a complex bubble called the biosphere, the only one so far known in the universe. Extending from the floor of the ocean to about six miles above sea level, the biosphere depends on the interaction of several large systems to process energy from the sun: the atmosphere (which provides oxygen), the hydrosphere (water in the ground and in the oceans), and the lithosphere (the land itself).

Several classification systems have been devised to organize Earth's life-forms. Most take into account temperature, climate, and neighboring life-forms within a region. The basic unit is called a biome, a geographic concept that can refer to areas on different continents that still share similar climates, terrains, and living things. Biomes are typically grouped according to dominant types of trees and grasses.

Although agriculture, urban development, and human population growth have altered the distribution of plant and animal species, biome classifications are based on the living things that would naturally exist in an area without human intervention. The

FOR MORE FACTS ON...

THE HISTORY AND PROCESS OF CLASSIFYING LIVING ORGANISMS see *Life-forms,* **CHAPTER 4, PAGES 132-3**

THE DIVERSITY OF LIVING THINGS ON EARTH see *Biodiversity,* **CHAPTER 4, PAGES 174-9**

presence of specific plants or animals is not as important as the forms of life involved: The rain forests of Africa and South America, for example, all contain vines and monkeys, though the individual species vary widely.

All Earth's biomes sum up into the biosphere—a dynamic, complex network that supports a wide variety of life, from minuscule bacteria to 80-foot blue whales, and the only one so far known in the universe.

G L O S S A R Y

Biome: The largest geographic biotic unit, a major community of plants and animals with similar life-forms and environmental conditions. It includes various communities and is named for the dominant type of vegetation.

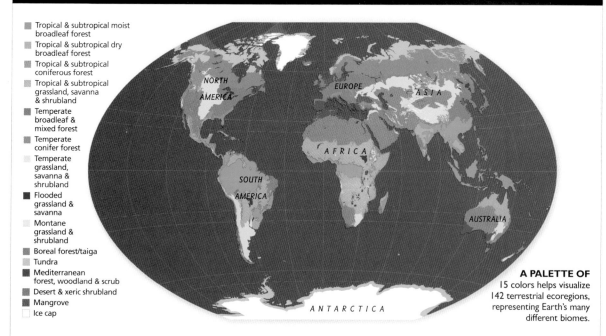

- Tropical & subtropical moist broadleaf forest
- Tropical & subtropical dry broadleaf forest
- Tropical & subtropical coniferous forest
- Tropical & subtropical grassland, savanna & shrubland
- Temperate broadleaf & mixed forest
- Temperate conifer forest
- Temperate grassland, savanna & shrubland
- Flooded grassland & savanna
- Montane grassland & shrubland
- Boreal forest/taiga
- Tundra
- Mediterranean forest, woodland & scrub
- Desert & xeric shrubland
- Mangrove
- Ice cap

A PALETTE OF 15 colors helps visualize 142 terrestrial ecoregions, representing Earth's many different biomes.

EARTH'S MANY ECOREGIONS

Political boundaries make one set of divisions in the world, nature another—and conservationists suggest we ignore politics to protect biodiversity.

Among the various classification systems in use, there are some broadly accepted categories. The U.S. Forest Service divides the planet into four basic types of land biome: forest, grassland, desert, and tundra. More specific classifications separate the tropical rain forests of South America from the temperate pine stands of the American South. Some biomes are limited in scale and unique in the life they support: Mangrove swamps, for instance, earn a classification all to themselves. Others cover vast areas of the planet but support comparatively little life—the sprawling deserts of North Africa and Asia, for example. These classifications are still subject to debate and reinterpretation.

CLICK IT: Ecoregions Map www.nationalgeographic.com/wildworld

FAST FACT Most life on Earth exists between about 650 feet below sea level and about 3.5 miles above it.

FOR MORE FACTS ON...

METHODS OF MAPPING EARTH'S PHENOMENA see *Geography,* **CHAPTER 1, PAGES 16-7, &** *The World in Maps,* **CHAPTER 1, PAGES 18-9**

SPECIFIC BIOMES see *Forests, Mangroves, Grassland & Savanna, Desert & Dry Shrubland, Tundra & Ice Cap, Aquatic Biomes,* **CHAPTER 5, PAGES 196-213**

Elm trees, California

FORESTS

LARGEST AREA OF FOREST

RUSSIA
2,957,203 square miles

CANADA
1,907,345 square miles

BRAZIL
1,884,179 square miles

UNITED STATES
1,142,824 square miles

DEMOCRATIC REPUBLIC OF CONGO
671,046 square miles

AUSTRALIA
559,848 square miles

CHINA
503,848 square miles

he world's temperate forests are characterized by a variety of deciduous trees—oak, hickory, beech, elm, willow, and others—that thrive during the mild growing season and survive the seasonal changes common across North America, central Asia, and western and central Europe. Temperatures in these areas can go below freezing during the winter months and top 90°F in the summer. The spring and summer provide a growing season as long as 200 days, with perhaps six frost-free months, during which species must store energy for the colder periods.

Depending on temperature and rainfall patterns, a temperate forest biome can also include evergreen trees, such as the coniferous pines found throughout the U.S. It also includes the temperate rain forests of the Pacific Northwest, which have the steady rainfall of tropical forests but cooler temperatures (though typically above freezing).

The canopy in temperate forests can be dense, but some vegetation grows at ground level. Animal life includes small ground-dwelling

FOR MORE FACTS ON...

THE BIOLOGY OF SHRUBS & TREES see *Shrubs,* **CHAPTER 4, PAGES 140-1,** & *Trees,* **CHAPTER 4, PAGES 142-3**
+
THE DEFINITION OF DECIDUOUS see *Plants: Shrubs,* **CHAPTER 4, PAGE 141**

mammals such as rabbits and skunks, large populations of deer, and predators such as bobcats, wolves, and foxes. Temperate forest animals adapt to winter with thick hair for warmth, foraging or food storage habits, and hibernation.

Leaves falling from deciduous trees enrich the soil, which has made the world's temperate forest regions valuable for agriculture. Timber from oak, elm, and other forest trees has long been used in construction. Beginning about 8,000 years ago, temper-

ate forests in Europe and China were harvested for use in ships and buildings. The hardwood forests in North America were largely exhausted by the end of the 19th century, meaning that the world contains less forest land now than in ages past.

ASPEN TREES in Colorado grow tall and straight. Their leafy canopy prevents significant forest undergrowth.

BLACK BEARS inhabit North American forests from Alaska to northern Mexico. They hibernate through cold winters.

WILD SUNFLOWERS sprout in the aftermath of a fire in California, a first step toward the forest's rebirth.

G L O S S A R Y

Deciduous: From the Latin *decidere*, to fall off. Tree species whose life cycles include the annual shedding of leaves. **/ Mycorhizae:** From Greek *mykes*, "fungus," + *rhiza*, "root." Fungi that help trees absorb nutrients more efficiently. **/ Vegetation profile:** Collection of smaller plants and shrubs in a forest that compete for resources beneath the trees.

WHEN DID AUTUMN COLORS EVOLVE?

Autumn leaves came into being at the start of the Cenozoic era, about 65 million years ago. After that, only equatorial areas faced the sun in a way to guarantee consistently high temperatures and steady rainfall. During much of the year elsewhere, there was not enough sunlight to support photosynthesis, and frost proved damaging to leaves. Deciduous species developed as a result, discarding thin leaves at the growing season's end.

MAPLE LEAVES, like these on a vine maple in Washington's Olympic State Park, display vibrant autumn reds.

CLICK IT: World's Biomes www.ucmp.berkeley.edu/exhibits/biomes

FAST FACT Kauri trees, on New Zealand's North Island, can live 2,000 years and reach between 145 and 180 feet tall.

FOR MORE FACTS ON...

WHY LEAVES CHANGE COLOR see *Plants: Trees,* **CHAPTER 4, PAGE 143**
+
ASIA, EUROPE & NORTH AMERICA in *Asia, Europe & North America,* **CHAPTER 9, PAGES 378-407, 414-23**

RAIN FORESTS

Tropical and subtropical rain forests present examples of how a hot, steady climate promotes remarkable diversity in plant growth.

Near the Earth's Equator, trade winds from different directions collide and create a zone of rising air that draws water up from the ground. Steady sunlight aids the process through evaporation and keeps temperatures high.

The result is little seasonal variation in temperature and nearly daily thunderstorms and rainfall. This climate gives rise to the tropical and subtropical forests, home of the world's most diverse collection of species.

The belt near the Equator itself includes the rain forests of South America, central Africa, and Asia—evergreen areas where broad-leaved,

straight-trunked trees dominate the landscape. Under such favorable conditions, trees grow so tall and lush that they create an aboveground canopy, which, because it blocks sunlight, limits ground vegetation. Animals thrive in this canopy, however. Arboreal animals such as monkeys are typical, and insects proliferate; insect-borne diseases like malaria and yellow fever are a constant threat.

Despite being under intense logging and development pressure, the rain forest zone remains the heart of world biodiversity, home to several million species including a hundred or

BUTTRESSED ROOTS of a tropical ceiba support a huge singular column and a canopy of leaves in the Guyana rain forest. Tallest trees of the Amazon, ceibas can reach a height of nearly 200 feet. The Maya believed a ceiba stood at Earth's center, making a connection to the spirit world above.

FOR MORE FACTS ON...

THE DEFINITION OF THE TROPICS see *Dividing Lines: Equator & Tropics*, **CHAPTER 1, PAGES 36-7**

THE DIVERSITY OF LIVING THINGS ON EARTH see *Biodiversity*, **CHAPTER 4, PAGES 174-5**

more different types of tree per square mile. Other typical vegetation includes orchids, vines, ferns, and mosses. Rain forests serve as the Earth's lungs, absorbing massive amounts of carbon dioxide and giving off oxygen.

By some definitions, the tropical/subtropical biome extends about 23° north and south of the Equator, a band wide enough to contain other types of forest. Trees are still the main life-form in those forests as well, with varieties depending on the pattern of precipitation. In the monsoon regions of Asia, western Africa, and South America, for example, where dry seasons alternate with heavy periods of rain, deciduous species predominate.

THE WHITE-FACED MONKEY occupies elevated tree branches in Costa Rica's Corcovado National Park, a haven for ecotourism.

BRILLIANT MASDEVALLIA ORCHIDS thrive in Colombia's humid cloud forest. Many orchids are epiphytic: parasites on trees.

A GREEN PARROT SNAKE slithers from the ground to low limbs in Costa Rican rain forests facing both the Caribbean and the Pacific.

G L O S S A R Y

Intertropical convergence zone: Area where the trade winds come together from different directions. **/ Stranglers:** Parasitic rain forest vines that can envelop an entire tree.

JUNGLE OR RAIN FOREST?

Jungles are often considered synonymous with rain forests, but in fact, jungles are areas within rain forests. Typically, the towering forest canopy that develops in a rain forest shields the ground from sunlight and limits the growth of lower-level vegetation. If a forest fire or other disruption creates a clearing, shrubs, grasses, and other pioneer species grow in such thick profusion that they become dense and impassable: a jungle.

RAIN FOREST UNDERSTORY GROWTH can be dense and viney, as in this section of the Mindo cloud forest on the west slope of the Andes Mountains in Ecuador.

CLICK IT: World Rain Forest Information www.rainforestweb.org

FAST FACT Rain forests consume about five times as much carbon dioxide per unit of area as temperate forests.

FOR MORE FACTS ON...

REPTILES & AMPHIBIANS OF THE RAIN FOREST see Reptiles, **CHAPTER 4, PAGES 160-1, &** Amphibians, **CHAPTER 4, PAGES 162-3**

PLANTS & ANIMALS THAT LIVE IN MANGROVE SWAMPS see Mangroves, **CHAPTER 5, PAGES 204-5**

BOREAL FORESTS

Encircling the northern part of the planet and covering about 17 percent of its surface, the northern boreal forests constitute the largest land-based biome. They stretch across Canada, Scandinavia, and Russia in a wide swath whose year-round residents have adapted to intense cold.

Moving poleward, forest cover becomes more sparse at this biome's northern extreme, gradually becom-ing an open expanse of tundra and then the polar region itself.

The climate of the boreal forest is subarctic, with a growing season of perhaps 130 days. Summers are short, but summer days see extended sun-light of up to nearly 24 hours at the summer solstice. Rainfall amounts to only two to three inches per month. Most of the annual precipitation comes as snow, from 15 to 40 inches annually. That precipitation level sup-ports a sometimes thick tree covering but only a limited number of species, making the boreal forest one of the least diverse biomes. Trees commonly found here are the evergreen conifers, such as pine, fir, and spruce, but they may be stunted by low precipitation.

Other plant and animal life is lim-ited in diversity, and the harsh climate has forced adaptations that include coloring changes during the year to migratory patterns forced by the onset

SPRUCE TREES stand tall amid the shrubbery bursting forth during the short span of a growing season in Alaska's Denali National Park. Warm weather coaxes grass to green up, trees to pollinate, and flowers to bloom despite nearby peaks, snow-covered year-round, on Mount McKinley.

FOR MORE FACTS ON...

THE CATEGORIES & CHARACTERISTICS OF SHRUBS & TREES see *Shrubs,* **CHAPTER 4, PAGES 140-1,** & *Trees,* **CHAPTER 4, PAGES 142-3**

+

THE DEFINITION OF EVERGREEN see *Plants: Shrubs,* **CHAPTER 4, PAGE 141**

of winter. The snowshoe hare, for example, changes color from summer to winter, going from gray or brown in the warm months to a pure white that lets it blend with the snow. The lynx has large feet with fur between its toes to help it walk more easily on the snow.

Moose are the largest mammals in the biome. Caribou here migrate the farthest distances of any North American mammal, moving in herds as large as 500,000 animals. The caribou and reindeer travel far north into the tundra regions in summer and then travel south as necessary in winter to find food.

This biome is also the summer home of flocks of migratory birds who feast on the swarms of insects that hatch in the boreal region in the warm months.

THE SNOWSHOE HARE'S coat changes color with the seasons: dirt brown in summer, snow white in winter for effective camouflage.

GRAY JAY, also known as Canada jay, lives in spruce and pine forests of North America, from Alaska to Newfoundland.

EVERGREEN TREES of the boreal forest grow in a characteristic shape, their branches making a peak that sheds snow efficiently.

G L O S S A R Y

Taiga: From the Russian, "little sticks." An alternative name for the boreal forest biome. **/ Spodosol:** Nutrient-poor, acidic soil present throughout the world's massive boreal forests. **/ Biomass:** The dry weight of organic matter.

BOREAL MOSSES

Plant life in the boreal forest is limited by cold, lack of precipitation, and the thick covering of evergreen trees—conditions just right for moss. A moss carpet covers as much as one-third of the boreal forest floor.

Mosses cling to trunks, rocks, and crags, from which they draw the tiny bit of moisture they need. Large wetlands in some boreal areas are formed by successive generations of moss, with one living layer growing on top of many dead and decaying ones.

LONGHOUSE RUINS, blanketed in a velvety green layer of moss, slowly return to nature in a former First Nations homesite on one of British Columbia's Queen Charlotte Islands.

CLICK IT: Taiga Rescue Network www.taigarescue.org

FAST FACT About two-thirds of the world's boreal forest is located in Siberia, in northern Russia.

FOR MORE FACTS ON...

MIGRATORY HABITS OF BOREAL FOREST DWELLERS see *Migration,* **CHAPTER 4, PAGES 172-3**

+

PLANTS & ANIMALS THAT INHABIT THE TUNDRA & ICE CAP BIOME see *Tundra & Ice Cap,* **CHAPTER 5, PAGES 210-1**

MEDITERRANEAN

Along a pair of bands between 30° and 40° north and south of the Equator lies what might be considered a niche biome, the Mediterranean shrublands and forests. Besides being limited by latitude, examples of this biome are found only on the west coast of continents and include parts of California, Chile, South Africa, and Australia. They also include the Mediterranean itself, where the sea's oceanlike effects maintain the climate eastward to Greece and the coastal areas of the Middle East.

This biome is characterized by hot, dry summers and mild, cool winters. Rain falls primarily in the winter months, when precipitation can total as much as 35 inches annually. The climate is largely governed by proximity to the ocean. In the summers, high-pressure "anticyclones" build over the sea and usher in months of clear skies and high temperatures. Low-pressure fronts and precipitation return in the winter, but temperatures are moderated by this biome's coastline position and distance from the polar air masses that concentrate over inland areas.

Mediterranean zones are island-like in their development, with unique sets of plants and trees that have adapted both to the climate and to repeated fires.

Around the Mediterranean itself, the shrubs are typically evergreen,

A LONE CYPRESS TREE braves wind, waves, and salt on a promontory near Pebble Beach, California, in one of the regions found in the band of biomes identified as Mediterranean forest and characterized by dry summers and cool winters. Here heat and precipitation are tempered by the sea.

FOR MORE FACTS ON...

TREES & THEIR DEFINING CHARACTERISTICS see *Plants: Trees,* **CHAPTER 4, PAGES 142-3**

COUNTRIES EDGING THE MEDITERRANEAN SEA see *Africa, Asia & Europe,* **CHAPTER 9, PAGES 360-407**

with hard, leathery leaves. Many have proved useful to human enterprise: aromatic spices such as sage, thyme, and rosemary. Mediterranean trees include pine, cedar, and olive. Important in ancient seafaring civilizations, all these species have been harvested for many centuries, so they are much less widespread than they once were.

Repeated fires have kept the Mediterranean zone of southern California dominated by shrubs as well, particularly sage and scrub oak. Plants like chamise and yucca have particularly adapted to survive fire, as has the closed-cone pine, whose seeds are protected in a resin coating that melts under heat to release them.

The climate in this biome is ideal for human habitation, so development is quickly encroaching on wild areas.

YUCCA PLANTS, with their thick, leathery leaves and deep taproot, survive frequent fires in California's Mediterranean forest zone.

WILD CATS—pumas or mountain lions—inhabit North and South American chaparral. An endangered lynx lives in Spain's shrublands.

THE DISTINCTIVE SILHOUETTES of ancient monkey puzzle trees, now endangered, rise above a stand of southern beech in Chile.

G L O S S A R Y

Niche biome: An area with distinctive climate and vegetation but more limited geographically than a typical biome. **/ Convergent evolution:** Development of similar traits in plants or animals that evolve independently, such as in different Mediterranean zones.

LOCAL NAMES, GLOBAL BIOME

Since the Mediterranean zones are narrowly defined coastal regions, these slices of habitat represent perhaps the most localized of all the biomes, which means that many local names have arisen for these scrublands.

Maquis is the name for these areas in Europe, a term referring broadly to areas of evergreen shrubs with a few scattered olive or fig trees.

Chaparral in California is named after its local scrub oak—known as *chapa* in Spanish.

In Chile, the word matorral refers to a strip of land set between the narrow country's mountains and its coastline. The word comes from the Spanish *mat,* for "shrub."

Fynbos in South Africa—which is Afrikaans for "fine bush"—describes the basic shrubby nature of the Mediterranean biome with extensive diversity in the form of dozens of endemic plant species.

No matter what the local name, the biome shows similar features around the globe: hot, dry summers; cool, rainy winters; a climate tempered by the sea; and wildlife, particularly plants, accustomed to the salt air.

CLICK IT: Forest Conservation Programme www.panda.org/about_wwf/what_we_do/forests/

FAST FACT Thanks to fire-suppression measures taken on California's Catalina and Santa Cruz Islands, shrubland is now developing into an "elfin" forest of small oaks.

FOR MORE FACTS ON...

SHRUBS & THEIR DEFINING CHARACTERISTICS see *Plants: Shrubs,* **CHAPTER 4, PAGES 140-1**
+
THE YUCCA PLANT & THE YUCCA MOTH see *Insects: Butterflies & Moths,* **CHAPTER 4, PAGE 153**

204

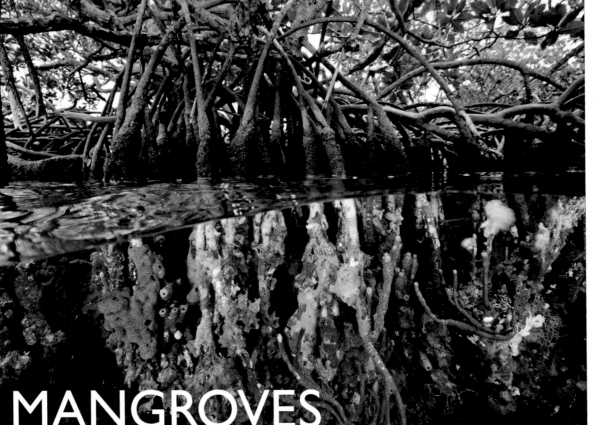

MANGROVES

ECOLOGICAL ADVANTAGES

SUSTAIN NUMEROUS SPECIES
such as protozoans, worms, barnacles,
oysters, and other invertebrates

PROVIDE NURSERY GROUNDS
for shrimp and fish

PROVIDE FEEDING GROUNDS
for birds and crocodiles

DELIVER ORGANIC MATTER
along food chain

PREVENT SHORELINE EROSION

SHIELD INLAND AREAS
from hurricane damage

CUSHION IMPACT
of tidal waves

order areas, where land gives way to water, are ecologically important, taking on many forms throughout the world. Estuaries like the Chesapeake Bay provide habitat for aquatic plants and animals. The massive bogs of the northern countries and the swamps of the tropical regions provide a sink for pollutants and a buffer against flooding and shoreline erosion.

One boundary area type is so unusual that it is often considered a biome unto itself: the mangrove swamp. Mangrove swamps exist at the border between fresh- and saltwater areas and are common in tropical and subtropical coastal areas, particularly along the Indian Ocean and Pacific coast of southern Asia, the Pacific coast of Mexico, and throughout the Caribbean.

There are dozens of species of mangrove tree. All exist in a unique relationship with the saturated earth in which they root. Mangroves grow in intertidal areas, land that is flooded as the tide moves in and muddy and soggy otherwise—conditions that would suffocate the root systems of most trees. To compensate, mangroves have developed an aboveground root system: a tangled, crisscrossing network that makes

FOR MORE FACTS ON...

THE DEFINITION OF THE TROPICS see *Dividing Lines: Equator & Tropics,* **CHAPTER 1, PAGES 36-7**

WHY THE TIDES OCCUR IN EARTH'S OCEANS see *Water: Oceans,* **CHAPTER 3, PAGES 112-5**

passage through these swamps virtually impossible for large animals.

Mangrove swamps are relatively rich and diverse in other life-forms. Algae and seaweeds grow from tree trunks and roots. Decaying mangrove leaves add nutrients to the mud, supporting plant life that, in turn, feeds a variety of crabs, shrimp, clams, snails, and other aquatic animals. The dense root system and foliage also provides food and protective cover for a variety of birds—herons, egrets, ibises, and less well-known species like the mangrove cuckoo.

AN ENDANGERED SPECIES, the proboscis monkey inhabits mangrove marshland along the Menanggul River in Sabah on Borneo.

MANGROVE SPECIES range from low shrubs to trees 200 feet high. There are 70 mangrove species in all.

ROSEATE SPOONBILL, native to the Americas, uses its beak to scoop up underwater prey while it stalks through the marshes.

GLOSSARY

Mangal: Name used by some researchers for mangrove swamps and other forested wetlands. **/ Halophytic:** From Greek *hals,* "salt" or "sea" + *phyton,* "plant." Vegetation that can live in a high-salt environment.

WHICH CREATURES TAKE TO THE MUD?

Mudskippers and mud lobsters are animals uniquely adapted to mangrove swamps. Mudskippers are fish that have developed the ability to propel themselves across the exposed mud at low tide, virtually walking along the ground in search of food. Mud lobsters burrow underground, creating cave systems beneath the mangrove trees and pushing deep, nutrient-rich mud to the surface.

TWO MUDSKIPPERS, propped up alertly, navigate the muddy environs of a Malaysian mangrove swamp. Mudskippers are amphibious fish, able to live on land and in water.

FAST FACT A single acre of red mangrove sheds about three tons of leaves a year.

FOR MORE FACTS ON...

WATER-DWELLING ANIMALS SUCH AS MOLLUSKS & FISH see *Mollusks,* **CHAPTER 4, PAGES 156-7, &** *Fish,* **CHAPTER 4, PAGES 158-9**
+
EVOLUTIONARY SUCCESSES & FAILURES see *Biodiversity,* **CHAPTER 4, PAGES 174-9**

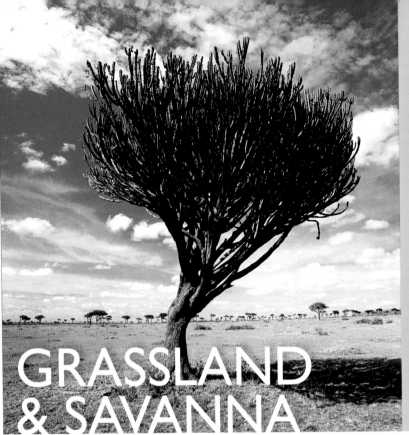

Candalabrum tree, Masai Mara National Reserve, Kenya

SAVANNA
Central Africa

VELD
South Africa

PUSZTA
Hungary

PLAINS
North America

PRAIRIE
north america

PAMPAS
South America

STEPPES
Russia

BUSH
Australia

GRASSLAND & SAVANNA

uring the Cenozoic era, some 65.5 million years ago, as temperatures fell in advance of the first Ice Age, rainfall became sparse across areas removed from both the Equator and the wetter, temperate coastal areas. Weather became more varied, with rainfall concentrated in a few months of the year, followed by a dry season. Ancient forests gave way to vast expanses covered primarily with grasses and shrubs— the areas known today as grasslands and savannas.

Grasslands and savannas are usually considered to represent one and the same biome, even though there are slight differences between them.

While rainfall can total as much as 35 to 50 inches annually in some of these generally dry regions, rain in grasslands or savannas falls inconsistently or only during a few months, which is why no forests can develop in these ecoregions. Savannas contain a few scattered trees, whereas grasslands are virtually treeless. Grassland areas see less annual rainfall, and temperature swings are more severe—from -40°F in the winter to over 100°F in the summer.

Savannas cover about half of Africa, and they represent large portions of South America, Australia, and India as well. Grasslands make up the prairies and plains of North America, the South African veld, the pampas of South America, the plains of Hungary, and the steppes of northern Asia.

In these regions, grasses provide an abundant food source for small and large mammals. Often only one or two grass species dominate in a given region.

Grassland and savanna biomes give rise to diverse animal life, such as that found in the African Serengeti. There, the arrival—or delay—of the seasonal rains directly affects the survival of newborn antelope and other animals. This, in turn, affects the food supply of larger predators like lions and leopards.

FOR MORE FACTS ON...

THE CENOZOIC ERA & OTHER SPANS OF GEOLOGIC TIME ON EARTH *see Ages of the Earth,* **CHAPTER 3, PAGES 94-5**

THE COMPONENTS OF SOIL *see Soil,* **CHAPTER 3, PAGES 96-7**

Soil quality is another feature that can be used to distinguish grasslands from savannas. Savannas typically have quick-draining, less fertile soil; grasslands have soil that holds nutrients from successive generations of decomposing roots. As a result, grassland areas have become important agricultural regions. Many have been converted for farming or grazing, meaning a net loss of these habitats around the world.

FEMALE PRONGHORNS graze watchfully, silhouetted against the Oregon sky.

DATE PALM TREES can bear edible fruit where other species would suffer from drought.

TINY BUILDERS of massive nests, termites ingest the cellulose of trees and lumber.

G L O S S A R Y

Climatic savanna: Savanna areas resulting from climatic conditions. **/ Edaphic savanna:** Savanna areas resulting from soil conditions and not entirely maintained by fire. **/ Derived savanna:** Savanna areas developing after humans have cleared and burned for planting, then departed.

WHAT ROLE DO WILDFIRES PLAY IN THE SAVANNA?

In the savanna, seasonal wildfires inhibit tree growth yet increase biodiversity. Fires break out during the dry season, sparked by lightning or, increasingly, by hunters or farmers clearing brush. They prevent trees from overtaking grasses as the dominant type of vegetation. Grasses and shrubs, which regenerate from underground roots, surge back when the rains return. Meanwhile the fire leaves behind dead and homeless insects, a banquet for the birds, and hiding places for small animals.

A RED-HOT BOUNDARY traces the progress of a fire in the Australian savanna. With alternating rainy and dry seasons, plants and animals of the savanna biome depend on fire.

CLICK IT: Savanna www.blueplanetbiomes.org/savanna.htm

FAST FACT African elephant herds have changed forest to grassland by stripping trees and smashing their trunks.

FOR MORE FACTS ON...

THE CLASSIFICATION & BIOLOGY OF INSECTS see Insects, **CHAPTER 4, PAGES 150-3**
+
WEATHER & TOPOGRAPHY see Weather, **CHAPTER 4, PAGES 182-3**

The sands of the Sahara, Niger

DESERT & DRY SHRUBLAND

LARGEST DESERTS

SAHARA / AFRICA
3.5 million square miles

ARABIAN / AFRICA
1 million square miles

GOBI / ASIA
500,000 square miles

PATAGONIAN / S. AMERICA
260,000 square miles

GREAT VICTORIA / AUSTRALIA
250,000 square miles

KALAHARI / AFRICA
220,000 square miles

GREAT BASIN / N. AMERICA
190,000 square miles

eserts cover about one-fifth of the Earth's surface. A single characteristic defines them: lack of rain. The dividing line is debatable. Some climatologists put it at about ten inches a year or less; others more than twice that. The amount of precipitation is so low and the temperatures so extreme that plants and animals struggle to survive. Special adaptation to heat and the lack of water are required.

The desert biome is subdivided into categories, depending on annual precipitation levels.

Hot and dry (or xeric) deserts, the largest category, include vast seas of sand like the Sahara in North Africa and the Mojave in the western United States, where precipitation is the least of all, typically concentrated in a few short bursts throughout the year. Areas of Chile and parts of the Sahara might receive as little as an inch of rainfall a year, sometimes none at all, while deserts in the western U.S. might receive ten or so inches. The climate is so dry and the air so warm that most precipitation evaporates before it hits ground. Evaporation rates

FOR MORE FACTS ON...

THE WATER CYCLE ON PLANET EARTH see *Water,* **CHAPTER 3, PAGE 111**
+
CURRENT WATER CRISES AROUND THE WORLD see *Threatened Planet: Water,* **CHAPTER 3, PAGES 126-7**

can sometimes exceed annual rainfall, forcing plants to adapt and rely more on conservation and atmospheric condensation than on precipitation.

The cloudless dry air contributes to wide daily temperature swings as well. Desert areas receive about twice as much solar radiation as more humid parts of the planet, and they lose about twice as much heat at night. Temperatures can range from 120°F to well below freezing.

Semiarid deserts and coastal deserts have slightly more rainfall and more moderate temperatures, but dryness still limits plant and animal life. Trees are sparse in any desert biome, but plants such as cactus have developed survival mechanisms in the form of narrow spiky leaves that help shade the plant and limit the loss of moisture through respiration. Plants like yucca, agave, and prickly pear exchange carbon dioxide and oxygen only during the night, when temperatures are cooler, an adaptation that also limits water loss.

GLOSSARY

Cold desert: Parts of Greenland and North America where annual precipitation levels resemble those of a desert. **/ Gibber:** Rock- and pebble-strewn, arid or semiarid regions in Australia, usually made of a hardened crust of soil cemented by silica resulting from mechanical, not chemical, weathering. **/ Wadi:** A streambed or riverbed that remains dry except during the season of heavy rains, when it carries water.

WHAT ARE HADLEY CELLS?

The lack of desert rain results partly from a pattern of air circulation described by George Hadley in 1735. In an effort to explain the direction of the trade winds, Hadley conjectured that air around the Equator will constantly rise and move toward the Poles as it warms, and then it will move back toward the Equator as it cools and falls, creating areas, cells, where air temperature and pressure are quite constant.

Hadley's theory does not work on a global scale, but Hadley cells do help explain atmospheric patterns around the Equator. Many of the world's deserts lie at the outer edge of these cells, beneath areas of dry air that have disgorged their moisture over tropical and subtropical forests.

CLICK IT: The Living Desert Zoo www.livingdesert.org

COLLARED PECCARY—whose tusks inspired its common name, javelina, Spanish for "spear"—eats cactus leaves and fruit.

GILA MONSTERS of the American Southwest and beaded lizards of the Mexican deserts are the world's only venomous lizards.

NIGHT HUNTING suits the wolf spider, resident of deserts in the Americas and Australia. During daytime heat, it remains in its burrow.

FAST FACT In the desert area of Cochones, Chile, it did not rain from 1919 to 1965.

FOR MORE FACTS ON...

WINDS ON EARTH & THE MANY EFFECTS THEY HAVE see Wind, CHAPTER 3, PAGES 106-7
+
REPTILES INCLUDING LIZARDS see Reptiles, CHAPTER 4, PAGES 160-1

WORLD TUNDRAS

ARCTIC TUNDRAS

North America / Northern Alaska, Canada, Greenland

Europe / Scandinavia

Asia / Siberia

ALPINE TUNDRAS

North America / Alaska, Canada, U.S., Mexico

Europe / Finland, Norway, Russia, Sweden

Asia / Himalaya, Japan

Africa / Mount Kilimanjaro

South America / Andes Mountains

TUNDRA & ICE CAP

At the extreme north and south regions of the planet, the trees of the boreal forest give way to tundra. Frigid and harsh, the tundra is among the least diverse of the Earth's biomes. It is characterized by sturdy mosses, lichens, and low-growing flowers and grasses that can survive through a short growing season, the perpetual night of the polar winter, and temperatures that average -30°F in the coldest months.

Tundra sweeps across the Arctic, from Alaska, through Canada, around the coast of Greenland, and covering the northern coast of Russia. Tundra also forms the coast of the frozen continent of Antarctica.

The tundra climate is dominated by large Arctic and Antarctic air masses. With the lack of any opposing frontal systems to draw moisture into the atmosphere, precipitation is limited to perhaps ten inches annually—conditions that prompt some climatologists to classify tundras as "cold desert."

Arctic tundra forms perhaps 10 percent of the Earth's surface, and includes a layer of permanently frozen soil called permafrost.

But that does not mean the biome is devoid of animal life by any means. Along with the ground cover of vegetation, the tundra is home to birds and mammals that have adapted to the severe climate.

Polar bears, the arctic fox, the arctic hare, and other species inhabit these frigid regions. Tiny lemmings eat grass and sedges in growing seasons and feed on roots during the winter. They burrow into the ground, store food seasonally, and fertilize the soil with their manure.

Caribou and reindeer migrate in massive herds through the world's tundra areas, as do flocks of birds that feed off of the area's summertime profusion of insects. Other tundra birds include raptors such as the snowy owl and the gyrfalcon.

FOR MORE FACTS ON...

THE DISTRIBUTION OF ICE THROUGHOUT PLANET EARTH see *Water: Ice,* **CHAPTER 3, PAGES 120-1**

THE BOREAL FOREST BIOME see *Boreal Forests,* **CHAPTER 5, PAGES 200-1**

WHAT IS PERMAFROST?

Permafrost, despite its name, is not always frozen. Soil composition, the presence of salt, and other factors can keep some of the ground from actually freezing, even as the temperature remains below the freezing point.

Across much of Alaska, Canada, Russia, and Antarctica, the ground is in fact frozen year-round, however, to depths of as much as 5,000 feet. A relatively thin active layer near the top may be subject to a yearly freeze-thaw cycle, allowing ground vegetation to survive.

As the planet warms, the effect of a meltdown in permafrost areas is a subject of debate. Some have speculated, for example, that a widespread thaw would release massive amounts of greenhouse gases now trapped in the permafrost into the atmosphere, further warming the planet.

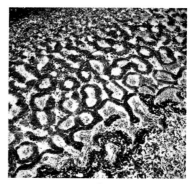

A MOTTLED MOIRÉ of snow and soil, the permafrost of Spitsbergen, Norway, is a terrestrial surface that freezes and thaws in predictable patterns every year.

GLOSSARY

Tundra: From the Finnish *tunturi*, "treeless plain." Treeless level or rolling terrain characterized by bare ground and rock or minimal vegetation: mosses, lichens, herbs, low shrubs. **/ Pingo:** From the Inuit *pingu*. A large mound in the tundra, caused by the cycle of freezing and thawing.

IN THE WAKE of an Arctic polar bear's passage southward, tracks etched in the snow are all that disturb the pristine white surface of the Devon Island ice cap in Canada's Northwest Territories.

ESSENTIAL ICE

Beyond the tundra—on the interior of Greenland and some Canadian lands, as well as throughout Antarctica—life and the food chain largely disappear, giving way to the polar ice caps, where the only living organisms are bacteria found inside the layers of ice.

These lifeless stretches are important to the planet's ecology, however. Water trapped in the massive ice sheets helps maintains sea levels, and large-scale melting could alter human geography by leaving some coastal communities underwater. Officials in some low-lying and storm-prone areas, such as Bangladesh, argue that they are already feeling the impact of such melting.

CLICK IT: Global Warming nationalgeographic.com/science/environment/global-warming/gw-overview.html

FAST FACT About 2 percent of the water on Earth is locked up in snow, ice, and glaciers.

FOR MORE FACTS ON...

THE BIOLOGICAL CLASSIFICATION OF LICHENS see *Fungi & Lichens,* **CHAPTER 4, PAGES 134-5**
+
THE FUTURE OF THE POLAR BEAR see *Biodiversity: Threatened Species,* **CHAPTER 4, PAGES 178-9**

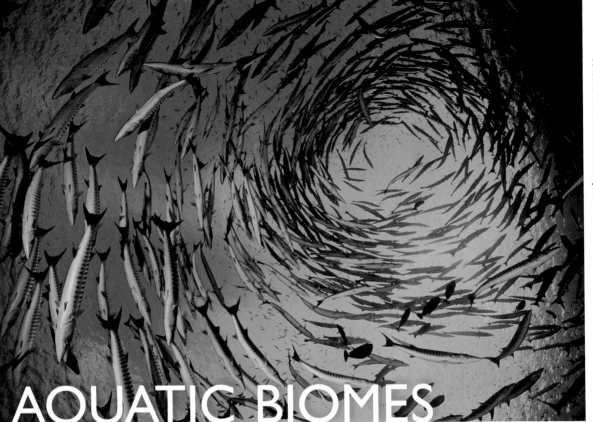

School of barracudas 60 feet deep, Solomon Islands

AQUATIC BIOMES

OCEAN FACTS

PACIFIC
Area: 58,925,815 square miles
Deepest point:
Mariana Trench, 35,994 feet

ATLANTIC
Area: 31,546,630 square miles
Deepest point:
Puerto Rico Trench, 28,232 feet

INDIAN
Area: 26,050,135 square miles
Deepest point:
Java Trench, 23,376 feet

ARCTIC
Area: 3,350,023 square miles
Deepest point:
Molloy Deep, 18,599 feet

he marine biomes include tidal estuaries, coral reefs, and ocean—about three-quarters of the planet in total, a dynamic system that is vital to sustaining the rest of Earth's life-forms. Oceans represent the largest portion of this biome by far and are divided into three zones: pelagic, commonly called the open sea, extending to about 13,000 feet below sea level; benthic, the ocean floor; and abyssal—dark, cold, and highly pressurized—from 13,000 to 20,000 feet below sea level.

Tidal estuaries represent the border area where bodies of salt water and fresh water meet—a mixing zone that supports a variety of aquatic plants and animals, from algae and seaweeds to fish, oysters, crabs, and numerous species of migratory waterfowl.

Coral reefs are distinctive habitats anchored by colonies of coral, marine invertebrate species that number in the thousands.

Freshwater habitats are found worldwide—small ponds, large glacial lakes, streams and rivers fed by snow-melt and rain—and support plants and animals adapted to low salt content.

FOR MORE FACTS ON...

BODIES OF WATER ON EARTH see *Water*, **CHAPTER 3, PAGES 110-21**
+
THE DIVERSITY OF LIFE ON EARTH see *Life-forms*, **CHAPTER 4, PAGES 132-3**, & *Biodiversity*, **CHAPTER 4, PAGES 174-9**

WHICH AQUATIC ECOREGIONS ARE IN DISTRESS?

From polar seas to tropical coral reefs, from desert wadis to mighty rivers, aquatic biomes are amazingly diverse. Numerous freshwater and marine ecosystems have been identified as needing special conservation attention, as indicated on this map.

Freshwater
- ■ Large lake
- ■ Large river
- ■ Large river delta
- ■ Large river headwater
- ■ Small lake
- ■ Small river basin
- ■ Xeric basin

Marine
- ▢ Temperate shelf & sea
- ▢ Coastal temperate upwelling
- ▢ Coastal tropical upwelling
- ▢ Coastal tropical coral
- ▢ Polar

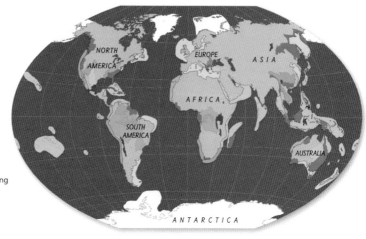

G L O S S A R Y

Euphotic: From the Greek *eu*, "good," + *phos*, "light." A term describing the uppermost zone of ocean water, from the surface down to about 260 feet below, where the sunlight penetrates powerfully enough to support photosynthesis.

COPEPODS, microscopic plankton, are food for ocean animals large and small. They measure up to 0.08 inch long, as shown in this image that compares them with the eye of a needle.

THE OCEAN, EARTH'S LIFEBLOOD

In many ways, the Earth depends on the ocean. Ocean salt water evaporates and fuels the precipitation cycle that provides fresh water for land-dwelling plants and animals. Microscopic phytoplankton are one of the planet's key energy sources: Through photosynthesis, they convert solar radiation into organic matter. Sitting at the base of a food chain that supports virtually all other marine life, they absorb carbon dioxide and produce perhaps as much as half the world's supply of oxygen.

CLICK IT: Marine Biology www.marinebio.org

WHAT IS CHEMOSYNTHESIS?

The abyssal zone forms a large portion of the ocean and might be considered a biome unto itself—a place where plant and animal communities have learned to exist without the source of energy used by the rest of the planet—light from the sun. Ocean-dwelling plankton and plants create organic matter by photosynthesis. But life in the abyss, where no light penetrates, requires a different set of rules. Here, bacteria perform chemosynthesis, converting sulfur into organic matter. The supply of sulfur is plentiful: Hydrothermal vents, formed from volcanic activity and the movement of tectonic plates, pump hydrogen sulfide to the ocean floor. The chemosynthetic bacteria form the basis of an entire deep-sea food chain, a biologic community supported by geothermal power.

FOR MORE FACTS ON...

HOW PHOTOSYNTHESIS WORKS see *Life Begins*, **CHAPTER 4, PAGE 131**
+
BACTERIA & RELATED MICROSCOPIC FORMS OF LIFE see *Bacteria, Protists & Archaea*, **CHAPTER 4, PAGES 148-9**

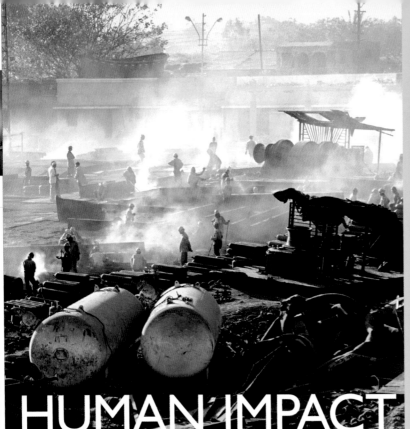

Cutting scrap metal, Alang, India

LARGEST CITIES

TOKYO, JAPAN
36.7 million

DELHI, INDIA
22.2 million

SÃO PAULO, BRAZIL
20.3 million

MUMBAI, INDIA
20 million

MEXICO CITY, MEXICO
19.5 million

NEW YORK-NEWARK, USA
19.4 million

SHANGHAI, CHINA
16.6 million

KOLKATA, INDIA
15.6 million

HUMAN IMPACT

he world's biomes are, in theory, a product of climate and nature, representing the characteristics of an area of the planet if it were simply left to grow without human intervention. But in fact, the biomes as they exist today have been influenced profoundly by the human presence, both in acute ways—through development and urbanization—and in more long-lasting ways—through dynamic changes like global warming.

Human impact is not strictly a modern phenomenon. Areas of the Amazon rain forest once thought to be pristine were in fact considerably altered by ancient communities for farming and fishing. Human settlement in Africa and Southeast Asia involved grazing and the use of fire to clear land, creating the savannas in areas that might otherwise have developed into forest land. The Mediterranean region, now considered shrubland, was once forested with pine, cedar, oak, and other trees prior to their harvest by ancient Greek and Roman civilizations. Expansive deciduous forests once covered Europe and China, now largely felled by humans clearing and harvesting the trees.

The long-term effects of global warming are a matter of debate, but many believe human-influenced climate change could cause an even more profound impact on the world's biomes than the direct change caused by chopping trees, planting food, and building cities. Organizations including the United Nations' Intergovernmental Panel on Climate Change have documented a gradual rise in temperatures in the permafrost areas of the Arctic Circle, a trend that, if continued, would alter the nature of the tundra biome—and beyond. Rising sea levels and changing salinity patterns could affect a niche biome like the coastal mangrove forests, while larger changes in weather patterns could enlarge the world's deserts.

FOR MORE FACTS ON...

THE HUMAN IMPACT ON EARTH AND ITS ENVIRONMENT see "Threatened Planet," **CHAPTER 3, PAGES 122-3**

THE HUMAN IMPACT ON ANIMAL & PLANT SPECIES see "Threatened Species," **CHAPTER 4, PAGES 178-9**

THE HUMAN FOOTPRINT

The rate of loss of biodiversity is one way to quantify human impact on the world's biomes. Maps of biodiversity show zones considered critical and endangered across much of North America and Europe—the heart of the industrialized world. China and India, recently industrialized, face intense population pressures that have drastically increased the amount of land under cultivation.

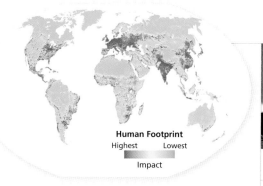

Human Footprint

Highest   Lowest

Impact

SOME REGIONS feel the impact of human civilization more intensely than others, reflecting longevity of habitation and population pressures.

G L O S S A R Y

CLICK IT: Human Footprint www.wcs.org/humanfootprint

Subclimax: Situation in which grazing, farming, or other dynamics prevent expectable climax plant species from taking root and dominating the landscape. **/ Heat islands:** Areas around the world experiencing higher temperature because of urbanization.

WHICH ECOREGIONS FEEL THE GREATEST IMPACT?

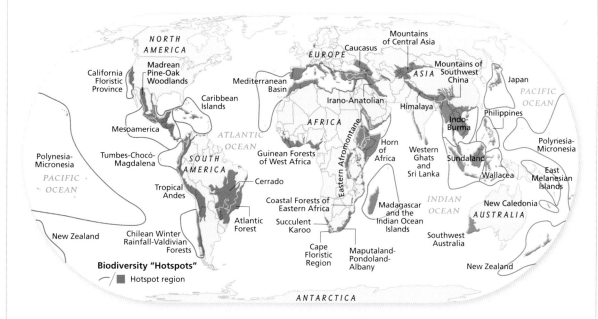

Biodiversity "Hotspots"

Hotspot region

THREATENED ECOREGIONS can be found around the world. Within this century, scientists say, half of all living species may disappear. Conservationists have identified 25 biodiversity "hot spots"—habitats for species found nowhere else in the world that are especially threatened. These hot spots contain the sole remaining habitats for 44 percent of all plant species and 35 percent of all invertebrate species.

FAST FACT China's temperate deciduous forests were cleared as many as 4,000 years ago.

FOR MORE FACTS ON...

THE GROWING HUMAN POPULATION ON EARTH see "World Population," **CHAPTER 6, PAGES 250-1**

URBANIZATION AND ITS EFFECTS ON EARTH see "Cities," **CHAPTER 6, PAGES 260-1**

Human Origins / Migration / The Hu
Gender / Language / Writing / Religio
/ Art / Music / Clothing / Food / A
Population / Transportation / Comme

THE HUMAN

n Family / Ethnicities / Race, Class &
Hinduism & Buddhism / Monotheism
ulture / Modern Agriculture / World
/ World Trade Today / Shelter / Cities

WORLD

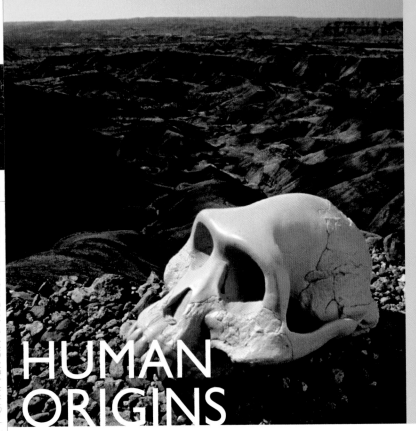

EARLY HOMINIDS

8 TO 6 MILLION YEARS AGO
Last common ancestor of chimpanzees and hominids

8 TO 6 MILLION YEARS AGO
Sahelanthropus tchadensis

5.8 MILLION YEARS AGO
Ardipithecus ramidus

4.2 MILLION YEARS AGO
Australopithecus anamensis

4 MILLION YEARS AGO
Australopithecus afarensis

3.5 MILLION YEARS AGO
Kenyanthropus playtops

3 MILLION YEARS AGO
Australopithecus africanus

HUMAN ORIGINS

oday, only one human species, *Homo sapiens,* exists, but over the course of human prehistory as many as 15 varieties of early human walked the Earth. Though the number of species and their relationships to one another are not settled, it seems clear that the earliest hominids—a term that describes all humans who ever lived—took their first steps in Africa.

They were (and we still are) primates, descended from a group of apes that also gave rise to gorillas and chimpanzees. Around 4 million years ago, something in the environment led the first hominids to leave the trees and walk upright, marking the official transition to human status. These early hominids are often grouped under the name Australopiths (from the term "southern ape") and include the genera *Ardipithecus, Australopithecus,* and *Paranthropus.* About 3.5 to 5 feet tall, they had apelike faces, with sloping foreheads and prominent jaws, but their canine teeth were small compared with an ape's and their hands featured long, flexible thumbs. The most famous fossil member of these early humans is the *Australopithecus afarensis* known fondly as "Lucy," whose partial skeleton was discovered in 1974. Her species, which lived in eastern Africa between 3 and 4 million years ago, is one leading candidate for being a direct ancestor of *Homo sapiens.*

Australopiths died out about 1.2 million years ago. By that time, their descendants, a new kind of hominid, were already roaming Africa: The genus *Homo,* which came into existence roughly 2.3 to 2.5 million years ago, was marked by a distinct increase in brain size. By 1.9 million years ago, these humans had tall skeletons like those of today's *Homo sapiens,* although their

FAST FACT *Homo erectus* built controlled fires as long as 790,000 years ago.

FOR MORE FACTS ON...

THE GEOLOGIC HISTORY OF PLANET EARTH *see Ages of the Earth,* **CHAPTER 3, PAGES 94-5**

EARLY LIFE-FORMS ON PLANET EARTH *see Life Begins,* **CHAPTER 4, PAGES 130-1**

skulls still featured sloping foreheads, prominent brows, and heavy jaws.

These late species of *Homo* also demonstrated another similarity to modern humans: the desire to explore new lands. Starting around 1.8 million years ago, the first great wave of human migration occurred when adventurous members of *Homo erectus* trekked out of Africa and into Europe and Asia. However, these hominids eventually died out and were not the direct ancestors of today's humans. That honor falls to the first members of our own genus, *Homo sapiens*, who appeared in East Africa about 200,000 years ago.

THE DETAILS OF HUMAN EVOLUTION are a subject of continuing study and debate, but the general sequence from an apelike proconsul of 23 to 15 million years ago (far left) through hominid forms to the present-day human posture (far right) is generally accepted by scientists today.

MITOCHONDRIAL EVE AND Y CHROMOSOME ADAM

The study of human DNA has increased our knowledge of human origins and migration. Although virtually all of our DNA is recombined with every generation, two parts of the genome remain mostly unshuffled. The Y chromosome is passed down virtually unchanged from father to son. DNA in the cell's mitochondria, on the other hand, is passed down only from mothers to children. Very rarely, but at a steady rate over time, a harmless mutation will occur in the DNA. This genetic marker will be carried through subsequent generations. Geneticists have traced the markers to the original pair of *Homo sapiens* ancestors, "Mitochondrial Eve" and "Y chromosome Adam," two Africans who lived about 60,000 and 150,000 years ago, respectively.

CLICK IT: Leakey Foundation www.leakeyfoundation.org

MARY LEAKEY / ANTHROPOLOGIST

The remarkable Leakey family has dominated the field of anthropology since the mid-20th century. Louis Leakey (1903–1972), born in Africa of English missionaries, was an early proponent of an African origin for modern humans. He and his wife, Mary (1913–1996), made the 1948 discovery of the skull of an apelike creature, *Proconsul africanus,* which gave evidence of a common ancestor of apes and humans. In 1959 Mary (left, in 1976) made an even more important discovery—*Paranthropus boisei* in Africa's Olduvai Gorge. In 1976 she found a trail of human footprints, 3.6 million years old, in Tanzania. Son Richard (b. 1944), an anthropologist and Kenyan politician, found the complete skeleton of a *Homo erectus* youth in 1985, and his wife, zoologist Meave Leakey (b. 1942), discovered some of the earliest Australopith skeletons ever found.

FOR MORE FACTS ON...

PRIMATE SPECIES & CHARACTERISTICS see *Mammals,* **CHAPTER 4, PAGES 166-7**
+
DNA STRUCTURE & HUMAN GENETICS see *Genetics,* **CHAPTER 8, PAGES 344-5**

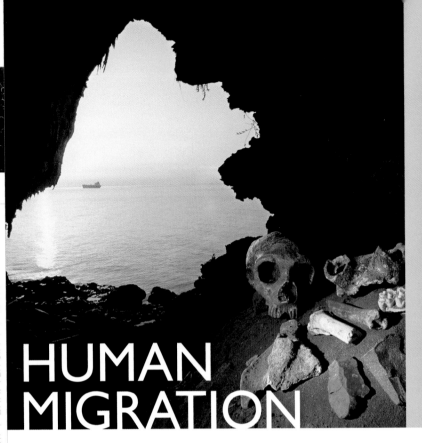

THE GENUS HOMO

2.5 MILLION YEARS AGO
Homo habilis

2.3 MILLION YEARS AGO
Homo rudolfensis

1.8 MILLION YEARS AGO
Homo erectus

800,000 YEARS AGO
Homo heidelbergensis

350,000 YEARS AGO
Homo neanderthalensis

200,000 YEARS AGO
Homo sapiens

HUMAN MIGRATION

About 60,000 years ago, a second great wave of migration took humans—now anatomically the modern species *Homo sapiens*—out of Africa. Within 10,000 years, they had made their way across thousands of miles to Australia by crossing land bridges exposed by the lower sea levels of the glacial Pleistocene. By 40,000 years ago, another wave of migrants had ventured into the Middle East and Near East, and by 30,000 years ago some of these hunters had followed antelopes and mammoths across the steppes into northern Asia and Europe.

As hunters spread through Siberia between 20,000 and 10,000 years ago, older groups began to develop more advanced cultures. Residents domesticated plants and began trading with shells and obsidian in the Middle East, shaped pottery in Japan, painted clothed human figures on rocks in Australia, and created sophisticated tools as well as bone animal carvings and cave paintings in Europe.

The last big wave of migration, from Siberia into North America, took place between 20,000 and 10,000 years ago (the precise date is much debated) when Asia and North America were connected by a thousand-mile-wide grassland. Asian migrants crossed this landmass and moved down the western edge of North America, reaching South America by 13,000 years ago.

Starting about 10,000 years ago, as the land grew warmer and wetter, hunter-gatherer societies around the world made the transition to agriculture, urban settlements, and writing.

FAST FACT Sometime between 150,000 and 50,000 years ago, the world's human population was as low as 10,000.

FOR MORE FACTS ON...

HUMAN PREHISTORY *in Prehistory 10,000 B.C.-3500 B.C.,* **CHAPTER 7, PAGES 264-5**

HUMAN MIGRATIONS *see Africa, Asia, Europe, Australia & Oceania, North America & South America,* **CHAPTER 9, PAGES 361, 379, 395, 409, 415 & 425**

HOW DO WE KNOW ABOUT HUMAN MIGRATION?

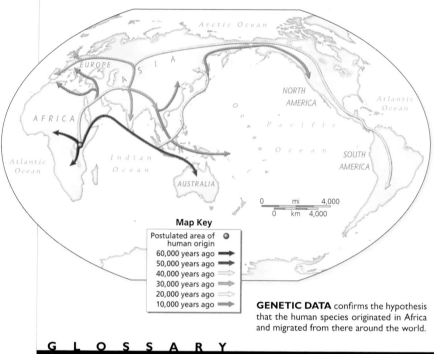

Map Key

Postulated area of human origin ●
60,000 years ago ➡
50,000 years ago ➡
40,000 years ago ⇒
30,000 years ago ⇒
20,000 years ago ⇒
10,000 years ago ⇒

GENETIC DATA confirms the hypothesis that the human species originated in Africa and migrated from there around the world.

In 2005 the National Geographic Society and IBM launched the Genographic Project to retrace the earliest human migrations through the use of DNA donated from people around the world. The project has provided details about both the origin and the later migrations that brought humans to occupy all corners of the globe. By calculating the pattern of genetic diversity in different populations, which arises when new mutations are introduced in each generation, geneticists are coming to understand both the age and ancestry of groups living in different geographic regions. From this work it is now widely accepted that humans originated in Africa and left that continent around 60,000 years ago to successfully populate the planet.

GLOSSARY

Genome: The entire set of chromosomes of an organism. / **Hominid:** Any member of the human lineage. / **Neolithic:** From the Greek *neos*, "new," + *lithikos*, "of stone." Relating to the latest period of the Stone Age, characterized by polished stone tools.

CLICK IT: ▶ The Genographic Project nationalgeographic.com/genographic

WHO WERE THE NEANDERTHALS?

As they moved into Europe and Eurasia some 30,000 years ago, modern humans may well have encountered another human species: Neanderthals. Descended from humans who left Africa in the first migration, Neanderthals were a hardy people whose stocky, muscular bodies helped them survive their cold environment. They walked upright, had larger brains than modern humans, produced tools, buried their dead with rituals, and may have been capable of speech.

Despite their adaptations to their chilly environs, or perhaps because of them, Neanderthals died out around the time *Homo sapiens* moved in, perhaps 28,000 years ago. Theories for their demise abound. They may have been unable to adapt to a changing, colder climate; they may have been "out-competed" by modern humans with better tools or a more flexible social organization that assigned gathering to female members. It's possible, though, that Neanderthals contributed to the modern human gene pool before they vanished. A study of Neanderthal DNA, extracted from a 45,000-year-old skeleton, is under way.

FOR MORE FACTS ON...

LANGUAGE CLASSIFICATIONS & DISTRIBUTION see *Language*, **CHAPTER 6, PAGES 228-31**
+
THE CREATION & DISCOVERY OF PREHISTORIC ART see *Art*, **CHAPTER 6, PAGES 238-9**

Sami family, Norway

THE HUMAN FAMILY

LIFE EXPECTANCIES

AT BIRTH

HIGHEST IN THE WORLD

COUNTRY	FEMALE	MALE
Japan	86	79
Australia	84	79
Switzerland	84	79
Iceland	83	80
Spain	84	78
Israel	83	79
Sweden	83	79

LOWEST IN THE WORLD

COUNTRY	FEMALE	MALE
Swaziland	39	40
Mozambique	42	42
Zambia	42	42
Angola	44	41
Sierra Leone	44	41

The family, which takes many forms across many cultures, is the fundamental unit of human society. Anthropologists traditionally define the nuclear family as consisting of adults of both sexes, joined in a socially approved sexual relationship, and one or more children, their own or adopted. Nuclear families share a residence, sometimes with their extended family, including members such as grandparents, aunts, and uncles, as well as in-laws, known as affinal relatives.

Of course, there are almost as many variations on this traditional family unit as there are families. Households may be headed by a single adult or by two of the same sex. The marital group may consist of one woman and multiple husbands (polyandry), as among some ethnic Tibetans, or one man and multiple wives (polygyny), found in Africa, the Middle East, and India, among other places. Kinship may be traced only through the female line, as in matrilineal systems, or only through males, as in patrilineal systems.

Despite their different forms, families tend to perform the same functions

FOR MORE FACTS ON...

KINSHIP, ETHNICITY & OTHER SOCIAL RELATIONSHIPS see Ethnicities, CHAPTER 6, PAGES 224-5

RELATIONSHIPS BASED ON TRADE see Commerce, CHAPTER 6, PAGES 254-7

across all cultures. As a stable unit, they arrange for the rearing and socialization of children; they care for the sick; they provide and share food, shelter, clothing, and security—both physical and emotional; and they enforce guidelines for procreation that encourage an enduring marital bond and prohibit incest. In modern, industrial societies, some of these roles and functions have fallen to the state, and extended families sharing the same household are increasingly rare. Even so, the basic structure of the family unit has remained surprisingly unchanged throughout the millennia.

G L O S S A R Y

Kinship: From Old English *cyn*, "family," "race," "kind," "nature." Socially recognized relationship between people related biologically or by marriage, adoption, or ritual. / **Affinal:** From Latin *affinis*, "bordering on." Kinship relationship based on marriage rather than blood.

MARGARET MEAD / ANTHROPOLOGIST

Margaret Mead (1901–1978), an American anthropologist, became a celebrity on the publication of her first book, *Coming of Age in Samoa*. "Because I was a woman and could hope for greater intimacy in working with girls, and because owing to a paucity of women ethnologists our knowledge of primitive girls is far slighter than our knowledge of boys, I chose to concentrate upon the adolescent girl in Samoa," she wrote. This book was followed by many others on culture and psychological development. Mead held various positions at the American Museum of Natural History, including curator of ethnology, and was an activist for women's rights and against nuclear proliferation. Although many of her anecdotal conclusions have been questioned, she is appreciated for bringing anthropology into the public consciousness.

" The mind is not sex-typed. "
—— MARGARET MEAD, 1972

RITES OF PASSAGE

Weddings and funerals, baptisms and bar mitzvahs, *quinceañeras* and baby showers—all are life cycle rituals of the modern world. All societies have rites and ceremonies that mark the most significant transitions of a human life: birth, sexual maturity, marriage, death.

Among the Blood Indians of Saskatchewan, Canada, for instance, male elders perform a naming ceremony for each infant in which they anoint the child with red ochre and raise it to the sun. The flowers and tossed rice of modern American weddings are lingering remnants of ancient fertility symbols. And ritual burials with attendant ceremony date back to the Neanderthals.

LATINO TEENAGERS in California celebrate a friend's *quinceañera*, a traditional observation of a young woman's coming of age.

FOR MORE FACTS ON...

NEANDERTHALS & HUMAN MIGRATION see *Human Migration*, **CHAPTER 6, PAGES 220-1**

SAMOAN HISTORY & ECONOMY see *Oceania & Australia*, **CHAPTER 9, PAGE 412**

THE HUMAN FAMILY

ETHNICITIES

Culture and ethnicity are intersecting concepts, different but overlapping ways to categorize human populations. Culture refers to a group's way of life, including the shared system of social meanings, values, and relations that is transmitted between generations. It incorporates such traits as language, religion, clothing, music, courtesy, legal systems, sports, tools—indeed, all learned behavior.

Ethnicity, which is a changeable and slippery concept of cultural distinctiveness, could be considered a subgroup of culture. It typically denotes a group of people who strongly identify themselves (or are identified by others, even against their will) as belonging together based on specific common traits they share. Such traits are largely involuntary—skin color, clan, or tribe membership, perceived or actual common ancestry, shared history or language, and even disability (such as deafness) or sexual orientation. Other traits may be chosen, abandoned, or changed. These include culture, religion or sect, age, dialect, marriage into a group, and so on.

Language is the most typical marker of ethnicity, but there are exceptions. Many speakers of Chinese cannot understand each other at all, for example, yet they may feel they all belong to the Han Chinese ethnic group. Many people, of course, consider themselves to be "hyphenated" members of more than one group, such as Italian Americans or Welsh Canadians.

As boundaries of ethnic identification keep shifting, is it virtually impossible to name and number all the ethnic groups in the world. Such a list, however, would have well over 10,000 entries. It would include the Mardu, approximately 700 Aboriginal people living in western Australia, as well as the Han, numbering over one billion in China. Large or small, each ethnic group regards itself as "a people."

MANY VARIATIONS in facial features, skin tones, and body proportions are found within the human family. Here, clockwise from upper left: Ainu (Japanese) woman, North American youth, Aboriginal (Australian) man and child, Mongolian girl, and Csango (Romanian) man.

FOR MORE FACTS ON...

OTHER FORMS OF CULTURAL IDENTITY see The Human Family: Race, Class & Gender, **CHAPTER 6, PAGES 226-7**

LANGUAGE see Language, **CHAPTER 6, PAGES 228-31**

WHAT CONNECTS US?

Kinship, a broader term than family, encompasses the social relationships between people who are related by blood, marriage, adoption, or other binding ritual. The term fictive kinship recognizes those who are given the roles and titles of kinship without actually being related. Godparents are the most obvious examples of fictive kin; acting as sponsors of a child at baptism and assuming a quasiparental role, godparents are so closely identified with the child's family in many cultures that marriage to a godchild or godparent's child is considered incest.

Other forms of fictive kinship include blood brothers (a bond sometimes sealed by the exchange of blood), "honorary" aunts and uncles, and even the "ghost husband" of the Nuer people of North Africa, the deceased spouse who remains a widow's legal mate even after she marries his living brother.

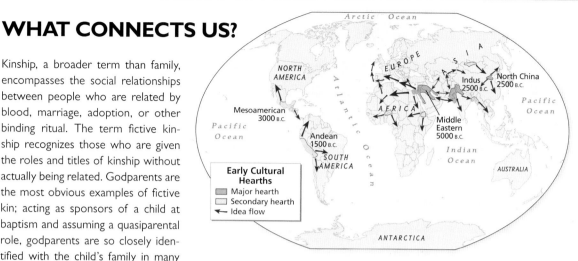

EARLY CULTURAL HEARTHS represent centers from which ideas and innovations sprang during the course of human history: the first cities, trading centers, and loci of intellectual advances.

FAST FACT Regions where cultural traits such as religion and agriculture originate are known as cultural hearths.

HOW DO WE NAME OUR CHILDREN?

Personal names are distinctive, yet very much a cultural product, and among the most obvious attributes of a particular culture or ethnicity.

In Western cultures, the typical pattern includes a given name, such as James or Katherine, a middle name, sometimes taken from a parental last name, such as Maxwell, and a hereditary family surname, such as Johnson.

But even this widespread practice has variations, such as among many Latin American families, in which each child carries two surnames inherited from each parent (such as Gabriel García Márquez). In Iceland, children's surnames are derived from a parent's first name; thus, the former prime minister Halldór Ásgrímsson is the son of a man whose given name was Ásgrímur.

Chinese, Korean, and Japanese names begin with the family name followed by a given name, such as Wen Jiabao. And in a few cultures, such as Java in Indonesia, individuals have one name only, as was the case for former president Suharto.

G L O S S A R Y

CLICK IT: Ethnicity & Race anthro.palomar.edu/ethnicity

Culture: From Latin *cultura*, "tilled" or "cultivated." An integrated pattern of human knowledge, belief, and behavior that is both a result of and integral to the human capacity for learning and transmitting knowledge to succeeding generations. **/ Ethnic group:** A social group or category of the population that, in a larger society, is set apart and bound together by common ties of language, nationality, or culture.

FOR MORE FACTS ON...

EARLY CIVILIZATIONS see *Mesopotamia 3500 B.C.- 500 B.C.,* **CHAPTER 7, PAGES 266-7, &** *Egypt 3000 B.C.-30 B.C.,* **CHAPTER 7, PAGES 268-9**

EARLY CIVILIZATIONS see *India 2500 B.C.-A.D. 500,* **CHAPTER 7, PAGES 270-71, &** *China 2200 B.C.-A.D. 500,* **CHAPTER 7, PAGES 272-3**

RACE, CLASS & GENDER

In many societies, and particularly in the West, people identify themselves and each other according to race, class, and gender. Although race and gender seem to have a basis in biology, all three of these distinctions are actually cultural ones.

The concept of race, for instance, typically groups people according to visible physical characteristics: skin color, stature, or facial features. But the definition of race has always been fluid and has also encompassed linguistic groups, religions, or nationalities (such as the "Polish race" or the "Jewish race"). Scholars attempting to categorize race have named anywhere from 3 to 60 races, but recently the biological basis for racial distinctions has been under question. Race is still a powerful idea, since human beings rely on group identity to maintain social structure.

Unlike race, social class has always been recognized as a cultural grouping, not a biological one. The idea of class—defined as a group of people with the same socioeconomic status—is a relatively new one. Until the late 18th century, social status was typically described in terms of "rank" or "order," reflecting the notion that people were born into their roles in the social hierarchy. Social and industrial revolutions largely replaced this idea with the concept of a grouping by wealth, employment, and education.

Simply put, the upper class possessed inherited wealth; the middle class consisted of white-collar workers and small-business owners; and the working class was characterized by blue-collar industrial and service workers with little property and lower levels of education. The boundaries between these apparent classes are considerably blurred.

Gender, different from a person's biological sex, refers to the way people assign themselves—and the ways others assign to them—skills and behavior associated with being masculine or feminine. In most societies, gender roles are traditionally defined and taught to each child consciously and unconsciously from birth.

IN TODAY'S URBAN CENTERS, like London (shown here), many races, multiple classes, all ages and genders meet.

FOR MORE FACTS ON...

FAMILY RELATIONSHIPS see *The Human Family,* **CHAPTER 6, PAGES 222-3**
+
GROWING URBANIZATION OF THE WORLD see *Cities,* **CHAPTER 6, PAGES 260-1**

WHAT IS RACE?

In recent years, DNA studies across all human populations have shown that humans cannot be divided into biological subgroups; humans, in fact, are remarkably homogeneous, genetically speaking. Of course, different groups in different locations share some physical characteristics, such as eye color or skull shape. Scientists call these phenotype differences. They come about because of local environmental adaptations, sexual selection (for instance, people in one culture may deem dark hair to be more attractive), and random genetic drift. However, these regional variations reflect only a tiny portion of the human genetic package and cannot be compartmentalized into any distinct genetic grouping. Individual differences are much greater than phenotype differences; one Maori woman is far more different from another Maori woman than Maoris, as a group, are different from Scandinavians.

GLOSSARY

Gender: A person's self-identity as masculine or feminine. **/ Phenotype:** All the observable characteristics of an organism, such as shape, size, color, and behavior, that result from the interaction of its genotype (total genetic makeup) with the environment.

THE HINDU CASTE SYSTEM

The caste system, found primarily among India's Hindus, separates a population into ranked, hereditary groups with distinct occupations. According to Hindu scripture, the four main castes, or varnas, sprang into being from the creator god's body: from the mouth came the Brahmans, from the arms the Kshatriyas, from the thighs the Vaishyas, and from the feet the Sudras.

Brahmans, which are the highest-ranking caste, were the priests and teachers; the Kshatriya, close to them in status, were rulers and warriors; Vaishyas were farmers and merchants; and slaves and serfs made up the lowest group, the Sudras. Some Hindus fell into an even lower-ranking group, whose members carried out unclean jobs such as the disposal of dead animals. These people, subject to intense discrimination, were known as untouchables, though now the term Dalit, meaning "downtrodden," is preferred. Discrimination against the Dalits is now illegal in India, and modern Hindu society is becoming more fluid. Nevertheless, the caste system still governs many jobs and marriages, particularly in rural India.

HINDU WEDDING PREPARATIONS among members of an upper caste in Mumbai, India, include festive dances. The women wear colorful silk saris and matching bracelets.

CLICK IT: Peoples of the World www.peoplesoftheworld.org

FAST FACT Mary Wollstonecraft's *Vindication of the Rights of Women,* 1792, is considered the first feminist tract.

FOR MORE FACTS ON...

THE HISTORY OF INDIA'S CASTE SYSTEM *see India 2500 B.C.-A.D. 500,* **CHAPTER 7, PAGE 271**

INDIA'S ECONOMY AND POPULATION *see Asia,* **CHAPTER 9, PAGE 386**

Bedouin storyteller, Sinai, Egypt

LANGUAGE

MOST SPEAKERS

MANDARIN CHINESE
874,000,000 speakers

HINDI
366,000,000 speakers

ENGLISH
341,000,000 speakers

SPANISH
322,000,000 speakers

BENGALI
207,000,000 speakers

PORTUGUESE
176,000,000 speakers

RUSSIAN
167,000,000 speakers

JAPANESE
125,000,000 speakers

How and when language emerged is a portion of our species's history that is still mysterious and hotly disputed. Language leaves behind no fossils and could not be recorded until the advent of writing, some 5,000 years ago. However, it seems reasonable to assume that language evolved along with early modern humans at least 100,000 years ago.

Once humans were using language, it came to occupy large, interconnected portions of the brain. Language and culture are inextricable: Each mirrors and extends the other. As separate human cultures evolved around the world, so did separate languages.

In our hunter-gatherer past we lived in small bands, an ideal scenario for language diversity. The pace of language change is such that within the space of just eight or ten generations, descendants of the same ancestors may already begin to have difficulty communicating.

In 2007, at least 6,912 distinct languages were spoken worldwide, but just 83 languages were distributed among 80 percent of the world's population. More than half of the world's languages are spoken by less than one percent of the population.

FOR MORE FACTS ON...

HUMAN EVOLUTION AFTER LANGUAGE AROSE *see Human Migration,* **CHAPTER 6, PAGES 220-1**
+
THE HUMAN BRAIN *see Mind & Brain,* **CHAPTER 8, PAGES 340-1**

HOW DO LANGUAGES DIE?

Many languages are rapidly becoming extinct. Of the almost 7,000 languages now in existence, only half may still be spoken by the end of this century. Languages such as Urarina (spoken by fewer than 3,000 people in the Amazon), Halkomelem (spoken by 200, in Canada), and Tofa (spoken by no more than 25 people, in Siberia) face a precarious and uncertain future.

Native speakers stop using their original language for a variety of reasons. They may favor a different language because it is more dominant, more prestigious, or more widely known. They may be motivated by official state policies to suppress speech or by social pressure to speak differently. Children worldwide experience subtle and overt pressures to switch to globally dominant languages.

When a language dies, much is lost: a unique knowledge of the planet and its creatures, a treasury of myths and poetry, and a window into the workings of the human brain. Language conservationists are working to revive those tongues that can still be saved and document those that cannot—before they vanish forever.

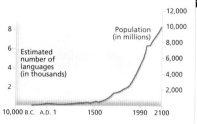

THE RATE OF LANGUAGE LOSS has picked up speed around the world in recent decades as influences associated with globalization make for a more homogeneous human experience.

GLOSSARY

Language: A system of conventional spoken or written symbols shared by people in a culture and used to communicate with one another. / **Myth:** A traditional story, ostensibly historical, told within a culture to explain a worldview, practice, belief, or natural phenomenon.

WHY MYTHS AND LEGENDS?

Myths encompass creation tales and stories of gods and mystical heroes; sagas and legends tell of great and dramatic historical events, such as the Trojan War; folktales are simpler stories of adventure or humor, often with a moral. All are vital carriers of cultural identity, informing each new generation about how its people understand the world and judge behavior. Though some stories from more dominant cultures have been written down, many others still depend upon oral transmission for their existence, and as such are inextricably intertwined with the language itself.

A RITUAL DANCE enacts ancient myths for Luvale boys coming of age in Zambia.

CLICK IT: Enduring Voices nationalgeographic.com/enduringvoices/

FAST FACT Only five members of Oklahoma's Yuchi Indians still speak their ancestral language.

FOR MORE FACTS ON...

MYTHS OF LIFE AFTER DEATH see Egypt 3000 B.C.-30 B.C., **CHAPTER 7, PAGE 269, &** South America Prehistory-1500, **CHAPTER 7, PAGE 291**

THE SWAHILI LANGUAGE see Africa 500-1500, **CHAPTER 7, PAGE 283**

LANGUAGE
WRITING

Writing, as best we can tell, was born from accounting. The earliest known use of symbols dates to about 8000 B.C. in Mesopotamia, when merchants made marks on clay tokens as bills of lading. In its earliest form, this writing used picture symbols, or pictographs, to denote particular meanings.

By 3300 B.C., these marks had become standardized into cuneiform script. The symbols began to represent sounds in spoken language, rather than just objects or concepts. The Akkadi-ans, Babylonians, and Assyrians adapted the script to their own languages. Almost 1,000 miles to the west, the Egyptians developed hieroglyphs that came to combine pictographs, word-signs, and syllabic symbols.

Between 1800 and 1300 B.C., Semitic peoples near the eastern Mediterranean developed an alphabet that borrowed from Egyptian hieroglyphs. This alphabet was revolutionary: Instead of requiring hundreds, if not thousands, of different signs, consonants in a spoken language were represented by single symbols. Because there are usually no more than 40 separate sounds in a spoken language, written communication was dramatically simplified. This system was adapted and modified by the Greeks, and the Greek alphabet became the basis for the Western alphabet now used around the world.

Meanwhile, in China some 4,000 years ago, a different system of writing arose, based on pictographs supplemented by ideograms that conveyed meaning. The writing was well suited to the diverse dialects spoken across China, since the symbols did not link to sounds. The system has changed little since it was codified in the third century B.C., making Chinese the oldest continuously used writing system in the world.

OVERSIZE BRUSH provides exercise and artistic expression to a man as he paints graceful pictogram characters on the sidewalk in China.

FOR MORE FACTS ON...

CARTOGRAPHY IN HUMAN HISTORY see The History of Mapping, **CHAPTER 1, PAGES 20-1**
+
THE EVOLUTION OF JAPANESE WRITING see Asia 500-1500, **CHAPTER 7, PAGE 285**

WHAT IS THE ROSETTA STONE?

Hieroglyphs are the written symbols that were used by scribes in ancient Egypt. While they appear to be pictures, or pictographs, they usually stood for sounds, or phonetics.

The hieroglyphic system of writing vanished from Egypt by about the fifth century A.D., and with it all knowledge of how to translate the complex symbols. Then, in 1799, a Frenchman in Rosetta, Egypt—now called Rashid—discovered a black granite stone from the second century B.C. that bore inscriptions in Egyptian hieroglyphic, Egyptian demotic (common script), and Greek. By comparing the symbols in the three different writing systems, he was able to begin to decipher the ancient Egyptian hieroglyphs, revealing a text written by priests in honor of the pharaoh.

THE ROSETTA STONE, created about 200 B.C., unlocked hieroglyphics.

WRITING SYSTEMS around the world differ in appearance and in their relation to spoken language. Some, like English, are phonetic; others, like Chinese, are ideographic. The name "Aristotle" looks remarkably different in nine different writing systems, as shown below.

GREEK	ΑΡΙΣΤΟΤΕΛΗΣ	ARABIC	ارسطوطاليس	JAPANESE	アリストテレス		
CYRILLIC	АРИСТОТЕЛЬ	HEBREW	אריסטו	HINDI	अरिस्टोटल		
AMHARIC	አርስጣጣሊስ	CHINESE	亞里士多德	THAI	อริสโตเติล		

CLICK IT: Chinese Calligraphy www.art-virtue.com/history

FAST FACT One out of every six people living in the world today speaks Mandarin Chinese as a native language.

MAJOR LANGUAGE FAMILIES

MANY WORLD LANGUAGES are related, like branches on a family tree.

- Afro-Asiatic
- Altaic
- Austro-Asiatic
- Austronesian
- Dravidian
- Indo-European
- Japanese/Korean
- Kam-Tai
- Niger-Congo
- Nilo-Saharan
- Sino-Tibetan
- Uralic
- Other

FOR MORE FACTS ON...

THE EARLIEST LEGAL DOCUMENT, HAMMURABI'S CODE see *Mesopotamia 3500 B.C.-500 B.C.,* **CHAPTER 7, PAGE 267**

ANCIENT EGYPTIAN CULTURE see *Egypt 3000 B.C.-30 B.C.,* **CHAPTER 7, PAGES 268-9**

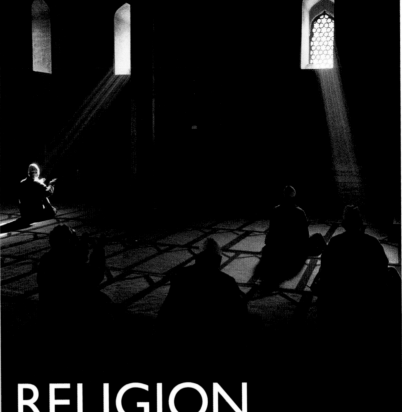

Muslims at prayer, Srinagar, Kashmir, India

MILESTONES OF RELIGION

70,000 B.C.
Neanderthals buried with ritual objects

10,000 B.C.
European cave paintings depict shamans

3000 B.C.
Egyptians build temples to creator god

2000 B.C.
Abraham leads Hebrews into Canaan

1500 B.C.
Hinduism begins as Aryans invade
the Indus Valley

1290 B.C.
Moses leads slaves out of Egypt

6TH CENTURY B.C.
Zoroaster brings monotheism to Persia

CIRCA 528 B.C.
Gautama Buddha receives enlightenment

CIRCA 500 B.C.
Confucius teaches moral principles

CIRCA A.D. 30
Jesus crucified in Judea

CIRCA A.D. 70
Four Christian Gospels are written

300–500
Buddhism spreads to China, Korea, Japan

610
Muhammad receives first revelations of
the Koran

1054
Christianity splits into Eastern and
Western branches

1517
Martin Luther begins Protestant
movement

RELIGION

he dawn of religion tens of thousands of years ago accompanied many other significant developments, such as the making of tools, control of fire, the beginnings of a symbol system, and art. Human remains dating back 70,000 years suggest that both Neanderthal humans and Paleolithic-era *Homo sapiens* may have placed objects in graves with the deceased.

Cave paintings at Trois Frères, in the French foothills of the Pyrenees, date from about 10,000 years ago. Among paintings of bison and horses, a fantastical biped with antlers, paws, and tail stares down. Art historians call him the Sorcerer, seeing in him the prototype of a man honored for his special connection to the unknown power beyond.

Half man, half beast, the Sorcerer embodies widespread early beliefs that animals embody great power and that humans must establish a spiritual connection to them in the struggle against the unknown. To some observers, the Sorcerer represents a shaman. Sometimes assisted by spirits or animal companions, shamans protect their communities by incorporating threats

FOR MORE FACTS ON...

EARLY HUMAN CHARACTERISTICS & MOVEMENT see *Human Migration,* **CHAPTER 6, PAGES 220-1**

EARLY HUMAN POTTERY & CAVE PAINTINGS see *Art,* **CHAPTER 6, PAGES 238-9**

into their own bodies. Shamanism is still found in Siberia, as well as in the Americas, India, and Australia.

Animism, another common early form of belief, lives on in religions such as Shintoism. The Kwakiutl of the Pacific Northwest wore masks of sacred animals to access their powers. Ancient Egyptians revered Bastet, a cat-headed goddess with a woman's body, representing the sun. Celtic people of pre-Christian Northern Europe revered the power dwelling in trees and associated deities with plant species: Cerridwen, the moon goddess, inhabited the birch, for example.

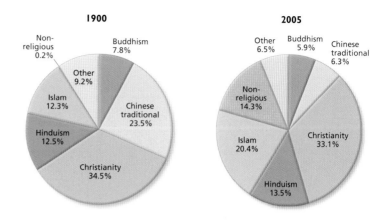

1900

Non-religious 0.2%
Buddhism 7.8%
Other 9.2%
Islam 12.3%
Chinese traditional 23.5%
Hinduism 12.5%
Christianity 34.5%

2005

Other 6.5%
Buddhism 5.9%
Chinese traditional 6.3%
Non-religious 14.3%
Christianity 33.1%
Islam 20.4%
Hinduism 13.5%

RELIGIOUS AFFILIATIONS WORLDWIDE reflect changing faith communities between 1900 and 2005. While the number of Christian and Hindu adherents has remained fairly constant, Islam has grown worldwide, as has the number who consider themselves nonreligious.

G L O S S A R Y

Magic: The use of supernatural forces to gain power over the natural world. **/ Animism:** A belief in spirits separable from bodies. **/ Shaman:** From a Siberian Tungus word, "to know." A charismatic individual believed able to control spirits and journey into the spirit world.

WHAT IS MAGICAL THINKING?

ENTRANCED BY THEIR BELIEFS, Haitian women engage in ritual bathing during a pilgrimage. Haitian religious practice blends magical elements of voodoo with Christian traditions.

Magical thinking underlies the practices of many forms of religion, including animism and shamanism. It is the belief that invisible energies connect living and nonliving things. Knocking on wood to ensure a hoped-for outcome, wearing a lucky shirt to class on exam day—these modern-day rituals reflect the same belief that small local actions influence distant uncontrollable events.

Sympathetic magic, the notion that like affects like, is a form of magical thinking. Sticking a needle into a voodoo doll, for example, is a way of invoking sympathetic magic. Hunters who eat the hearts of their bravest prey and gamblers who expect a win after a streak of losses are also believing in magical influences.

FAST FACT Fire is a sacred element in many belief systems, including Zoroastrianism and the Maya religion.

FOR MORE FACTS ON...

HINDUISM, BUDDHISM, JUDAISM, CHRISTIANITY & ISLAM see Hinduism & Buddhism, **CHAPTER 6, PAGES 234-5,** & Monotheism, **CHAPTER 6, PAGES 236-7**
+
RELIGIONS OF THE MAYA & INCA see Mesoamerica Prehistory-1500, **CHAPTER 7, PAGES 288-9,** & South America Prehistory-1500, **CHAPTER 7, PAGES 290-1**

RELIGION

HINDUISM & BUDDHISM

Two of the world's five major religions blossomed on the Asian subcontinent of India. Hinduism, oldest of the five, was brought to the Indus Valley perhaps 3,500 years ago by Aryan tribes from Central Asia. It diffused eastward toward the Ganges Valley and to much of Southeast Asia including Malaysia and Indonesia; about 80 percent of India's one billion people are Hindu.

The Aryans brought with them the sacred writings called the Vedas. These writings explore the central concept of reincarnation, in which an individual is reborn into a caste based on the karma or totality of actions during his or her prior life. The ultimate power and spiritual source of the universe is the Brahman, and Hinduism urges its practitioners to achieve spiritual liberation through knowledge of this final reality.

Hinduism is a diverse religion, with differing sects and practices and a variety of gods, including Vishnu, Shiva, and Shakti—although these are usually seen as aspects of the Brahman. Indian society has been shaped by Hinduism, especially in its caste system, which defines social and religious status.

Buddhism, the other major religion with roots in Asia, is an offshoot of Hinduism based on the teachings of the prophet Siddhartha Gautama (later called the Buddha, or "Enlightened One"), born in the sixth century B.C. Missionaries carried Buddhism from the borders of what are now India and Nepal, where Siddhartha was born, to eastern Asia following the conversion of Asoka, Emperor of India, around 261 B.C.

The Buddha adopted the idea of karma from Hinduism, but not its gods. He taught that desire brings suffering, so to escape from suffering and the cycle of rebirth, practitioners must meditate and live according to moral precepts. Those rules can be found in the Eightfold Path: right intent, right concentration, right views, right speech, right conduct, right livelihood, right effort, and right mindfulness. Different branches of Buddhism have developed over time, including Theravada Buddhism, a more conservative branch, and Mahayana Buddhism, which includes Zen Buddhism.

Buddhism spread through Asia, including to China and Japan, where it merged with the traditional religion Shinto, which venerates ancestors. Zen Buddhism arose in China in the sixth century A.D. and developed further in Japan. Zen teaches that enlightenment is attained not through good deeds or study but through meditation.

BATHING IN THE GANGES at sunrise, as this man is doing in Varanasi, India, is a holy act for the Hindu faithful. Many begin every day by performing this ritual.

FOR MORE FACTS ON...

THE CASTE SYSTEM & EARLY HISTORY OF INDIA see *India 2500 B.C.-A.D. 500,* **CHAPTER 7, PAGES 270-1**

THE EARLY HISTORY OF CHINA see *China 2200 B.C.-A.D. 500,* **CHAPTER 7, PAGES 272-3**

HINDU DEITIES

The varieties of Hinduism recognize many gods with many names, but most modern Hindus believe that the gods are all different aspects of the one supreme god, Brahman. Prominent among these are Vishnu, protector of the world, who appears in human form in a variety of heroic avatars, including Rama and Krishna; Shiva, representing both fertility and destruction; and Shakti, his consort and the mother goddess.

The Hindu gods have many names and aspects and are associated with a wide range of animals, emotions, and natural forces, both creative and destructive. Shakti, for instance, is known as Durga, Parvati, Ambika, and Kali; she can be shown as a frightening figure with many arms, riding a tiger, or as the benevolent goddess Lakshi, consort of Vishnu.

Ganesha, portrayed as an elephant riding a mouse, is called the lord of success and destroyer of obstacles.

EFFIGIES OF GANESHA, the elephant-headed god, line up in preparation for India's ten-day festival, Ganesh Chaturthi, when Hindus chant, sing, dance, and immerse their colorful idols into the sea or river, asking Ganesha to brighten their lives for another year.

CLICK IT: Hinduism www.bbc.co.uk/religion/religions/hinduism

FAST FACT Tibetan Buddhists believe that each Dalai Lama, their spiritual leader, is a reincarnation of the previous one.

SIDDHARTHA GAUTAMA / THE BUDDHA

Siddhartha Gautama, founder of Buddhism (ca 560-ca 480 B.C.), was born a prince in the foothills south of the Himalaya. The sheltered youth grew up unaware of the larger world. Only when he finally ventured outside the palace did he see suffering: a man doubled over with sickness, a man decrepit with age, and a corpse. Renouncing his worldly goods, Gautama traveled the Ganges plain, begging for food. After six years of deprivation, near death, he sat down under a fig tree beside the Nairanjana River near Uruvela, called Bodh Gaya today. There he achieved enlightenment and realized the Four Noble Truths: Existence is suffering; there is a cause of suffering; by eliminating the cause, one can end suffering; and there is a path by which one can end suffering. He began to preach and drew disciples before dying at the age of 80.

FOR MORE FACTS ON...

MYTH IN HUMAN CULTURE see Language, **CHAPTER 6, PAGE 229**

THE HISTORY & ECONOMIES OF ASIAN COUNTRIES see Asia, **CHAPTER 9, PAGES 379-93**

RELIGION

MONOTHEISM

The three major monotheistic religions—Judaism, Christianity, and Islam—started in the Middle East and, despite their differences, share many key beliefs and some prophets.

Judaism traces its origins to the biblical patriarch Abraham, who lived sometime between 2100 and 1500 B.C. The religious heart of Judaism lies in Jerusalem, in present-day Israel. Driven from the area by ancient Romans in the Diaspora of the first century, Jews dispersed throughout the world. Subject to frequent persecution over the centuries, as many as six million Jews were murdered during the 20th-century Holocaust. In 1948, the state of Israel was established as a Jewish homeland, although large Jewish populations also exist in many major European and American cities.

Christianity evolved from Judaism with the teachings of Jesus, a Jew born in Bethlehem about 2,000 years ago. The actual calendar date of his birth is elusive—somewhere between 6 B.C. and A.D. 1. Jesus' disciples believed he was the son of God and the promised messiah, or *christos* in Greek, whose death and resurrection promise salvation to his followers. Christianity spread to Europe with the proselytizing of the Apostle Paul and other missionaries and the conversion of Constantine, emperor of Rome, eventually spreading around the world with European missionaries during later ages of exploration and empire. Christianity now has three major divisions: Roman Catholicism, Eastern Orthodoxy, and Protestantism.

Islam is the most recent of the religions originating in the Middle East. It evolved in reaction to the polytheistic beliefs of early inhabitants of the Arabian Peninsula. By the sixth century A.D., Arabs were feeling the influences of three surrounding monotheistic religions—Judaism, Christianity, and Zoroastrianism (an influential faith founded by the Persian prophet Zarathustra). Into this world was born the founder of Islam, the prophet Muhammad, around A.D. 570. Muhammad taught that there was only one god, Allah; revelations passed on to Muhammad were written down as the Koran over a period of years. The moral obligations of all Muslims are summed up in Five Pillars of Islam: prayer, charity, pilgrimage, fasting, and belief in God and his prophets.

Islam has two main branches, Sunni and Shiite, which separated during the seventh century in a dispute over the legacy of leadership. Sunnis compose about 84 percent of all Muslims and dominate the Arabian Peninsula and northern Africa. Shiites form the majority in Iran and Iraq.

ORTHODOX JEWS, some wearing prayer shawls and all with covered heads, practice devotion at Jerusalem's Western Wall during the Passover holiday.

FOR MORE FACTS ON...

THE ANCIENT MIDDLE EAST see *Mesopotamia 3500 B.C.-500 B.C.,* **CHAPTER 7, PAGE 267**

JUDAISM & CHRISTIANITY IN ANCIENT ROME see *Rome 500 B.C.-A.D. 500,* **CHAPTER 7, PAGE 277**

THREE PROPHETS, THREE RELIGIONS, ONE GOD

Abraham, Jesus, and Muhammad—these three men, prophets and teachers, are held to be the founders of three major world religions: Judaism, Christianity, and Islam.

The Jewish patriarch Abraham lived in the second millennium B.C. Genesis, the first book of the Bible, tells how the devout 75-year-old man and his wife traveled to Canaan, where God promised him that his descendants would form a great nation. That nation took its name from Abraham's grandson, Jacob, also called Israel.

Jesus of Nazareth was a Galilean Jew born around A.D. 1. Jesus became a traveling preacher and healer, attracting many followers. Arrested by Roman authorities in Jerusalem, he was crucified around A.D. 30. His followers believed that he rose from the

MEMBERS OF THE CHURCH OF ZION in Durban, South Africa, perform a baptism in the Indian Ocean, enacting one of the rituals shared by all Christians, no matter what denomination.

dead, proving his divinity. They traveled and spread his teachings.

Muhammad was born in Mecca around 570. One night he saw a vision and heard a voice demanding obedience to the one god, Allah, and dictating scripture, which he transcribed: the Koran. Fearful for his life, Muhammad fled Mecca but later returned to take the city peacefully.

CLICK IT: Audio Koran www.quranexplorer.com

FAST FACT Muslims believe that the Arabic text of the Koran is the one authentic version.

THE BIBLE AND THE KORAN

The Jewish Bible consists of 24 books, written by many authors in Hebrew and Aramaic, and divided into three sections: the Torah (the first five books), the Prophets, and the Writings.

The Christian Bible begins with these writings, organized into 39 books, and calls them the Old Testament. It adds the New Testament, originally written in Greek, which describes the life and teachings of Jesus Christ and the history of the early church.

The Koran, the holy book of Islam, is held to be the word of God as revealed to Muhammad in stages over 20 years. The Koran is divided into 114 chapters, called suras, most in rhymed Arabic prose. It teaches that there is only one God, Allah, and contains many directives about moral conduct in daily life. Study of the Koran is a key part of Muslim education.

PRAYER FROM THE KORAN is one of the Five Pillars of Islam, practices required of every Muslim. Visiting Mecca, seasonal fasting, almsgiving, and profession of faith are the others.

FOR MORE FACTS ON...

THE HISTORY OF ISLAM see *Middle Ages 500-1000*, **CHAPTER 7, PAGES 278-9**

THE PROTESTANT REFORMATION see *Renaissance & Reformation 1500-1650*, **CHAPTER 7, PAGES 294-5**

Museumgoers and Picasso's "Dora Maar au Chat"

ART

Expressing oneself through art seems a universal human impulse, while the style of that expression is one of the distinguishing marks of a culture. As difficult as it is to define, art typically involves a skilled, imaginative creator, whose creation is pleasing to the senses and often symbolically significant or useful. Art can be verbal, as in poetry, storytelling, or literature, or can take the form of music and dance.

The oldest stories, passed down orally, may be lost to us now, but thanks to writing, tales such as the *Epic of Gilgamesh* (from the second millennium B.C.) or the *Iliad* (about the eighth century B.C.) entered the record and still hold meaning today.

Visual art dates back 30,000 years, when Paleolithic humans decorated themselves with beads and shells. Then as now, skilled artisans often mixed aesthetic effect with symbolic meaning. In an existence that centered around hunting, ancient Australians carved animal and bird tracks into their rocks; early cave artists in Lascaux, France, painted or engraved more than 2,000 real and mythical animals. Ancient Africans created stirring masks, highly stylized depictions of animals and spirits that allow the wearer to embody the spiritual power of those beings.

Even when creating tools or kitchen items, people seem unable to resist decorating or shaping them for beauty. Ancient hunters carved the ivory handles of their knives. Ming dynasty ceramists embellished plates with graceful dragons. Modern Pueblo Indians incorporate traditional motifs into their carved and painted pots.

The Western fine arts tradition values beauty and message. Once heavily influenced by Christianity and classical mythology, painting and sculpture has more recently moved toward personal expression and abstraction.

FOR MORE FACTS ON...

TOOLMAKING IN HUMAN HISTORY see *Human Migration*, **CHAPTER 6, PAGES 220-1, &** *Prehistory 10,000 B.C.-3500 B.C.*, **CHAPTER 7, PAGES 264-5**

ANCIENT ART OF CHINA see *China 2200 B.C.-A.D. 500*, **CHAPTER 7, PAGE 273**

WHEN WAS POTTERY FIRST MADE?

Humans have probably been molding clay—one of the most widely available materials in the world—since the earliest times. The era of ceramics began, however, only after the discovery that very high heat renders clay hard enough to be impervious to water. As societies grew more complex and settled, the need for ways to store water, food, and other commodities increased.

In Japan, the Jomon people were making ceramics as early as 11,000 B.C. By about the seventh millennium B.C., kilns were in use in the Middle East and China, achieving temperatures above 1832°F. Mesopotamians were the first to develop true glazes, though the art of glazing arguably reached its highest expression in the celadon and three-color glazes of medieval China. In the New World, although potters never reached the heights of technology seen

MAYA COVERED BOWL, found at Tikal, representing the potter's art of Mesoamerica around A.D. 400.

elsewhere, Moche, Maya, Aztec, and Puebloan artists created a diversity of expressive figurines and glazed vessels.

CLICK IT: Altamira Cave Paintings grupos.unican.es/arte/ingles/prehist/paleo/b

FAST FACT Bronze sculpture, virtually indestructible, may outlast all other human artwork.

THE WORLD'S FIRST ARTISTS

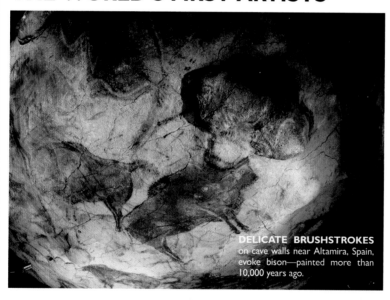

DELICATE BRUSHSTROKES on cave walls near Altamira, Spain, evoke bison—painted more than 10,000 years ago.

When Spanish nobleman Marcelino Sanz de Sautuola described the paintings he discovered in a cave in Altamira, contemporaries declared the whole thing a modern fraud. Subsequent finds confirmed the validity of his claims and proved that Paleolithic people were skilled artists.

Early artists used stone tools to engrave shapes into rock walls. They used pigments from hematite, manganese dioxide, and evergreens to achieve red, yellow, brown, and black colors. Brushes were made from feathers, leaves, and animal hair. Artists also used blowpipes to spray paint around hands and stencils.

GLOSSARY

Aesthetic: From Greek *aisthanesthai*, "to perceive" or "to feel." Relating to beauty or pleasing appearance. **/ Ceramics:** Objects created from such naturally occurring raw materials as clay minerals and quartz sand by shaping the material and then hardening it by firing at high temperatures.

FOR MORE FACTS ON...

EARLY AFRICAN STATUARY see Africa 500-1500, **CHAPTER 7, PAGE 283**

EARLY AMERICAN STATUARY see Oceania & North America Prehistory to 1500, **CHAPTER 7, PAGE 287**

Musicians on All Saints' Day, Toledo, Bolivia

MUSIC

INSTRUMENT FAMILIES

STRINGS
Balalaika (Russia)
Guzheng (China)
Oud (Turkey, Greece, N. Africa)
Sitar (India)

WIND
Bagpipes (Scotland)
Didgeridoo (Australia)
Mijwiz (Syria, Lebanon, Palestine)
Shofar (Middle East)

PERCUSSION
Castanets (Spain)
Maracas (Latin America)
Gong (Tibet, China)

KEYBOARD
Harmonium (Britain)
Kalimba (Africa)
Synthesizer (World)

Music is found across all cultures and all historical periods. The human voice was surely one of the earliest musical instruments; others may have developed from utensils and tools such as hollowed gourds or hunting bows. By 4000 B.C., Egyptians were playing harps and flutes; Hinduism's Vedic hymns, still chanted today, date back at least 3,000 years. Music is an integral form of ritual; it tells stories, bonds communities, fuels dancing, animates theater—and simply entertains.

In Papua New Guinea, the Kaluli people capture birdsong in their songs and drumming. A symphony orchestra does the same thing with a few more instruments when it performs Beethoven's *Pastoral* Symphony.

In general, whether created by the Kaluli or Beethoven, all music shares basic elements: tone or pitch, rhythm, melody, and tone color (the quality of the sound that distinguishes a violin from, say, a flute). The dominance of one element over another, the kinds of instruments used, and the musical scales and forms can vary dramatically from culture to culture.

FOR MORE FACTS ON...

THE PLACE OF MYTH & STORYTELLING IN HUMAN CULTURE see *Language*, **CHAPTER 6, PAGE 229**

HINDUISM see *Hinduism & Buddhism*, **CHAPTER 6, PAGES 234-5**

Western music, for instance, makes substantial use of harmony, while Asian music generally eschews harmony in favor of complex melody. Asian music is distinguished by the use of flutes, gongs, and plucked strings; African music by polyrhythmic drumming and close harmony; Arab music by complex vocal poetry.

Musical styles have increasingly spread across national boundaries, however. The slave trade brought African music to the New World, for example, fueling America's gospel, ragtime, and jazz. In the 19th century, Western composers began to seek out and incorporate elements from diverse cultures into their serious musical compositions.

With the advent of recording technology, then mass media, and then the Internet and MP3 players, the globalization of music has greatly accelerated. Western music now pervades the East, while Eastern sounds contribute to the scores to popular Hollywood films.

"World music" is a category known to music listeners today. A blend of indigenous, pop, and experimental music, it is the sound of the 21st century.

CLICK IT: Music of the World nationalgeographic.com/worldmusic

FAST FACT Medieval musicians considered an augmented fourth, as in C to F-sharp, to be "the devil in music."

BÉLA BARTÓK / COMPOSER

Béla Bartók (1881–1945), born in Hungary, was said to be able to play 40 folk songs on the piano by the age of four. As a young man, he was inspired by the new nationalistic fervor in eastern Europe to seek out authentic folk music. With fellow composer Zoltán Kodály, in the early years of the 20th century Bartók traveled through the countryside of Hungary, Romania, Bulgaria, Serbia, and other nations in search of music as it was actually performed by everyday people. Using wax recording cylinders that could be played back on the Edison phonograph, Bartók and Kodály recorded hundreds of folk tunes. The irregular rhythms and unusual scales and modes that they heard made their way into some of their most famous compositions.

WHAT IS A MUSICAL SCALE?

Musical traditions from different parts of the world derive their distinctive characters from their scales: the pattern of relationships among the baseline notes used. Traditional Western music uses a diatonic scale, a succession of seven steps—five whole steps and two half steps, or twelve equal half steps—that make up an octave. Asian music typically uses a pentatonic scale based on five pitches per octave (which can be sounded on the five black keys in a piano's octave). Indian music is also based on seven notes, but their relationships change depending on the style of music. Fine distinctions also abound in Islamic music, in which seven basic whole and half steps can be augmented by tones not found in Western scales.

MUSICAL NOTATION is an art form itself, as displayed in this page from a score for an operatic aria, handwritten by Mozart.

FOR MORE FACTS ON...

THE ROLE OF ART IN HUMAN CULTURE & THROUGH HISTORY see *Art*, **CHAPTER 6, PAGES 238-9**

THE USE OF COMPUTERS IN TODAY'S WORLD see *Computer Science*, **CHAPTER 8, PAGES 346-9**

TEXTILE TIME LINE

5000 B.C.
Cotton weaving in Pakistan, India & Africa

5000 B.C.
Flax weaving in Egypt

2700 B.C.
Silkworm cocoon thread used to weave cloth in China

500 B.C.
Spinning wheel developed in India

1790
Water-powered spinning mill in the U.S.

1910
Rayon developed

1938
Nylon developed

1952
Polyester developed

CLOTHING

The desire to drape skins and cloth around our bodies is a distinctly human one, shared by no other animal. Certainly clothing provides protection from the elements, but people in even the balmiest climes usually wear some sort of garments. The "fig leaf" theory holds that humans adopt clothing out of modesty, hiding taboo body parts from view; other experts believe that clothing is a form of sexual display. Possibly all of these apply to some degree in most cultures. But what seems clear is that clothing is both a symbol of identity and a visible indicator of social and economic status.

Given the perishable nature of animal skins and textiles, few examples of early human clothing remain. Sculptures, artwork, and ancient tools tell us that, in northern regions at least, Neolithic people wore clothing made of sewn animal skins, including sealskin. By about 8000 B.C., people had learned to weave textiles, possibly picking up the technique from basketweaving.

The earliest materials came from wild plants such as flax (which produces linen) and hemp; later came wool from sheep, cotton from India and Peru, and silk from China. Weaving and dyeing rapidly became an art form, visible in the exquisitely sheer linens of ancient Egypt and the delicately embroidered silks of early China. International trade in textiles started as early as the Phoenicians and remains a powerful economic force today. In the 20th century, chemists began to synthesize textiles, giving us durable, flexible—but not necessarily more attractive—fabrics ranging from nylon to Kevlar.

Fashion has long been a serious matter in hierarchical societies and was often regulated by sumptuary laws that sought to reduce frivolous spending

FOR MORE FACTS ON...

CLASS STRUCTURE IN HUMAN SOCIETY see *Race, Class & Gender,* **CHAPTER 6, PAGES 226-7**

TRADE & COMMERCE see *Commerce,* **CHAPTER 6, PAGES 254-5**

and keep social classes in line. By law, matrons in the Roman republic could wear no more than half an ounce of gold; in 1377, English king Edward III decreed that no one below the rank of knight could wear fur. Only the upper classes in medieval China wore long robes; members of the imperial court could wear the dragon robe. In many societies, fashions change from the top; upper classes adopt a style intended to differentiate them from lower orders. Inevitably, the lower classes begin to imitate the style, at which point the upper classes must invent new fashions to keep their status evident.

Until recently, clothing styles were clear markers of nationality; a Japanese kimono or an Inuit parka was an instant indicator of national origin. But increasing internationalization has broken down national barriers to fashion. Clothing around the world has become more Westernized, more casual, and less gender specific. Fashion, however, continues to change rapidly, and remains a potent symbol of identity.

FAST FACT In the 19th century, women's corsets were sometimes so tight that they deformed the rib cage and organs.

THE STATUS OF SILK

By 3000 B.C. the Chinese had discovered that the filament covering a silkworm cocoon could be unwound and woven into fabric. China guarded the secret of sericulture until about A.D. 300. By then, through Korean weavers migrating from China, Japan had learned the technique and soon mastered weaving and dyeing. Traders had also carried silk into Europe along the 4,000-mile Silk Road; Roman law forbade men from wearing the fabric, perceived as too feminine. Two Persian monks smuggled silkworms to Constantinople in the sixth century, and the art of silk production came to Europe. It flourished there until World War II, after which China and Japan regained their domination of silk production. Silk remains a mark of luxury and status.

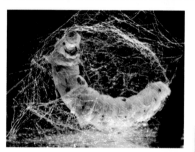

A SINGLE MULBERRY SILKWORM grows to a length of less than three inches, but it can weave a cocoon whose silken thread, when unwound, measures more than a mile.

CLICK IT: History of Silk www.silk.org.uk/history.htm

NECK RINGS, symbol of beauty and belonging, glisten on a Padaung woman from Thailand.

THE GLINT OF JEWELRY

One of the oldest of all human arts, jewelry is found in every human society and dates back to the earliest days of *Homo sapiens.* Perforated shells, some dyed red, have been found in North African caves and may be 80,000 years old. Paleolithic burials in Europe included jewelry of bone, shell, and amber. Metalworking and advanced toolmaking introduced gold, silver, bronze, and gems into jewelry, often to magnificent effect, as seen, for instance, in the spectacular pectoral necklace found in King Tut's tomb. Jewelry has been used as adornment, talisman, status symbol, expression of wealth, portable trading item, or money. Tuareg women in Africa, for example, wear their wealth on their bodies in bracelets and necklaces; in the West, a band on the left ring finger indicates the wearer is married.

FOR MORE FACTS ON...

MOTHS & THEIR COCOONS see *Butterflies & Moths,* **CHAPTER 4, PAGES** 152-3
+
THE EARLY DAYS OF THE HUMAN SPECIES see *Human Origins,* **CHAPTER 6, PAGES** 218-9, & *Human Migration,* **CHAPTER 6, PAGES** 220-1

Navajo woman, New Mexico, holding corn and cota, an herb used for tea

FOOD

WORLD'S TOP CROPS

SUGARCANE

MAIZE

WHEAT

RICE

POTATOES

SUGAR BEETS

SOYBEAN

OIL PALM FRUIT

BARLEY

TOMATOES

ood is a physical necessity. In human society, it is a cultural force as well. Early humans were hunters and gatherers, entailing cooperation and a division of labor, perhaps between male hunters and female gatherers. Our ancestors learned to make food preparation tools of increasing sophistication. Their diet was high in energy, about one-third of their calories coming from fats, one-third from proteins, and one-third from carbohydrates. The act of cooking and sharing a meal reinforced family and community bonds.

Between 10,000 B.C. and 3000 B.C., peoples in the Middle East, Southeast Asia, and other regions of Asia, Africa, and Europe underwent the first great revolution in human culture: the development of agriculture. They learned to domesticate sheep, pigs, and cattle and to grow crops, such as wheat, barley, rice, oats, millet, and flax. Farmers produced surpluses. People began to gather in villages, towns, and city-states, dividing into specialized occupations and forming social hierarchies based on wealth. Their diet diversified as different groups eagerly traded foods.

FOR MORE FACTS ON...

EARLY HUMANS see *Human Migration*, **CHAPTER 6, PAGES 220-1**

THE DEVELOPMENT AND HISTORY OF FOOD CROPS see *Agriculture*, **CHAPTER 6, PAGES 246-9**

Christopher Columbus and the other great travelers of the age of exploration inaugurated the next great transformation in food: the transfer of foods from the New World to the Old, and vice versa. Items such as tomatoes, potatoes, pineapples, and peanuts were brought to Europe, Asia, and Africa from the Americas; wheat, oats, sugarcane, and animals such as horses and sheep came to the Americas from Europe. Europeans learned to love hot chocolate and to smoke tobacco; Americans began to drink coffee and rum, made from sugar harvested on plantations in the West Indies.

By the 20th century, mechanized agriculture and especially the "green revolution"—the huge increase in production of high-yield grains in developing countries—had created an abundance of food, though unequally distributed.

Free-flowing food trade has begun to erase boundaries, with people around the world increasingly sharing a diet high in processed sugars, salt, dairy products, and meat.

CLICK IT: USDA Foreign Agricultural Service www.fas.usda.gov

FAST FACT Daily caloric intake for American women was 1,542 in 1971 and 1,877 in 2000 (1,600 is recommended).

FOODS THAT FEED THE WORLD

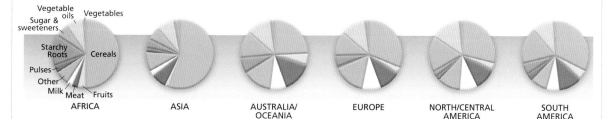

Vegetable oils · Vegetables · Sugar & sweeteners · Starchy Roots · Cereals · Pulses · Other · Milk · Meat · Fruits

AFRICA ASIA AUSTRALIA/OCEANIA EUROPE NORTH/CENTRAL AMERICA SOUTH AMERICA

Indicates breakdown of per-capita calorie supply

CEREALS, SWEETS, AND STARCHES dominate the world's diet. Rice, a labor-intensive plant, is the staple for about half the world's people. Wheat, best in temperate climates, is Earth's most widely cultivated grain. Corn (or maize), a staple in prehistoric Mexico and Peru, has spread around the world. Sugar and sweeteners form a surprisingly large part of the world's diet—particularly in the Americas, where they make up about a fifth of daily caloric consumption. Meat and milk make up about a fifth of the daily menu in developed countries.

YOU WANT FRIES WITH THAT?

Globalization is rapidly erasing the boundaries between nations' cuisines, with most countries in the world moving toward the Western-pattern diet: energy-dense meals rich in meat, dairy, and processed sugars. Many people think of this as the "fast-food diet," because providers such as McDonald's and KFC (Kentucky Fried Chicken) not only champion these kinds of high-fat, high-sugar meals, but are among the world's most widespread restaurant chains: McDonald's alone has more than 31,000 restaurants in 120 countries. As this diet has spread around the world, so has obesity. Approximately 1.6 billion adults are overweight and 400 million are obese, with the most rapid increase coming among low- and middle-income urban populations.

McDONALD'S and other American fast-food franchises have spread globally, obscuring long-held local food traditions.

FOR MORE FACTS ON...

CHANGES IN WORLD POPULATION see *World Population*, **CHAPTER 6, PAGES 250-1**

COLUMBUS & THE AGE OF EXPLORATION see *World Navigation 1492-1522*, **CHAPTER 7, PAGES 292-3**

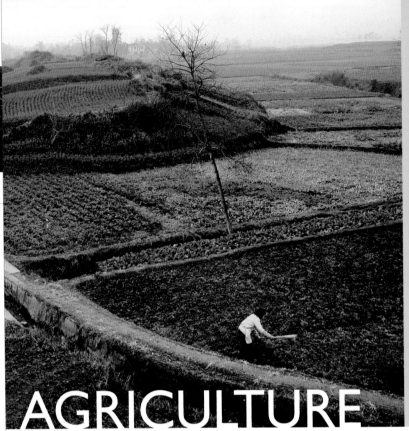

Preparing to plant lettuce, Sichuan Province, China

9000-7000 B.C.
Wheat and barley, sheep, and goats raised in Fertile Crescent

7000-3000 B.C.
Maize, squash, and other crops cultivated in Americas

6500 B.C.
Cattle domesticated in Greece

6000-5000 B.C.
Millet and rice harvested in China

5500 B.C.
Irrigation established in Mesopotamia

2500 B.C.
Grain agriculture helps Indus River Valley civilization evolve in Asia

A.D. 800
Open-field planting in western Europe

AGRICULTURE

Humans have been farming for only a brief part of their history. Until about 10,000 years ago, people fed themselves by hunting wild animals and gathering wild plants. Even today, some isolated peoples subsist this way. The shift to cultivating crops and domesticating wild animals marked a profound transition in human culture, one that led to the rise of cities, writing, and hierarchical societies, as well as plagues and technology.

Agriculture arose independently in at least five areas of the world: the Fertile Crescent, China, Mesoamerica, the Andes, and eastern North America. In the Fertile Crescent, hunters harvested grain with flint knives and began to herd sheep and goats for food and clothing. Attempts such as scattering seeds to enlarge production or controlling the feeding and breeding of herd animals laid the foundations of an agricultural society. In northern China, millet cultivation, silkworm farming, and the domestication of both pigs and dogs characterized village life from about the seventh millennium B.C. Mesoamerican farmers developed seed crops such as maize, beans, and squash during the sixth millennium B.C. Crops and farming techniques spread especially rapidly from the Middle East to Europe and Asia, given similar growing conditions and a relative lack of geographical barriers, whereas in South America and Africa diffusion may have been hampered by differing climates and obstacles such as deserts and jungles.

In Asia and Europe, the invention of the plow made possible the use of draft animals, the development of larger fields, and the cultivation of heavier soils. Organized agriculture everywhere encouraged larger settlements and growing populations. When one family could feed 20 others, people were free to specialize in other occupations and develop organized societies.

FOR MORE FACTS ON...

DESERT & JUNGLE CLIMATES see Climate, **CHAPTER 5, PAGES 192-3, &** Rain Forests, **CHAPTER 5, PAGES 198-9**

THE TRANSITION TO AGRICULTURE see Human Migration, **CHAPTER 6, PAGES 220-1**

WHEN WERE ANIMALS DOMESTICATED?

In the history of agriculture, the domestication of animals is as important as the domestication of plants. They provide transportation, military might, and companionship. Dogs were probably the first animals domesticated, bred from wolves as long as 12,000 years ago to accompany early hunters. By 9000 B.C. or so, Middle Eastern nomads began to breed sheep and goats for meat. Not long afterward, perhaps by 7000 B.C., Asian farmers domesticated cattle and pigs. Early civilizations soon bred cats as mousers; in Egypt, they gained sacred status. From 3000 to 1500 B.C., transport animals begin to appear: horses in Asia, asses in Egypt, camels in north Africa and Asia, and llamas and alpacas in South America. In the next centuries, poultry, bees, and rabbits began to be domesticated too.

CHICKENS, a double-duty food source, may have evolved from Asian jungle fowl domesticated as early as 3000 B.C. Eggs have been gathered and eaten by humans for tens of thousands of years.

CLICK IT: Food in History www.foodtimeline.org

FAST FACT Einkorn, an ancient wheat, was gathered by humans in the Stone Age, 10,000 B.C., and possibly earlier.

RICE CULTIVATION dates back to well before 5000 B.C. in East Asia, where Chinese farmers living in the delta of the Yangtze River cultivated rice in irrigated fields. The labor-intensive work is partially mechanized now in much of the world, but in Asia, where most rice is grown, it is still nurtured and harvested by hand. A grass, rice grows in stands of water called paddies. Rice represents a staple food for more than half the world. It is the endosperm—the heart of the seed—that humans eat.

G L O S S A R Y

Cultivation: Loosening and breaking up (tilling) of the soil around existing plants. **/ Subsistence farming:** A form of farming in which nearly all the crops or livestock raised are used to maintain the farmer and his family, leaving little surplus for sale or trade.

FOR MORE FACTS ON...

THE IMPORTANCE OF DIVERSITY AMONG EARTH'S SPECIES see Biodiversity, **CHAPTER 4, PAGES 174-5**

THE POPULATION, ECONOMY & HISTORY OF CHINA see Asia, **CHAPTER 9, PAGE 392**

MODERN

By the 17th century, commercial (for-profit) agriculture began to overtake subsistence farming in Europe and its colonies. Enclosed fields, improvements in breeding stock and seeds, crop rotation, and the introduction of new foods from the Americas all boosted yields and drove down the price of food. By the 19th century, mechanization—the cotton gin, the threshing machine, and more—brought about a revolution not only in farming, but also in the workforce in more developed parts of the world. The new machines drastically reduced the number of workers needed per acre, driving countless rural families off farms and freeing up a labor supply that was quickly absorbed by industrializing societies. Mechanization only increased over the 20th century, introducing scores of petroleum-hungry machines into farming, making it a highly productive but energy-intensive business.

Agriculture in today's developed world is more rightly termed agri-business. The total number of farms in the United States declined in the last half of the 20th century from 5.5 million to 2.2 million, while the average farm size rose from 200 acres to 436. Fewer than 3 percent of American and Canadian workers are farmers now; the figure is 9 percent in Europe. In the less developed world, smaller subsistence farms still feed many families. Over 60 percent of workers in Asia and sub-Saharan Africa are farmers; the average farm size in India is 5 acres. Growing populations and civil wars have led to famines in some of these areas, even while the United States—the world's largest producer of agricultural goods—exports a food surplus.

Recently, new technologies have been reshaping agriculture, particularly in the developed world. The computer revolution introduced digital controls for irrigation, the application of pesticides, and harvesting. Sometimes referred to as the Third Agricultural Revolution, recent innovations—fertilizers, hybrid seeds, agrochemicals, and recombinant DNA techniques for genetically altering crops—have increased productivity further. However, agriculture's dependence on oil, the world's limited supply of arable land, shortages of groundwater, and the erosion of delicate environments, among other issues, will make the task of feeding the world a challenging one in the 21st century.

GPS TECHNOLOGY installed in his tractor helps an Illinois farmer track his path as he spreads fertilizer and sprays herbicides.

FOR MORE FACTS ON...

GLOBAL POSITIONING SYSTEM (GPS) & HOW IT WORKS see *Advances in Mapping*, **CHAPTER 1, PAGES 28-9**
+
DNA & GENETIC ENGINEERING see *Genetics*, **CHAPTER 8, PAGES 344-5**

WHAT WAS THE GREEN REVOLUTION?

During and shortly after World War II, the Rockefeller Foundation led efforts to boost agricultural productivity in developing countries by applying science to the selective breeding of high-yield, high-protein "miracle crops." These efforts produced many new strains of fast-growing rice and wheat. Miracle crops often yielded two or three harvests per year, compared with one for most traditional breeds, and each crop was two to three times larger; often they were more drought and disease resistant as well. Critics pointed out that the crops often required more water, fertilizer, pesticides, and money than indigenous crops, increasing costs for small farmers. However, the results were indisputable. In the 1960s, these crops were introduced to such rapidly growing countries as Mexico, India, the Philippines, Indonesia, Bangladesh, and Egypt. Asian rice productivity almost doubled, and green revolution crops accounted for most of the world's agricultural productivity gains in the 1960s and 1970s and for 80 percent in the 1980s.

MASS PRODUCTION depends on top technology. Here an Iowa combine reaps 27,000 bushels—over 750 tons—of corn in one harvest.

GLOSSARY

Aquaculture: The rearing of fish, shellfish, and some aquatic plants to supplement the natural supply. **/ Hybrid:** From Latin *ibrida*, "mongrel." Offspring of parents that differ in genetically determined traits; usually refers to animals or plants resulting from a cross between two races, breeds, strains, or varieties of the same species accomplished by human intervention.

THE FUTURE OF FISH FARMING

One of the fastest-growing areas of food production in the world is aquaculture, or fish farming—the controlled breeding, raising, and harvesting of fish and the cultivation of seaweed. Techniques for fish farming date back some 4,000 years in China.

About 90 percent of aquaculture occurs in developing countries, with China accounting for a bit more than two-thirds of the world's total output. Aquaculture now produces 40 percent of the fish that people eat around the world; experts project that by 2010, fish farming may overtake cattle ranching as a world food source.

A CHINESE FISH FARMER stands proudly amid a swirl of catfish he has grown.

CLICK IT: UN Food and Agriculture Organization www.fao.org

FAST FACT Americans eat about eight ounces of meat a day—twice the world average.

FOR MORE FACTS ON...

THE BIOLOGY & ANATOMY OF FISH see *Fish*, **CHAPTER 4, PAGES 158-9**
+
THE GROWING WORLD POPULATION see *World Population*, **CHAPTER 6, PAGES 250-1**

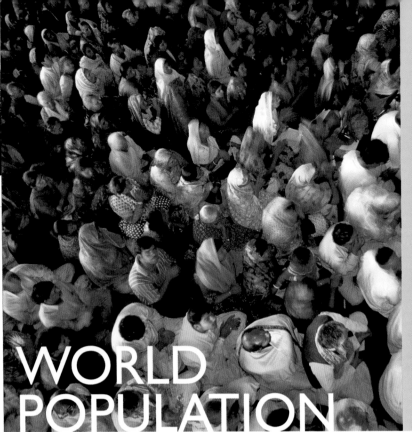

HIGHEST FERTILITY RATES

AVERAGE BIRTHS
PER WOMAN'S LIFETIME

GUINEA-BISSAU / 7.1

NIGER / 7.1

EAST TIMOR / 7.0

AFGHANISTAN / 6.8

ANGOLA / 6.8

BURUNDI / 6.8

LIBERIA / 6.8

SOMALIA / 6.8

DEMOCRATIC REPUBLIC
OF CONGO / 6.7

MALI / 6.6

WORLD POPULATION

From around 8000 B.C. to the mid-17th century, the world's population grew slowly from 10 million to 500 million. The human presence on Earth was limited by the planet's carrying capacity—its ability to sustain human life on the available land. Then, beginning in the 19th century, the industrial revolution, huge increases in agricultural productivity, and great strides in health care brought about an explosion in human numbers.

From one billion people in the early 1800s, the population expanded with increasing speed, reaching 6.6 billion in 2007. More than one-third of that total lives in two countries, China and India, with populations of 1.3 billion and 1.1 billion respectively.

The growth equation is simple: Births minus deaths equals the rate of natural increase. At a 2007 annual rate of 1.2 percent, population growth worldwide translates by 2050 to a total of 9.3 billion human beings. Much of that increase is taking place in less developed countries: Sub-Saharan African countries such as Mali, Niger, and Uganda have rates of increase over 3 percent. In the more developed world, by contrast, rates are typically low or even declining. Russia and Germany, among others, will see their populations drop over the coming decades.

Country populations also grow or shrink due to migration. Immigration to industrialized countries has been on the rise since the 1980s. Canada's foreign-born population is close to 20 percent, and immigrants make up well over 10 percent of populations in the United States and Ireland. Small, wealthy countries

FAST FACT The total number of humans born since 50,000 B.C. is estimated at 105.7 billion.

FOR MORE FACTS ON...

EARLY HUMAN MIGRATION see Human Migration, CHAPTER 6, PAGES 220-1
+
URBANIZATION IN RECENT TIMES see Cities, CHAPTER 6, PAGES 260-1

such as Qatar or Singapore draw foreign workers in droves; poorer nations in war-torn regions, such as Botswana, swell with refugees as well as job seekers.

NEWBORNS ABOUND at the Xining Children Hospital, Qinghai Province, China. Chinese population experts predict a small baby boom in the coming years. Already 110,000,000 children under six live in China.

FAST FACT By 2050, India will be the world's most populous country, with 1.7 billion people.

THOMAS MALTHUS / POLITICAL ECONOMIST

Born into a society that believed in steady human progress, Englishman Thomas Robert Malthus (1766-1834) took a dimmer view. A professor of history and political economy, Malthus published *An Essay on the Principles of Population as It Affects the Future Improvement of Society* in 1798, which notes that although the populations tend to grow geometrically—exponentially—food supplies increase arithmetically, at a constant absolute rate. Clearly, he said, the future holds famine, unless populations could be held in check by such means as war, disease, and abstinence. Malthus understandably failed to foresee the agricultural revolution or the advent of widespread contraception. Nevertheless, his views continue to be influential among economists and policymakers in a world beset by rapid population growth, war, and famine.

> Population, when unchecked, increases in a geometrical ratio. Subsistence increases only in an arithmetical ratio. — **THOMAS MALTHUS, 1798**

THE AGING WORLD

Although populations continue to grow, fertility rates on average have dropped. This, combined with improvements in health care and life expectancy, means that the world's population is an aging one, particularly in industrialized countries. By 2050, 26 percent of Europe's population will be over 65, as will be 21 percent of North America's. These countries will face the problem of having a dwindling workforce supporting a populace in need of more health care, even while countries at the other end of the spectrum will contend with many young mouths to feed and educate. Every country, in the end, will face the same challenge of nurturing a changing population with limited resources.

POLISH ELDERS meet at a park in Krakow and pass their time playing—or commenting on—a game of cards.

FOR MORE FACTS ON...

WORLD HISTORY IN MALTHUS'S TIME see *Revolutions 1600-1800, Nationalism 1790-1900 & The Industrial Revolution 1765-1900*, **CHAPTER 7, PAGES 298-303**

ADVANCES IN MEDICINE see *Medical Science*, **CHAPTER 8, PAGES 338-45**

Traffic jam, Bangkok, Thailand

TRANSPORTATION

TRANSPORT TIME LINE

CIRCA 3500 B.C.
First known wheel, Mesopotamia

3000 B.C.
Egyptians build sailing ships

A.D. 1769
Cugnot invents steam-propelled vehicle

1783
Montgolfier brothers fly hot-air balloon

1807
Fulton operates successful steamboat

1885-1886
Daimler & Benz build gas-powered auto

1903
Wilbur and Orville Wright fly airplane

ransportation shapes the world: Along with communications, it forms a global net that connects each person to the next, one city to another, and every country to every other country. Transportation routes, such as roads, waterways, and airways, as well as vehicles—feet, carts, steamships, jets— are vital to the functioning and spread of every civilization.

A country's economy depends on reliable transportation for its trade. Cities spread out along roads, rivers, and rails. Information travels along the same routes, as do armies, who depend on roads as much as they do weapons in their campaigns. Until the 20th century, these routes were by land or water. With the invention of powered flight, the air became an open road as well.

The earliest way of traveling was undoubtedly by foot, and humans' earliest means of transporting goods was carrying loads on their back or head. By 4000 B.C., people were using domesticated animals for transport, a method greatly improved in some parts of the world by the invention of the wheel, which was probably first developed in Mesopotamia around 3500 B.C.

FOR MORE FACTS ON...

MAPS & THEIR ROLE IN HUMAN TRANSPORTATION see *The History of Mapping & Mapmaking,* **CHAPTER 1, PAGES 20-1, 24-9**
+
ANIMAL MIGRATION see *Migration,* **CHAPTER 4, PAGES 172-3**

Until the 19th century, animals were the engines of land transportation. But with the invention of the steam engine and the internal combustion engine, railroads and automobiles revolutionized travel and trade. More than 600 million cars and trucks travel the world today.

Water has always been a fast and economical mode of travel, and even today it remains a primary mover of heavy goods. The importance of waterways to human civilization can be seen on any map: Virtually all of the world's major cities are located on coastlines or rivers. As early as 7000 B.C., people were building dugout canoes; long-distance sailing ships were common by about 3000 B.C. Steam and internal combustion engines greatly boosted the speed and efficiency of ships in the 19th and 20th centuries. Until the 1950s, ships were the chief means of overseas passenger travel. Now most oceangoing vessels are used to carry heavy cargo or for military transport.

JET AIRCRAFT picked up speed rapidly during the Cold War era. The fastest supersonic craft was the Lockheed SR-71 Blackbird (above), which logged 24 years of service with the Air Force. On its final flight, in March 1990, the two-seat titanium Blackbird set a speed record by flying from Los Angeles to Washington, D.C., in 1 hour, 4 minutes, 20 seconds—an average of 2,124 miles an hour.

Although the Montgolfier brothers and their successors took flight in balloons in the 18th century, air travel was not practical until the invention of powered flight in 1903. Within ten years, the commercial aviation business had begun. Two world wars spurred rapid technological advances, including the advent of jet aircraft in 1939. In 1958, Pan American World Airways began transatlantic passenger service and air travel blossomed. Passenger volume worldwide is forecast to reach 2.8 billion annually by 2018.

CLICK IT: On the Move americanhistory.si.edu/onthemove

FAST FACT The Wright brothers' first successful flight lasted only 12 seconds.

HOW DID HUMANS BUILD WITHOUT WHEELS?

Once ancient builders had the wheel, they could transport heavy materials to their building sites. Yet even before the wheel, civilizations managed to build huge, heavy structures, such as Egypt's pyramids or Britain's stone circles. How did they do it?

Most theories involve a combination of water transport, sledges, ramps, rolling logs, and brute force. The 2.5-ton blocks of sandstone, granite, and other materials that built the pyramids could have been floated on barges down the Nile from their quarries—but on land they would have to have been dragged on sleds, perhaps over wooden rollers. Once at the building site, workers probably had to drag the stones up ramps. The mysterious folk who built Britain's Neolithic monument Stonehenge may have used similar techniques. Some of its massive stones were quarried in Wales, 240 miles away. The builders may have used rafts, sledges, log rollers, and serious muscle power to bring the stones to Salisbury Plain.

FOR MORE FACTS ON...

CITIES AS GATEWAYS OF TRADE & TRANSPORTATION see Cities, **CHAPTER 6, PAGE 261**

ENGINEERING ACCOMPLISHMENTS ANCIENT & MODERN see Physical Science: Engineering, **CHAPTER 8, PAGES 332-3**

Fruit vendors in Old City, Jerusalem

BIGGEST FOOD COMPANIES
(NOT RANK-ORDERED)

NESTLE S.A.
Switzerland

KRAFT FOODS, INC.
USA (Illinois)

CONAGRA, INC.
USA (Nebraska)

PEPSICO, INC.
USA (New York)

UNILEVER PIC
UK & Netherlands

ARCHER DANIELS MIDLAND
USA (Illinois)

COMMERCE

Trade—the traffic in goods—has been a social and economic institution since prehistoric times. In the form of gift, barter, or sale, trade can take place between individuals, clans, companies, or countries. It is closely linked to transportation, so the people who have dominated world trade have typically dominated its trade routes as well.

Phoenicians were among the world's great early trade powers. From about 1200 B.C., Phoenician galleys dominated shipping in the Mediterranean for more than a thousand years. Their wares, including bronze, gold, ivory and glass artifacts, textiles, and furniture, have been found from one end of the Mediterranean to the other.

To the east, the Chinese of the Han dynasty began to spread out across overland caravan routes. Flourishing from 200 B.C. to A.D. 200 and again about 1,000 years later, these routes eventually linked Asia to Europe and came to be known as the Silk Road. More than silk traveled these routes, however. Asian traders bought spices like cinnamon, cloves, and nutmeg to Europeans; Mediterranean merchants traded wools, gold, silver, glassware, olive oil, and wine.

The Vikings, better known as raiders, were traders as well. In the early Middle Ages they traveled along the coasts and rivers into what is now Russia. They carried furs, amber, jewelry, and glass throughout northern Europe. In the south, the Crusades opened up the Near East and the Silk Road routes to Venetian traders, among them the inimitable Polo family.

With the age of exploration and the opening of sea lanes to Asia, commerce and national power became even more closely linked. In the 17th and 18th centuries, companies dedicated to trade with Asia were formed in Europe, most notably the Dutch and the English East India Companies.

FOR MORE FACTS ON...

EARLY MAPS FOR TRADE & TRAVEL see The World in Maps & The History of Mapping, **CHAPTER 1, PAGES 18-21**

TRADE IN MEDIEVAL TIMES see Middle Ages 500-1500, **CHAPTER 7, PAGES 278-81**

These organizations were practically countries in their own right, exercising sovereign powers, administering colonies, and waging war. The Dutch East India Company exercised a trade monopoly in Indonesia, the Malay Peninsula, Ceylon, the Malabar Coast of India, Japan, and South Africa in the 1600s. In the 18th century the English East India Company established a monopoly in India and China, maintaining political control over most of India until the Indian Mutiny of 1857. New economic theories, industrialization, and revolutions in transportation and communications have begun to change the face, but not the underlying nature, of world trade.

GLOSSARY

Commerce: The exchange of economic goods on a large scale. **/ Monopoly:** The exclusive possession of a market by a supplier of a product or service for which there is no substitute.

WHAT IS CURRENCY?

In prehistoric times—and even in some contemporary African societies—cattle were used as currency. By 1200 B.C., the Chinese used cowrie shells; 200 years later, they began to circulate metal versions, the first coins. Round, stamped coins of precious metals appeared in Turkey, Greece, and the Roman Empire beginning in 500 B.C.

In A.D. 806, China created the first paper money. Marco Polo described with admiration the Chinese paper money he encountered in the 13th century; Europe did not use paper currency until the 17th century. China also experienced the hazards of easily printed currency early on: Medieval Mongol rulers printed so much that it became virtually valueless, a problem still plaguing many inflation-racked countries today.

CURRENCY typically means metal coins and paper money to modern users, but any agreed-upon item, arbitrary and consistent, can suffice as a symbol of monetary value.

CLICK IT: Silk Road Foundation www.silk-road.com

FAST FACT Bricks of compressed tea leaves, sometimes glued with yak dung, once served as currency in parts of Asia.

LOCAL TRADE

Barter—a moneyless trading system still prevalent in traditional societies—is the oldest form of commerce. Almost anything can be bartered: labor for food, cattle for sheep. But the person doing the bartering must put time and effort into finding a partner willing to trade. Bartering exists today, supported by the Internet (and taxed, when possible, by the government).

CHINESE FARMERS discuss the price of a calf: Local economies continue despite the growing prevalence of international commerce.

FOR MORE FACTS ON...

HUMAN PREHISTORY see Human Migration, **CHAPTER 6, PAGES 220-1**
+
IMPERIALISM & TRADE see Imperialism: Middle East & Africa 1500-1900 & Imperialism: Asia & Pacific 1750-1900, **CHAPTER 7, PAGES 304-7**

COMMERCE

WORLD TRADE TODAY

The mercantilism of the 17th and 18th centuries, in which countries sought to accumulate wealth and territory through dominance of trade, has given way in recent years to an interdependent web of associations in which countries promote trade in order to build their economies. Few nations now could survive without trade with other countries, and for some, international trade makes up more than half the national income. This exchange of goods and services benefits trading partners by allowing them to export the goods that they are best at producing and import those that are best produced abroad. The greatest amount of trade occurs between the richest countries, demonstrating what economists call the gravity equation: Like attraction between two masses, the volume of trade between two countries is proportional to the size of their economies and the distance between them.

Richer countries typically exchange different varieties of similar manufactured goods, such as automobiles. When higher income regions trade with lower income regions, the richer countries usually provide more complex goods, such as electronic equipment, while low-income countries provide primary goods such as minerals. Smaller, poorer countries are more likely to be dependent on exporting a single commodity, such as coffee or petroleum. In general, poor, labor-abundant countries tend to export labor-intensive goods, such as textiles and shoes, and the countries rich in arable land will export foods such as grains.

Germany, the United States, and China, with its rapidly growing economy, now lead the globe in the total value of their merchandise exports. In general, the value of a country's imports is close to the value of its exports. The exception is the United States, which, driven by huge consumer demand in the early 21st century, imported far more than it exported. The result of such a trade imbalance has been a large trade deficit.

CRUDE OIL OPTIONS TRADER at the New York Mercantile Exchange yells out a bid. Even the most sophisticated marketplaces still teem with human emotion.

FOR MORE FACTS ON...

THE INTERNET AS A FORCE FOR INTERNATIONAL COMMUNICATIONS see The Internet, **CHAPTER 8, PAGES 348-9**
+
UNIONS, AGREEMENTS & ASSOCIATIONS AMONG COUNTRIES OF THE WORLD see Nations & Alliances, **CHAPTER 9, PAGES 358-9**

OUTSOURCING

Although outsourcing, or hiring outside contractors to perform jobs that could be done by employees, has been much in the news in recent years, it is nothing new to business.

In recent years outsourcing has been increasingly linked to offshoring, the use of contract labor from other countries. This form of outsourcing is driven by differences in labor costs, since workers in countries such as China or India typically make a small percentage of the wages paid in the most developed countries.

Facilitated by the 24-hour connections of the Internet, service jobs such as customer call centers have long been popular forms of international outsourcing.

Increasingly, jobs in areas like financial management and information technology are also going to well-

CALL CENTER RESPONDENTS live and work in Mohali, Punjab, India, but they answer service questions from American users of Quark software.

educated workers in countries such as India. Outsourcing and offshoring continue to be controversial topics in many developed countries, where local workers feel they are losing jobs to foreign competitors.

CLICK IT: World Trade Organization www.wto.org

GLOSSARY

Manufacturing: From Latin *manu*, "hand," + *factus*, "completed" or "accomplished." The fabrication or assembly of components into finished products on a large scale. **/ Mercantilism:** A policy influential in Europe from the 16th century to the 18th century that called for government regulation of a nation's economy in order to increase its power at the expense of rival nations.

WHO INVENTED CONTAINERIZATION?

American businessman Malcolm McLean started out as a truck driver hauling farm goods during the Depression, but he ultimately developed a system that revolutionized world trade: containerization.

McLean recognized that unloading trucks and ships crate by crate was

slow and inefficient. He saw that cargo could be packed and shipped far more easily if goods were packed into separate, detachable freight containers that could be hauled by trucks or trains without being emptied.

Containerization soon broke down transport barriers and created

vast networks comprising merchant ships, rail, and road links. Standardized units whose shipping costs fall as their payload increases, containers have greatly reduced time and costs in shipping; a shipment from Hong Kong to New York that took 50 days in 1970 now takes just 17.

FAST FACT The United States accounts for about one-fifth of the world's imports of fuel.

FOR MORE FACTS ON...

THE HISTORY & VARIETY OF MODES OF TRANSPORTATION see *Transportation,* **CHAPTER 6, PAGES 252-3**

+

THE ECONOMY OF HONG KONG see *Asia,* **CHAPTER 9, PAGE 392**

258

SHELTER

TALLEST BUILDINGS

BURJ DUBAI / 3,117 FEET
Dubai, United Arab Emirates

TAIPEI 101 / 1,669 FEET
Taipei, Taiwan

BUSAN LOTTE TOWER / 1,620 FEET
Busan, South Korea

SHANGHAI WORLD FINANCIAL CENTER / 1,614 FEET
Shanghai, China

ABRAJ AL BAIT TOWERS / 1,591 FEET
Mecca, Saudi Arabia

INTERNATIONAL COMMERCE CENTRE / 1,588 FEET
Hong Kong, China

As they have done with other necessities of life, humans have taken the need for shelter and turned it into a social statement and an art form. At its most basic, human shelter must provide protection against the elements, a place to sleep, a location for a fire, access to the outside, and a light source. Yet even cave dwellers more than 30,000 years ago went so far as to decorate the walls of their caves with exquisite images of bears, lions, mammoths, and humans.

As civilizations grew up around centers of trade and agriculture, human shelters came to reflect a host of influences. They incorporated their environment in both their plans and their materials: mud bricks in the ancient (and modern) Middle East, wood in the forested realms of Europe and North America, or limestone in the Karst regions of China.

They also reflected social and economic status. By the Middle Ages, wealthy landowners built themselves large castles and palaces that served as social centers, defensive fortifications, and visible exemplars of power,

FOR MORE FACTS ON...

TREES & FORESTS see *Trees,* **CHAPTER 4, PAGES 142-3,** & *Forests,* **CHAPTER 5, PAGES 196-203**

THE MIDDLE AGES see *Middle Ages 500-1500,* **CHAPTER 7, PAGES 278-81**

while peasants shared their single-room dwellings—built with straw and mud—with their animals. The social extremes of Europe in the 17th and 18th centuries found their greatest symbol in the palace of Versailles, the French royal residence, a complex of extravagant buildings on 37,000 acres that could house 5,000 inhabitants (mostly servants).

Grand palaces also formed visible displays of imperial power in Asia, but everyday houses exemplified the spiritual and social philosophies of the average family. Chinese houses were (and often still are) built facing south and oriented toward local mountains and streams according to the practice of feng shui, which seeks to maximize nature's positive influences on the inhabitants. Houses in China were typically built around an inner courtyard, without windows to the outside, to protect a family's privacy.

In the Western world, the industrial revolution brought new technologies and an expanding middle class. These prospering workers built themselves more standardized, comfortable, single-family houses, even while the poor crowded into tenements. Improved transportation routes soon spawned suburbs, with larger houses standing on more land. Technology brought heating, lighting, and indoor plumbing to the masses, while steel and elevators made tall apartment buildings possible.

Contemporary building techniques and materials have made housing more comfortable for much of the world, but the rules that governed the ancient Romans still apply to 21st-century dwellings: Wealth, occupation, and social status still play a part in shaping human shelters, from the favelas of Rio de Janeiro to the Mc-Mansions of the American suburb.

GLOSSARY

Feng shui: From the Chinese, "wind" + "water." A traditional Chinese method of arranging the human and social world in auspicious alignment with the forces of the cosmos. **/ Tepee:** From the Dakota, "to dwell." A tall conical tent dwelling used by the Plains Indians of North America.

HAVE YURT, WILL TRAVEL

Homes need not be anchored to the ground. Nomadic peoples around the world have perfected portable, practical dwellings that can be packed up and moved on short notice. The nomads of Mongolia and Kyrgyzstan, for instance, live in ergonomic round structures of felt on wood lattices, called yurts or gers. These can be rapidly disassembled, packed into a truck or onto a camel's back, and transported to a new place. The camel-herding Tuareg of Niger also move frequently. Their sturdy tents, supported on curved sticks, are built and owned by the women of the community. Evenki reindeer herders also live in canvas or deerskin-covered tepees that they pack up and move as they follow their herds.

The simple, efficient construction of these kinds of portable homes has changed little over the generations.

A HOUSE IN THE ROUND, the ger—still a common dwelling in Mongolia—is constructed of a wood frame and fabric covering.

CLICK IT: Great Buildings Collection www.greatbuildings.com

FAST FACT The Kombai of Papua New Guinea live as high as a hundred feet in the air in wood-and-vine tree houses.

FOR MORE FACTS ON...

THE TREND TOWARD URBANIZATION *The Industrial Revolution 1765-1900,* **CHAPTER 7, PAGE 303**

URBAN LIFE *see Cities,* **CHAPTER 6, PAGES 260-1**

Times Square, New York

CITIES

alf of the world now lives in cities. Between 1960 and 2007, city dwellers more than tripled in number, from 1 billion to 3.3 billion, while the world population roughly doubled, from just over 3 billion to 6.6 billion. Analysts predict 6.4 billion urban dwellers by 2050—86 percent of the population in more developed countries and 67 percent in less developed nations. China and India will account for one-third of the increase.

Clearly, the world's cities are growing in both size and number.

In 1975 there were 174 urban agglomerations of 1 to 5 million people and 17 urban areas of 5 to 10 million. Today there are approximately 360 metropolitan areas of 1 to 5 million and 30 metropolitan areas of 5 to 10 million.

City size is not the only factor in deciding which areas become dominant in the world. Ever since the advent of merchant capitalism in the 15th century, certain cities, known as world cities, have played key roles in the world's economy. In earlier centuries, these were such cities as Berlin, Venice, and Lisbon. Today, with the globalization of the economy, the roles of world cities are less about imperial power and more about multinational corporate organization, international banking and finance, and the work of international agencies.

These influential cities do include some of the largest in the world, including London, New York, and Tokyo. But they also include Brussels, Chicago, Frankfurt, Los Angeles, Paris, Singapore, Zurich, and Washington, D.C. These world cities are centers of authority, containing specialized firms and expert professionals. They channel their nation's resources into the global economy and transmit the impulses of globalization back to national centers—pivotal points in the reorganization of global space.

FOR MORE FACTS ON...

THE RAPID EXPANSION OF THE WORLD'S POPULATION see World Population, CHAPTER 6, PAGES 250-1

THE GREAT CITIES OF AFRICA see Africa, CHAPTER 9, PAGE 371

YESTERDAY'S GATEWAY CITIES, TODAY'S HISTORY

Some of the world's biggest and most prosperous urban centers arose during the 17th century as gateway cities—cities that because of their location served as links between one country or region and others.

Gateway cities include Boston, Charleston, Savannah, Recife, and Rio de Janeiro in the Americas; Luanda and Cape Town in Africa; Aden in Yemen; Goa and Colombo around the Indian Ocean; and Malacca, Manila, and Macau in East Asia.

Protected by fortifications and European naval power, they began as trading posts and colonial administrative centers. Before long they developed their own manufacturing industries and commercial and financial services. As colonies developed, many gateways grew rapidly, becoming major population centers as well as important markets for imported European goods.

CLICK IT: Shelter for All—United Nations Settlement Programme www.unhabitat.org

SHANTYTOWNS

The unprecedented rates of urban growth in developing regions have been driven by rural push—overpopulation and the unemployment in the countryside—rather than by the pull of resources of towns and cities. Many cities, particularly in developing countries, have added more people than they have jobs or housing. This overurbanization creates instant slums, characterized by shacks, open sewers, and squatter settlements. Typically, well over one-third of the population of major cities in less developed countries lives in these unofficial settlements. The shantytown of Dharavi in Mumbai, India, contains 600,000 people in tin shacks on just one square mile of land—land said to be worth ten billion dollars. The favelas of Rio de Janeiro, over 500 squatter settlements on the city's hillsides, have housed the poor for generations. Housing shortages in Cairo, Egypt, have driven as many as one million poor Cairenes to live in "cities of the dead" among the tombs of Cairo's cemeteries. Occupants in these ramshackle settlements pay no rent and do not own the land, but in some cities they have developed a sense of community ties and a viable, if difficult, way of life.

WITH HOUSES built right up to the water line, this favela, or shantytown, represents the precarious edge of urban sprawl in Manaus, Brazil, a city of more than a million on the Amazon.

FAST FACT More than 20,000 Chinese leave the countryside to settle in urban areas every day.

FOR MORE FACTS ON...

HOUSING see Shelter, **CHAPTER 6, PAGES 258-9**

HISTORY OF THE 17TH CENTURY see Renaissance & Reformation 1500-1650 & A New World 1500-1775, **CHAPTER 7, PAGES 294-7**

Prehistory / Mesopotamia / Egypt
Rome / Middle Ages / Africa /
/ Mesoamerica / South America
& Reformation / A New World / Re
Revolution / Imperialism / Worl

WORLD

India / China / Greece & Persia /
Asia / Oceania & North America
/ World Navigation / Renaissance
lution / Nationalism / The Industrial
Wars / Cold War / Globalization

HISTORY

Egyptian vase, circa 3600 B.C.

MAJOR PERIODS
OF HISTORY

ANCIENT HISTORY
3500 B.C.–A.D. 500
From the rise of Sumer in
Mesopotamia and the beginning of
writing to the fall of Rome

MEDIEVAL HISTORY
A.D. 500–1500
The Middle Ages, through the time Columbus and other European mariners
reached the Americas

MODERN HISTORY
1500–present
An era of expanding European empires
and then two world wars

PREHISTORY
10,000 B.C.–3500 B.C.

round 10,000 B.C. the Ice Age waned, the planet began warming, and humans had to adapt. They did so with great ingenuity. Many of the larger mammals on which people had relied for food died out as a result of global warming and overhunting. At the same time, edible plants flourished in places that had once been too cold or dry to support them.

By 8000 B.C., people in some parts of the world had moved beyond gathering plants to cultivating them. They domesticated animals, too. Eventually, people who practiced agriculture in fertile areas raised enough food to support specialists involved in various trades, fostering the growth of complex societies.

Some of the earliest settlements arose in a region called the Fertile Crescent, extending from Mesopotamia to the eastern Mediterranean coast. By 7000 B.C., about 2,000 inhabitants—more than ten times as many as found in a typical hunter-gatherer band—lived in Jericho, near the Jordan River. There

and in other such towns lived people involved in nonagricultural trades, including merchants and potters.

By 6500 B.C., artisans at the town of Çatal Hüyük in Anatolia (modern-day Turkey) were hard-firing pots in kilns. The potter's wheel, developed later, may have inspired wheeled vehicles.

Artisans in Anatolia and Mesopotamia also pioneered the craft of smelting copper. This led to the development of bronze and ushered in a new technological era, the Bronze Age, which succeeded the Stone Age. By 3500 B.C., advances in agriculture, metallurgy, and other crafts had laid the foundation in Mesopotamia for the emergence of cities and the rise of civilization.

FAST FACT The cultivation of rice began in Southeast Asia around 7000 B.C.

FOR MORE FACTS ON...

MIGRATION TRENDS & CHARACTERISTICS OF THE EARLIEST HUMANS see Human Migration, CHAPTER 6, PAGES 220-1
+
CROP DOMESTICATION & THE EVOLUTION OF AGRICULTURE see Agriculture, CHAPTER 6, PAGES 246-7

WHAT DO B.C. AND A.D. MEAN?

B.C. stands for "before Christ" and A.D. stands for *anno Domini,* Latin for "in the year of the Lord." Both terms originated when scholars took the year in which they thought Jesus Christ was born as the basis for dating events. But if, as the Gospel of Matthew indicates, Jesus was an infant when King Herod the Great of Judea died, then he was born just before 4 B.C.

Some historians prefer C.E. and B.C.E. ("Common Era" and "before the Common Era"). Dates in the two systems are identical, and B.C. and A.D. are still widely used, including in this book.

THIS CUNEIFORM TABLET from Iraq, seventh century B.C., tells of a great flood in the *Epic of Gilgamesh.*

CLICK IT: Stone Age Institute www.stoneageinstitute.org

FAST FACT Jericho, founded around 9000 B.C., is one of the world's oldest communities and its oldest known walled town.

THE THREE AGES OF HUMAN PREHISTORY

In Greek mythology, the ages of man were stages of decline for humanity, beginning with the idyllic Golden Age of old and continuing through the violent Bronze Age to the corrupt Iron Age. Today, historians use similar terms, but they have a different way of defining the ages of human prehistory, based on technological advances.

THE STONE AGE was the first phase in human technological development. It is divided into three periods: the Paleolithic, the Mesolithic, and the Neolithic, each period representing new advances in tool manufacture. The Neolithic, or New Stone Age, began around 10,000 years ago and witnessed the production of better stone implements and the introduction of tools and weapons made of copper and other metals.

THE BRONZE AGE followed, a period delineated by the developing technique of metalsmithing: mixing molten copper with tin or other alloys to produce metal tools. In Greece and China, the Bronze Age dates from about 3000 B.C.; in the British Isles, it did not occur until about 1900 B.C. Distinctive inventions of the Bronze Age include the wheel and ox-drawn plow, greatly increasing agricultural potential.

THE IRON AGE, which began around 1200 B.C. in Europe and 600 B.C. in China, was distinguished by iron tools and weapons, more durable and widely available because iron ore was more plentiful than the tin needed to produce bronze. Production of iron tools and weapons seems to have been accompanied by increased patterns of permanent settlement, and the great cities of the ancient world date back to this period.

G L O S S A R Y

Domestication: The process of adapting wild animals and plants to make them more useful to people. **/ Metallurgy:** Art and science of extracting metals from their ores and modifying the metals for use.

FOR MORE FACTS ON...

LANGUAGE AMONG EARLY HUMANS see *Language,* **CHAPTER 6, PAGES 228-31**

MODERN TECHNOLOGY see *Physical Science: Engineering, Medical Science: Surgery & Nanotechnology,* **CHAPTER 8, PAGES 332-3, 342-3, 350-1**

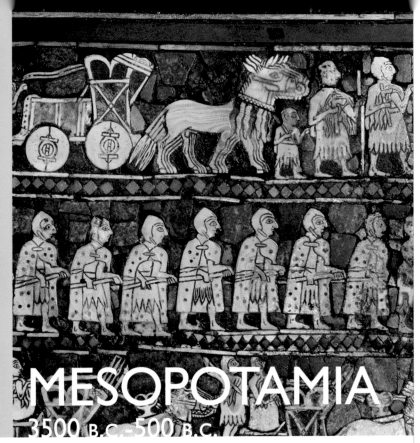

Royal Standard of Ur, a mosaic from ancient Sumeria, circa 2500 B.C.

ANCIENT MIDDLE EAST

CIRCA 3500 B.C.
Sumerians develop cities

CIRCA 2900 B.C.
Powerful city-states emerge in Sumer

2334 B.C.
King Sargon of Akkad conquers Sumer

1792 B.C.
Hammurabi establishes
Babylonian Empire

CIRCA 900 B.C.
Assyrians expand in
northern Mesopotamia

539 B.C.
Cyrus the Great of Persia
conquers Babylonians

MESOPOTAMIA
3500 B.C.–500 B.C.

Marking the dawn of human civilization, ancient cultures built impressive cities or ceremonial centers adorned with fine works of art and architecture. All had strong rulers capable of commanding the services of thousands for public projects or military campaigns. Most used writing to keep records, codify laws, and preserve wisdom and lore in the form of literature.

The world's first civilization arose in southern Mesopotamia, where the Tigris and Euphrates converged to form a fertile floodplain. Here the Sumerians dug canals to bring river water to their fields in the dry season.

Building and maintaining that irrigation system required strong leadership and yielded agricultural surpluses that fed people in emerging Sumerian cities, where merchants and artisans pursued their trades. Surplus grain was stored in temples, and scribes kept accounts by drawing pictographs of common objects such as sheaves of grain. Over time, those pictographs evolved into abstract characters known as cuneiform, inscribed in clay with a stylus. Sumerian scribes used this form of writing not just for bookkeeping but also to inscribe on clay tablets their laws and legends, thus preserving a record of their civilization for posterity.

By 2900 B.C., Sumerian cities were expanding into city-states that controlled surrounding villages. Warfare between rival city-states such as Ur and Uruk, which had more than 50,000 inhabitants, took its toll. In 2334 B.C.

FAST FACT Assyrian armies numbered up to 200,000 men and were divided into several divisions: cavalry, light infantry armed with bows, and heavy infantry armed with swords and spears.

FOR MORE FACTS ON...

THE IMPORTANCE OF CITIES IN HUMAN CULTURE see *Cities*, **CHAPTER 6, PAGES 260-1**

MATHEMATICAL ADVANCES MADE BY THE ANCIENT BABYLONIANS see *Counting & Measurement*, **CHAPTER 8, PAGE 323**

the Sumerians were conquered by Sargon of Akkad, a land to their north, who forged an empire reaching from the Persian Gulf to the Mediterranean. His dynasty was short-lived, but later Mesopotamian rulers followed. Among them was Hammurabi, from Babylon, who united Mesopotamia under his authority and codified the laws of his realm. The Babylonian Empire he fostered was shattered in 1595 B.C. by the Hittites, invaders from the northwest. Their collapse around 1200 B.C. left a void in the region that was later filled by the Assyrians, who wielded iron weapons and ruled with an iron first.

In 612 B.C., Babylonians overthrew the Assyrians and regained power. Storming Jerusalem, they carried captive Jews off to Babylon but yielded to superior force in 539 B.C. when Persians led by Cyrus the Great overran the region and went on to forge the largest empire the world had yet witnessed—from northern India to Egypt.

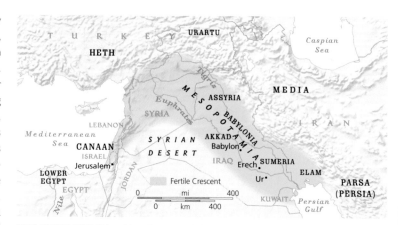

THE MIDDLE EAST, or Near East, extends from the southern and eastern Mediterranean to Iraq, once called Mesopotamia. Centers of civilization clustered in this fertile land in ancient times.

WHAT IS THE MIDDLE EAST?

Because the Middle East straddles two continents, armies, migrants, merchants, and ideas have long moved steadily through the region.

In ancient times, this was the Fertile Crescent, the cradle of civilization, and the birthplace of Judaism and Christianity. In medieval times, it gave rise to Islam.

In recent times, the discovery of vast oil reserves and the establishment of Israel in this largely Muslim region have made the Middle East one of the world's most hotly contested areas.

FAST FACT Some Sumerians sold themselves or members of their family into slavery to escape poverty or debt.

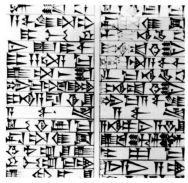

IMPRESSIONS IN CLAY evolved into the first system of writing, such as those shown in this transcription of Hammurabi's Code.

WHAT WAS HAMMURABI'S CODE?

Hammurabi's Code is a collection of laws written during the reign of Hammurabi in the 18th century B.C. and recorded on a stela, a stone marker, in the temple of the Babylonian god Marduk. It was discovered in 1901.

By modern standards, the laws set forth by Hammurabi seem harsh. "If the wife of a man is caught lying with another man," Hammurabi's Code decreed, authorities "shall bind the two and cast them into the water." Yet the very act of putting laws in writing protected people from arbitrary punishment. If defendants felt they had not received justice under the law, they could appeal to Hammurabi, who included as part of his legal code, inscribed on the stela, these words: "Let the oppressed man who has a cause come into the presence of my statue and read carefully."

FOR MORE FACTS ON...

MEDICAL PRACTICES CITED IN HAMMURABI'S CODE see Medical Science: Surgery, **CHAPTER 8, PAGE 342**

COUNTRIES IN THE MIDDLE EAST TODAY see Asia, **CHAPTER 9, PAGES 380-3**

Camels and riders silhouetted against pyramids in Giza, Egypt

EGYPT 3000 B.C.-30 B.C.

ANCIENT EGYPT

CIRCA 3000 B.C.
King Narmer unifies Upper and Lower Egypt (the Nile Delta)

CIRCA 2700 B.C. / OLD KINGDOM
Egyptian pharaohs begin constructing huge pyramids

CIRCA 2550 B.C.
Pharaoh orders Great Pyramid at Giza

CIRCA 2050 B.C. / MIDDLE KINGDOM
After drought and famine, order is restored

CIRCA 1630 B.C.
Hyksos invade Nile Delta

CIRCA 1550 B.C. / NEW KINGDOM
Theban rule begins

gypt's Nile Valley was one of the most fertile places in the ancient world. Each summer, monsoon rains swelled the Nile and flooded surrounding fields, depositing a rich layer of silt. In prehistoric times, people settled along the river and began cultivating wheat and barley and building rafts of papyrus. Around 3000 B.C., a king from Upper Egypt led forces into the Nile Delta and conquered Lower Egypt, founding the first of more than 30 dynasties that would rule this land over the next 3,000 years.

Rulers from Thebes (today's Luxor) inaugurated the Middle Kingdom around 2050 B.C.—a time of expansion when Egyptian troops conquered much of Nubia (Sudan). Lords of Thebes also repelled an invasion by warriors called Hyksos around 1630 B.C. Thebes emerged as capital of the New Kingdom (ca 1550 B.C.-1070 B.C.), when Egypt reached the height of its power. New Kingdom rulers such as Ramses II sent armies against the Hittites and other Middle Eastern rivals. By 1000 B.C., however, Egypt was losing strength. In centuries to come, it fell subject to one foreign power after another.

FOR MORE FACTS ON...

EGYPTIAN ASTRONOMY AS THE BASIS FOR TODAY'S CALENDAR see Telling Time, CHAPTER 8, PAGE 325
+
THE COUNTRY OF EGYPT TODAY see Africa, CHAPTER 9, PAGE 364

WHO WERE THE PHARAOHS?

Along the Nile River, irrigation allowed Egyptian farmers to increase the amount of land under cultivation and to produce enough food to support people involved in other pursuits, including priests and rulers. Powerful men called pharaohs—a term meaning "great house"—collected taxes in the form of grain and drafted troops and laborers for military campaigns and public projects. Over time, the term "pharaoh" came to mean both the king and his palace.

Around 2700 B.C., Egypt entered its first great age of power and prosperity, known as the Old Kingdom, marked by the construction of massive royal tombs like the Great Pyramid at Giza, completed around 2500 B.C. Pyramids symbolized the soaring ambitions of pharaohs, who identified with the sun god Re. One text written in hieroglyphs by a royal scribe promised that the pharaoh's spirit would rise up from the pyramid and "ascend to heaven as the eye of Re"—inspiring the image on the American dollar bill.

WHAT'S A MUMMY?

Egyptians sought to preserve the body after death, fearing that the wandering soul might be lost if it had no corpse to return to. Mummification, preparing the body of the dead by removing perishable internal organs and embalming the remains, was a practice originally confined to royalty. Poor people buried their dead in the sand, which inhibited decay.

In later times, however, many Egyptians were mummified and buried in coffins on which spells were inscribed to ward off evil and launch the spirit safely on its heavenly journey. "I shall sail rightly in my bark," reads one such verse. "I am lord of eternity in the crossing of the sky." Mummified animals were buried as offerings to deities such as the cat goddess, Bastet.

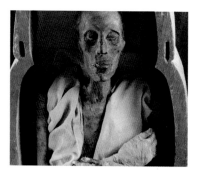

THE MUMMY of Ramses II, who reigned in Egypt for 67 years, from 1279 to 1213 B.C., now lies on display in the Cairo Museum.

G L O S S A R Y

Monsoon: Major wind system that seasonally reverses its direction. **/ Tribute:** A required contribution or payment made by subjects to their ruler. **/ Dynasty:** A succession of rulers belonging to the same family or group.

RAMSES II / PHARAOH OF EGYPT

It was not uncommon for Egyptian kings to have numerous wives and offspring, but Ramses II went to extremes by fathering more than 100 children during his long reign. His principal wife, Queen Nefertari, had to share him with many secondary wives, including his sister. (Incestuous unions were common within the royal family.) Secondary wives sometimes lived together with their children in households called harems and performed useful tasks such as weaving. After battling Hittites at Kadesh in Syria in 1285 B.C., Ramses made peace with the Hittite king by engaging to wed his eldest daughter. He then prayed to the gods to see her safely to Egypt: "May you not send rain, icy blast or snow, until the marvel you have decreed for me shall reach me!"

FOR MORE FACTS ON...

THE PLACE OF MYTH IN HUMAN HISTORY see Language, **CHAPTER 6, PAGE 229**

THE PYRAMIDS & OTHER WONDERS OF THE ANCIENT WORLD see Engineering, **CHAPTER 8, PAGE 333**

ANCIENT INDIA

CIRCA 2500 B.C.
Harappan civilization develops

CIRCA 700 B.C.
Upanishads, Hindu scripture, composed

CIRCA 560 B.C.
Siddhartha Gautama, founder
of Buddhism, is born in India

327 B.C.
Alexander the Great invades India

321 B.C.
Maurya dynasty is founded

A.D. 320
Gupta dynasty is founded

Priest-king figurine from Mohenjo Daro, circa 2000 B.C.

INDIA
2500 B.C.–A.D. 500

n India, as in Egypt and Mesopotamia, civilization arose in a fertile floodplain—in this case, the Indus River Valley. Abundant harvests from irrigated fields there fed the growth of cities such as Mohenjo Daro and Harappa, which gave its name to the Harappan civilization that emerged around 2500 B.C. Those cities were laid out on plans with standardized housing for the common people, larger residences for the elite, and a sanitation system with bathrooms linked to sewers.

Seasonal flooding helped nourish the fields but was sometimes catastrophic. Mohenjo Daro had to be rebuilt at least nine times. Ruinous floods may have contributed to the decline of Harappan civilization after 2000 B.C., when the cities were abandoned.

Around 1500 B.C., invaders called Aryans entered the valley through mountain passes from Afghanistan and Iran (named for the Aryans). Gradually, Aryan rulers called rajas expanded from the Indus Valley into the lush Ganges Valley and formed more than a dozen states or kingdoms across northern India. Aryan doctrines were questioned and reinterpreted by Indian philosophers such as Siddhartha Gautama, known to his followers as the Buddha, or Enlightened One, and the teachers who composed the Upanishads.

Around 520 B.C., Persians conquered the Indus Valley and made it a province of their empire. Two centuries later, Alexander the Great took control here but withdrew after his troops rebelled.

Alexander's departure left behind a power vacuum that was soon filled by Chandragupta Maurya, who came from the wealthy kingdom of Magadha in the Ganges Valley. He and his descendants forged an empire that covered all of the Indian subcontinent except its southern tip. That empire reached its peak with the conquests of Ashoka, who, after establishing his

FAST FACT Sanskrit, an ancient Indian language still used by Hindu scholars, is related to Greek, Latin, German, and English—all belonging to the Indo-European language family.

FOR MORE FACTS ON...

EARLY RELIGIONS OF INDIA see *Hinduism & Buddhism* **CHAPTER 6, PAGES 234-5**
+
CITIES IN HUMAN CULTURE see *Cities,* **CHAPTER 6, PAGES 260-1**

expanded reign, renounced violence and embraced Buddhism.

Ashoka died around 235 B.C., and India fractured into competing kingdoms. In the fourth century A.D. another ruler from Magadha, called Chandra Gupta in honor of Chandragupta Maurya, begin reunifying India. Under the Gupta dynasty, trade, crafts, science, medicine, and the arts flourished. By now, Hinduism was the dominant faith. Doctrines such as reincarnation were enshrined in sacred texts like the Bhagavad Gita. The Gupta dynasty declined around A.D. 450 as nomads from Central Asia invaded India.

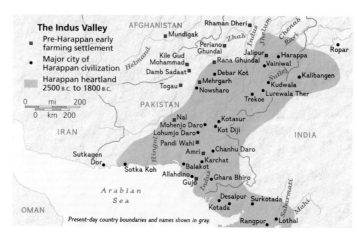

The Indus Valley
- Pre-Harappan early farming settlement
- Major city of Harappan civilization
- Harappan heartland 2500 B.C. to 1800 B.C.

Present-day country boundaries and names shown in gray.

THE RICH INDUS RIVER VALLEY in today's Pakistan and northwestern India cradled a remarkably sophisticated society in the third and second millennium B.C. Remains of ancient cities suggest an organized economy, social hierarchy, and civic infrastructure.

WHAT'S THE CASTE SYSTEM?

India's caste system had its origins in the class system of the Aryans, who invaded India around 1500 B.C. and long dominated the country.

At the top of the Aryan social hierarchy were priests known as Brahmans, followed by a ruling warrior class, commoners such as merchants and landowners, and an underclass of laborers and peasants. The lowest of the low were so-called untouchables, who performed tasks considered unclean such as butchering animals.

Over time an elaborate caste system evolved, with hundreds of occupational groups ranked according to social status. Children were to take up the work of their parents and to marry within their caste. Although individuals had little opportunity to advance socially, the caste to which they belonged sometimes rose in status as its members gained wealth and political power.

ASHOKA / PROMOTER OF BUDDHISM IN INDIA

Like the Roman emperor Constantine, whose conversion spread Christianity through the Mediterranean world, the Indian emperor Ashoka (ca 265 B.C.-235 B.C.) embraced Buddhism and promoted its teachings across Asia. Ashoka underwent his conversion after a brutal campaign of conquest in which his troops claimed tens of thousands of lives. Renouncing violence, he devoted himself to peaceful pursuits, including founding hospitals and building roads and inns to promote travel and trade. He preached religious tolerance and stressed principles such as mercy, compassion, and kindness to animals, appealing to Indians of various sects, who believed that all creatures had souls. By supporting Buddhist monasteries and missionaries, he helped the faith he espoused advance beyond India to Tibet, Southeast Asia, and China.

FOR MORE FACTS ON...

INDIA'S CASTE SYSTEM *see Race, Class & Gender,* **CHAPTER 6, PAGES 226-7**

GEOGRAPHY & NATIONAL PRODUCTS OF INDIA TODAY *see Asia,* **CHAPTER 9, PAGE 386**

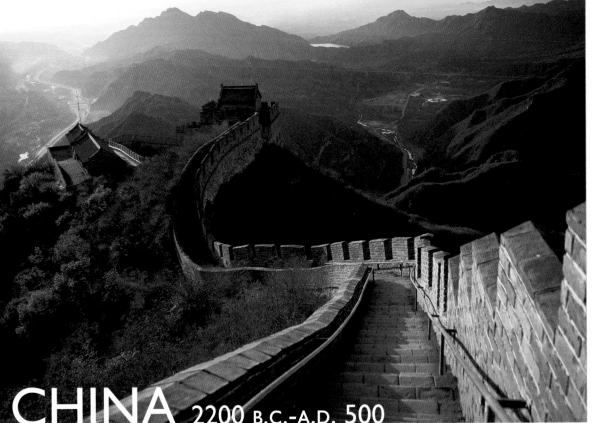

Great Wall of China, Juyongguan, near Beijing

CHINA 2200 B.C.–A.D. 500

ANCIENT CHINA

CIRCA 2200 B.C.
Civilization emerges along Yellow River

CIRCA 1750 B.C.
Shang dynasty begins

CIRCA 1100 B.C.
Zhou dynasty begins and expands south

CIRCA 550 B.C.
Philosopher Confucius is born

403 B.C.
Period of the Warring States

221-206 B.C.
Qin Shi Huangdi is emperor of China

A.D. 220
Han dynasty collapses

China's first kings came to power along the Yellow River, so called for the yellow soil along its banks. That rich soil was fertile, but it clogged the river and caused floods. Chinese chronicles credit a king named Yu with taming the river's floods and founding the Xia dynasty. Rulers mobilized laborers for flood-control projects and grew stronger in the process.

Beginning around 1750 B.C., the Shang dynasty succeeded the Xia and expanded beyond the Yellow River Valley. Around their cities, the Chinese built defensive walls up to 35 feet thick, made of earth rammed between a frame of timbers. At the Shang capital, Anyang, from about 1300 B.C., villages and workshops for bronze smiths and other artisans surrounded the royal district. Like other ancient civilizations, the Chinese became highly stratified, with great gaps in wealth and status between rulers or nobles, peasants or slaves.

Around 1100 B.C., challengers from western China overthrew the Shang and founded the Zhou dynasty, whose rulers claimed they had a mandate from heaven to govern China as

FOR MORE FACTS ON...

SOIL CLASSIFICATIONS & ELEMENTS THAT MAKE SOIL FERTILE *see Soil,* **CHAPTER 3, PAGES 96-7**

THE IMPORTANT ROLE OF THE WORLD'S RIVERS *see Rivers,* **CHAPTER 3, PAGES 116-7**

long as they did so wisely and justly. Their kingdom reached southward to the fertile Yangtze River Valley, where rice was cultivated. To rule that vast domain, they relied on local lords, who had their own troops and equipped them with iron weapons. By the fifth century B.C., Zhou rulers had lost control of those lords, and their kingdom was splitting into rival states.

After nearly 200 years of strife, known as the Period of the Warring States, the ruler of the strongest state, Qin, unified China and took the title Qin Shi Huangdi (First Emperor). The heavy demands he placed on the populace led to a rebellion after the First Emperor's death, ushering in the Han dynasty in 206 B.C., which lasted more than four centuries.

Han emperors governed China with the help of officials schooled in the teachings of Confucius, a philosopher born around 550 B.C. who urged rulers to lead by moral example. "Approach your duties with reverence and be trustworthy," Confucius advised; "employ the labor of the common people only in the right seasons." Han rulers did not always follow that advice. Peasants remained desperately poor and were often conscripted to serve on the empire's expanding frontiers, from Vietnam to the Korean peninsula. Late Han emperors faced uprisings, and in A.D. 220 the dynasty came to an end.

BRONZE EFFIGIES of ancestral spirits allowed veneration of ancestors, an ancient tradition in China. Confucius urged his followers to revere their parents and honor them after death. Many Chinese did so by making offerings of food and wine to ancestral spirits.

China fractured into rival kingdoms and was menaced by invaders from Central Asia, who were advancing on several fronts and threatening other empires around the world.

FAST FACT Emperor Qin Shi Huangdi wanted to link defensive barriers in northern China into one wall that measured 10,000 li—roughly 3,000 miles—in length. Ultimately, the Great Wall was expanded to a total of more than 4,000 miles.

WHO WAS CHINA'S FIRST EMPEROR?

Many of history's great empire-builders were more feared than admired. Qin Shi Huangdi, the man who laid the foundation for imperial China, was no exception. He executed his critics, burned their writings, and forced millions to work on public projects, including the defensive barrier that became the Great Wall of China. He also built roads, standardized laws and coinage, and instituted a common script that allowed Chinese ethnic groups who spoke many different languages to communicate in writing.

When this accomplished and dreaded ruler died in 210 B.C., he was buried in an immense tomb surrounded by the bodies of slaves sacrificed for the occasion. Arrayed within the tomb were also thousands of lifelike soldiers molded of clay with great artistry, an army that would never tire.

A FIERCE WARRIOR, one among an estimated 8,000, stands guard in the tomb of Emperor Qin Shi Huangdi near Xi'an, China. The entire underground terra-cotta army was not discovered until the 1970s.

FOR MORE FACTS ON...

THE IMPORTANCE OF ANCESTORS, FAMILY & KINSHIP see The Human Family, **CHAPTER 6, PAGES 222-3**

METALLURGY DURING THE BRONZE AGE see Prehistory 10,000 B.C.-3500 B.C., **CHAPTER 7, PAGE 265**

Greek temple ruins, Aphrodisias, Turkey

274

GREECE & PERSIA
1600 B.C.–A.D. 500

CLASSICAL PERIOD

CIRCA 1600 B.C.
Mycenaeans occupy Crete

558 B.C.
Cyrus becomes king of Persia

480–479 B.C.
Greeks defeat Persians;
Greco-Persian Wars end

404 B.C.
Sparta defeats Athens;
Peloponnesian War ends

336 B.C.
Alexander takes power

323 B.C.
Death of Alexander the Great

n 500 B.C., Greeks living along the eastern shore of the Aegean Sea rebelled against their Persian masters, setting at odds two of the world's most accomplished societies. Greek civilization went back more than a thousand years to the time when Mycenaeans swept down from the north and occupied mainland Greece and islands such as Crete, home to the Minoans, maritime traders who built splendid palaces.

Heirs to Mycenaean and Minoan traditions, Greeks established powerful city-states like Athens and Sparta and planted colonies on distant shores.

The Persians rose to glory under Cyrus the Great and his successors, who forged an immense empire from the Indus River to the Nile and the Black Sea. Emperor Darius, who took power in 522 B.C., divided this realm into provinces and appointed men to govern and collect taxes, which paid for a grand capital at Persepolis and a road to Ephesus on the Aegean Sea.

FAST FACT In the Athenian democracy, only free adult males born in Athens voted. Neither women, nor slaves, nor foreigners could vote.

FOR MORE FACTS ON...

THE COUNTRIES OF GREECE & IRAN TODAY see Europe, **CHAPTER 9, PAGE 405,** & Asia, **CHAPTER 9, PAGE 386**

HOW THE ANCIENT GREEKS MEASURED THE EARTH see Dividing Lines, **CHAPTER 1, PAGE 31**

When Greek cities rebelled against Darius, Athens came to their aid and repulsed Persian forces at Marathon in 490 B.C. Darius's successor, Xerxes, then raised a huge army, but Athenians, united with Spartans and other Greeks, shattered the Persian fleet in 480 and defeated Xerxes' army a year later—the end of Persian expansion and the dawn of a golden age for Greece. Athens fostered democracy by granting all adult male citizens the right to vote, and the works of its artists, playwrights, poets, and philosophers formed the basis of classical Western culture.

Macedonians led by King Philip II conquered Greece in 338 B.C. and went on to attack Persia under the king's ambitious son, Alexander the Great. Schooled in Greek like other noble Macedonians, Alexander made the Persian Empire his own.

After his death at age 32, Alexander's empire was divided among his top generals, and Greek learning

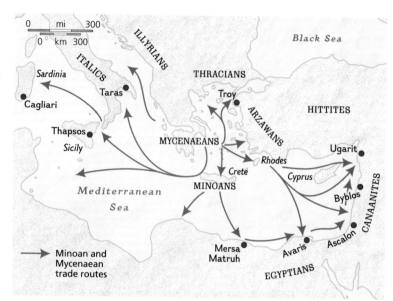

FROM GREECE AND NEARBY ISLANDS, passages of trade and conquest spread out in all directions. First the Minoans and then the Mycenaeans dominated Mediterranean trade routes. Eventually the Phoenicians, living on the coast of today's Lebanon, gained dominance in the region.

became part of the cultural heritage of the Middle East. That legacy outlasted the Roman Empire, which crumbled in the fifth century A.D., leaving the Byzantine Empire in control around the eastern Mediterranean.

CLICK IT: Ancient Greece www.ancient-greece.org

G L O S S A R Y

Democracy: From the Greek *demos*, "people," + *kratos*, "rule." Form of government in which supreme power is vested in the people and exercised by them directly or indirectly through a system of representation usually involving periodic free elections.

ALEXANDER THE GREAT / HERO OF ANCIENT GREECE

Tutored in his youth by the philosopher Aristotle, Alexander the Great (356 B.C.-323 B.C.) loved Greek culture and considered himself a Greek hero, claiming descent from the Homeric hero Achilles, legendary leader of the assault on Troy. Some Greeks, however, viewed the Macedonian-born Alexander as a foreign despot. Soon after he took the throne, he faced a rebellion from the Greek city of Thebes and razed it to the ground, slaughtering thousands and enslaving others. Not until he waged war on the Persians, archenemies of the Greeks, did he become their champion. Greeks living under Persian rule hailed him as a liberator. After conquering the Persian Empire, he founded cities on the Greek model. Chief among them was Alexandria, in Egypt.

FOR MORE FACTS ON...

EARLY METHODS OF MAPMAKING & NAVIGATION see *Navigation*, **CHAPTER 1, PAGES 38-9**
+
CULTURAL CENTERS IN THE ANCIENT MIDDLE EAST see *Mesopotamia 3500 B.C.-500 B.C.*, **CHAPTER 7, PAGE 267**

Colosseum, Rome, built first century A.D.

ANCIENT ROME

509 B.C.
Rome establishes republic

264-146 B.C.
Punic Wars with Carthage

44 B.C.
Julius Caesar assassinated

31 B.C.
First Roman emperor, Augustus

A.D. 117
Empire reaches peak under Trajan

A.D. 330
Constantine founds Constantinople

A.D. 476
Rome falls to Germanic invaders

ROME 500 B.C.-A.D. 500

uilt on hills above the Tiber River, Rome began its phenomenal ascent to power in 509 B.C. when it won independence from the Etruscans, who had long dominated the area. After ousting their Etruscan king, Romans created a republic in which aristocrats called patricians elected two consuls to lead them for a year.

Consuls were guided by aristocrats in the senate, leaving the common people, called plebeians, powerless. Plebeians eventually won the right to elect tribunes and one of the two consuls. Although social tensions persisted, plebeians now had a stake in Rome's success, and so they served dutifully in Roman legions, often receiving land in areas they conquered.

By 265 B.C., Romans had gained control of the Italian peninsula and were eyeing Sicily. Opponents who submitted to their authority were treated generously, and some became Roman citizens. Those who remained defiant were crushed.

No rival proved more defiant than Carthage, a North African city of Phoenician origin that controlled Spain and other lands around the western Mediterranean and clashed with Rome over Sicily in the first of three Punic Wars. Despite heroic efforts by the general Hannibal, Carthage was ultimately defeated. After burning the city to the ground in 146 B.C., Romans reportedly plowed its ashes under with salt so that nothing would grow there again. By 100 B.C., the Romans had conquered Greece and were masters of the Mediterranean.

The wealth and prestige Roman generals gained through conquest allowed them to defy the senate and impose their will politically. After defeating the Gauls in France, Julius Caesar returned to Rome in 49 B.C., seized power, and ruled as dictator. His assassination in 44 B.C. by conspirators who hoped to preserve the republic triggered a bloody civil war. This struggle ended in 31 B.C. when Caesar's nephew Gaius Octavius defeated Mark Antony and his ally, Queen Cleopatra of Egypt, and took

FAST FACT At its height, Rome had a population of more than one million, making it the largest city in the ancient world.

FOR MORE FACTS ON...

THE CALENDAR USED IN ANCIENT ROME *see Telling Time,* **CHAPTER 8, PAGE 324**
+
THE GEOGRAPHY & ECONOMICS OF ITALY TODAY *see Europe,* **CHAPTER 9, PAGE 404**

the title Augustus ("revered one"). As Rome's first emperor, he wielded absolute power. His successors likewise expanded the empire, which by the second century A.D. stretched from Mesopotamia to Britain.

This huge realm came under stress in the third century as invaders began pouring across Roman frontiers. As the crisis deepened, Christianity—whose adherents rejected the cult of the divine emperor and worshipped a higher authority—won greater acceptance. When the emperor Constantine embraced Christianity and moved his capital in A.D. 330 to Constantinople, a more defensible place, Rome lost its aura of invincibility. In the fifth century, Huns advancing from Central Asia into eastern Europe displaced Vandals, Visigoths, and other Germanic tribes, who then overwhelmed Italy. Rome fell in 476, leaving what remained of the Roman world to Constantinople and the Byzantine Empire.

ROMULUS AND REMUS, fabled founders of the city of Rome, were said to have been raised by a she-wolf.

JEWS, CHRISTIANS, AND ROME

During the first century A.D., Jews in Judea, a Roman province, chafed under Roman rule. The emperor was hailed as a god, but Jews, who worshipped one supreme God, were forbidden to serve idols. Some hoped for a messiah, or savior, to free them from Roman rule. Jesus of Nazareth offered no resistance to Rome but foretold a kingdom of God surpassing any empire on earth. After his death, both Christians, who believed he was the Messiah, and Jews faced persecution. After a Jewish revolt, Romans sacked Jerusalem in A.D. 70 and destroyed its temple.

CLICK IT: Forum Romanum www.forumromanum.org

 No one is so brave that he is not disturbed by something unexpected.
—— JULIUS CAESAR, CIRCA 55 B.C.

JULIUS CAESAR / ROMAN GENERAL & DICTATOR

Julius Caesar (100 B.C.-44 B.C.) rose to power by subduing the Gauls, a Celtic people living on either side of the Alps. Celtic culture originated around 1000 B.C. along the upper Danube River and spread across France to northern Italy and Spain and the British Isles. Celts mastered ironworking and were formidable warriors but lacked unity. Caesar recruited Gauls in northern Italy to bolster his legions, and then he crushed defiant Gauls in France led by Vercingetorix, who was hauled off to Rome in chains and eventually executed. Caesar captured an estimated one million Gauls and sold them as slaves, amassing a huge fortune, which he used to purchase the loyalty of troops and maintain power. From Gaul, he went on to military victories in Britain and Egypt. He became dictator in 46 B.C. but was assassinated two years later.

FOR MORE FACTS ON...

JUDAISM & CHRISTIANITY see Religion: Monotheism, **CHAPTER 6, PAGES 236-7**

THE BYZANTINE EMPIRE AFTER THE FALL OF ROME see Middle Ages 500-1000, **CHAPTER 7, PAGES 278-9**

Hagia Sophia, Istanbul, Turkey, built A.D. 537

MIDDLE AGES 500-1000

EARLY MIDDLE AGES

630
Muhammad and followers take Mecca

661
Ali killed; Umayyad dynasty founded

732
Martel defeats Muslims at Battle of Tours

750
Abbasid dynasty founded in Baghdad

800
Charlemagne crowned emperor in Rome

962
Otto I becomes Holy Roman Emperor

The Middle Ages began with the collapse of the Roman Empire around 500 and ended around 1500 with exploration of the New World. The early Middle Ages have been called the Dark Ages—an era when Germanic tribes overran Roman provinces, leaving few written records to shed light on events. The Byzantine Empire, however, based in Constantinople, flourished and expanded under Emperor Justinian.

His realm nearly encircled the Mediterranean by the time he died in 565. Thereafter, Byzantine power slowly declined as his successors lost control of Italy—where Christians recognized the bishop of Rome rather than the Byzantine patriarch as their spiritual father, or pope—and lost ground to Muslim rulers who were forging their own empire.

Islam arose in Mecca, where the Arab prophet Muhammad was born

FAST FACT Hagia Sophia, completed in Constantinople in 537 under the Byzantine emperor Justinian, was the largest Christian cathedral in the world until Ottoman Turks conquered the city in 1453 and converted it into a mosque.

FOR MORE FACTS ON...

THE ANCIENT CITY OF ROME & THE ROMAN EMPIRE see Rome 500 B.C.-A.D. 500, **CHAPTER 7, PAGES 276-7**

ROMAN & BYZANTINE ART & LITERATURE IN THE RENAISSANCE see Renaissance & Reformation 1500-1650, **CHAPTER 7, PAGE 294**

around 570. Traveling widely as a merchant, he came in contact with Jews and Christians. When he was around 40, he experienced a revelation in which he recognized Allah (God) as supreme and all-encompassing and embraced Islam, which means submission to Allah. "There is no God but Allah," Muslims declared ever after, "and Muhammad is his prophet." In 630, he and his followers returned from exile and conquered Mecca, whose holiest shrine, the Kaaba, became the required pilgrimage of devout Muslims.

After Muhammad died in 632, rulers called caliphs united Arabia under Islam and spread their faith through conquest and conversion.

By the eighth century, the Islamic world extended across North Africa to Spain. In 750, Abu al-Abbas overthrew the Umayyad dynasty, whose caliphs ruled from Damascus, and founded the Abbasid dynasty, based in Baghdad. Scholars flocked there from many lands to study the Koran as well as classical works by Persian, Greek, and Indian sages, including treatises on medicine and mathematics. Arabic numerals and algebra were among the gifts of Muslim scholars to modern science.

Western Europe was divided among various Germanic tribes until the rise of Charlemagne, who became king of the Franks in 768 and extended his domain beyond France and Germany to Italy and northern Spain, where Roman Catholic Franks halted the advance of Islam. Charlemagne was crowned emperor in Rome in 800 by Pope Leo III, but his empire fractured after he died. Europe remained a feudal society in which serfs owed duties to their lords, who in turn served as vassals to higher nobility. In some places, kings arose: For example, Alfred of Wessex reclaimed part of Britain from invading Vikings—adventurers from Scandinavia who ranged far in their longships, raiding, trading, and colonizing places such as Iceland and Normandy, named for the Norsemen who settled there.

CLICK IT: Islamic History www.islamfortoday.com/history.htm

GLOSSARY

Patriarch: From the Latin *pater,* father. A revered religious leader in the Christian tradition; the term is applied to biblical figures such as Abraham and to leaders of the Eastern Orthodox Church. **/ Feudalism:** Social system prevalent in Europe in the early Middle Ages, where each district was ruled by a duke, count, or other noble who offered protection and property to dependents called vassals in exchange for loyalty and service.

SHIITE AND SUNNI MUSLIMS

After the death of Muhammad, disputes arose among his followers as to who should become the leader of the religion of Islam. Some supported his cousin and son-in-law, Ali, as caliph, or religious leader. Others—including Aisha, Muhammad's last wife—favored other candidates.

Ali became the fourth caliph in 656 and ruled the Islamic world until he was assassinated in 661. Muslims known as Shiites (from *shiat-u-Ali,* the party of Ali) believed that only a descendant of Ali should be caliph and opposed the Umayyad dynasty that took power after he died.

Sunni Muslims—named for the *sunnah,* or practice, of Muhammad himself —accepted as legitimate caliphs those who were just and devout, whether or not they descended from Muhammad. The two groups differed in ritual and doctrine and perpetuated a lasting division within the world of Islam.

MOSES AND MUHAMMAD converse with the archangel Gabriel in this 16th-century Turkish illuminated manuscript. Muhammad, the rightmost of the central three figures, wears a veil over his face. According to Islamic law, no portrayal may reveal the face of the Prophet Muhammad.

FOR MORE FACTS ON...

THE HISTORY & BELIEFS OF ISLAM see *Religion: Monotheism,* **CHAPTER 6, PAGES 236-7**

VIKING EXPEDITIONS TO THE NEW WORLD see *World Navigation 1492-1522,* **CHAPTER 7, PAGE 293**

1000-1500

During the late Middle Ages, Christian Europeans clashed with Muslims in the Middle East. The Crusades that led to war in the Holy Land resulted from divisions within both worlds.

By 1000, Seljuk Turks from Central Asia were pouring into the Middle East and converting to Islam. In 1055, a Turk named Tughril Beg became sultan (chieftain) in Baghdad. He and his successors embarked on conquests, capturing Syria and Palestine from the Fatimids—a rival Muslim dynasty—and advancing into Anatolia (Turkey), where they defeated Byzantine forces.

In response, the Byzantine emperor sought help from western Europe. The Eastern Orthodox Church had recently broken with the Roman Catholic Church, and Pope Urban II in Rome hoped to regain authority in the eastern Mediterranean by securing Jerusalem and other sites in the Holy Land sacred to Christians as well as Muslims. In 1095, he called for a crusade against the Turks. The turmoil in the Middle East had made it unsafe for Christians to make pilgrimages there, and many Catholics blamed the Turks and answered the pope's call.

The First Crusade began badly when a zealot named Peter the Hermit led an undisciplined army to a disastrous defeat. Meanwhile, nobles in France were assembling a stronger fighting force that succeeded in capturing Jerusalem in 1099. Bands of crusaders then carved out states along the eastern Mediterranean. The capture of one such state by Turks prompted the Second Crusade in 1147, which made no gains. In 1171 the sultan Saladin wrested Egypt from the Fatimids and went on to reclaim Jerusalem for Muslims in 1187. Later Catholic crusaders were unable to win the Holy Land back and turned against Orthodox Christians in Constantinople, sacking that city in 1204 and leaving the Byzantine Empire vulnerable to future assaults by Turks.

Although the Crusades failed militarily, they introduced Europeans to alluring goods from Asia and opened trade routes. Italian city-states such as Venice and Florence prospered through trade with Asia, and Marco Polo and other merchants journeyed to China.

In 1453, Ottoman Turks conquered Constantinople and tightened their grip on overland trade with Asia. Seeking maritime routes to the Far East, Europeans sailed around Africa and crossed the Atlantic to the New World.

THIRTEENTH-CENTURY CRUSADERS, shown crossing the Bosporus in this painting, believed that they were fighting a holy war in their quest to conquer the Islamic Middle East.

FAST FACT By the time the Crusades began in 1095, Muslim conquests in the Middle East, North Africa, and Spain had reduced the scope of the Christian world by two-thirds.

FOR MORE FACTS ON...

MAPMAKING IN THE AGE OF THE CRUSADES see *The History of Mapping,* **CHAPTER 1, PAGES 20-1**

THE EARLY PERIOD OF THE MIDDLE AGES see *Middle Ages 500-1000,* **CHAPTER 7, PAGES 278-9**

WHAT WAS THE BUBONIC PLAGUE?

MEDIEVAL PHYSICIANS wore protective clothing to try to save their own health while treating victims of the plague.

The bubonic plague is a fatal disease carried by fleas that infested rodents. In 1347, it reached Europe from Asia and wreaked havoc. The characteristic symptom was swelling of the lymph nodes, also called buboes (hence the name). The disease was also known as the "black death," referring to the dark sores that covered the bodies of victims before they died.

The Black Death of Europe, one of the most widespread outbreaks of plague in history, decimated populations during the 14th century. This fearful pandemic killed more than 20 million people in Europe and reduced the population there by at least one-fourth. Outbreaks caused hysteria. In some places, Christians blamed Jews for the plague and attacked them.

In the long run, Europe proved remarkably resilient. Those who survived the Black Death lived to seek a better existence. The primary method of treatment for the plague was isolation, and these measures that evolved into higher quality hospitals and medical treatments. The ensuing labor shortage meant workers could command higher wages, and their standard of living rose. By 1450, kingdoms such as France, England, and Spain—where Islam gave way to Christianity—were gaining strength politically and economically and would soon wield power around the globe.

G L O S S A R Y

Pandemic: From Greek *pan* + *demos,* "all people." A disease affecting a wide area and a large percentage of that area's population.
/ Chivalry: From French *cheval,* "horse." The knightly class of feudal times; knights or fully armed and mounted fighting men, hence the gallantry and honor expected of knights.

 To sacrifice what you are and to live without belief—that is a fate more terrible than dying.
— **JOAN OF ARC, 1431**

JOAN OF ARC / MYSTIC, MILITARY HERO & MARTYR

No hero loomed larger during the Hundred Years' War than the young woman known as Joan of Arc (1412-1431), a farmer's daughter who inspired French resistance to English forces occupying northern France in the early 1400s. A mystic who heard the voices of saints, she sometimes wore men's clothing and believed that God had ordered her to expel the English from France. She urged on French troops, who defeated the English at Orleans in 1429, advancing the cause of young King Charles VII. A year later she was captured at Compiègne, in northern France, while leading troops against the Duke of Burgundy, a French ally of the English, and was tried as a heretic. In 1431, at the age of 19, she was burned at the stake. She remained a hero to foes of the English, who were ultimately forced out of France.

FOR MORE FACTS ON...

THE ORIGINS OF CHRISTIANITY & ISLAM see *Monotheism,* **CHAPTER 6, PAGES 236-7**
+
THE HISTORY OF MEDICINE & ITS BATTLE AGAINST DISEASE see *Medical Science,* **CHAPTER 8, PAGES 338-9**

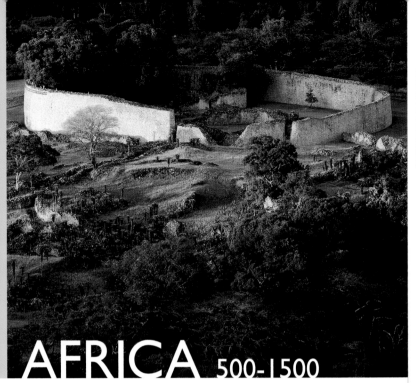

Ruins of Great Zimbabwe

ANCIENT AFRICA

CIRCA 800
Muslim caravans cross Sahara

CIRCA 900
Muslims reach Mogadishu in East Africa

1235
Mali ruler Sundiata starts empire in West Africa, absorbing Ghana

1324
Mali's Mansa Musa treks to Mecca

1441
Portuguese begin taking slaves from West Africa

1464
Songhai ruler Sunni Ali starts empire in West Africa, absorbing Mali

AFRICA 500-1500

Africa underwent rapid economic and political development during the Middle Ages as trade developed by caravan between the Mediterranean coast and West Africa and by ship between lands around the Indian Ocean and East Africa. By 750, Egypt and other North African countries that were once part of the Roman or Byzantine Empires had come under Muslim rule. Some people there adhered to other faiths, notably Ethiopians in isolated areas who remained Christian.

By the ninth century, Muslim merchants were crossing the Sahara by camel from the Mediterranean coast to trade with people living in West Africa along the Senegal and Niger Rivers, a fertile area that gave rise to powerful states. That trade benefited the emerging kingdom of Ghana, which obtained cloth, salt, weapons, and other goods from Muslim merchants in exchange for gold, ivory, and slaves. (Africa was just one source of slaves—a word derived from Slavs, many of whom were seized in eastern Europe and enslaved.) The rulers of Ghana converted to Islam but were slow to abandon such traditional religious practices as praying to images of ancestral spirits or nature gods. Great artistry and devotion went into crafting masks and other ritual objects honoring those spirits.

Contact with the Islamic world brought prosperity and power to Ghana, which expanded before coming under attack by nomads sweeping down from the Sahara around 1200. Those disruptive raids allowed the Mali Empire to absorb Ghana and surrounding areas. The Mali emperor Mansa Musa, who took power in 1312 and reigned for a quarter century, was a devout Muslim and helped make his capital, Timbuktu, a great center of Islamic culture. In the mid-1400s, Mali was in turn absorbed by the Songhai Empire, which dominated West Africa for more than a century before suffering a devastating defeat by troops from Morocco and collapsing.

In East Africa, Muslim merchants arriving by sea at ports like Mogadishu and Mombasa encountered Swahilis, or

FOR MORE FACTS ON...

THE GEOGRAPHY OF THE CONTINENT OF AFRICA see *Africa*, **CHAPTER 9, PAGES 360-1**

THE COUNTRIES OF AFRICA TODAY, INCLUDING GHANA see *Africa*, **CHAPTER 9, PAGES 362-77**

"coasters," who embraced Islam and incorporated Arabic and Persian words into their language as their prosperous towns grew into city-states. Swahili merchants served as middlemen, trading to merchants from abroad goods they obtained from Africans in the interior.

Some inland kingdoms flourished as a result, notably Zimbabwe, whose imposing capital, Great Zimbabwe, was graced with impressive stone architecture and home to nearly 20,000 people. Like kingdoms in West Africa, Zimbabwe flourished by selling slaves as well as gold and ivory.

But the slave trade did not become a consuming and catastrophic business in Africa until Europeans began shipping black Africans across the Atlantic. By the late 1400s, Portuguese traders were exporting a few thousand slaves each year—a mere trickle compared with the massive transports to come.

WHAT IS SWAHILI?

The Swahili language is the most widely spoken language in Africa today, where it is a first or second language for millions living in East and central Africa. It evolved on the so-called Swahili coast of Africa—the eastern coastline, edging the Indian Ocean, from Tanzania to Kenya.

Along this coast, native Bantu speakers came into contact with merchants or colonists from Arabia, Persia, and other lands. They absorbed words from foreigners and created

Swahili, an amalgam of many different languages.

In Swahili, for example, the numbers six (sita), seven (saba), and nine (tisa) are borrowed from Arabic, whereas the other numbers from one through ten are of Bantu origin. The Swahili word for tea (chai) is of Persian origin. Other terms have been acquired from Europeans, including the words meaning table (meza, from Portuguese), bus (basi, from English), and school (shule, from German).

CLAY STATUETTES found by archaeologists at Jenne-jeno, an Iron Age city of Mali in West Africa, may represent ancestral spirits.

CLICK IT: Swahili Language & Culture www.glcom.com/hassan

FAST FACT The English word "safari" originates from the Swahili word for journey or expedition.

MANSA MUSA / EMPEROR, TRAVELER & TRADER

The Mali emperor Mansa Musa became a legendary figure in the Islamic world when he made a spectacular pilgrimage to Mecca in 1324, taking with him more than 1,000 followers and 100 camels, each carrying 300 pounds of gold. According to one Arab chronicler, he disbursed so much gold in Egypt that he caused the value of that precious metal to plummet. He greatly impressed the Arabs, but their culture made an even deeper impression on him. Returning to his capital Timbuktu, he brought with him an Arabic library and an Arab architect, who built a mosque and palace there. Under Mansa Musa, Timbuktu became to Africa what Baghdad was to the Middle East—a haven for Muslim scholars, artists, and poets.

FOR MORE FACTS ON...

LANGUAGES OF THE WORLD see Language, **CHAPTER 6, PAGES 228-31**

TRADE & COMMERCE AS AN ELEMENT OF HUMAN SOCIETY see Commerce, **CHAPTER 6, PAGES 254-7**

284

Buddhist observances at temple ruins, Angkor Wat, Cambodia

ASIA 500-1500

EARLY ASIA

606
Buddhist King Harsha rules in India

618
China's Tang dynasty begins

794
Japanese imperial court at Heian (Kyoto)

960
China's Song dynasty arises

1113
Khmer king begins Angkor Wat

1279
Kublai Khan ends China's Song dynasty

1368
Mongol rule ends in China; Ming dynasty begins

n Asia as in Europe and other regions, faith loomed large during the Middle Ages, but Asian societies held diverse beliefs. Most people in India, for example, were Hindus, but the Indus Valley region to the north was ruled in the early seventh century by a devout Buddhist, King Harsha, and was later conquered by Muslims, who eventually converted much of what is now Pakistan to Islam.

Indian merchants brought various goods, customs, and beliefs to Southeast Asia. Rulers of Funan, in southern Indochina, called themselves rajas, worshipped Hindu deities, and adopted Sanskrit. After Funan collapsed, Khmers took power in Cambodia and embraced Hinduism and later Buddhism. Beginning around 900, Khmer rulers built monuments to both faiths there, including the great 12th-century Hindu shrine, Angkor Wat.

In China, Buddhism coexisted with Confucianism. Following the short-lived Sui dynasty, emperors of the Tang dynasty endorsed Confucian ideals and required office-seekers to show knowledge of Confucian texts in civil service examinations. China flourished under the Tang dynasty and the

FOR MORE FACTS ON...

THE HISTORY OF CIVILIZATION IN THE INDUS RIVER VALLEY see *India 2500 b.c.-a.d. 500*, **CHAPTER 7, PAGES 270-1**
+
THE GEOGRAPHY OF ASIA see *Asia*, **CHAPTER 9, PAGES 378-9**

Song dynasty that succeeded it. Chinese inventors devised the magnetic compass, gunpowder, and porcelain, the country's most prized export.

Korea resisted subjugation by China but was greatly influenced by Chinese culture, as was Japan. Literature and the arts flourished at Japan's imperial court at Heian (Kyoto) in the tenth century. In later centuries, a feudal system developed in which samurai warriors served as vassals to provincial lords, who in turn served as vassals to a military governor called the shogun.

A turbulent new age dawned in Asia when Mongols united under Genghis Khan in 1206, conquering northern China and lands to the west. Khan's grandson Kublai Khan completed the conquest of China but failed to take Japan. Mongols overran Russia and much of the Middle East before the Black Death ravaged their realm in the 14th century. In China, Mongol rule gave way to the Ming dynasty. In the Middle East, Turks regained control, first under the conqueror Tamerlane and then under the Ottomans.

THE TALE OF GENJI, written in the 11th century by Murasaki Shikibu, a lady of the Japanese court, chronicles romantic adventures.

HOW DID JAPANESE WRITING EVOLVE?

The Japanese had no written language when they first came under China's influence, and they readily adopted the Chinese script. Japanese scribes and scholars spent years mastering its complexities by studying and copying Chinese texts.

In the ninth century, however, a much simpler phonetic Japanese script called *kana* was introduced. It could be acquired without lengthy schooling and was learned by women as well as men. Used first for private diaries or love notes, kana soon became the preferred language for Japanese poetry and prose.

Two remarkable works written by women around A.D. 1000—*The Tale of Genji* by Murasaki Shikibu and the *Pillow Book* of Sei Shonagon—represent the starting point for Japanese fiction. The authors used their own language to describe the society they lived in. Their artistic efforts helped create a new literary form in the Japanese language: the novel.

CLICK IT: Tale of Genji www.taleofgenji.org

GENGHIS KHAN / MONGOL CONQUEROR

The man known as Genghis Khan—or Universal Ruler—was the son of a Mongol chieftain who was poisoned by a rival band, leaving the boy he named Temujin to fend for himself. Mongols led a hard life, moving frequently on horseback. As Temujin grew up, he continued to be harried by his father's enemies. In time, he crushed that hostile band by killing all the males taller than a cart axle, so it was said, and enslaving the women and children. He united the many Mongol tribes under his authority, killing his own brother for opposing him. In forging an empire, he combined terror with diplomacy, killing those who resisted him but sparing foes who yielded without a fight and welcoming to his court talented men of various faiths.

FOR MORE FACTS ON...

THE VARIETIES OF WRITTEN LANGUAGE IN THE WORLD TODAY see Language: Writing, **CHAPTER 6, PAGES 230-1**

THE COUNTRIES OF ASIA TODAY INCLUDING KOREA, CHINA & JAPAN see Asia, **CHAPTER 9, PAGES 380-93**

Giant *moai*, stone figures, Easter Island

OCEANIA & NORTH AMERICA
PREHISTORY TO 1500

PRECOLUMBIAN

CIRCA 700
Polynesians settle New Zealand

CIRCA 800
Hohokam culture develops,
American Southwest

CIRCA 1000
Norse reach Newfoundland;
Mississippian culture emerges,
North American Midwest

CIRCA 1100
Anasazi culture peaks,
American Southwest

CIRCA 1200
Polynesian society, Easter Island

CIRCA 1300
Anasazi abandon cliff dwellings;
Mississippian culture declines

ong before European navigators fanned out around the globe in about 1500, societies had developed in lands unknown to people of the Old World and had achieved significant accomplishments of knowledge and culture. Between 15,000 and 20,000 years ago, people crossed from Siberia to Alaska on a land bridge that formed as sea levels lowered during the Ice Age.

By 9000 B.C., humans had reached the southern tip of South America. Throughout the Americas, small bands of people subsisted by hunting and gathering until around 3000 B.C., when maize, or corn, was domesticated.

The cultivation of corn, beans, squash, and other crops spread northward over time, allowing some tribes in the present United States to develop complex societies whose chiefs were buried surrounded by treasure in huge mounds. The first such cultures, the Adena and Hopewell, developed in the Ohio River Valley between 500 and 100 B.C., but the greatest of the mound builders were the Mississippians, who flourished in the Mississippi River Valley and parts of the Southeast from around 1000 to 1300.

FOR MORE FACTS ON...

PATHWAYS OF HUMAN MIGRATION see *Human Migration*, **CHAPTER 6, PAGES 220-1**

THE IMPORTANCE OF AGRICULTURE IN EARLY HUMAN HISTORY see *Agriculture*, **CHAPTER 6, PAGES 246-7**

Their most imposing settlement was Cahokia, near modern-day St. Louis. At its peak, as many as 20,000 people lived there around massive burial mounds. Like the rulers of other ancient civilizations, chiefs here were honored at death like gods. One ruler received a majestic grave offering of 20,000 shell beads and was buried with at least 60 other people, some of whom were evidently sacrificed.

Mississippian society declined at about the same time that Native Americans called Puebloan or Anasazi (ancient ones) abandoned their home sites in the Southwest. They left behind other remarkable monuments, including an urban complex of multistory dwellings and kivas (underground ceremonial chambers) in New Mexico's Chaco Canyon. Prolonged drought may have caused the ancient Puebloans to abandon this area and move first to cliff dwellings at higher and wetter areas like Mesa Verde and later to permanent water sources like the Rio Grande, where Pueblo society arose in the 14th century.

The most isolated societies were those of the Polynesians, whose ancestors left Australia and New Guinea around 2000 B.C. and began colonizing distant Pacific islands such as Samoa and Tahiti. Intrepid seafarers who migrated in outrigger canoes, taking with them dogs and pigs and crops like yams and breadfruit, they reached Hawaii around 100 B.C. and may have reached Easter Island as early as 500 B.C., although recent evidence suggests a date later by centuries. Polynesians were led by hereditary chiefs.

The Rapa Nui people on Easter Island raised huge stone monoliths representing gods and godlike chiefs.

ANCIENT CLIFF DWELLINGS in the North American Southwest only hint at the sophisticated society of the Puebloan people.

WHAT DO WE KNOW OF EARLY AMERICANS?

MARBLE FIGURES found by archaeologists at Etowah, a Mississippian site in present-day Georgia, came from mounds that formed part of a burial complex with stairs, walkways, and a plaza.

North of present-day Mexico, no great empires developed. Tribes subsisted by hunting buffalo or other game, best accomplished by small and highly mobile bands whose chiefs had little authority beyond their immediate camp circles. Settled groups like the Mississippians living in fertile areas, however, developed a political system resembling feudalism. Local chiefs in outlying villages recognized the ruler at ceremonial centers like Cahokia as their overlord, to whom they owed duties in the form of crops, labor, or military service. Those required to labor on the great burial mounds at Cahokia may have considered it a sacred obligation, for Mississippian rulers were earthly representatives of the sun god—the paramount force on which all life depended.

CLICK IT: Places of Power www.sacredsites.com

FAST FACT Mississippian culture was still in evidence when Spanish conquistador Hernando de Soto reached North America in the 16th century and found people worshipping the sun god at temples atop burial mounds.

FOR MORE FACTS ON...

POTTERY & OTHER EARLY ART FORMS see Art, **CHAPTER 6, PAGES 238-9**

OCEANIA & NORTH AMERICA TODAY see Australia & Oceania, **CHAPTER 9, PAGES 408-33,** & North America, **CHAPTER 9, PAGES 414-23**

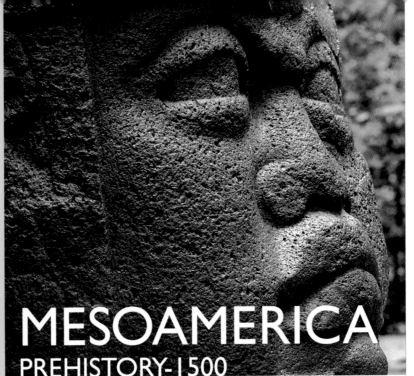

Olmec stone head, La Venta, Mexico, created circa 1000 B.C.

ANCIENT AMERICAS

CIRCA 600
Maya civilization reaches peak

683
Maya ruler Pacal buried at Palenque

CIRCA 900
Maya civilization collapses

CIRCA 1170
Mexico's Toltec Empire ends

1325
Aztec found Tenochtitlan (Mexico City)

1428
Itzcoatl expands Aztec Empire

MESOAMERICA
PREHISTORY-1500

uring Europe's Middle Ages, several powerful Native American societies with similar beliefs and customs flourished in Mesoamerica, a region extending from the Valley of Mexico, embracing what is now Mexico City, to north of the Isthmus of Panama. The cultural foundation for those societies was laid in ancient times by the Olmec people.

The Olmec lived in southern Mexico near the Gulf Coast and built great ceremonial centers at San Lorenzo and La Venta featuring earthen pyramids, stone temples, and ball courts where a game of ritual significance was played. Massive stone heads thought to represent Olmec rulers were erected there and inscribed with cryptic pictographs called glyphs.

Olmec culture died out with the destruction of La Venta around 400 B.C., but it strongly influenced the Maya living around the Yucatán Peninsula. Maya civilization reached its peak around A.D. 600 as rival city-states like Palenque, Copán, and Tikal expanded and vied for supremacy, much as Athens and Sparta did in ancient Greece.

Maya kings and queens looked to the movements of stars to determine when to attack rivals. Captives taken in such "star wars" were often sacrificed to honor gods whom the Maya credited for their success. The blood of royalty was considered especially appealing to the gods, and Maya rulers sometimes drew their own blood as offerings. High population densities in Maya cities strained the resources of outlying areas and caused resentments and rebellions that contributed to the collapse of this civilization around 900.

Among the trading partners of the Maya were merchants from Teotihuacan in the fertile Valley of Mexico. By the sixth century, this great urban center was home to more than 150,000 people, many of them artisans who produced goods for export. Like Maya city-states, populous Teotihuacan strained the resources of the surrounding area and eventually collapsed, coming to a fiery end around 700.

The Valley of Mexico was later dominated by the warlike Toltecs, who sacrificed captives in droves at their capital, Tula, and made demands

FOR MORE FACTS ON...

THE MIDDLE AGES IN THE MEDITERRANEAN WORLD see Middle Ages 500-1500, **CHAPTER 7, PAGES 278-81**
+
TODAY'S MESOAMERICA see North America & South America, **CHAPTER 9, PAGES 414-23 & 424-9**

for tribute that grew onerous for their subjects when drought struck the area in the 12th century. Around 1170, rebels destroyed Tula and brought down the Toltec Empire.

Following in the Toltec path were the mighty Aztec, who entered the Valley of Mexico from the north and forged their own empire in the 15th century based at Tenochtitlan, a majestic capital built where Mexico City now stands. Like the Maya, Aztec studied the heavens, kept intricate calendars, and preserved their lore in writing. Kings celebrated their coronations by waging war and taking captives, who were sacrificed by the thousands atop the Great Pyramid in Tenochtitlan to seek divine blessings. Some Aztec rivals became trusted allies, but other groups were forced to pay heavy tribute, fueling resentments that Spanish invaders would later exploit to divide and conquer the Aztec Empire.

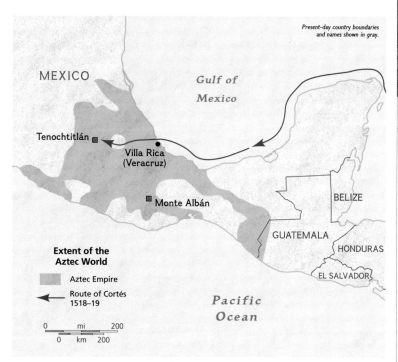

Present-day country boundaries and names shown in gray.

MEXICO

Gulf of Mexico

Tenochtitlán

Villa Rica (Veracruz)

Monte Albán

BELIZE

GUATEMALA

HONDURAS

EL SALVADOR

Pacific Ocean

Extent of the Aztec World

Aztec Empire

Route of Cortés 1518–19

0 mi 200
0 km 200

THE AZTEC EMPIRE covered much of central and southern Mexico when the Spanish conquistador Hernán Cortés arrived. Cortés sailed from Cuba south through the Gulf of Mexico and reached Tenochtitlan, the Aztec capital, in 1519. He and his soldiers remained there and finally conquered the Aztec Empire in 1521.

THE MAYA BALL GAME

Great ball courts take center stage in the remains of Maya cities such as Tikal, Copán, and Chichén Itzá.

A ritual ball game played by the Maya people in these ball courts evoked a mythic contest in which lords of the underworld defeated and killed the maize god, who returned to life as a cornstalk, offering people sustenance. Losers in the ball game were sacrificed in the belief that their blood would nourish the earth and renew the blessings of the maize god and other Maya deities.

Teams of two men each played the game, using a solid rubber sphere about the size of a human head. (In legend, the lords of the underworld used a skull as their ball.) Wearing protective gear, players struck the ball with their hips and shoulders. The object may have been to propel the ball through a hoop on the opposing team's side.

CARVED STONE DISK portraying a Maya ball player and dated A.D. 591 was found among the ruins of Chinkultic, a minor Maya city.

CLICK IT: The Maya Code www.pbs.org/wgbh/nova/mayacode

FOR MORE FACTS ON...

EARLY RELIGIOUS BELIEFS & PRACTICES see Religion, **CHAPTER 6, PAGES 232-3**

THE ERA OF EXPLORATION INCLUDING THE CONQUISTADORES see World Navigation 1492-1522, **CHAPTER 7, PAGES 292-3**

Ruins of Machu Picchu, the Inca capital, Peru

SOUTH AMERICA
PREHISTORY-1500

EARLY SOUTH AMERICA

CIRCA 500
In Peru, Moche reach peak of power and Nasca create line drawings

CIRCA 1400
Inca begin forging an empire

1438
Inca ruler Pachacuti expands empire through reforms and conquests

1471
Pachacuti abdicates in favor of his son, who completes conquest of the Chimú

CIRCA 1500
Inca Empire reaches its greatest extent

The most significant historical developments in South America in ancient and medieval times occurred in what is now Peru. By 500 B.C., the ceremonial center of Chavín de Huántar, high in the Peruvian Andes, attracted pilgrims from a wide area, who worshipped at shrines to the jaguar god and the spirits of other rain forest animals. Most likely, the Chavín cult leaders came from the rain forest and found a following among people living along the western slopes, for whom water flowing down from the mountains was a source of wonder and fertility.

By A.D. 500, a well-organized state had emerged along the Moche River in northern Peru, where massive irrigation projects increased the amount of land under cultivation and fed the growth of a complex society with an aristocratic elite. Gifted artists produced glittering masks of gold and copper that were buried with Moche warlords along with captives sacrificed for the occasion. Moche potters crafted decorative clay vessels that offered

FOR MORE FACTS ON...

EARLY RELIGIONS & MAGICAL THINKING see *Religion,* **CHAPTER 6, PAGES 232-3**

THE COUNTRIES OF SOUTH AMERICA TODAY see *South America,* **CHAPTER 9, PAGES 424-9**

a vivid tableau of their society, including scenes of helmeted warriors clubbing their enemies. Pyramids made of millions of adobe bricks and decorated with splendid wall paintings suggest that Moche society was approaching the grandeur of Mesoamerican civilizations before it declined around 600, perhaps because of drought, floods, or other natural causes. A similar fate befell the Nasca, who lived south of the Moche in an arid region made fruitful by irrigation. They left behind monumental line drawings in the desert that could be viewed in their entirety only from above and may have been intended for spirits in heaven.

Around 1000, the promising Moche River Valley gave birth to another accomplished society, the Chimú, whose capital of Chan Chan had nearly 30,000 inhabitants. Around 1300, Chimú rulers embarked on conquests that brought more than 600 miles of the Peruvian coast under their control before they fell to a superior power—the Inca. Those conquerors began their imperial quest around 1400 when they outgrew the confines of the Cusco Valley high in the Andes. They owed much of their success to the dynamic ruler Pachacuti, or He Who Transforms the Earth. The Inca had no script but kept meticulous records by tying knots on strings. All people had to serve the state periodically as soldiers, farmers, or laborers, working on projects like the remarkable Inca highway system, which had two main arteries, one along the coast and another along the Andes, with way stations a day's journey apart. By 1500, the well-organized Inca Empire extended for 2,500 miles from present-day Ecuador southward to Chile and embraced nearly 100 ethnic groups.

WHO DID THE INCA SACRIFICE?

On rare occasions, such as a king's inauguration, the Inca sacrificed as many as 200 young people to their gods. More often, they sacrificed llamas or made offerings of food. Every day Inca priests offered cornmeal to honor the sun god. "Eat this, Lord Sun," they proclaimed, "so that you will know that we are your children." The Inca also worshipped several female deities, including Earth Mother and Moon Mother, wife of the sun god. Devotees known as Chosen Women lived in seclusion at shrines and temples and wove richly embroidered fabrics.

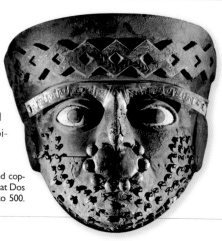

AFTERLIFE RICHES like this gold and copper mask filled three Moche tombs found at Dos Cabezas, Peru, inhabited from A.D. 150 to 500.

WHO BUILT MACHU PICCHU?

When Pachacuti came to power in 1438, the Inca were quickly expanding, but he did much to enhance and consolidate their empire. All the wealth he and future kings acquired during their reigns, he decreed, would be devoted to housing and caring for their mummified remains. This practice reinforced the idea that the ruler was immortal. It also forced each new ruler to make his own fortune and reputation through conquest. When Pachacuti abdicated in favor of his son in 1471, the young king did just that, completing the conquest of the Chimú begun by his father. Pachacuti forced some defeated groups to resettle near the Inca homeland, where they were closely watched. Loyal subjects were sent to colonize newly conquered territory. Before stepping down as emperor, he built Machu Picchu, a majestic mountaintop retreat and ceremonial center near the Inca capital, Cusco.

FAST FACT Many Nasca geoglyphs—shapes etched in the dry pampa rock—measure more than 1,000 feet tall.

FOR MORE FACTS ON...

THE MANY VARIETIES OF BUILDINGS & SHELTER see Shelter, CHAPTER 6, PAGES 258-9
+
GEOGRAPHY & ECONOMY OF PERU TODAY see South America, CHAPTER 9, PAGE 427

EXPLORATIONS

1492
Columbus reaches Caribbean from Spain

1497
Cabot explores Newfoundland

1498
Da Gama pioneers ocean route to Asia

1502
Columbus takes fourth and final voyage

1504
Vespucci's travel accounts published,
naming New World

1522
Magellan's crew reaches Spain:
first circumnavigation

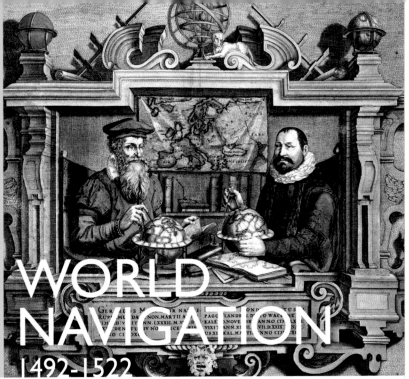

WORLD NAVIGATION
1492-1522

Gerardus Mercator and Jodocus Hondius, early cartographers

he world entered the modern era around 1500 as Europeans sailed around the globe and began colonizing newly discovered lands. They made this leap by applying lessons learned during the late Middle Ages, when trade with the Middle East and Far East gave them incentives to venture abroad and improve their navigational techniques.

Before 1500, most accomplished mariners were non-Europeans, such as Zheng He, a Chinese admiral who in the early 1400s took seven voyages that ranged as far as Africa and the Persian Gulf. China's rulers grew isolationist, though, and their navy dwindled.

The Ottoman Empire profited from the maritime skill and naval resources of the Arab world, but Middle Easterners already had access to the Far East by land and sea and did not need new routes to acquire prized goods.

Western Europeans, however, could obtain those commodities directly only by pursuing uncharted paths. That profit motive and the desire to spread Christianity led rulers to encourage maritime exploration, fostering the growth of vast European empires.

Leading the way were Portugal and Spain, assisted by Italy. In the mid-1400s Prince Henry the Navigator of Portugal founded a school devoted to improving navigation and sponsoring expeditions along the West African coast. Portuguese mariners traded for slaves and gold there and continued around Africa to India, first reached by sea from Portugal by Vasco da Gama in 1498. This proved to be the best route between Europe and the Far East, but efforts to find a shorter path by crossing the Atlantic revealed new lands.

In 1492, Italian Christopher Columbus, backed by Spain's King Ferdinand and Queen Isabella, reached the Caribbean, which he believed was the Indies. Another Italian exploring for Spain, Amerigo Vespucci, concluded a decade later that what lay across the Atlantic was in fact a New World, eventually called America in his honor. Earth's extent became clear when the expedition launched by Ferdinand Magellan in 1519—and completed after his death—rounded South America, crossed the Pacific, and reached Europe in 1522, circumnavigating the globe.

FOR MORE FACTS ON...

MAPS & INSTRUMENTS USED BY EARLY NAVIGATORS see *The History of Mapping & Mapmaking,* **CHAPTER 1, PAGES 20-1, 24-5**

THE CHALLENGES OF EARLY NAVIGATION see *Navigation,* **CHAPTER 1, PAGES 38-9**

ADVANCES IN NAVIGATION

In navigating the globe, European mariners drew on technology and know-how from other regions and earlier times. The magnetic compass and the stern-post rudder, for example, first appeared in medieval China and probably reached Europe through the Middle East, although such inventions sometimes arose independently in various parts of the world. The astrolabe and other devices used to calculate latitude by measuring the angle of the sun above the horizon at noon were of ancient origin and were refined by Arab navigators, from whom Portuguese mariners acquired the technology.

Astute sailors and scholars reckoned that the Earth was round long before Christopher Columbus acted on that principle. The crucial question that remained to be answered in his day was just how extensive the globe was. Columbus grossly underestimated how far one would have to travel west to reach Asia—an error that led him to great discoveries.

COLUMBUS'S FLEET, the *Nina,* the *Pinta,* and the *Santa Maria,* reached the Caribbean from Spain in nine weeks. Expecting to reach Asia, they named their destination the "West Indies."

CLICK IT: Columbus Navigation www.columbusnavigation.com

FAST FACT Columbus was not the first European to sail to the New World; Vikings had already crossed the Atlantic, coasted Greenland, and reached Newfoundland around A.D. 1000. Leif Eriksson may have traveled as far south as Cape Cod.

 Oct. 11, course to west and southwest. Heavier sea than they had known. . . . At two hours after midnight land appeared. — **CHRISTOPHER COLUMBUS, 1492**

CHRISTOPHER COLUMBUS / EXPLORER & COLONIZER

Columbus (1451-1506) made landfall on the island of Hispaniola (now Haiti and the Dominican Republic) in 1492, and launched global European expansion by colonizing the Caribbean. Returning to Hispaniola in 1493, Columbus found sailors he had left behind there dead and the fort they occupied destroyed. Undeterred, he settled the island in earnest and subjugated the Taino Indians who lived there. Tainos who refused to pay tribute to Spanish colonists were killed or captured. In 1496 Columbus shipped nearly 500 captives to Spain, where those who survived the voyage were sold as slaves in violation of a royal edict. He and his colonists found little gold in the Caribbean, but their efforts led to further New World conquests that brought enormous wealth to Spain and made it the world's greatest power in the 16th century.

FOR MORE FACTS ON...

CHANGING WORLDVIEWS BASED ON CHANGES IN KNOWLEDGE see *Scientific Worldviews,* **CHAPTER 8, PAGES 326-7**
+
COUNTRIES IN THE AMERICAS TODAY see *North America & South America,* **CHAPTER 9, PAGES 414-29**

RENAISSANCE & REFORMATION 1500-1650

NEW IDEAS

1517
Martin Luther issues 95 theses

1534
Henry VIII establishes Church of England

1536
Calvin begins ministry in Switzerland

1543
Copernicus claims Earth orbits the sun

1558
Elizabeth I crowned queen of England

1588
Spanish Armada launched

1648
Thirty Years' War ends;
Protestants gain freedom of worship

he Renaissance had its origins in the late Middle Ages. Merchants in 14th-century Florence and other thriving Italian city-states served as patrons of artists and poets, who drew inspiration from the past. They took inspiration from classical Greek and Roman literature preserved in Catholic monasteries and in the libraries of Byzantium and the Islamic world.

Among those nurtured in Florence were poet Dante Alighieri, painter Giotto di Bondone, and scholar Petrarch. Their works served as a bridge between Europe's age of faith and the humanism of the Renaissance, which reached its peak in the 1500s with the achievements of artist Michelangelo and Leonardo da Vinci—painter, inventor, and scientist.

Humanists shared the conviction that nothing was too mysterious or sacred to be grasped by the human intellect and imagination. Renaissance scientists questioned ideas such as the cosmology in which Earth was the center of the universe. This marked the beginning of a scientific revolution that would ultimately refute basic articles of faith, like the biblical story of creation.

FOR MORE FACTS ON...

THE HISTORY OF THE MIDDLE AGES see Middle Ages, **CHAPTER 7, PAGES 278-81**

CHANGING VIEWS OF THE UNIVERSE & EARTH'S POSITION IN IT see Scientific Worldviews, **CHAPTER 8, PAGES 326-7**

WHAT WAS THE REFORMATION?

The Protestant Reformation began in 1517 when Martin Luther, a German monk, protested practices such as the sale of indulgences, pardoning people for their sins. Rejecting the authority of the pope and the priesthood, Protestants ordained ministers who lived much like their parishioners and who preached in their own tongue—instead of Latin—using Bibles published on printing presses like that devised by Johannes Gutenberg of Germany in the 15th century. Printing and the use of native languages also fostered the work of great Renaissance writers like the English poet and playwright William Shakespeare.

Protestantism flourished in urban areas in northern Europe, where many literate people questioned Catholic doctrine based on their reading of the Bible. Conflict ensued between Catholic Spain and northern Protestant countries. In 1618 German Protestants rebelled against the Habsburg dynasty that ruled both Spain and the Holy Roman Empire. Their actions launched the Thirty Years' War, which ended when the Habsburgs granted religious freedom to their German subjects.

LONDON'S GLOBE THEATRE, built in 1598 and home to Shakespeare, burned down in 1613, set afire by a staged cannon shot.

GLOSSARY

Classical: From the Latin *classicus,* "of the highest class, superior." Pertaining to ancient Greece and Rome. **/ Puritanism:** Movement in the late 16th and 17th centuries that sought to "purify" the Church of England, leading to civil war in England and to the founding of colonies in North America.

 To be a king and wear a crown is more glorious to them that see it than it is pleasure to them that bear it. — **QUEEN ELIZABETH I, 1601**

ELIZABETH I / QUEEN OF ENGLAND

Queen Elizabeth I (1533-1603), who ruled England from 1558 until her death, was a product of the Reformation. Her father, King Henry VIII, had broken with Rome in 1533 because he desperately wanted a male heir and the pope would not let him divorce his queen, Catherine of Aragon, and marry Anne Boleyn, who later gave birth to Elizabeth. As queen, Elizabeth steered a middle course between Catholicism and Puritanism and upheld a moderate form of Protestantism. Known as the Virgin Queen, she preserved England's sovereignty by rejecting foreign suitors, including King Philip II of Spain, who later sent an armada in the hopes of conquering England and restoring Catholic rule. By repelling that fleet, England emerged as a major power, capable of competing with the mighty Spanish Empire.

FAST FACT Italy, which gave birth to the Renaissance, was divided into 250 city-states, fostering competition and innovation that made those such as Florence and Venice centers of power, wealth, learning, and artistry.

FOR MORE FACTS ON...

THE ORIGINS & HISTORY OF CHRISTIANITY see *Religion: Monotheism,* **CHAPTER 6, PAGES 236-7**

THE ROLE OF ART IN HUMAN CULTURE see *Art,* **CHAPTER 6, PAGES 238-9**

A NEW WORLD 1500-1775

NORTH AMERICA

1541
Cartier founds Quebec

1565
Spanish colonists found St. Augustine

1607
English colonists found Jamestown

1620
English Pilgrims found Plymouth

1664
English seize port at New Amsterdam, renaming it New York

1682
La Salle claims Louisiana for France

1763
France surrenders North American territories to Britain

Spain took the lead in colonizing the New World, bringing vast areas under its authority. Colonization of the Caribbean, begun by Columbus, devastated Indians there, who were all but wiped out by smallpox and other imported diseases. When there was no more gold to extract, colonists took to raising sugarcane, bringing in so many slaves that the population became largely African.

Spanish conquistadores enriched both themselves and the crown by defeating and plundering the Aztec and Inca Empires. After helping to colonize Cuba, Hernán Cortés sailed for Mexico in 1519 with 600 men and turned Indians against the Aztec. Attacking Tenochtitlan in 1521 during a smallpox epidemic, Cortés sacked and burned the Aztec capital and founded Mexi-

co City in its place. Francisco Pizarro used similar tactics in Peru to conquer the Inca and seize their capital, Cusco, in 1533. Vast amounts of silver poured into Spanish coffers from South America and Mexico, but conquistadores who ventured north of Mexico found no great wealth or native empires. Colonization there was left to Spanish monks and settlers who founded

FOR MORE FACTS ON...

CHRISTOPHER COLUMBUS & HIS NEW WORLD VOYAGES see World Navigation 1492-1522, **CHAPTER 7, PAGE 293**

COUNTRIES IN THE AMERICAS TODAY see North America & South America, **CHAPTER 9, PAGES 414-29**

isolated missions and towns. In 1680, Pueblo Indians in New Mexico drove the Spaniards out. When colonists returned, they reached an accommodation with Pueblos, who served with them in expeditions against hostile tribes. Throughout the Spanish-American Empire, colonists lived closely among Indians and depended on their labor.

A different pattern prevailed in England's North American colonies. In Virginia, where the first permanent settlement was founded at Jamestown in 1607, colonists clashed with Algonquian Indians and held them off. Rather than using Indian laborers to raise crops like tobacco, colonists used indentured servants from England or slaves from Africa. The Puritans who settled Massachusetts also displaced Indians and encroached on their land, triggering a fiery uprising in 1675 in which warriors killed some 600 colonists before the English defeated them with the help of the powerful Iroquois tribe. In time, the Iroquois too would lose out to Anglo-American settlers.

Colonists arrived in such large numbers from England that they supplanted not only Indians but also other Europeans, including the Dutch who settled New York before the English took control there in 1664. Their chief rivals in North America were the French, who began colonizing Canada in earnest in 1608.

French settlers were relatively few in number, but they forged alliances with Indians that gave France a vast

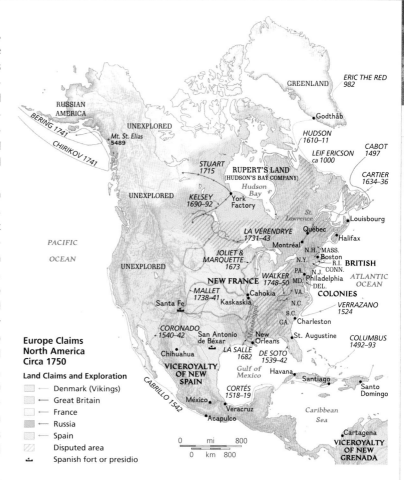

Europe Claims North America Circa 1750

Land Claims and Exploration

- ← Denmark (Vikings)
- ← Great Britain
- ← France
- ← Russia
- ← Spain
- Disputed area
- Spanish fort or presidio

EUROPEAN COLONIAL POWERS carved up the New World, claiming land and vying for wealth, resources, and control. Their legacies live on in regional customs and national languages.

area of influence extending from Canada down the Mississippi River to New Orleans.

In 1713 France lost Newfoundland, Nova Scotia, and other territory to Great Britain—as England was known after its union with Scotland in 1709—before surrendering its remaining claims in North America to the British at the conclusion of the French and Indian War in 1763. For all its might, Britain could not prevent its American colonies from rebelling in 1775 and winning independence.

CLICK IT: Historic Jamestowne historicjamestowne.org

FAST FACT Spanish ships carrying treasure home from the Americas were subject to attack by British buccaneers and pirates from other lands and traveled in fleets of ten for protection.

FOR MORE FACTS ON...

NATIVE CULTURES OF MESOAMERICA & SOUTH AMERICA see *Mesoamerica Preshitory-1500 & South America Preshitory-1500*, **CHAPTER 7, PAGES 288-91**

THE AMERICAN REVOLUTION see *Revolution 1600-1800*, **CHAPTER 7, PAGES 298-9**

Boston Massacre, Boston, Massachusets, 1770

TIME OF TURMOIL

1649
Charles I executed, English Civil War

1688
England's Glorious Revolution;
monarch now subject to Parliament

1689
Locke publishes theory of natural rights

1762
Rousseau publishes *Social Contract*

1776
American colonies declare independence;
Adam Smith publishes *Wealth of Nations*

1789
French Revolution begins

REVOLUTION
1600-1800

Engrav'd Printed & Sold by PAUL REVERE *BOSTON*

The Enlightenment, an intellectual movement, grew out of the Renaissance and favored rational inquiry over established dogma. Enlightenment thinkers took their cue from the French philosopher and mathematician René Descartes, who wrote in 1637 that his first rule was "never to accept a thing as true until I knew it as such without a single doubt."

The idea of testing hypotheses was essential to the scientific method, refined in the late 1600s by English physicist Isaac Newton. The Enlightenment also spawned political revolutions as freethinkers toppled old regimes.

Political philosophers of the Enlightenment analyzed how society worked. Adam Smith of Scotland concluded that self-interest benefited society by fostering economic competition and that restricting competition (for example, granting royal monopolies to companies) harmed society. John Locke of England argued that people owe loyalty to their government only as long as their rights are protected. French philosopher Jean-Jacques Rousseau, author of *The Social Contract*, argued that only a republic could preserve liberty.

Despite the threat such ideas posed to the established order, some European monarchs tried to rule in enlightened fashion. Catherine the Great of Russia improved education among nobility and ended some of the worst abuses of serfs, while Prussia's Frederick the Great promoted religious tolerance and established a civil service. But such enlightened despots were as intent on maintaining power as absolute monarchs like France's King Louis XIV, who died after reigning for 71 years.

The rival monarchies of Europe clashed frequently during the 18th century, setting British troops and colonists in North America against the French and their Indian allies. To help pay for that costly war, the British imposed the Stamp Act on colonists, one of several measures that led Americans to defy King George III and declare independence in 1776. Similar resentments in France against King Louis XVI and taxes he imposed to cover debts incurred in past wars triggered a bloody revolution there and gave birth to a republic based on the Enlightenment ideals of liberty, equality, and fraternity.

FOR MORE FACTS ON...

SCIENCE OF THE ENLIGHTENMENT *see Physical Science & Chemistry,* **CHAPTER 8, PAGES 328-9, 334-5**

TRADE & ECONOMIC COMPETITION IN THE 21ST CENTURY *see World Trade Today,* **CHAPTER 6, PAGES 256-7**

LIBERTY, EQUALITY, FRATERNITY—OR DEATH

Unlike the Americans, who formed a legislature resembling the British Parliament after rebelling against King George III, the French had no strong parliamentary tradition to draw on when they rose up against King Louis XVI. Deeply in debt, King Louis in 1789 convened the Estates-General, an assembly that had not met in 175 years. Traditionally, the first two estates—the clergy and the nobility—had dominated, but in this crisis commoners who made up the Third Estate took charge and formed the National Assembly, whose members declared that all men are "born and remain free and equal in rights." The king accepted this declaration only after women of Paris took up arms and marched on his palace at Versailles. In 1792 revolutionaries abolished the monarchy and proclaimed a republic. One revolutionary group, the Jacobins,

MAXIMILIEN ROBESPIERRE, a mastermind of the French Revolution, was violently arrested and executed by guillotine the very next day. This 19th-century painting imagines his arrest.

then launched a Reign of Terror, executing King Louis and Queen Marie-Antoinette and thousands of so-called counterrevolutionaries. In the conservative reaction that followed, Jacobins were seized and put to death.

FAST FACT The palace of King Louis XIV of France at Versailles was Europe's largest, with 1,400 fountains, 230 acres of gardens, and an extravagant hall of mirrors more than 200 feet long with 70 windows overlooking the gardens.

HOW DID PHILOSOPHY INFLUENCE REVOLUTION?

The political philosophy of Englishman John Locke had a profound impact on Thomas Jefferson and the American Revolution. Born in England in 1632, Locke witnessed two revolutions during his lifetime. The first, in which his father participated, was a struggle between Puritans in Parliament and King Charles I, who was executed in 1649. The second, in which Locke took part, ended in 1688 when the Protestant monarchs Queen Mary II and King William III supplanted the Catholic King James II and accepted a Bill of Rights making the crown subject to Parliament. This Glorious Revolution exemplified Locke's view that rulers must respond to the will of the people. For Jefferson, born in colonial Virginia in 1743 and educated at the College of William and Mary, Locke's ideas helped justify the American rebellion against King George III. Jefferson drew on Locke when he asserted in the Declaration of Independence that governments derive "their just powers from the consent of the governed" and that when a government denies people their rights, they have the right "to alter or abolish it."

FOR MORE FACTS ON...

SOCIAL CLASSES & THEIR ROLE IN HUMAN SOCIETY see *The Human Family: Race, Class & Gender,* **CHAPTER 6, PAGES 226-7**

THE COUNTRY OF FRANCE TODAY see *Europe,* **CHAPTER 9, PAGES 398**

NATIONALISM 1790–1900

EARLY MODERN TIMES

1804
Napoleon Bonaparte becomes emperor of France

1810
Rebellions against Spain

1815
Congress of Vienna convenes

1829
Greece wins independence

1848
Revolutions in European countries

1861
Russian Tsar Alexander II abolishes serfdom

he French Revolution shook Europe to its very foundations. No monarch could risk ignoring the will of the people. Napoleon Bonaparte, who crowned himself emperor of France in 1804, recognized the spirit of the times and, despite his dictatorial leanings, granted legal rights to citizens, instituted public education, and reformed the tax system.

Yet he muzzled the press, jailed opponents, and handpicked the legislature. He was a nationalist, not a revolutionary. His hard-fighting and triumphant citizen army was devoted to him but even more devoted to France.

Napoleon met with defeat and disaster when he invaded Russia in 1812. The allied powers opposing him tried to restore the old order in Europe by pledging to defend established monarchies. But nationalist fervor could not be suppressed.

Greeks won independence from the Ottoman Empire in 1829, encouraging other groups to seek rights or freedom. In 1848 revolutionary fervor peaked in cities like Paris, Vienna, and Berlin, and the *Communist Manifesto* was published. Yet rising nationalism

FOR MORE FACTS ON...

THE FRENCH REVOLUTION, LEADING UP TO NAPOLEON'S REIGN see *Revolutions 1600–1800*, **CHAPTER 7, PAGES 298-9**

KARL MARX & THE COMMUNIST MANIFESTO see *The Industrial Revolution 1765–1900*, **CHAPTER 7, PAGES 302-3**

did not bring radical changes or democratic reforms. Germany was unified by the Prussian statesman Otto von Bismarck, who launched wars of expansion that forged a new German empire. Legislatures with limited powers were introduced in many monarchies, including Germany, newly unified Italy, Austria-Hungary, and Russia.

Nationalism also had a strong cultural impact. As education became widely available, women emerged as leading figures in literature and began pressing for rights. Women had figured prominently in the French Revolution until the Reign of Terror, when they were excluded from politics. Among those executed in the Terror was Olympe de Gouges, author of the Declaration of the Rights of Woman. Around the same time, Mary Wollstonecraft of England published *A Vindication of the Rights of Woman*. By the mid-19th century, women were seeking the vote in Britain and the United States—granted first by New Zealand in 1893.

THE UNITED STATES, at first a confederation, gradually became a coherent nation, guided by its Constitution, created during a convention in Philadelphia in 1787 (above). Early Presidents used powers granted by the Constitution to expand America greatly through treaties and conflicts. The acquisition of western territories set northern and southern states at odds over whether slavery should expand westward. The Civil War erupted in 1861, and victory for the Union cleared the way for America's emergence as a great power with a strong central government and a united citizenry.

CLICK IT: Napoleon www.pbs.org/empires/napoleon

FAST FACT Of the 600,000 troops who invaded Russia under Napoleon in 1812 and were exposed to cold and famine, fewer than 40,000 made it back to France.

> Let us without fear lay the cornerstone of South American freedom. To hesitate is to die. — **SIMÓN BOLÍVAR, 1811**

SIMÓN BOLÍVAR / LIBERATOR & NATION-BUILDER

As the Spanish Empire declined, Latin American countries followed the example of the U.S. and sought independence. In 1810, rebellions broke out in Mexico and South America, where Simón Bolívar of Venezuela (1783-1830) led the way. By the 1820s, all of Latin America was free, including Brazil, which separated from Portugal. But the political future of the region remained uncertain. Bolívar stepped down in 1826 as dictator of Peru after founding Bolivia, named for him. He remained president of Gran Colombia—now Colombia, Ecuador, Panama, and Venezuela. In 1828, faced with a rebellion, he assumed dictatorial powers to prevent Gran Colombia from splitting into small, weak states that might be dominated by imperial powers. He abdicated and died in 1830, and Gran Colombia died with him, breaking apart as he had feared.

FOR MORE FACTS ON...

GENDER AS A SOCIAL DETERMINANT see *The Human Family: Race, Class & Gender*, **CHAPTER 6, PAGES 226-7**

+

THE COUNTRIES OF LATIN AMERICA TODAY see *North America & South America*, **CHAPTER 9, PAGES 417-9, 426-9**

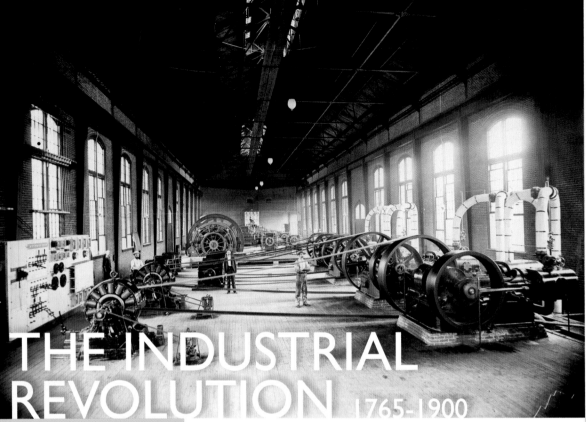

Generators for the B&O Railroad's electric plant, Baltimore, Maryland, 1895

THE INDUSTRIAL REVOLUTION 1765–1900

TECHNOLOGY MILESTONES

1769
Watt patents steam engine

1844
Morse sends first telegraph message

1856
Bessemer improves steel production

1876
Bell invents the telephone

1879
Edison perfects incandescent lightbulb

1892
Diesel patents internal combustion engine

1895
Marconi pioneers wireless telegraphy

The industrial revolution began in Great Britain, which had large deposits of iron ore and coal—the fuel on which modern industry first depended—and a political system that encouraged private enterprise and investment. Britain also had a thriving cottage industry from which a new business economy could evolve. For instance, workers spun and wove wool and cotton by hand at home.

After James Watt perfected the steam engine in the 1760s and steam power was applied to spinning and weaving, the textile industry boomed. Cottages gave way to factories, and the productivity of workers soared, producing profits and attracting investors, which allowed companies to purchase equipment and build more factories. Steam-powered locomotives, introduced in the early 1800s, linked factories to cities, ports, and coal mines. During the 19th century, the industrial revolution spread across Europe and reached other parts of the world, including the United States and Japan.

The initial impact of industrialization was traumatic. Protesters known as

FOR MORE FACTS ON...

MINERALS & ORE FROM PLANET EARTH see *Earth's Elements & Rocks & Minerals,* **CHAPTER 3, PAGES 90-3**

ADVANCES IN TECHNOLOGY see *Physical Science: Engineering,* **CHAPTER 8, PAGES 332-3**

Luddites sabotaged machinery, fearing widespread unemployment. Children toiled 12 hours a day in mills, exposed to choking dust and machines that mangled arms and legs. A visitor to Manchester, England, in 1842 likened the city's many amputees to an "army just returned from a campaign." Industrialization and overcrowding left cities cloaked in coal smoke and teeming with sewage and other filth that caused plagues such as cholera. Efforts to form unions or go on strike were thwarted. Proposed remedies for these ills ranged from the utopian socialism of Robert Owen—a British manufacturer who established model industrial commu-nities in Scotland and Indiana—to the communism of Karl Marx—a German political philosopher who collaborated with Friedrich Engels in 1848 to pro-duce the *Communist Manifesto,* which forecast a class struggle that would lead to a dictatorship of the proletariat and ultimately to a classless society. What Marx did not foresee were the gains laborers would make as indus-trial, scientific, and political advances improved living and working conditions and brought employees higher wages and shorter hours.

In 1831, Englishman Michael Fara-day discovered that moving a magnet through a coiled wire produces an electric current. This led to the elec-trification of entire cities by the late 1800s and the use of electronic signals to communicate by telegraph, tele-phone, and radio, pioneered by Gug-lielmo Marconi of Italy in the 1890s. Around the same time, Rudolf Diesel of Germany and others perfected the oil-fueled internal combustion engine, which supplanted steam power in fac-tories and ships and ushered in the age of automobiles and airplanes. These momentous developments gave indus-trialized societies huge advantages over preindustrial societies and left much of the world under the influence or con-trol of a small number of great powers.

FAST FACT The world's largest cities in 1900 were in heavily industrialized nations, with London leading with its population of 6.5 million, followed by New York, Paris, and Berlin.

URBANIZATION

The industrial revolution caused mas-sive migrations to urban areas, where most factories were located. In 1800 only one in five people in Great Britain lived in a town or city. By mid-century more than half the population occupied urban areas. Mechanization and other agricultural improvements made it pos-sible for fewer farms to feed large num-bers of people holding industrial jobs. And international trade, facilitated by steamships and railroads, allowed na-tions to import food. Cities in the early stages of the industrial revolution were disease-ridden, but advances such as chlorinated water, and improved sew-age systems eventually allowed millions of people to live and work together in close proximity safely.

INDUSTRIALIZATION meant a denser concentration of people and industry in the world's cities, leading to overcrowding and pollution, problems that persist into the 21st century.

FOR MORE FACTS ON...

THE EFFECT OF HUMAN DEVELOPMENT ON PLANET EARTH see *Human Impact,* **CHAPTER 5, PAGES 214-5**

THE IMPORTANCE OF CITIES IN HUMAN CULTURE & HISTORY see *Cities,* **CHAPTER 6, PAGES 260-1**

304

France's Empress Eugenie presiding over opening of Suez Canal, Egypt, 1869

IMPERIALISM
MIDDLE EAST & AFRICA 1500-1900

EMPIRE BUILDING

1520
Ottoman Empire at its peak

1652
Dutch found trading post at
Cape Town, South Africa

1798
France invades Egypt

1830
France occupies Algiers

1882
Britain takes control of Egypt

1884
Conference of Western Powers in Berlin
to divide up Africa

1889
Britain battle Boers for South Africa

mpires have existed since ancient times, but modern imperialism began when Europeans colonized the Americas and other distant regions and forged global empires. Colonialism was the most common form of imperialism. But technologically advanced nations could also dominate less advanced countries economically without colonizing them.

In the Middle East, European powers competed with the Ottoman Empire, which expanded in the 15th century. Under Sultan Suleyman I, who took power in 1520, the Ottoman Empire reached its peak, extending from Hungary to the Persian Gulf and across North Africa from Cairo to Algiers.

In 1571, five years after Suleyman died, the Ottoman navy was defeated on the coast of Greece by an allied Christian fleet sent by Venice and Spain. More serious setbacks lay ahead for sultans as European empires grew wealthier and modernized their armed forces. The Ottoman Empire began to crumble in 1798 when Napoleon's troops invaded Egypt. The British then took firm control of Egypt in 1882 to put down a nationalist uprising there

FOR MORE FACTS ON...

THE MIDDLE EAST IN WORLD HISTORY see *Mesopotamia 3500 b.c.-500 b.c.,* **CHAPTER 7, PAGES 266-7**

NAPOLEON & HIS ROLE IN SHAPING MODERN EUROPE see *Nationalism 1790-1900,* **CHAPTER 7, PAGES 300-1**

and protect the recently constructed Suez Canal. By then, Greece had won independence and Ottomans were losing other territory to the Russian and Austro-Hungarian Empires.

European imperialism had the most wrenching impact in Africa. First Portuguese slave traders built coastal forts, and then the French and British became involved in that ruinous trade. In pursuit of gold, ivory, and other riches, European involvement deepened. Portugal invaded the Congo and Angola. The Dutch established a trading post at Cape Town in 1652 and went on to colonize South Africa. Other African countries controlled by Great Britain—which ruled the world's largest empire in the 19th century—included Nigeria and Rhodesia (now Zambia and Zimbabwe). The rest of the continent was divided among older powers like France and Portugal and newer ones like Belgium, Italy, and Germany.

Empires In 1900
- British
- French
- Russian
- German
- Dutch
- Danish
- Italian
- Portuguese
- American (U.S.)
- Spanish
- Japanese
- Ottoman

THE SUN NEVER SET on the British Empire in 1900 because Britain had imperial hold over territories more broadly located in the world than any other colonial power. Numerous other European countries held colonial territories at this moment in history, the peak of imperialism.

FAST FACT By 1900, the British Empire embraced nearly one-fourth of the world and some 400 million people.

ENDING THE SLAVE TRADE

Various factors combined to bring the slave trade to an end in the early 1800s. Slaves resisted their masters by rebelling or refusing to work hard, and overproduced crops like sugarcane fell in value. The industrial revolution also demonstrated that employers paying low wages to free laborers could reap greater profits than plantation owners could. Some concluded that slavery no longer made economic sense; others argued that it was morally abhorrent. By 1814, France, Great Britain, and the United States had outlawed the importation of slaves, and they would abolish slavery over the next half century.

ELEPHANT TUSK IVORY was a leading commodity collected in East Africa and traded to European markets for high prices.

FOR MORE FACTS ON...

TRADE & ITS ROLE IN HUMAN CULTURE see *Commerce*, **CHAPTER 6, PAGES 254-7**

THE CONTINENT OF AFRICA & ITS COUNTRIES TODAY see *Africa*, **CHAPTER 9, PAGES 360-77**

ASIA & PACIFIC 1750-1900

British domination in India dated to the 1700s, when the East India Company established forts and trading posts. India's once mighty Mughal (Mogul) Empire—founded in the early 1500s by Babur, a Muslim conqueror of Turkish and Mongol ancestry—had fractured as Hindus rebelled, leaving local rulers to contend with the British.

In 1757 British forces ousted the ruler of Bengal, who was accused of killing British prisoners by confining them to a dungeon in Calcutta called the Black Hole and replaced him with a compliant ruler, setting a precedent for the takeover of other Indian states. In 1857 the British Army put down a mutiny by Indian troops called sepoys and imposed direct imperial rule. India provided Britain with cotton and other raw materials and served as a market for British manufactured goods such as cotton fabric, exported to India in such quantity that its native textile industry withered.

Among the items British traders exported from India was opium, which was then sold illegally in China. When China tried to halt that trade in 1839, British gunships intervened and crushed the antiquated Chinese fleet, forcing China to sign a treaty legalizing the opium trade and granting Britain control of Hong Kong.

This blatant exercise of imperial power came as a humiliating blow to China's own emperor, whose Qing dynasty had supplanted the Ming dynasty in the 17th century when Manchurian invaders called Manchus took power. The Manchus were further discredited in 1900 by the Boxer Rebellion, an uprising against foreigners that ended when foreign troops intervened. With China debilitated, European powers were free to occupy Southeast Asia. Britain took Burma and Malaysia, France claimed Indochina, and the Dutch expanded their control over the East Indies.

Japan escaped foreign domination by becoming an imperial power itself. Shocked when an American fleet entered Tokyo Bay (known then as Edo Bay) in 1853 to demand access, the Japanese restored imperial rule under Emperor Meiji and modernized their society by industrializing and building powerful armed forces that defeated China in 1895 and occupied Taiwan and other territories.

CMDR. MATTHEW PERRY'S steam-powered warships arrived in the harbor of Edo (now Tokyo) in 1853, intending to secure a military foothold. Japanese artists commented nonverbally.

FAST FACT Australia's Aborigines, who had occupied that continent for more than 30,000 years, lost half their population within 50 years of the arrival of British colonists in 1788.

FOR MORE FACTS ON...

THE EARLY HISTORY OF CHINA & JAPAN see *China 2200 B.C.-A.D. 500 & Asia 500-1500,* **CHAPTER 7, PAGES 272-3, 284-5**

THE COUNTRIES OF ASIA & THE PACIFIC TODAY see *Asia & Australia & Oceania,* **CHAPTER 9, PAGES 378-93, 408-13**

COLONIZING THE PACIFIC ISLANDS

The imperial land grab extended to remote Pacific islands when Captain James Cook explored for Britain. Many islands in the Pacific were too small for major colonization efforts such as Britain undertook in Australia and New Zealand, settled in the early 1800s despite opposition from the indigenous Maoris. But imperial powers seeking naval bases or trading stations in the Pacific competed even for tiny islands. France took over the Marquesas and made Tahiti a colony. Germany vied for control of Samoa and purchased the Carolines and Marianas from Spain. The U.S. annexed Hawaii and then seized the Philippines and Guam from Spain in a war fought over Cuba in 1898.

HAWAII BECAME A U.S. TERRITORY in 1898, the occasion celebrated by a naval honor guard marching in front of Iolani Palace in Honolulu. Many native Hawaiians opposed the annexation.

G L O S S A R Y

Imperialism: State policy of extending power and dominion, especially by direct territorial acquisition or by gaining political and economic control of other areas. **/ Annexation:** A formal act whereby a state proclaims its sovereignty over territory hitherto outside its domain; a unilateral act made effective by actual possession and legitimized by general recognition, frequently preceded by conquest and military occupation.

 Great events make me quiet and calm; it is only trifles that irritate my nerves.
— **QUEEN VICTORIA, 1848**

VICTORIA / QUEEN OF THE BRITISH EMPIRE

In 1876 Britain's Queen Victoria (1819-1901) received a new title in which she took particular pride: Empress of India. Since ascending to the throne at the age of 18, she had taken a keen interest in the growth of the British Empire, and India became the jewel in her crown, as symbolized by the fabled 105-carat Kohinoor diamond, presented to her when she became the country's empress. She was an unapologetic imperialist. Even as she asserted her own authority and Britain's on the world stage, however, she presided over the dawning of a new age as Britain began to allow colonies a measure of autonomy. One of her last acts before she died in 1901 was to sign a bill recognizing Australia as a self-governing dominion.

FOR MORE FACTS ON...

THE GEOGRAPHY OF HAWAII see Landforms: Islands, **CHAPTER 3, PAGE 103**
+
IMPERLIASM IN THE MIDDLE EAST & AFRICA see Imperialism: Middle East & Africa 1500-1900, **CHAPTER 7, PAGES 304-5**

British machine gunners, Battle of Somme, France, 1916

WORLD WARS
WORLD WAR I 1900-18

THE GREAT WAR

1905
Russians rebel against Tsar Nicholas II

1907
France, Britain, and Russia become allies

1908
Austria-Hungary annexes Bosnia

1914
Franz Ferdinand of Austria-Hungary
assassinated; World War I begins

1915
Italy sides with the Allies

1917
U.S. joins the Allies;
Bolsheviks seize power in Russia

1918
War ends

y the early 20th century, industrialism, nationalism, and imperialism had generated explosive rivalries among the world's great powers. Germany and France had been sharply at odds since the Franco-Prussian War, which ended in 1871 when France surrendered the disputed borderlands of Alsace and Lorraine. That core rivalry expanded in years to come.

Germany joined Austria-Hungary and Italy in the Triple Alliance, and France joined Great Britain and Russia in the Triple Entente. These alliances, combined with technological advances in weaponry, set the stage for a conflict of unprecedented scope and severity.

In the Balkans, Austria-Hungary and Russia competed as the Ottoman Empire lost control. In 1908 Austria-Hungary annexed Bosnia. Russia supported neighboring Serbia, which aided rebellious Serbs in Bosnia. In June 1914 Archduke Franz Ferdinand, heir to the Austro-Hungarian throne, was assassinated by a Serbian nationalist in the Bosnian capital. Austria-Hungary blamed Serbia, and Russia came to Serbia's defense. Germany then joined its ally Austria-Hungary against Russia and

FOR MORE FACTS ON...

INDUSTRIALIZATION LEADING UP TO WORLD WAR I see *The Industrial Revolution 1765-1900*, **CHAPTER 7, PAGES 302-3**

ALLIANCES AMONG NATIONS see *Nations & Alliances*, **CHAPTER 9, PAGES 358-9**

planned to defeat the French quickly before the Russians could mobilize for war. In early August, days after Austria-Hungary declared war on Serbia and Russia began mobilizing, Germany invaded Belgium and headed to France—thus engaging Britain.

German hopes for quick victory were dashed when French and British troops held fast in northern France. Both sides tried to break the stalemate, but attackers suffered terrible losses, struggling through minefields and barbed wire under machine-gun fire. German and Austro-Hungarian forces fared better against the Russians but fell short of victory. Ottoman Turks joined with Germany and Austria-Hungary to form the Central Powers, and Italy left that coalition in 1915 to join the Allies.

Conflict spread to the Middle East, where Arabs joined the Allies in battling the Turks. India contributed to the Allied cause, hoping to be rewarded by Britain with independence or dominion status. Japan joined the Allies, hoping to seize Germany's Pacific possessions.

In April 1917 the U.S. entered the war in response to German U-boat attacks in the Atlantic, boosting Allied strength just before Russia withdrew from the war. American forces with tanks helped the Allies thwart a German offensive. On November 11, 1918, Germany signed an armistice, bringing the war to an end.

PERSHING'S ROLE IN WORLD WAR I

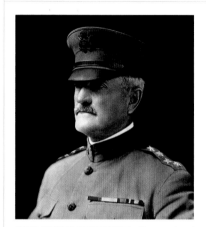

GEN. JOHN J. PERSHING had been assigned to pursue Mexican revolutionary Pancho Villa when the U.S. entered World War I.

Gen. John J. Pershing led the American Expeditionary Force (AEF), which helped secure victory for the Allies in 1918. He began his military career three decades earlier, fighting defiant Indians in the American West.

Known as Black Jack because he commanded African-American troops, Pershing later served in campaigns that signaled the emergence of the U.S. as a world power, including the occupation of the Philippines.

In 1917 he was stationed in Mexico, and he might have been remembered as a Yankee imperialist whose presence incited a second Mexican-American War had not President Woodrow Wilson reassigned him to the AEF, whose success raised the U.S. to new heights internationally.

CLICK IT: World War I www.firstworldwar.com

THE BOLSHEVIK REVOLUTION

By 1917, the imperial regime of Russian Tsar Nicholas II was near collapse. German forces were advancing into Russia, demoralizing the populace and discrediting the tsar. In March, Nicholas abdicated in favor of a provisional government that continued the war effort. Revolutionary councils, or soviets, urged an end to the war, and exiled communist leader Vladimir Lenin returned through Germany aided by German authorities who hoped he would take charge and make peace on their terms—which he did. He and his Bolsheviks seized power in November and agreed to an armistice with Germany. In 1918, members of the royal family were shot to death by Lenin's order.

THE TSAR and his family were probably killed in 1918, as recent DNA tests seem to confirm.

FOR MORE FACTS ON...

IMPERIALISM UP THROUGH THE 19TH CENTURY *see Imperialism,* **CHAPTER 7, PAGES 304-7**

THE CONTINENT OF EUROPE & ITS COUNTRIES TODAY *see Europe,* **CHAPTER 9, PAGES 394-407**

FRAGILE PEACE 1919-29

When diplomats and heads of state gathered in Paris in 1919, they faced the task of bringing order to a world convulsed by the collapse of empires. The Central Powers lost their imperial domains and became the struggling nations of Germany, Austria, Hungary, and Turkey. With Russia in revolutionary turmoil, the leaders of France, Britain, the U.S., and Italy made up the "Big Four" in Paris. At the talks, U.S. President Woodrow Wilson proposed a League of Nations to resolve future disputes and self-determination for ethnic groups aspiring to nationhood.

Wilson's hopes for a just and lasting peace were not realized. He failed to win U.S. Senate approval for America's entry into the League of Nations. Britain and France retained their colonies and acquired new dependencies in the Middle East, challenging the principle of self-determination and tempting rivals to enter the imperial contest. New nations such as Yugoslavia and Czechoslovakia and rehabilitated nations such as Poland emerged, many of which were politically weak, making them takeover targets for expansive powers.

Peace terms imposed on Germany under the Treaty of Versailles weakened that nation's fledgling Weimar Republic, whose leaders had to accept blame for the war and pay reparations. Italy left Paris before the peace conference was over, feeling slighted by the remaining "Big Three," and resentment contributed to the rise of Benito Mussolini, who took power in 1922 and promised imperial glory. His fascist dictatorship represented a right-wing alternative to the communist regime Vladimir Lenin. Victory enabled Lenin to reconstitute the old Russian empire under a new name, the Union of Soviet Socialist Republics, and eliminate political opposition through surveillance by secret police and show trials of dissidents. After Lenin's 1924 death, one-party rule degenerated into one-man rule when Joseph Stalin fastened his grip on the Communist Party and Soviet society as a whole.

Despite these ominous political developments, the 1920s were largely peaceful and increasingly prosperous as the American economy boomed and U.S. investment helped European nations recover from the war. Automobiles and electrical appliances became available in advanced nations, and radio broadcasts, phonographs, and films proliferated, creating an international popular culture that drew much of its energy from the U.S. Jazz music of African-American origin gained such wide appeal that some referred to this postwar era as the jazz age. But dreams of a cooperative world where democratic allies would set the tone and go unchallenged were shattered by the onset of the Great Depression.

CHARLES LINDBERGH LANDED at Croydon Airport, London, completing his historic transatlantic one-man flight on May 21, 1927, and became a world hero.

FOR MORE FACTS ON...

WORLD WAR I *see World Wars: World War I,* **CHAPTER 7, PAGES 310-1**

INTERNATIONAL ALLIANCES *see Nations & Alliances,* **CHAPTER 9, PAGES 358-9**

REVOLUTION IN CHINA

Once a great world power, China played little part in World War I or the peace negotiations that followed because it was caught up in a revolution that began in 1911, when its emperor abdicated under pressure, and continued for nearly four decades. Sun Yat-sen, founder of the Kuomintang (Nationalist People's Party), proclaimed China a republic in 1912 but could not hold the country together. Although he was not a communist, Sun Yat-sen welcomed Soviet aid in the early 1920s as he struggled to subdue warlords and unite China under his rule. In return for Moscow's help, he granted several Chinese communists high positions in his party.

After Sun Yat-sen's death in 1925, however, his ambitious aide, Chiang Kai-shek, gained control of the Kuomintang with support from conservatives and broke with the Soviets, expelling communists from the Nationalist Party and entering into a long and bitter contest with them for control of China.

CHIANG KAI-SHEK (left) meets with Wang Ching Wei, a Bolshevik representative, in 1925.

CLICK IT: The Roaring Twenties www.1920-30.com

G L O S S A R Y

Reparations: Payment in money or materials by a nation defeated in war. **/ Fascism:** From Italian *fascio*, "group" or "bundle." Philosophy of government that stresses the primacy and glory of the state, unquestioning obedience to its leader, and harsh suppression of dissent; different from communism in its protection of business- and land-owning elites and its preservation of class systems.

> " Non-cooperation is not a passive state, it is an intensely active state—more active than physical resistance or violence. **— MAHATMA GANDHI, 1922** "

MAHATMA GANDHI / NONVIOLENT ACTIVIST

In 1919, as the principle of self-determination was being debated at the Peace Conference in Paris, opposition to British rule in India crystallized around Mohandas Gandhi (1869-1948), known to admirers as the Mahatma (great soul). Gandhi drew on his Hindu faith and other beliefs to propose *satyagraha*: a philosophy of nonviolent resistance using moral pressure to induce opponents to change their ways. Aroused by legislation denying legal rights to political prisoners, Gandhi called for peaceful dissent. On April 13, British troops opened fire on unarmed demonstrators at Amritsar, killing nearly 400 people. Gandhi responded by organizing a boycott of British goods and institutions in India and urging acts of nonviolent civil disobedience. His movement placed mounting pressure on the British to grant India independence.

FAST FACT By 1924 the Ford Model T, produced on assembly lines perfected by American industrialist Henry Ford, accounted for one-half of the world's automobiles.

FOR MORE FACTS ON...

REVOLUTIONS ELSEWHERE IN THE WORLD see *Revolutions 1600-1800*, **CHAPTER 7, PAGES 298-9**

THE COUNTRIES OF INDIA & CHINA TODAY see *Asia*, **CHAPTER 9, PAGES 386, 392**

DEPRESSION 1929-39

America's booming economy of the 1920s helped finance the recovery of war-torn Europe. But the boom came to an end in late 1929 with the crash of the stock market, a disaster that sent shock waves around the world.

On "Black Thursday," October 24, 1929, shareholders panicked and began unloading at any price. By month's end stocks had lost nearly half their value since early September. Stunned by the crash, consumers cut back, causing businesses to slash production and lay off workers. The number of Americans unemployed rose to 5 million in 1930 and 13 million a year later.

By 1932, people were losing trust in banks and stashing money away at home. That November, Republican incumbent Herbert Hoover lost the presidential election to Democrat Franklin Roosevelt, who promised "a new deal for Americans." Roosevelt stabilized the banking system and sought to promote economic recovery by creating agencies such as the Civilian Conservation Corps. His New Deal did not end the Great Depression, but it avoided the political upheaval seen in other nations.

The crash on Wall Street destabilized Germany as nervous American investors demanded repayment of loans. Unemployment doubled there between 1929 and 1930, and the Communist Party and Adolf Hitler's National Socialist (Nazi) Party made big gains in the nation's legislature. Blaming Germany's woes on communists and Jews, Hitler rose to power through the electoral process and then claimed emergency powers in 1933. He drew lessons from Italy's Benito Mussolini and sought to revive Germany by building a new empire he called the Third Reich. France and Britain, fearful of renewed war, allowed Hitler to defy the Versailles Treaty in 1936 and reoccupy the Rhineland.

Soviet dictator Joseph Stalin tried to strengthen his regime by launching a brutal Five-Year Plan in 1929 aimed at collectivizing agriculture and spurring industrialization. To eliminate opposition, he carried out ruinous purges in the 1930s in which millions of people were executed or sent to labor camps.

During the Spanish Civil War, which began in 1936, Stalin gave military aid to Republicans fighting Nationalists led by Gen. Francisco Franco, who prevailed with support from Hitler and Mussolini. This coincided with strife in Asia as economic turmoil in Japan weakened the constitutional government there and increased the clout of military leaders, who favored imperial expansion. In 1937, Japanese forces invaded China, offering a grim preview of the global struggle to come.

DEPOSITORS THRONG a New York City branch of the American Union Bank, fearful for their investments, in 1931. While some had predicted that the Crash of 1929 was a single unfortunate event, banks kept closing as the Depression deepened.

FOR MORE FACTS ON...

ECONOMICS & REVOLUTION IN EARLIER CENTURIES see *Revolutions 1600-1800*, **CHAPTER 7, PAGES 298-9**

MARX & THE ORIGINS OF COMMUNISM see *Nationalism 1790-1900 & The Industrial Revolution 1765-1900*, **CHAPTER 7, PAGES 300-3**

THE POWER OF AIR POWER

Not long after Orville and Wilbur Wright's pioneering flight at Kitty Hawk, North Carolina, in 1903, the U.S. armed forces found military uses for aircraft.

During World War I, pilots often flew reconnaissance missions and sometimes dueled with rivals in aerial dogfights. A few aviators carried out strategic bombing raids on cities or factories, but early aircraft lacked the range and capacity to do much damage to population centers.

After the war, advances such as the introduction of powerful radial engines on monoplanes allowed aircraft to carry big payloads to distant targets and raised the specter of massive destruction from the air. Germany made a big investment in air power in the 1930s and tested its Luftwaffe (air force) in the Spanish Civil War. A German air raid on the Spanish village of Guernica in April 1937 killed nearly one-third of its 5,000 inhabitants and drew a memo-

A GERMAN BOMBARDIER readies his pineapple-size bomb during World War II.

rable protest from Spanish painter Pablo Picasso, whose "Guernica" depicts tortured figures looking skyward in terror.

GLOSSARY

Economic depression: A major business cycle downswing, characterized by sharply reduced industrial production, widespread unemployment, serious declines or cessations of growth in construction activity, and great reductions in international trade and capital movements.

HITLER: FROM ONE WAR TO ANOTHER

AT THE AGE OF 34, Adolf Hitler spent nine months in prison, accused of treason after fomenting rebellion among Bavarian soldiers against the prevailing Weimar Republic.

Adolf Hitler, born in Austria in 1889, developed political views that were shaped by his experiences during the First World War and the defeat Germany suffered in 1918. At his first military screening, he was rejected for lack of physical vigor, but the demands of war changed the requirements, and in 1914 he joined the Bavarian Reserve Infantry. Awarded two Iron Crosses for bravery during World War I, Hitler believed that if Germans had all been as loyal to the cause as he had been, the country would have won the war.

He blamed Germany's collapse on revolutionaries who rose up in early November 1918 and caused Kaiser Wilhelm II to abdicate, although Germany had in fact already

lost the war when that uprising began. Overlooking the contributions of patriotic German Jews to the war effort, Hitler portrayed the November revolution as a "Jewish Bolshevik" conspiracy and made Jews scapegoats for Germany's downfall.

These ideas evolved into a social philosophy. Misreading history, Hitler concluded that Germany could avenge its humiliation and dominate Europe if it regained its will to victory and eliminated those he accused of betraying the nation. His success in selling this myth to the public led to the Holocaust, in which millions of Jews were murdered, and exposed Germany and the world to even greater calamity in the Second World War than it suffered in the First.

FOR MORE FACTS ON...

MILITARY AIR PHOTOGRAPHY & ITS INFLUENCE ON MAPS see Mapmaking: Modern Maps, **CHAPTER 1, PAGES 26-7**

THE HISTORY & BELIEFS OF JUDAISM see Religion: Monotheism, **CHAPTER 6, PAGES 236-7**

WORLD WAR II 1938-45

Hitler set the stage for World War II in 1938 by annexing Austria and demanding that Czechoslovakia cede the Sudetenland, an ethnically German area. Czechoslovakia refused and sought support from France and Britain. Meeting at Munich, the Allies accepted Hitler's claim to the Sudetenland in exchange for his pledge to make no more territorial demands.

Promising "peace in our time," British Prime Minister Neville Chamberlain appeared so eager to appease Germany that Hitler figured he would tolerate further aggression. When German troops seized all of Czechoslovakia in early 1939, the Allies pledged to defend Poland against attack. Hitler then strengthened ties with his Axis partner Mussolini. The alliances in Europe were similar to those before the First World War with one crucial exception: The Allies could not count on Russian support. After signing a non-aggression pact with Stalin, Hitler sent troops into Poland on September 1, 1939, launching the most destructive war in history.

After conquering Poland in less than a month, German forces went on to defeat France in June 1940.

Hitler expected Britain to come to terms, but newly appointed Prime Minister Winston Churchill vowed never to surrender. Aided by radar, British pilots countered onslaughts by the Luftwaffe and forced Hitler to scrub a planned invasion that fall.

The war widened in 1941 as Hitler invaded North Africa, the Balkans, and the Soviet Union, breaking his pact with Stalin and targeting Jews and other ethnic groups. Nazi officials went on to impose their Final Solution by forcing Jews into camps and killing nearly six million by the war's end.

In December 1941 Soviets struck back at the invading Germans, who received no help from Japan, which had joined the Axis in 1940. Instead of targeting the Soviets, Japan attacked the U.S. at Pearl Harbor in Hawaii and went on to seize the Philippines from the Americans and Burma, Singapore, Malaya, and other colonies from the British.

The uncoordinated Axis offensives of 1941 brought the Soviet Union and the United States, two nations with huge populations and industrial potential, into the war on the Allied side. This proved decisive when Germany and Japan failed to win quickly and faced prolonged struggles. Allied triumphs in 1942 at Midway in the Pacific, El Alamein in North Africa, and

FAST FACT In the long run, 30 nations from five continents participated militarily in World War II.

FOR MORE FACTS ON...

ADOLF HITLER & HIS ROLE IN WORLD WAR II see *World Wars: Depression 1929-39,* **CHAPTER 7, PAGE 313**

BRITISH COLONIZATION see *Imperialism,* **CHAPTER 7, PAGES 304-7**

Stalingrad in the Soviet Union left the Axis on the defensive.

In 1943 American and British forces invaded Italy and drove Mussolini from power. In 1944 Allied troops landed at Normandy on June 6 and went on to liberate Paris and enter Germany from the west as Soviets advanced from the east. Berlin fell on April 30, 1945, and Hitler committed suicide, leading to Germany's unconditional surrender.

Japan, having lost the Philippines and other occupied territory to advancing American troops, surrendered after the U.S. Air Force obliterated the Japanese cities of Hiroshima and Nagasaki in August by dropping a single atomic bomb on each target.

THE ATOM BOMBS that ended World War II resulted from breakthroughs by leading scientists: Albert Einstein, Ernest Rutherford, James Chadwick, and Enrico Fermi. Einstein and Fermi, who had fled to the U.S. to escape fascism, produced the first controlled, self-sustaining nuclear chain reaction at the University of Chicago in 1942 by exposing uranium to a beam of neutrons. This experiment led to atomic weapons such as "Little Boy" (above), dropped on Hiroshima, Japan, on August 6, 1945.

FAST FACT The Second World War claimed the lives of more than 50 million soldiers and civilians.

CHURCHILL & ROOSEVELT: PARTNERS IN VICTORY

AT YALTA in February 1945, Allied leaders Winston Churchill, Franklin Roosevelt, and Joseph Stalin agreed to end the war and redivide Europe.

The productive partnership between Allied leaders Churchill and Roosevelt stood in marked contrast to the relationship between Hitler and Mussolini, who resented the overbearing German dictator and tried to assert himself by launching unsuccessful campaigns in North Africa and the Balkans.

Roosevelt offered Churchill military aid that helped keep Britain in the fight when Hitler appeared on the verge of conquering Europe. Churchill's determined resistance to Nazi aggression inspired the American President and public and helped clear the way for Roosevelt's policy of Europe First—which gave the war against Germany priority over the struggle against Japan. Whereas Hitler received little help from Mussolini and had to commit German troops to hold Italy, the cordial give-and-take between Roosevelt and Churchill translated into effective military cooperation.

FOR MORE FACTS ON...

CONTEMPORARY IDEAS IN PHYSICS see *Physical Science: Physics*, **CHAPTER 8, PAGES 330-1**

THE COUNTRY OF GERMANY TODAY see *Europe*, **CHAPTER 9, PAGE 399**

LATE 20TH CENTURY

1949
Soviet Union explodes atomic bomb;
Communists take over China

1961
Berlin Wall constructed

1962
Cuban Missile Crisis resolved

1985
Gorbachev restructures Soviet economy

1989
Berlin Wall falls

1991
Cold War ends as Soviet Union disbands

COLD WAR
1945-1991

n 1946, as the Soviet Union installed communist regimes in East Germany, Poland, and other European countries occupied during World War II, Winston Churchill declared that an "iron curtain has descended across the continent." In the so-called Cold War, the U.S. and U.S.S.R. emerged as leaders of opposing alliances. This coincided with decolonization around the world: Germany, Japan, and Italy lost colonies when defeated by the Allies, and Britain and France freed colonies under pressure from independence movements.

Some former colonies like Korea, partitioned in 1945 when Japan lost control there, gained in importance during the Cold War, which expanded when Mao Zedong won control of China in 1949 and aligned with the Soviet Union.

In 1950 North Korea, with Chinese and Soviet backing, invaded South Korea, defended by the U.S. and its allies. War continued there until 1953 when the prewar boundary was restored.

A much longer conflict unfolded in Vietnam when France tried to regain control there. Aided by China and the Soviet Union, Vietnamese communists led by Ho Chi Minh defeated the French in 1954. The U.S. stepped in to aid South Vietnam against communists, remaining involved militarily for nearly two decades. After losing more than 50,000 troops, the U.S. withdrew, leaving Vietnam under communist rule.

In Europe, the U.S. forged a stronger alliance with its North Atlantic Treaty Organization (NATO) partners than Moscow did with its Warsaw Pact satellites. Soviet Premier Nikita Khrushchev sent in troops to crush a revolt in Hungary in 1956. In 1962 he gave missiles to Cuba after a failed U.S.-backed coup against Fidel Castro. The world faced the threat of nuclear war when President John F. Kennedy

FAST FACT The United Nations (UN), which had 51 member nations when it was founded in 1945, gained more than 100 additional members by 1990, most of them former colonies.

FOR MORE FACTS ON...

COLONIZATION IN THE 19TH CENTURY see *Imperialism*, **CHAPTER 7, PAGES 304-7**

ALLIANCES AMONG COUNTRIES OF THE WORLD TODAY see *Nations & Alliances*, **CHAPTER 9, PAGES 358-9**

demanded removal of those missiles, but Khrushchev complied in exchange for assurances that the U.S. would withdraw its missiles from Turkey and cease efforts to overthrow Castro.

The superpowers also vied in the Middle East, where Soviet aid helped Egypt and Syria challenge Israel, backed by the U.S. Victories by Israel in 1967 and 1973 reduced Soviet influence in the region but aggravated the ongoing Arab-Israeli dispute over the fate of Palestinians in Israeli-controlled areas.

By the 1980s, Moscow could no longer afford the Cold War, and Soviet Premier Mikhail Gorbachev admitted as much by withdrawing troops from Afghanistan, pursuing détente with the West, and promoting glasnost, or greater freedom within the Soviet system. As restraints were eased, Poland and other satellites broke free.

A failed coup in 1991 by hardliners in Moscow, who ousted Gorbachev before giving way to reformer Boris Yeltsin, led to the breakup of the Soviet Union.

JOHN F. KENNEDY was the President of the United States through the Cold War years, from 1961 until his assassination in November 1963.

FIDEL CASTRO led a successful revolution in Cuba in 1959 and then went on to lead the island nation for almost 50 years, until 2008.

NIKITA KHRUSHCHEV was the head of the Communist Party in the Soviet Union and effectively the country's leader, from 1958 to 1964.

G L O S S A R Y

Iron Curtain: Coined by Winston Churchill, 1946. Political, military, and ideological barrier established by the Soviet Union after World War II to isolate its dependent Eastern European allies from the West.

 Letting a hundred flowers blossom and a hundred schools of thought contend is the policy for . . . a flourishing culture in our land. —— **MAO ZEDONG, 1957**

MAO ZEDONG / COMMUNIST LEADER OF CHINA

The communist regime of Mao Zedong (1893-1976), leader of the People's Republic of China, distributed land to peasants, provided education and health care for the poor, and advanced rights for women. But his wider efforts proved disastrous. In 1958, his Great Leap Forward diverted effort from agriculture to industry and contributed to a famine that killed millions. Mao initiated the Cultural Revolution, during which many dissidents were sentenced to hard labor and some killed. After his death in 1976, leaders loosened economic restraints, allowing capitalism to develop. Mao's enduring legacy to China was nationalism. By breaking with the Soviet Union, he asserted China's independence and set the stage for relations with the U.S. and other powers that once dominated China but now acknowledged it as an equal.

FOR MORE FACTS ON...

THE USE OF THE ATOM BOMB IN WORLD WAR II see *World War II 1938-1945,* **CHAPTER 7, PAGE 315**

THE HISTORY OF CHINA see *China 2200 B.C.-A.D. 500 & Asia 500-1500,* **CHAPTER 7, PAGES 272-3, 284-5**

Man on the street, and Ronald McDonald, Beijing, China

INTO THE 21ST CENTURY

1991
U.S.-led coalition ousts Iraq from Kuwait

1992
U.S., Canada, and Mexico sign NAFTA

1999
EU introduces new currency: the euro

2001
Terrorists attack U.S. World Trade Center and Pentagon

2003
U.S. and Britain invade Iraq

2005
Kyoto Protocol to curb global warming

GLOBALIZATION
1991–PRESENT

Globalization accelerated in the last years of the 20th century, signaled by the rise of international bodies like the World Trade Organization and the European Union, fueled by multinational economic treaties like the North American Free Trade Agreement, and spurred on by technological advances like the Internet.

Some of the world's worst trouble spots in the 1990s were nations created when empires collapsed. After ethnically divided Yugoslavia, forged in 1919, broke up in 1990, Serbian troops entered Croatia and Bosnia to support Serbian minorities there. UN peacekeepers failed to prevent ethnic cleansing by Serbian forces, who murdered thousands and drove many from their homes. In 1994 the UN and the Organization of African Unity proved powerless to stop genocide in Rwanda, where militants belonging to the Hutu majority attacked the once dominant Tutsi minority.

The legacy of colonialism also contributed to strife in the Middle East, where Iraqi dictator Saddam Hussein used deadly force to hold together his country, formed after British troops seized Baghdad from Ottoman Turks during World War I and left minority Sunni Muslims in authority. Hussein, a Sunni, faced opposition from Shiites and Kurds, whom he targeted with chemical weapons. After he invaded oil-rich Kuwait, the U.S. led a coalition to oust Iraqi forces in 1991.

In 2001, in response to the attacks on September 11, President George W. Bush sent troops into Afghanistan to root out al Qaeda, the group responsible for the attacks, and proclaimed a war on terror. Acting on later discredited reports of weapons of mass destruction, American and British troops seized Iraq in 2003 and toppled Hussein. Critics faulted Bush's administration for acting without UN approval.

Whether international bodies representing many countries with diverse interests can halt aggression or deal with pressing environmental threats remains to be seen. Not until the world withstands severe financial or political shocks without losing cohesion can the trend of global cooperation be considered the dawning of a new age.

FOR MORE FACTS ON...

COMMERCE & ITS IMPORTANCE IN HUMAN CULTURE see Commerce, CHAPTER 6, PAGES 254-7
+
THE UNITED NATIONS see Nations & Alliances, CHAPTER 9, PAGE 359

9-11-2001

On September 11, 2001, a cadre of Saudi Arabian and Egyptian men, members of Osama bin Laden's al Qaeda international terrorist organization, commandeered four airliners taking off from U.S. airports. They flew two of them into the twin towers of New York's World Trade Center and a third into the Pentagon, headquarters for the U.S. Department of Defense in Washington, D.C. The fourth jet crashed in a Pennsylvania field after passengers rushed the hijackers in an effort to retake the plane. Never had a single terrorist attack taken so many lives—more than 3,000. Terrorism is not new, but in a world connected by globalization, it has grown more powerful and far-reaching; and in a world of high-powered technology, it is all the more terrifying.

IMAGE OF TERROR: Terrorists hijacked jets on September 11, 2001, flying two into New York's World Trade Center (above) and one into Washington's Pentagon. Another crashed in a Pennsylvania field. About 3,000 people, plus 400 rescue workers, died. All 19 terrorists died as well.

 No one is born hating another person because of the color of his skin, or his background, or his religion. People learn to hate. **— NELSON MANDELA, 1995**

NELSON MANDELA / PRESIDENT OF SOUTH AFRICA

Born in 1918 to a tribal chief in South Africa, Nelson Mandela went on to dismantle the strict policy of racial segregation and discrimination known as apartheid and become president in 1994—the first leader of his country elected by people of all races. As a young lawyer, Mandela joined the African National Congress (ANC), a black nationalist organization that organized protests against apartheid. Outlawed in 1960, the ANC formed a military wing, led by Mandela, who was arrested in 1962. He remained in prison until 1990, when released by President F. W. de Klerk, leader of the all-white National Party. Mandela and de Klerk then entered into negotiations that brought apartheid to an end and earned them the Nobel Peace Prize in 1993. As president, Mandela enacted a new democratic constitution.

FAST FACT The value of all exports around the world increased from $1.9 trillion in 1985 to $6.3 trillion in 2000.

FOR MORE FACTS ON...

RACE & ETHNICITY AS ELEMENTS IN HUMAN CULTURE see The Human Family: Ethnicities & The Human Family: Race, Class & Gender, **CHAPTER 6, PAGES 224-7**

THE COUNTRY OF SOUTH AFRICA TODAY see Africa, **CHAPTER 9, PAGE 377**

Counting & Measurement/Te
Physical Science / Physics / E
Medical Science / Mind & Brain
Science/Internet/Nanotechnolo

SCIENCE & TE

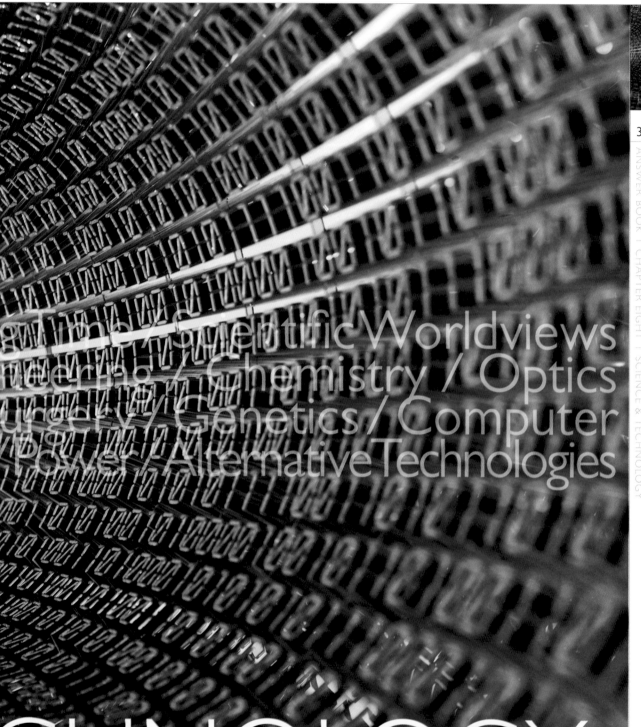

Time / Scientific Worldviews
...neering / Chemistry / Optics
...urgery / Genetics / Computer
...Power / Alternative Technologies

...CHNOLOGY

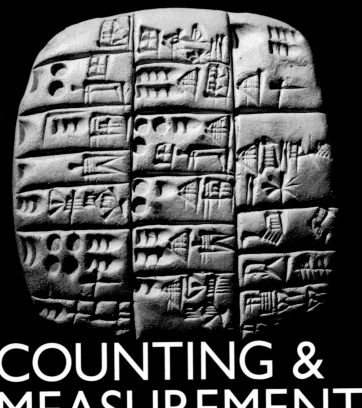

Cuneiform tally of sheep and goats, ancient Sumeria, circa 3500 B.C.

COUNTING

8000 B.C.
Tally marks used in Congo region

7500 B.C.
Sumerians track grain, animals,
and valuables with clay tokens

3400 B.C.
Egyptians use marks up to
nine and special symbol for ten

CIRCA 3100 B.C.
Symbols on clay tablets in Sumeria use
a wedge for one, a circle for ten;
Babylonian base-60 system expresses
quantity by symbol and position

300 B.C.
Hindu-Arabic numerals in India
include zero as placeholder

50 B.C.
Base-10 system with numerals
akin to ours used in India

COUNTING & MEASUREMENT

Systems for counting and measuring are among the oldest and most basic human innovations. Both major cultures and minor tribes have developed their own ways to quantify the world, from the rough scratches found on a 10,000-year-old bone in Africa's Congo region to the advanced number theories of ancient Greek and Arab civilizations.

While we live in an age of standardization, with units like the meter globally understood, early methods for counting and measuring were seemingly arbitrary. Some Aboriginal tribes in Australia and New Guinea used a counting system based on twos: for example, the number five becomes two and two and one. Those at the tip of South America base their counting system on three and four. The most systematic early counting methods emerged in ancient Egypt and Mesopotamia between 3400 and 3000 B.C., where groupings based on the number ten allowed a way to express larger and larger quantities and helped the development of complex administrative and record keeping systems. The primacy of the number 10 endures as a foundation for mathematics, though counting by 12 (a dozen) or by 20 (a score) echoes those earlier methods.

Determining length, weight, volume, distance, or other quantities—measurement—requires special units of comparison for each, and the earliest efforts also seem inexact today. The cubit, used by the ancient Egyptians to measure length, was based on the length of a human arm from

FAST FACT The carat, used as a unit of weight for precious gems, was originally based on the weight of certain seeds, but it has been standardized to equal 0.2 gram.

elbow to fingertip. Romans calculated a mile as a thousand double-steps of a soldier. Weight often involved comparison to stones or grains.

An early effort at standardization was made by French Emperor Charlemagne when he ruled that the foot would be the length of his own foot. The French offered an even more profound standardization when they developed the metric system during the French Revolution.

Based on meters, liters, and grams, this same metric system is in daily use now throughout the world—with one notable exception. In the U.S., the standard system of measurement still relies on gallons, pounds, and other units developed in imperial England,

NUMBERS PREDICT FUTURES on New York's Times Square, where stock exchange averages from Wall Street appear in brilliant colors, constantly updated to reflect a changing market.

even though England has itself adopted the metric system. In the 21st century, measurement has been standardized on the atomic scale. A meter is now defined as the distance light travels in a vacuum in 1/299,792,458 of a second.

FAST FACT The metric system originally calculated the meter—its basic unit—as one ten-millionth of the distance from the Equator to the North Pole.

WHO WERE THE EARLY MATHEMATICIANS?

With a flourishing agricultural economy, ancient Babylon, located in modern-day Iraq, was one of the first societies complex enough to need modern record keeping. The ancient Babylonians were therefore among the first to develop a sophisticated counting system.

They developed positional numbering—the system whereby not only a symbol but also its position relative to other symbols expresses value. Positional numbering allowed large quantities to be expressed with simple symbols pressed into clay tablets. The Babylonian sexagesimal, or base-60, system grouped numbers by sets of 60—60^2, 60^3, and so on—just as modern counting uses the symbol 1 for sets of 10: 10^2 (100), 10^3 (1,000).

Clay tablets have come down through history that clearly show the Babylonians' advanced understanding of numbers. The tablet known as Plimpton 322 shows a sequence of numbers that appear to express the equation "$x^2 + y^2 = z^2$." In other words, the Babylonians had a version of what would later be called the Pythagorean theorem.

GLOSSARY

Base number: An arbitrarily chosen whole number greater than 1 in terms of which any number can be expressed as a sum of that base raised to various powers. Systems through history have used different numbers as their group unit, or base, but over time the decimal system—a base-10 system—overshadowed all others. **/ Sunya:** From the Sanskrit for "vacant." In positional number systems, a symbol is required to mark the place of a power of the base not actually occurring. Hindus developed the *sunya*, a dot or small circle, the first use of the concept of zero.

FOR MORE FACTS ON...

THE INFLUENCE OF MATHEMATICS IN ANCIENT BABYLON ON MAPMAKING see *Dividing Lines*, **CHAPTER 1, PAGE 31**

CHARLEMAGNE & HIS INFLUENCE ON WORLD HISTORY see *Middle Ages 500-1000*, **CHAPTER 7, PAGES 278-9**

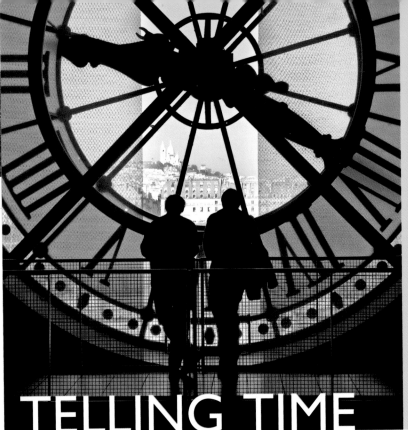

CLOCKS & CALENDARS

CIRCA 3000 B.C.
Egyptians develop 365-day year

CIRCA 2700 B.C.
Sumerians use sun & moon for calendars

CIRCA 1600 B.C.
Chaldeans chart stars: the first zodiac

46 B.C.
Romans add an extra day (leap day)
to every fourth year of Egyptian calendar

A.D. 1582
Pope Gregory XIII refines calendar

1951
First atomic clock uses cesium

1967
Second redefined as frequency of
radiation emitted under certain
conditions by cesium-133

TELLING TIME

ur sense of time is connected to biology and astronomy—the patterns of nature and the patterns of the universe. Living things react to natural cycles. Animals migrate and breed, tides rise and fall, plants bloom— and from early on, people have noticed the correlation of those events with the movements of the sun, moon, and stars.

The technology developed to organize time, however, is as much about the future as it is about the present and past. It gives individuals and societies the ability to anticipate when important events are likely to occur and to decide when certain things should happen in response. Knowing that animals migrate when it turns cold is one thing; advance knowledge of when that is likely to occur informs the hunting plan.

Clocks and calendars are the tools that allow this sort of rhythmic planning. They evolved over thousands of years as people studied patterns in the Earth and sky and began associating changes in the weather or other phenomena with the positions of heavenly bodies. The basic divisions of our modern calendar remain astronomical: A day is the time it takes Earth to spin on its axis; a year is the time it takes Earth to orbit around the sun; and a month roughly reflects the time it takes for the moon to pass through its cycle of phases.

The first calendar emerged in Sumeria almost 5,000 years ago and used the position of the sun and moon to coordinate agriculture and religious rituals and sacrifices. The Chinese, Maya, Greek, and Roman civilizations all developed calendars suited to their own societies and view of the world. The Romans, for example, used an eight-day week as the basic unit for reckoning time, a period reflecting the rhythm of their commerce, for every eighth day was market day.

FOR MORE FACTS ON...

HOW TIME INFLUENCES MAPS & MAPS RECKON WITH TIME see *Time Zones*, **CHAPTER 1, PAGES 32-3**
+
THE INTERACTION OF ASTRONOMY & CALENDARS see *Constellations*, **CHAPTER 2, PAGES 46-7**

The basis for the modern calendar was developed by Egyptian astronomical observations, which by 1300 B.C. had grown sophisticated enough to chart 43 constellations and planets and to predict eclipses. The Egyptians, who closely tied such phenomena to their sun-worshipping religion, devised the 365-day year admired in ancient Greece and still in use today.

Clocks are used for short-term measurements of time. Sundials and hourglasses were early tools for tracking the passing of time throughout the day. In China, as early as the 11th century A.D., an oversize water-powered clock tower, designed by polymath Su Sung, used mechanical means to measure the day. Today's wristwatches are powered by microchips or the resonance of a quartz crystal, while computers and cell phones are tied into networks that electronically update internal clocks.

POPE GREGORY XIII / CREATOR OF THE CALENDAR

For centuries Europe used the Julian calendar, put in place by Julius Caesar, which gave us the now familiar names of the months but which was off by about 11 minutes a year. By 1582, after 1,600 years, the error had grown to the equivalent of about ten days. After gathering calculations made by a group of mathematicians and astronomers, Pope Gregory XIII (1502-1585) ordered by decree that October 5, 1582, would become October 15, 1582. The result is the Gregorian calendar that we still use today. Gregory also refined the leap year by adding one day to February every four years excepting years divisible by 100 (unless also divisible by 400) to correct the calendar and match Earth's actual 365.24199-day annual trip around the sun.

GREENWICH MEAN TIME

As transportation and communication grew faster in the 1800s, coordinating events between different locations became problematic. High noon in one city is not concurrent with high noon in a city far to the east or the west. This issue was particularly nettlesome for officials trying to coordinate the schedule for the United States' expanding railroads.

In 1883 they recommended a standardized system that separated the globe into 24 time zones, each covering 15 degrees of longitude and differing from the adjacent zone by one hour. The Royal Greenwich Observatory in suburban London became the location used around the world to fix the prime meridian—the longitudinal line assigned 0°—and Greenwich mean time gradually became the world's reference point for synchronizing watches.

A QUARTZ CRYSTAL shaped like a tiny tuning fork vibrates at a known frequency when exposed to an alternating electric current inside every quartz watch. The interaction of electrical and mechanical properties is called the piezoelectric effect.

FAST FACT The earliest known timekeeping device was the gnomon, a rudimentary sundial developed by about 3500 B.C.

FOR MORE FACTS ON...

GREENWICH & THE PRIME MERIDIAN see Dividing Lines, **CHAPTER 1, PAGES 30-1**
+
THE HISTORY & CULTURE OF ANCIENT EGYPT see Egypt 3000 B.C. 30 B.C., **CHAPTER 7, PAGES 268-9**

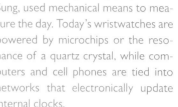

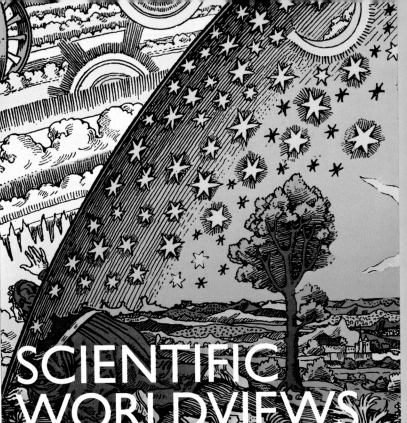

MYTHIC WORLDVIEWS

ANCIENT GREEK
Uranus and Gaia, Sky and Earth, gave birth to the Titans, including Zeus

MAYA
Earth floats on a giant crocodile with 13 layers of heaven above and 9 layers of underworld below

AUSTRALIAN ABORIGINAL
Sun Mother, guided by the Father of All Spirits, walked across Earth and created living things, then became the sun

HINDU
Brahma, the Divine Being, hatched from an egg and created Heaven and Earth from the egg's remains

ONEIDA NATIVE AMERICAN
Sky Woman fell through the heavens onto a mud-covered turtle and gave birth to twins, Good Spirit and Evil Spirit

SCIENTIFIC WORLDVIEWS

G reek mathematician Pythagoras, born around 560 B.C., offered the earliest scientific worldview with his idea that all things could be understood as relationships among numbers. Roughly 150 years later, Aristotle fleshed out Pythagoras's worldview when he described the mechanics of the planets and the stars. The challenge of demystifying the workings of our universe still faces today's astrophysicists as they seek to grasp the universe's shape, origin, and future.

Aristotle understood that Earth was round, based on its shadow during a lunar eclipse, but he believed that Earth was at the center of everything, with 56 spheres rotating around it. About 500 years later Claudius Ptolemy, the last of the great Greek astronomers, compounded the confusion. By proposing that Earth's axis tilts, he could keep it at the center of planetary and stellar orbits but still accurately predict the motion of the sun and moon.

In the 16th century, Nicholas Copernicus argued that Earth, like other planets, rotates around the sun. Decades later, Galileo Galilei, using a rudimentary telescope, made observations that supported Copernicus's claims. Publishing at the height of the Roman Catholic Church's Inquisition, Galileo was tried for heresy.

In the late 1600s, Sir Isaac Newton outlined the basic laws of planetary motion, including the description of gravity as the universal glue. Though

FAST FACT Launched by NASA in 2001, the Wilkinson Microwave Anisotropy Probe continues hunting for evidence about the state of the early universe.

FOR MORE FACTS ON...

PTOLEMY & ANCIENT GEOGRAPHY see Geography, CHAPTER 1, PAGES 16-7
+
ASTRONOMICAL OBSERVATION PAST & PRESENT see Observation, CHAPTER 2, PAGES 68-71

profound in their effects on science overall, Newton's laws did not apply to a problem posed by Albert Einstein in the early 1900s: What if the observer is moving? If two trains are moving at the same speed, passengers on one perceive the other as standing still. Einstein developed theories about gravity and the unity of space and time that fixed inaccuracies in Newtonian mechanical theories. Einstein's work led to more discoveries, such as Edwin Hubble's observation that the universe is expanding—an insight that supports the big bang theory that the universe started with a cosmic eruption from an infinitely dense singularity into which time and space were compacted.

GLOSSARY

Doppler effect: Named for Austrian physicist A. C. E. Doppler (1803–1853). Apparent difference in frequency of sound or light as the source moves toward or away from an observer, central to the finding that galaxies are receding from each other.

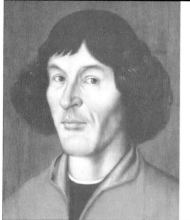

NICOLAUS COPERNICUS / ASTRONOMER

Born to a merchant family in Torun, Poland, Nicolaus Copernicus (1473-1543) studied church (canon) law and medicine. His pursuit of astronomy, however, unraveled humankind's understanding of the universe. He completed his *Commentary on the Theories of the Motions of Heavenly Objects from Their Arrangements* in 1514, placing Earth in orbit around the sun—not only contradicting giants such as Aristotle, but also defying Catholic orthodoxy. A student of canon law and the nephew of a bishop, Copernicus was sensitive to the implications of his claim. Though encouraged by the church officials of his day, he waited 30 years to publish his work, which, along with correcting previous mistakes, was a triumph of the emerging scientific method.

HOW DID EINSTEIN RESHAPE OUR WORLDVIEW?

By the early 1900s, scientists had established that the speed of light was a constant, which challenged the classical theory that velocity is additive: A swimmer moving at one mile an hour in a two-mile-an-hour current travels three miles an hour, but light beamed from a moving train still travels 186,000 miles per second. Albert Einstein developed equations showing that space and time, the other variables involved in velocity, change as objects approach the speed of light. Astronomical observations eventually confirmed this, as did experiments on airplanes that showed time does slow as speed increases.

Einstein's special and general theories of relativity unified the three dimensions of space with a fourth dimension of time; explained the interchangeability of mass and energy through the famous equation $E=mc^2$; and recast gravity as a force that acts by bending space—phenomena relevant only across massive distances and high speeds—but that helped unlock some very practical forces, such as nuclear power.

HOAG'S OBJECT and other galactic objects now glimpsed by the Hubble telescope have added new knowledge about the formation of the universe, further shaping our worldview.

FOR MORE FACTS ON...

MAPS IN THE TIME OF COPERNICUS see *The History of Mapping,* **CHAPTER 1, PAGES 20-1**
+
THE NEWEST COSMIC WORLDVIEW see *The New Solar System,* **CHAPTER 2, PAGES 52-3**

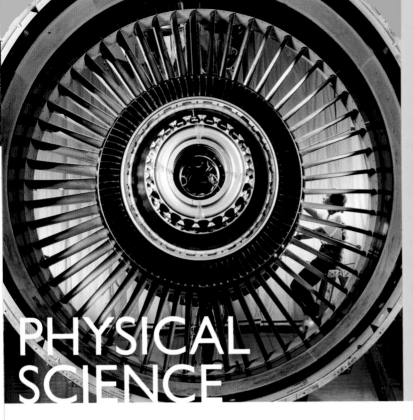

Manufacturing a jet engine

NEWTON'S THREE LAWS OF MOTION

FIRST LAW
An object at rest or in motion stays as is unless acted upon by an external force

SECOND LAW
The external force upon a body equals the body's mass times its acceleration

THIRD LAW
For every action there is an equal and opposite reaction

PHYSICAL SCIENCE

The basic concept of mechanics is that a force applied at one point can overcome friction, gravity, and other forms of resistance to produce motion at another. This physical law has been long understood, and inventors have devised machines in order to amplify the effect, allowing larger amounts of resistance to be overcome with less power.

Archimedes, a Greek mathematician, made early strides in understanding the mathematics underlying physics. Legend has it that while bathing he was inspired by observing the displacement of water. His insights helped in hydraulics and in the basic principles of leverage as well: He determined that the force needed to leverage an object declined with its distance from a fulcrum.

In the 1500s Nicolaus Copernicus and, subsequently, Galileo Galilei and Johannes Kepler revolutionized humankind's understanding of the solar system and the rules regarding planetary motion. Their work relied not just on astronomical observations but on experiments with moving bodies and an understanding of inertia and the effects of force over distance.

In 1665 Sir Isaac Newton began two decades of thought and experimentation that resulted in a set of universal laws of physical science. Culminating with the 1687 publication of his *Philosophiae Naturalis Principia Mathematica*, Newton provided the mathematics of how objects, including the planets, move and interact—tools and concepts still vital to science and engineering today.

FAST FACT Mechanics now requires three separate sets of theory: Einstein's relativistic theories for galactic distances, quantum mechanics for subatomic behavior, and Newtonian mechanics for everyday objects.

FOR MORE FACTS ON...

THE HISTORY & CULTURE OF ANCIENT GREECE see *Greece & Persia 1600 B.C.-A.D. 500*, **CHAPTER 7, PAGES 274-5**
+
EVER CHANGING WORLDVIEWS see *Scientific Worldviews*, **CHAPTER 8, PAGES 326-7**

WHAT IS WORK?

Scientists have refined and expanded on Newton's laws and their implications, but all mechanics is fundamentally about motion. Closely related to all three of Newton's laws of motion is the concept of work.

To a scientist, work necessarily involves motion, which is produced in a given body by an external force that is applied at least partly in the direction of movement and that is measured as a transfer of energy between the objects. Thus work might involve compressing a gas, rotating a shaft, applying leverage, or countless other movements or operations necessary in a society that depends on machines.

Two other concepts critical to Newton's laws of motion are force and inertia. Force is any action that has the ability to maintain, alter, or distort the motion of an object. Force has magnitude and direction. Inertia is a property inherent in a body by which it opposes any impulse to begin or change in movement.

A NEWTONIAN DEFINITION of work, given in terms of force and inertia, applies to many realms of the physical world—including the efforts of this 1943 prison work crew.

CLICK IT: Mechanical Engineering memagazine.org

G L O S S A R Y

Archimedean screw: Spiral-shaped pipe that raises water when rotated, attributed to Archimedes and used by Romans for water management. **/ Newton:** Named for Sir Isaac Newton (1643–1727). The unit of force necessary to provide a mass of one kilogram with an acceleration of one meter per second per second.

WHAT IS HYDRAULICS?

French mathematician and philosopher Blaise Pascal laid the foundation for modern hydraulics, which studies the special properties of liquids. Pascal in the mid-1600s determined that the pressure applied to a liquid in a confined space is transferred equally throughout the substance. This principle, which allows the transfer and amplification of force through liquid-filled chambers, has broad applications. Pascal himself invented the syringe and the hydraulic press, and hydraulic systems are common in today's automobile braking and steering systems.

Decades later, Swiss physicist Daniel Bernoulli examined the properties of water in motion, showing that pressure decreases with velocity—a fact that explains the movement of water through pipes, and, since air rushing across a wing is subject to the same rule, is basic to aerodynamics and flight.

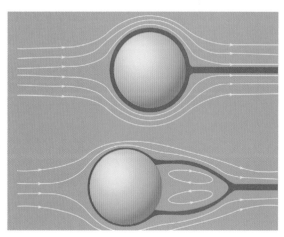

BERNOULLI'S PRINCIPLE, named for the Swiss scientist Daniel Bernoulli, describes the movement of fluids (shown in yellow) around moving objects (green spheres). Essential to airplane design, Bernoulli's principle helps engineers analyze turbulence (yellow ovals in lower right).

FOR MORE FACTS ON...

THE PLACE OF AIR TRAVEL IN THE HISTORY OF TRANSPORTATION see Transportation, **CHAPTER 6, PAGES 252-3**

THE ENLIGHTENMENT & ITS PHILOSOPHICAL IMPACT see Revolution 1600-1800, **CHAPTER 7, PAGES 298-9**

PHYSICS

Physics is the study of what the world is made of—the underlying "stuff" that gets turned into stars, planets, and people—and how it functions. It thus serves as a set of ground rules for chemistry, biology, and other sciences.

Early natural philosophers (as scientists once were called) relied largely on argument as opposed to experiment, with Chinese, Indian, and Greek theorists proposing different basic ideas about the nature of matter. The debate was particularly vibrant in Greece around the fifth century B.C., when Parmenides' followers—who argued that all in nature came from combinations of earth, air, fire, and water—debated those of Democritus—who believed the world was made of invisible, indivisible units he named atoms.

In the late 18th and early 19th centuries, this debate was resolved in Democritus's favor when Henry Cavendish and Antoine Lavoisier showed that both water and air could be broken down into other components, one of which Lavoisier named hydrogen. Based on those and other findings, English schoolteacher John Dalton surmised that substances were made of basic elements, or atoms. Early in the 20th century Ernest Rutherford argued that even atoms have parts: protons, neutrons, and electrons.

Scientists then posed the question, What holds this all together? Beginning in 1864 James Clerk Maxwell developed equations showing that electricity and magnetism act together to produce electromagnetic waves. Electromagnetism is now recognized as one of four basic forces that hold matter together, along with so-called strong and weak forces, which act on the subatomic scale, and gravity, which acts across cosmic distances.

The foundation for quantum mechanics, a field based on the knowledge that the basic particles of matter behave more like waves, was laid by researchers such as Niels Bohr and Werner Heisenberg in the 20th century. Quantum mechanics united electromagnetism and light with atomic structure.

WITH 100 TRILLION WATTS of power, this particle beam fusion accelerator at the Sandia National Laboratories in New Mexico can ignite a controlled thermonuclear fusion reaction.

FOR MORE FACTS ON...

THE ELEMENTS THAT MAKE UP PLANET EARTH see Earth's Elements, **CHAPTER 3, PAGES 90-1**

THE ELEMENTS THAT MAKE UP EARTH'S ATMOSPHERE see Earth's Atmosphere, **CHAPTER 3, PAGES 104-5**

WHAT IS STRING THEORY?

The search for a common thread by which to explain the universe has turned into just that—a theory stating that gravity, electromagnetism, and the strong and weak forces that hold atoms together all connect through the vibrations of infinitesimal strings of energy.

Though without empirical proof so far, string theory is rooted in 1960s research that found that the mathematical model describing the bond between protons and neutrons suggested energy to be a vibrating filament. String theorists hypothesize that this connective tissue works across as many as eleven dimensions—all but three so small they cannot be seen.

FAST FACT The resonating filaments of energy postulated in string theory measure about a millionth of a billionth of a billionth of a billionth of a centimeter in size.

WHAT IS A QUARK?

Early models of the atom were fairly simple, with neutrons and protons forming a nucleus and negatively charged electrons orbiting in what seemed like a tiny solar system. In the early 1930s, however, analysis of cosmic rays and experiments with particle accelerators began revealing new particles by the dozen.

American physicist Murray Gell-Mann in the early 1960s conjectured that protons and neutrons were made of even more fundamental particles, which he dubbed quarks, a word borrowed from a James Joyce novel. He suggested that six "flavors" of quark were needed to explain atomic behavior—up, down, top, bottom, charm, and strange. All six have since been identified through experimentation. Carrying a fraction of the charge of an electron, the up and down quark are the constituents of protons and neutrons.

CLICK IT: String Theory www.superstringtheory.com

 If *A* is a success in life, then *A* equals *x* plus *y* plus *z*. Work is *x*; *y* is play; and *z* is keeping your mouth shut. **— ALBERT EINSTEIN, 1950**

ALBERT EINSTEIN / RELATIVITY THEORIST

Born in Ulm, Germany, Albert Einstein (1879-1955) studied at the Zurich Polytechnic Institute and was working as a patent examiner in Bern when, at age 26, his articles on special relativity were published in the German journal *Annalen der Physik*. The work had its origins in a thought experiment he had conducted at age 16, when he imagined riding on a beam of light and puzzling about how, even though the speed of light is a constant, a parallel beam would have seemed stationary. Einstein's theories of special and general relativity ultimately united matter with energy and space with time. They redefined how gravity works. And they also helped usher in the age of atomic energy and weapons.

FOR MORE FACTS ON...

THE HISTORY OF THE ATOM BOMB DURING WORLD WAR II see *World War II 1938-1945*, **CHAPTER 7, PAGES 314-5**

HOW EINSTEIN'S IDEAS RESHAPED OUR WORLDVIEW see *Scientific Worldviews*, **CHAPTER 8, PAGE 327**

ENGINEERING

Engineering involves the application of energy to material to create something—a building, a monument, a network of computers. An applied pursuit, it allowed early builders to use initial discoveries about mechanics and chemistry to create structures that remain standing thousands of years later.

Imhotep, who built the Step Pyramid in Saqqara, Egypt, in 2550 B.C., is the first builder recognized by name. Vitruvius's volume *De Architectura*, published in Rome in the first century A.D., laid out an extensive array of building methods and materials put to use in the Colosseum and the network of aqueducts. Roman *agrimensors*, or surveyors, used basic math, plumb lines, levels, and right angles to lay boundaries for what was then the world's greatest empire.

More than a thousand years later, a high level of applied mathematics and materials science went into the construction of Gothic cathedrals and other structures, as revealed in the sketches by Villard de Honnecourt in France. Then, as now, however, the engineering talent of that day was often diverted from architectural projects to military applications: catapults, siege tools, and other machines of war.

Engineering was traditionally concerned with buildings and public projects like roads, docks, and lighthouses. English engineer John Smeaton apparently coined the term "civil engineer" in 1782, marking new directions for engineering as it began to feel the influence of the scientific and industrial revolutions. New technologies evolved that were capable of unlocking and putting to use the forces of electricity, chemistry, heat, and, ultimately, the atom.

It is hard to separate the history of engineering from the history of invention—of John Smeaton's development in the 1750s of a mortar that would set underwater, for example; of the improvements James Watt made in the steam engine at the dawn of the industrial revolution, during the 1770s; of Alexander Graham Bell's telephone and Thomas Edison's electric light in the last decades of the 19th century. The 20th century saw numerous inventions and advances added to the list of each discipline, as an understanding of the atom created demand for a generation of nuclear engineers and as the advent of the computer gave rise to a host of new engineering specializations: software programmers, chip designers, and network architects.

THE GOLDEN GATE BRIDGE of San Francisco, an engineering accomplishment completed in 1937, was an early example of long-span suspension bridges.

FOR MORE FACTS ON...

ANCIENT PYRAMID BUILDERS see Egypt 3000 B.C.-30 B.C., **CHAPTER 7, PAGES 268-9, &** South America Prehistory to 1500, **CHAPTER 7, PAGES 290-1**

THE CONSTRUCTION OF THE GREAT WALL OF CHINA see China 2200 B.C.-A.D. 500, **CHAPTER 7, PAGES 272-3**

ENGINEERING MATERIALS FOR STRENGTH

Engineering advances continue to make new inroads in the traditional field of building. The advent of synthetic materials has given engineers ever greater leeway, changing certain guiding principles of design.

If early builders sought solidity—the wide base of the pyramids or the keystone at the top of an arch—as a way to balance a structure's internal forces, modern engineers have instead found safety in motion.

Modern bridges are built to allow for the expansion and contraction of materials as temperatures change. Modern skyscrapers rest on layers of rubber and include ball bearings under columns to let the buildings sway and dissipate the effects of high wind and earthquakes. Newly engineered materials, often alloys or combinations of metals manipulated at the molecular level, are now designed with strength and flexibility in mind.

CLICK IT: Great Engineering www.greatachievements.org

G L O S S A R Y

Thermodynamics: The science of the relationship between heat, work, temperature, and energy. **/ Systems engineering:** A branch of engineering that uses knowledge from various other branches of engineering and science in the planning and development of more abstract systems such as work-flow or risk assessment.

SEVEN WONDERS OF THE ANCIENT WORLD

Even if builders' scientific knowledge was rudimentary, it took remarkable skill and planning to build the structures known as the Seven Wonders of the Ancient World.

The Pyramids of Giza are the only extant ancient wonder. The mathematical precision of their design is undisputed, although the exact method of construction remains unknown. Remnants of the 350-by-180-foot Temple of Artemis remain on site in Turkey, and fragments of the Mausoleum of Halicarnassus are in the British Museum. The other ancient engineering wonders have been lost. They include the 105-foot-tall bronze Colossus of Rhodes, which stood near the harbor of the ancient Greek city until an earthquake toppled it, and the 350-foot-tall Pharos of Alexandria lighthouse. The 40-foot-tall statue of Zeus at Olympia was built in 430 B.C.

The last, the Hanging Gardens of Babylon, remains a subject of debate, with research as to its location continuing.

AN ANCIENT ENGINEERING MARVEL, Turkey's Temple of Artemis was probably built in the sixth century B.C. It dwarfed the Parthenon. Alexander the Great admired it in 333 B.C. Five hundred years later, it was leveled by the Goths. Only one of its columns still stands.

FAST FACT Ancient Egyptians are thought to have used a system of water trenches to ensure the pyramids were level.

FOR MORE FACTS ON...

THE DEVELOPMENT OF NUMBERS & COUNTING SYSTEMS see *Counting & Measurement,* **CHAPTER 8, PAGES 322-3**

COMPUTERS AS TOOLS FOR DESIGN & CALCULATION see *Computer Science,* **CHAPTER 8, PAGES 346-7**

CHEMISTRY

People manipulated substances found in nature long before chemistry became an organized pursuit. Ancient weapons, ceramics, and other artifacts demonstrate a practical knowledge of chemical reactions despite little understanding of how they worked.

Early philosophers theorized that everything was made of foundational substances like earth, air, water, and fire. Overlap between chemistry as a modern science and the durable pseudoscience known as alchemy remained until the scientific revolution was well under way. Even Sir Isaac Newton toyed with the idea of synthesizing gold. So did Robert Boyle, considered a founder of modern chemistry in the 1600s for his intent experimental approach and his rejection of the old Greek ideas in favor of a more universal theory of matter.

Chemistry in Boyle's day focused on the study of gases. Boyle's law, for example, describes the inverse relation between the volume and pressure of a gas. Over time, particular attention turned to the process of combustion. By the 18th century, theories about combustion focused on phlogiston, hypothesized by German physician George Ernst Stahl as the substance that allowed things to burn.

The phlogiston theory did not satisfy Antoine Lavoisier, a French chemist who used advances in measurement to analyze the constituent parts of different substances. He noticed that sulfur and phosphorus weighed more after combustion than before, a finding inconsistent with the idea that their phlogiston had been consumed. English chemist Joseph Priestley had been experimenting with a gas whose presence made candles burn more brightly and whose absence killed small animals. Lavoisier identified the gas, which he called oxygen, as the key to combustion—and breathing. The combined work of Lavoisier, Priestley, English aristocrat Henry Cavendish, and Scottish chemist Joseph Black set the stage for modern atomic and chemical theory.

Late 19th and early 20th century advances in physics helped answer another basic question: Why do atoms stick together in the first place? Discovery of the electron focused the search on an electrical basis for the bond. Niels Bohr's quantum mechanics and Linus Pauling's chemical research indicated that an atom's furthermost, or valence, electrons control its ability to combine with other atoms. Advances in analytical equipment and industrial methods produced a veritable explosion of practical discoveries and synthetic chemical inventions that continues to this day, spinning fabrics and plastics from petroleum and unraveling the complicated chemical processes that support life.

THOMAS EDISON'S LABORATORY, circa 1915, in West Orange, New Jersey, where the great scientist and his "muckers," as he called his assistants, worked 55-hour weeks.

FOR MORE FACTS ON...

JOSEPH PRIESTLEY & THE DISCOVERY OF OXYGEN see Earth's Atmosphere, **CHAPTER 3, PAGE 105**

THE HISTORY & CULTURE OF ANCIENT GREECE see Greece & Persia 1600 B.C.-A.D. 500, **CHAPTER 7, PAGES 274-5**

HOW DOES THE PERIODIC TABLE WORK?

Charting the elements for a textbook in the late 1860s, Russian chemist Dmitry Mendeleyev noticed similarities in groups of elements based on their atomic weight: Each element resembled the eighth to follow it. That insight led him to outline the periodic table still in use today. By arraying elements in rows and columns, placing like substances in vertical groups, Mendeleyev accurately predicted that other elements would eventually be discovered. Later the chart was reorganized to reflect the proton count in an atom's nucleus—an element's atomic number. It now contains 92 natural elements and others produced by human-made nuclear reactions.

EVERY ELEMENT is represented by its atomic number, alphabetical symbol, and atomic weight in the periodic table.

G L O S S A R Y

Superconductivity: The complete disappearance of electrical resistance in various solids when they are cooled below a characteristic temperature. Superconductors repel magnetic fields and have many industrial applications.

> " This discovery was one of the most spiritual experiences that any of us in the original team of five has ever experienced. — **RICHARD E. SMALLEY, 1996** "

RICHARD SMALLEY / DISCOVERER OF FULLERENE

The challenge inherent in Dmitry Mendeleyev's first, incomplete periodic table remains ongoing, and in 1985 Richard Smalley (1943-2005) was among a trio of chemists who discovered a new and potentially revolutionary form of natural carbon. Vaporizing graphite rods with lasers in helium gas produced circular, beautifully symmetrical structures containing 60 carbon atoms. These spherical structures were named fullerenes, or buckyballs, recalling the geodesic dome structure invented by American architect R. Buckminster Fuller. Smalley, who shared the 1996 Nobel Prize in chemistry for the discovery, became a leading proponent of nanotechnology. It is estimated that materials made of fullerene could be 50 to 100 times stronger than steel at a fraction of the weight.

FULLERENES are molecules made of 60 carbon atoms and shaped either as a cage (right) or a cylinder. The cage-shaped fullerene atoms are called buckyballs; the cylinder-shaped ones, nanotubes. Nanotubes conduct heat and electricity and show great tensile strength. The element, discovered only in 1985, was named for the visionary architect R. Buckminster Fuller.

FAST FACT Lord Kelvin established absolute zero as the point at which further cooling is impossible (-459.67°F).

FOR MORE FACTS ON...

THE PERIODIC TABLE & THE ELEMENTS OF PLANET EARTH see *Earth's Elements,* **CHAPTER 3, PAGES 90-1**

+

MANIPULATING MATTER AT THE ATOMIC LEVEL see *Nanotechnology,* **CHAPTER 8, PAGES 350-1**

OPTICS

The formal study of light began as an effort to explain vision, which early Greek thinkers associated with a ray emitted from the human eye. A surviving work from Euclid, the Greek geometrician, laid out basic concepts of perspective, using straight lines to show why objects at a distance appear shorter or slower than they actually are.

Eleventh-century Islamic scholar Abu Ali al Hasan ibn al-Haytham—known also by the Latinized name Alhazen—revisited the work done by Euclid and Ptolemy and advanced the study of reflection, refraction, and color. He argued that light moves out in all directions from illuminated objects and that vision results when light enters the eye.

Thanks to better glass-grinding techniques in the late 16th and 17th centuries, researchers including Dutch mathematician Willebrord Snel noticed that light bent as it passed through a lens or fluid. Although his contemporaries believed the speed of light to be infinite, Danish astronomer Ole Rømer in 1676 used telescopic observations of Jupiter's moons to estimate the speed of light as 140,000 miles a second. Around the same time, Sir Isaac Newton used prisms to demonstrate that white light could be separated into a spectrum of basic colors. He believed that light was made of particles, whereas Dutch mathematician Christiaan Huygens described light as a wave.

The particle versus wave debate advanced in the 1800s. English physician Thomas Young's experiments with vision suggested wavelike behavior, since sources of light seemed to cancel out or reinforce each other. Scottish physicist James Clerk Maxwell's research united the forces of electricity and magnetism and showed that the same equations described light. Maxwell posited that both visible light and the invisible forces of electromagnetism fell along a single spectrum.

The arrival of quantum physics in the late 19th and early 20th century prompted the next leap in understanding light. By studying the emission of electrons from a grid hit by a beam of light—known as the photoelectric effect—Albert Einstein concluded that light came from what he called photons, emitted as electrons changed their orbit around an atomic nucleus and then jumped back to their original state. Though Einstein's finding seemed to favor the particle theory of light, further experiments showed that light and matter itself behave both as waves and as particles.

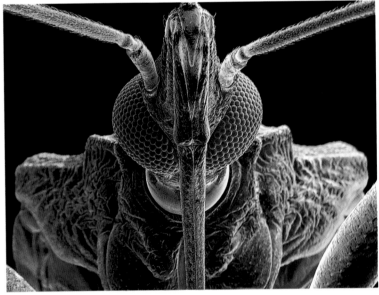

A SCANNING ELECTRON MICROSCOPE creates images of minuscule objects, like an insect's face (above), by shooting a beam of electrons and collecting those that scatter back from the specimen's surface. The instrument changes light into electric current and amplifies it by a factor of 10,000 or more.

FOR MORE FACTS ON...

THE SUN, EARTH'S ULTIMATE LIGHT SOURCE see The Sun, **CHAPTER 2, PAGES 54-7**

THE NATURE OF LIGHT ON EARTH see Earth's Atmosphere & Light, **CHAPTER 3, PAGES 104-5, 108-9**

HOW DO LASERS WORK?

Einstein's work on the photoelectric effect led to the laser, an acronym for "light amplification by stimulated emission of radiation." Typically, as electrons are excited from one quantum state to another, they emit a single photon when jumping back. But Einstein predicted that when an already excited atom was hit with the right type of stimulus, it would give off two identical photons. Subsequent experiments showed that certain source materials, such as ruby, not only did that but also emitted photons that were perfectly coherent—not scattered like the emissions of a flashlight, but all of the same wavelength and amplitude.

These powerfully focused beams are now commonplace, found in grocery store scanners, handheld pointers, and cutting instruments from the hospital operating room to the shop floors of heavy industry.

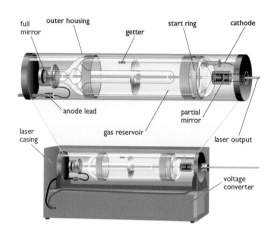

BY PASSING LIGHT through a casing designed to produce multiple photons of the same phase, wavelength, and direction, a laser creates a coherent, narrow beam of light with useful properties.

WHAT IS HOLOGRAPHY?

Holography was invented in 1948 as a way to create refined images by splitting a light source and bouncing part of it off of an image to a photographic plate while the other part went straight to the plate to form a sort of background. In 1964 the process became of practical interest when Emmett Norman Leith and a colleague at the University of Michigan thought of using lasers to etch three-dimensional images. The powerful source improved a process that had been of largely academic interest. Holographs are now in wide use—found on credit cards and currency, as a way to protect against fraud, and employed in engineering, medicine, and other fields.

NEW TRENDS IN OPTICS

Ever more precise manipulation of photons of light may help researchers devise quantum computers—exponentially faster than today's supercomputers and capable of protecting data with quantum cryptographic techniques.

Nonlinear optics originated in 1961. When researchers passed high-intensity light through a crystal, they noted that at least some of it doubled in frequency. That frequency-doubling effect has led to advances in information processing, computing, and physical analysis. Resonance-ionization spectroscopy, for example, pairs pulsed lasers with nonlinear optical devices to create analytical machines that are sensitive at the level of a single atom.

LASERS HELP GEOLOGISTS measure minute changes in the dimensions of the Long Valley Caldera at California's Mammoth Lakes, recently affected by seismic activity.

FOR MORE FACTS ON...

THE INFLUENCE OF EINSTEIN ON MODERN PHYSICS see Scientific Worldviews, **CHAPTER 8, PAGES 326-7, &** Physics, **CHAPTER 8, PAGES 330-1**

THE USE OF LASERS IN SURGERY see Surgery, **CHAPTER 8, PAGE 342**

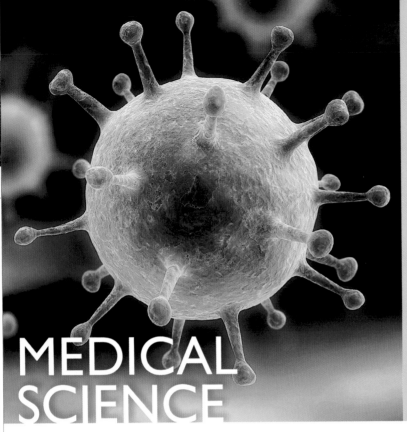

Virus particle

HIGHEST IN WORLD

Marshall Islands / 15.4%

United States of America / 15.2%

Timor-Leste / 13.7%

Micronesia / 13.5%

LOWEST IN WORLD

Indonesia / 2.1%

Pakistan / 2.1%

Republic of the Congo / 1.9%

Angola / 1.8%

MEDICAL SCIENCE

t may be the world's first medical text: a 65-foot-long papyrus scroll dating to 1550 B.C. that outlines more than 700 remedies Egyptian practitioners used for everything from tumors to crocodile bites. If nothing else, the Ebers Papyrus, named for the German Egyptologist who acquired it in 1872, showed an early urge to understand the human body and fix its problems.

Greek physician Alcmaeon is credited with the first human dissection, which took place around 500 B.C. Hippocrates, living about a century later, is considered the first practicing physician—legendary for focusing on patient care, which is why today physicians take the so-called Hippocratic oath, promising to do all they can to save the lives and benefit the health of their patients.

Second-century physician Claudius Galenus, or Galen, a brilliant healer, founded experimental physiology. He believed that disease stemmed from imbalances in bodily humors, a theory that held sway for millennia even as dissection became widespread. Swiss physician Paracelsus is credited with being the first to challenge this theory, when his observations in the 16th century about lung problems among miners connected disease with external causes.

In the 17th century English physician William Harvey described the circulation of blood through the heart and body, and Dutch microscopist Antoni van Leeuwenhoek observed red blood cells.

More than a century later, germ theory developed as scientists such as Louis Pasteur, Joseph Lister, and Robert Koch identified the microbes responsible for specific diseases and began developing methods of sterilization and treatment. Infections, long a cause of death, came to be better understood and controlled thanks to the 20th-century development of antibiotics such as penicillin.

FOR MORE FACTS ON...

PASTEUR & HIS DISCOVERIES IN MICROBIOLOGY see *Bacteria, Protists & Archaea*, **CHAPTER 4, PAGE 149**

ANCIENT EGYPTIAN HISTORY & CULTURE see *Egypt 3000 B.C.-30 B.C.*, **CHAPTER 7, PAGES 268-9**

WHAT IS MRSA?

Antibiotics have saved countless lives, but their widespread use may prompt bacteria to mutate and develop resistance to them. Methicillin-resistant *Staphylococcus aureus,* or MRSA, may be just such a bug. MRSA caused an estimated 94,000 infections and 19,000 deaths in 2005 alone. Most MRSA infections occur at hospitals. Awareness about MRSA spiked in 2007 after the death of some children prompted schools to close for disinfection. Basic hygiene, such as keeping wounds bandaged and not sharing towels or personal items, is an effective defense.

GLOSSARY

Apoptosis: From Greek *apo + ptosis,* "falling from." The process by which a body routinely kills off and replaces damaged or used-up cells—sloughing off dead skin, for example—at a rate of perhaps 70 billion cells a day; it may have a role in therapies to prevent cancer.

WHAT IS STEM CELL THERAPY?

Early in the formation of a fetus, the embryo contains versatile genetic material known as stem cells. These nondifferentiated cells gradually produce both other stem cells and the tissue that forms the rest of the body. Research indicates that stem cells, cultivated from an early-stage embryo called a blastocyst, could replace cells damaged by heart disease, diabetes, Parkinson's disease, or other illnesses.

Because the embryo is destroyed in the process of extracting stem cells, stem cell research has raised ethical concerns. Researchers are now seeking alternative sources for stem cells. Hematopoietic (blood-forming) stem cells from the umbilical cords of newborns are also being used on an experimental basis to treat blood diseases such as leukemia and lymphoma.

WHAT IS HIV/AIDS?

HIV, the human immunodeficiency virus, degrades the immune system, causes acquired immune deficiency syndrome (AIDS), and leaves the body vulnerable to disease. HIV affects about 33 million people worldwide and has been a top public health concern for 30 years. Though still incurable, HIV can be suppressed with drugs, yet only 2 million of the 7.1 million people needing treatment in low- and middle-income countries have access to them. HIV may have entered the human population in the first half of the century in equatorial Africa, possibly through the consumption of chimpanzees infected with the simian immunodeficiency virus. Researchers conjecture that it spread from Africa, still the hardest-hit continent, to Haiti.

ANTIRETROVIRAL DRUGS made in Bangkok, Thailand (above), are designed to combat the human immunodeficiency virus (opposite).

CLICK IT: Centers for Disease Control and Prevention www.cdc.gov

FAST FACT First identified in the U.S. in 1981, HIV is believed to have entered the country between 1969 and 1972.

FOR MORE FACTS ON...

ALEXANDER FLEMING & HIS DISCOVERY OF PENICILLIN see *Fungi & Lichens,* **CHAPTER 4, PAGE 135**
+
DISEASE IN HISTORY: THE BUBONIC PLAGUE see *Middle Ages: 1000-1500,* **CHAPTER 7, PAGE 281**

MIND & BRAIN

As early as the sixth century B.C., a Greek physician performing a dissection noticed the connection between the optic nerve and the brain. Anatomical research through the Renaissance gradually mapped the connections between the brain, the spinal column, and the nerves that carry neural signals throughout the body. Religious and philosophical worldviews tended to separate mind and body, but advances in anatomy suggested that the two were intimately connected.

In the late 18th century, Italian professor Luigi Galvani applied static electric charges to the muscles of dead frogs and made them twitch—a feat that provided evidence for the idea that intention and perhaps even the lifeforce itself had a physical basis. For decades after, the study and clinical use of electricity in the body was called galvanism in his honor.

These efforts to understand how the brain sends its signals evolved into today's neuroscience, a field that has begun to provide anatomical and biochemical explanations and treatments for problems once thought to be purely psychological—involving emotions and attitudes, not organic processes.

In the late 19th and early 20th centuries, Spanish physician and anatomist Santiago Ramón y Cajal made painstaking descriptions of the nervous system, distinguishing the basic nerve cell, or neuron, through use of a silver nitrate stain. Numbering in the billions, neurons in the human body carry messages via neurotransmitter chemicals, released from cell to cell across a vast network. Depending on the chemical mix and the origin of the message, the signals might regulate the autonomic work of internal organs or get interpreted as dreams.

Early research linked different parts of the brain to different activities—higher level functions to the cerebral cortex, language in the left hemisphere, memory in the right. Advances in electromagnetic imaging refined the study even further. Researchers at the University of Pennsylvania in 2005, for example, used functional magnetic resonance imaging to document increased blood flow to the prefrontal cortex of people subjected to stress. Research into the role of neurotransmitters has linked chemicals such as dopamine and serotonin to different diseases and disorders—the basis for antidepressants.

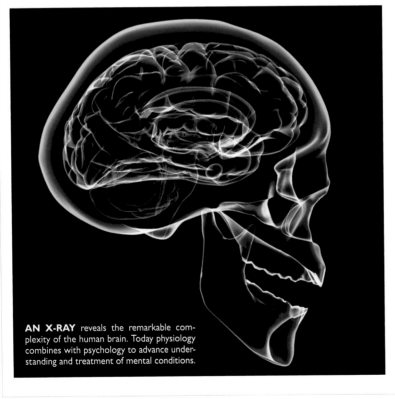

AN X-RAY reveals the remarkable complexity of the human brain. Today physiology combines with psychology to advance understanding and treatment of mental conditions.

FOR MORE FACTS ON...

THE ANIMAL WITH THE BIGGEST BRAIN see Animal Curiosities, **CHAPTER 4, PAGE 170**

ADVANCES IN IMAGING TECHNIQUES see Physical Science: Optics, **CHAPTER 8, PAGES 336-7**

WHAT ARE THE MOST COMMON MENTAL ILLNESSES?

Mental illness can range from mild neuroses, universal to the human condition and often not needing treatment, to dangerous breaks with reality. Like schizophrenia, bipolar disorder is one of the more serious category of disease known as psychosis. Some psychoses appear rooted in genetics and may involve imbalances in brain chemistry. Personality disorders, such as narcissism and borderline personality disorder, involve persistent antisocial acts and are thought to involve biochemical and social influences that immunize individuals to the emotions that check behavior.

Alzheimer's disease is a degenerative brain disease resulting in degraded mental capacity in the elderly. Autism, which is increasingly diagnosed among children, can involve disrupted development of speech, inappropriate social behavior, and extreme sensitivity to environmental change.

THE CHALLENGE OF DEPRESSION

Lobotomy, a controversial surgery, disconnected the prefrontal lobe, center of emotion and social behavior, from the brain. It was pioneered in the 1930s by Portuguese neurologist António Egas Moniz for use with patients suffering severe mental illness.

Today such challenges are treated with antidepressants, which increase available serotonin or norepinephrine—chemicals whose contact with nerve cells improves mood—by inhibiting the tendency for nerve cells to absorb or deactivate those chemicals.

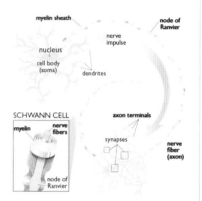

A NEURON, OR NERVE CELL, typically has one axon—the portion of the cell that carries impulses elsewhere—by which it connects with other neurons or with muscle or gland cells.

FAST FACT One human being's network of neurons, laid end to end, might extend as far as three million miles.

WHOSE IDEAS SHAPED MODERN PSYCHOLOGY?

THE FOUNDER of modern-day psychoanalysis, Sigmund Freud described an individual as divided into an impulsive id, the ego of everyday life, and a controlling superego.

BREAKING with Freud, Carl Jung emphasized culturally or even biologically inherent thought patterns, which he called archetypes, as the forces driving behavior.

ANTHROPOLOGIST Claude Lévi-Strauss saw people as governed by unspoken structures and underlying social rules, such as taboos and kinship.

ORIGINATOR of behaviorism, B. F. Skinner believed that rewards and punishment shape behavior and developed a system of gratification and withholding as a way to raise children.

CHILD PSYCHOLOGIST Jean Piaget argued that the years leading up to cognition and self-awareness determine much about the rest of a person's life.

FOR MORE FACTS ON...

VARIETIES OF LIFE-FORMS see Biodiversity, **CHAPTER 4, PAGES 174-5**

BONDS THAT CONNECT HUMANS IN FAMILY & SOCIETY see The Human Family, **CHAPTER 6, PAGES 222-7**

SURGERY

Treating illness by using tools to remove or manipulate parts of the human body is an old idea. Prehistoric skulls have been found with holes bored into them—a primitive escape hatch, presumably, for the evil spirits or vapors on which disease was blamed. The Code of Hammurabi, written in the 18th century B.C. and outlining the laws governing ancient Babylon, included what were perhaps the first penalties for surgical malpractice: Doctors who killed a patient when draining an abscess had their hands cut off.

Given the likelihood of infection at the time, even minor operations carried high risks, but that doesn't mean all early surgery failed. Indian doctors, beginning centuries before the birth of Christ, successfully removed tumors and performed amputations and other operations. They developed dozens of metal tools, relied on alcohol to dull the patient, and controlled bleeding with hot oil and tar.

Notable practitioners over the next few centuries included Ambroise Paré in the 1500s, a surgeon to kings and an innovator who used ligature, instead of painful cauterization, to tie off wounds. In the late 1700s, English surgeon John Hunter built up extensive experimental knowledge, establishing surgery as a reputable profession.

But scant knowledge about infection, anatomy, and the causes of disease kept surgery rudimentary until the 19th century, when two separate discoveries liberated its potential. William Thomas Morton, in a demonstration at Massachusetts General Hospital in 1846, showed how ether could be used as a general anesthetic, relieving the patient's pain and giving the surgeon more leeway. Crawford Williamson Long had performed the first such operation in Georgia several years earlier, but Morton's demonstration helped the concept spread.

Two decades later, Scottish surgeon Joseph Lister, inspired by the bacteriological discoveries of Louis Pasteur, began covering wounds with a germ barrier of carbolic acid. By the end of the century, surgeons had successfully attacked cancers by removing parts of the stomach and bowel, and appendectomy had become the standard treatment for appendicitis.

The 20th century brought even more radical change through technology. Surgeons could plan operations using x-rays and other images and could rely on the extreme heat of lasers, the extreme cold of cryogenics, or the small size of fiber optics to perform ever more exacting procedures. It became possible for surgeons to monitor and sustain a patient's breathing and blood flow with advanced machinery. They could also not just remove body parts but replace them—either with human substitutes or artificial items manufactured from plastics and metals.

LASER BEAMS are proving to have multiple uses in medicine today: Laser treatments range from repairing detached retinas to healing superficial bladder cancer.

FOR MORE FACTS ON...

THE CODE OF HAMMURABI see *Mesopotamia 3500 B.C.-500 B.C.,* **CHAPTER 7, PAGE 267**

THE HISTORY & CULTURE OF INDIA see *India 2500 B.C.-A.D. 500,* **CHAPTER 7, PAGES 270-1**

WHAT IS LAPAROSCOPY?

Advances in fiber-optic technology and the miniaturization of video equipment have revolutionized surgery. Procedures that once required major incisions, general anesthetics, and long recoveries can now be done with local numbing and a small slit or two.

Laparoscopy is performed on major abdominal organs by means of a tube called an endoscope, fitted with a fiber-optic light, a video device, and minuscule surgical instruments. The video device, slid into the abdominal cavity through a small incision, provides visual guidance as the surgeon manipulates tools also inserted through small incisions. Tubal ligations, appendectomies, gall bladder removal procedures, and many other operations can now be accomplished through laparoscopy.

Arthroscopy uses similar technologies to examine and treat joints and bones.

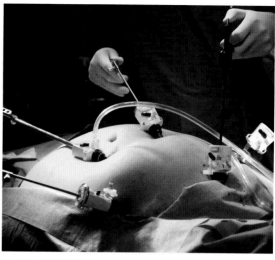

A GASTRIC BYPASS now requires several small incisions rather than major abdominal surgery. Carbon dioxide gas inflates the area around the organs of concern, making way for miniaturized instruments and a camera to picture every surgical move.

FAST FACT Surgical lasers can generate heat up to 10,000°F on a pinhead-size spot, sealing blood vessels and sterilizing.

SURGICAL ROBOTS and virtual computer technology are changing medical practice. Robotic surgical tools (above) increase precision. In 1998, heart surgeons at Paris's Broussais Hospital performed the first robotic surgery. New technology allows an enhanced views and precise control of instruments.

THERAPEUTIC HYPOTHERMIA

Hypothermia—a drop in body temperature significantly below normal—can be life threatening, as in the case of overexposure to severe wintry conditions. But in some cases, like that of Kevin Everett of the Buffalo Bills, hypothermia can be a lifesaver.

Everett fell to the ground with a potentially crippling spinal cord injury during a 2007 football game. Doctors treating him on the field immediately injected his body with a cooling fluid. At the hospital, they inserted a cooling catheter to lower his body temperature by roughly five degrees, at the same time proceeding with surgery to fix his fractured spine. Despite fears that he would be paralyzed, Everett has regained his ability to walk, and advocates of therapeutic hypothermia feel his lowered body temperature may have made the difference.

Therapeutic hypothermia is still a controversial procedure: The side effects of excessive cooling include heart problems, blood clotting, and increased infection risk. On the other hand, supporters claim, it slows down cell damage, swelling, and other destructive processes well enough that it can mean successful surgery after a catastrophic injury.

CLICK IT: World Health Organization www.who.int

FOR MORE FACTS ON...

HOW LASERS WORK see Physical Science: Optics, **CHAPTER 8, PAGE 337**

INTERNATIONAL EFFORTS SUCH AS THE WORLD HEALTH ORGANIZATION see Nations & Alliances, **CHAPTER 9, PAGES 358-9**

GENETICS

They may not have known why it was so, but Babylonian herdsmen and farmers knew that certain traits were passed down among animals. Clay tablets from the era show they also knew how to cross-pollinate date palm trees.

The formal study of genetics did not begin until the mid-1800s, however, when Austrian botanist and monk Gregor Mendel experimented with pea plants in a monastery garden. Meticulously cross-pollinating peas with different traits, such as seed col-

or, he discovered that first-generation offspring didn't mix the characteristics of the two parent samples but displayed discrete traits of one or the other. Mixing a red-flowered pea with a white-flowered pea, for example, would produce not pink-flowered offspring, but rather red-flowered ones. Moreover, whiteness recurred in successive generations, meaning that the trait had not been lost but was being passed along in latent form.

Ignored at the time, Mendel's work described the basic laws of heredity. It

was not until the early 20th century that experiments, particularly with the cells of fruit flies, confirmed the existence of chromosomes as carriers of genetic information. Then, in 1941, geneticist George Beadle and biochemist Edward Tatum showed that genes were not simply passive carriers of information; they also functioned at a cellular level as a code for the production of proteins. Three years later, a team including bacteriologist Oswald Avery, geneticist Colin M. MacLeod, and biologist Maclyn McCarty began unlocking the composition of genes, determining that they were made of deoxyribonucleic acid, or DNA.

The pace of discovery since then has been furious. In 1953, biophysicists James D. Watson and Francis Crick proposed the double-helix structure of DNA—two strands of the material, knit together by four base chemicals. Since then scientists have identified specific genes within a DNA strand, connected those genes to character traits, spliced genes, and cloned or replicated them. These successes have led to new treatments for cancer, allowed doctors to address certain birth defects through gene therapy, given biotechnologists the tools to grow new medicines, and made it possible for forensic scientists to confirm individual identities with biological evidence.

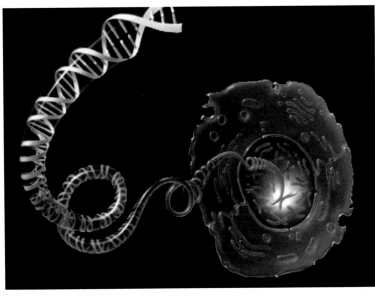

DNA, A DOUBLE-HELIX MOLECULE, resides deep in the nucleus of every cell of the human body. It is organized into chromosomes, which transmit genetic information from birth to death and from generation to generation.

FAST FACT Stem cells, medically useful in regenerating an array of tissues, may be available from human teeth.

FOR MORE FACTS ON...

DNA & ELEMENTS ESSENTIAL FOR LIFE ON EARTH see Earth's Elements, **CHAPTER 3, PAGE 91**

THE VARIETY OF LIFE-FORMS ON EARTH see Life-forms & Biodiversity, **CHAPTER 4, PAGES 132-3, 174-7**

MAPPING THE HUMAN GENOME

The goal of modern genetics has been mapping the human genome—the detailed structure of our own DNA. The effort to do that was largely complete by 2003, yielding a guide to the more than three billion base pairs of chemicals that compose the rungs of a double helix–shaped ladder and give the coded instructions for the manufacture of protein. Though there are still gaps in the map, the Human Genome Project found that those base pairs make up some 30,000 distinct human genes. So far, the function of about half of those genes has been identified, but researchers continue to search for those that play a role in illnesses such as cardiovascular disease, diabetes, and various cancers.

One new tool, the HapMap catalog, uses geographically diverse blood samples to trace regional variations in DNA and may speed research into the roots of some health problems.

HUMAN GENOME LAB researchers use ultraviolet light to view DNA strands.

CLICK IT: Genome Programs genomics.energy.gov

G L O S S A R Y

Restriction enzymes: Developed in 1969 by Hamilton O. Smith, these snip DNA at specific locations, giving researchers the ability to cleave the molecule at the beginning and end of a gene. **/ Gene therapy:** The introduction of a normal gene into an individual's genetic material in order to repair a mutation or avoid an inherited disease.

WHAT IS GENETIC ENGINEERING?

Genetic engineering has been around for as long as farmers have cross-pollinated plants, but it moved to a new level in 1973, when biochemists Stanley N. Cohen and Herbert W. Boyer inserted altered DNA into *E. coli* bacteria. This procedure, termed recombinant DNA, is now the principal method of genetic engineering, widely used in industry and agriculture.

Taking the next step, scientists have created full strands of synthetic DNA in the laboratory. By customizing that genetic code and placing it into a living cell, researchers envision using bacteria as tiny manufacturing factories, producing ethanol fuel, synthetic fibers, or other products.

WHO DISCOVERED THE DOUBLE HELIX?

The Nobel Prize in physiology or medicine in 1962 went to physicist Francis Crick, molecular biologist James Watson, and biophysicist Maurice Wilkins for deciphering the structure of DNA. But the full story includes critical work by another research scientist.

X-ray crystallography performed in the 1950s by Rosalind Franklin began to show

DNA's twisting molecular structure. Wilkins, Franklin's former research partner, provided Crick and Watson with copies of her images, which, combined with their research, revealed the architecture of DNA.

ROSALIND FRANKLIN, a London microbiologist, contributed essential information on the path leading to Watson and Crick's prizewinning discovery.

FOR MORE FACTS ON...

BACTERIA see *Bacteria, Protists & Archaea,* **CHAPTER 4, PAGES 148-9**

+

HOW HUMAN GENETICS HELPS TRACK HUMAN HISTORY see *Human Migration,* **CHAPTER 6, PAGES 220-1**

TIME LINE

1100 B.C.
The abacus: beads on a wire

A.D. 1671
Leibniz's Step Reckoner:
a gear-driven computing machine

1804
Jacquard's loom:
punched cards that executed designs

1823
Babbage's Analytical Engine:
the first computer, never built

1854
Boole's symbolic logic:
key to computer programming

1943
Turing's Colossus:
the first programmable computer

1946
ENIAC:
the first modern computer

COMPUTER SCIENCE

From slow beginnings, computers have developed the speed and complexity by which they process billions of pieces of information in a second and solve problems beyond practical human reach. The first computing devices were simple—beginning with the abacus, a rectangular array of beads mounted on rods, used since at least 1100 B.C. for basic arithmetic.

During the Renaissance, innovators from Leonardo da Vinci to Gottfried Leibniz and Blaise Pascal designed or built machines that could add and subtract. (Leibniz's Step Reckoner even multiplied.) But the 1800s saw the first machines that could translate programmed instructions, store information, and branch through alternative processes depending on prior outcomes. Joseph-Marie Jacquard, a French weaver, developed a loom that used punched cards to execute complicated designs. In the 1820s, Englishman Charles Babbage envisioned a steam-driven Analytical Engine that would store a thousand large numbers, decipher punch-card instructions, switch operations based on outcomes, and feed results to a printer.

Babbage's wonder was never built, but in the 1930s inventors like Howard Aiken and John Vincent Atanasoff began using vacuum tubes and electronic circuits to build increasingly powerful machines. They also experimented with expressing instructions in binary code, reducing information to 1s and 0s. That work culminated in the World War II–era development by Alan Turing of the Colossus, a code-cracking machine. In 1946, the room-size Electronic Numerical Integrator and Computer (ENIAC) became the first modern computer in operation. By 1964, integrated circuits helped move computers into the commercial world, with IBM's first mainframe office computer. A decade later, microprocessors made machines faster and smaller.

FOR MORE FACTS ON...

THE RENAISSANCE see Renaissance & Reformation 1500-1650, **CHAPTER 7, PAGES 294-5**

EARLY HUMAN METHODS OF CALCULATION see Counting & Measurement, **CHAPTER 8, PAGES 322-3**

VIRTUAL REALITY

Stroll into a retirement home and you might find a crowd gathered at the television "bowling" or "boxing." Though the movements resemble those used in sports, these players are using a hand-held device to control the movements of a character generated by Nintendo's Wii gaming system. The urge to create artificial worlds can be seen in many 20th-century experiments that used cinematic and other technologies to fool the senses. Computers allowed an even deeper immersion into artificial environments, with the development of gloves, helmets, and other devices to send information to a subject and to translate instructions back—a system of early interest to the military for its applications in flight and battle simulation. Today, virtual reality has developed along even broader lines: Products like the Wii provide a direct sensory link between human and machine, and "massively multiplayer" games like Second Life establish sophisticated on-line communities in which thousands interact through computerized avatars.

THE WORLD'S FIRST MODERN COMPUTER, ENIAC—an acronym for Electronic Numerical Integrator and Computer—required an entire room at the University of Pennsylvania. Shown here in 1946, it generated 150 kilowatts of heat and could perform a record 5,000 additions per minute.

G L O S S A R Y

Turing machine: Named for its inventor, English mathematician Alan Turing (1912–1954). A hypothetical device that consisted of a tape and reader providing input and output, a storage memory, and a central processor. **/ Boolean algebra:** Named for English mathematician George Boole (1815–1864). A system, essential to computer programming, that reduces decision-making to three operations: "and," "or," and "not."

AUGUSTA ADA BYRON / COMPUTER PROGRAMMER

Lady Byron discouraged her daughter, Augusta Ada (1815–1852), from becoming a poet like her renegade father, Lord Byron, and made sure she learned mathematics and science. The young woman became interested in the inventions of Charles Babbage, not fully appreciated by his contemporaries. Ada Byron understood that Babbage's Analytical Engine—a steam-driven mill programmed by punch cards, able to do arithmetic—could go beyond mere mechanics to mimic thought. She wrote proposals for and predictions of the machine's capabilities, including a description of how it might calculate Bernoulli numbers. For this, Ada (who, marrying, became the Countess of Lovelace) is known as the first computer programmer.

CLICK IT: Computer History Museum www.computerhistory.org

FAST FACT The IBM-developed Blue Gene/L computer at Lawrence Livermore National Laboratory in California can perform 478.2 trillion operations per second.

FOR MORE FACTS ON...

BUSINESS & COMMERCE IN THE 21ST CENTURY see *World Trade Today,* **CHAPTER 6, PAGES 256-7**
+
THE ERA OF WORLD WAR II see *World War II 1938-1945,* **CHAPTER 7, PAGES 314-5**

THE INTERNET

The "network of networks" that connects computers throughout the world has its origins in a problem that arose as the machines became more sophisticated in the 1950s: How can many users in a large organization share computational power? Programmers figured out how to break information into small packets that could be routed through different available circuits, and ever faster computers reassembled the packets more and more quickly.

The defense and airline industries first took advantage of networks in the 1950s, with the Pentagon adopting a new computer-based command and control system and American Airlines teaming with IBM on the Sabre passenger reservation system.

In 1969, the Defense Advanced Research Projects Agency (DARPA) established the Advanced Research Projects Agency Network, ARPA-NET, the precursor to today's Internet. Through ARPANET, major U.S. government and university research computers shared computing power and information. ARPANET programmers developed packet switching and other basic tools for sending messages and transferring files, such as simple mail transfer protocol (SMTP) and file transfer protocol (FTP).

In the 1970s, DARPA commissioned work on "internetting," that is, communication among computer networks. Researchers Vinton Cerf and Robert Kahn developed two important methods: the transmission control protocol (TCP), which established rules for collecting and reassembling data packets, and the Internet protocol (IP), which routed data to the correct endpoint by providing numerical addresses for interconnected machines.

In the 1980s, other government agencies and universities began tapping into the system. The National Science Foundation funded supercomputing centers at five universities, with a so-called backbone connecting them nationally. Gradually the system opened up to commercial networks, which now largely oversee a collection of regional network access points (NAPs). The exploding set of numbered addresses, meanwhile, is administered by the non-profit Internet Corporation for Assigned Names and Numbers.

As access expanded, so did ease of use. Swiss researcher Tim Berners-Lee developed hypertext transfer protocol (HTTP) in the early 1990s, which allowed various elements—graphics, imagery, and text—to be collected together into a "page" with links and references to other pages. Pages accessible through this growing World Wide Web were identified by a textual label, called a universal resource locator (URL). At the University of Illinois, Marc Andreessen developed Mosaic, the world's first Web "browser"— software by which computer users can view pages and navigate the Internet with the use of a computer mouse.

ELECTRONS ZING through nodes on a miniature circuit board at the heart of every one of the world's more than 300 million computers.

FOR MORE FACTS ON...

TODAY'S MULTINATIONAL BUSINESSES see Commerce: World Trade Today, **CHAPTER 6, PAGES 256-7**

COMPUTER TECHNOLOGY see Computer Science, **CHAPTER 8, PAGES 346-7**

NAVIGATING THE INTERNET

When you enter a website address into your computer's Internet browser, the browser launches an exchange of information with computers around the world to identify the site's numerical IP address and connect to the computer hosting it. The information flows first to a "point of presence" computer maintained by an Internet service provider (ISP)—the company that connects your home or office to the Internet. From there, it travels to a broader NAP, where networks connect to each other and to the Internet's even larger trunk, or backbone—fiber-optic lines.

Eventually the request reaches a group of computers called root servers and domain name servers; they function as the Internet's address book. Maintained by private companies and government agencies, the servers pass around the query until one of them identifies the location of the requested website and returns the

information needed to connect to it and receive images and text from it.

Although the computers involved may be spread around the globe, the process typically takes only seconds to complete.

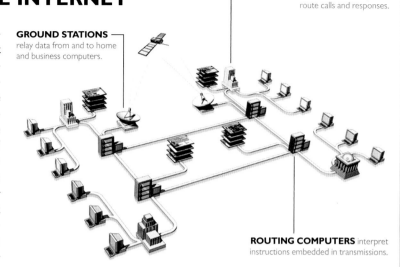

GATEWAY computers route calls and responses.

GROUND STATIONS relay data from and to home and business computers.

ROUTING COMPUTERS interpret instructions embedded in transmissions.

A TYPICAL NETWORK connects businesses, homes, universities, and government agencies. Powerful gateway computers operated by service providers connect different wide-area networks. Satellites and home lines relay data and messages between computers. Routing computers along the way decode instructions on the transmissions that tell how and where to send the messages.

CLICK IT: Internet Past and Future www.elon.edu/predictions

FAST FACT In 1996, 45 million people used the Internet worldwide. By 2008, as many as 1.4 billion used it.

VINTON CERF & ROBERT KAHN / INTERNET INVENTORS

As a student at UCLA in the 1960s, Vinton Cerf (b. 1943) employed the concept of packet switching to create the communication system for ARPANET, allowing government and university research computers a way to talk to each other. In the early 1970s, electrical engineer Robert Kahn (b. 1938) recruited Cerf to further government work at the Information Techniques Program Office, where Kahn was working on what was conceived of as a "network of networks." Together, they laid the foundation for the Internet, creating the TCP/IP that helped ensure packets of information were properly disassembled and reassembled in the correct location. Cerf in particular pushed for public access to the Internet, helping MCI develop the first commercial e-mail service and working with nonprofits involved with information and Internet policy.

FOR MORE FACTS ON...

NATURAL SATELLITES see Moons, **CHAPTER 2, PAGES 64-5**

CONNECTIONS BETWEEN THE WORLD'S COUNTRIES TODAY see Nations & Alliances, **CHAPTER 9, PAGES 358-9**

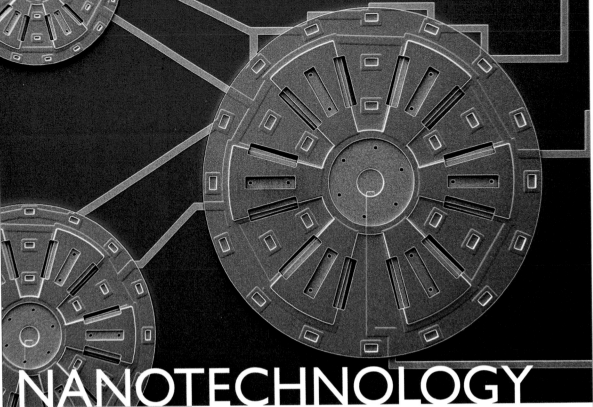

A micro-electro-mechanical (MEMS) valve device

NANOTECHNOLOGY

FOR COMPARISON

1 NANOMETER (NM) =
One-billionth of a meter

6 BONDED CARBON ATOMS =
1 nm in width

THE HEAD OF A PIN =
1 million nm across

1 INCH = 25,400,000 nm

1 RED BLOOD CELL =
Approx. 7,000 nm in width
and 2,000 nm in height

1 VIRUS =
Approx. 100 nm in diameter

The pure gold in a wedding band creates a symbol of permanence and stability. But medieval artisans knew that mixing super-small amounts of glass with gold could create different colors and effects. Their work is considered a primitive application of nanotechnology—the art of manipulating matter a few atoms at a time. Nanotechnology works on an almost unimaginably small dimension, using the nanometer, a billionth of a meter, as a basic measurement.

Substances often act differently on an atomic scale than they do in larger quantities, when fewer atoms are at the surface of the overall structure and the forces of Newtonian physics come to dominate. At the atomic level, magnetic and other properties can be exaggerated, bonds among atoms are stronger, and catalytic reactions become more dynamic.

Nanotechnologists precisely engineer small groups of atoms and then assemble those groups into larger structures. They foresee the treatment of tumors or genetic malignancies with "molecular machines" that root

FOR MORE FACTS ON...

THE CHEMICAL COMPOSITION OF PLANET EARTH see *Earth's Elements*, **CHAPTER 3, PAGES 90-1**

ENGINEERING ACCOMPLISHMENTS PAST & PRESENT see *Engineering*, **CHAPTER 8, PAGES 332-3**

out bad cells or viral DNA sequences. Researchers at MIT found that after severing the optic nerve of hamsters, an injection of nanoparticle peptides created a scaffold that allowed the severed nerve to regenerate and sight to be recovered. Already, filters made with nanoscale particles are being used to purify drinking water.

The techniques used to manipulate materials at the nanoscale are not that different, conceptually, from those involved in everyday manufacturing. Advances in microprocessor production—the creation of thousands of circuits on silicon wafers through optical lithography, or etching with light—already allows engineers to work at a scale of less than 100 nanometers. It may allow even smaller scale work if more intense light or x-rays are used.

Other nanotechniques rely on small-scale chemical or physical processes to let material build up an atom at a time. The way materials attract or repel each other at the atomic scale—perhaps in the presence of a magnet or an electric current—allows researchers to grow carbon nanotubes, for example, or quantum dots, which may prove useful in a variety of applications.

In 2006, products incorporating nanotechnology generated $50 billion in sales. Some project that the global market for nanotechnology will reach over $3 trillion by 2015.

THANKS TO TINY MEMS—micro-electro-mechanical systems—laser scanners read bar codes 40 times faster.

G L O S S A R Y

Nanoparticle: From Greek *nanos*, "dwarf." Matter at the scale of atoms or groups of atoms, measured in nanometers, or billionths of a meter. **/ Dendrimer:** From Greek *dendros* + *meros*, "tree" + "part." Artificially made molecule, long and thin with a hollow core, with promise of many applications, including delivery of drugs to a specific part of the body—a tumor site, for example.

HEAD OF A PIN?

Quantum physicist Richard P. Feynman gave the world a glimpse of (small) things to come when in a 1959 lecture he proposed inscribing the *Encyclopedia Britannica* on the head of a pin.

A typical copy of the encyclopedia covered an area about 25,000 times as large as a pinhead. Reducing the size by that amount would still allow letters and pictures to be constructed out of dots about 32 atoms wide—small, to be sure, but in Feynman's view, not insubstantial.

Today's nanotechnologists have created tools to work on an even smaller scale. Using a tool like a small, rapidly vibrating quartz tuning fork, IBM scientists recently calculated how much push it takes to move an atom of cobalt over a surface of copper: 17 piconewtons, about two-billionths the force needed to lift a penny.

WITH A MINUTE TIP made of ceramic or silicon, an atomic force microscope probes atoms, allowing nanotechnologists to study the structure of phenomena such as corrosion.

CLICK IT: Nanotechnology Now www.nanotech-now.com

FAST FACT Human fingernails grow at a rate of one nanometer per second.

FOR MORE FACTS ON...

THE PHYSICS OF ATOMS & SUBATOMIC PARTICLES *see Physics*, CHAPTER 8, PAGES 330-1

+

ENGINEERING FULLERENE, A 60-ATOM MOLECULE *see Chemistry*, CHAPTER 8, PAGES 334-5

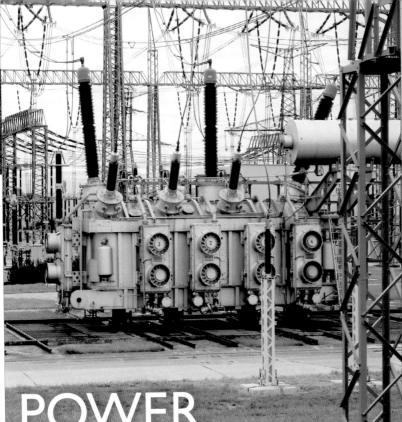

ENERGY USE
ANNUAL USE;
UNITS = ONE MILLION TONS OF OIL

AUSTRALIA & OCEANIA / 182.9
1.7% of world total

AFRICA / 344.4
3.1% of world total

SOUTH & CENTRAL AMERICA / 552.9
5.0% of world total

NORTH AMERICA / 2838.6
25.6% of world total

EUROPE / 2840.8
25.6% of world total

ASIA / 4339.8
39.0% of world total

POWER

ower involves converting one form of energy into another. That conversion is constantly under way: Energy from the sun is harnessed by plants through photosynthesis, and our bodies convert energy-rich carbohydrates into motion. Since prehistory, people have tapped outside sources of power, such as draft animals, to enable them to do more work. The first non-animal power source may have been fire, with which burning wood or waste was translated into heat for warmth and cooking.

The earliest evidence of mechanized power production dates from the first century B.C., in Greece, with the use of waterwheels. Capturing the gravity-generated force of water rushing down a stream (or on the surging tide), waterwheels powered industry for centuries, grinding meal, sawing logs, weaving cloth, operating pumps, and driving the bellows in forges and furnaces.

In the mountainous region between Iran and Afghanistan, a different form of energy conversion took root: the windmill, designed to turn the force of the wind into mechanical work. Arabic writings in the ninth century A.D. referred to Persian millers who had fixed horizontal sails to a vertical shaft to turn a millstone.

These early sources of power were all sustainable: They converted power into energy without consuming the original resource. But they were also limited geographically, operational only in places with a steady flow of water or a steady wind, and unpredictable to the extent that seasonal weather changes could determine available power.

FAST FACT The world's largest hydroelectric dam is the Itaipu dam on the Paraná River of Brazil and Paraguay.

FOR MORE FACTS ON...

HOW DAMS GENERATE ELECTRICITY see Water: Lakes, **CHAPTER 3, PAGE 119**

PHOTOSYNTHESIS & HOW PLANTS USE SOLAR ENERGY see Life Begins, **CHAPTER 4, PAGE 131**

With the coal-burning steam engines and harnessed electricity that made possible the industrial revolution, humankind entered the era of nonrenewable resources. The focus shifted to thermal energy and the force of combustion, whether by generated steam driving engines and turbines or by contained explosions driving internal combustion engines.

Today large hydroelectric plants are used to turn massive turbines. But there are environmental limitations to such projects, since they require blocking the natural course of rivers and flooding large tracts of land. The effects of China's mammoth Three Gorges Dam across the Yangtze River, for example, are yet to be seen. The largest hydroelectric project in the world, it will provide one-ninth of all the electricity used in China. Its excavation displaced 1.4 million people, and the project is now blamed for increased soil erosion, pollution, and other problems both upstream and down.

CLICK IT: Green Guide www.thegreenguide.com

POWER THROUGH THE AGES

Humans may have used fire as early as 1,420,000 B.C., but not until the Neolithic era, 7000 B.C., did we learn to create friction and kindle a blaze. That development allowed the clearing of land and the creation of fertilizer ash for agriculture; it also promoted advances in material and metalworking as humans learned how to fire clay into pottery and mold iron into tools.

Water has provided power for many centuries as well. Once Michael Faraday showed that a magnet rotating around a wire coil generated electricity, water went from being a direct source of mechanical power to the force driving mammoth turbines to generate electrical power.

The first significant use of hydroelectric power came in 1880, when a turbine powered lamps at a Michigan chair factory. Hydroelectric power accounted for roughly 40 percent of the U.S.'s electricity in the early 1900s.

DAMS GENERATE ELECTRICITY by training moving water across turbine blades. Hydroelectric power plants produce nearly 20 percent of all electricity used around the world today. Arizona's Glen Canyon Dam (above) turns a 15-million-gallon-a-minute flow into 1.3 million kilowatts of electricity.

COOLING TOWERS rise above the coal-powered Drax Power Station near Selby, England. While environmentalists decry the carbon emissions produced by coal-burning power plants, countries around the world are building them in numbers: More than 500 new coal-fired generating plants were built between 2002 and 2006 worldwide.

POWER TODAY

Petroleum products represent the most prevalent power source used in the world today.

Natural gas is growing in its use around the world as a source of power for generating electricity. It is favored because it emits less sulfur dioxide, carbon dioxide, and particulates than oil when burned.

Coal, which has long been the primary combustible for energy generation in the Western world, is now growing in use throughout developing countries of Asia. China and the U.S. are the world's dominant coal consumers.

Nuclear energy accounts for the smallest portion of the world's power generation, owing to the high cost of building plants and troubling safety and waste issues.

· FOR MORE FACTS ON...

THE CONSEQUENCES OF POLLUTION see *Threatened Planet: Air*, **CHAPTER 3, PAGES 124-5**

THE INDUSTRIAL REVOLUTION see *The Industrial Revolution 1765-1900*, **CHAPTER 7, PAGES 302-3**

ALTERNATIVE TECHNOLOGIES

Though still small, contributors to the world's electrical grid, wind, geothermal, biomass, solar, and fuel cell technologies may nonetheless represent the power of the future, given the economic, geo-political, and environmental costs of power generation in operation today.

Wind power has been used for centuries, but instead of turning mill-stones it now involves large, fanlike blades geared to turn turbines. Wind farms, concentrated installations of power-generating wind turbines, have found their most extensive use in Cali-fornia. Wind power plants operate in northern Europe, Saudi Arabia, and India, and more have been proposed for the U.S., offshore on the Atlantic coast and on the midwestern plains.

Geothermal systems tap Earth's underground heat. Like sunlight, this is a free and limitless resource, but one that for large-scale use requires the user to be near an area where volcanic activity or radioactive decay is producing heat close enough to the surface to be used efficiently. Single dwellings can benefit from geothermal heat just by conscientious design.

Biomass fuels are typically distilled from corn, sugarcane, or other plants high in sugar. They have recently gained popularity, but the local and global economic effects of redirecting agricultural production for fuel rather than food raises concerns, as does the amount of fossil fuels used to grow such crops.

Solar energy reaches Earth at a rate about 200,000 times the daily capacity of existing power plants, and available technology harnesses it for heat or electricity. Solar pan-els work by absorbing heat from the sun and transferring it into circulat-ing fluid. Photovoltaic cells made of silicon, boron, and other substances convert sunlight into electricity. As with geothermal energy, individual buildings can be designed to benefit from the sun's heat without com-plex equipment, a technique called passive solar.

Fuel cell technologies hold great promise. Research agencies, private companies, and the world's major au-tomobile manufacturers are exploring these new ways of converting chemical energy directly to electricity, possibly providing a battery-operated alterna-tive to the conventional automobile.

WIND AND SUNLIGHT are free—and, in many parts of the world, abundant—sources of energy that can be captured by new technologies and transformed into electricity. Denmark's Horns Rev wind farm (left) generates power with 80 offshore windmills. A solar park in Leipzig, Germany (right), the world's largest, uses more than 30,000 photovoltaic modules to generate electricity for about 1,800 households.

CLICK IT: Alternative Energy News www.alternative-energy-news.info

FOR MORE FACTS ON...

THE SUN & THE ENERGY IT GENERATES see The Sun, **CHAPTER 2, PAGES 54-7**

CATEGORIES & CHARACTERISTICS OF THE WINDS ON PLANET EARTH see Wind, **CHAPTER 3, PAGES 106-7**

WHAT IS GEOTHERMAL ENERGY?

BATHERS LUXURIATE in the geothermal spa of the Blue Lagoon in Grindavík, Iceland.

Temperatures at the center of the Earth may reach as high as 7000°F. That energy radiates out in the form of underground hot springs, volcanoes, geysers, fumaroles, and other geologic phenomena, and it has become an important source of power in more than 20 countries of the world, including New Zealand, Japan, Iceland, Mexico, and the United States.

The oldest modern geothermal power system was built in Larderello, Italy, in 1904, and it still operates today. Reykjavík, Iceland, uses geothermal energy for district heating in the city, which has significantly cut back on pollution. The first U.S. city to install geothermal district heating was Boise, Idaho. The world's largest geothermal development is the Geysers, north of San Francisco, a complex of 22 power plants that serves 725,000 homes.

Major geothermal plants are limited to sites where sources of underground heat are intense and shallow enough to be tapped economically. By contrast, geothermal heat pumps take advantage of the Earth's relatively constant temperature even ten feet belowground—a way to produce air that is, relative to the surface, cooler in the summer and warmer in the winter.

G L O S S A R Y

Fuel cell: A device that converts a fuel's chemical energy into electricity. **/ Photovoltaic:** From the Greek *photos*, "light" + the English *volt*, a unit of energy named for Alessandro Volta (1745–1827), an Italian physicist. A device that converts energy from sunlight into electricity.

ETHANOL OR GOBAR? CHOOSE YOUR FUEL

Since the late 1970s—following two oil embargoes—autos and trucks in the U.S. have been able to burn a mixture of gas and up to 10 percent ethanol, a combustible fuel manufactured from sugar-rich agricultural products like corn. As oil prices escalated, U.S. ethanol production tripled between 2000 and 2006, to an estimated 5.4 billion gallons, surpassing Brazil's production of sugarcane-based ethanol.

An alternative to fossil fuel, corn-based ethanol has problems of its own—evident in rising food prices, concerns about land use, and controversy over the amount of fuel, fertilizer, and other resources used in the growing process. Cellulosic ethanol, derived from scrub grasses and waste products with high cellulose content, has been advocated as an alternative to the alternative.

GOBAR, COW DUNG IN HINDI, may be the fuel of the future. When sealed in an airtight chamber, bacteria present in fecal matter break down the waste, releasing a refineable gas that is about 70 percent methane. The remaining solids serve as fertilizer. Gobar power also reduces the need to burn wood, leaving trees to absorb carbon dioxide.

FAST FACT The United States is the world's largest producer of geothermal power. About 90 percent of it comes from California's 33 geothermal plants.

FOR MORE FACTS ON...

THE IMPACT OF HUMAN CIVILIZATION ON EARTH see *Human Impact,* **CHAPTER 5, PAGES 214-5**
+
THE FUTURE OF AGRICULTURE see *Agriculture: Modern,* **CHAPTER 6, PAGES 248-9**

COUNTRIES

of the WORLD

ina / Armenia / Australia / Austria / Azerbaijan / Bahamas / Bahrain / Bangladesh
Herzegovina / Botswana / Brazil / Brunei / Bulgaria / Burkina Faso / Burundi
Chile / China / Colombia / Comoros / Congo / Costa Rica / Côte d'Ivoire
o / Denmark / Djibouti / Dominica / Dominican Republic / Ecuador / Egypt
France / Gabon / Gambia / Georgia / Germany / Ghana / Greece / Grenada
celand / India / Indonesia / Iran / Iraq / Ireland / Israel / Italy / Jamaica / Japan
ia / Lebanon / Lesotho / Liberia / Libya / Liechtenstein / Lithuania / Luxembourg
hall Islands / Mauritania / Mauritius / Mexico / Micronesia / Moldova / Monaco
epal / Netherlands / New Zealand / Nicaragua / Niger / Nigeria / North Korea
Peru / Philippines / Poland / Portugal / Qatar / Romania / Russia / Rwanda
an Marino / São Tomé and Príncipe / Saudi Arabia / Senegal / Serbia / Seychelles
frica / South Korea / Spain / Sri Lanka / Sudan / Suriname / Swaziland / Sweden
rinidad and Tobago / Tunisia / Turkey / Turkmenistan / Tuvalu / Uganda / Ukraine
Vanuatu / Vatican City / Venezuela / Vietnam / Yemen / Zambia / Zimbabwe

United Nations headquarters, New York

NATIONS & ALLIANCES

INTERNATIONAL ALLIANCES

North Atlantic Treaty Organization
(NATO)
Formed in 1949

European Union
(EU)
Originated in 1950

Organization of the Petroleum Exporting Countries
(OPEC)
Formed in 1960

Organisation for Economic Co-operation and Development
(OECD)
Formed in 1961

Association of Southeast Asian Nations
(ASEAN)
Formed in 1967

Boundaries that have demarcated the world for centuries are shifting, even vanishing. Globalization—the international integration of governments, companies, and peoples—is occurring in economic, social, and political spheres. Nowhere is it seen more than in the European Union, an international organization of 27 individual countries that began in the 1950s as a free trade area among 6 of those. Now it has evolved with the goal of furthering European political and economic integration.

The Maastricht Treaty in 1992 marked the beginning of today's European Union (EU). This treaty presented an agenda for the incorporation of a unified European currency, the euro. Initially reserved for financial markets and businesses, the euro was introduced for public use in 2002.

EU members also agreed to seek unified foreign and security policies and to find ways to eliminate border controls among members. While individual members retain veto rights in areas such as taxation, Europe has achieved an unprecedented level of international integration.

IS IT A NATION, A STATE, OR A COUNTRY?

What distinguishes a nation from a state or a country?

The most formal of the three words, "state" refers to a place with a unified political identity. A state is an independent political unit, able to claim its own jurisdiction over a defined territory. A state is recognized by the rest of the world as legally able to control the affairs of its land and people.

A "nation" does not depend on location or political identity. It is a distinct society of people dedicated to a region. Generally, a nation is an ethnic group that shares a distinctive language, religion, and history.

The word "country" conveys power and identity but is used less formally and, of the three terms, most commonly. A country can consist entirely of one nation of people, but more often than not, multiple nations coexist within one state or country. While a nation may abide by its own legal procedures, its decisions hold no broader validity unless granted by surrounding states.

The world's changing perception of boundaries includes an increasing number of international alliances despite the cornucopia of countries, cultures, and languages scattered across the globe. Some are casual, while others represent official political stances. In all cases, the parties involved are generally dedicated to a common cause. Examples include the Association of Southeast Asian Nations, formed in 1967; the Organisation for Economic Co-operation and Development, a 1961 expansion of the Organisation for European Economic Co-operation; and NATO, the North Atlantic Treaty Organization, which dates back to 1949.

THE UN GENERAL ASSEMBLY includes all 192 member states, each with one vote. They meet from September to December.

WHAT ABOUT ANTARCTICA?

Antarctica's identity has long been under debate. It is a large mass of land that does not lie within the boundaries of any other continent—since it is itself a continent—nor does it function as the dependency of any other single state. It does not exist as an independent country; it does not have native inhabitants. So what is Antarctica, and who governs it? In the late 1950s, 12 countries with a significant research and exploration presence there took part in a conference of diplomacy. The resulting Antarctic Treaty, which came into force in 1961, was originally ratified by those 12 countries, representing all six inhabited continents: Argentina, Australia, Belgium, Chile, France, Japan, New Zealand, Norway, South Africa, the Soviet Union (now Russia), the United Kingdom, and the United States. Since that time, 33 more states have joined by demonstrating scientific interest and activity in the region. According to the treaty, no state holds sovereignty in Antarctica. Military bases and maneuvers are not allowed; scientific exploration and collaboration are encouraged. So far, the treaty stands as a shining example of long-term international cooperation, and it will persist as long as those involved allow.

TUNISIA
p. 363

p. 362 MOROCCO

Western
Sahara
(Morocco)

ALGERIA
p. 363

LIBYA
p. 362

EGYPT
p. 364

SENEGAL
p. 368

MAURITANIA
p. 363

MALI
p. 363

NIGER
p. 364

CHAD
p. 364

SUDAN
p. 364

ERITREA
p. 365

CAPE
VERDE
p. 366

GAMBIA
p. 368

GUINEA-
BISSAU
p. 368

GUINEA
p. 368

BURKINA
FASO
p. 370

NIGERIA
p. 372

DJIBOUTI
p. 365

ETHIOPIA
p. 365

SIERRA
LEONE
p. 370

COTE
D'IVOIRE
p. 370

GHANA
p. 371

BENIN
p. 372

CAMEROON
p. 373

CENTRAL
AFRICAN REPUBLIC
p. 366

SOMALIA

p. 365

LIBERIA
p. 370

TOGO
p. 371

EQUATORIAL GUINEA
p. 372

UGANDA
p. 367

KENYA
p. 369

SAO TOME
AND PRINCIPE
p. 372

GABON
p. 373

DEMOCRATIC

REPUBLIC

OF THE

CONGO
p. 366

RWANDA
p. 367

BURUNDI
p. 367

p. 366

Cabinda
(Angola)

CONGO

TANZANIA
p. 373

SEYCHELLES
p. 373

MALAWI
p. 374

COMOROS
p. 375

ANGOLA
p. 374

ZAMBIA
p. 374

MAP KEY

LIBERIA   Country name and page number
p. 370   where country facts can be found

ZIMBABWE
p. 374

MOZAMBIQUE

p. 375

MADAGASCAR

p. 376

MAUR
p. 376

NAMIBIA
p. 376

BOTSWANA
p. 376

SWAZILAND
p. 377

SOUTH
AFRICA
p. 377

LESOTHO
p. 377

AFRICA

Second largest continent after Asia, Africa accounts for a fifth of the world's land surface. Bulging to the west and surrounded by oceans and seas, Africa can be considered underpopulated because despite its size, only slightly more than 10 percent of the world's population lives here.

Stretching 5,000 miles from north to south and 4,600 miles from east to west, Africa rises from narrow coastal strips to form a gigantic plateau. Its coastline has limited harbors and few bays and inlets. Though formed by a series of expansive uplands, Africa has few true mountain chains. To the southeast, the Ethiopian highlands form a broad area of high topography. Perpetual ice and snow crown Mount Kilimanjaro, the continent's highest point at 19,340 feet.

The East African Rift System is the continent's most dramatic geologic feature. This great rent begins in the Red Sea and then cuts southward to form a stunning landscapes of lakes, volcanoes, and deep valleys. The Great Rift Valley, a region of active plate tectonics, marks the divide where East Africa is being pulled away.

Dividing the continent, the Sahara covers more than a quarter of Africa's surface. Watered regions of lakes and rivers lie south of the Sahel, a vast semi-arid zone of short grasses that spans the continent south of the Sahara. Most of Africa is savanna—

high, rolling, grassy plains. The Great Escarpment in southern Africa, a plateau that falls off to the coastal strip, is best represented by the stark, highly eroded Drakensberg Range, which reaches altitudes over 11,400 feet.

Madagascar, fourth largest island in the world, lies east of the main continent and is remarkable for its flora and fauna, including medicinal plants and lemur species.

Africa's great rivers include the Niger, Congo, and Zambezi, each regionally important for internal transport and fishing. The Nile, the world's longest river, originates south of the Equator and flows north-northeast before finally delivering its life-giving waters into the Mediterranean. Wildlife still abounds in eastern and southern Africa, but hundreds of plant and animal species live precariously close to extinction.

THE HUMAN FOOTPRINT

IN 1987 MOLECULAR BIOLOGIST Rebecca Cann introduced her revolutionary findings on genetic lineages around the world. Her work suggested that all humans share a common ancestor, known as Mitochondrial Eve, a hypothetical human who lived in sub-Saharan Africa. / Archaeological and genetic evidence suggest the first hunter-gatherers left their sub-Saharan homeland for the East African savanna and, in times of drastic climate fluctuation, migrated to the coast. Meanwhile, distant inland populations were probably struggling in East and central Africa to survive on the changing savannas. / The analysis of DNA from populations in North Africa and the Middle East confirms that when the climate shifted, our ancestors headed for greener pastures. The first modern humans migrated northward before the Sahara expanded. The genetic lineages of these Paleolithic hunter-gatherers survive today in some North African populations.

WIND SCULPTS GRACEFUL ARABESQUES in the distinctively red sand of the dunes of Erq Bourarhet in Algeria's Sahara. This region, also called the Tiguentourine Erg, stretches south to the border with Libya. Hard to pinpoint, the boundary is the archetypal line drawn in the sand.

MOROCCO

KINGDOM OF MOROCCO

AREA 274,461 SQ. MI. ▮ POPULATION 34,859,000 ▮ CAPITAL RABAT (POP. 1,793,000) ▮ LITERACY 52% ▮ LIFE EXPECTANCY 72 ▮ CURRENCY MOROCCAN DIRHAM ▮ GDP PER CAPITA $4,000 ▮ ECONOMY IND: PHOSPHATE ROCK MINING & PROCESSING, FOOD PROCESSING, LEATHER GOODS, TEXTILES. AGR: BARLEY, WHEAT, CITRUS, WINE, LIVESTOCK. EXP: CLOTHING, FISH, INORGANIC CHEMICALS, TRANSISTORS, CRUDE MINERALS, FERTILIZERS.

Dominated by the Atlas Mountains, which separate fertile coastal regions from the Sahara, Morocco is primarily a nation of farmers, although most Moroccans live in coastal cities.

Drought, unemployment, disputes over the phosphate-rich Western Sahara: All have taxed the country. Sporadic warfare continues between the Moroccan Army and the Algerian-backed Polisario (the Western Sahara independence movement). Morocco is one of three kingdoms left on the continent, the other two being Lesotho and Swaziland, smaller countries in the south.

LIBYA

GREAT SOCIALIST PEOPLE'S LIBYAN ARAB JAMAHIRIYA

AREA 679,362 SQ. MI. ▮ POPULATION 6,310,434 ▮ CAPITAL TRIPOLI (POP. 2,327,000) ▮ LITERACY 83% ▮ LIFE EXPECTANCY 77 ▮ CURRENCY LIBYAN DINAR ▮ GDP PER CAPITA $14,400 ▮ ECONOMY IND: PETROLEUM, FOOD PROCESSING, TEXTILES, HANDICRAFTS, CEMENT. AGR: WHEAT, BARLEY, OLIVES, DATES, CATTLE. EXP: CRUDE OIL, REFINED PETROLEUM PRODUCTS.

Water-poor, oil-rich Libya has the highest per capita income of continental Africa. Most Libyans live on the Mediterranean coast. The largest water development project ever devised, the Great Man-Made River Project, brings water from aquifers under the Sahara to the coastal cities. Since 1969 this former Italian colony, independent since 1951, has been an authoritarian socialist state under Muammar Qaddafi—whose backing of terrorism led to a U.S. bombing in 1986 and UN sanctions in 1992. In 2011, anti-Qaddafi forces rebelled and a NATO-led, UN-sanctioned coalition sought to protect civilians during the strife.

ALGERIA

PEOPLE'S DEMOCRATIC REPUBLIC OF ALGERIA

AREA 919,595 SQ. MI. ▊ POPULATION 34,178,000 ▊ CAPITAL ALGIERS (POP. 3,574,000) ▊ LITERACY 70% ▊ LIFE EXPECTANCY 74 ▊ CURRENCY ALGERIAN DINAR ▊ GDP PER CAPITA $7,000 ▊ ECONOMY IND: PETROLEUM, NATURAL GAS, LIGHT INDUSTRIES, MINING. AGR: WHEAT, BARLEY, OATS, GRAPES, SHEEP. EXP: PETROLEUM, NATURAL GAS, PETROLEUM PRODUCTS.

Algeria, on the Mediterranean coast, is the second largest African country. The Sahara covers more than four-fifths of its territory, and in its desert region, inhabitants concentrate in scattered oases. More than 90 percent of Algerians live along the coast. The northern slopes of the Atlas Mountains, which cross Algeria east to west along the coast, receive good winter rainfall.

Independence from France was achieved in 1962. A socialist-style, military-dominated government pinned its hopes on huge oil and natural gas reserves in the Algerian Sahara. But low petroleum prices, a high birthrate, and austere policies produced an economic crisis, prompting many Algerians to emigrate. Since 1991 Algerian politics have been dominated by violence between the military and Islamic militants.

TUNISIA

TUNISIAN REPUBLIC

AREA 63,170 SQ. MI. ▊ POPULATION 10,486,000 ▊ CAPITAL TUNIS (POP. 1,996,000) ▊ LITERACY 74% ▊ LIFE EXPECTANCY 76 ▊ CURRENCY TUNISIAN DINAR ▊ GDP PER CAPITA $7,900 ▊ ECONOMY IND: PETROLEUM, MINING, TOURISM, TEXTILES, FOOTWEAR. AGR: OLIVES, GRAIN, DAIRY. EXP: TEXTILES, MECHANICAL GOODS, PHOSPHATES & CHEMICALS, AGRICULTURAL PRODUCTS.

Gaining independence in 1956 after 75 years under France, this North African nation was ruled by President for Life Habib Bourguiba until his ouster in 1987. Political and economic reforms have since pulled Tunisia from collapse. The fluctuating economy is based on agriculture, as well as phosphates and petroleum. Its sunny Mediterranean coast and the nation's ancient history, preserved at Carthage, make for a robust tourist industry.

MAURITANIA

ISLAMIC REPUBLIC OF MAURITANIA

AREA 397,955 SQ. MI. ▊ POPULATION 3,129,000 ▊ CAPITAL NOUAKCHOTT (POP. 600,000) ▊ LITERACY 60% ▊ LIFE EXPECTANCY 54 ▊ CURRENCY OUGUIYA ▊ GDP PER CAPITA $2,100 ▊ ECONOMY IND: FISH PROCESSING, MINING OF IRON ORE & GYPSUM. AGR: DATES, MILLET, SORGHUM, RICE. CATTLE. EXP: IRON ORE, FISH & FISH PRODUCTS, GOLD.

Part of French West Africa until gaining independence in 1960, Mauritania is influenced by Arab and African cultures. Horticulture is largely confined to the Sénégal River's floodplain, straining relations with the country of Senegal over use of the river. Some of the world's richest fishing grounds lie off the coast.

The population is still largely dependent on agriculture and livestock, even though recurring droughts have forced most nomads and many subsistence farmers into the cities. Further strains are the result of internal racial divisions between blacks and Arabs.

MALI

REPUBLIC OF MALI

AREA 478,841 SQ. MI. ▊ POPULATION 12,667,000 ▊ CAPITAL BAMAKO (POP. 1,708,000) ▊ LITERACY 46% ▊ LIFE EXPECTANCY 50 ▊ CURRENCY CFA FRANC ▊ GDP PER CAPITA $1,200 ▊ ECONOMY IND: FOOD PROCESSING, CONSTRUCTION, PHOSPHATE, GOLD MINING. AGR: COTTON, MILLET, RICE, CORN, CATTLE. EXP: GOLD.

The landlocked West African country of Mali is mostly desert or semidesert. Trans-Saharan caravans once enriched Timbuktu and Gao, trading hubs on the Niger River. About 90 percent of the population is Muslim.

Mali's inhabitants—descendants of the empires of Ghana, Malinke, and Songhai—came under French rule in the late 19th century and gained independence in 1960. In the 1980s economic woes worsened by drought and famine led to deregulation and privatization. Desertification forces nomadic herders south to the subsistence farming belt. With increased gold mining operations, Mali is becoming a major gold exporter.

NIGER

REPUBLIC OF NIGER

AREA 489,191 SQ. MI. ▮ POPULATION 15,306,000 ▮ CAPITAL NIAMEY (POP. 1,027,000) ▮ LITERACY 29% ▮ LIFE EXPECTANCY 53 ▮ CURRENCY CFA FRANC ▮ GDP PER CAPITA $700 ▮ ECONOMY IND: URANIUM MINING, CEMENT, BRICK, TEXTILES. AGR: COWPEAS, COTTON, PEANUTS, MILLET, CATTLE. EXP: URANIUM ORE, LIVESTOCK, COWPEAS, ONIONS.

Landlocked in western Africa, Niger uses the Niger River as a link to the sea. Most people live in the southern savanna; the north is all Sahara. While free elections have restored democracy, falling world demand for Niger's valuable uranium has exacerbated economic problems. At the mercy of drought and desertification, Niger relies on foreign aid.

CHAD

REPUBLIC OF CHAD

AREA 495,755 SQ. MI. ▮ POPULATION 10,329,000 ▮ CAPITAL N'DJAMENA (POP. 1,127,000) ▮ LITERACY 26% ▮ LIFE EXPECTANCY 48 ▮ CURRENCY CFA FRANC ▮ GDP PER CAPITA $1,600 ▮ ECONOMY IND: OIL, COTTON TEXTILES, MEAT PACKING, BEER BREWING, NATRON (SODIUM CARBONATE). AGR: COTTON, SORGHUM, MILLET, PEANUTS, CATTLE. EXP: COTTON, CATTLE, GUM ARABIC.

Landlocked Chad contains fertile lowlands in the south and arid land and desert in the north. Chad suffers from tensions between the African-Christian south and the Arab-Muslim north and east. A border dispute with Libya went to the United Nations' International Court of Justice; the court ruled in favor of Chad. The start of large-scale oil production in 2004 helped the economy of Chad, one of Africa's poorest countries.

A REBEL FIGHTER watches the village of Chero Kasi burn, set ablaze by Janjaweed militiamen in Darfur, Sudan, in September 2004.

EGYPT

ARAB REPUBLIC OF EGYPT

AREA 386,874 SQ. MI. ▮ POPULATION 83,083,000 ▮ CAPITAL CAIRO (POP. 12,503,000) ▮ LITERACY 71% ▮ LIFE EXPECTANCY 72 ▮ CURRENCY EGYPTIAN POUND ▮ GDP PER CAPITA $5,400 ▮ ECONOMY IND: TEXTILES, FOOD PROCESSING, TOURISM, CHEMICALS. AGR: COTTON, RICE, CORN, WHEAT, CATTLE. EXP: CRUDE OIL & PETROLEUM PRODUCTS, COTTON, TEXTILES, CHEMICALS.

Located in northeast Africa, Egypt controls the Suez Canal, the shortest sea link between the Indian Ocean and the Mediterranean Sea. The country is defined by the Nile, which flows out of central Africa to the Mediterranean, and by desert: a mountainous desert to the east, dry desert to the west, and the vast Sahara to the south. About 95 percent of Egyptians live along the Nile, on less than 5 percent of Egypt's land. Most are Muslim Arabs, but there is a sizable Coptic Christian population. An ally of the West, the government is democratic but authoritarian, seeking to control Islamism and political dissent.

SUDAN

REPUBLIC OF THE SUDAN (SOUTH SUDAN)

AREA 967,500 SQ. MI. ▮ POPULATION 41,088,000 ▮ CAPITAL KHARTOUM (POP. 5,185,000) ▮ LITERACY 61% ▮ LIFE EXPECTANCY 51 ▮ CURRENCY SUDANESE DINAR ▮ GDP PER CAPITA $2,500 ▮ ECONOMY IND: OIL, COTTON GINNING, TEXTILES, CEMENT, EDIBLE OILS, SUGAR, SOAP DISTILLING, SHOES, PETROLEUM, REFINING. AGR: COTTON, GROUNDNUTS (PEANUTS), SORGHUM, MILLET, WHEAT, SHEEP. EXP: OIL & PETROLEUM PRODUCTS, COTTON, SESAME, LIVESTOCK, GROUNDNUTS.

Sudan is dominated by the Nile. Mountains rise along Sudan's Red Sea coast and its western border with Chad. Muslim Arabs, 39 percent of the population, control the government. Africans make up 52 percent. Sudan's government has functioned as a military dictatorship since the 1989 military coup led by Omar al-Bashir. UN peacekeeping troops have struggled to stabilize the Darfur region. Civil war has continued, heightened by the discovery of oil fields in the south, and in 2011 the Republic of South Sudan separated as an independent country.

 # ETHIOPIA

FEDERAL DEMOCRATIC REPUBLIC OF ETHIOPIA

AREA 437,600 SQ. MI. ▮ POPULATION 85,237,000 ▮ CAPITAL ADDIS ABABA (POP. 3,453,000) ▮ LITERACY 43% ▮ LIFE EXPECTANCY 55 ▮ CURRENCY BIRR ▮ GDP PER CAPITA $800 ▮ ECONOMY IND: FOOD PROCESSING, BEVERAGES, TEXTILES, CHEMICALS. AGR: CEREALS, PULSES, COFFEE, OILSEED, CATTLE, HIDES. EXP: COFFEE, QAT, GOLD, LEATHER PRODUCTS, LIVE ANIMALS, OILSEEDS.

Ethiopia is a landlocked country in northeastern Africa. It has a high central plateau split diagonally by the Great Rift Valley. The western highlands get summer rainfall; the lowlands and eastern highlands are hot and dry. Most people live in the western highlands, where the capital, Addis Ababa, is located. The population is almost evenly split between Christians and Muslims.

Most Ethiopians are farmers and herders, but deforestation, drought, and soil degradation have caused crop failures and famine. A 30-year civil war between the government and rebel forces aligned with Eritrean nationalists ended in 1991, and in 1993 Eritrea became independent, cutting off Ethiopia's access to the Red Sea.

 # SOMALIA

SOMALIA

AREA 246,201 SQ. MI. ▮ POPULATION 9,832,000 ▮ CAPITAL MOGADISHU (POP. 1,500,000) ▮ LITERACY 38% ▮ LIFE EXPECTANCY 50 ▮ CURRENCY SOMALI SHILLING ▮ GDP PER CAPITA $600 ▮ ECONOMY IND: A FEW LIGHT INDUSTRIES, INC. SUGAR REFINING, TEXTILES, PETROLEUM REFINING (MOSTLY SHUT DOWN). AGR: BANANAS, SORGHUM, CORN, COCONUTS, CATTLE, FISH. EXP: LIVESTOCK, BANANAS, HIDES, FISH, CHARCOAL.

Somalia is flat in the south, with mountains in the north. In 1960 northern British Somaliland voted to join southern Italian Somaliland to create Somalia. Somalis are one of the most homogeneous peoples in Africa, but unity is thwarted by clan-based rivalries. Somalia has been without a national government after civil war ended its dictatorship in 1991. It now has a transitional parliamentary federal government. The independent "Republic of Somaliland," while acknowledged, is not officially recognized internationally, as efforts continue to reunify Somalia.

SEEKING TO SLOW DESERTIFICATION in Somalia, volunteers work with pitchfork and shovel, tipping new cactus plants into arid soil.

 # ERITREA

STATE OF ERITREA

AREA 46,774 SQ. MI. ▮ POPULATION 5,647,000 ▮ CAPITAL ASMARA (POP. 556,000) ▮ LITERACY 59% ▮ LIFE EXPECTANCY 62 ▮ CURRENCY NAKFA ▮ GDP PER CAPITA $1,000 ▮ ECONOMY IND: FOOD PROCESSING, BEVERAGES, CLOTHING, TEXTILES. AGR: SORGHUM, LENTILS, VEGETABLES, CORN, LIVESTOCK, FISH. EXP: LIVESTOCK, SORGHUM, TEXTILES, FOOD, SMALL MANUFACTURING.

Eritrea, a former Italian colony in northeast Africa, was annexed by Ethiopian Emperor Haile Selassie in 1962, despite a UN-administered federation to the contrary, touching off decades of bitter warfare. In 1993 Eritrea achieved independence from its dominating neighbor. After independence, Eritrea plunged into war with Yemen and then Ethiopia over land disputes. A peace agreement in 2000 established a UN-patrolled buffer zone along the Eritrean-Ethiopian border.

 # DJIBOUTI

REPUBLIC OF DJIBOUTI

AREA 8,958 SQ. MI. ▮ POPULATION 516,000 ▮ CAPITAL DJIBOUTI (POP. 502,000) ▮ LITERACY 68% ▮ LIFE EXPECTANCY 43 ▮ CURRENCY DJIBOUTIAN FRANC ▮ GDP PER CAPITA $3,700 ▮ ECONOMY IND: CONSTRUCTION, AGRICULTURAL PROCESSING. AGR: FRUITS, VEGETABLES, GOATS. EXP: REEXPORTS, HIDES & SKINS, COFFEE (IN TRANSIT).

A gateway for Red Sea shipping, Djibouti was a French territory until 1977; a French naval base and garrison generate about half the country's income today. The capital of this resource-poor nation profits as a regional banking center with a free port and modern air facilities. Terminus of the railway from Addis Ababa, it handles much of Ethiopia's trade.

A civil war in the early 1990s ended with a power-sharing agreement between the two main ethnic groups, the Issa of Somali origin and the Afar of Ethiopian origin.

CAPE VERDE

REPUBLIC OF CAPE VERDE

AREA 1,558 SQ. MI. ▮ POPULATION 429,000 ▮ CAPITAL PRAIA (POP. 107,000) ▮ LITERACY 77% ▮ LIFE EXPECTANCY 72 ▮ CURRENCY CAPE VERDEAN ESCUDO ▮ GDP PER CAPITA $3,800 ▮ ECONOMY IND: FOOD & BEVERAGES, FISH PROCESSING, SHOES & GARMENTS, SALT MINING. AGR: BANANAS, CORN, BEANS, SWEET POTATOES, FISH. EXP: FUEL, SHOES, GARMENTS, FISH, HIDES.

Off the coast of West Africa, Cape Verde comprises ten volcanic islands and five islets. The islands were uninhabited until they were discovered by the Portuguese in 1456. Independence from Portugal occurred in 1975. African culture is most evident on the island of São Tiago, where half the population lives. Cape Verde enjoys a stable democratic system. Though freshwater shortages hinder agriculture, tourism is an expanding industry.

CENTRAL AFRICAN REPUBLIC

CENTRAL AFRICAN REPUBLIC

AREA 240,535 SQ. MI. ▮ POPULATION 4,511,000 ▮ CAPITAL BANGUI (POP. 698,000) ▮ LITERACY 49% ▮ LIFE EXPECTANCY 45 ▮ CURRENCY CFA FRANC ▮ GDP PER CAPITA $700 ▮ ECONOMY IND: DIAMOND MINING, LOGGING, BREWING, TEXTILES. AGR: COTTON, COFFEE, TOBACCO, MANIOC (TAPIOCA), TIMBER. EXP: DIAMONDS, TIMBER, COTTON, COFFEE, TOBACCO.

The Central African Republic, found deep in the heart of Africa, was part of French Equatorial Africa before independence in 1960. Most of the country is savanna plateau, with rain forests in the south. The economy remains in poor condition. This is one of the world's least developed countries, with most of the population engaged in subsistence farming. Timber and uncut diamonds are sources of export revenue. Political instability continued with a coup and rebellions in 2003.

GLOSSARY

Coup: From the French *couper*, "to cut" or "to chop." An abrupt, generally violent, overthrow of a functioning government by a small faction that involves control of any armed or military elements. Rather than acting as a movement for social, economic, or political change, a coup typically results only in the replacement of leading government personnel.

CONGO

REPUBLIC OF THE CONGO

AREA 132,047 SQ. MI. ▮ POPULATION 4,013,000 ▮ CAPITAL BRAZZAVILLE (POP. 1,505,000) ▮ LITERACY 84% ▮ LIFE EXPECTANCY 54 ▮ CURRENCY CFA FRANC ▮ GDP PER CAPITA $4,000 ▮ ECONOMY IND: PETROLEUM EXTRACTION, CEMENT, LUMBER, BREWING, SUGAR, PALM OIL, SOAP. AGR: CASSAVA (TAPIOCA), SUGAR, RICE, CORN, FOREST PRODUCTS. EXP: PETROLEUM, LUMBER, PLYWOOD, SUGAR, CACAO.

Astride the Equator, Congo has a small population that is concentrated in the southwest, with a virtually uninhabited jungle in the north. Most people live in or between Brazzaville, the capital, and Pointe-Noire, Congo's port city and focus for the oil industry. Since achieving independence in 1960, the country has been hampered by political turmoil. After almost three decades of Marxist rule, Congo adopted a multiparty, democratic system in 1992. Conflict in the late 1990s derailed democracy, but a new constitution in 2002 brings the promise of stability.

DEMOCRATIC REPUBLIC OF THE CONGO

DEMOCRATIC REPUBLIC OF THE CONGO

AREA 905,365 SQ. MI. ▮ POPULATION 68,693,000 ▮ CAPITAL KINSHASA (POP. 9,052,000) ▮ LITERACY 67% ▮ LIFE EXPECTANCY 54 ▮ CURRENCY CONGOLESE FRANC ▮ GDP PER CAPITA $600 ▮ ECONOMY IND: MINING (DIAMONDS, COPPER, ZINC), MINERAL PROCESSING, CONSUMER PRODUCTS. AGR: COFFEE, SUGAR, PALM OIL, RUBBER, WOOD PRODUCTS. EXP: DIAMONDS, COPPER, CRUDE OIL, COFFEE, COBALT.

Within the Democratic Republic of the Congo, the Congo River flows through a land rich in minerals, fertile farmlands, and rain forests. The forested river basin, 60 percent of the nation's area, is a communication barrier between the western capital, Kinshasa, the mountainous east, and the southern highlands. As many as 250 ethnic groups speaking some 700 local languages and dialects endure one of the world's lowest living standards. War, government corruption, neglected public services, and depressed copper and coffee markets are contributing factors.

 # RWANDA

REPUBLIC OF RWANDA

AREA 10,169 SQ. MI. ▌ POPULATION 10,473,000 ▌ CAPITAL KIGALI
(POP. 947,000) ▌ LITERACY 70% ▌ LIFE EXPECTANCY 51 ▌
CURRENCY RWANDAN FRANC ▌ GDP PER CAPITA $900 ▌
ECONOMY IND: CEMENT, AGRICULTURAL PRODUCTS,
SMALL-SCALE BEVERAGES, SOAP. AGR: COFFEE, TEA, PYRETHRUM,
BANANAS, LIVESTOCK.

Rwanda, just south of the Equator in central Africa, is a mountainous land. This tiny, landlocked country is one of the continent's most densely populated. Rwanda gained independence from Belgium in 1962. Conflict and civil war between ethnic Hutus and Tutsis have marked the country's history. In 1994 the genocide of some 800,000 Tutsis by Hutus occurred before Tutsi forces could gain control of Rwanda. Hutu militias fled Rwanda and continued to attack Tutsis from outposts in Zaire until Rwandan forces invaded Zaire in 1997—where they remained until 2002, when the Democratic Republic of the Congo (formerly Zaire) agreed to help Tutsis disarm Hutu gunmen.

BURUNDI

REPUBLIC OF BURUNDI

AREA 10,747 SQ. MI. ▌ POPULATION 8,988,000 ▌ CAPITAL
BUJUMBURA 378,000 ▌ LITERACY 59% ▌ LIFE EXPECTANCY 52 ▌
CURRENCY BURUNDI FRANC ▌ GDP PER CAPITA $500 ▌ ECONOMY
IND: LIGHT CONSUMER GOODS (BLANKETS, SHOES, SOAP),
ASSEMBLY OF IMPORTED COMPONENTS. AGR: COFFEE, COTTON,
TEA, CORN, BEEF. EXP: COFFEE, TEA, SUGAR, COTTON, HIDES.

Poor, densely populated, landlocked, and small, Burundi lies just south of the Equator in central Africa. From the capital, Bujumbura, on Lake Tanganyika, a great escarpment rises to fertile highlands. Agriculture employs 90 percent of the people, mostly subsistence farmers. Since gaining independence from Belgium in 1962, Burundi has been plagued by ethnic conflict between the majority Hutus and the Tutsis, who, although only 14 percent of the population, tend to dominate the government and army. A 2003 new government and 2006 cease-fire offer hope for peace.

 # UGANDA

REPUBLIC OF UGANDA

AREA 93,104 SQ. MI. ▌ POPULATION 32,370,000 ▌ CAPITAL KAMPALA
(POP. 1,597,000) ▌ LITERACY 67% ▌ LIFE EXPECTANCY 53 ▌ CURRENCY
UGANDAN SHILLING ▌ GDP PER CAPITA $1,200 ▌ ECONOMY IND:
SUGAR, BREWING, TOBACCO, COTTON TEXTILES, CEMENT.

Uganda, a landlocked country in East Africa, consists of savanna plateau with mountains and lakes. Key features of this former British protectorate are Lake Victoria—the largest lake in Africa—and the Ruwenzori Mountains.

Uganda gained independence in 1962, but it suffered under militaristic regimes until 1996 brought the institution of popular election. An insurgent militia, known as the Lord's Resistance Army, continues to operate, terrorizing northern Uganda and abducting some 20,000 children and making them soldiers. Fertile soil keeps farms and coffee plantations flourishing, but AIDS, epidemic in some areas, may now be the country's greatest enemy.

A HOARD OF LAND MINES discovered and defused in Rwanda's Volcanoes National Park demonstrates how human violence pervades one of the world's few habitats populated by the mountain gorilla.

 GUINEA

REPUBLIC OF GUINEA

AREA 94,926 SQ. MI. ❙ POPULATION 10,058,000 ❙ CAPITAL CONAKRY (POP. 1,645,000) ❙ LITERACY 30% ❙ LIFE EXPECTANCY 57 ❙ CURRENCY GUINEAN FRANC ❙ GDP PER CAPITA $1,100 ❙ ECONOMY IND: BAUXITE, GOLD, DIAMONDS, ALUMINA REFINING, LIGHT MANUFAC-TURING. ❙ AGR: RICE, COFFEE, PINEAPPLES, PALM KERNELS, CATTLE, TIMBER. EXP: BAUXITE, ALUMINA, GOLD, DIAMONDS, COFFEE.

Facing the Atlantic Ocean in West Africa, Guinea is a country with a narrow coastal plain and interior highlands that are forested in the southeast. After it gained independence from France in 1958, repressive socialist rule plunged the country into economic ruin. A 1984 coup brought in a military government until 1990, after which Guinea began the transition to a multiparty democratic system. Liberal-ized commercial policies, plus diamonds and gold, diversify an economy overly dependent on the bauxite industry.

GAMBIA

REPUBLIC OF THE GAMBIA

AREA 4,361 SQ. MI. ❙ POPULATION 1,783,000 ❙ CAPITAL BANJUL (POP. 372,000) ❙ LITERACY 40% ❙ LIFE EXPECTANCY 55 ❙ CURRENCY DALASI ❙ GDP PER CAPITA $1,300 ❙ ECONOMY IND: PROCESSING PEANUTS, FISH, HIDES, TOURISM, BEVERAGES, AGRICULTURAL MACHINERY ASSEMBLY. AGR: RICE, MILLET, SORGHUM, PEANUTS, CATTLE. EXP: PEANUT PRODUCTS, FISH, COTTON LINT, PALM KERNELS.

Gambia, in West Africa, is a small, narrow country with an outlet to the Atlantic Ocean. In 1588 Britain purchased trading rights to this territory from Portugal. Independence came in 1965. After nearly 30 years of democratic rule, Gambia's president was ousted by a military coup in 1994. The constitution was rewritten and approved by national referendum in August 1996, and constitutional rule was reestablished in January 1997. Most people are subsis-tence farmers; the main export is groundnuts (peanuts).

GLOSSARY

International Monetary Fund (IMF): A specialized United Nations agency that secures international monetary cooperation, stabilizing currency exchange rates and expanding international access to hard currency. **/ World Bank:** A specialized United Nations agency that designs financial projects to enhance economic development and realize a free-market economy, often working with the IMF and World Trade Organization.

 SENEGAL

REPUBLIC OF SENEGAL

AREA 75,955 SQ. MI. ❙ POPULATION 13,711,000 ❙ CAPITAL DAKAR (POP. 2,856,000) ❙ LITERACY 39% ❙ LIFE EXPECTANCY 59 ❙ CUR-RENCY CFA FRANC ❙ GDP PER CAPITA $1,600 ❙ ECONOMY IND: AGRICULTURAL & FISH PROCESSING, PHOSPHATE MINING, FERTIL-IZER PRODUCTION, PETROLEUM REFINING. AGR: PEANUTS, MILLET, CORN, SORGHUM, CATTLE, FISH. EXP: FISH, PEANUTS, PETROLEUM PRODUCTS, PHOSPHATES, COTTON.

Senegal lies on West Africa's Atlantic coast. This river-laced land of marshes and plains, once ruled by Wolof chieftains, became one of the first multiparty democra-cies in today's Africa. The moderate socialist government has initiated economic reforms. A deep natural harbor at Dakar makes this cosmopolitan city a major West African port. Peanuts from the drought-prone in-terior are an important export.

 GUINEA-BISSAU

REPUBLIC OF GUINEA-BISSAU

AREA 13,948 SQ. MI. ❙ POPULATION 1,534,000 ❙ CAPITAL BISSAU (POP. 336,000) ❙ LITERACY 42% ❙ LIFE EXPECTANCY 48 ❙ CURRENCY CFA FRANC ❙ GDP PER CAPITA $600 ❙ ECONOMY IND: AGRICULTURAL PRODUCTS PROCESSING, BEER, SOFT DRINKS. AGR: RICE, CORN, BEANS, CASSAVA (TAPIOCA), TIMBER, FISH. EXP: CASHEW NUTS, SHRIMP, PEANUTS, PALM KERNELS, SAWN LUMBER.

Guinea-Bissau's swampy coastal forests change to grasslands in the east. In 1994 the country's first multiparty elections were held. An army uprising four years later led to a bloody civil war, severely damaging the nation's infrastructure. The president was assassinated in 2009 and replaced by an elect-ed leader in July of that year. Guinea-Bissau is among the world's least developed countries, with most people engaged in subsistence agriculture and fishing.

KOFI ANNAN / FORMER UN SECRETARY-GENERAL

Kofi Annan served as the seventh secretary-general of the United Nations, from 1997 to 2007. He was born in Ghana in 1938, and his grandfathers and uncle were tribal chiefs among the Asante and Fante people. His father worked as an export manager in the cocoa industry. Annan studied at the University of Science and Technology in Kumasi, Ghana, and earned an economics degree from Macalester College in Minnesota, as well as an M.S. degree in management from the Massachusetts Institute of Technology. He joined the World Health Organization as a budget officer in 1962 and joined the staff of the United Nations in 1987. For his work toward a more organized and peaceful world, he received the Nobel Peace Prize in 2001.

> "What matters is that the strong as well as the weak agree to be bound by the same rules, to treat each other with the same respect. —— **KOFI ANNAN, 2006**

KENYA

REPUBLIC OF KENYA

AREA 224,081 SQ. MI. ▌ POPULATION 39,003,000 ▌ CAPITAL NAIROBI (POP. 3,363,000) ▌ LITERACY 85% ▌ LIFE EXPECTANCY 58 ▌ CURRENCY KENYAN SHILLING ▌ GDP PER CAPITA $1,600 ▌ ECONOMY IND: SMALL-SCALE CONSUMER GOODS (PLASTIC, FURNITURE), AGRICULTURAL PRODUCTS PROCESSING, OIL REFINING.

Kenya rises from a low coastal plain on the Indian Ocean to mountains and plateaus at its center. In its basic framework, Kenya is divided into a number of geographic regions: the Rift Valley and associated highlands, the eastern plateau, the coast, the Lake Victoria basin, and the arid northern and southern regions. The Rift Valley divides the highland region into two areas: the western Mau Escarpment and the eastern Aberdare Range. Free enterprise and political debate have contributed to Kenya's status as one of Africa's most stable nations since its independence from Britain in 1963. The nation moved to a multiparty system in the late 1990s. Tourism is essential to the economy. Intense competition for arable land drives thousands to cities, where unemployment is high.

A PAIR OF RETICULATED GIRAFFES, mother and young, stand silhouetted against the clouds in Kenya's Masai Mara National Reserve, nearly 600 square miles of protected land within the Great Rift Valley.

SIERRA LEONE

REPUBLIC OF SIERRA LEONE

AREA 27,699 SQ. MI. ▮ POPULATION 6,440,000 ▮ CAPITAL FREETOWN (POP. 894,000) ▮ LITERACY 35% ▮ LIFE EXPECTANCY 41 ▮ CURRENCY LEONE ▮ GDP PER CAPITA $700 ▮ ECONOMY IND: MINING (DIAMONDS), SMALL-SCALE MANUFACTURING (BEVERAGES, TEXTILES), PETROLEUM REFINING. AGR: RICE, COFFEE, CACAO, PALM KERNELS, POULTRY, FISH.

Sierra Leone is on the Atlantic coast of West Africa, with coastal swamps rising to interior plateaus and mountains. It was named by a 15th-century Portuguese explorer; Sierra Leone means "Lion Mountain." It was a British colony from the early 19th century until 1961. In the 1990s democratically elected leaders were overthrown but subsequently regained power, and major hostilities have demoralized the population and destabilized the economy. In 2002 Sierra Leone emerged from a decade of civil war, with the help of some 17,000 UN peacekeepers.

CÔTE D'IVOIRE (IVORY COAST)

REPUBLIC OF CÔTE D'IVOIRE

AREA 124,503 SQ. MI. ▮ POPULATION 20,617,000 ▮ ADMINISTRATIVE CAPITAL ABIDJAN (POP. 4,175,000), LEGISLATIVE CAPITAL YAMOUSSOUKRO (POP. 416,000) ▮ LITERACY 49% ▮ LIFE EXPECTANCY 55 ▮ CURRENCY CFA FRANC ▮ GDP PER CAPITA $1,800 ▮ ECONOMY IND: FOODSTUFFS, BEVERAGES, WOOD PRODUCTS, OIL REFINING, TRUCK & BUS ASSEMBLY. AGR: COFFEE, CACAO, BANANAS, PALM KERNELS, TIMBER.

Côte d'Ivoire's geography ranges from beaches and forests in the south to a savanna plateau in the north. Muslims (40 percent) live mostly in the north, Christians (35 percent) in the south. The country has 60 ethnic groups, the largest being the Baoule, whose dominance in running the country since independence is a major issue. The first multiparty elections were held in 1990. In 2002 a failed coup turned into a rebellion. This crisis contributed further to the swiftly declining economy, even as unemployment and urban migration increased.

BURKINA FASO

BURKINA FASO

AREA 105,869 SQ. MI. ▮ POPULATION 15,746,000 ▮ CAPITAL OUAGADOUGOU (POP. 1,324,000) ▮ LITERACY 22% ▮ LIFE EXPECTANCY 53 ▮ CURRENCY CFA FRANC ▮ GDP PER CAPITA $1,200 ▮ ECONOMY IND: COTTON LINT, BEVERAGES, AGRICULTURAL PROCESSING, SOAP. AGR: COTTON, PEANUTS, SHEA NUTS, SESAME, LIVESTOCK. EXP: COTTON, LIVESTOCK, GOLD.

The landlocked country of Burkina Faso—which contains desert in the north and savanna in the center and south—is home to 63 ethnic groups. Formerly known as Upper Volta, the French colony gained independence in 1960. Its mostly agricultural economy has been hurt by droughts and political instability. Parks protect the largest elephant population in West Africa and other wildlife.

LIBERIA

REPUBLIC OF LIBERIA

AREA 43,000 SQ. MI. ▮ POPULATION 3,442,000 ▮ CAPITAL MONROVIA (POP. 1,185,000) ▮ LITERACY 58% ▮ LIFE EXPECTANCY 42 ▮ CURRENCY LIBERIAN DOLLAR ▮ GDP PER CAPITA $500 ▮ ECONOMY IND: RUBBER PROCESSING, PALM OIL PROCESSING, TIMBER, DIAMONDS. AGR: RUBBER, COFFEE, CACAO, RICE, SHEEP, TIMBER.

Freed American slaves began settling on the West African coast in 1820. In 1847 Liberia was declared an independent republic—Africa's first under a constitution modeled on that of the United States. In 1999 the government of Charles Taylor was accused of supporting rebels in Sierra Leone, and it fought a border war with Guinea in 2000. Taylor was forced into exile in 2003, and the government has worked to rebuild the nation.

GHANA

REPUBLIC OF GHANA

AREA 92,100 SQ. MI. ▮ POPULATION 23,832,000 ▮ CAPITAL ACCRA (POP. 2,332,000) ▮ LITERACY 58% ▮ LIFE EXPECTANCY 60 ▮ CURRENCY CEDI ▮ GDP PER CAPITA $1,500 ▮ ECONOMY IND: MINING, LUMBERING, LIGHT MANUFACTURING, ALUMINUM SMELTING. AGR: CACAO, RICE, COFFEE, CASSAVA (TAPIOCA), TIMBER. EXP: GOLD, CACAO, TIMBER, TUNA, BAUXITE.

Ghana, in West Africa, emcompasses most of the area formerly known as the Gold Coast. It is a land of plains and low plateaus covered by rain forests in the west and Lake Volta in the east. After Ghana's independence from Britain in 1957, President Kwame Nkrumah emerged as a leading spokesman for Pan-Africanism. A series of military coups brought Jerry Rawlings to power in 1981. Multiparty democracy started with the new 1992 constitution. In December 2000, for the first time in its history, Ghana witnessed the election of an opposition party.

AFRICA'S GREAT CITIES

CAIRO, EGYPT
Ancient capital, Africa's largest city
POP. 12,503,000

LAGOS, NIGERIA
Second largest in Africa
POP. 10,572,000

KINSHASA, DEMOCRATIC REPUBLIC OF THE CONGO
Formerly Leopoldville
POP. 9,052,000

ABIDJAN, COTE D'IVOIRE
Administrative capital and commercial hub
POP. 4,175,000

NAIROBI, KENYA
East Africa's center of commerce
POP. 3,363,000

CAPE TOWN, SOUTH AFRICA
Harbor for Cape of Good Hope
POP. 3,357,000

CASABLANCA, MOROCCO
North African seaport
POP. 3,267,000

STRAINING OFF THE OIL extracted from shea or karite nuts, a woman in Burkina Faso performs one of the many arduous steps in manufacturing shea butter. Women from her country produced 20 tons in 2007.

TOGO

TOGOLESE REPUBLIC

AREA 21,925 SQ. MI. ▮ POPULATION 6,020,000 ▮ CAPITAL LOMÉ (POP. 1,669,000) ▮ LITERACY 61% ▮ LIFE EXPECTANCY 59 ▮ CURRENCY CFA FRANC ▮ GDP PER CAPITA $900 ▮ ECONOMY IND: PHOSPHATE MINING, AGRICULTURAL PROCESSING, CEMENT, HANDICRAFTS. AGR: COFFEE, CACAO, COTTON, YAMS, LIVESTOCK, FISH. EXP: REEXPORTS, COTTON, PHOSPHATES, COFFEE, CACAO.

Togo is a long, narrow country in West Africa, with an interior plateau rising to mountains in the north. In 1922 the eastern part of the German protectorate of Togoland passed into French hands; 38 years later, in 1960, it became independent. Military rule finally yielded to some democratic reforms amid civil unrest in the 1990s. Togo is a poor country agriculturally. Electoral fraud and human rights abuses led many of Togo's citizens to emigrate, but demographic gains in recent years have improved life there.

BENIN

REPUBLIC OF BENIN

AREA 43,484 SQ. MI. ▌ POPULATION 8,792,000 ▌ CAPITAL PORTO-NOVO (POP. 238,000) ▌ LITERACY 35% ▌ LIFE EXPECTANCY 59 ▌ CURRENCY CFA FRANC ▌ GDP PER CAPITA $1,500 ▌ ECONOMY IND: TEXTILES, FOOD PROCESSING, CHEMICAL PRODUCTION, CONSTRUCTION MATERIALS. AGR: COTTON, CORN, CASSAVA (TAPIOCA), YAMS, LIVESTOCK. EXP: COTTON, CRUDE OIL, PALM PRODUCTS, CACAO.

Until the 1940s, slaves were this country's main export. After independence from France in 1960, Benin—then called Dahomey—was plagued by many coups; in 1975 a Marxist military government renamed the nation Benin. About 42 African ethnic groups live in Benin, with most of the population living in the south. In 1989 the government renounced Marxism. Since then it has held numerous free elections. The agricultural economy is based largely on cotton.

EQUATORIAL GUINEA

REPUBLIC OF EQUATORIAL GUINEA

AREA 10,831 SQ. MI. ▌ POPULATION 633,000 ▌ CAPITAL MALABO (POP. 95,000) ▌ LITERACY 87% ▌ LIFE EXPECTANCY 62 ▌ CURRENCY CFA FRANC ▌ GDP PER CAPITA $31,400 ▌ ECONOMY IND: PETROLEUM, FISHING, SAWMILLING, NATURAL GAS. AGR: COFFEE, COCOA, RICE, YAMS, LIVESTOCK, TIMBER. EXP: PETROLEUM, METHANOL, TIMBER, CACAO.

A small country on the west coast of central Africa, Equatorial Guinea comprises the mainland territory of Río Muni and five volcanic islands. After independence from Spain in 1968, it fell under the rule of Francisco Macías Nguema, who plunged it into ruin. He was overthrown and executed in 1979 by his nephew. President Obiang Nguema Mbasogo continues the family dictatorship, and there is widespread civil unrest over flawed elections. New oil wealth masks widespread poverty and economic stagnation.

CLICK IT: Africa's People & Places www3.nationalgeographic.com/places/continents/continent_africa.html

NIGERIA

FEDERAL REPUBLIC OF NIGERIA

AREA 356,669 SQ. MI. ▌ POPULATION 149,229,000 ▌ CAPITAL ABUJA (POP. 1,994,000) ▌ LITERACY 68% ▌ LIFE EXPECTANCY 47 ▌ CURRENCY NAIRA ▌ GDP PER CAPITA $2,300 ▌ ECONOMY IND: CRUDE OIL, COAL, TIN, COLUMBITE, PALM OIL, PEANUTS, COTTON, RUBBER. AGR: CACAO, PEANUTS, PALM OIL, CORN, CATTLE, TIMBER, FISH. EXP: PETROLEUM & PETROLEUM PRODUCTS, CACAO, RUBBER.

Nigeria, Africa's most populous country, changes in terrain from the oil-rich Niger Delta in the south to rain forests inland and high savanna-covered plateaus in the north. The population is diverse, with 250 ethnic groups—Hausa-Fulani, Yoruba, and Igbo the largest. After decades of military coups, free elections were held in 1999. Oil and gas account for 95 percent of export earnings, and national gross domestic product increased in 2007 and 2008. Badly managed agriculture and a poor transportation infrastructure hinder development.

SÃO TOMÉ & PRINCIPE

DEMOCRATIC REPUBLIC OF SÃO TOMÉ & PRINCIPE

AREA 386 SQ. MI. ▌ POPULATION 213,000 ▌ CAPITAL SÃO TOMÉ (POP. 54,000) ▌ LITERACY 85% ▌ LIFE EXPECTANCY 68 ▌ CURRENCY DOBRA ▌ GDP PER CAPITA $1,300 ▌ ECONOMY IND: LIGHT CONSTRUCTION, TEXTILES, SOAP, BEER, FISH PROCESSING, TIMBER. AGR: CACAO, COCONUTS, PALM KERNELS, COPRA, POULTRY, FISH. EXP: CACAO, COPRA, COFFEE, PALM OIL.

In the 15th century, Portuguese navigators discovered these two volcanic islands off the coast of West Africa in the Gulf of Guinea. São Tomé is the larger of the islands, containing 90 percent of the population. This, the continent's smallest nation, gained independence from Portugal in 1975. In 1991 the formerly Marxist government made a complete transition to democracy. The new leaders have moved to liberalize the economy and reduce dependence on plantation crops. New offshore oil discoveries could translate into substantial oil revenue.

TANZANIA

UNITED REPUBLIC OF TANZANIA

AREA 364,900 SQ. MI. ▌ POPULATION 41,049,000 ▌ ADMINISTRATIVE CAPITAL DAR ES SALAAM (POP. 3,319,000), LEGISLATIVE CAPITAL DODOMA (POP. 155,000) ▌ LITERACY 69% ▌ LIFE EXPECTANCY 52 ▌ CURRENCY TANZANIAN SHILLING ▌ GDP PER CAPITA $1,300 ▌ ECONOMY IND: AGRICULTURAL PROCESSING (SUGAR, BEER, CIGARETTES, SISAL TWINE), DIAMOND & GOLD MINING, OIL REFINING. AGR: COFFEE, SISAL, TEA, COTTON, CATTLE. EXP: GOLD, COFFEE, CASHEW NUTS, MANUFACTURING, COTTON.

Tanzania, the largest country in East Africa, includes the islands of Zanzibar, Pemba, and Mafia and contains Africa's highest point, Kilimanjaro. Tanganyika, a British-controlled UN trust territory, gained independence in 1961; and Zanzibar, a British protectorate, became independent in 1963. The two united in 1964, and a multiparty system was established in 1992.

Most Tanzanians farm or fish at subsistence levels; in many areas tse-tse fly infestation hampers successful animal husbandry. Deteriorating roads and railways and high energy costs are major problems. Fourteen percent of the country's land is protected; the two national parks are rich in wildlife, although poaching endangers some species.

GABON

GABONESE REPUBLIC

AREA 103,347 SQ. MI. ▌ POPULATION 1,515,000 ▌ CAPITAL LIBREVILLE (POP. 611,000) ▌ LITERACY 63% ▌ LIFE EXPECTANCY 53 ▌ CURRENCY CFA FRANC ▌ GDP PER CAPITA $14,400 ▌ ECONOMY IND: PETROLEUM EXTRACTION & REFINING, MANGANESE & GOLD MINING, CHEMICALS. AGR: CACAO, COFFEE, SUGAR, PALM OIL, CATTLE, OKOUME (A TROPICAL SOFTWOOD), FISH. EXP: CRUDE OIL, TIMBER, MANGANESE, URANIUM.

Gabon sits on the Equator in western Africa. Oil, timber, and manganese earn this thinly settled republic one of the highest per capita incomes in Africa. However, the income is largely oil money going to a few; most live by subsistence farming. Independent from France since 1960, it was mostly a one-party state until 1991, when a new constitution brought multiparty democracy. In 2002 the country created 13 new national parks, some 11 percent of Gabon's area, to protect its forests from logging.

CAMEROON

REPUBLIC OF CAMEROON

AREA 183,569 SQ. MI. ▌ POPULATION 18,879,000 ▌ CAPITAL YAOUNDÉ (POP. 1,787,000) ▌ LITERACY 68% ▌ LIFE EXPECTANCY 54 ▌ CURRENCY CFA FRANC ▌ GDP PER CAPITA $2,300 ▌ ECONOMY IND: PETROLEUM PRODUCTION & REFINING, FOOD PROCESSING, LIGHT CONSUMER GOODS, TEXTILES. AGR: COFFEE, CACAO, COTTON, RUBBER, LIVESTOCK, TIMBER. EXP: CRUDE OIL & PETROLEUM PRODUCTS, LUMBER, CACAO, ALUMINUM.

The landscape of Cameroon, in West Africa, is a mixture of desert plains in the north, mountains in the central regions, and tropical rain forest in the south. Along its western border are mountains, including the volcanic Cameroon Mountain. The Republic of Cameroon is a union of two former United Nations trust territories: French Cameroun and southern British Cameroons.

While oil earnings have helped fund industrial expansion, price fluctuations of export commodities have forced austerity. After the 1990 legalization of opposition parties, the government adopted IMF and World Bank programs to increase business investment and to foster efficiency in agriculture and trade. The Chad-Cameroon oil pipeline brings new business to Cameroon's port of Kribi.

SEYCHELLES

REPUBLIC OF SEYCHELLES

AREA 176 SQ. MI. ▌ POPULATION 85,000 ▌ CAPITAL VICTORIA (POP. 25,000) ▌ LITERACY 92% ▌ LIFE EXPECTANCY 73 ▌ CURRENCY SEYCHELLES RUPEE ▌ GDP PER CAPITA $17,000 ▌ ECONOMY IND: FISHING, TOURISM, PROCESSING OF COCONUTS & VANILLA, COIR (COCONUT FIBER) ROPE. AGR: COCONUTS, CINNAMON, VANILLA, SWEET POTATOES, BROILER CHICKENS, TUNA. EXP: CANNED TUNA, FROZEN FISH, CINNAMON BARK, COPRA, PETROLEUM PRODUCTS (REEXPORTS).

The Republic of Seychelles, some 115 islands in the Indian Ocean, achieved independence from Britain in1976. An international airport opened in 1971 on the largest island, Mahé, increasing tourism, Seychelles' economic mainstay. An estimated 88 percent of the population lives on Mahé. After 15 years of one-party rule, the first elections in the country's history were held in 1993.

ANSWER BOOK | CHAPTER NINE | COUNTRIES OF THE WORLD

ZIMBABWE

REPUBLIC OF ZIMBABWE

AREA 150,872 SQ. MI. ▌ POPULATION 11,393,000 ▌ CAPITAL HARARE (POP. 1,663,000) ▌ LITERACY 91% ▌ LIFE EXPECTANCY 46 ▌ CURRENCY ZIMBABWEAN DOLLAR ▌ GDP PER CAPITA $200 ▌ ECONOMY IND: MINING (COAL, GOLD), STEEL, WOOD PRODUCTS, CEMENT, CHEMICALS. AGR: CORN, COTTON, TOBACCO, WHEAT, CATTLE. EXP: TOBACCO, GOLD, FERRO-ALLOYS, TEXTILES, CLOTHING.

This plateau country in southern Africa's interior declared independence from Britain as Rhodesia in 1965 under a white minority government. International sanctions and guerrilla warfare led to a legitimately independent Zimbabwe in 1980. Although nominally a multiparty state, the party of President Robert Mugabe has dominated the political system.

The economy centers on farming, mining, and manufacturing. Land redistribution is a charged issue. Mugabe's government began seizing all white-owned commercial agricultural land in 2000. African settlers were dumped on the land without government support. This chaotic land reform is causing massive declines in food production and famine.

ZAMBIA

REPUBLIC OF ZAMBIA

AREA 290,586 SQ. MI. ▌ POPULATION 11,863,000 ▌ CAPITAL LUSAKA (POP. 1,421,000) ▌ LITERACY 81% ▌ LIFE EXPECTANCY 39 ▌ CURRENCY ZAMBIAN KWACHA ▌ GDP PER CAPITA $1,500 ▌ ECONOMY IND: COPPER MINING & PROCESSING, CONSTRUCTION, FOODSTUFFS, BEVERAGES. AGR: CORN, SORGHUM, RICE, PEANUTS, CATTLE. EXP: COPPER, COBALT, ELECTRICITY, TOBACCO, FLOWERS.

Landlocked Zambia occupies an elevated plateau in central Africa. The Zambezi River flows through north to south, its Victoria Falls on the southern border. With huge copper reserves and fertile farmland, Zambia was optimistic after independence from Britain in 1964, but plunging copper prices and rising transport costs caused economic decline. Zambia's first multiparty elections in 19 years were held in 1991. More than 70 percent of Zambians live in poverty, and rising unemployment and the spread of AIDS are serious problems.

ANGOLA

REPUBLIC OF ANGOLA

AREA 481,354 SQ. MI. ▌ POPULATION 12,799,000 ▌ CAPITAL LUANDA (POP. 4,775,000) ▌ LITERACY 67% ▌ LIFE EXPECTANCY 38 ▌ CURRENCY KWANZA ▌ GDP PER CAPITA $8,800 ▌ ECONOMY IND: PETROLEUM, DIAMONDS, IRON ORE, PHOSPHATES, FELDSPAR, BAUXITE, URANIUM, GOLD. AGR: BANANAS, SUGARCANE, COFFEE, SISAL, LIVESTOCK, FOREST PRODUCTS, FISH. EXP: CRUDE OIL, DIAMONDS, REFINED PETROLEUM PRODUCTS, GAS.

Angola lies on the Atlantic coast of southwestern Africa; its northern province, Cabinda, is separated from the rest of the country by a small part of the Democratic Republic of the Congo and the Congo River. Angola's narrow coastal plain rises to a high interior plateau with rain forests in the north and dry savanna in the south. Originally a Portuguese colony, Angola won independence in 1975 after 14 years of guerrilla war. After 16 years of ensuing civil war, a peace agreement made elections possible in 1991. The elections were disputed, however, and the conflict renewed. The 27-year-long civil war finally ended in 2002.

MALAWI

REPUBLIC OF MALAWI

AREA 45,747 SQ. MI. ▌ POPULATION 14,269,000 ▌ CAPITAL LILONGWE (POP. 587,000) ▌ LITERACY 63% ▌ LIFE EXPECTANCY 44 ▌ CURRENCY MALAWIAN KWACHA ▌ GDP PER CAPITA $800 ▌ ECONOMY IND: TOBACCO, TEA, SUGAR, SAWMILL PRODUCTS. AGR: TOBACCO, SUGARCANE, COTTON, TEA, PEANUTS, CATTLE. EXP: TOBACCO, TEA, SUGAR, COTTON, COFFEE.

Malawi lies tucked inside in southeast Africa, with Lake Malawi taking up about a fifth of the landscape. Independent from Britain since 1964, it endured the one-party rule of President for Life Hastings Kamuzu Banda for more than 25 years. Democratic elections in 1994 ushered in new leadership. Transportation costs for exports skyrocketed as a result of civil war in adjacent Mozambique, disrupting rail links to the sea. Since the 1992 peace accord in Mozambique, rail links have been reestablished, and Malawi is slowly recovering.

SEEKING SARDINES AFTER SUNDOWN, Malawian fishermen hang lanterns to lure fish into their traps. Many living near Cape Maclear, a rocky headland jutting out into Lake Malawi, depend on a small fish called usipa, caught in abundance and dried on racks in the sun.

MOZAMBIQUE

REPUBLIC OF MOZAMBIQUE

AREA 308,642 SQ. MI. ▮ POPULATION 21,669,000 ▮ CAPITAL MAPUTO (POP. 1,621,000) ▮ LITERACY 48% ▮ LIFE EXPECTANCY 41 ▮ CURRENCY METICAL ▮ GDP PER CAPITA $900 ▮ ECONOMY IND: FOOD, BEVERAGES, CHEMICALS, ALUMINUM, PETROLEUM PRODUCTS, TEXTILES. ▮ AGR: COTTON, CASHEW NUTS, SUGARCANE, TEA, BEEF. EXP: ALUMINUM, PRAWNS, CASHEW NUTS, COTTON, SUGAR.

Mozambique, on the east coast of southern Africa, is mainly a savanna plateau, with highlands to the north. Infusions of aid are essential to a country devastated by decades of war, drought, and floods. Mozambique won independence from Portugal in 1975 and became a one-party state allied to the Soviet bloc, but a democratic constitution was adopted in 1990. In 1994 multiparty elections ushered in a new government. Production of food and manufactured goods is steadily increasing, and a large-scale aluminum smelter started in 2000. Solid economic success bodes well for the future.

COMOROS

UNION OF THE COMOROS

AREA 719 SQ. MI. ▮ POPULATION 752,000 ▮ CAPITAL MORONI (POP. 53,000) ▮ LITERACY 57% ▮ LIFE EXPECTANCY 63 ▮ CURRENCY COMORAN FRANC ▮ GDP PER CAPITA $1,000 ▮ ECONOMY IND: TOURISM, PERFUME DISTILLATION. AGR: VANILLA, CLOVES, PERFUME ESSENCES, COPRA. EXP: VANILLA, YLANG-YLANG, CLOVES, PERFUME OIL, COPRA.

The Comoros are volcanic islands in the Mozambique Channel between northern Madagascar and Africa. In 1975 three of the islands voted for independence from France; the fourth, Mayotte, elected to remain a dependency. More than 20 attempted coups since independence have created great instability. In 1997 the islands of Anjouan and Mohéli declared independence, but a new federal constitution in 2001 brought the islands back together.

Most inhabitants make their living from subsistence agriculture or fishing; exports include vanilla and essences used in the manufacture of perfumes.

MADAGASCAR

REPUBLIC OF MADAGASCAR

AREA 226,658 SQ. MI. ▮ POPULATION 20,654,000 ▮ CAPITAL ANTANANARIVO (POP. 1,877,000) ▮ LITERACY 69% ▮ LIFE EXPECTANCY 63 ▮ CURRENCY MALAGASY FRANC ▮ GDP PER CAPITA $1,000 ▮ ECONOMY IND: MEAT PROCESSING, SOAP, BREWERIES, TANNERIES. AGR: COFFEE, VANILLA, SUGARCANE, CLOVES, LIVESTOCK PRODUCTS. EXP: COFFEE, VANILLA, SHELLFISH, SUGAR, COTTON CLOTH, CHROMITE, PETROLEUM PRODUCTS.

Off Africa's southeast coast in the Indian Ocean, Madagascar contains a stunning diversity of plant and animal species found nowhere else. It has a mountainous central plateau and coastal plains. Most of the population depends on subsistence farming, based on rice and cattle, with coffee, vanilla, and seafood being important exports. Independence from France came in 1960. In 1990, after decades of Marxism, Madagascar lifted a ban on opposition parties, and a new president was elected in 1993. Environmental degradation is a major concern as damaging agricultural practices cause deforestation, soil erosion, and desertification.

MAURITIUS

REPUBLIC OF MAURITIUS

AREA 788 SQ. MI. ▮ POPULATION 1,284,000 ▮ CAPITAL PORT LOUIS (POP. 143,000) ▮ LITERACY 84% ▮ LIFE EXPECTANCY 74 ▮ CURRENCY MAURITIAN RUPEE ▮ GDP PER CAPITA $12,100 ▮ ECONOMY IND: FOOD PROCESSING (LARGELY SUGAR MILLING), TEXTILES, CLOTHING, CHEMICALS, METAL PRODUCTS. AGR: SUGARCANE, TEA, CORN, POTATOES, BANANAS, CATTLE, FISH. EXP: CLOTHING & TEXTILES, SUGAR, CUT FLOWERS, MOLASSES.

The island country of Mauritius lies in the Indian Ocean east of Madagascar. The volcanic main island of Mauritius is ringed by coral reefs; there are some 20 smaller islands. The islands were ruled in turn by the Dutch, French, and British, whose legacy includes a parliamentary form of government. Independence came in 1968. Diversifying sugarcane farming with manufacturing and tourism strengthens the nation—a blend of Africans, Indians (40 percent of the population), Europeans, and Chinese. With approximately 1,500 people per square mile, Mauritius is the most densely populated country in Africa.

NAMIBIA

REPUBLIC OF NAMIBIA

AREA 318,261 SQ. MI. ▮ POPULATION 2,109,000 ▮ CAPITAL WINDHOEK (POP. 237,000) ▮ LITERACY 85% ▮ LIFE EXPECTANCY 51 ▮ CURRENCY NAMIBIAN DOLLAR, SOUTH AFRICAN RAND ▮ GDP PER CAPITA $5,400 ▮ ECONOMY IND: MEATPACKING, FISH PROCESSING, DAIRY PRODUCTS, MINING (DIAMONDS, LEAD, ZINC). AGR: MILLET, SORGHUM, PEANUTS, LIVESTOCK, FISH. EXP: DIAMONDS, COPPER, GOLD, ZINC, LEAD.

Namibia is a large, sparsely populated country on Africa's southwest coast. Its low population can be attributed to its harsh geography—the coastal Namib Desert, central semiarid mountains, and Kalahari Desert east of the mountains. Independence from South Africa was achieved in 1990. Reflecting its colonial past, the population is 80 to 90 percent Christian. The multiparty, multiracial democracy inherits an economy based on mining (mostly diamonds), sheep and cattle ranching, and fishing.

BOTSWANA

REPUBLIC OF BOTSWANA

AREA 224,607 SQ. MI. ▮ POPULATION 1,991,000 ▮ CAPITAL GABORONE (POP. 199,000) ▮ LITERACY 81% ▮ LIFE EXPECTANCY 62 ▮ CURRENCY PULA ▮ GDP PER CAPITA $13,300 ▮ ECONOMY IND: DIAMONDS, COPPER, NICKEL, SALT, SODA ASH, POTASH, LIVESTOCK PROCESSING, TEXTILES. AGR: SORGHUM, MAIZE, MILLET, LIVESTOCK. EXP: DIAMONDS, COPPER, NICKEL, SODA ASH, MEAT.

Landlocked Botswana enjoys a mild climate in the east; the Kalahari Desert dominates the west and south. The Okavango Delta and Chobe National Park in the north are areas of outstanding natural beauty, rich in animal life. Stable and prosperous, Botswana has blossomed since independence from Britain in 1966. It is Africa's longest continuous democracy and one of the world's biggest diamond producers. Unlike many other countries in Africa, Botswana has put much of its mining revenues into social and economic infrastructure.

SOUTH AFRICA
REPUBLIC OF SOUTH AFRICA

AREA 470,693 SQ. MI. ∎ POPULATION 49,052,000 ∎
ADMINISTRATIVE CAPITAL PRETORIA (POP. 1,409,000),
JUDICIAL CAPITAL BLOEMFONTEIN (POP. 381,000),
CAPE TOWN (LEGISLATIVE CAPITAL, POP. 3,357,000) ∎
LITERACY 86% ∎ LIFE EXPECTANCY 49 ∎ CURRENCY RAND ∎
GDP PER CAPITA $10,000 ∎ ECONOMY IND: MINING (PLATINUM,
GOLD, CHROMIUM) AUTOMOBILE ASSEMBLY, METALWORKING,
MACHINERY. AGR: CORN, WHEAT, SUGARCANE, FRUITS,
BEEF. EXP: GOLD, DIAMONDS, PLATINUM, OTHER METALS &
MINERALS, MACHINERY & EQUIPMENT.

Boasting Africa's largest and most developed economy, South Africa produces high-tech equipment and is a world leader in the output of gold and diamonds. From 1948 to 1991 South Africa's political system was dominated by apartheid, a policy of segregation that isolated blacks in so-called homelands and overcrowded townships. In 1989 the government began dismantling apartheid. The first multiracial parliament was elected in 1994. In the 21st century, South Africa is a democratic country. The government recognizes 11 official languages. Today, South Africa is making up for decades of social disruption, but high unemployment and the AIDS epidemic threaten economic progress.

LESOTHO
KINGDOM OF LESOTHO

AREA 11,720 SQ. MI. ∎ POPULATION 2,131,000 ∎ CAPITAL MASERU (POP.
170,000) ∎ LITERACY 85% ∎ LIFE EXPECTANCY 40 ∎ CURRENCY LOTI,
SOUTH AFRICAN RAND ∎ GDP PER CAPITA $1,600 ∎ ECONOMY IND:
FOOD, BEVERAGES, TEXTILES, APPAREL ASSEMBLY, HANDICRAFTS.
AGR: CORN, WHEAT, PULSES, SORGHUM, LIVESTOCK. EXP: MANUFAC-
TURING (CLOTHING, FOOTWEAR, ROAD VEHICLES), WOOL, MOHAIR.

In the early 19th century, Basuto Chief Moshoeshoe united tribes in this mountainous land surrounded by South Africa. Lesotho became independent from Britain in 1966; in 1993 it became a constitutional monarchy. Water is its major natural resource: A large hydropower plant, completed in 1998, helps the economy expand through the sale of water to South Africa.

SWAZILAND
KINGDOM OF SWAZILAND

AREA 6,704 SQ. MI. ∎ POPULATION 1,124,000 ∎ ADMINISTRATIVE
CAPITAL MBABANE (POP. 70,000), LEGISLATIVE & ROYAL CAPITAL
LOBAMBA (POP. 4,400) ∎ LITERACY 82% ∎ LIFE EXPECTANCY 32 ∎
CURRENCY LILANGENI ∎ GDP PER CAPITA $5,100 ∎ ECONOMY IND:
MINING (COAL), WOOD PULP, SUGAR, SOFT DRINK CONCENTRATES.
AGR: SUGARCANE, COTTON, CORN, TOBACCO, CATTLE. EXP: SOFT
DRINK CONCENTRATES, SUGAR, WOOD PULP, COTTON YARN.

Swaziland, which is located in southern Africa, consists mostly of high plateaus and mountains. In 1949 the British government rejected a South African request for the control of this small, landlocked nation. Independence was granted in 1968. The king is an absolute monarch with supreme executive, legislative, and judicial powers. Nearly 60 percent of Swazi territory is held by the crown.

TINY BROOKESIAS, the world's smallest chameleons, inhabit Nosy Mangabe, an island preserve in Madagascar's Masoala National Park.

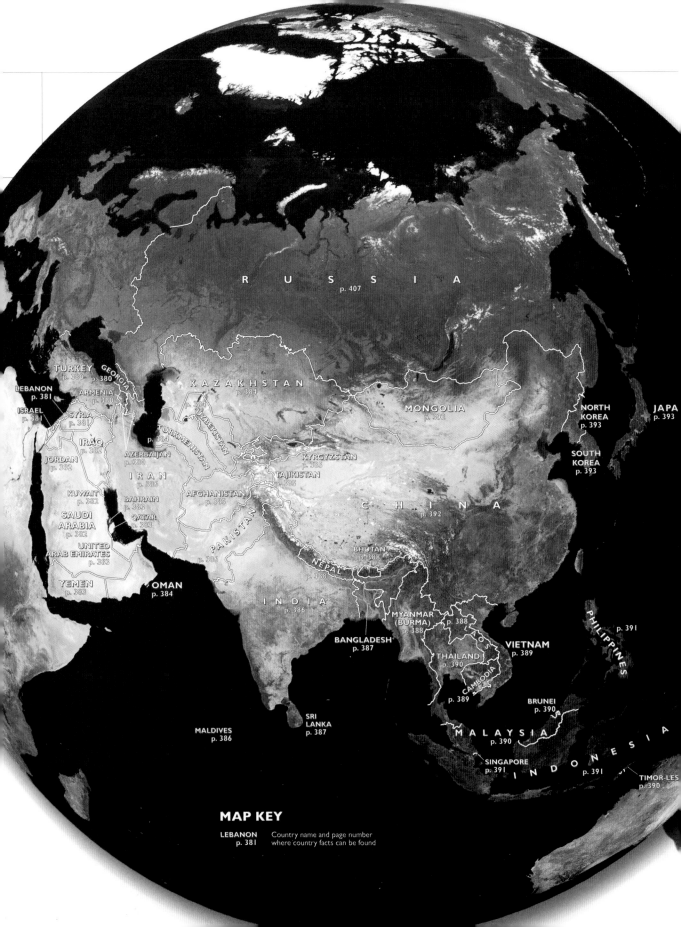

R U S S I A
p. 407

TURKEY
p. 380

GEORGIA
p. 380

LEBANON
p. 381

ARMENIA
p. 380

ISRAEL
p. 381

SYRIA
p. 381

IRAQ
p. 382

JORDAN
p. 382

KUWAIT
p. 382

SAUDI
ARABIA
p. 382

BAHRAIN
p. 388

QATAR
p. 388

UNITED
ARAB EMIRATES
p. 383

YEMEN
p. 383

OMAN
p. 384

AZERBAIJAN
p. 380

UZBEKISTAN
p. 384

TURKMENISTAN
p. 384

IRAN
p. 386

AFGHANISTAN
p. 385

PAKISTAN
p. 386

KAZAKHSTAN
p. 381

KYRGYZSTAN
p. 385

TAJIKISTAN
p. 385

MONGOLIA
p. 392

C H I N A
p. 392

NEPAL
p. 388

BHUTAN
p. 388

INDIA
p. 386

BANGLADESH
p. 387

MYANMAR
(BURMA)
p. 388

LAOS
p. 388

THAILAND
p. 390

CAMBODIA
p. 389

VIETNAM
p. 389

NORTH
KOREA
p. 393

SOUTH
KOREA
p. 393

JAPAN
p. 393

PHILIPPINES
p. 391

BRUNEI
p. 390

M A L A Y S I A
p. 390

SINGAPORE
p. 391

I N D O N E S I A
p. 391

TIMOR-LES
p. 390

MALDIVES
p. 386

SRI
LANKA
p. 387

MAP KEY

LEBANON
p. 381   Country name and page number
where country facts can be found

ASIA

Occupying four-fifths of the Eurasian landmass, the continent of Asia stretches from the Pacific Ocean to the Ural Mountains and the Black Sea. It is Earth's largest continent, containing 30 percent of the planet's land surface.

Asia's geographic extremes allow it to claim many world records. Mount Everest is the planet's highest point, while the Dead Sea is the lowest. A site in Assam, India, receives 39 feet of rain each year, making it the planet's wettest spot, and Siberia's Lake Baikal plunges over a mile (5,371 feet), making it the world's deepest lake. The Caspian Sea is the world's largest lake—more than quadruple the area of Lake Superior.

Asia has a lengthy coastline, and all but 12 of the continent's countries have direct access to the ocean. These landlocked states form a great band across the middle latitudes of the continent, comprising deserts, mountains, and plateaus. The vast Tibetan Plateau gives rise to Asia's vital rivers: the Yellow, Yangzi, Indus, Ganges, Salween, and Mekong. At the continent's heart lies a convergence of the world's mightiest mountains: Himalaya, Karakoram, Hindu Kush, Pamir, and Kunlun.

Asia also includes island countries like Japan, the Philippines, Indonesia, and Sri Lanka, as well as many of the world's major islands, such as Borneo, Sumatra, Honshu, Celebes, and Java.

Asia displays continuing geologic activity. Volcanoes form a chain along the entire Pacific edge, from Siberia's Kamchatka Peninsula to the islands of the Philippines and Indonesia. In addition, earthquakes rattle China, Japan, and West Asia.

To the north grow boreal forests of conifers—the taiga. Beyond the taiga lie frozen expanses of tundra. Siberia reaches deep inside the Arctic Circle and fills the continent's northern quarter. Cyclones and monsoon winds bring annual rains to thickly populated regions of South and Southeast Asia. These wet, green domains support some of the world's last rain forests and amazing numbers of plants.

Human impact through agriculture, animal grazing, forestry, pollution, and industrialization has altered much of Asia's landscape and still threatens the natural realm.

THE HUMAN FOOTPRINT

PREDOMINANT GENETIC PATTERNS seen today suggest that once agriculture developed, some of the early farmers moved out of the fertile crescent of the Tigris and Euphrates River basins and into central Asia. Europe, East Asia, India, and the Americas were all populated by migrations originating from the Eurasian heartland. If Africa was the cradle of humanity, central Asia was its nursery. *I* Rice farming in East Asia led to another large population ex-

pansion. The spread of agriculture to Japan, Taiwan, and Southeast Asia parallels the genetic patterns of the people living there. *I* As agriculturalists moved south—through the mainland and toward the islands of Indonesia—they found people already inhabiting the area. In Southeast Asia, the earliest populations lived in large farming communities, where they dominated the landscape with terraced rice farms but lived in both cultural and geographical isolation.

TURKEY

REPUBLIC OF TURKEY

AREA 300,948 SQ. MI. ▮ POPULATION 76,806,000 ▮ CAPITAL ANKARA (POP. 3,908,000) ▮ LITERACY 87% ▮ LIFE EXPECTANCY 72 ▮ CURRENCY TURKISH LIRA ▮ GDP PER CAPITA $12,000 ▮ ECONOMY IND: TEXTILES, FOOD PROCESSING, AUTOS, MINING, STEEL, PETROLEUM. AGR: TOBACCO, COTTON, GRAIN, OLIVES, LIVESTOCK. EXP: APPAREL, FOOD, TEXTILES, METAL MANUFACTURING, TRANSPORT EQUIPMENT.

Straddling Europe and Asia, Turkey acts as a bridge between West and East. The portion of Turkey's land in Europe may be small, but the country's largest city, Istanbul, is there. The Asian part of Turkey is dominated by the dry plateau of Anatolia, where coastal areas consist of fertile lowlands. The country, especially northern Turkey, suffers from severe earthquakes. In 1999 Turkey gained approval as a candidate country for membership in the European Union. Most of its trade is with Europe, and many European vacationers come to Turkey for the climate, fine beaches, resorts, Roman ruins, and Crusader castles.

 # GEORGIA

GEORGIA

AREA 26,911 SQ. MI. ▮ POPULATION 4,616,000 ▮ CAPITAL TBILISI (POP. 1,108,000) ▮ LITERACY 100% ▮ LIFE EXPECTANCY 77 ▮ CURRENCY LARI ▮ GDP PER CAPITA $4,700 ▮ ECONOMY IND: STEEL, AIRCRAFT, MACHINE TOOLS, ELECTRICAL APPLIANCES. MINING. AGR: CITRUS, GRAPES, TEA, HAZELNUTS, LIVESTOCK. EXP: SCRAP METAL, MACHINERY, CHEMICALS, FUEL REEXPORTS, CITRUS FRUITS, TEA.

Georgia, on the Black Sea, is geographically in Asia—the mountains forming its northern border serve as the boundary between Europe and Asia. Rich in farmland and minerals, rugged Georgia is wedged between the Caucasus Mountains and the Lesser Caucasus. Over the centuries it has been an object of rivalry between Persia, Turkey, and Russia and was annexed by Russia in the 19th century.

After independence came in 1991, ethnic strife caused Georgia to lose control of South Ossetia and Abkhazia. Both regions enjoyed autonomy during Soviet rule, and both allied with Russia to separate from Georgia. The UN works to resolve these separatist disputes.

ARMENIA

REPUBLIC OF ARMENIA

AREA 11,484 SQ. MI. ▮ POPULATION 2,967,000 ▮ CAPITAL YEREVAN (POP. 1,102,000) ▮ LITERACY 99% ▮ LIFE EXPECTANCY 73 ▮ CURRENCY DRAM ▮ GDP PER CAPITA $6,400 ▮ ECONOMY IND: METAL-CUTTING MACHINE TOOLS, FORGING-PRESSING MACHINES, ELECTRIC MOTORS, TIRES. AGR: FRUIT (ESPECIALLY GRAPES), VEGETABLES, LIVESTOCK. EXP: DIAMONDS, MINERAL PRODUCTS, FOODSTUFFS, ENERGY.

The smallest former Soviet republic, Armenia sits landlocked and earthquake-ridden in rugged mountains. In A.D. 301, Armenia became the first Christian nation; today it is almost surrounded by Islamic nations. During World War I the Ottoman Turks brutally forced out Armenians, causing a diaspora to foreign havens. Armenia gained independence in 1918 but succumbed to a Red Army invasion in 1920. In 1988, a conflict with Azerbaijan over Nagorno-Karabakh (a region with 140,000 ethnic Armenians) erupted. By 1994 Armenians had defeated Azeri forces and had control of Nagorno-Karabakh—but the dispute remains unresolved.

 # AZERBAIJAN

REPUBLIC OF AZERBAIJAN

AREA 33,436 SQ. MI. ▮ POPULATION 8,239,000 ▮ CAPITAL BAKU (POP. 1,931,000) ▮ LITERACY 99% ▮ LIFE EXPECTANCY 67 ▮ CURRENCY AZERBAIJANI MANAT ▮ GDP PER CAPITA $3,700 ▮ ECONOMY IND: PETROLEUM & NATURAL GAS, PETROLEUM PRODUCTS, OIL FIELD EQUIPMENT, STEEL. AGR: COTTON, GRAIN, RICE, GRAPES, CATTLE. EXP: OIL & GAS, MACHINERY, COTTON, FOODSTUFFS.

South of Russia, Azerbaijan is on the west coast of the Caspian Sea; the Caucasus Mountains define its northwestern border. South and west of Baku, the oil-rich capital, lie extensive lowlands, often below sea level. To the west, separated from the main part of the country by Armenia, is the autonomous region of Naxçivan.

When the Soviet Union collapsed, Azerbaijan was one of the first republics to declare independence, escalating the war over Nagorno-Karabakh, a predominately ethnic Armenian region. A cease-fire was reached in 1994 after some 30,000 deaths and hundreds of thousands of displacements, but Armenian forces retain control.

ISRAEL
STATE OF ISRAEL

AREA 8,550 SQ. MI. ▌ POPULATION 7,234,000 ▌ CAPITAL JERUSALEM (POP. 692,300) ▌ LITERACY 97% ▌ LIFE EXPECTANCY 81 ▌ CURRENCY NEW ISRAELI SHEKEL ▌ GDP PER CAPITA $28,800 ▌ ECONOMY IND: HIGH-TECHNOLOGY PROJECTS, WOOD & PAPER PRODUCTS, POTASH & PHOSPHATES, FOOD. AGR: CITRUS, VEGETABLES, COTTON, BEEF. EXP: MACHINERY & EQUIPMENT, SOFTWARE, CUT DIAMONDS, AGRICULTURAL PRODUCTS, CHEMICALS.

A narrow strip of land on the Mediterranean coast, Israel has four principal regions: the coastal plain, the eastern mountains, the southern Negev Desert, and the Jordan Valley. The dry eastern interior includes the Dead Sea. Israel's population is about 77 percent Jewish; most of the remainder is Arab.

Israel ended its occupation of the Sinai Peninsula in 1982. After an extended rebellion, a 1993 accord granted Palestinian self-rule in the Gaza Strip and the West Bank. Israel also annexed the Golan Heights, although Syria still claims this territory. Peace with Palestine and Syria seemed close at the turn of the millennium, but violence again erupted.

LEBANON
LEBANESE REPUBLIC

AREA 4,036 SQ. MI. ▌ POPULATION 4,018,000 ▌ CAPITAL BEIRUT (POP. 1,941,000) ▌ LITERACY 87% ▌ LIFE EXPECTANCY 74 ▌ CURRENCY LEBANESE POUND ▌ GDP PER CAPITA $11,000 ▌ ECONOMY IND: BANKING, FOOD PROCESSING, JEWELRY, CEMENT, TEXTILES, MINERAL & CHEMICAL PRODUCTS. AGR: CITRUS, GRAPES, TOMATOES, APPLES, SHEEP. EXP: FOODSTUFFS & TOBACCO, TEXTILES, CHEMICALS, PRECIOUS STONES, METAL PRODUCTS.

Lebanon is a small, mountainous country in the Middle East. After independence from France in 1943, it prospered as a banking, resort, and university center. Muslims represent about two-thirds of the resident population, the rest being Christian. No census has been taken since 1932 due to political sensitivity over religious affiliation. Fighting between Christian and Muslim militias escalated into civil war from 1975 to 1991. Democracy was restored in 1992— allocating government positions based on religion.

SYRIA
SYRIAN ARAB REPUBLIC

AREA 71,498 SQ. MI. ▌ POPULATION 20,178,000 ▌ CAPITAL DAMASCUS (POP. 2,675,000) ▌ LITERACY 80% ▌ LIFE EXPECTANCY 71 ▌ CURRENCY SYRIAN POUND ▌ GDP PER CAPITA $4,800 ▌ ECONOMY IND: PETROLEUM, TEXTILES, FOOD PROCESSING, BEVERAGES. AGR: WHEAT, BARLEY, COTTON, LENTILS, BEEF. EXP: CRUDE OIL, PETROLEUM PRODUCTS, FRUITS & VEGETABLES, COTTON FIBER, CLOTHING.

Syria is in southwest Asia in the heart of the Middle East. The Mediterranean coastal plain is backed by a low range of hills, followed by a vast interior desert plateau. Most people live near the coast or near the Euphrates River, which brings life to the desert plateau.

Syrians are mostly Arab; about 9 percent are Kurds, living mainly in Syria's northeast corner. The Alawite-controlled Baath (Renaissance) Party has ruled Syria since 1963. Part of the Ottoman Empire for four centuries, Syria came under French mandate in 1920 and gained independence in 1946. The 30-year rule of Hafez al-Assad was marked by authoritarian government, an anti-Israel policy, and military intervention in Lebanon. Bashar al-Assad succeeded his father as president in 2000 and continues his father's policies.

JEWS, CHRISTIANS, AND MUSLIMS visit the mausoleum said to hold the tomb of Abraham, patriarch of monotheism, in Hebron on Israel's West Bank.

IRAQ

REPUBLIC OF IRAQ

AREA 168,754 SQ. MI. ▌ POPULATION 28,946,000 ▌ CAPITAL BAGHDAD (POP. 5,891,000) ▌ LITERACY 74% ▌ LIFE EXPECTANCY 70 ▌ CURRENCY IRAQI DINAR ▌ GDP PER CAPITA $4,000 ▌ ECONOMY IND: PETROLEUM, CHEMICALS, TEXTILES, CONSTRUCTION MATERIALS. AGR: WHEAT, BARLEY, RICE, VEGETABLES, CATTLE. EXP: CRUDE OIL.

Known in ancient times as Mesopotamia, Iraq's lands once held some of the world's earliest civilizations such as Sumer and Babylon. These lands also compose much of the Fertile Crescent. Iraq is bordered by numerous countries on all sides as well as the Persian Gulf in the south. Iraq's lands split into three physiographic regions: the wooded northeastern highlands, the Syrian Desert, and the lowlands watered by the Euphrates and Tigris Rivers. Many of its southern marshes were drained by Saddam Hussein after the Gulf War, however, leaving barren desert land. Iraq is one of the top four countries in rich oil reserves. Iraq's diverse population includes some 20 million Arabs and about 4 million Kurds.

JORDAN

HASHEMITE KINGDOM OF JORDAN

AREA 34,495 SQ. MI. ▌ POPULATION 6,343,000 ▌ CAPITAL AMMAN (POP. 1,106,000) ▌ LITERACY 90% ▌ LIFE EXPECTANCY 79 ▌ CURRENCY JORDANIAN DINAR ▌ GDP PER CAPITA $5,000 ▌ ECONOMY IND: PHOSPHATE MINING, PHARMACEUTICALS, PETROLEUM REFINING, CEMENT, POTASH. AGR: WHEAT, BARLEY, CITRUS, TOMATOES, SHEEP. EXP: PHOSPHATES, FERTILIZERS, POTASH, AGRICULTURAL PRODUCTS, MANUFACTURING.

Located on desert plateaus, Jordan has only a short coast on the Gulf of Aqaba. Much of Jordan's landscape lies eroded, primarily from wind. The Jordan Valley, often referred to as the Ghor, is the lowest natural point on the Earth's surface as it reaches the Dead Sea, dropping to an average of 1,312 feet below sea level. The 1994 peace treaty between Israel and Jordan over the conflict involving the territory of former Palestine set Jordan's western boundary along the Jordan River, the Dead Sea, and the Wadi Araba. However, the final form of the boundary is yet to be made.

KUWAIT

STATE OF KUWAIT

AREA 6,880 SQ. MI. ▌ POPULATION 2,691,000 ▌ CAPITAL KUWAIT CITY (POP. 2,305,000) ▌ LITERACY 93% ▌ LIFE EXPECTANCY 78 ▌ CURRENCY KUWAITI DINAR ▌ GDP PER CAPITA $57,400 ▌ ECONOMY IND: PETROLEUM, PETROCHEMICALS, DESALINATION, FOOD PROCESSING. AGR: PRACTICALLY NO CROPS, FISH. EXP: OIL & REFINED PRODUCTS, FERTILIZERS.

A small, oil-rich country on the Persian Gulf, Kuwait is flat and arid, but oil wealth makes this an attractive place for immigrants. Kuwaiti Arabs make up 45 percent of the population, with other Arabs 35 percent and non-Arabs 20 percent. Full independence from British rule was achieved in 1961. Iraq invaded Kuwait in 1990, but a U.S.-led coalition routed Iraqi forces. Kuwait was the principal platform for U.S. military operations against Saddam Hussein in 2003.

SAUDI ARABIA

KINGDOM OF SAUDI ARABIA

AREA 756,985 SQ. MI. ▌ POPULATION 28,687,000 ▌ CAPITAL RIYADH (POP. 4,856,000) ▌ LITERACY 79% ▌ LIFE EXPECTANCY 76 ▌ CURRENCY SAUDI RIYAL ▌ GDP PER CAPITA $20,700 ▌ ECONOMY IND: CRUDE OIL PRODUCTION, PETROLEUM REFINING, BASIC PETROCHEMICALS, CEMENT. AGR: WHEAT, BARLEY, TOMATOES, MELONS, MUTTON. EXP: PETROLEUM & PETROLEUM PRODUCTS.

Saudi Arabia occupies most of the Arabian Peninsula, but 95 percent of the land is desert. Mountains running parallel to the Red Sea slope down to plains along the Persian Gulf. Below the arid landscape, oil has made this desert kingdom one of the wealthiest nations in the world. Recent efforts at economic diversification have emphasized manufacturing and irrigated farming, but water supplies are limited.

Relations with the United States were strained after the September 11, 2001, terrorist attacks, carried out in part by Saudi citizens. In this conservative society, underpinned by Islamic law, or sharia, women live in veiled segregation. Saudi Arabia is keeper of Islam's most sacred cities, Mecca and Medina.

YEMEN

REPUBLIC OF YEMEN

AREA 207,286 SQ. MI. ▌POPULATION 23,823,000 ▌CAPITAL SANAA (POP. 2,345,000) ▌LITERACY 50% ▌LIFE EXPECTANCY 63 ▌CURRENCY YEMENI RIAL ▌GDP PER CAPITA $2,400 ▌ECONOMY IND: CRUDE OIL PRODUCTION & PETROLEUM REFINING, SMALL-SCALE PRODUCTION OF COTTON TEXTILES & LEATHER GOODS. AGR: GRAIN, FRUITS, VEGETABLES, PULSES, DAIRY PRODUCTS, FISH. EXP: CRUDE OIL, COFFEE, DRIED & SALTED FISH.

Ancient kingdoms flourished in southwestern Arabia (now Yemen), a crossroads of trade from the Orient and Africa to the Mediterranean. Marib, capital of Saba (biblical Sheba), was the queen city of incense; nearby a huge dam irrigated thousands of hectares of farmland. Today a new dam and oil pump life into Marib. In Yemen's highlands volcanic soils yield cereal crops. Most coffee groves have been replaced by fields of qat, chewed as a stimulant. Yemen's modest oil reserves provide most of the revenue, but it is the poorest country in the Middle East.

UNITED ARAB EMIRATES

UNITED ARAB EMIRATES

AREA 30,000 SQ. MI. ▌POPULATION 4,798,000 ▌CAPITAL ABU DHABI (POP. 475,000) ▌LITERACY 78% ▌LIFE EXPECTANCY 76 ▌CURRENCY EMIRATI DIRHAM ▌GDP PER CAPITA $40,000 ▌ECONOMY IND: PETROLEUM, FISHING, PETROCHEMICALS, CONSTRUCTION MATERIALS. AGR: DATES, VEGETABLES, WATERMELONS, POULTRY, FISH. EXP: CRUDE OIL, NATURAL GAS, REEXPORTS, DRIED FISH, DATES.

Seven sheikhdoms on the Arabian Peninsula combined to form a federation, the United Arab Emirates, after Britain pulled out of this barren coastal region in 1971. The United Arab Emirates, often referred to as the UAE, comprises Abu Dhabi, seat of the federal government and the oil capital; Dubayy (Dubai), the main port and commercial-industrial hub; Ajman; Umm al Qaywayn; Ras al Khaymah; Al Fujayrah; and Sharjah. Oil, discovered in 1958, is the major income earner. Oil wealth also attracted foreign workers. A favorite destination for tourists, the country has a liberal attitude toward other cultures and beliefs.

FAST FACT People first drank coffee in Yemen in the 11th century; mocha was named for its Red Sea port, Al Mukha.

QATAR

STATE OF QATAR

AREA 4,448 SQ. MI. ▌POPULATION 833,000 ▌CAPITAL DOHA (POP. 286,000) ▌LITERACY 89% ▌LIFE EXPECTANCY 75 ▌CURRENCY QATARI RIAL ▌GDP PER CAPITA $103,500 ▌ECONOMY IND: CRUDE OIL PRODUCTION & REFINING, FERTILIZERS, PETROCHEMICALS, STEEL REINFORCING BARS, CEMENT. AGR: FRUITS, VEGETABLES, POULTRY, DAIRY PRODUCTS, BEEF, FISH. EXP: PETROLEUM PRODUCTS, FERTILIZERS, STEEL.

Dominated by the Atlas Mountains, Qatar occupies a peninsula that extends into the Persian Gulf. This oil-rich nation, under British protection until 1971, chose not to join the United Arab Emirates. Qatar has exported oil since 1949, and as reserves decline, the nation has turned to its natural gas reserves. The North Field is the largest single reservoir of natural gas in the world. The current emir has instituted political reforms, including allowing women to vote and hold office.

BAHRAIN

KINGDOM OF BAHRAIN

AREA 277 SQ. MI. ▌POPULATION 728,000 ▌CAPITAL MANAMA (POP. 139,000) ▌LITERACY 87% ▌LIFE EXPECTANCY 75 ▌CURRENCY BAHRAINI DINAR ▌GDP PER CAPITA $37,200 ▌ECONOMY IND: PETROLEUM PROCESSING & REFINING, ALUMINUM SMELTING, OFFSHORE BANKING, SHIP REPAIRING, TOURISM. AGR: FRUIT, VEGETABLES, POULTRY, SHRIMP. EXP: PETROLEUM & PETROLEUM PRODUCTS, ALUMINUM, TEXTILES.

Bahrain consists of 33 islands in the Persian Gulf (Arabian Gulf). Since the 1930s the oil industry has replaced pearl diving, and Bahrain has become a financial and communications hub. It is connected to Saudi Arabia by the King Fahd Causeway. Since independence from Britain in 1971, there has been conflict between the ruling Sunni tribe and the Shiite majority. A new constitution in 2002 provided for an elected parliament and gave women the right to vote and stand as candidates.

KAZAKHSTAN

REPUBLIC OF KAZAKHSTAN

AREA 1,049,155 SQ. MI. ❚ POPULATION 15,399,000 ❚ CAPITAL ASTANA (POP. 332,000) ❚ LITERACY 100% ❚ LIFE EXPECTANCY 68 ❚ CURRENCY TENGE ❚ GDP PER CAPITA $11,500 ❚ ECONOMY IND: OIL, COAL, IRON ORE, MANGANESE, CHROMITE, LEAD, ZINC, COPPER, TITANIUM. AGR: GRAIN (MOSTLY SPRING WHEAT), COTTON, LIVESTOCK. EXP: OIL & OIL PRODUCTS, FERROUS METALS, CHEMICALS, MACHINERY, GRAIN.

Stretching across Central Asia, Kazakhstan is a landlocked and arid land. Flat in the west, it rises to high mountains in the east. Kazakhstan declared independence from the U.S.S.R. in 1991, but Russia still uses the Baykonur Cosmodrome in Kazakhstan, which was the principal site for Soviet space launches and which hosts the world's oldest and largest spaceport. The nation confronts a legacy of environmental abuse left behind by the Soviets and is facing ecological disaster in the Aral Sea area. Kazakhstan is trying to preserve the northern part of the sea in order to prevent desertification. The country enjoys strong economic growth because of its large oil, gas, and mineral reserves.

TURKMENISTAN

TURKMENISTAN

AREA 188,456 SQ. MI. ❚ POPULATION 4,885,000 ❚ CAPITAL ASHGABAT (POP. 574,000) ❚ LITERACY 99% ❚ LIFE EXPECTANCY 68 ❚ CURRENCY TURKMEN MANAT ❚ GDP PER CAPITA $6,100 ❚ ECONOMY IND: NATURAL GAS, OIL, PETROLEUM PRODUCTS, TEXTILES. AGR: COTTON, GRAIN, LIVESTOCK. EXP: GAS, OIL, COTTON FIBER, TEXTILES.

Turkmenistan is a desert nation. Nomadic for centuries, the people of Turkmenistan gained independence from Russia in 1991. The country's hope lies in its sector of the Caspian Sea, where oil and natural gas fields are concentrated. Unfortunately, development of gas exports is hampered by a lack of gas-pipeline routes out of this landlocked country. Disputes between Azerbaijan, Iran, Kazakhstan, Russia, and Turkmenistan over the Caspian Sea seabed and maritime boundaries limit international investment in new gas fields and pipelines. Revenue from oil and gas production benefits few because of an authoritarian government.

UZBEKISTAN

REPUBLIC OF UZBEKISTAN

AREA 172,742 SQ. MI. ❚ POPULATION 27,606,000 ❚ CAPITAL TASHKENT (POP. 2,247,000) ❚ LITERACY 99% ❚ LIFE EXPECTANCY 72 ❚ CURRENCY UZBEKISTANI SUM ❚ GDP PER CAPITA $2,600 ❚ ECONOMY IND: TEXTILES, FOOD PROCESSING, MACHINE BUILDING, METALLURGY, NATURAL GAS. AGR: COTTON, VEGETABLES, FRUITS, GRAIN, LIVESTOCK. EXP: COTTON, GOLD, ENERGY PRODUCTS, MINERAL FERTILIZERS, FERROUS METALS.

Uzbekistan is a landlocked country dominated by the Qizilqum desert. Uzbeks descend from Turkic people and are rooted in the Sunni Muslim faith. About 80 percent of the country is flat desert, with mountain ranges rising in the far southeast and northeast. The Fergana Valley in the northeast is the country's most fertile region, containing many cities and industries. Uzbekistan is still one of the largest exporters of cotton, and the world's largest open-pit gold mine is at Muruntau in the Qizilqum desert. However, the economic climate is poor because of smothering state control. The already authoritarian government is becoming more rigid as it is threatened by Islamist groups.

OMAN

SULTANATE OF OMAN

AREA 119,500 SQ. MI. ❚ POPULATION 3,418,000 ❚ CAPITAL MUSCAT (POP. 638,000) ❚ LITERACY 81% ❚ LIFE EXPECTANCY 74 ❚ CURRENCY OMANI RIAL ❚ GDP PER CAPITA $20,200 ❚ ECONOMY IND: CRUDE OIL PRODUCTION & REFINING, NATURAL GAS PRODUCTION, CONSTRUCTION. AGR: DATES, LIMES, BANANAS, ALFALFA, CAMELS, FISH. EXP: PETROLEUM, REEXPORTS, FISH, METALS, TEXTILES.

At the mouth of the Persian Gulf and in the path of trade routes to East Africa and the Orient lies Oman. After the mid-19th century, power struggles weakened the sultanate, strengthening bonds to Britain. In 1970 British-educated Qaboos bin Said al-Said deposed his father as sultan and began modernizing the country. Oman allows the United States to use port and air base facilities. Profits from oil, exported since 1967, have financed roads, schools, and hospitals. The majority of Omanis still farm or fish, and protection of fisheries and coastal zones is promoted.

TAJIKISTAN

REPUBLIC OF TAJIKISTAN

AREA 55,251 SQ. MI. ▌ POPULATION 7,349,000 ▌ CAPITAL DUSHANBE (POP. 554,000) ▌ LITERACY 100% ▌ LIFE EXPECTANCY 65 ▌ CURRENCY SOMONI ▌ GDP PER CAPITA $2,100 ▌ ECONOMY IND: ALUMINUM, ZINC, LEAD, CHEMICALS & FERTILIZERS. AGR: COTTON, GRAIN, FRUITS, GRAPES, VEGETABLES, CATTLE, SHEEP, GOATS. EXP: ALUMINUM, ELECTRICITY, COTTON, FRUITS, VEGETABLE OIL, TEXTILES.

Mountains cover more than 90 percent of this Central Asian republic. Within its borders is the former Soviet Union's highest peak, commonly known as Communism Peak. Shortly after independence in 1991, Tajikistan endured a five-year civil war between the Moscow-backed government and the Islamist-led opposition. A peace agreement was signed in 1997, but the political turmoil has depressed the economy. Tajikistan relies heavily on Russian assistance, and there are some 23,000 Russian troops guarding Tajikistan's borders—against weapons, drugs, and Islamic extremists.

KYRGYZSTAN

KYRGYZ REPUBLIC

AREA 77,182 SQ. MI. ▌ POPULATION 5,432,000 ▌ CAPITAL BISHKEK (POP. 869,000) ▌ LITERACY 99% ▌ LIFE EXPECTANCY 69 ▌ CURRENCY KYRGYZSTANI SOM ▌ GDP PER CAPITA $2,100 ▌ ECONOMY IND: SMALL MACHINERY, TEXTILES, FOOD PROCESSING, CEMENT, SHOES, LOGS. AGR: TOBACCO, COTTON, POTATOES, VEGETABLES, SHEEP. EXP: COTTON, WOOL, MEAT, TOBACCO, GOLD, MERCURY, URANIUM, NATURAL GAS.

A rugged nation in Central Asia, Kyrgyzstan shares the snowcapped Tian Shan with China. Some three quarters of the region is mountainous. In their mountain fastness, the nomadic Kyrgyz people, a Turkic-speaking community with loose ties to Islam, bred horses, cattle, and yaks for centuries. The Kyrgyz came under tsarist Russian rule during the 19th century, and thousands of Slavic farmers migrated into the region. Kyrgyzstan gained independence in 1991. Raising livestock still remains the main agricultural activity today.

AFGHANISTAN

ISLAMIC REPUBLIC OF AFGHANISTAN

AREA 251,773 SQ. MI. ▌ POPULATION 33,610,000 ▌ CAPITAL KABUL (POP. 3,768,000) ▌ LITERACY 28% ▌ LIFE EXPECTANCY 45 ▌ CURRENCY AFGHANI ▌ GDP PER CAPITA $800 ▌ ECONOMY IND: SMALL-SCALE PRODUCTION OF TEXTILES, SOAP, FURNITURE, SHOES. AGR: OPIUM, WHEAT, FRUITS, NUTS, WOOL. EXP: OPIUM, FRUITS & NUTS, HANDWOVEN CARPETS, WOOL, COTTON.

Afghanistan is a country of ethnic minorities. The northern plains and valleys are home to Tajiks and Uzbeks. Pashtuns inhabit the desert-dominated southern plateaus. The Hazara live in the central highlands. After decades of war, Afghanistan is rebuilding its economy, which is mostly agricultural, and attempting to stabilize its government. The Taliban government, which harbored Osama bin Laden after the September 11, 2001, attacks, was overthrown by Afghan and international forces. Afghanistan remains a hot spot of international military action.

EASTERN ORTHODOX FAITHFUL gather to celebrate on Epiphany, a winter holiday, near the village of Sosnovka, some 50 miles outside Bishkuk, the capital of Kyrgyzstan.

PAKISTAN

ISLAMIC REPUBLIC OF PAKISTAN

AREA 307,374 SQ. MI. ▮ POPULATION 176,243,000 ▮ CAPITAL ISLAMABAD (POP. 851,000) ▮ LITERACY 50% ▮ LIFE EXPECTANCY 64 ▮ CURRENCY PAKISTANI RUPEE ▮ GDP PER CAPITA $2,600 ▮ ECONOMY IND: TEXTILES & APPAREL, FOOD PROCESSING, BEVERAGES, CONSTRUCTION MATERIALS. AGR: COTTON, WHEAT, RICE, SUGARCANE, MILK. EXP: TEXTILES, RICE, LEATHER, SPORTS GOODS, CARPETS & RUGS.

The eastern and southern parts of Pakistan are dominated by the Indus River and its tributaries. West of the Indus, the land becomes increasingly arid and mountainous. To the north are the great mountains of the Hindu Kush and Karakoram. Agriculture is concentrated in the extensively irrigated Indus Basin. Despite an increase in cotton, wheat, and rice production, feeding the growing population is a challenge. Other problems include continuing tension and a presumed nuclear arms rivalry with India, violence by Islamist militants, and a growing trade in heroin.

IRAN

ISLAMIC REPUBLIC OF IRAN

AREA 1,024,020 SQ. MI. ▮ POPULATION 66,429,000 ▮ CAPITAL TEHRAN (POP. 8,221,000) ▮ LITERACY 77% ▮ LIFE EXPECTANCY 71 ▮ CURRENCY IRANIAN RIAL ▮ GDP PER CAPITA $12,800 ▮ ECONOMY IND: PETROLEUM, PETROCHEMICALS, FERTILIZERS, CAUSTIC SODA, TEXTILES, CEMENT AND OTHER CONSTRUCTION MATERIALS, FOOD PROCESSING (ESP. SUGAR & VEGETABLE OIL), FERROUS AND NON-FERROUS METAL FABRICATION, ARMAMENTS. EXP: PETROLEUM, CHEMICAL PRODUCTS, FRUITS AND NUTS, CARPETS.

An extremely arid country, Iran's central plateau is ringed by heavily eroded mountain ranges, most prominently the Zagros Mountains in the north and the Elburz, or Alborz, Mountains in the south. Most people live off the land, although internal migration from the more rural areas to cities has become a large trend. Almost a third of the country's border consists of seacoast. Iran has a young population, with nearly 40 percent of the people 15 years of age or younger. A leader in the Islamic world, Iran's 1979 constitution established the country as an Islamic republic in which the clergy dominate the executive, parliamentary, and judiciary bodies.

INDIA

REPUBLIC OF INDIA

AREA 1,269,221 SQ. MI. ▮ POPULATION 1,166,079,000 ▮ CAPITAL NEW DELHI (POP. 295,000) ▮ LITERACY 61% ▮ LIFE EXPECTANCY 70 ▮ CURRENCY INDIAN RUPEE ▮ GDP PER CAPITA $2,800 ▮ ECONOMY IND: TEXTILES, CHEMICALS, FOOD PROCESSING, STEEL, TRANSPORTATION EQUIPMENT, CEMENT, MINING. AGR: RICE, WHEAT, OILSEED, COTTON, CATTLE, FISH. EXP: TEXTILE GOODS, GEMS & JEWELRY, ENGINEERING GOODS, CHEMICALS, LEATHER MANUFACTURING.

The South Asian country of India is a land of great contrasts in geography. The barren, snow-capped Himalaya rises along its northern border. South of the Himalaya lies the low, fertile Ganges Plain. The Great Indian Desert lies in the west, but eastern India receives some of the highest rainfall in the world during the monsoon season.

India has a massive population, and although the majority of people are Hindu, India also has one of the world's largest Muslim populations. The Hindu caste system reflects economic and religious hierarchies. One of six Indians is a dalit, or untouchable, the lowest rank in the Hindu caste system and one that has received government protections in recent years. India has a burgeoning middle class and has made great strides in engineering and information technology.

MALDIVES

REPUBLIC OF MALDIVES

AREA 115 SQ. MI. ▮ POPULATION 396,000 ▮ CAPITAL MALE (POP. 83,000) ▮ LITERACY 96% ▮ LIFE EXPECTANCY 74 ▮ CURRENCY RUFIYAA ▮ GDP PER CAPITA $5,000 ▮ ECONOMY IND: FISH PROCESSING, TOURISM, SHIPPING, BOAT BUILDING, COCONUT PROCESSING. AGR: COCONUTS, CORN, SWEET POTATOES, FISH. EXP: FISH, CLOTHING.

The island nation of Maldives is south of India in the Indian Ocean. The islands are small, and none rise more than 6 feet above sea level. Like necklaces draped along an undersea plateau, 1,200 coral islands—about 200 of which are inhabited—form the Maldives. In 1968, three years after independence from Britain, the sultanate gave way to an Islamic republic. Tourism and fishing sustain the economy. Maldives sustained damage from the December 2004 tsunami.

BENAZIR BHUTTO / PAKISTANI REFORM LEADER

The daughter of Zulfikar Ali Bhutto, Benazir Bhutto became the figurehead of her father's political party, the Pakistan People's Party, after his execution in 1979. Returning to Pakistan after years of exile, she quickly rose as the most prominent political figure opposing then-military dictator Mohammad Zia-ul-Haq. After Zia's death, she won the position of prime minister in 1988—becoming the first woman leader of a Muslim nation. Her government was twice dismissed, however, on charges of corruption. Under threat of arrest, Bhutto fell into self-imposed exile in London and Dubai in the late 1990s. Bhutto was granted amnesty in 2007, and she returned to Karachi, only to be assassinated two months later in a suicide attack.

" We are prepared to risk our lives. We're prepared to risk our liberty. But we're not prepared to surrender this great nation to militants. — **BENAZIR BHUTTO, 2007 "**

FAST FACT Hindi is India's national language, but there are 14 other official languages and more than 1,500 dialects.

SRI LANKA
DEMOCRATIC SOCIALIST REPUBLIC OF SRI LANKA

AREA 25,299 SQ. MI. ▌ POPULATION 21,325,000 ▌ CAPITAL COLOMBO (POP. 648,000) ▌ LITERACY 91% ▌ LIFE EXPECTANCY 75 ▌ CURRENCY SRI LANKAN RUPEE ▌ GDP PER CAPITA $4,300 ▌ ECONOMY IND: RUBBER PROCESSING, TEA, COCONUTS, OTHER AGRICULTURAL COMMODITIES, CLOTHING, CEMENT. AGR: RICE, SUGARCANE, GRAINS, PULSES, MILK. EXP: TEXTILES & APPAREL, TEA, DIAMONDS, COCONUT PRODUCTS, PETROLEUM PRODUCTS.

Sri Lanka, known as Ceylon until 1972, is a tropical island lying near the southern tip of India and the Equator. From the coast, the land rises to a central plateau, where tea plantations are found. Population density is highest in the island's southwest corner, where Colombo, the capital, is located. After 450 years under European rule, Ceylon gained its independence from the United Kingdom in 1948. Some among the Tamil Hindu minority have argued for a separate state, which is not supported by the Sinhalese Buddhist majority. Decades of civil war have had a negative impact on economic growth, which depends on tea and garment manufacture. Fighting continues between the government and Tamil rebels.

BANGLADESH
PEOPLE'S REPUBLIC OF BANGLADESH

AREA 56,977 SQ. MI. ▌ POPULATION 156,051,000 ▌ CAPITAL DHAKA (POP. 14,796,000) ▌ LITERACY 48% ▌ LIFE EXPECTANCY 60 ▌ CURRENCY TAKA ▌ GDP PER CAPITA $1,500 ▌ ECONOMY IND: COTTON TEXTILES, JUTE, GARMENTS, TEA PROCESSING. AGR: RICE, JUTE, TEA, WHEAT, BEEF. EXP: GARMENTS, JUTE & JUTE GOODS, LEATHER, FROZEN FISH & SEAFOOD.

Bangladesh is a low-lying country formed by the alluvial plain of the river system formed by the Ganges and the Brahmaputra. The rivers' annual floods bring silt to renew farmland fertility, often creating new islands in the delta that are quickly claimed as farmland. Much of the land is barely above sea level, with the exception of hills east and south of Chittagong. The monsoon winds come in summer, bringing heavy rainfall and cyclones, which at times cause storm surges that smash into the delta, sweeping people, livestock, and crops from the lowlands. Deforestation worsens flooding downstream. The government protects the Sundarbans mangrove forest—one of the largest in the world and home to threatened species like the Bengal tiger.

388

NEPAL

FEDERAL DEMOCRATIC REPUBLIC OF NEPAL

AREA 56,827 SQ. MI. ▮ POPULATION 28,563,000 ▮ CAPITAL KATHMANDU (POP. 1,029,000) ▮ LITERACY 49% ▮ LIFE EXPECTANCY 65 ▮ CURRENCY NEPALESE RUPEE ▮ GDP PER CAPITA $1,100 ▮ ECONOMY IND: TOURISM, CARPETS, TEXTILES, SMALL RICE, JUTE, SUGAR, OILSEED MILLS, CIGARETTES, CEMENT & BRICK PRODUCTION. AGR: RICE, CORN, WHEAT, SUGARCANE, MILK. EXP: CARPETS, CLOTHING, LEATHER GOODS, JUTE GOODS, GRAIN.

Nepal lies between China and India in South Asia. Political instability in this country has prevented economic growth, and Nepal remains one of the world's poorest countries. Most Nepalese live in the central, hilly region and in the southern plain known as the Terai. The cutting of trees for fuel causes erosion. Rivers that spring from the Himalaya generate electricity for local use and potentially for export. Nepal possesses the greatest altitude variation on Earth, from the lowlands near sea level to Mount Everest. Sherpas benefit from the mountaineering boom and tourism in the Everest region, owning much of the lodging and transportation. After 240 years under the Shah dynasty, Nepal abolished its monarchy and became a republic in May 2008.

LAOS

LAO PEOPLE'S DEMOCRATIC REPUBLIC

AREA 91,429 SQ. MI. ▮ POPULATION 6,835,000 ▮ CAPITAL VIENTIANE (POP. 716,000) ▮ LITERACY 69% ▮ LIFE EXPECTANCY 69 ▮ CURRENCY KIP ▮ GDP PER CAPITA $2,100 ▮ ECONOMY IND: TIN & GYPSUM MINING, TIMBER, ELECTRIC POWER, AGRICULTURAL PROCESSING. AGR: SWEET POTATOES, VEGETABLES, CORN, COFFEE, WATER BUFFALO. EXP: WOOD PRODUCTS, GARMENTS, ELECTRICITY, COFFEE, TIN.

Laos is a landlocked, mountainous country. Agriculture, primarily subsistence farming, dominates the economy. Most people live in the valleys of the Mekong River and its tributaries, where the fertile floodplains provide a suitable environment for growing rice. Laos is one of the few remaining communist states, its economy hampered by poor roads, no railroad, and limited access to electricity.

MYANMAR (BURMA)

REPUBLIC OF THE UNION OF MYANMAR

AREA 261,218 SQ. MI. ▮ POPULATION 48,138,000 ▮ CAPITAL YANGON (POP. 4,348,000) ▮ LITERACY 90% ▮ LIFE EXPECTANCY 63 ▮ CURRENCY KYAT ▮ GDP PER CAPITA $1,200 ▮ ECONOMY IND: AGRICULTURAL PROCESSING, KNIT & WOVEN APPAREL, WOOD & WOOD PRODUCTS, COPPER, TIN, TUNGSTEN, IRON, GEMS, JADE. AGR: RICE, PULSES, BEANS, SESAME, HARDWOOD (TEAK), FISH. EXP: GAS, WOOD PRODUCTS, PULSES, BEANS, FISH, RICE.

Myanmar's Ayeyarwady Basin is surrounded by forested mountains and plateaus. Most people live in the fertile valley and delta of the Ayeyarwady River. The majority of Myanmar's people are Burmans, although minorities are dominant in border and mountainous areas. Myanmar, which gained independence from Britain in 1948, has been ruled by military governments since 1962. It is a resource-rich country with a strong agricultural base, but military rule prevents economic development. The isolationist government's response to Cyclone Nargis in 2008 drew international attention and criticism.

BHUTAN

KINGDOM OF BHUTAN

AREA 17,954 SQ. MI. ▮ POPULATION 691,000 ▮ CAPITAL THIMPHU (POP. 35,000) ▮ LITERACY 47% ▮ LIFE EXPECTANCY 66 ▮ CURRENCY NGULTRUM, INDIAN RUPEE ▮ GDP PER CAPITA $5,600 ▮ ECONOMY IND: CEMENT, WOOD PRODUCTS, PROCESSED FRUITS, ALCOHOLIC BEVERAGES. AGR: RICE, CORN, ROOT CROPS, CITRUS, DAIRY PRODUCTS. EXP: ELECTRICITY (TO INDIA), CARDAMOM, GYPSUM, TIMBER, HANDICRAFTS.

Bhutan is a tiny, remote, and impoverished country between two powerful neighbors, India and China. This conservative Buddhist kingdom high in the Himalaya had no paved roads until the 1960s, was off-limits to foreigners until 1974, and launched television service only in 1999. Fertile valleys (less than 10 percent of the land) feed all the Bhutanese. Bhutan's ancient Buddhist culture and mountain scenery make it attractive for tourists, whose numbers are limited by the government.

VIETNAMESE WOMEN in traditional conical straw hats pass by a Westernized shopping center in Ho Chi Minh City. After two decades of reforms, Vietnam is enjoying prosperity. Per capita income doubled during the first five years of the 21st century.

CAMBODIA

KINGDOM OF CAMBODIA

AREA 69,898 SQ. MI. ▮ POPULATION 14,494,000 ▮ CAPITAL PHNOM PENH (POP. 1,657,000) ▮ LITERACY 74% ▮ LIFE EXPECTANCY 62 ▮ CURRENCY RIEL ▮ GDP PER CAPITA $2,000 ▮ ECONOMY IND: TOURISM, GARMENTS, RICE MILLING, FISHING, WOOD & WOOD PRODUCTS. AGR: RICE, RUBBER, CORN, VEGETABLES. EXP: TIMBER, GARMENTS, RUBBER, RICE, FISH.

Cambodia is a mostly flat and forested land. Independence from France came in 1953. It is believed that under the rule of Saloth Sar (Pol Pot) and the Khmer Rouge from 1975 to 1979, more than a million people were killed or died as a result of the government's so-called reforms. In 2004, Norodom Sihamoni became king, leading the constitutional monarchy and introducing democratic reforms. Cambodia enjoys relative stability today, but subsistence farming employs 75 percent of the workforce and many live in poverty. Cambodians hope that tourism to Angkor Wat will bring prosperity.

VIETNAM

SOCIALIST REPUBLIC OF VIETNAM

AREA 127,844 SQ. MI. ▮ POPULATION 86,968,000 ▮ CAPITAL HANOI (POP. 4,723,000) ▮ LITERACY 90% ▮ LIFE EXPECTANCY 72 ▮ CURRENCY DONG ▮ GDP PER CAPITA $2,800 ▮ ECONOMY IND: FOOD PROCESSING, GARMENTS, SHOES, MACHINE BUILDING. AGR: PADDY RICE, CORN, POTATOES, RUBBER, POULTRY, FISH. EXP: CRUDE OIL, MARINE PRODUCTS, RICE, COFFEE, RUBBER.

Vietnam's northern lowlands are separated from the Mekong Delta in the south by coastal plains backed by the forested Annam highlands. Armed struggle won independence from France in 1954. For two decades South Vietnam and North Vietnam fought, with other countries—especially France and the United States—participating. In 1975 South Vietnam fell and was reunified under a communist regime. Vietnam saw dramatic economic progress throughout most of the 1990s. A stock exchange was launched in 2000, and foreign investment has since increased.

THAILAND

KINGDOM OF THAILAND

AREA 198,115 SQ. MI. ∎ POPULATION 65,905,000 ∎ CAPITAL BANGKOK (POP. 6,918,000) ∎ LITERACY 93% ∎ LIFE EXPECTANCY 73 ∎ CURRENCY BAHT ∎ GDP PER CAPITA $8,500 ∎ ECONOMY IND: TOURISM, TEXTILES & GARMENTS, AGRICULTURAL PROCESSING, BEVERAGES, TOBACCO, CEMENT. AGR: RICE, CASSAVA (TAPIOCA), RUBBER, CORN. EXP: COMPUTERS, TRANSISTORS, SEAFOOD, CLOTHING, RICE.

Thailand is dominated by the Chao Phraya River basin. To the east rises the Khorat Plateau, a sandstone plateau with poor soils supporting grasses and woodlands. The southern region is hilly and forested. High, rugged mountains lie throughout northern Thailand, where the rich soils in the remote mountain valleys yield profitable crops of opium poppies. The largely homogeneous population is mostly ethnic Thai and Buddhist. Democracy is returning to Thailand after a 2006 military coup and the government is enjoying a fast-growing economy. Social problems are linked to opium production, heroin trafficking, and a great number of Burmese refugees.

TIMOR-LESTE

DEMOCRATIC REPUBLIC OF TIMOR-LESTE
(EAST TIMOR)

AREA 5,640 SQ. MI. ∎ POPULATION 1,132,000 ∎ CAPITAL DILI (POP. 49,000) ∎ LITERACY 59% ∎ LIFE EXPECTANCY 67 ∎ CURRENCY US DOLLAR ∎ GDP PER CAPITA $2,400 ∎ ECONOMY IND: PRINTING, SOAP MANUFACTURING, HANDICRAFTS, WOVEN CLOTH. AGR: COFFEE, RICE, MAIZE, CASSAVA. EXP: COFFEE, SANDALWOOD, MARBLE.

Timor-Leste, a Portuguese colony until 1975, shares the island of Timor with Indonesia. When the Portuguese left, Indonesia invaded and annexed East Timor. The UN condemned the occupation, and a Nobel Prize for Peace was given to East Timorese José Ramos-Horta for his work toward independence and peace. In 1999 a UN-organized referendum showed that most East Timorese wanted independence. Indonesian militias caused severe damage after the vote, but the UN guided East Timor to independence in 2002. Oil in the Timor Sea promises future revenue.

MALAYSIA

MALAYSIA

AREA 127,355 SQ. MI. ∎ POPULATION 25,716,000 ∎ CAPITAL KUALA LUMPUR (POP. 1,519,000) ∎ LITERACY 89% ∎ LIFE EXPECTANCY 73 ∎ CURRENCY RINGGIT ∎ GDP PER CAPITA $15,300 ∎ ECONOMY IND: RUBBER & OIL, PALM PROCESSING & MANUFACTURING, LIGHT MANUFACTURING INDUSTRY, LOGGING, PETROLEUM PRODUCTION & REFINING. AGR: RUBBER, PALM OIL, CACAO, RICE. EXP: ELECTRONIC EQUIPMENT, PETROLEUM & LIQUEFIED NATURAL GAS, WOOD & WOOD PRODUCTS, PALM OIL.

Comprising the territories of Malaya, Sarawak, and Sabah, Malaysia stretches from peninsular Malaysia to northeastern Borneo. Central mountains divide peninsular Malaysia, separating the eastern coast, with its sheltered beaches and bays, from the western plains. Sarawak and Sabah share the island of Borneo with Indonesia and Brunei, where swamps rise to jungle-covered mountains.

Malaysia is one of the world's largest exporters of semiconductors, electrical goods, and appliances. The government, a federal democracy with a ceremonial king, plans to build on its already successful semiconductor industry to make Malaysia a leading producer and developer of high-tech products.

BRUNEI

BRUNEI DARUSSALAM

AREA 2,226 SQ. MI. ∎ POPULATION 388,000 ∎ CAPITAL BANDAR SERI BEGAWAN (POP. 61,000) ∎ LITERACY 93% ∎ LIFE EXPECTANCY 76 ∎ CURRENCY BRUNEIAN DOLLAR ∎ GDP PER CAPITA $53,100 ∎ ECONOMY IND: PETROLEUM, PETROLEUM REFINING, LIQUEFIED NATURAL GAS, CONSTRUCTION. AGR: RICE, VEGETABLES, FRUITS, POULTRY. EXP: CRUDE OIL, NATURAL GAS, REFINED PRODUCTS.

A small country, Brunei is located on the island of Borneo in Southeast Asia. Consisting of just two jungle enclaves, Brunei won its independence in 1984 after almost a century as a British protectorate. The people of this Muslim sultanate—rich in oil and natural gas—enjoy high subsidies and generous health care. Brunei has an absolute monarchy and a hereditary nobility, with the sultan awarding titles to commoners.

INDONESIA

REPUBLIC OF INDONESIA

AREA 742,308 SQ. MI. ▮ POPULATION 240,272,000 ▮ CAPITAL
JAKARTA (POP. 9,703,000) ▮ LITERACY 90% ▮ LIFE EXPECTANCY 71
▮ CURRENCY INDONESIAN RUPIAH ▮ GDP PER CAPITA $3,900 ▮
ECONOMY IND: PETROLEUM & NATURAL GAS, TEXTILES, APPAREL,
FOOTWEAR, MINING, CEMENT, CHEMICAL FERTILIZERS. AGR: RICE,
CASSAVA (TAPIOCA), PEANUTS, RUBBER, POULTRY. EXP: OIL & GAS,
ELECTRICAL APPLIANCES, PLYWOOD, TEXTILES, RUBBER.

Indonesia is an archipelago of 17,508 islands between the
Indian and Pacific Oceans. The islands are mountainous
with dense rain forests; some have active volcanoes. The
democratic government faces problems such as militant
Islamic groups, religious conflict between Muslims and
Christians, and terrorist actions. Export earnings from oil
and natural gas help the economy, and Indonesia is a member of the Organization of Petroleum Exporting Countries
(OPEC). Tourists come to see the rich diversity of plants
and wildlife, some of which exist nowhere else.

DESIGNED BY ARGENTINE-AMERICAN architect César Pelli,
the Petronas Towers stand in Kuala Lumpur, the capital of Malaysia. At
88 stories—1,482 feet—they are the tallest twin towers in the world.

 # PHILIPPINES

REPUBLIC OF THE PHILIPPINES

AREA 115,831 SQ. MI. ▮ POPULATION 97,977,000 ▮ CAPITAL MANILA
(POP. 11,662,000) ▮ LITERACY 93% ▮ LIFE EXPECTANCY 71 ▮ CUR-
RENCY PHILIPPINE PESO ▮ GDP PER CAPITA $3,300 ▮ ECONOMY
IND: TEXTILES, PHARMACEUTICALS, CHEMICALS, WOOD PROD-
UCTS. AGR: RICE, COCONUTS, CORN, SUGARCANE, PORK, FISH.
EXP: ELECTRONIC EQUIPMENT, MACHINERY & TRANSPORT EQUIP-
MENT, GARMENTS, COCONUT PRODUCTS.

The Philippine Islands lie between the South China Sea
and the Pacific Ocean. Independence came in 1946,
when Japanese occupation ended. In 1986 President Ferdinand Marcos was compelled to hold an election and
Corazon Aquino, widow of a murdered opposition leader, became president. Although just north of the world's
largest Muslim state, Indonesia, the population of the
Philippines is about 94 percent Christian. The economy
is increasingly dependent on remittances—in 2007,
the country received more than $13 billion from
over eight million Filipinos working abroad.

 # SINGAPORE

REPUBLIC OF SINGAPORE

AREA 430 SQ. MI. ▮ POPULATION 4,658,000 ▮ CAPITAL SINGAPORE
(POP. 4,592,000) ▮ LITERACY 93% ▮ LIFE EXPECTANCY 82 ▮
CURRENCY SINGAPORE DOLLAR ▮ GDP PER CAPITA $53,000 ▮
ECONOMY IND: ELECTRONICS, CHEMICALS, FINANCIAL SER-
VICES, OIL DRILLING EQUIPMENT, PETROLEUM REFINING, RUBBER
PROCESSING AND RUBBER PRODUCTS, PROCESSED FOOD AND
BEVERAGES, SHIP REPAIR, OFFSHORE PLATFORM CONSTRUCTION,
LIFE SCIENCES, ENTREPOT TRADE. AGR: RUBBER, COPRA, FRUIT,
ORCHIDS, VEGETABLES, POULTRY, EGGS, FISH, ORNAMENTAL FISH
EXP: MACHINERY AND EQUIPMENT (INCLUDING ELECTRONICS),
CONSUMER GOODS, CHEMICALS, MINERAL FUELS.

The country of Singapore, which consists of Singapore
Island and some 50 smaller tropical islands, is located at
the tip of the Malay Peninsula. More than 3,000 multinational companies have offices on the main island, located
at the entrance to the Strait of Malacca, which is the shortest sea route between the Indian Ocean and the South
China Sea. As a trade center of the British Empire, Singapore attracted thousands of Chinese settlers, who now
make up a majority of the population. Independent
since 1965, Singapore is Southeast Asia's financial
hub and the world's busiest container port.

CHINA

PEOPLE'S REPUBLIC OF CHINA

AREA 3,705,405 SQ. MI. ∎ POPULATION 1,388,613,000 ∎ CAPITAL BEIJING (POP. 11,741,000) ∎ LITERACY 91% ∎ LIFE EXPECTANCY 74 ∎ CURRENCY YUAN (ALSO REFERRED TO AS THE RENMINBI) ∎ GDP PER CAPITA $6,000 ∎ ECONOMY IND: IRON & STEEL, COAL, MACHINE BUILDING, ARMAMENTS, TEXTILES & APPAREL, PETROLEUM, CEMENT. AGR: RICE, WHEAT, POTATOES, SORGHUM, PORK, FISH. EXP: MACHINERY & EQUIPMENT, TEXTILES & CLOTHING, FOOTWEAR, TOYS & SPORTING GOODS, MINERAL FUELS.

China's geography is highly diverse, with hills, plains, and river deltas in the east and deserts, high plateaus, and mountains in the west. China has reformed its economy and allowed competition, and today has the world's highest rate of growth. Politically it still maintains strict control over its people. Chinese rule over Tibet remains controversial, and political issues with Taiwan remain unresolved. China regained Hong Kong from Britain in 1997 and Macau from Portugal in 1999. In 2003 China became only the third nation (after Russia and the U.S.) to launch a manned spaceflight. The Sichuan Province suffered extensive damages and casualties from a severe earthquake in May 2008, only months before Beijing hosted the summer Olympics.

MONGOLIA

MONGOLIA

AREA 603,909 SQ. MI. ∎ POPULATION 3,041,000 ∎ CAPITAL ULAANBAATAR (POP. 919,000) ∎ LITERACY 98% ∎ LIFE EXPECTANCY 68 ∎ CURRENCY TOGROG/TUGRIK ∎ GDP PER CAPITA $3,200 ∎ ECONOMY IND: CONSTRUCTION MATERIALS, MINING, OIL, FOOD & BEVERAGES, PROCESSING OF ANIMAL PRODUCTS. AGR: WHEAT, BARLEY, POTATOES, FORAGE CROPS, SHEEP. EXP: COPPER, GOLD, LIVESTOCK, ANIMAL PRODUCTS, CASHMERE, WOOL, HIDES.

Landlocked between two larger countries—Russia and China—Mongolia is one of the world's highest countries, with an average elevation of 5,180 feet. Mongolia suffers extreme temperatures, and southern Mongolia is dominated by the Gobi desert. Mongolia became a communist country in 1924, but in 1990 multiparty elections were held. Copper, cashmere, and gold exports help the economy, although poverty remains a major concern.

HONG KONG

CITY OF WORLD COMMERCE

Hong Kong, which functions as both a city and special administrative zone, is located in southeastern China. The zone comprises the 29-square-mile island of Hong Kong, the Kowloon peninsula, and the New Territories—a mountainous mass of land abutting Kowloon. The core of Hong Kong lies at the foot of Victoria Peak, part of an extensive granite range blanketing the island. Hong Kong centers on a natural deepwater harbor, making it one of the world's biggest container shipping ports. Hong Kong's landmass continues to increase through land reclamation.

Hong Kong's economy depends on its role as a trade center and a shipping and banking emporium. Other common occupations include farming and fishing. Since the expiration of Britain's lease on Hong Kong in 1997, China has agreed to give Hong Kong virtual autonomy for a period of 50 years.

TAIWAN

ISLAND OF PROSPERITY

Taiwan, located off the Chinese coast, has a fertile plain along the west coast that rises to high mountain ranges. It is an island of 13,885 square miles with an estimated population of 22,974,000.

After civil war in China between Communist and Nationalist forces, the latter retreated to Taiwan in 1949. Formally known as the Republic of China, Taiwan made the transition from an authoritarian state to a multiparty democracy in the early 1990s. The Democratic Progressive Party won the presidential election in 2000, ending the Nationalist Party's 55-year monopoly.

Politically, most world countries and the UN acknowledge Taiwan as one of 23 provinces of China. The relationship between China and Taiwan remains awkward. Taiwan is one of the world's largest suppliers of computer technology. The ambitious Taipei 101 building, the world's tallest when built in 2004, reflects the island's economic success.

NORTH KOREA

DEMOCRATIC PEOPLE'S REPUBLIC OF KOREA

AREA 46,540 SQ. MI. ▮ POPULATION 22,665,000 ▮ CAPITAL PYONG-YANG (POP. 3,346,000) ▮ LITERACY 99% ▮ LIFE EXPECTANCY 72 ▮ CURRENCY NORTH KOREAN WON ▮ GDP PER CAPITA $11,700 ▮ ECONOMY IND: MILITARY PRODUCTS, MACHINE BUILDING, ELECTRIC POWER, CHEMICALS, MINING. AGR: RICE, CORN, POTATOES, SOYBEANS, CATTLE. EXP: MINERALS, METALLURGICAL PRODUCTS, MANUFACTURING (INC. ARMAMENTS), TEXTILES.

North Korea occupies the northern part of the Korean peninsula; mountains cover more than 80 percent of the land. Korea was first divided in 1945, with Soviet troops occupying the north and the United States the south. North Korea functions as one of the few remaining communist states. It devotes large amounts of money to the military, while its people suffer from chronic food shortages. Despite severe shortages of food and electricity, North Korea maintains the world's fourth largest army, a nuclear weapons program, and missiles that threaten South Korea and Japan.

SOUTH KOREA

REPUBLIC OF KOREA

AREA 38,321 SQ. MI. ▮ POPULATION 48,509,000 ▮ CAPITAL SEOUL (POP. 9,762,000) ▮ LITERACY 98% ▮ LIFE EXPECTANCY 79 ▮ CURRENCY SOUTH KOREAN WON ▮ GDP PER CAPITA $26,000 ▮ ECONOMY IND: ELECTRONICS, AUTOMOBILE PRODUCTION, CHEMICALS, SHIPBUILDING, STEEL, TEXTILES. AGR: RICE, ROOT CROPS, BARLEY, VEGETABLES, CATTLE, FISH. EXP: ELECTRONIC PRODUCTS, MACHINERY & EQUIPMENT, MOTOR VEHICLES, STEEL, SHIPS, TEXTILES.

South Korea consists of the southern half of the Korean peninsula and islands off the western and southern coasts. The terrain is mountainous, though less rugged than that of North Korea. This capitalist country is a major exporter of cars, consumer electronics, and computer components. The economic growth following the Asian financial crisis lasted until the mid to late 2000s. The government, a multiparty democracy, seeks peace initiatives and trade with the unpredictable North Korean regime. Road and railway projects to link the two Koreas are under way.

JAPAN

JAPAN

AREA 145,902 SQ. MI. ▮ POPULATION 127,079,000 ▮ CAPITAL TOKYO (POP. 36,094,000) ▮ LITERACY 99% ▮ LIFE EXPECTANCY 82 ▮ CURRENCY YEN ▮ GDP PER CAPITA $34,200 ▮ ECONOMY IND: MOTOR VEHICLES, ELECTRONIC EQUIPMENT, MACHINE TOOLS, STEEL & NONFERROUS METALS. AGR: RICE, SUGAR BEETS, VEGETABLES, FRUIT, PORK, FISH. EXP: MOTOR VEHICLES, SEMICONDUCTORS, OFFICE MACHINERY, CHEMICALS.

Japan, a country of islands, extends along the Pacific coast of Asia. More than 4,000 smaller islands surround the four largest. About 73 percent of Japan is mountainous, and all its major cities, except the ancient capital of Kyoto, cling to narrow coastal plains. Japan is democratic and outward-looking. Amid rumors of governmental incompetence, elections in 2007 brought an end to the 52-year dominance of the Liberal Democrating Party. Among the top three exporters of manufactured goods, the nation has the second largest economy after that of the United States. Japan faces the challenges of an aging population, a rising inequality of wealth, the changing role of women in society, and growing concern about security and the environment. Current problems include unemployment and low economic growth. Despite international opposition, Japan continues to support whaling.

A MAIKO—an apprentice geisha—wears traditional garb and makeup en route by sedan to an appointment in Kyoto, Japan.

AUSTRIA—p. 400
CROATIA—p. 402
CZECH REPUBLIC—p. 400
HUNGARY—p. 401
ITALY—p. 404
LIECHTENSTEIN—p. 400
MONACO—p. 399
SERBIA—p. 403
SLOVAKIA—p. 401
SLOVENIA—p. 402

ICELAND
p. 396

DENMARK
p. 397

IRELAND
p. 397

p. 397
UNITED
KINGDOM

p. 398 NETHERLANDS

p. 398 BELGIUM

p. 398 LUXEMBOURG

p. 398 FRANCE

p. 399 SWITZERLAND

PORTUGAL
p. 404

SPAIN
p. 404

ANDORRA
p. 404

MONACO

SAN
MARINO
p. 405

VATICAN
CITY
p. 405

p. 405 MALTA

p. 396

NORWAY

SWEDEN

FINLAND

p. 396

p. 396

Kaliningrad
(Russia)

GERMANY

p. 399

p. 400
POLAND

CZECH
REP.

LIECH.

AUSTRIA

SLOVENIA

CROATIA

ITALY

SLOVAKIA

HUNGARY

ROMANIA
p. 401

SERBIA

GREECE
p. 405

BOSNIA &
HERZEGOVINA
p. 402

ALBANIA
p. 403

MONTENEGRO
p. 403

ESTONIA p. 406
LATVIA p. 406
LITHUANIA p. 406

BELARUS
p. 406

UKRAINE

MOLDOVA p. 407

BULGARIA p. 402

KOSOVO p. 401

MACEDONIA
p. 403

CYPRUS
p. 405

RUSSIA
p. 407

p. 407

MAP KEY

IRELAND   Country name and page number
p. 397   where country facts can be found

EUROPE

The world's second smallest continent, after Australia, Europe is a cluster of peninsulas and islands that extends northwest of Asia. Despite its northern location, most of Europe enjoys a mild climate tempered by warm ocean currents.

With an area of about four million square miles, Europe is bounded by the Arctic and Atlantic Oceans and the Mediterranean, Black, and Caspian Seas. The traditional land boundary follows the Ural Mountains south across Russia from the Arctic Ocean via the Ural River to the Caspian Sea and then continues west along the crest of the Caucasus Mountains between the Caspian and Black Seas. Waterways linking the Black Sea to the Mediterranean place a small part of Turkey in Europe.

Two mountain systems lie between icy tundra and boreal forest in the far north and the warm, dry, hilly Mediterranean south.

Ancient highlands, worn down by Ice Age glaciers, arc southwestward from Scandinavia through the British Isles, to the Iberian Peninsula. An Alpine system spreads east to west across southern Europe. Still pushing upward from a collision of tectonic plates, these mountains include the Carpathians, the Alps, and the Pyrenees. The high point is Mont Blanc, shared by France and Italy.

Three major navigable rivers—the Danube, the Rhine, and the Rhône—rise in the Alps. Europe's longest river is the Volga, flowing southeast across Russia and into the Caspian Sea. Movements in Earth's crust cause earthquakes and volcanic eruptions in southern Europe and Iceland. The best known volcanoes are Vesuvius, Etna, and Stromboli, all found in Italy.

Between Europe's two mountain systems, a rolling, fertile plain stretches from the Pyrenees to the Urals. Some of the world's greatest cities are on this plain, including Paris, Berlin, and Moscow. Huge industrial areas house much of Europe's dense population.

Environmental problems are often international. Acid rain from England affects Swedish lakes. Damage is widespread from a nuclear accident in Ukraine. The Danube and Rhine Rivers spread industrial pollution downstream. Regional solutions, when possible, hold the most promise.

THE HUMAN FOOTPRINT

AROUND 30,000 YEARS AGO the Eurasian steppes extended from today's Germany and France to China and Korea. Through this land a new DNA mutation—a distinctive genetic marker—was carried by the first major wave of humans inhabiting the fertile region. That marker is now found in over 70 percent of Western European men. **/** Scientists named these early Europeans the Cro-Magnons, after the cave where their first specimens were found. More such sites have been found, suggesting a population boom. **/** Expanding ice sheets forced these early Europeans south. During the glacial maximum, all Northern Europe, most of Canada, and the northern half of the West Siberian Plain were covered by ice. Humans moved closer to the temperate Mediterranean. Once temperatures warmed, and the ice retreated, people migrated northward again. Much of Western Europe's current gene pool descends directly from these early survivors.

ICELAND

REPUBLIC OF ICELAND

AREA 39,769 SQ. MI. ▌ POPULATION 307,000 ▌ CAPITAL REYKJAVÍK (POP. 184,000) ▌ LITERACY 99% ▌ LIFE EXPECTANCY 81 ▌ CURRENCY ICELANDIC KRONA ▌ GDP PER CAPITA $39,900 ▌ ECONOMY IND: FISH PROCESSING, ALUMINUM SMELTING, FERROSILICON PRODUCTION, GEOTHERMAL POWER. AGR: POTATOES, GREEN VEGETABLES, POULTRY, PORK, FISH. EXP: FISH & FISH PRODUCTS, ANIMAL PRODUCTS, ALUMINUM, DIATOMITE, FERROSILICON.

A volcanic island, Iceland is Europe's westernmost country and home to the world's northernmost capital city, Reykjavík. Although glaciers cover more than a tenth of the island, the Gulf Stream and warm southwesterly winds moderate the climate—most residents occupy the country's southwest. Under the Danish crown for more than 500 years, the country became a republic in 1944. Almost all of its electricity and heating come from hydroelectric power and geothermal water reserves. Explosive geysers, relaxing geothermal spas, glacier-fed waterfalls like Gullfoss (Golden Falls), and whalewatching attract more than 270,000 visitors a year.

NORWAY

KINGDOM OF NORWAY

AREA 125,004 SQ. MI. ▌ POPULATION 4,661,000 ▌ CAPITAL OSLO (POP. 858,000) ▌ LITERACY 100% ▌ LIFE EXPECTANCY 80 ▌ CURRENCY NORWEGIAN KRONE ▌ GDP PER CAPITA $55,200 ▌ ECONOMY IND: PETROLEUM & GAS, FOOD PROCESSING, SHIPBUILDING, PULP & PAPER PRODUCTS. AGR: BARLEY, WHEAT, POTATOES, PORK, FISH. EXP: PETROLEUM & PETROLEUM PRODUCTS, MACHINERY & EQUIPMENT, METALS, CHEMICALS, SHIPS, FISH.

Norway, including the Arctic islands of Svalbard and Jan Mayen, is partitioned by mountains and has a fjord-gashed shoreline. Norway draws its strength from the sea. Its merchant and oil-tanker fleets are among the world's largest, and its fishing flotilla lands Western Europe's biggest catch. Wealth from North Sea oil and gas subsidizes public health and welfare programs. Norway is the world's third largest oil exporter. A member of NATO, the UN, and the European Free Trade Association, Norway voted against joining the European Union in 1994. It has frequently held the top spot on the UN's quality-of-life index.

SWEDEN

KINGDOM OF SWEDEN

AREA 173,732 SQ. MI. ▌ POPULATION 9,060,000 ▌ CAPITAL STOCKHOLM (POP. 1,285,000) ▌ LITERACY 99% ▌ LIFE EXPECTANCY 81 ▌ CURRENCY SWEDISH KRONA ▌ GDP PER CAPITA $38,500 ▌ ECONOMY IND: IRON & STEEL, PRECISION EQUIPMENT, WOOD & PAPER PRODUCTS, PROCESSED FOODS. AGR: BARLEY, WHEAT, SUGAR BEETS, MEAT. EXP: MACHINERY, MOTOR VEHICLES, PAPER PRODUCTS, PULP & WOOD, IRON & STEEL PRODUCTS, CHEMICALS.

Armed neutrality has kept Sweden out of war for nearly two centuries. Low unemployment, a low birthrate, and one of the world's highest life expectancies have characterized modern Sweden. Success has been credited to a blending of socialism and capitalism, including cooperation between the government and labor unions. High taxes finance advanced social programs, from education to health and child care and paid paternal leave. Sweden joined the EU in 1995. Inflation is low and unemployment is down. Radioactive fallout from Chernobyl underscored Sweden's resolve to dismantle its nuclear power plants, a process that began in 1997.

FINLAND

REPUBLIC OF FINLAND

AREA 130,558 SQ. MI. ▌ POPULATION 5,250,000 ▌ CAPITAL HELSINKI (POP. 1,139,000) ▌ LITERACY 100% ▌ LIFE EXPECTANCY 79 ▌ CURRENCY EURO ▌ GDP PER CAPITA $37,200 ▌ ECONOMY IND: METAL PRODUCTS, ELECTRONICS, SHIP-BUILDING, PULP & PAPER, COPPER REFINING. AGR: BARLEY, WHEAT, SUGAR BEETS, POTATOES, DAIRY CATTLE, FISH. EXP: MACHINERY & EQUIPMENT, CHEMICALS, METALS, TIMBER, PAPER, PULP.

Finland is low-lying in the south and center with mountains in the north. One quarter of its territory lies north of the Arctic Circle, and the country experiences long, harsh winters. Coniferous forests and more than 180,000 lakes grace Finland, which maintains a fleet of icebreakers to keep ports open during the long winters. The Finns declared independence in 1917 but lost territory to the Soviets in World War II. Close economic ties between the two nations existed until the U.S.S.R. was dissolved. Since then Finland has strengthened links with Europe by joining the EU. Helsinki is a center for international diplomacy.

DENMARK

KINGDOM OF DENMARK

AREA 16,640 SQ. MI. ▮ POPULATION 5,501,000 ▮ CAPITAL COPEN-HAGEN (POP. 1,087,000) ▮ LITERACY 99% ▮ LIFE EXPECTANCY 78 ▮ CURRENCY DANISH KRONE ▮ GDP PER CAPITA $37,400 ▮ ECONOMY IND: FOOD PROCESSING, MACHINERY & EQUIPMENT, TEXTILES & CLOTHING, CHEMICAL PRODUCTS. AGR: BARLEY, WHEAT, POTA-TOES, SUGAR BEETS, PORK, FISH. EXP: MACHINERY & INSTRUMENTS, MEAT & MEAT PRODUCTS, DAIRY PRODUCTS, FISH, CHEMICALS.

Denmark consists of the mainland of Jutland and 406 islands. Fertile farmland covers 64 percent of the country, which is among the flattest in the world. Membership in the European Union gives Denmark ready access to markets for its pork and dairy products. However, Danes rejected adopting the euro currency in 2000. The Kingdom of Denmark, a constitutional monarchy, includes the self-governing territories of the Faroe Islands and Greenland.

IRELAND

IRELAND

AREA 27,133 SQ. MI. ▮ POPULATION 4,203,000 ▮ CAPITAL DUBLIN (POP. 1,098,000) ▮ LITERACY 98% ▮ LIFE EXPECTANCY 78 ▮ CUR-RENCY EURO ▮ GDP PER CAPITA $46,200 ▮ ECONOMY IND: FOOD PRODUCTS, BREWING, TEXTILES, CLOTHING, CHEMICALS, PHAR-MACEUTICALS. AGR: TURNIPS, BARLEY, POTATOES, SUGAR BEETS, BEEF. EXP: MACHINERY & EQUIPMENT, COMPUTERS, CHEMICALS, PHARMACEUTICALS, LIVE ANIMALS.

A North Atlantic island west of Great Britian, Ireland features mountains in the west and interior lowlands, with numerous hills, lakes, and bogs. The Republic of Ireland occupies most of the island; Northern Ireland is part of the United Kingdom. In 1921, 26 Roman Catholic counties—which made up five-sixths of the island's area—won independence, while Northern Ireland remained under British control. After years of anti-British violence, a peace agreement was signed by Northern Ireland, Britain, and Ireland in 1998—with Ireland giving up its claim to Northern Ireland. The country's growth promotes trade, foreign investment, and industries such as electronics.

UNITED KINGDOM

UNITED KINGDOM OF GREAT BRITAIN AND NORTHERN IRELAND

AREA 93,788 SQ. MI. ▮ POPULATION 61,113,000 ▮ CAPITAL LONDON (POP. 8,607,000) ▮ LITERACY 99% ▮ LIFE EXPECTANCY 79 ▮ CURRENCY BRITISH POUND ▮ GDP PER CAPITA $36,600 ▮ ECONOMY IND: MACHINE TOOLS, ELECTRIC POWER EQUIPMENT, AUTOMATION EQUIPMENT, RAILROAD EQUIPMENT, SHIPBUILDING. AGR: CEREALS, OILSEED, POTATOES, VEGETABLES, CATTLE, FISH. EXP: MANUFAC-TURED GOODS, FUELS, CHEMICALS, FOOD, BEVERAGES, TOBACCO.

Separated from the rest of the European continent by the North Sea and English Channel, the United Kingdom's constitutional monarchy is often referred to as Great Britain. Technically speaking, the island comprising England, Wales, and Scotland is Great Britain; the UK includes Northern Ireland as well.

Scotland's coastline is littered with lochs and firths. Southern Scotland features rolling moorlands, while the central lowlands rise to meet the Grampian Mountains in the north. England's gently rolling downs and wide plains stretch from the southern coastal cliffs. The eastern coastal lowlands stretch northward, while the rugged northern highlands are met by the central plains. Wales, to the west, is bound by water in three directions and is largely mountainous. Northern Ireland is also mountainous. Farming and the manufacture of textiles, paper, and furniture are among its major industries.

MEMBERS OF THE EUROPEAN UNION

AUSTRIA	FINLAND	MALTA
BELGIUM	FRANCE	NETHERLANDS
BULGARIA	GERMANY	POLAND
CYPRUS	GREECE	PORTUGAL
CZECH REPUBLIC	HUNGARY	ROMANIA
DENMARK	IRELAND	SLOVAKIA
ESTONIA	ITALY	SLOVENIA
	LATVIA	SPAIN
	LITHUANIA	SWEDEN
	LUXEMBOURG	UNITED KINGDOM

NETHERLANDS

KINGDOM OF THE NETHERLANDS

AREA 16,034 SQ. MI. ▌ POPULATION 16,716,000 ▌ CAPITAL AMSTER-
DAM (POP. 1,044,000) ▌ LITERACY 99% ▌ LIFE EXPECTANCY 79 ▌
CURRENCY EURO ▌ GDP PER CAPITA $40,300 ▌ ECONOMY IND:
AGROINDUSTRIES, METAL & ENGINEERING PRODUCTS, ELECTRICAL
MACHINERY & EQUIPMENT, CHEMICALS. AGR: GRAINS, POTATOES,
SUGAR BEETS, FRUITS, LIVESTOCK. EXP: MACHINERY & EQUIPMENT,
CHEMICALS, FUELS, FOODSTUFFS.

The Netherlands faces the North Sea in western Europe.
Today more than 1,491 miles of dikes shield the low, flat
land, most which lies below sea level. Without the existing
dikes, 65 percent of the country would be flooded daily.
About 60 percent of the country is farmed. Tourism is important, and many visitors come to see Dutch art, architecture, and flowers—tulips are a major industry. The country
comprises 12 provinces, including North and South Holland.

LUXEMBOURG

GRAND DUCHY OF LUXEMBOURG

AREA 998 SQ. MI. ▌ POPULATION 492,000 ▌ CAPITAL LUXEMBOURG
(POP. 77,000) ▌ LITERACY 100% ▌ LIFE EXPECTANCY 79 ▌ CURRENCY
EURO ▌ GDP PER CAPITA $81,100 ▌ ECONOMY IND: BANKING, IRON
& STEEL, FOOD PROCESSING, CHEMICALS. AGR: BARLEY, OATS, POTA-
TOES, WHEAT, LIVESTOCK PRODUCTS. EXP: MACHINERY & EQUIP-
MENT, STEEL PRODUCTS, CHEMICALS, RUBBER PRODUCTS, GLASS.

Luxembourg, a landlocked country, has heavily forested
hills in the north and open, rolling countryside in the
south. It became a member of a customs union in 1948
that evolved into today's European Union. Although it is
small in size, Luxembourg's central location, political stability, and multilingual population have proved advantageous
to it as a financial center, as have tax incentives. Foreign
investment in light manufacturing and services has offset
the decline in steel, once the nation's major industry.

FAST FACT Five of the world's smallest countries are in Europe: Vatican City, Monaco, San Marino, Liechtenstein, and Malta.

 BELGIUM

KINGDOM OF BELGIUM

AREA 11,787 SQ. MI. ▌ POPULATION 10,414,000 ▌ CAPITAL BRUSSELS
(POP. 1,744,000) ▌ LITERACY 99% ▌ LIFE EXPECTANCY 79 ▌ CURREN-
CY EURO ▌ GDP PER CAPITA $37,500 ▌ ECONOMY IND: ENGINEER-
ING & METAL PRODUCTS, MOTOR VEHICLE ASSEMBLY, PROCESSED
FOOD & BEVERAGES, CHEMICALS. AGR: SUGAR BEETS, FRESH
VEGETABLES, FRUITS, GRAIN, BEEF. EXP: MACHINERY & EQUIPMENT,
CHEMICALS, DIAMONDS, METALS & METAL PRODUCTS.

Belgium, in Western Europe, is flat except for the hilly
and forested southeast region. In 1994 Belgium became
a federal state, giving political representation to its Dutch,
French, and German cultures. Brussels is the headquarters of the European Union and the North Atlantic Treaty
Organization. Bolstered by a strong economy, Belgium
can compete in the new single-currency European mar-
ketplace. It is the world's largest producer of azaleas.
Antwerp is the diamond capital of the world. Tourism also plays an important role in the economy.

 FRANCE

FRENCH REPUBLIC

AREA 210,026 SQ. MI. ▌ POPULATION 64,058,000 ▌ CAPITAL PARIS
(POP. 9,958,000) ▌ LITERACY 99% ▌ LIFE EXPECTANCY 81 ▌ CURRENCY
EURO ▌ GDP PER CAPITA $32,700 ▌ ECONOMY IND: MACHINERY,
CHEMICALS, AUTOMOBILES, METALLURGY, AIRCRAFT, ELECTRONICS,
TEXTILES. AGR: WHEAT, CEREALS, SUGAR BEETS, POTATOES, BEEF,
FISH. EXP: MACHINERY & TRANSPORTATION EQUIPMENT, AIRCRAFT,
PLASTICS, CHEMICALS, PHARMACEUTICALS, FOOD.

Fertile plains cover two-thirds of France. The mountain
ranges in the south include the Alps and Pyrenees. France's
forests are a source of environmental and scenic wealth. The
north is humid and cool; the south is dry and warm. France
is the world's largest producer of wine and sets a fast pace
in telecommunications, biotechnology, and aerospace.
Coal and steel industries are concentrated in the northeast. Overseas departments (officially part of France)
with their own elected governments include French
Guiana, Guadeloupe, Martinique, and Réunion.

MONACO

PRINCIPALITY OF MONACO

AREA 1 SQ. MI. ▮ POPULATION 33,000 ▮ CAPITAL MONACO (POP. 33,000) ▮ LITERACY 99% ▮ LIFE EXPECTANCY 80 ▮ CURRENCY EURO ▮ GDP PER CAPITA $30,000 ▮ ECONOMY IND: TOURISM, BANKING, CONSTRUCTION, SMALL-SCALE INDUSTRIAL & CONSUMER PRODUCTS. AGR: NA. EXP: NA.

Monaco occupies a mostly rocky strip of land on France's Mediterranean coast. An unparalleled luxury resort since the mid-19th century, Monaco has a reputation that belies its size. Millions visit each year for the beachfront hotels, the yacht harbor, the Opera House, and the famous Monte Carlo Casino. Wealthy residents benefit from no income tax. The House of Grimaldi has ruled since 1297, except between 1793 and 1814. Tourism and gambling drive the economy, but Monaco is also a major banking center.

GERMANY

FEDERAL REPUBLIC OF GERMANY

AREA 137,847 SQ. MI. ▮ POPULATION 82,330,000 ▮ CAPITAL BERLIN (POP. 3,423,000) ▮ LITERACY 99% ▮ LIFE EXPECTANCY 79 ▮ CURRENCY EURO ▮ GDP PER CAPITA $34,800 ▮ ECONOMY IND: IRON, STEEL, COAL, CEMENT, CHEMICALS, MACHINERY, VEHICLES, MACHINE TOOLS, ELECTRONICS. AGR: POTATOES, WHEAT, BARLEY, SUGAR BEETS, CATTLE. EXP: MACHINERY, VEHICLES, CHEMICALS, METALS & MANUFACTURING, FOODSTUFFS, TEXTILES.

Germany's fertile northern plains stretch south from the North and Baltic Seas, changing to central highlands and then rising to the rugged Schwarzwald (Black Forest) in the southwest and the Alps in the far south. Some German industry is known internationally (Daimler, Siemens, and Volkswagen). On November 9, 1989, East Germans breached the Berlin Wall. A year later, on October 3, 1990, Germany was reborn. Rejoining the populations of East and West Germany after 45 years of separation by both the military and the Berlin Wall has been difficult. Eastern Germany's economy remains weak; the population is declining as young people go west for jobs. High taxes and wages also make economic growth difficult.

SWITZERLAND

SWISS CONFEDERATION

AREA 15,940 SQ. MI. ▮ POPULATION 7,604,000 ▮ CAPITAL BERN (POP. 320,000) ▮ LITERACY 99% ▮ LIFE EXPECTANCY 81 ▮ CURRENCY SWISS FRANC ▮ GDP PER CAPITA $40,900 ▮ ECONOMY IND: MACHINERY, CHEMICALS, WATCHES, TEXTILES, PRECISION INSTRUMENTS. AGR: GRAINS, FRUITS & VEGETABLES, MEAT. EXP: MACHINERY, CHEMICALS, METALS, WATCHES, AGRICULTURAL PRODUCTS.

The Alps in the south and east and the Jura Mountains in the northwest delineate the Mittelland plateau in the center of Switzerland. A history of political stability and expertise in technology and commerce explain a postindustrial economy with one of the highest per capita incomes in the world. Switzerland competes in global markets with exports that make up almost half of the nation's economy; in a 2001 referendum, however, the Swiss voted against joining the European Union. Civil defense measures and a strong militia back up the Swiss policy of permanent neutrality. Switzerland is firmly committed to world peace, and in 2002 became a member of the United Nations.

LANDLOCKED, MOUNTAINOUS Switzerland boasts picture-postcard vistas, a rich intellectual heritage, and a lively economy.

POLAND

REPUBLIC OF POLAND

AREA 120,728 SQ. MI. ▮ POPULATION 38,483,000 ▮ CAPITAL WARSAW (POP. 1,724,000) ▮ LITERACY 100% ▮ LIFE EXPECTANCY 76 ▮ CURRENCY ZLOTY ▮ GDP PER CAPITA $17,300 ▮ ECONOMY IND: MACHINE BUILDING, IRON & STEEL, COAL MINING, CHEMICALS, SHIPBUILDING. AGR: POTATOES, FRUITS, VEGETABLES, WHEAT, POULTRY. EXP: MACHINERY & TRANSPORT EQUIPMENT, INTERMEDIATE MANUFACTURED GOODS.

Poland is the largest country in central Europe. Buffered by the Baltic Sea in the north and the Carpathian Mountains in the south, Poland enjoys no such natural protection to the east and west. In 1989 Solidarity swept Poland's first free elections in more than 40 years and began moving the U.S.S.R.'s largest, most populous satellite toward democracy and free enterprise. It was the first Eastern European country to overthrow communist rule. Poland joined NATO in 1999. It then developed a market-oriented economy and joined the European Union in 2004.

 # AUSTRIA

REPUBLIC OF AUSTRIA

AREA 32,378 SQ. MI. ▮ POPULATION 8,210,000 ▮ CAPITAL VIENNA (POP. 2,385,000) ▮ LITERACY 98% ▮ LIFE EXPECTANCY 80 ▮ CURRENCY EURO ▮ GDP PER CAPITA $39,200 ▮ ECONOMY IND: CONSTRUCTION, MACHINERY, VEHICLES & PARTS, FOOD. AGR: GRAINS, POTATOES, SUGAR BEETS, WINE, DAIRY PRODUCTS, LUMBER. EXP: MACHINERY & EQUIPMENT, MOTOR VEHICLES & PARTS, PAPER, METAL GOODS, CHEMICALS, IRON ORE, OIL, TIMBER.

Bordering eight countries, Austria is mountainous in the south and west. Fertile lowlands in the east are part of the Danube River basin. Natural grandeur lures visitors to Tirol and the Hohe Tauern National Park—the largest protected natural area in Central Europe. Austria was accepted into the European Union (EU) in 1995. Manufacturing, powered by hydroelectricity, drives the nation's export trade; Austria also profits from iron ore, oil, and timber. Austria is one of the most forested countries in Europe with almost half its territory covered in forest.

 # CZECH REPUBLIC

CZECH REPUBLIC (CZECHIA)

AREA 30,450 SQ. MI. ▮ POPULATION 10,212,000 ▮ CAPITAL PRAGUE 1,160,000 ▮ LITERACY 99% ▮ LIFE EXPECTANCY 77 ▮ CURRENCY CZECH KORUNA ▮ GDP PER CAPITA $26,100 ▮ ECONOMY IND: METALLURGY, MACHINERY & EQUIPMENT, MOTOR VEHICLES, GLASS, ARMAMENTS. AGR: WHEAT, POTATOES, SUGAR BEETS, HOPS, PIGS. EXP: MACHINERY & TRANSPORT EQUIPMENT, INTERMEDIATE MANUFACTURING, CHEMICALS, RAW MATERIALS, FUEL.

Within the Czech Republic, Bohemia is a plateau surrounded by mountains, while Moravia, to the east, is mostly hills and lowlands. With the end of the Austro-Hungarian Empire, Czechs and Slovaks came together to create Czechoslovakia, although the two were separated during World War II. Communists took charge of a reunited Czechoslovakia in 1948, only to be forced out in 1989. After its break with the Slovak Republic, the Czech nation rapidly privatized state-owned businesses. Although the political and financial crises of 1997 eroded somewhat the country's stability and prosperity, the Czech Republic succeeded in becoming a NATO member in 1999 and a European Union member in 2004.

 # LIECHTENSTEIN

PRINCIPALITY OF LIECHTENSTEIN

AREA 62 SQ. MI. ▮ POPULATION 35,000 ▮ CAPITAL VADUZ (POP. 5,000) ▮ LITERACY 100% ▮ LIFE EXPECTANCY 80 ▮ CURRENCY SWISS FRANC ▮ GDP PER CAPITA $118,000 ▮ ECONOMY IND: ELECTRONICS, METAL MANUFACTURING, DENTAL PRODUCTS, CERAMICS, PHARMACEUTICALS. AGR: WHEAT, BARLEY, CORN, POTATOES, LIVESTOCK. EXP: SMALL SPECIALTY MACHINERY, CONNECTORS FOR AUDIO & VIDEO, PARTS FOR MOTOR VEHICLES, DENTAL PRODUCTS.

This tiny independent state lies between Switzerland and Austria. The eastern part of the country contains the rugged foothills of the Rhätikon Mountains; the western the Rhine River floodplains. Founded in 1719 as a part of the Holy Roman Empire, Liechtenstein gained independence in 1866. Because of liberal tax policies and banking laws, it counts more companies than citizens. It contains no university and one prison and employs one judge.

 **HUNGARY**

REPUBLIC OF HUNGARY

AREA 35,919 SQ. MI. ▌ POPULATION 9,906,000 ▌ CAPITAL BUDAPEST (POP. 1,664,000) ▌ LITERACY 99% ▌ LIFE EXPECTANCY 73 ▌ CURRENCY FORINT ▌ GDP PER CAPITA $19,800 ▌ ECONOMY IND: MINING, METALLURGY, CONSTRUCTION MATERIALS, PROCESSED FOODS, TEXTILES, CHEMICALS. AGR: WHEAT, CORN, SUNFLOWER SEED, POTATOES, SUGAR BEETS, PIGS. EXP: MACHINERY & EQUIPMENT, OTHER MANUFACTURING, FOOD PRODUCTS, RAW MATERIALS.

The Danube River flows north to south through the middle of Hungary, splitting this landlocked central European country almost in half. Fertile plains lie east of the Danube, with hills to the west and north. In 1989, after decades of communist leadership, the government abolished censorship, dismantled barriers along the Austrian border, and called for privatization of industry, religious freedom, and free elections. Now a member of NATO, Hungary also joined the European Union in 2004. Foreign investment and private companies are flourishing. However, Hungary saw increased political tension and public protests in response to recent economic crises and the government's failure to acknowledge and avert the crises.

 **KOSOVO**

REPUBLIC OF KOSOVO

AREA 4,203 SQ. MI. ▌ POPULATION 1,804,838 ▌ CAPITAL PRISHTINA (POP. 560,000) ▌ LITERACY 92% ▌ CURRENCY EURO ▌ GDP PER CAPITA $2,300 ▌ ECONOMY IND: MINERAL MINING, CONSTRUCTION MATERIALS, BASE METALS, LEATHER, MACHINERY, APPLIANCES. EXP: MINING AND PROCESSED METAL PRODUCTS, SCRAP METALS, LEATHER PRODUCTS, MACHINERY, APPLIANCES.

This mountainous country encompasses the fertile valleys of Kosovo and Metohija. Its population is almost 90 percent Albanian. Major occupations include forestry, livestock raising, the mining of lead and various other metals, and farming. Since its settlement by the Slavs in the seventh century, Kosovo has changed hands a number of times. After years of conflict with Serbian troops, Kosovo declared independence in 2008. Although its independence is disputed by Serbia, it is recognized by many nations including the United States.

 **SLOVAKIA**

SLOVAK REPUBLIC

AREA 18,932 SQ. MI. ▌ POPULATION 5,463,000 ▌ CAPITAL BRATISLAVA (POP. 425,000) ▌ LITERACY 100% ▌ LIFE EXPECTANCY 75 ▌ CURRENCY EURO ▌ GDP PER CAPITA $21,900 ▌ ECONOMY IND: METAL & METAL PRODUCTS, FOOD & BEVERAGES, ELECTRICITY, GAS. AGR: GRAINS, POTATOES, SUGAR BEETS, HOPS, PIGS, FOREST PRODUCTS. EXP: MACHINERY & TRANSPORT EQUIPMENT, MISCELLANEOUS MANUFACTURED GOODS.

A landlocked country in central Europe, Slovakia is mostly mountainous except for southern lowlands along the Danube, where the capital, Bratislava, is found. This country's split from the more affluent, industrialized Czech Republic in 1993 was prompted by Slovak nationalism and grievances over rapid economic reforms instituted by the Czechoslovak government in Prague—reforms that left many Slovaks without jobs. Slovakia's industrial economy is market oriented. It joined NATO and the European Union in 2004.

 ROMANIA

ROMANIA

AREA 92,043 SQ. MI. ▌ POPULATION 22,215,000 ▌ CAPITAL BUCHAREST (POP. 1,947,000) ▌ LITERACY 97% ▌ LIFE EXPECTANCY 72 ▌ CURRENCY LEU ▌ GDP PER CAPITA $12,200 ▌ ECONOMY IND: TEXTILES & FOOTWEAR, LIGHT MACHINERY & AUTO ASSEMBLY, MINING, TIMBER. AGR: WHEAT, CORN, BARLEY, SUGAR BEETS, EGGS. EXP: TEXTILES & FOOTWEAR, METALS & METAL PRODUCTS, MACHINERY & EQUIPMENT, MINERALS & FUELS.

Romania lies on the Black Sea coast of southeastern Europe. The Carpathian Mountains and the Transylvanian Alps divide the country into three physical and historical regions: Wallachia in the south, Moldavia in the northeast, and Transylvania in the country's center. The majority of the people are Romanian (90 percent), but the Hungarian minority, living in the Transylvanian basin, numbers some 1.7 million. Since the revolution in 1989, which resulted in the execution of President Ceausescu and his wife, subsequent governments have been laboring under massive foreign debt. Significant public and private corruption impede economic growth and undercut public trust in new democratic institutions. Romania joined NATO in 2004 and the EU in 2007.

BOSNIA & HERZEGOVINA

BOSNIA AND HERZEGOVINA

AREA 19,741 SQ. MI. ▌POPULATION 4,613,000 ▌CAPITAL SARAJEVO (POP. 579,000) ▌LITERACY 97 ▌LIFE EXPECTANCY 79 ▌CURRENCY MARKA ▌GDP PER CAPITA $6,500 ▌ECONOMY IND: STEEL, COAL, IRON ORE, LEAD, ZINC, MANGANESE, BAUXITE, VEHICLE ASSEMBLY. AGR: WHEAT, CORN, FRUITS, VEGETABLES, LIVESTOCK. EXP: METALS, CLOTHING, WOOD PRODUCTS.

In mountainous southeastern Europe, Bosnia's Muslims, or Bosniacs, trace their ancestry to Christian Slavs who converted to Islam under the Ottomans for tax and land-holding advantages. Yugoslavia recognized Bosniacs as a separate people in 1969. Muslim Slavs and Roman Catholic Croats voted in early 1992 for independence from Yugoslavia, which most Eastern Orthodox Serbs fiercely opposed. In the ensuing 1992-95 civil war, some 250,000 people died. The Dayton Peace Accords ended the war and partitioned the country into a Muslim-Croat region and a Serbian region, now the Republic of Serbia. High unemployment and ethnic tensions continue.

SLOVENIA

REPUBLIC OF SLOVENIA

AREA 7,827 SQ. MI. ▌POPULATION 2,006,000 ▌CAPITAL LJUBLJANA (POP. 256,000) ▌LITERACY 100% ▌LIFE EXPECTANCY 77 ▌CURRENCY EURO ▌GDP PER CAPITA $29,500 ▌ECONOMY IND: FERROUS METALLURGY & ALUMINUM PRODUCTS, LEAD & ZINC SMELTING, ELECTRONICS, TRUCKS. AGR: POTATOES, HOPS, WHEAT, SUGAR BEETS, CATTLE. EXP: MANUFACTURED GOODS, MACHINERY & TRANSPORT EQUIPMENT, CHEMICALS, FOOD.

Slovenia, an Alpine-mountain state in southern Europe consisting mainly of Roman Catholic Slovenes, joined the Kingdom of Serbs, Croats, and Slovenes—subsequently named Yugoslavia—in 1918. Slovenia proclaimed its independence in June 1991, prompting a ten-day conflict that brought defeat to the Serb-dominated Yugoslav Army. It is the most prosperous of the former Yugoslav republics. Its Western outlook and economic stability won Slovenia membership in both NATO and the EU in 2004.

BULGARIA

REPUBLIC OF BULGARIA

AREA 42,855 SQ. MI. ▌POPULATION 7,205,000 ▌CAPITAL SOFIA (POP. 1,212,000) ▌LITERACY 98% ▌LIFE EXPECTANCY 73 ▌CURRENCY LEV ▌GDP PER CAPITA $12,900 ▌ECONOMY IND: ELECTRICITY, GAS & WATER, FOOD, BEVERAGES, TOBACCO. AGR: VEGETABLES, FRUITS, TOBACCO, LIVESTOCK. EXP: CLOTHING, FOOTWEAR, IRON & STEEL, MACHINERY & EQUIPMENT.

Bulgaria, in southeastern Europe, is dominated by rugged mountains, except for the Danube lowland in the north that it shares with Romania. Rich farmland in the Danube Valley, 80 miles of sandy beaches on the Black Sea, and mountainous terrain characterize one of Eastern Europe's least densely populated nations. Most of the population is urban; about 83 percent Orthodox Christians, and some 12 percent Muslim. The Rhodope Mountains, along the border with Greece, are home to many Muslims, including an ethnic Turkish minority.

CROATIA

REPUBLIC OF CROATIA

AREA 21,831 SQ. MI. ▌POPULATION 4,489,000 ▌CAPITAL ZAGREB (POP. 688,000) ▌LITERACY 98% ▌LIFE EXPECTANCY 75 ▌CURRENCY KUNA ▌GDP PER CAPITA $16,100 ▌ECONOMY IND: CHEMICALS & PLASTICS, MACHINE TOOLS, FABRICATED METAL, ELECTRONICS. AGR: WHEAT, CORN, SUGAR BEETS, SUNFLOWER SEED, LIVESTOCK. EXP: TRANSPORT EQUIPMENT, TEXTILES, CHEMICALS, FOODSTUFFS, FUELS.

A crescent-shaped country in southeast Europe, Croatia extends from the fertile plains of the Danube to the mountainous coast of the Adriatic Sea. In the Adriatic, Croatia has 1,185 islands—many are major tourist areas. The 1991-95 civil war between Croats and Serbs caused massive damage to cities and industries. War halted the tourist trade and cut industrial output, including a lucrative shipbuilding business. Since the war, Croatia has progressed politically and economically; it is a candidate for European Union membership. Corruption among government officials and prosecution of war criminals are some of the concerns facing Croatians today.

SERBIA

REPUBLIC OF SERBIA

AREA 41,375 SQ. MI. ▮ POPULATION 7,379,000 ▮ CAPITAL BELGRADE (POP. 1,096,000) ▮ LITERACY 96% ▮ LIFE EXPECTANCY 74 ▮ CURRENCY SERBIAN DINAR ▮ GDP PER CAPITA $10,900 ▮ ECONOMY IND: SUGAR, AGRICULTURAL MACHINERY, ELECTRICAL & COMMUNICATION EQUIPMENT, PAPER & PULP, LEAD. AGR: WHEAT, MAIZE, SUGAR BEETS, SUNFLOWER, RASPBERRIES. EXP: MANUFACTURED GOODS, FOOD & LIVE ANIMALS, MACHINERY & TRANSPORT EQUIPMENT.

Serbia is hidden within a number of mountain systems, its slopes dragging northward toward the Danube and Sava Rivers. Plains dominate the northern Vojvodina region, while hills and mountains characterize central Serbia. Serbia and Montenegro replaced Yugoslavia on the map in 2003, although the two countries split in 2006 to become two individual independent states. Two years later, after talks between the Serbs and Kosovars failed to produce results, Kosovo formally seceded from Serbia.

 ALBANIA

REPUBLIC OF ALBANIA

AREA 11,100 SQ. MI. ▮ POPULATION 3,639,000 ▮ CAPITAL TIRANA (POP. 367,000) ▮ LITERACY 99% ▮ LIFE EXPECTANCY 78 ▮ CURRENCY LEK ▮ GDP PER CAPITA $6,000 ▮ ECONOMY IND: FOOD PROCESSING, TEXTILES & CLOTHING, LUMBER, OIL. AGR: WHEAT, CORN, POTATOES, VEGETABLES, MEAT. EXP: TEXTILES & FOOTWEAR, ASPHALT, METALS & METALLIC ORES, CRUDE OIL.

Albania lies along the Adriatic Sea in southeastern Europe. The narrow coastal plain rises to mountains that reach 9,000 feet and cover most of the country. These mountains are rich in mineral resources such as chrome, iron, nickel, and copper; however, mining requires investment that Albania lacks. It is one of the poorest countries in Europe. It suffered from more than 40 years of communist rule, which ended in 1991. War in neighboring Kosovo brought 480,000 ethnic Albanian refugees into Albania in 1999, straining the country's resources. The largely agricultural economy is growing thanks to remittances from Albanian workers abroad, most of whom live in Greece and Italy. Albania is actively pursuing membership in the European Union and joined NATO in 2009.

 MONTENEGRO

MONTENEGRO

AREA 8,715 SQ. MI. ▮ POPULATION 672,000 ▮ CAPITAL PODGORICA (POP. 136,473) ▮ LITERACY 96% ▮ LIFE EXPECTANCY 75 ▮ CURRENCY EURO ▮ GDP PER CAPITA $9,700 ▮ ECONOMY IND: STEELMAKING, ALUMINUM, AGRICULTURAL PROCESSING, CONSUMER GOODS, TOURISM. AGR: GRAINS, TOBACCO, POTATOES, CITRUS FRUITS, OLIVES. EXP: MINING & PROCESSED METAL PRODUCTS, SCRAP METALS, LEATHER PRODUCTS, MACHINERY, APPLIANCES.

Montenegro is located in the Balkans in the southern Alps. Its name, "Black Mountain," mostly likely refers to Mount Lovcen, near the Adriatic Sea. Southwestern Montenegro consists of arid hills while the eastern districts contain sizable forests and grassy uplands, providing much more fertile ground. Montenegro's coastal plain is quite narrow at only one to four miles wide, disappearing completely in the north as the mountain peaks suddenly rise. For the large part of the 20th century Montenegro existed as a piece of Yugoslavia. From 2003 to 2006 it functioned as an element of the federated union of Serbia and Montenegro. It gained full independence from Serbia in June 2006 and is now governed by independent executive, legislative, and judicial branches.

 **MACEDONIA**

REPUBLIC OF MACEDONIA

AREA 9,928 SQ. MI. ▮ POPULATION 2,067,000 ▮ CAPITAL SKOPJE (POP. 447,000) ▮ LITERACY 96 ▮ LIFE EXPECTANCY 75 ▮ CURRENCY MACEDONIAN DENAR ▮ GDP PER CAPITA $9,000 ▮ ECONOMY IND: COAL, METALLIC CHROMIUM, LEAD, ZINC, FERRONICKEL, TEXTILES. AGR: RICE, TOBACCO, WHEAT, CORN, BEEF. EXP: FOOD, BEVERAGES, TOBACCO, MISCELLANEOUS MANUFACTURING, IRON & STEEL.

Macedonia is a landlocked and predominantly mountainous country which proclaimed its independence from Yugoslavia in September 1991. The UN officially calls it "The Former Yugoslav Republic of Macedonia" because Greece fears that using "Macedonia" might imply territorial ambitions toward the Greek region of Macedonia. The democratic government faced a 2001 rebellion launched by ethnic Albanians, 25 percent of the population. Negotiations led to making Albanian an official language and providing other minority rights.

FAST FACT Vatican City, the Holy See of the Roman Catholic Church, maintains diplomatic relations with 150 countries.

404

ANSWER BOOK I CHAPTER NINE I COUNTRIES OF THE WORLD

PORTUGAL

PORTUGUESE REPUBLIC

AREA 35,655 SQ. MI. ▮ POPULATION 10,708,000 ▮ CAPITAL LISBON (POP. 2,890,000) ▮ LITERACY 93% ▮ LIFE EXPECTANCY 78 ▮ CURRENCY EURO ▮ GDP PER CAPITA $22,000 ▮ ECONOMY IND: TEXTILES & FOOTWEAR, WOOD PULP, PAPER, CORK, METALWORKING. AGR: GRAIN, POTATOES, OLIVES, GRAPES, SHEEP. EXP: CLOTHING & FOOT-WEAR, MACHINERY, CHEMICALS, CORK & PAPER PRODUCTS, HIDES.

Portugal, with its long Atlantic coast, lies on the western coast of the Iberian Peninsula, making it the most westerly country on the European mainland. The land consists of highland forests in the north and rolling lowland in the south. It tends to be wetter and cooler in the north. The south can be hot and parched, and it is dotted with reservoirs to conserve water. Most people live along the coast, with a third of the population living in the urban areas of Lisbon and Porto. A coup in 1974 ended 42 years of dictatorship, and Portugal joined the European Union in 1986.

SPAIN

KINGDOM OF SPAIN

AREA 195,363 SQ. MI. ▮ POPULATION 40,525,000 ▮ CAPITAL MADRID (POP. 5,764,000) ▮ LITERACY 98% ▮ LIFE EXPECTANCY 80 ▮ CURRENCY EURO ▮ GDP PER CAPITA $34,600 ▮ ECONOMY IND: TEXTILES & APPAREL, FOOD & BEVERAGES, METALS & METAL MANUFACTURING, CHEMICALS. AGR: GRAIN, VEGETABLES, OLIVES, WINE GRAPES, BEEF, FISH. EXP: MACHINERY, MOTOR VEHICLES, FOODSTUFFS, OTHER CONSUMER GOODS.

Spain occupies most of the Iberian Peninsula in southwest Europe, and its territory includes the Balearic Islands in the Mediterranean and the Canary Islands in the Atlantic. Much of the mainland is high plateau, with mountain ranges, including the Pyrenees, in the north. The plateau experiences hot summers and cold winters; it is cooler and wetter to the north. The Socialist Party under Felipe González Márquez led Spain into the European Union in 1986. Unemployment has been a problem, but recent economic growth makes the country's future outlook positive. The government has had to contend with Basque separatists, who have at times resorted to violence.

ANDORRA

PRINCIPALITY OF ANDORRA

AREA 181 SQ. MI. ▮ POPULATION 84,000 ▮ CAPITAL ANDORRA LA VELLA (POP. 21,000) ▮ LITERACY 100% ▮ LIFE EXPECTANCY 83 ▮ CURRENCY EURO ▮ GDP PER CAPITA $42,500 ▮ ECONOMY IND: TOURISM, CATTLE RAISING, TIMBER, BANKING. AGR: RYE, WHEAT, BARLEY, OATS, SHEEP. EXP: TOBACCO PRODUCTS, FURNITURE.

Tiny Andorra sits almost hidden in the high Pyrenees between France and Spain. A co-principality since the 13th century, mountainous Andorra has two princes as heads of state: France's president and Spain's Bishop of La Seu d'Urgell (a historic town just south of Andorra). It adopted a democratic constitution in 1993, creating a parliament and limiting the power of the co-princes. The economy is based on tax-free shopping, tourism, and international banking.

ITALY

ITALIAN REPUBLIC

AREA 116,345 SQ. MI. ▮ POPULATION 58,126,000 ▮ CAPITAL ROME (POP. 3,333,000) ▮ LITERACY 98% ▮ LIFE EXPECTANCY 80 ▮ CURRENCY EURO ▮ GDP PER CAPITA $31,000 ▮ ECONOMY IND: TOURISM, MACHINERY, IRON & STEEL, CHEMICALS. AGR: FRUITS, VEGETABLES, GRAPES, POTATOES, BEEF, FISH. EXP: ENGINEERING PRODUCTS, TEXTILES & CLOTHING, PRODUCTION MACHINERY, MOTOR VEHICLES, TRANS-PORT EQUIPMENT.

Italy consists of a mountainous peninsula extending into the Mediterranean Sea; it includes the islands of Sicily, Sardinia, and about 70 other smaller islands. The Alps form Italy's border with France, Switzerland, Austria, and Slovenia. Most of Italy has warm, dry summers and mild winters, with northern Italy experiencing colder, wetter winters. Some notable active volcanoes—Vesuvius, Etna, and Stromboli—are found here. Italy's economic strength is in the processing and manufacturing of goods, primarily in small and medium size family-owned firms, although it has to import almost all its raw materials and energy. A founding member of both NATO and the European Union, Italy boasts a superb transportation system, from airports to high-speed trains, which connects it to the rest of Europe.

VATICAN CITY
VATICAN CITY

AREA 0.4 SQ. MI. ▮ POPULATION 826 ▮ LITERACY 100%
▮ LIFE EXPECTANCY 78 ▮ CURRENCY EURO ▮ GDP PER
CAPITA $25,500 ▮ ECONOMY IND: PRINTING, BANKING
AND FINANCIAL ACTIVITIES, PRODUCTION OF COINS,
MEDALS, POSTAGE STAMPS.

Vatican City is a triangular territory on the west bank of
the Tiber River and located within the city of Rome. From
this state, the pope ministers to a flock of more than a billion Roman Catholics. The Lateran Treaty between Italy
and the Holy See created an independent Vatican City in
1929. The pope is elected by the College of Cardinals and
serves for life. The civil government of the Vatican is run
by a lay governor and council appointed by the pope.

GREECE
HELLENIC REPUBLIC

AREA 50,949 SQ. MI. ▮ POPULATION 10,737,000 ▮ CAPITAL ATHENS
(POP. 3,256,000) ▮ LITERACY 96% ▮ LIFE EXPECTANCY 80 ▮ CURRENCY
EURO ▮ GDP PER CAPITA $32,000 ▮ ECONOMY IND: TOURISM, FOOD
& TOBACCO PROCESSING, TEXTILES, CHEMICALS. AGR: WHEAT,
CORN, BARLEY, SUGAR BEETS, BEEF. EXP: FOOD & BEVERAGES,
MANUFACTURED GOODS, PETROLEUM PRODUCTS, CHEMICALS.

Greece, on the Balkan Peninsula in southeastern Europe,
is mostly dry and mountainous, with a large mainland and
over 1,400 islands. The unique ecosystems of the Prespa
Lakes region and the dense woodlands of the Rhodope
Mountains have been set aside as international preserves.

Greece gained independence from Turkish rule in
1830. Scarred by Nazi occupation during World War II
and an ensuing civil war, the nation endured seven years
of military dictatorship from 1967 to 1974. This was
followed by an elected government and new constitution. Greece's membership in the European Union has
helped stimulate industry, agriculture, and shipping, and
the country's maritime fleet is the largest in Europe. Recent economic growth has helped Greece somewhat
overcome its position as one of the poorest of the
EU countries in terms of per capita income.

MALTA
REPUBLIC OF MALTA

AREA 196 SQ. MI. ▮ POPULATION 405,000 ▮ CAPITAL VALLETTA
(POP. 7,137) ▮ LITERACY 93% ▮ LIFE EXPECTANCY 79 ▮ CURRENCY
EURO ▮ GDP PER CAPITA $24,200 ▮ ECONOMY IND: TOURISM, ELEC-
TRONICS, SHIP BUILDING, CONSTRUCTION, FOOD & BEVERAGES,
PHARMACEUTICALS. AGR: VEGETABLES, FRUIT, GRAIN, FLOWERS,
PORK, MILK, POULTRY, EGGS. EXP: MACHINERY.

The island nation of Malta holds a strategic position, midway
between Europe and Africa. Sixteenth-century Crusaders
met Suleyman the Magnificent here; Malta withstood Axis
bombs during World War II as well. Malta won independence from Britain in 1964 and joined the EU in 2004.

SAN MARINO
REPUBLIC OF SAN MARINO

AREA 24 SQ. MI. ▮ POPULATION 30,000 ▮ CAPITAL SAN MARINO
(POP. 5,000) ▮ LITERACY 96% ▮ LIFE EXPECTANCY 82 ▮ CURRENCY
EURO ▮ GDP PER CAPITA $41,900 ▮ ECONOMY IND: TOURISM,
BANKING, TEXTILES, ELECTRONICS. AGR: WHEAT, GRAPES, CORN,
OLIVES, CATTLE. EXP: STONE, LIME, WOOD, CHESTNUTS, WINE.

A medieval city-state and the world's oldest republic, San
Marino perches on a mountain in north-central Italy. It
takes pride in its finely minted coins, ceremonial guard,
and postage stamps. Well-preserved castles and sweeping Adriatic vistas enchant 3.5 million visitors a year.

CYPRUS
REPUBLIC OF CYPRUS

AREA 3,572 SQ. MI. ▮ POPULATION 797,000 ▮ CAPITAL NICOSIA (POP.
205,000) ▮ LITERACY 98% ▮ LIFE EXPECTANCY 78 ▮ CURRENCY EURO
▮ GDP PER CAPITA $28,600 ▮ ECONOMY IND: FOOD, BEVERAGES,
TEXTILES, CHEMICALS. AGR: POTATOES, CITRUS, VEGETABLES,
BARLEY. EXP: CITRUS, POTATOES, PHARMACEUTICALS, CEMENT,
TEXTILES.

The island of Cyprus was divided in 1974 when Turkish troops invaded to stop plans for enosis (union) with
Greece. The UN patrols the border. The northern
Turkish Republic of Northern Cyprus is not recognized by the UN. The island joined the EU in 2004.

ESTONIA
REPUBLIC OF ESTONIA

AREA 17,462 SQ. MI. ▮ POPULATION 1,299,000 ▮ CAPITAL TALLINN (POP. 391,000) ▮ LITERACY 100% ▮ LIFE EXPECTANCY 73 ▮ CURRENCY EURO ▮ GDP PER CAPITA $21,200 ▮ ECONOMY IND: ENGINEER-ING, ELECTRONICS, WOOD & WOOD PRODUCTS, TEXTILES. AGR: POTATOES, VEGETABLES, LIVESTOCK & DAIRY PRODUCTS, FISH. EXP: MACHINERY & EQUIPMENT, WOOD & PAPER, TEXTILES, FOOD PRODUCTS, FURNITURE.

Estonia, smallest in population of the former Soviet repub-lics, is a low-lying land on the Baltic Sea with 1,500 lakes and plenty of forests. Independence blossomed briefly between 1918 and 1940 after centuries of German, Swedish, and Rus-sian rule. During World War II it was invaded first by Rus-sian troops, then Germans, and then Russians again, forcing Estonia into the Soviet Union in 1944. The country gained independence, however, in 1991. As a stable democracy with a market economy that grew at a rate of about 10 per-cent in 2005 and 2006, Estonia looks west for trade and se-curity. It became a member of the EU and NATO in 2004.

LATVIA
REPUBLIC OF LATVIA

AREA 24,938 SQ. MI. ▮ POPULATION 2,232,000 ▮ CAPITAL RIGA (POP. 733,000) ▮ LITERACY 100% ▮ LIFE EXPECTANCY 72 ▮ CURRENCY LATVIAN LAT ▮ GDP PER CAPITA $17,800 ▮ ECONOMY IND: BUSES, VANS, STREET & RAILROAD CARS, SYNTHETIC FIBERS. AGR: GRAIN, SUGAR BEETS, POTATOES, VEGETABLES, BEEF, FISH. EXP: WOOD & WOOD PRODUCTS, MACHINERY & EQUIPMENT, METALS, TEXTILES.

Flat and forested, Latvia lies on the Baltic Sea in northern Europe. Few former Soviet republics experienced a more profound shift in character during their 50 years of domina-tion than this Baltic country. From 1939 to 1989 the pro-portion of ethnic Latvians in Latvia dropped from 73 to 52 percent, due to heavy Russian immigration and Latvian em-igration. Since independence in 1991, Latvian ethnicity has started to rebound, and Latvians now constitute 58 percent of the population—Russians are 30 percent. An indus-trial country with trade ties to the West, Latvia joined NATO and the European Union in 2004.

LITHUANIA
REPUBLIC OF LITHUANIA

AREA 25,212 SQ. MI. ▮ POPULATION 3,555,000 ▮ CAPITAL VILNIUS (POP. 549,000) ▮ LITERACY 100% ▮ LIFE EXPECTANCY 75 ▮ CURRENCY LITAS ▮ GDP PER CAPITA $17,700 ▮ ECONOMY IND: METAL-CUTTING MACHINE TOOLS, ELECTRIC MOTORS, TELEVISION SETS, REFRIGERA-TORS & FREEZERS. AGR: GRAIN, POTATOES, SUGAR BEETS, FLAX, BEEF, FISH. EXP: MINERAL PRODUCTS, TEXTILES & CLOTHING, MACHINERY & EQUIPMENT, CHEMICALS.

Lithuania is in northern Europe, on the eastern shores of the Baltic Sea. The landscape consists of gently rolling plains and extensive forests. Beginning its quest for independence at about the same time as movements in the other Baltic re-publics of Estonia and Latvia, Lithuania quickly surged ahead. In March 1990 democratically elected representatives voted for independence, lost in 1940 with annexation by the Soviet Union. Lithuania, embracing market reform since indepen-dence, joined both the European Union and NATO in 2004.

BELARUS
REPUBLIC OF BELARUS

AREA 80,153 SQ. MI. ▮ POPULATION 9,649,000 ▮ CAPITAL MINSK (POP. 1,846,000) ▮ LITERACY 100% ▮ LIFE EXPECTANCY 71 ▮ CUR-RENCY BELARUSIAN RUBLE ▮ GDP PER CAPITA $11,800 ▮ ECONOMY IND: METAL-CUTTING MACHINE TOOLS, TRACTORS, TRUCKS, EARTHMOVERS. AGR: GRAIN, POTATOES, VEGETABLES, SUGAR-BEETS, BEEF. EXP: MACHINERY & EQUIPMENT, MINERAL PRODUCTS, CHEMICALS, METALS, TEXTILES.

Belarus consists of flat lowlands separated by low hills and uplands. Forests cover a third of this republic, and the Pinsk Marshes occupy much of the south. Since the 1986 nuclear disaster at Chernobyl, Belarusians continue to suffer from high incidences of cancer and birth defects, and about 25 percent of the land is considered uninhabitable. With inde-pendence in 1991 came economic decline. The government continues to stifle democracy and oppose privatization of state enterprises. Belarus remains heavily dependent on Rus-sia, especially for energy. Minsk is the administrative head-quarters for the Commonwealth of Independent States, and Belarus uses this organization to seek greater economic and political integration with Russia.

UKRAINE

UKRAINE

AREA 233,090 SQ. MI. ▮ POPULATION 45,700,000 ▮ CAPITAL KIEV (POP. 2,748,000) ▮ LITERACY 99% ▮ LIFE EXPECTANCY 68 ▮ CURRENCY HRYVNIA ▮ GDP PER CAPITA $6,900 ▮ ECONOMY IND: COAL, ELECTRIC POWER, FERROUS & NONFERROUS METALS, MACHINERY & TRANSPORT EQUIPMENT. AGR: GRAIN, SUGAR BEETS, SUNFLOWER SEED, BEEF. EXP: FERROUS & NONFERROUS METALS, FUEL & PETROLEUM PRODUCTS, CHEMICALS, MACHINERY & TRANSPORT EQUIPMENT.

The Carpathian Mountains rise in the west and the Crimean Mountains in the south, but the heartland of Ukraine is the rich flat earth that stretches for 1,000 miles—the steppe. Ukraine also has huge deposits of coal and iron that feed heavy industry. In 1991, 90 percent of Ukrainians voted for independence, in effect dissolving the Soviet Union. Now Ukraine faces ongoing border disputes with Russia. In 2001 the country destroyed its last Soviet-era nuclear missile silo, and in 2002 it announced plans to join NATO. Ukraine faced civil war in 2004, after opposition candidate Viktor Yushchenko was poisoned and election results were contested. Yushchenko was inaugurated in January 2005.

MOLDOVA

REPUBLIC OF MOLDOVA

AREA 13,050 SQ. MI. ▮ POPULATION 4,321,000 ▮ CAPITAL CHISINAU (POP. 662,000) ▮ LITERACY 99% ▮ LIFE EXPECTANCY 71 ▮ CURRENCY MOLDOVAN LEU ▮ GDP PER CAPITA $2,500 ▮ ECONOMY IND: FOOD PROCESSING, AGRICULTURAL MACHINERY, FOUNDRY EQUIPMENT, REFRIGERATORS & FREEZERS. AGR: VEGETABLES, FRUITS, WINE, GRAIN, BEEF. EXP: FOODSTUFFS, TEXTILES, MACHINERY.

Landlocked Moldova consists of hilly grassland drained by the Prut and Dniester Rivers. Mainly agricultural, most of the land was in Romania before World War II. Soviets annexed Moldova in 1940; Russians and Ukrainians settled in the industrial region east of the Dniester (Transdniestria). After Moldova gained independence in 1991, Transdniestria seceded, making Tiraspol its capital. Moldova does not recognize Transdniestria's independence.

RUSSIA

RUSSIAN FEDERATION

AREA 6,592,850 SQ. MI. ▮ POPULATION 140,041,000 ▮ CAPITAL MOSCOW (POP. 10,495,000) ▮ LITERACY 99% ▮ LIFE EXPECTANCY 66 ▮ CURRENCY RUSSIAN RUBLE ▮ GDP PER CAPITA $15,800 ▮ ECONOMY IND: MINING & EXTRACTIVE INDUSTRIES, MACHINE BUILDING, SHIPBUILDING, ROAD & RAIL TRANSPORTATION EQUIPMENT, COMMUNICATIONS EQUIPMENT. AGR: GRAIN, SUGAR BEETS, SUNFLOWER SEED, VEGETABLES, BEEF. EXP: PETROLEUM & PETROLEUM PRODUCTS, NATURAL GAS, WOOD & WOOD PRODUCTS, METALS, FUR.

Stretching from Europe to Asia, Russia is the heartland of the former Soviet Union. Today Russia is a democratic federation. The country has rich mineral and energy resources. The mighty Volga, Europe's longest river, flows from northern Russia into the Caspian Sea. Siberia encompasses more than half the territory but is home to less than 20 percent of the population. Siberian workers toil at prying natural gas, oil, coal, gold, and diamonds from the frozen earth. Commodities such as fur and timber also earn coveted foreign currency. The Soviet Union dissolved after a failed coup in 1991, yielding Russia and 14 independent republics. Russia seeks to maintain its economic influence on resources and to confront separatism at home.

HUNDREDS OF THOUSANDS OF CROSSES adorn the Hill of Crosses, north of Siauliai, Lithuania, a Christian pilgrimage destination.

Northern
Mariana
Islands
(U.S.)

Hawai'i
(U.S.)

MARSHALL
ISLANDS
p. 413

PALAU
p. 413

FEDERATED STATES OF MICRONESIA
p. 410

NAURU
p. 413

K I R I B A T
p. 412

PAPUA
NEW
GUINEA
p. 410

SOLOMON
ISLANDS
p. 411

TUVALU
p. 412

VANUATU
p. 411

SAMOA
p. 412

American Samoa
(U.S.)

FIJI
ISLANDS
p. 411

TONGA
p. 412

New Caledonia
(France)

A U S T R A L I A
p. 410

NEW
ZEALAND
p. 410

MAP KEY

PALAU
p. 413

Country name and page number
where country facts can be found

AUSTRALIA & OCEANIA

Australia is the smallest, lowest, flattest, and—apart from Antarctica—driest continent on the planet. Off its northeastern coast lies the Great Barrier Reef, the largest coral reef in the world, with an area of 135,000 square miles. Other islands in the region are generally considered part of the Australian continent.

Australia can be divided into the Western Plateau, the Central Lowlands, and the Eastern Highlands. Central Australia is relatively flat. A third of the country is desert, a third scrub and steppe. Sand dunes and stony deserts mark the continent's great tableland.

Australia's rivers often end in salt lakes. Dry for much of each year, they become beds of salt and mud. The Eastern Highlands rise from central Australia toward a series of high plateaus, the highest part around Mount Kosciuszko. The Great Escarpment runs from northern Queensland to the Victoria border in the south.

Tasmania lies off Australia's southeastern coast. To the east is New Zealand, which is composed of the North and the South Islands. Mountainous in comparison to Australia, New Zealand receives considerably more rain, making its climate cooler and more temperate.

Oceania designates the central and south Pacific regions, including Australia, New Zealand, and the islands of Melanesia, Micronesia, and Polynesia—more than 10,000 in all. Polynesia encompasses islands from New Zealand in the southwest, to Easter Island in the east, and Hawai'i in the north. Micronesia also includes many islands.

THE HUMAN FOOTPRINT

WHEN HUMANS ARRIVED in Southeast Asia, glaciers had trapped water and exposed an overland passageway that allowed short migrations to Australia and Papua New Guinea, which at the time were a single landmass (Sahul). Genetic work with Pacific populations shows that their ancestors arrived along the South Asia coastline within a few thousand years of leaving Africa. *I* Meanwhile, explorers reached the Polynesian islands, completing the greatest migration in human history. Early farming peoples migrated to nearby islands—Indonesia, the Philippines, and Taiwan. Competition for space fueled rivalries, and some took to the Pacific, either going from Taiwan east or proceeding slowly through Melanesia. *I* The first settlers in the region were the Lapita people. Using Fiji as a base, these people colonized many of the Pacific islands and may even have established contact with coastal South America. Their expansion stopped suddenly after Tonga and Samoa.

ench
ynesia
ance)

 AUSTRALIA

COMMONWEALTH OF AUSTRALIA

AREA 2,969,906 SQ. MI. ▌ POPULATION 21,263,000 ▌ CAPITAL CANBERRA (POP. 373,000) ▌ LITERACY 99% ▌ LIFE EXPECTANCY 82 ▌ CURRENCY AUSTRALIAN DOLLAR ▌ GDP PER CAPITA $38,100 ▌ ECONOMY IND: MINING, INDUSTRIAL & TRANSPORTATION EQUIPMENT, FOOD PROCESSING, CHEMICALS, STEEL. AGR: WHEAT, BARLEY, SUGARCANE, FRUITS, CATTLE. EXP: COAL, GOLD, MEAT, WOOL, ALUMINA, IRON ORE.

An island continent, Australia combines a wide variety of landscapes. Most people reside along the southeast coast because winds from the southeast release rain there—leaving the interior beyond the mountains arid or semiarid. Vegetation ranges from rain forests in the far north to steppes and deserts in the vast interior of the Outback. The Murray-Darling River Basin, covering about 14 percent of the continent, helps sustain wheat and wool industries. Like Canada, Australia is a federal parliamentary state and a member of the British Commonwealth. Since Capt. James Cook's landing on what he dubbed New South Wales in 1770, relationships between Aboriginals and European settlers and their descendants have been marked by injustices and violence. Contemporary political concerns include restoring native land, improving the living conditions of rural Aboriginal children, and addressing environmental concerns, especially drought.

 **MICRONESIA**

FEDERATED STATES OF MICRONESIA

AREA 271 SQ. MI. ▌ POPULATION 107,000 ▌ CAPITAL PALIKIR (POP. 7,000) ▌ LITERACY 89% ▌ LIFE EXPECTANCY 71 ▌ CURRENCY US DOLLAR ▌ GDP PER CAPITA $2,200 ▌ ECONOMY IND: TOURISM, CONSTRUCTION, FISH PROCESSING, SPECIALIZED AQUACULTURE, CRAFT ITEMS FROM SHELL, WOOD & PEARLS. AGR: BLACK PEPPER, TROPICAL FRUITS & VEGETABLES, COCONUTS, CASSAVA (TAPIOCA), PIGS. EXP: FISH, GARMENTS, BANANAS, BLACK PEPPER.

Micronesia consists of the Caroline Islands Archipelago. In 1899 Spain sold the islands to Germany. Japan later occupied the region and fortified the islands just before World War II. In 1986 these 600 islands and atolls became self-governing in free association with the United States. American aid is crucial to the islands' economy.

NEW ZEALAND

NEW ZEALAND

AREA 104,454 SQ. MI. ▌ POPULATION 4,213,000 ▌ CAPITAL WELLINGTON (POP. 343,000) ▌ LITERACY 99% ▌ LIFE EXPECTANCY 80 ▌ CURRENCY NEW ZEALAND DOLLAR ▌ GDP PER CAPITA $27,900 ▌ ECONOMY IND: FOOD PROCESSING, WOOD & PAPER PRODUCTS, TEXTILES, MACHINERY. AGR: WHEAT, BARLEY, POTATOES, PULSES, WOOL, FISH. EXP: DAIRY PRODUCTS, MEAT, WOOD & WOOD PRODUCTS, FISH, CHEMICALS, WOOL.

New Zealand, known to the indigenous Maori as Aotearoa, is a fertile and mountainous island cluster in the southwestern Pacific. Snowy peaks, fjord-scarred shores, and pastures dotted with sheep define this country. New Zealand, peopled mostly by descendants of British settlers, is a parliamentary democracy modeled on that of the United Kingdom. The indigenous Maori constitute about 8 percent of New Zealanders; recent immigrants—who come primarily from Samoa and Fiji—give Auckland one of the world's largest Polynesian populations. An area of economic growth is tourism: Almost 2.5 million international tourists visited New Zealand in 2007.

 PAPUA NEW GUINEA

INDEPENDENT STATE OF PAPUA NEW GUINEA

AREA 178,703 SQ. MI. ▌ POPULATION 6,057,000 ▌ CAPITAL PORT MORESBY (POP. 275,000) ▌ LITERACY 57% ▌ LIFE EXPECTANCY 66 ▌ CURRENCY KINA ▌ GDP PER CAPITA $2,900 ▌ ECONOMY IND: COPRA CRUSHING, PALM OIL PROCESSING, PLYWOOD PRODUCTION, WOOD CHIP PRODUCTION. AGR: COFFEE, CACAO, COCONUTS, PALM KERNELS, POULTRY. EXP: OIL, GOLD, COPPER ORE, LOGS.

Papua New Guinea is an island country in the western Pacific. An abundance of minerals and petroleum brightens the outlook for this tropical nation, comprising eastern New Guinea and many small islands—including Bougainville and the Bismarck Archipelago. A patchwork of mountains, jungles, and swamplands, the country is home to some 700 Papuan and Melanesian tribes, each with its own language. Most of the inhabitants are subsistence farmers, although some grow cash crops. More than 850 distinct indigenous languages—more than 10 percent of all known languages on Earth—are found on this island.

SOLOMON ISLANDS

SOLOMON ISLANDS

AREA 10,954 SQ. MI. ▌ POPULATION 596,000 ▌ CAPITAL HONIARA (POP. 56,000) ▌ LITERACY 62% ▌ LIFE EXPECTANCY 74 ▌ CURRENCY SOLOMON ISLANDS DOLLAR ▌ GDP PER CAPITA $1,900 ▌ ECONOMY IND: FISH (TUNA), MINING, TIMBER. AGR: CACAO, COCONUTS, PALM KERNELS, RICE, CATTLE, TIMBER, FISH. EXP: TIMBER, FISH, COPRA, PALM OIL.

Northeast of Australia in the South Pacific, the Solomon Islands chain consists of six main islands that are volcanic, mountainous, and forested. Guadalcanal, known to many as the site of fierce battles between Japan and the United States during World War II, is the most populous island. About 95 percent of the islanders are Melanesians, who speak some 120 indigenous languages. Ethnic tension between natives of Guadalcanal and settlers from nearby Malaita Island escalated into an armed conflict that lasted from 1998 until 2003, when an Australian-led peacekeeping force restored order.

 # VANUATU

REPUBLIC OF VANUATU

AREA 4,707 SQ. MI. ▌ POPULATION 219,000 ▌ CAPITAL PORT VILA (POP. 34,000) ▌ LITERACY 74% ▌ LIFE EXPECTANCY 64 ▌ CURRENCY VATU ▌ GDP PER CAPITA $4,600 ▌ ECONOMY IND: FOOD & FISH FREEZING, WOOD PROCESSING, MEAT CANNING. AGR: COPRA, COCONUTS, CACAO, COFFEE, FISH. EXP: COPRA, BEEF, CACAO, TIMBER, KAVA.

France and the United Kingdom jointly administered some 80 South Pacific islands known as the New Hebrides for 74 years until their independence in 1980. The country was renamed Vanuatu—"Our Land Forever." During World War II the U.S. launched attacks from here against Japanese troops in the Solomon Islands and New Guinea, inspiring James Michener's *Tales of the South Pacific*. Tourism augments income from copra, tuna processing, meat canning, and timber sales. South American hardwoods have been introduced to expand forests.

 # FIJI

REPUBLIC OF FIJI

AREA 7,095 SQ. MI. ▌ POPULATION 945,000 ▌ CAPITAL SUVA (POP. 210,000) ▌ LITERACY 94% ▌ LIFE EXPECTANCY 71 ▌ CURRENCY FIJIAN DOLLAR ▌ GDP PER CAPITA $3,900 ▌ ECONOMY IND: TOURISM, SUGAR, CLOTHING, COPRA. AGR: SUGARCANE, COCONUTS, CASSAVA (TAPIOCA), RICE, CATTLE, FISH. EXP: SUGAR, GARMENTS, GOLD, TIMBER, FISH.

The Fiji islands comprise 332 islands in the South Pacific, adorned with beaches, coral gardens, and rain forests. Most people live on the largest island, Viti Levu, where the capital, Suva, is located. After 96 years as a British colony, Fiji gained independence in 1970. During British rule, indentured servants from India came to work in the sugarcane fields. Indo-Fijians, who currently constitute 37 percent of the population, are mostly Hindu, whereas the majority of native Fijians are mostly Christian. Tensions between the communities caused two coups in 1987, one in 2000, and another in December 2007, after which Fiji's membership in the Commonwealth of Nations was suspended.

A HEADDRESS MADE of feathers and leaves, a necklace made of seashells, and colorful face paints ready this woman for a tribal sing in Garoka, Papua, New Guinea.

HOME TO MORE THAN 200 species of coral, the National Park of American Samoa is the only U.S. national park below the Equator. Ten Samoan villages lease the land to the United States Park Service.

KIRIBATI

REPUBLIC OF KIRIBATI

AREA 313 SQ. MI. ▮ POPULATION 113,000 ▮ CAPITAL TARAWA (POP. 42,000) ▮ LITERACY NA ▮ LIFE EXPECTANCY 63 ▮ CURRENCY AUSTRALIAN DOLLAR ▮ GDP PER CAPITA $3,200 ▮ ECONOMY IND: FISHING, HANDICRAFTS. AGR: COPRA, TARO, BREADFRUIT, SWEET POTATOES, FISH. EXP: COPRA, COCONUTS, SEAWEED, FISH.

Scattered over nearly two million square miles, these 33 islands were formerly the Gilberts of the British Gilbert and Ellice Islands Colony and became the Republic of Kiribati in 1979. The country relies on foreign financial aid, particularly from the U.K. and Japan, in addition to revenues from fishing and copra. As its phosphate reserves diminish, the island has been forced to rely on a reserve trust. Remittances from citizens now working abroad augment the economy.

In 2008 Kiribati announced that it was doubling the size of its Phoenix Islands Protected Area. This is now the world's largest protected marine area. These 164,200 square miles include eight coral atolls and are home to more than 120 species of coral and 520 species of fish.

TUVALU

TUVALU

AREA 10 SQ. MI. ▮ POPULATION 12,000 ▮ CAPITAL FUNAFUTI (POP. 6,000) ▮ LITERACY NA ▮ LIFE EXPECTANCY 69 ▮ CURRENCY AUSTRALIAN DOLLAR, TUVALUAN DOLLAR ▮ GDP PER CAPITA $1,600 ▮ ECONOMY IND: FISHING, TOURISM, COPRA. AGR: COCONUTS, FISH. EXP: COPRA, FISH.

This cluster of South Pacific atolls, once a component of the Gilbert and Ellice Islands Colony, achieved independence from Britain and joined the Commonwealth in 1978. Agriculture is limited due to poor soils and lack of fresh water. Mainstays are fishing, sales of copra and postage stamps, and remittances from Tuvaluans working abroad. Revenue also comes from a trust fund created by the U.K. and Pacific-area sponsors.

SAMOA

INDEPENDENT STATE OF SAMOA

AREA 1,093 SQ. MI. ▮ POPULATION 220,000 ▮ CAPITAL APIA (POP. 40,000) ▮ LITERACY 100% ▮ LIFE EXPECTANCY 72 ▮ CURRENCY TALA ▮ GDP PER CAPITA $4,900 ▮ ECONOMY IND: FOOD PROCESSING, BUILDING MATERIALS, AUTO PARTS. AGR: COCONUTS, BANANAS, TARO, YAMS. EXP: FISH, COCONUT OIL & CREAM, COPRA, TARO.

Western political institutions and Polynesian social structure combine in Samoa, whose location at the crossroads of South Pacific shipping lanes attracted European powers. Germany took over the western part of the Samoan archipelago in 1900. After World War I, New Zealand administered the islands until they became independent in 1962. Membership in the Commonwealth came in 1970. An enlarged airport brings growing numbers of tourists.

TONGA

KINGDOM OF TONGA

AREA 289 SQ. MI. ▮ POPULATION 121,000 ▮ CAPITAL NUKU'ALOFA (POP. 35,000) ▮ LITERACY 99% ▮ LIFE EXPECTANCY 71 ▮ CURRENCY PA'ANGA ▮ GDP PER CAPITA $4,600 ▮ ECONOMY IND: TOURISM, FISHING. AGR: SQUASH, COCONUTS, COPRA, BANANAS, FISH. EXP: SQUASH, FISH, VANILLA BEANS, ROOT CROPS.

The ruler of this last remaining Polynesian kingdom in the South Pacific traces his lineage back a thousand years. The 169 islands, 36 of them inhabited, were under British protection for 70 years, until independence came in 1970.

Compulsory primary education has created a high literacy rate. The economy relies on agriculture and, increasingly, tourism and light industry.

 **PALAU**

REPUBLIC OF PALAU

AREA 189 SQ. MI. ▮ POPULATION 21,000 ▮ CAPITAL KOROR (POP. 14,000) ▮ LITERACY 92% ▮ LIFE EXPECTANCY 71 ▮ CURRENCY US DOLLAR ▮ GDP PER CAPITA $8,100 ▮ ECONOMY IND: TOURISM, CRAFT ITEMS, CONSTRUCTION, GARMENT MAKING. AGR: COCONUTS, COPRA, CASSAVA (TAPIOCA), SWEET POTATOES. EXP: SHELLFISH, TUNA, COPRA, GARMENTS.

Located in the western Pacific Ocean, Palau is an archipelago of more than 300 islands. It was a Japanese stronghold during World War II, and after that period, in 1947, the United Nations assigned the administration of these islands to the United States. The territory has thus been tied economically to the U.S., and it became an independent nation in October 1994.

About 70 percent of the population lives in the capital city of Koror on the island of Koror. Tourism is the country's main industry, with the rich marine environment providing opportunities for snorkeling and scuba diving.

 **NAURU**

REPUBLIC OF NAURU

AREA 8 SQ. MI. ▮ POPULATION 14,000 ▮ CAPITAL YAREN (POP. 670) ▮ LITERACY NA ▮ LIFE EXPECTANCY 64 ▮ CURRENCY AUSTRALIAN DOLLAR ▮ GDP PER CAPITA $5,000 ▮ ECONOMY IND: PHOSPHATE MINING, OFFSHORE BANKING, COCONUT PRODUCTS. AGR: COCONUTS. EXP: PHOSPHATES.

Nauru is a small oval-shaped island in the western Pacific. The interior phosphate plateau, representing 60 percent of the land area, has been extensively mined, leaving a jagged and pitted landscape. Germany annexed Nauru in 1888, and Australia took it over in 1914. After World War II it was a joint trust territory of Australia, Britain, and New Zealand until it became independent in 1968. Phosphate exports earned economic stability for the country, but deposits are severely depleted.

CLICK IT Bikini Atoll www.bikiniatoll.com

 MARSHALL ISLANDS

REPUBLIC OF THE MARSHALL ISLANDS

AREA 70 SQ. MI. ▮ POPULATION 65,000 ▮ CAPITAL MAJURO (POP. 25,000) ▮ LITERACY 94% ▮ LIFE EXPECTANCY 71 ▮ CURRENCY US DOLLAR ▮ GDP PER CAPITA $2,500 ▮ ECONOMY IND: COPRA, FISH, TOURISM, CRAFT ITEMS FROM SHELL, WOOD & PEARLS. AGR: COCONUTS, TOMATOES, MELONS, TARO, PIGS. EXP: COPRA CAKE, COCONUT OIL, HANDICRAFTS, FISH.

Tropical islands in the western Pacific, the Marshall Islands form two parallel island groups, the Ratak and Ralik (Sunrise and Sunset) Chains. These atolls, reefs, and islets include Kwajalein, a test range for U.S. missiles and home to the world's largest lagoon, and Enewetak, where the United States exploded the first hydrogen bomb in 1952. Bikini Atoll is still uninhabitable because of past nuclear tests. In 1986 the former trust territory became self-governing in free association with the United States, which is responsible for its defense and foreign affairs. More than 60 percent of the country's budget comes from U.S. aid.

A CONCRETE DOME on Runit, one of the Marshall Islands, covers soil made radioactive by nuclear tests conducted by the United States in the 1940s and 1950s.

Greenland
(Denmark)

Alaska
(U.S.)

C A N A D A
p. 416

U N I T E D   S T A T E S
p. 416

M E X I C O

p. 417

MAP KEY

HAITI
p. 421   Country name and page number
where country facts can be found

Puerto Rico
(U.S.)

ANTIGUA &
BARBUDA
p. 420

BAHAMAS
p. 419

DOMINICAN
REPUBLIC
p. 420

DOMINICA p. 42

ST. LUCIA p. 42

BARBADOS
p. 422

CUBA
p. 418

JAMAICA
p. 420

HAITI
p. 421

ST. KITTS
& NEVIS
p. 420

ST. VINCENT
THE GRENAD
p. 423

p. 417
BELIZE

HONDURAS
p. 417

GRENADA
p. 423

TRINIDAD &
TOBAGO
p. 423

p. 417 GUATEMALA

NICARAGUA p. 418

EL SALVADOR
p. 418

COSTA
RICA
p. 419

PANAMA
p. 418

NORTH AMERICA

From the world's largest island (Greenland) and the world's greatest concentration of fresh water (the Great Lakes) to such spectacular geographic features as the Grand Canyon and Niagara Falls, North America holds a wealth of superlatives. It is also home to Earth's largest and tallest trees (the redwoods of California) and many of its biggest animals (grizzly bears, moose, and bison).

The continent is known as well for dramatic extremes of climate—from 134°F recorded in Death Valley to -87°F logged on Greenland's wind-swept ice cap.

North America encompasses 9.45 million square miles, reaching from Greenland to Panama. Deeply indented with inlets and bays, North America has a remarkably long coastline. Surrounded by water—the Atlantic, Pacific, and Arctic Oceans, the Gulf of Mexico, and the Caribbean Sea—the continent was isolated for millions of years. Into North America's coastal waters pour a number of mighty rivers, including the Saint Lawrence, Rio Grande, Yukon, and Mississippi.

Three geologic features dominate this landmass: the Canadian Shield, the great Western Cordillera, and a colossal flatland that embraces the Great Plains, the Mississippi-Missouri River basin, and most of the Great Lakes region. Other major components include the Appalachian Mountains and the predominantly volcanic islands of the Caribbean Sea.

The continent has an equally diverse biological heritage, but many plant and animal populations declined as the human population grew and spread across the continent.

THE HUMAN FOOTPRINT

SOME 35,000 YEARS AGO, migrations in southern Siberia brought people to the Arctic. Shorter, stockier frames better equipped for the cold became the norm. Wearing footwear and warm clothing, humans followed reindeer across the tundra into lands never before visited by their kind. **/** The timing and location of migrations into the Americas remain hotly disputed. The earliest groups likely came across a land bridge created between Asia and today's Alaska during the last glacial maximum. When ice sheets parted briefly, small groups of hunter-gathers crossed into the Americas. **/** Findings in New Mexico show that humans have lived there for at least 11,000 years. These artifacts characterize Clovis, a prehistoric culture believed by some archaeologists to be the source from which all indigenous Americans descended. Sites in Chile have been dated at 12,500 years old, however, indicating human habitation there earlier than the first Clovis emergence.

WATER CASCADES 167 feet down Horseshoe Falls, the Canadian portion of Niagara Falls, on the Ontario–New York border.

 # CANADA

CANADA

AREA 3,855,101 SQ. MI. ▌ POPULATION 33,487,000 ▌ CAPITAL OTTAWA (POP. 1,182,000) ▌ LITERACY 99% ▌ LIFE EXPECTANCY 81 ▌ CURRENCY CANADIAN DOLLAR ▌ GDP PER CAPITA $39,300 ▌ ECONOMY IND: TRANSPORTATION EQUIPMENT, CHEMICALS, PROCESSED & UNPROCESSED MINERALS, FOOD PRODUCTS. AGR: WHEAT, BARLEY, OILSEED, TOBACCO, DAIRY PRODUCTS, FOREST PRODUCTS, FISH. EXP: MOTOR VEHICLES & PARTS, INDUSTRIAL MACHINERY, AIRCRAFT, TELECOMMUNICATIONS EQUIPMENT, CHEMICALS, TIMBER, CRUDE PETROLEUM.

Canada reigns as the world's second largest country in area after Russia. A vast region of swamps, lakes, and rock, known as the Canadian Shield, radiates out from Hudson Bay, covering half of the country. Because of subarctic climates in the Canadian Shield and the western mountains, an estimated 90 percent of Canadians live within 100 miles of the U.S. border.

Officially bilingual, Canada is a multicultural society, most of the population being of British or French descent, while 2 percent are First Nations, or native, peoples. Other minorities include Italians, Germans, Ukrainians, and Chinese. Most Canadians live in four areas: southern Ontario, the Montreal region, Vancouver city and southern Vancouver Island, and the Calgary-Edmonton corridor. The economy has a large manufacturing base, and the 1994 North American Free Trade Agreement (NAFTA) brought an economic boom.

 # UNITED STATES

UNITED STATES OF AMERICA

AREA 3,794,083 SQ. MI. ▌ POPULATION 307,212,000 ▌ CAPITAL WASHINGTON, D.C. (POP. 4,464,000) ▌ LITERACY 99% ▌ LIFE EXPECTANCY 78 ▌ CURRENCY US DOLLAR ▌ GDP PER CAPITA $47,000 ▌ ECONOMY IND: PETROLEUM, STEEL, MOTOR VEHICLES, AEROSPACE, TELECOMMUNICATIONS, CHEMICALS, ELECTRONICS. AGR: WHEAT, CORN, OTHER GRAINS, FRUITS, BEEF, FOREST PRODUCTS, FISH. EXP: CAPITAL GOODS, AUTOMOBILES, INDUSTRIAL SUPPLIES & RAW MATERIALS, CONSUMER GOODS, AGRICULTURAL PRODUCTS.

The continental United States can be divided into seven physiographic regions, from east to west: the Atlantic-Gulf Coastal Plain, the Appalachian Highlands, the Interior Plains, the Interior Highlands, the Rocky Mountain System, the Intermontane Region, and the Pacific Mountain System. The country also has a broad range of climates, varying from the tropical rain forest of Hawaii to the subarctic and tundra climates of Alaska.

In 1776, after years of British rule, the 13 original colonies declared independence. A federal republic was set up with a constitution in 1787. Since then, America's territory has rapidly expanded. The Louisiana Purchase in 1803, for example, practically doubled the land owned by the United States at the time. As a result, the number of states has also increased considerably, expanding to include 50 separate states. The year 1959 brought statehood to Alaska and Hawaii, the last two territories to become states.

COMMONWEALTHS & TERRITORIES OF THE U.S.

AMERICAN SAMOA
BAKER ISLAND
GUAM
GUANTANAMO BAY
HOWLAND ISLAND
JARVIS ISLAND
JOHNSTON ATOLL
KINGMAN REEF
MIDWAY ISLANDS
NAVASSA ISLAND
NORTHERN MARIANA ISLANDS
PALMYRA ATOLL
PUERTO RICO
VIRGIN ISLANDS
WAKE ISLAND

BELIZE

BELIZE

AREA 8,867 SQ. MI. ▌ POPULATION 308,000 ▌ CAPITAL BELMOPAN (POP. 9,000) ▌ LITERACY 77% ▌ LIFE EXPECTANCY 68 ▌ CURRENCY BELIZEAN DOLLAR ▌ GDP PER CAPITA $8,600 ▌ ECONOMY IND: GARMENT PRODUCTION, FOOD PROCESSING, TOURISM, CONSTRUCTION. AGR: BANANAS, COCA, CITRUS, SUGAR, FISH, LUMBER. EXP: SUGAR, BANANAS, CITRUS, CLOTHING, FISH PRODUCTS.

Belize lies along the Caribbean coast of Central America. English is the official language, but Spanish is widely spoken. Peace and plentiful land attract refugees from troubled neighboring countries. Tourists flock to see Maya ruins like Altun Ha; wildlife such as jaguars, howler monkeys, and toucans; and the Western Hemisphere's longest coral reef.

 # MEXICO

UNITED MEXICAN STATES

AREA 758,449 SQ. MI. ▌ POPULATION 111,212,000 ▌ CAPITAL MEXICO CITY (POP. 19,485,000) ▌ LITERACY 91% ▌ LIFE EXPECTANCY 76 ▌ CURRENCY MEXICAN PESO ▌ GDP PER CAPITA $14,200 ▌ ECONOMY IND: FOOD & BEVERAGES, TOBACCO, CHEMICALS, IRON & STEEL. AGR: CORN, WHEAT, SOYBEANS, RICE, BEEF, WOOD PRODUCTS. EXP: MANUFACTURED GOODS, OIL & OIL PRODUCTS, SILVER, FRUITS, VEGETABLES.

Mexico's coastal plains rise to a central plateau. Northern Mexico is desertlike, while the south is a mountainous jungle. Most Mexicans are of mixed Spanish and Indian descent, but about 30 percent are Indian. The nation is blessed with abundant minerals, advanced technology, and a huge workforce. Tax reform, privatization of state-run industries, and more-open trade policies have improved competitiveness and boosted exports. Education funding is increasing, and authority is shifting from the federal to state governments to improve accountability. Oil and gas provide a third of the government's revenue; agriculture remains an important employer. Mexico's system of *ejidos*, communal farms, was reformed in the 1990s to promote private investment and large-scale agriculture. The North American Free Trade Agreement (NAFTA, 1994) makes Mexico dependent on exports to the U.S., and a downturn in U.S. business results in little or no growth in the Mexican economy.

 # GUATEMALA

REPUBLIC OF GUATEMALA

AREA 42,042 SQ. MI. ▌ POPULATION 13,277,000 ▌ CAPITAL GUATEMALA CITY (POP. 1,104,000) ▌ LITERACY 69% ▌ LIFE EXPECTANCY 70 ▌ CURRENCY QUETZAL, US DOLLAR, OTHERS ALLOWED ▌ GDP PER CAPITA $5,200 ▌ ECONOMY IND: SUGAR, TEXTILES & CLOTHING, FURNITURE, CHEMICALS. AGR: SUGARCANE, CORN, BANANAS, COFFEE, CATTLE. EXP: COFFEE, SUGAR, BANANAS, FRUITS & VEGETABLES, CARDAMOM, MEAT.

Guatemala is a heavily forested and mountainous nation with coasts on both the Pacific and the Caribbean. More than half of Guatemalans descended from the indigenous Maya peoples; most live in the highlands and retain traditional dress, customs, and language. The rest of the population, known as Ladinos (mostly of mixed Maya-Spanish ancestry), speak Spanish and wear Western clothing. Conflict between these two cultures led to warfare between guerrillas and the government lasting years and costing hundreds of thousands of lives. In September 1996 the government and the guerrillas finally agreed on terms to end the 36-year-long civil war. The democratic government faces problems of crime, illiteracy, and poverty, but it is making progress in moving the economy.

HONDURAS

REPUBLIC OF HONDURAS

AREA 43,433 SQ. MI. ▌ POPULATION 7,793,000 ▌ CAPITAL TEGUCIGALPA (POP. 1,022,000) ▌ LITERACY 80% ▌ LIFE EXPECTANCY 69 ▌ CURRENCY LEMPIRA ▌ GDP PER CAPITA $4,400 ▌ ECONOMY IND: SUGAR, COFFEE, TEXTILES, CLOTHING. AGR: BANANAS, COFFEE, CITRUS, BEEF, TIMBER, SHRIMP. EXP: COFFEE, BANANAS, SHRIMP, LOBSTER, MEAT.

Honduras is mountainous and forested—although widespread slash-and-burn subsistence farming is destroying many forests. The largely mestizo (Spanish-Indian) population speaks Spanish, with English common on the northern coast and Bay Islands. Maya ruins at Copán help diversify the economy with tourist revenue. Although agricultural products, mostly bananas and coffee, are plentiful, they have failed to enliven the economy of this tenuous democracy. The U.S.-dependent economy suffered in the 2008 financial crisis.

418

EL SALVADOR

REPUBLIC OF EL SALVADOR

AREA 8,124 SQ. MI. ▮ POPULATION 7,185,000 ▮ CAPITAL SAN SALVADOR (POP. 1,520,000) ▮ LITERACY 80% ▮ LIFE EXPECTANCY 72 ▮ CURRENCY US DOLLAR ▮ GDP PER CAPITA $6,200 ▮ ECONOMY IND: FOOD PROCESSING, BEVERAGES, PETROLEUM, CHEMICALS. AGR: COFFEE, SUGAR, CORN, RICE, SHRIMP, BEEF. EXP: OFFSHORE ASSEMBLY EXPORTS, COFFEE, SUGAR, SHRIMP, TEXTILES, CHEMICALS, ELECTRICITY.

The smallest and most densely populated country in Central America, El Salvador adjoins the Pacific in a narrow coastal plain, backed by a volcanic mountain chain and a fertile plateau. About 90 percent of Salvadorans are mestizo; 9 percent claim Spanish descent. The rich volcanic soils have supported coffee plantations with a few rich landowners and a subjugated peasant population. Economic inequality led to the 1980-92 civil war; many Salvadorans, rich and poor, fled to the United States. El Salvador's democratic government has shown success in adding manufacturing jobs but faces the challenges of poverty, crime, and natural disasters.

NICARAGUA

REPUBLIC OF NICARAGUA

AREA 50,193 SQ. MI. ▮ POPULATION 5,891,000 ▮ CAPITAL MANAGUA (POP. 944,000) ▮ LITERACY 68% ▮ LIFE EXPECTANCY 72 ▮ CURRENCY GOLD CORDOBA ▮ GDP PER CAPITA $2,900 ▮ ECONOMY IND: FOOD PROCESSING, CHEMICALS, MACHINERY & METAL PRODUCTS, TEXTILES. AGR: COFFEE, BANANAS, SUGARCANE, COTTON, BEEF, VEAL. EXP: COFFEE, SHRIMP & LOBSTER, COTTON, TOBACCO, BANANAS.

Natural disasters and the consequences of civil war have harassed this largest Central American country. Volcanoes and earthquakes along the Pacific coast are a constant threat, and hurricanes hit the low-lying Caribbean coast. With the Sandinistas' overthrow of Anastasio Somoza in 1979, ending his family's 42-year dictatorship, Nicaragua came under the control of a junta. Eight years of civil war between the Sandinista regime and the U.S.-funded rebels (contras) ended in 1988. Peace brought democracy, but poverty and corruption are major problems.

 CUBA

REPUBLIC OF CUBA

AREA 42,803 SQ. MI. ▮ POPULATION 11,452,000 ▮ CAPITAL HAVANA (POP. 2,159,000) ▮ LITERACY 100% ▮ LIFE EXPECTANCY 77 ▮ CURRENCY CUBAN PESO ▮ GDP PER CAPITA $9,500 ▮ ECONOMY IND: SUGAR, PETROLEUM, TOBACCO, CHEMICALS. AGR: SUGAR, TOBACCO, CITRUS, COFFEE, LIVESTOCK. EXP: SUGAR, NICKEL, TOBACCO, FISH, MEDICAL PRODUCTS.

The Republic of Cuba comprises more than 4,000 islands and cays; the main island is the largest in the West Indies. By the mid-1800s its sugar plantations were satisfying a third of world demand. The economy crashed after Cuba was abandoned by the former U.S.S.R. and Eastern European trading partners in the early 1990s, and food and energy were tightly rationed. Today, despite a trade embargo enforced by the U.S., Cuba's economy is improving. Cuba's natural beauty draws millions of tourists, with many coming to see the thousands of plant and animal species that live nowhere else on Earth. In southeastern Cuba, the U.S. maintains a presence at Guantanamo Bay; a 1934 treaty grants a perpetual lease, voided only by mutual consent or by U.S. abandonment of the naval base.

PANAMA

REPUBLIC OF PANAMA

AREA 29,157 SQ. MI. ▮ POPULATION 3,360,000 ▮ CAPITAL PANAMA CITY (POP. 1,379,000) ▮ LITERACY 92% ▮ LIFE EXPECTANCY 77 ▮ CURRENCY BALBOA, US DOLLAR ▮ GDP PER CAPITA $11,600 ▮ ECONOMY IND: CONSTRUCTION, PETROLEUM REFINING, BREWING, CEMENT & OTHER CONSTRUCTION MATERIALS. AGR: BANANAS, RICE, CORN, COFFEE, LIVESTOCK, SHRIMP. EXP: BANANAS, SHRIMP, SUGAR, COFFEE, CLOTHING.

Panama is a narrow land bridge connecting North and South America. The Panama Canal, built by the United States after Panama's independence from Colombia in 1903, joins the Atlantic and Pacific Oceans. In 1989 U.S. troops overthrew Gen. Manuel Noriega, following his indictment for complicity in drug trafficking. Panama's first woman president, Mireya Moscoso, was elected in 1999, the year that Panama assumed full control of the canal.

RAINBOWS, THATCHED-ROOF COTTAGES, and new red shoes make for simple pleasures in Manicaragua, Cuba, in the Villa Clara Province, an agricultural region in the center of the island. Known for its fine tobacco and distinctively flavorful coffee beans, Manicaragua presides over a fertile inland valley.

 # BAHAMAS

COMMONWEALTH OF THE BAHAMAS

AREA 5,382 SQ. MI. ▌ POPULATION 309,000 ▌ CAPITAL NASSAU (POP. 222,000) ▌ LITERACY 96% ▌ LIFE EXPECTANCY 66 ▌ CURRENCY BAHAMIAN DOLLAR ▌ GDP PER CAPITA $28,600 ▌ ECONOMY IND: TOURISM, BANKING, E-COMMERCE, CEMENT, OIL REFINING & SHIPPING. AGR: CITRUS, VEGETABLES, POULTRY. EXP: FISH & CRAWFISH, RUM, SALT, CHEMICALS, FRUIT & VEGETABLES.

The Bahamas, 700 islands and 2,400 cays, dot the Atlantic Ocean from Florida almost to Haiti. Only 30 of the islands are inhabited. When Columbus first set foot in the New World on San Salvador in 1492, the Arawak Indians were the only inhabitants there. Today, about 85 percent of Bahamians are of African heritage. New Providence, one of the smallest of the major islands, is home to almost 70 percent of the population. Tourism brings more than three billion dollars annually. International banking and investment management augment the economy, with more than 400 banking institutions from 36 countries.

COSTA RICA

REPUBLIC OF COSTA RICA

AREA 19,730 SQ. MI. ▌ POPULATION 4,254,000 ▌ CAPITAL SAN JOSÉ (POP. 1,374,000) ▌ LITERACY 95% ▌ LIFE EXPECTANCY 78 ▌ CURRENCY COSTA RICAN COLON ▌ GDP PER CAPITA $11,600 ▌ ECONOMY IND: MICRO-PROCESSORS, FOOD PROCESSING, TEXTILES & CLOTHING, CONSTRUCTION MATERIALS. AGR: COFFEE, PINEAPPLES, BANANAS, SUGAR, BEEF, TIMBER. EXP: COFFEE, BANANAS, SUGAR, PINEAPPLES, TEXTILES.

Costa Rica has coastlines on both the Caribbean Sea and the Pacific Ocean. The country's tropical coastal plains rise to mountains, active volcanoes, and a temperate central plateau where most people live. (San José, the capital, is here.) Costa Rica enjoys continuing stability after a century of almost uninterrupted democratic government. Tourism, which has overtaken bananas as Costa Rica's leading foreign exchange earner, bolsters the economy. A quarter of the land has protected status; the beauty of rain forest preserves draws more and more visitors.

FAST FACT Columbus named Nevis for the Spanish word for snow after observing the island's cloud-shrouded peak.

420

ANSWER BOOK | CHAPTER NINE | COUNTRIES OF THE WORLD

SAINT KITTS & NEVIS

FEDERATION OF SAINT KITTS & NEVIS

AREA 104 SQ. MI. ▌ POPULATION 40,000 ▌ CAPITAL BASSETERRE (POP. 13,000) ▌ LITERACY 98% ▌ LIFE EXPECTANCY 73 ▌ CURRENCY EAST CARIBBEAN DOLLAR ▌ GDP PER CAPITA $19,700 ▌ ECONOMY IND: SUGAR PROCESSING, TOURISM, COTTON, SALT. AGR: SUGARCANE, RICE, YAMS, VEGETABLES, FISH. EXP: MACHINERY, FOOD, ELECTRONICS, BEVERAGES, TOBACCO.

The twin islands of Saint Kitts and Nevis are both volcanic, with sandy beaches and a warm, wet climate. Once known as the Gibraltar of the West Indies, the massive 17th-century fortress atop Brimstone Hill on St. Kitts recalls colonial occupation. Independent of Britain since 1983, the two-island nation is diversifying the economy away from sugar toward tourism, banking, and light manufacturing. The island of Nevis has been pursuing the constitutional process of secession since 1996.

DOMINICAN REPUBLIC

DOMINICAN REPUBLIC

AREA 18,704 SQ. MI. ▌ POPULATION 9,650,000 ▌ CAPITAL SANTO DOMINGO (POP. 2,298,000) ▌ LITERACY 87% ▌ LIFE EXPECTANCY 74 ▌ CURRENCY DOMINICAN PESO ▌ GDP PER CAPITA $8,100 ▌ ECONOMY IND: TOURISM, SUGAR PROCESSING, FERRONICKEL & GOLD MINING, TEXTILES. AGR: SUGARCANE, COFFEE, COTTON, CACAO, CATTLE. EXP: FERRONICKEL, SUGAR, GOLD, SILVER, COFFEE.

Two-thirds of Hispaniola, the Dominican Republic is the second largest country, after Cuba, in the West Indies. This mountainous land includes Pico Duarte—the highest point in the Caribbean. Colonized in 1493 by Spaniards, it offered the first chartered university, hospital, cathedral, and monastery in the Americas. Santo Domingo, founded in 1496, is the oldest European settlement in the Western Hemisphere. The nation, independent since 1844, is a democracy, economically dependent on agriculture and tourism.

CLICK IT: National Geographic Travel & Cultures travel.nationalgeographic.com/places

JAMAICA

JAMAICA

AREA 4,244 SQ. MI. ▌ POPULATION 2,826,000 ▌ CAPITAL KINGSTON (POP. 575,000) ▌ LITERACY 88% ▌ LIFE EXPECTANCY 74 ▌ CURRENCY JAMAICAN DOLLAR ▌ GDP PER CAPITA $7,400 ▌ ECONOMY IND: TOURISM, BAUXITE, TEXTILES, FOOD PROCESSING. AGR: SUGARCANE, BANANAS, COFFEE, CITRUS, POULTRY. EXP: ALUMINA, BAUXITE, SUGAR, BANANAS, RUM.

Columbus landed on this mountainous island just south of Cuba in 1494, and the Spanish soon brought in slaves as the native Taino Indians died out—today more than 90 percent of the population is of African descent. The British seized the island in 1655, granting independence in 1962. Tourism is a steady, but reliance on unpredictably priced commodities, such as bauxite, causes uneven economic growth. The island is a major transit point for South American cocaine en route to the U.S. and Europe.

ANTIGUA & BARBUDA

ANTIGUA AND BARBUDA

AREA 171 SQ. MI. ▌ POPULATION 86,000 ▌ CAPITAL ST. JOHN'S (POP. 28,000) ▌ LITERACY 86% ▌ LIFE EXPECTANCY 75 ▌ CURRENCY EAST CARIBBEAN DOLLAR ▌ GDP PER CAPITA $19,000 ▌ ECONOMY IND: TOURISM, CONSTRUCTION, LIGHT MANUFACTURING. AGR: COTTON, FRUITS, VEGETABLES, BANANAS, LIVESTOCK. EXP: PETROLEUM PRODUCTS, MANUFACTURING, MACHINERY & TRANSPORT EQUIPMENT, FOOD & LIVE ANIMALS.

Antigua and Barbuda, small islands in the eastern Caribbean, were colonized by the English in 1632. Sugar plantations ruled the economy, and African slaves were brought in as laborers. Independent of Britain since 1981, this three-island nation remains within the Commonwealth. Antigua, one of the first Caribbean islands to promote tourism, in the early 1960s, is the wealthiest. Barbuda seeks to balance resort development with protection of its varied wildlife. Tiny Redonda is uninhabited.

THE POOREST COUNTRY in the Western Hemisphere, still Haiti has a fruitful climate. Here workers harvest the yield from a massive tomato farm established in Haiti by USAid, a U.S. governmental agency dedicated to supporting economic growth, global health, and humanitarian assistance worldwide.

 ## HAITI

REPUBLIC OF HAITI

AREA 10,714 SQ. MI. ▮ POPULATION 9,036,000 ▮ CAPITAL PORT-AU-PRINCE (POP. 2,209,000) ▮ LITERACY 53% ▮ LIFE EXPECTANCY 61 ▮ CURRENCY GOURDE ▮ GDP PER CAPITA $1,300 ▮ ECONOMY IND: SUGAR REFINING, FLOUR MILLING, TEXTILES, CEMENT. AGR: COFFEE, MANGOES, SUGARCANE, RICE, WOOD. EXP: MANUFACTURING, COFFEE, OILS, COCOA.

After a slave revolt against the French in 1804, Haiti (the western third of Hispaniola) became the first Caribbean state to achieve independence and the first black republic in the Americas. Mountainous with a tropical climate, it is the poorest country in the Americas due to decades of violence and instability. There is a huge income gap between the Creole-speaking black majority and the French-speaking mulattos who, though only 5 percent of the population, control most of the wealth. As Haiti celebrated 200 years of independence, a rebellion toppled the government in February 2004. A democratically elected president and parliament took the helm in 2006.

 ## DOMINICA

COMMONWEALTH OF DOMINICA

AREA 290 SQ. MI. ▮ POPULATION 73,000 ▮ CAPITAL ROSEAU (POP. 27,000) ▮ LITERACY 94% ▮ LIFE EXPECTANCY 76 ▮ CURRENCY EAST CARIBBEAN DOLLAR ▮ GDP PER CAPITA $9,900 ▮ ECONOMY IND: SOAP, COCONUT OIL, TOURISM, COPRA. AGR: BANANAS, CITRUS, MANGOES, ROOT CROPS. EXP: BANANAS, SOAP, BAY OIL, VEGETABLES, GRAPEFRUIT.

Mountainous, densely forested, with waterfalls and exotic birds, much of Dominica is protected as national wilderness. Volcanic activity provides boiling pools, geysers, and black-sand beaches. Most Dominicans are descendants of African slaves brought in by colonial planters. Independent from Britain since 1978, Dominica remains poor and dependent on banana exports. Governments, including that of Mary Eugenia Charles, the first female prime minister in the West Indies, have sought to broaden the economic base with tourism and light industry. Home to 3,000 Carib Indians, Dominica is the last bastion of this once populous Caribbean tribe.

BETWEEN BOW AND PEAK, a yawl sails by the Pitons, St. Lucia's signature pair of mountains. Two volcanic plugs shoot straight up out of the water, reaching more than 2,000 feet above sea level. Hot sulfur springs bubble partway up their slopes. UNESCO has designated them a World Heritage Site.

 # BARBADOS

BARBADOS

AREA 166 SQ. MI. ▮ POPULATION 285,000 ▮ CAPITAL BRIDGETOWN (POP. 140,000) ▮ LITERACY 100% ▮ LIFE EXPECTANCY 74 ▮ CURRENCY BARBADIAN DOLLAR ▮ GDP PER CAPITA $19,300 ▮ ECONOMY IND: TOURISM, SUGAR, LIGHT MANUFACTURING, COMPONENT ASSEMBLY FOR EXPORT. AGR: SUGARCANE, VEGETABLES, COTTON. EXP: SUGAR & MOLASSES, RUM, OTHER FOODS & BEVERAGES, CHEMICALS.

Barbados is the most easterly of the Caribbean islands and first in line for seasonal hurricanes. The west coast has white sandy beaches and calm water, but the east coast faces the turbulent Atlantic. Settled by the British in 1627, it won independence in 1966 but retains a strong British flavor. With more than 1,705 people per square mile, Barbados is one of the world's most densely populated nations. It has a stable democracy and a relatively prosperous economy, based largely on tourism and sugar. The grapefruit originates from Barbados.

 # SAINT LUCIA

SAINT LUCIA

AREA 238 SQ. MI. ▮ POPULATION 160,000 ▮ CAPITAL CASTRIES (POP. 14,000) ▮ LITERACY 90% ▮ LIFE EXPECTANCY 76 ▮ CURRENCY EAST CARIBBEAN DOLLAR ▮ GDP PER CAPITA $11,300 ▮ ECONOMY IND: CLOTHING, ASSEMBLY OF ELECTRONIC COMPONENTS, BEVERAGES, CORRUGATED CARDBOARD BOXES. AGR: BANANAS, COCONUTS, VEGETABLES, CITRUS. EXP: BANANAS, CLOTHING, CACAO, VEGETABLES.

A tropical island in the eastern Caribbean Sea, Saint Lucia gained independence from Britain in 1979. Tropical forests cloak a mountainous interior flanked by twin volcanic peaks, known as the Pitons. Carib Indians inhabited the island before it was invaded by buccaneers in the 1500s, but none are found on the island today. Dutch, French, and British all settled here. Oil trans-shipment via a U.S.-built terminal and the export of manufactured goods supplement agriculture and tourism. The government is challenged by unemployment and drug-related crime.

TRINIDAD & TOBAGO

REPUBLIC OF TRINIDAD & TOBAGO

AREA 1,980 SQ. MI. ▌ POPULATION 1,230,000 ▌ CAPITAL PORT-OF-SPAIN (POP. 55,000) ▌ LITERACY 99% ▌ LIFE EXPECTANCY 71 ▌ CURRENCY TRINIDAD & TOBAGO DOLLAR ▌ GDP PER CAPITA $18,600 ▌ ECONOMY IND: PETROLEUM, CHEMICALS, TOURISM, FOOD PROCESSING. AGR: CACAO, SUGARCANE, RICE, CITRUS, POULTRY. EXP: PETROLEUM & PETROLEUM PRODUCTS, CHEMICALS, STEEL PRODUCTS, FERTILIZER.

Trinidad and Tobago are the southernmost islands of the Caribbean chain. The Spanish were present on Trinidad from Columbus's arrival in 1498. The British took possession in 1802 and held power until 1962. While geographically close, the islands are far apart in their tempo of life: Steel-band music and a multiethnic population, including many of African and East Indian descent, give flamboyant Trinidad a fast beat; small farms and quiet resorts give scenic Tobago a slower rhythm. In addition to having reserves of oil and natural gas, Trinidad—which is more than 16 times as large as Tobago—contains Pitch Lake, a huge asphalt deposit. High priorities for the economy are increased gas production, aggressive promotion of foreign investment, and industrial and agricultural diversification.

ST. GEORGE'S, GRENADA, flattened by Hurricane Ivan in 2004, rebuilt quickly; the town hosted the 2007 Cricket World Cup.

SAINT VINCENT & THE GRENADINES

SAINT VINCENT & THE GRENADINES

AREA 150 SQ. MI. ▌ POPULATION 105,000 ▌ CAPITAL KINGSTOWN (POP. 29,000) ▌ LITERACY 96% ▌ LIFE EXPECTANCY 74 ▌ CURRENCY EAST CARIBBEAN DOLLAR ▌ GDP PER CAPITA $10,500 ▌ ECONOMY IND: FOOD PROCESSING, CEMENT, FURNITURE, CLOTHING, STARCH. AGR: BANANAS, COCONUTS, SWEET POTATOES, SPICES, CATTLE, FISH. EXP: BANANAS, DASHEEN (TARO), ARROWROOT STARCH, TENNIS RACKETS.

This eastern Caribbean country consists of volcanic St. Vincent island and the Grenadines, 32 smaller islands and cays. St. Vincent is hilly with rich volcanic soils, and its volcano, Soufrière, last erupted in 1979—the year of independence from Britain. Two hydroelectric plants help power St. Vincent's diversifying economy, dependent in part on exports of bananas and arrowroot, which is valuable as a starch in carbonless copy paper. Tourism is of growing importance.

GRENADA

GRENADA

AREA 133 SQ. MI. ▌ POPULATION 91,000 ▌ CAPITAL ST. GEORGE'S (POP. 33,000) ▌ LITERACY 96% ▌ LIFE EXPECTANCY 66 ▌ CURRENCY EAST CARIBBEAN DOLLAR ▌ GDP PER CAPITA $13,400 ▌ ECONOMY IND: FOOD & BEVERAGES, TEXTILES, LIGHT ASSEMBLY OPERATIONS, TOURISM. AGR: BANANAS, CACAO, NUTMEG, MACE. EXP: BANANAS, CACAO, NUTMEG, FRUITS & VEGETABLES.

Grenada, located in the southeastern Caribbean, is made up of the islands of Grenada, Carriacou, and Petite Martinique. Most Grenadians are of African descent. Grenada, the largest and most populous of the islands, is popularly known as "The Spice of the Caribbean." In the 20th century, nutmeg overtook sugar and cacao as the island's primary crop. Small farms replaced sugar plantations, slavery was abolished in 1833, and today the sweet smells of nutmeg and other spices waft on balmy breezes. Independence from Britain came in 1974; a military coup in 1983 brought a U.S.-Caribbean force that restored democracy.

VENEZUELA
p. 426

GUYANA p. 426
SURINAME p. 426
French Guiana
(France)

COLOMBIA
p. 426

ECUADOR
p. 427

P E R U

p. 427

B R A Z I L
p. 428

BOLIVIA
p. 428

PARAGUAY
p. 429

MAP KEY

URUGUAY
p. 429

Country name and page number
where country facts can be found

C H I L E

p. 428

A R G E N T I N A

p. 428

URUGUAY
p. 429

SOUTH AMERICA

With a base along the Caribbean coast and an apex at Cape Horn, South America is shaped like an elongated triangle. Embracing an area of nearly 6.9 million square miles, the continent is bounded by the Atlantic Ocean, the Pacific Ocean, and the Caribbean Sea. Its only connection to North America is the narrow Isthmus of Panama. In the south, the Drake Passage separates South America from Antarctica.

Other than in the extreme south, South America has a regular coastline and relatively few islands, although its offshore elements are distinctive: frigid Tierra del Fuego, the battle-torn Falklands (Malvinas), the biologically wondrous Galápagos, the spectacular fjord country of southern Chile, and the untamed Marajó Island in the Amazon delta.

The Andes mountains, the Amazon Basin, and a wide southern plain dominate the mainland. The Andes, which run from northern Colombia to southern Chile and Argentina, are the world's longest mountain range. South America's hydrology is astounding: Rainwater spilling off the Andes creates the Amazon River, which sustains the world's largest rain forest.

The Amazon is not the world's longest river, yet it carries more water than the next ten biggest rivers in the world combined. In addition, spilling off a tabletop mountain in the north is Angel Falls, the world's highest cascade.

Among the other geographic oddities of this continent are windswept Patagonia and the super-dry Atacama Desert, which often goes without rain for hundreds of years. The Pantanal region of southern Brazil is among the Earth's great wetlands.

THE HUMAN FOOTPRINT

WITHIN A FEW MILLENNIA, humans had migrated 12,000 miles—from the Arctic Northwest to the southern tip of Tierra del Fuego. By 6,000 years ago, humans were cultivating maize in lowland Mesoamerica. Cities coalesced around 1200 B.C. into the first Mesoamerican civilization, the Olmec, whose culture flourished for 800 years. Next the Maya and Aztec civilizations developed, with sophisticated mathematical systems and written languages. Many of today's Mesoamericans directly descend from these cultures. / Hunter-gatherer communities exploited the jungles along the Amazon and Orinoco Rivers, but crops did poorly in such light- and nutrient-poor environments. / Spring runoff from the Andes flooded the semiarid valleys of Peru, where as many as 25 groups terraced and irrigated. By the 13th century, the Inca had incorporated western South America into a kingdom, maintaining control and providing security with decentralized power.

COLOMBIA

REPUBLIC OF COLOMBIA

AREA 440,831 SQ. MI. ▍ POPULATION 45,644,000 ▍ CAPITAL BOGOTÁ (POP. 8,320,000) ▍ LITERACY 90% ▍ LIFE EXPECTANCY 73 ▍ CURRENCY COLOMBIAN PESO ▍ GDP PER CAPITA $8,900 ▍ ECONOMY IND: TEXTILES, FOOD PROCESSING, OIL, CLOTHING & FOOTWEAR. AGR: COFFEE, CUT FLOWERS, BANANAS, RICE, FOREST PRODUCTS. EXP: PETROLEUM, COFFEE, COAL, APPAREL, BANANAS, CUT FLOWERS.

The only South American country with coastlines on both the Caribbean and the Pacific shores, Colombia's terrain is characterized by three mighty Andean cordilleras, which separate the western coastal lowlands from the eastern jungles. It contains both hot, wet rain forests and snow-encrusted mountains. Most people live in the Andean interior, which is the cultivation center for coffee, Colombia's major crop. The majority of Colombia's territory, however, lies in the tropical lowlands to the east of the Andes. Savannas, or *llanos*, fill northern Colombia, and are largely devoted to cattle grazing, while the southeastern rain forests produce wood products.

VENEZUELA

BOLIVARIAN REPUBLIC OF VENEZUELA

AREA 352,144 SQ. MI. ▍ POPULATION 26,815,000 ▍ CAPITAL CARACAS 3,098,000 ▍ LITERACY 93% ▍ LIFE EXPECTANCY 74 ▍ CURRENCY BOLIVAR ▍ GDP PER CAPITA $13,500 ▍ ECONOMY IND: PETROLEUM, IRON ORE MINING, CONSTRUCTION MATERIALS, FOOD PROCESSING. AGR: CORN, SORGHUM, SUGARCANE, RICE, BEEF, FISH. EXP: PETROLEUM, BAUXITE & ALUMINUM, STEEL, CHEMICALS, AGRICULTURAL PRODUCTS.

Venezuela contains an incredibly diverse physiographic identity. Its topography can be divided three ways into the lowland plains, the mountains, and the interior forested uplands. Its landscape in general is even more variable, however, containing islands and coastal plains, lowlands and highlands, hills, valleys, and mountain ranges. The population clusters primarily in the cities on the mountain range near the Caribbean coast. For the first half of the 20th century, Venezuela was ruled by military strongmen who promoted the oil industry. To this day, oil revenues represent roughly 90 percent of export earnings. Democratically elected governments have held sway since 1959.

SURINAME

REPUBLIC OF SURINAME

AREA 63,037 SQ. MI. ▍ POPULATION 481,000 ▍ CAPITAL PARAMARIBO (POP. 253,000) ▍ LITERACY 90% ▍ LIFE EXPECTANCY 90 ▍ CURRENCY SURINAMESE GUILDER ▍ GDP PER CAPITA $8,900 ▍ ECONOMY IND: BAUXITE & GOLD MINING, ALUMINA PRODUCTION, OIL, LUMBERING, FOOD PROCESSING. AGR: PADDY RICE, BANANAS, PALM KERNELS, BEEF, FOREST PRODUCTS, SHRIMP. EXP: ALUMINA, CRUDE OIL, LUMBER, SHRIMP & FISH, RICE.

Suriname is a small, but ethnically diverse, country along South America's northern coast. Formerly known as Dutch Guiana, Suriname gained independence in 1975. Most Surinamers—descendants of African slaves and Indian or Indonesian servants brought over by the Dutch—live in the northern coastal plain. Access to the interior rain forest is limited. Bauxite mining and alumina exports dominate trade; inexpensive power from the Afobaka hydroelectric plant helps the economy.

GUYANA

CO-OPERATIVE REPUBLIC OF GUYANA

AREA 83,000 SQ. MI. ▍ POPULATION 773,000 ▍ CAPITAL GEORGETOWN (POP. 231,000) ▍ LITERACY 99% ▍ LIFE EXPECTANCY 67 ▍ CURRENCY GUYANESE DOLLAR ▍ GDP PER CAPITA $3,900 ▍ ECONOMY IND: BAUXITE, SUGAR, RICE MILLING, TIMBER, TEXTILES. AGR: SUGAR, RICE, WHEAT, VEGETABLE OILS, BEEF, SHRIMP. EXP: SUGAR, GOLD, BAUXITE/ALUMINA, RICE, SHRIMP.

Tropical rain forest shrouds more than 80 percent of this former British colony on the north coast of South America. During 150 years of rule, Britain imported Africans and East Indians as laborers, and Guyana forged close trade ties with the Caribbean. Since independence in 1966, the Guyanese have supported a parliamentary system. Guyana's high debt burden to foreign creditors and territorial disputes with Suriname and Venezuela continue to hamper the government.

FOR MORE THAN 2,000 YEARS, silver was the ruling commodity in the Peruvian Andes. As recently as 2007, in fact, Peru led the world in silver production. Often the precious metal is cast into brick-size bullions, fetching high prices on the world market.

ECUADOR

REPUBLIC OF ECUADOR

AREA 109,483 SQ. MI. ▌ POPULATION 14,573,000 ▌ CAPITAL QUITO (POP. 1,846,000) ▌ LITERACY 91% ▌ LIFE EXPECTANCY 75 ▌ CURRENCY US DOLLAR ▌ GDP PER CAPITA $7,500 ▌ ECONOMY IND: PETROLEUM, FOOD PROCESSING, TEXTILES, METAL WORK. AGR: BANANAS, COFFEE, CACAO, RICE, CATTLE, BALSA WOOD, FISH. EXP: PETROLEUM, BANANAS, SHRIMP, COFFEE, CACAO.

Located along the Equator, Ecuador contains four distinct and contrasting regions. The Costa, or coastal plain, grows enough bananas to make Ecuador the world's largest fruit exporter. The Sierra, or Andean uplands, offers productive farmland. Oil from the Oriente, jungles east of the Andes, enriches the economy. The Galápagos Islands to the west bring tourism revenue with their unique wildlife. The country is also divided ethnically. About 7 percent of the population is of European descent, about a quarter belong to indigenous cultures, and the rest are mostly of mixed ethnicity. Regional and ethnic issues contribute to political instability for Ecuador's democracy.

PERU

REPUBLIC OF PERU

AREA 496,224 SQ. MI. ▌ POPULATION 29,547,000 ▌ CAPITAL LIMA (POP. 8,375,000) ▌ LITERACY 93% ▌ LIFE EXPECTANCY 71 ▌ CURRENCY NUEVO SOL ▌ GDP PER CAPITA $8,400 ▌ ECONOMY IND: MINING OF METALS, PETROLEUM, FISHING, TEXTILES, CLOTHING. AGR: COFFEE, COTTON, SUGARCANE, RICE, POULTRY. EXP: FISH & FISH PRODUCTS, GOLD, COPPER, ZINC, CRUDE PETROLEUM & BY-PRODUCTS.

Peru lies on the Pacific coast just south of the Equator. The western seaboard is desert, making Lima an oasis. The Andean highlands occupy about a third of the country. Today Peru ranks among the world's top producers of silver, copper, lead, and zinc. Its petroleum industry is one of the world's oldest, and its fisheries are among the world's richest. Peru's recent history has seen it switch between periods of democracy and dictatorship. The desperate poverty of the Indian population gave rise to the ruthless Maoist guerrilla organization Sendero Luminoso (Shining Path). The guerrillas were largely defeated, but problems with poverty and illegal coca production persist.

 BOLIVIA

REPUBLIC OF BOLIVIA

AREA 424,164 SQ. MI. ▐ POPULATION 9,775,000 ▐ ADMINISTRATIVE CAPITAL LA PAZ (POP. 1,642,000), CONSTITUTIONAL CAPITAL SUCRE (POP. 212,000) ▐ LITERACY 87% ▐ LIFE EXPECTANCY 67 ▐ CURRENCY BOLIVIANO ▐ GDP PER CAPITA $4,500 ▐ ECONOMY IND: MINING, SMELTING, PETROLEUM, FOOD & BEVERAGES. AGR: SOYBEANS, COFFEE, COCA, COTTON, TIMBER. EXP: SOYBEANS, NATURAL GAS, ZINC, GOLD, WOOD.

Bolivia is mountainous and landlocked. Many of Bolivia's people are subsistence farmers on the Altiplano. Here La Paz sprawls amid snowy peaks near Lake Titicaca. The waters of the lake help warm the air. Otherwise La Paz, the world's highest capital city, would not be inhabitable. Bolivia's Madidi National Park includes everything from Andean glaciers to rain forests, which helps Indians develop ecotourism. Large natural gas deposits and expansion of soybean cultivation help the economy. But a historic boundary dispute with Chile and cocaine from the Cochabamba area plague the government.

 BRAZIL

FEDERATIVE REPUBLIC OF BRAZIL

AREA 3,300,169 SQ. MI. ▐ POPULATION 198,739,000 ▐ CAPITAL BRASÍLIA (POP. 3,938,000) ▐ LITERACY 89% ▐ LIFE EXPECTANCY 72 ▐ CURRENCY REAL ▐ GDP PER CAPITA $10,100 ▐ ECONOMY IND: TEXTILES, SHOES, CHEMICALS, CEMENT, LUMBER, IRON ORE. AGR: COFFEE, SOYBEANS, WHEAT, RICE, BEEF. EXP: TRANSPORT EQUIPMENT, IRON ORE, SOYBEANS, FOOTWEAR, COFFEE.

Brazil contains nearly half of South America's area and people. Over half of the population is of European origin; almost as many are black or of mixed-race, a legacy of the slave trade. Less than one percent are from indigenous groups. Southeastern Brazil includes São Paulo and Rio de Janeiro, the economic hub of Brazil. South of São Paulo is a rich agricultural region. Northeastern Brazil stretches from Maranhão in the north down to Bahia. Despite past wealth, this is a poor, drought-prone region. However, tourism has been growing, while the government is making progress in conserving the tropical rain forest and protecting the indigenous people.

 CHILE

REPUBLIC OF CHILE

AREA 291,930 SQ. MI. ▐ POPULATION 16,602,000 ▐ CAPITAL SANTIAGO (POP. 5,879,000) ▐ LITERACY 96% ▐ LIFE EXPECTANCY 77 ▐ CURRENCY CHILEAN PESO ▐ GDP PER CAPITA $14,900 ▐ ECONOMY IND: COPPER, OTHER MINERALS, FOODSTUFFS, FISH PROCESSING, IRON & STEEL. AGR: WHEAT, CORN, GRAPES, BEANS, BEEF, FISH, TIMBER. EXP: COPPER, FISH, FRUITS, PAPER & PULP, CHEMICALS.

Chile extends down the west coast of South America, wedged between the ocean and a mountain chain and straddling a tectonically unstable region. Mountains cover 80 percent of the land. Most Chileans are of European or mixed European and indigenous ancestry—only about 5 percent are indigenous (mostly Mapuche). After 16 years of dictatorship under Gen. Augusto Pinochet, democracy was restored in 1989. Privatization of industries and increased agricultural exports have boosted the economy. The Chuquicamata and Escondida copper mines rank as the world's largest. Tourism is a major business; a popular attraction is Easter Island.

ARGENTINA

ARGENTINE REPUBLIC

AREA 1,073,518 SQ. MI. ▐ POPULATION 40,914,000 ▐ CAPITAL BUENOS AIRES (POP. 13,089,000) ▐ LITERACY 97% ▐ LIFE EXPECTANCY 77 ▐ CURRENCY ARGENTINE PESO ▐ GDP PER CAPITA $14,200 ▐ ECONOMY IND: FOOD PROCESSING, MOTOR VEHICLES, CONSUMER DURABLES, TEXTILES. AGR: SUNFLOWER SEEDS, LEMONS, SOYBEANS, LIVESTOCK. EXP: EDIBLE OILS, FUELS & ENERGY, CEREALS, FEED, MOTOR VEHICLES.

Argentina's heartland is a broad grassy plain called the Pampas. The Andes—with Aconcagua, the highest peak in the Western Hemisphere—mark Argentina's western edge. Gently rolling plains extend eastward toward the sea. Northeast Argentina features rain forests and the Iguazú Falls. South of the Pampas, dry and windswept Patagonia stretches to the southernmost tip of South America with the world's southernmost city, Ushuaia. Since its days as a military dictatorship ended in the early 1980s, much has been won: greater freedom of the press, tolerance of opposition, and increased foreign investment. Unemployment, however, plagues the economy.

MICHELLE BACHELET / ADVOCATE FOR WOMEN

After her father, a Chilean air force general, was arrested for resisting the military coup led by Augusto Pinochet, Michelle Bachelet was also arrested and tortured before her 1975 release into exile. She lived in Europe, active in socialism, until her return in 1979, when she finished her medical degree. Bachelet became involved in politics after Pinochet's ousting in 1990; four years later, she was named an adviser to the minister for health. In 2000, Bachelet became health minister and two years later was appointed to lead the defense ministry. The 2005 Socialist presidential candidate, she won and held that office from 2006 to 2010. In 2010 she became executive director of the newly established UN Women.

> " I know exactly how it feels to be a refugee in a strange country. I know it because I lived that—I also was a refugee. — **MICHELLE BACHELET, 2008** "

GLOSSARY

Pampas: From the Quechua for "flat surface." Vast grassland plains, especially those in Argentina and elsewhere in South America. / **Mestizo:** From the Spanish for "mixed." A person of mixed ancestry; in Central and South America, a person of combined Indian and European extraction.

PARAGUAY

REPUBLIC OF PARAGUAY

AREA 157,048 SQ. MI. ▊ POPULATION 6,996,000 ▊ CAPITAL ASUNCIÓN (POP. 2,030,000) ▊ LITERACY 94% ▊ LIFE EXPECTANCY 76 ▊ CURRENCY GUARANI ▊ GDP PER CAPITA $4,200 ▊ ECONOMY IND: SUGAR, CEMENT, TEXTILES, BEVERAGES. AGR: COTTON, SUGARCANE, SOYBEANS, CORN, BEEF, TIMBER. EXP: SOYBEANS, FEED, COTTON, MEAT, EDIBLE OILS.

Paraguay, landlocked in central South America, is divided by the Paraguay River into a hilly, forested east and a flat plain (known as the Chaco) in the west. The Chaco, marshy near the river and turning to semidesert farther west, contains 60 percent of the country but only 2 percent of the people. Paraguayans are mostly a mixture of Spanish and Guaraní Indian. Paraguay possesses plenty of electric power thanks to hydroelectric dams such as Itaipú, the world's largest, built and operated jointly with Brazil. Democracy replaced dictatorship by 1993, but the government still faces problems with a poor agricultural population and rapid deforestation.

URUGUAY

ORIENTAL REPUBLIC OF URUGUAY

AREA 68,037 SQ. MI. ▊ POPULATION 3,494,000 ▊ CAPITAL MONTEVIDEO (POP. 1,504,000) ▊ LITERACY 98% ▊ LIFE EXPECTANCY 76 ▊ CURRENCY URUGUAYAN PESO ▊ GDP PER CAPITA $12,200 ▊ ECONOMY IND: FOOD PROCESSING, ELECTRICAL MACHINERY, TRANSPORTATION EQUIPMENT, PETROLEUM PRODUCTS. AGR: RICE, WHEAT, CORN, BARLEY, LIVESTOCK, FISH. EXP: MEAT, RICE, LEATHER PRODUCTS, WOOL, VEHICLES.

Situated below Brazil on the Atlantic coast of southeastern South America, Uruguay consists mostly of low, rolling grasslands. Ranchers raise cattle and sheep on the well-watered pastures. Uruguay has one of the highest urbanization and literacy rates—as well as the lowest poverty and population growth rates—in South America. Still, high unemployment leads many Uruguayans to emigrate to places like Spain for better job opportunities. Uruguay's economy remains dependent on agriculture. Economic diversification, including development of hydroelectric power, has spread optimism.

INDEX

Boldface indicates illustrations

FAST FACT Benjamin Franklin was first to record the course, speed, temperature, and depth of the Gulf Stream.

431

ANSWER BOOK | INDEX

FAST FACT The weight of the Antarctic ice cap deforms Earth's shape.

FAST FACT Dark matter makes up at least 75 percent of the universe's mass.

435

ANSWER BOOK | INDEX

FAST FACT Earth's core is about the size of the planet Mars.

439

ANSWER BOOK | INDEX

FAST FACT Portugal provides at least half the world's supply of cork.

FAST FACT The exposed rocks of the Canadian Shield at Hudson Bay are 3.5 billion years old.

ILLUSTRATIONS

1, Jim Richardson; 2, Amit Bhargava/CORBIS; 3, Stephen Alvarez/NationalGeographicStock.com; 4-5, George F. Mobley; 6, Tim Laman/NationalGeographicStock.com; 7, Robert B. Haas; 8, Jodi Cobb/NationalGeographicStock.com; 9, Cary Sol Wolinsky; 10, Michael Poliza/NationalGeographicStock.com; 11, John Henry Claude Wilson/Robert Harding World Imagery/CORBIS; 14-15, Data courtesy Marc Imhoff of NASA GSFC and Christopher Elvidge of NOAA NGDC. Image by Craig Mayhew and Robert Simmon, NASA GSFC; 16, Bruce Dale; 17, Hulton Archive/Getty Images; 18, The Granger Collection, NY; 20, Gerard Mercator/Getty Images; 21, Bridgeman Art Library/Getty Images; 22, Hiroyuki Matsumoto/Getty Images; 23 (UP), Library of Congress, Geography & Map Division; 23 (LO), James L. Stanfield; 24, Chris Hondros/Getty Images; 25 (UP), Library of Congress, Geography & Map Division; 25 (LO LE), Irina Tischenko/Shutterstock; 25 (LO CTR LE), Stephen Coburn/Shutterstock; 25 (LO CTR RT), Goncalo Veloso de Figueiredo/Shutterstock; 25 (LO RT), Paul Cowan/Shutterstock; 27 (UP), Stapleton Collection/CORBIS; 27 (LO), Richard Ward/Getty Images; 28, NASA/CORBIS; 29, © Encyclopædia Britannica, Inc., used under license; 30, Dennis di Cicco/CORBIS; 31, Library of Congress, Geography & Map Division; 35, Popperfoto/Getty Images; 36, B. Anthony Stewart; 37, © Encyclopædia Britannica, Inc., used under license; 38, Gordon Wiltsie/NationalGeographicStock.com; 39 (UP), Hulton Archive/Getty Images; 39 (LO), Library of Congress, Geography & Map Division; 40-41, NASA/JPL-Caltech/Harvard-Smithsonian CfA; 42, NASA, ESA, and S. Beckwith (STScI) and the HUDF Team; 43 (UP), David A. Hardy/Photo Researchers, Inc.; 43 (LO), WMAP Science Team, NASA; 44, Credit for Hubble Image: NASA, ESA, N. Smith (University of California, Berkeley), and The Hubble Heritage Team (STScI/AURA) Credit for CTIO Image: N. Smith (University of California, Berkeley) and NOAO/AURA/NSF; 45 (LE), Barron Storey; 45 (RT), David A. Aguilar; 46, NASA, ESA and AURA/Caltech; 48, Bill Schoening, Vanessa Harvey/REU program/NOAO/AURA/NSF ; 49 (UP LE), NASA, Rogier Windhorst (Arizona State University, Tempe, AZ), and the Hubble mid-UV team; 49 (UP CTR LE), NASA, ESA, and The Hubble Heritage Team (STScI/AURA); 49 (UP CTR RT), NASA, ESA, and The Hubble Heritage Team (STScI/AURA); 49 (UP RT), NASA, ESA, and The Hubble Heritage Team (STScI/AURA)-ESA/Hubble Collaboration; 49 (LO), NASA; 50, Rob Wood; 51 (UP), Mike Marsland/WireImage/Getty Images; 51 (LO), David A. Hardy/Photo Researchers, Inc.; 52, NASA, ESA, J. Clarke (Boston University), and Z. Levay (STScI); 53, David A. Aguilar; 54, Ralph Lee Hopkins/NationalGeographicStock.com; 55 (UP), NASA/SOHO/AFP/Getty Images; 55 (LO), Peter Lloyd; 56, NASA/Newsmakers/Getty Images; 57 (UP), Naval Research Laboratory and NASA; 57 (LO), Mike Agliolo/Photo Researchers, Inc.; 58, David A. Aguilar; 60, David Aguilar; 61 (UP), Detlev van Ravenswaay/Photo Researchers, Inc.; 61 (LO), NASA-JPL; 62, NASA-JPL; 63 (UP), David Aguilar; 63 (LO), NASA; 64, NASA; 65 (UP), Rafael Pacheco/Shutterstock; 65 (LO), David A. Aguilar; 66, Ali Jarekji/Reuters/CORBIS; 67 (UP), NASA-JPL; 67 (LO), Lowell Observatory/NOAO/AURA/NSF; 68, Jim Richardson; 69 (UP), Robert Harding/Getty Images; 69 (CTR), Kean Collection/Getty Images; 69 (LO), British Museum, London/Bridgeman Art Library/Getty Images; 70, Robert W. Madden; 71 (UP LE), NASA; 71 (UP RT), Courtesy David A. Aguilar; 71 (LO), Jon Brenneis/Time Life Pictures/Getty Images; 72, NASA Marshall Space Flight Center (NASA-MSFC); 73 (UP), Neil A. Armstrong/NASA; 73 (LO), Popperfoto/Getty Images; 74, NASA; 75 (UP), NASA-JPL, Art by Corby Waste; 75 (LO), NASA; 76, 77, David A. Aguilar; 78-79, NASA; 80, NASA, ESA, and the Hubble Heritage Team (STScI/AURA)-ESA/Hubble Collaboration; 81, Tibor Toth; 82, Henning Dalhoff/Bonnier Publications/Photo

Researchers, Inc.; 83 (UP), James King-Holmes/Photo Researchers, Inc.; 83 (LO), Wikipedia; 84, Michael Fay/NationalGeographicStock.com; 85 (UP), Christopher R. Scotese/PALEOMAP Project; 85 (LO), SPL/Photo Researchers, Inc.; 86, Karen Kasmauski; 87 (UP), USGS; 87 (LO), © Encyclopædia Britannica, Inc., used under license; 88, Lester Lefkowitz/Getty Images; 89, Gary Hincks/Photo Researchers, Inc.; 90, Geoff Tompkinson/Photo Researchers, Inc.; 91 (UP), 3D4Medical.com/Getty Images; 91 (LO), Novosti/Photo Researchers, Inc.; 92, Ralph Lee Hopkins/NationalGeographicStock.com; 93 (UP LE), William Allen; 93 (UP CTR), Walter M. Edwards; 93 (UP RT), Raymond Gehman/NationalGeographicStock.com; 93 (LO), ChrisOrr.com and XNR Productions; 94, O. Louis Mazzatenta; 95, Joseph Graham, William Newman, and John Stacy, USGS; 96, Jacana/Photo Researchers, Inc.; 97 (UP), Michael Hampshire; 97 (LO), Jodi Cobb; 98, Handout/Malacanang/Reuters/CORBIS; 99 (UP), Shusei Nagaoka; 99 (LO ALL), Susan Sanford, Planet Earth; 100, George F. Mobley; 101 (UP LE), ChrisOrr.com; 101 (UP CTR LE), ChrisOrr.com; 101 (UP CTR), ChrisOrr.com; 101 (UP CTR RT), ChrisOrr.com; 101 (UP RT), ChrisOrr.com; 101 (LO LE), Robert E. Hynes; 101 (LO RT), Robert E. Hynes; 102, Jason Edwards/NationalGeographicStock.com; 103 (UP), David Doubilet; 103 (LO), Gary Hincks/Photo Researchers, Inc.; 104, Karsten Schneider/Photo Researchers, Inc.; 105 (UP), CORBIS; 105 (LO), © Encyclopædia Britannica, Inc., used under license; 106, Annie Griffiths Belt/NationalGeographicStock.com; 107, ChrisOrr.com and XNR Productions; 108, Randy Olson; 109 (UP), BSIP/Photo Researchers, Inc.; 109 (LO), Paul Nicklen/NationalGeographicStock.com; 110, James P. Blair; 111, © Encyclopædia Britannica, Inc., used under license; 112, World Ocean Floor Panorama, Bruce C. Heezen and Marie Tharp, 1977, Copyright by Marie Tharp 1977/2003. Reproduced by permission of Marie Tharp Maps, LLC, 8 Edward Street, Sparkill, New York 10976; 113 (UP), Courtesy Robert M. Carey, NOAA; 113 (LO), Bettmann/CORBIS; 114, Maria Stenzel; 115 (UP), © Encyclopædia Britannica, Inc., used under license; 116, Nicolas Reynard; 117 (UP), CORBIS; 117 (LO), Steven Fick/Canadian Geographic; 118, Sarah Leen/NationalGeographicStock.com; 119 (UP), © Encyclopædia Britannica, Inc., used under license; 119 (LO), Jim Richardson; 120 (UP), James D. Balog; 120 (LO), Carsten Peter/NationalGeographicStock.com; 121 (UP ALL), Steven Fick; 121 (LO), Ralph Lee Hopkins/NationalGeographicStock.com; 122, James P. Blair; 123 (UP), Comma Image/Jupiter Images; 123 (LO), Dennis Finley; 124, Robert Landau/CORBIS; 125 (UP ALL), Image courtesy the TOMS science team & and the Scientific Visualization Studio, NASA GSFC; 125 (LO), © Encyclopædia Britannica, Inc., used under license ; 126, Ashley Cooper/CORBIS; 127, Hong Jin-Hwan/AFP/Getty Images; 128-129, Chris Johns, NGS; 130, Piotr Naskrecki/Minden Pictures/NationalGeographicStock.com; 131, © Encyclopædia Britannica, Inc., used under license; 132, Jason Edwards/NationalGeographicStock.com; 133 (UP), Sam Abell; 133 (LO), Mansell/Time Life Pictures/Getty Images; 134, James P. Blair/NationalGeographicStock.com; 135 (UP), Baron/Getty Images; 135 (LO), Hal Horwitz/CORBIS; 136, Melissa Farlow; 137 (UP), Nicole Duplaix/NationalGeographicStock.com; 137 (LO), © Encyclopædia Britannica, Inc., used under license; 138, H. Edward Kim; 139 (UP), Simone End/Getty Images; 139 (LO), © Encyclopædia Britannica, Inc., used under license; 140, Sam Abell; 141 (UP), Michael and Patricia Fogden/Minden Pictures/NationalGeographicStock.com; 141 (CTR), Joel Sartore/NationalGeographicStock.com; 141 (LO), BananaStock/Jupiter Images; 142, Robert F. Sisson; 143 (UP), Robert W. Madden; 143 (LO), Chris McGrath/Getty Images; 144, Karen Kasmauski; 145 (UP), James L. Stanfield; 145 (LO), Darlyne A. Murawski/NationalGeographicStock.com;

CONTRIBUTORS

CATHERINE HERBERT HOWELL CHAPTERS 1, 2, 3 & 4 /

An anthropologist by training and formerly a National Geographic staff member, Catherine Herbert Howell is the author of *Flora Mirabilis: How Plants Have Shaped World Knowledge, Health, Wealth & Beauty.* She has contributed to dozens of other National Geographic books, including many children's books on science and nature. She lives in Arlington, Virginia.

HOWARD SCHNEIDER CHAPTERS 5 & 8 /

Howard Schneider is a journalist with the *Washington Post* currently reporting from Jerusalem, Israel. He has also served as economics editor and chief of the paper's bureau in Cairo, Egypt, and has written on fitness and physiology for the paper's Health section.

PATRICIA S. DANIELS CHAPTER 6 /

Patricia S. Daniels is a freelance writer specializing in history, science, and geography. Most recently she contributed to the National Geographic Society's *New Solar System, Body: The Complete Human*; and *1000 Events That Shaped the World.*

STEPHEN G. HYSLOP CHAPTER 7 /

Stephen G. Hyslop is the author of *Eyewitness to the Civil War, Bound for Santa Fe*, and, with Patricia S. Daniels, *Almanac of World History.* Formerly an editor at Time-Life Books, he has contributed to many other volumes on American and world history, and his articles have appeared in *American History, World War II*, and the History Channel magazine.

KATHRYN THORNTON FOREWORD /

Kathryn Thornton was a NASA astronaut from 1985 to 1996. She flew four missions, including the first Hubble Space Telescope service mission, and logged 975 hours in space including 21 extravehicular hours. She is a professor of mechanical and aerospace engineering at the University of Virginia in Charlottesville.

JAN NIJMAN CONSULTING GEOGRAPHER /

Jan Nijman is professor of geography and regional studies and director of the urban studies program at the University of Miami. He specializes in issues of global urbanization and does fieldwork in Mumbai, India; Accra, Ghana; Amsterdam, The Netherlands; and Miami, Florida.

ANSWER BOOK

PUBLISHED BY THE NATIONAL GEOGRAPHIC SOCIETY

John M. Fahey, Jr., *Chairman of the Board and Chief Executive Officer*
Timothy T. Kelly, *President*
Declan Moore, *Executive Vice President; President, Publishing*
Melina Gerosa Bellows, *Executive Vice President, Chief Creative
  Officer, Books, Kids, and Family*

PREPARED BY THE BOOK DIVISION

Barbara Brownell Grogan, *Vice President and Editor in Chief*
Jonathan Halling, *Design Director, Books and Children's Publishing*
Marianne R. Koszorus, *Design Director, Books*
R. Gary Colbert, *Production Director*
Jennifer A. Thornton, *Managing Editor*
Meredith C. Wilcox, *Administrative Director, Illustrations*

STAFF FOR THIS BOOK

Susan Tyler Hitchcock, *Project Editor*
Sam Serebin, *Art Director*
Jennifer Conrad Seidel, *Text Editor*
Kevin Eans, *Illustrations Editor*
Betsy Towner, *Researcher*
Matt Chwastyk, Steven D. Gardner, Michael McNey,
  and Mapping Specialists, *Map Research and Production*
Catherine Herbert Howell, *Developmental Editor
  and Contributing Writer*
Patricia S. Daniels, *Contributing Writer*
Stephen G. Hyslop, *Contributing Writer*
Howard Schneider, *Contributing Writer*
Jan Nijman, *Consulting Geographer*
Mike Horenstein, *Production Project Manager*
Marshall Kiker, *Illustrations Specialist*
Al Morrow, Noelle Weber, *Design Assistants*
Stephanie Hanlon Handy, Heidi Egloff, *Editorial Assistants*

MANUFACTURING AND QUALITY MANAGEMENT

Christopher A. Liedel, *Chief Financial Officer*
Phillip L. Schlosser, *Senior Vice President*
Chris Brown, *Technical Director*
Nicole Elliott, *Manager*
Rachel Faulise, *Manager*
Robert L. Barr, *Manager*

*Many of the definitions in Glossary features are derived
from content provided by Encyclopædia Britannica, Inc.*

The National Geographic Society is one of the world's largest non-profit scientific and educational organizations. Founded in 1888 to "increase and diffuse geographic knowledge," the Society's mission is to inspire people to care about the planet. It reaches more than 400 million people worldwide each month through its official journal, *National Geographic*, and other magazines; National Geographic Channel; television documentaries; music; radio; films; books; DVDs; maps; exhibitions; live events; school publishing programs; interactive media; and merchandise. National Geographic has funded more than 9,600 scientific research, conservation and exploration projects and supports an education program promoting geographic literacy. For more information, visit www.nationalgeographic.com.

For more information, please call 1-800-NGS LINE (647-5463) or write to the following address:

National Geographic Society
1145 17th Street N.W.
Washington, D.C. 20036-4688 U.S.A.

Visit us online at www.nationalgeographic.com

For information about special discounts for bulk purchases, please contact National Geographic Books Special Sales: ngspecsales@ngs.org

For rights or permissions inquiries, please contact National Geographic Books Subsidiary Rights: ngbookrights@ngs.org

First paperback printing 2011

ISBN 978-1-4262-0892-8

The Library of Congress has cataloged the hardcover edition as follows:
Answer Book: Fast Facts About Our World
p. cm.
Includes index.
ISBN 978-1-4262-0345-9 (regular ed.) -- ISBN 978-1-4262-0346-6 (deluxe ed.)
1. Geography--Handbooks, manuals, etc. 2. World history--Handbooks, manuals, etc. 3. Civilization, Ancient--Handbooks, manuals, etc. 4. Civilization, Medieval--Handbooks, manuals, etc. 5. Civilization, Modern--Handbooks, manuals, etc. 6. Science--Handbooks, manuals, etc. 7. Technology--Handbooks, manuals, etc. 8. Economics--Handbooks, manuals, etc. 9. Political science--Handbooks, manuals, etc. I. National Geographic Society (U.S.)
G123.W67 2009
910--dc22
2008030627

Printed in United States of America

11/QGT-CML/1